PORTFOLIO MANAGEMENT IN PRACTICE

Volume 3

CFA Institute is the premier association for investment professionals around the world, with over 170,000 members more than 160 countries. Since 1963 the organization has developed and administered the renowned Chartered Financial Analyst Program. With a rich history of leading the investment profession, CFA Institute has set the highest standards in ethics, education, and professional excellence within the global investment community, and is the foremost authority on investment profession conduct and practice.

Each book in the CFA Institute Investment Series is geared toward industry practitioners along with graduate-level finance students and covers the most important topics in the industry. The authors of these cutting-edge books are themselves industry professionals and academics and bring their wealth of knowledge and expertise to this series.

PORTFOLIO MANAGEMENT IN PRACTICE

Volume 3

Equity Portfolio Management

WILEY

PREFACE

We are pleased to bring you Equity Portfolio Management, Volume 3 of Portfolio Management in Practice. This series of three volumes serves as a particularly important resource for investment professionals who recognize that portfolio management is an integrated set of activities. The topic coverage in the three volumes is organized according to a well-articulated portfolio management decision-making process. This organizing principle—in addition to the breadth of coverage, the currency and quality of content, and its meticulous pedagogy—distinguishes the three volumes in Portfolio Management in Practice series of volumes from other investment texts that deal with portfolio management.

The content was developed in partnership by a team of distinguished academics and practitioners, chosen for their acknowledged expertise in the field, and guided by CFA Institute. It is written specifically with the investment practitioner in mind and is replete with examples and practice problems that reinforce the learning outcomes and demonstrate real-world applicability.

The CFA Program curriculum, from which the content of this book was drawn, is subjected to a rigorous review process to assure that it is:

- faithful to the findings of our ongoing industry practice analysis
- Valuable to members, employers, and investors
- Globally relevant
- Generalist (as opposed to specialist) in nature
- replete with sufficient examples and practice opportunities
- Pedagogically sound

The accompanying workbook is a useful reference that provides Learning Outcome Statements, which describe exactly what readers will learn and be able to demonstrate after mastering the accompanying material. additionally, the workbook has summary overviews and practice problems for each chapter.

We hope you will find this and other books in the CFA Institute Investment Series helpful in your efforts to grow your investment knowledge, whether you are a relatively new entrant or an experienced veteran striving to keep up to date in the ever-changing market environment. CFA Institute, as a long-term committed participant in the investment profession and a not-for-profit global membership association, is pleased to provide you with this opportunity.

CONTENTS

CHAPTER 4
PASSIVE EQUITY INVESTING

95

CHAPTER 7
Active Equity Investing: Portfolio Construction 271

ACKNOWLEDGMENTS

Special thanks to all the reviewers, advisors, and question writers who helped to ensure high practical relevance, technical correctness, and understandability of the material presented here.

We would like to thank the many others who played a role in the conception and production of this book: the Curriculum and Learning Experience team at CFA Institute with special thanks to the curriculum directors, past and present, who worked with the authors and reviewers to produce the chapters in this book, the Practice Analysis team at CFA Institute, and the Publishing and Technology team for bringing this book to production.

ABOUT THE CFA INSTITUTE INVESTMENT SERIES

CFA Institute is pleased to provide the CFA Institute Investment Series, which covers major areas in the field of investments. We provide this best-in-class series for the same reason we have been chartering investment professionals for more than 45 years: to lead the investment profession globally by setting the highest standards of ethics, education, and professional excellence.

The books in the CFA Institute Investment Series contain practical, globally relevant material. They are intended both for those contemplating entry into the extremely competitive field of investment management as well as for those seeking a means of keeping their knowledge fresh and up to date. This series was designed to be user friendly and highly relevant.

We hope you find this series helpful in your efforts to grow your investment knowledge, whether you are a relatively new entrant or an experienced veteran ethically bound to keep up to date in the ever-changing market environment. As a long-term, committed participant in the investment profession and a not-for-profit global membership association, CFA Institute is pleased to provide you with this opportunity.

THE TEXTS

Corporate Finance: A Practical Approach is a solid foundation for those looking to achieve lasting business growth. In today's competitive business environment, companies must find innovative ways to enable rapid and sustainable growth. This text equips readers with the foundational knowledge and tools for making smart business decisions and formulating strategies to maximize company value. It covers everything from managing relationships between stakeholders to evaluating merger and acquisition bids, as well as the companies behind them. Through extensive use of real-world examples, readers will gain critical perspective into interpreting corporate financial data, evaluating projects, and allocating funds in ways that increase corporate value. Readers will gain insights into the tools and strategies used in modern corporate financial management.

Equity Asset Valuation is a particularly cogent and important resource for anyone involved in estimating the value of securities and understanding security pricing. A well-informed professional knows that the common forms of equity valuation—dividend discount modeling, free cash flow modeling, price/earnings modeling, and residual income modeling—can all be reconciled with one another under certain assumptions. With a deep understanding of the underlying assumptions, the professional investor can better understand what other investors assume when calculating their valuation estimates. This text has a global orientation, including emerging markets.

Fixed Income Analysis has been at the forefront of new concepts in recent years, and this particular text offers some of the most recent material for the seasoned professional who is not a fixed-income specialist. The application of option and derivative technology to the once staid province of fixed income has helped contribute to an explosion of thought in this area. Professionals have been challenged to stay up to speed with credit derivatives, swaptions, collateralized mortgage securities, mortgage-backed securities, and other vehicles, and this explosion of products has strained the world's financial markets and tested central banks to provide sufficient oversight. Armed with a thorough grasp of the new exposures, the professional investor is much better able to anticipate and understand the challenges our central bankers and markets face.

International Financial Statement Analysis is designed to address the ever-increasing need for investment professionals and students to think about financial statement analysis from a global perspective. The text is a practically oriented introduction to financial statement analysis that is distinguished by its combination of a true international orientation, a structured presentation style, and abundant illustrations and tools covering concepts as they are introduced in the text. The authors cover this discipline comprehensively and with an eye to ensuring the reader's success at all levels in the complex world of financial statement analysis.

Investments: Principles of Portfolio and Equity Analysis provides an accessible yet rigorous introduction to portfolio and equity analysis. Portfolio planning and portfolio management are presented within a context of up-to-date, global coverage of security markets, trading, and market-related concepts and products. The essentials of equity analysis and valuation are explained in detail and profusely illustrated. The book includes coverage of practitioner-important but often neglected topics, such as industry analysis. Throughout, the focus is on the practical application of key concepts with examples drawn from both emerging and developed markets. Each chapter affords the reader many opportunities to self-check his or her understanding of topics.

All books in the CFA Institute Investment Series are available through all major booksellers. And, all titles are available on the Wiley Custom Select platform at http://customselect. wiley.com/ where individual chapters for all the books may be mixed and matched to create custom textbooks for the classroom.

CHAPTER 1

OVERVIEW OF EQUITY SECURITIES

Ryan C. Fuhrmann, CFA
Asjeet S. Lamba, PhD, CFA

LEARNING OUTCOMES

The candidate should be able to:

- describe characteristics of types of equity securities;
- describe differences in voting rights and other ownership characteristics among different equity classes;
- distinguish between public and private equity securities;
- describe methods for investing in non-domestic equity securities;
- compare the risk and return characteristics of different types of equity securities;
- explain the role of equity securities in the financing of a company's assets;
- distinguish between the market value and book value of equity securities;
- compare a company's cost of equity, its (accounting) return on equity, and investors' required rates of return.

1. INTRODUCTION

Equity securities represent ownership claims on a company's net assets. As an asset class, equity plays a fundamental role in investment analysis and portfolio management because it represents a significant portion of many individual and institutional investment portfolios.

The study of equity securities is important for many reasons. First, the decision on how much of a client's portfolio to allocate to equities affects the risk and return characteristics of the entire portfolio. Second, different types of equity securities have different ownership claims on a company's net assets, which affect their risk and return characteristics in different ways. Finally, variations in the features of equity securities are reflected in their market prices, so it is important to understand the valuation implications of these features.

This chapter provides an overview of equity securities and their different features and establishes the background required to analyze and value equity securities in a global context. It addresses the following questions:

- What distinguishes common shares from preference shares, and what purposes do these securities serve in financing a company's operations?
- What are convertible preference shares, and why are they often used to raise equity for unseasoned or highly risky companies?
- What are private equity securities, and how do they differ from public equity securities?
- What are depository receipts and their various types, and what is the rationale for investing in them?
- What are the risk factors involved in investing in equity securities?
- How do equity securities create company value?
- What is the relationship between a company's cost of equity, its return on equity, and investors' required rate of return?

The remainder of this chapter is organized as follows. Section 2 provides an overview of global equity markets and their historical performance. Section 3 examines the different types and characteristics of equity securities, and Section 4 outlines the differences between public and private equity securities. Section 5 provides an overview of the various types of equity securities listed and traded in global markets. Section 6 discusses the risk and return characteristics of equity securities. Section 7 examines the role of equity securities in creating company value and the relationship between a company's cost of equity, its return on equity, and investors' required rate of return. The final section summarizes the chapter.

2. EQUITY SECURITIES IN GLOBAL FINANCIAL MARKETS

This section highlights the relative importance and performance of equity securities as an asset class. We examine the total market capitalization and trading volume of global equity markets and the prevalence of equity ownership across various geographic regions. We also examine historical returns on equities and compare them to the returns on government bonds and bills.

Exhibit 1 summarizes the contributions of selected countries and geographic regions to global gross domestic product (GDP) and global equity market capitalization. Analysts may examine the relationship between equity market capitalization and GDP as a rough indicator of whether the global equity market (or a specific country's or region's equity market) is under, over, or fairly valued, particularly compared to its long-run average.

Exhibit 1 illustrates the significant value that investors attach to publicly traded equities relative to the sum of goods and services produced globally every year. It shows the continued significance, and the potential over-representation, of US equity markets relative to their contribution to global GDP. That is, while US equity markets contribute around 51 percent to the total capitalization of global equity markets, their contribution to the global GDP is only around 25 percent. Following the stock market turmoil in 2008, however, the market capitalization to GDP ratio of the United States fell to 59 percent, which is significantly lower than its long-run average of 79 percent.

As equity markets outside the United States develop and become increasingly global, their total capitalization levels are expected to grow closer to their respective world GDP contributions. Therefore, it is important to understand and analyze equity securities from a global perspective.

EXHIBIT 1   Country and Regional Contributions to Global GDP and Equity Market Capitalization (2017)

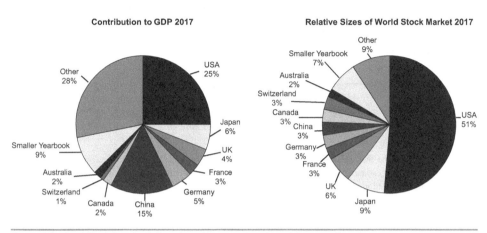

Sources: The WorldBank Databank (2017), and Dimson, Marsh, and Staunton (2018).

Exhibit 2 lists the top 10 equity markets at the end of 2017 based on total market capitalization (in billions of US dollars), trading volume, and the number of listed companies.[1] Note that the rankings differ based on the criteria used. For example, the top three markets based on total market capitalization are the NYSE Euronext (US), NASDAQ OMX, and the Japan Exchange Group; however, the top three markets based on total US dollar trading volume are the Nasdaq OMX, NYSE Euronext (US), and the Shenzhen Stock Exchange, respectively.[2]

EXHIBIT 2   Equity Markets Ranked by Total Market Capitalization at the End of 2017 (Billions of US Dollars)

Rank	Name of Market	Total US Dollar Market Capitalization	Total US Dollar Trading Volume	Number of Listed Companies
1	NYSE Euronext (US)	$22,081.4	$16,140.1	2,286
2	NASDAQ OMX	$10,039.4	$33,407.1	2,949
3	Japan Exchange Group[a]	$6,220.0	$6,612.1	3,604
4	Shanghai Stock Exchange	$5,084.4	$7,589.3	1,396
5	Euronext[b]	$4,393.0	$1,981.6	1,255
6	Hong Kong Exchanges	$4,350.5	$1,958.8	2,118
7	Shenzhen Stock Exchanges	$3,617.9	$9,219.7	2,089

---

[1]The market capitalization of an individual stock is computed as the share price multiplied by the number of shares outstanding. The total market capitalization of an equity market is the sum of the market capitalizations of each individual stock listed on that market. Similarly, the total trading volume of an equity market is computed by value weighting the total trading volume of each individual stock listed on that market. Total dollar trading volume is computed as the average share price multiplied by the number of shares traded.

[2]NASDAQ is the acronym for the National Association of Securities Dealers Automated Quotations.

Rank	Name of Market	Total US Dollar Market Capitalization	Total US Dollar Trading Volume	Number of Listed Companies
8	National Stock Exchange of India	$2,351.5	$1,013.3	1,897
9	BSE Limited[c]	$2,331.6	$183.0	5,616
10	Deutsche Börse	$2,262.2	$1,497.9	499

Notes:

[a] Japan Exchange Group is the merged entity containing the Tokyo Stock Exchange and Osaka Securities Exchange.

[b] From 2001, includes Netherlands, France, England, Belgium, and Portugal.

[c] Bombay Stock Exchange.

Source: Adapted from the *World Federation of Exchanges 2017 Report* (see http://www.world-exchanges.org). Note that market capitalization by company is calculated by multiplying its stock price by the number of shares outstanding. The market's overall capitalization is the aggregate of the market capitalizations of all companies traded on that market. The number of listed companies includes both domestic and foreign companies whose shares trade on these markets.

Exhibit 3 compares the *real* (or inflation-adjusted) compounded returns on government bonds, government bills, and equity securities in 21 countries plus the world index ("Wld"), the world ex-US ("WxU"), and Europe ("Eur") during the 118 years 1900–2017.[3] In real terms, government bonds and bills have essentially kept pace with the inflation rate, earning annualized real returns of less than 2 percent in most countries.[4] By comparison, real returns in equity markets have generally been around 3.5 percent per year in most markets—with a world average return of around 5.2 percent and a world average return excluding the United States just under 5 percent. During this period, South Africa and Australia were the best performing markets followed by the United States, New Zealand, and Sweden.

EXHIBIT 3   Real Returns on Global Equity Securities, Bonds, and Bills During 1900–2017

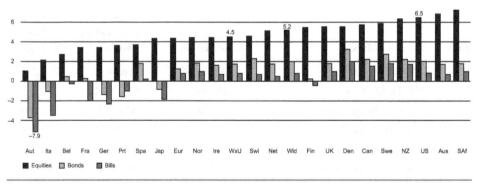

Source: Dimson, Marsh, and Staunton (2018).

Exhibit 4 shows the annualized real returns on major asset classes for the world index over 1900–2017.

---

[3] The real return for a security is approximated by taking the nominal return and subtracting the observed inflation rate in that country.

[4] The exceptions are Austria, Belgium, Finland, France, Germany, Portugal, and Italy—where the average real returns on government bonds and/or bills have been negative. In general, that performance reflects the very high inflation rates in these countries during the World War years.

EXHIBIT 4   Annualized Real Returns on Asset Classes for the World Index, 1900–2017

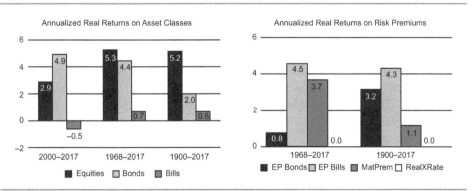

Source: Dimson, Marsh, and Staunton (2018).

The volatility in asset market returns is further highlighted in Exhibit 5, which shows the annualized risk premia for equity relative to bonds (EP Bonds), and equity relative to treasury bills (EP Bills). Maturity premium for government bond returns relative to treasury bill returns (Mat Prem) is also shown.

These observations and historical data are consistent with the concept that the return on securities is directly related to risk level. That is, equity securities have higher risk levels when compared with government bonds and bills, they earn higher rates of return to compensate investors for these higher risk levels, and they also tend to be more volatile over time.

EXHIBIT 5   Annualized Real Returns on Asset Classes and Risk Premiums for the World Index since 1900–2017

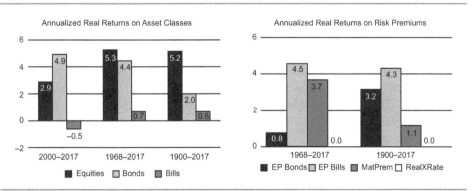

Notes: Equities are total returns, including reinvested dividend income. Bonds are total return, including reinvested coupons, on long-term government bonds. Bills denotes the total return, including any income, from Treasury bills. All returns are adjusted for inflation and are expressed as geometric mean returns. EP bonds denotes the equity risk premium relative to long-term government bonds. EP Bills denotes the equity premium relative to Treasury bills. MatPrem denotes the maturity premium for government bond returns relative to bill returns. RealXRate denotes the real (inflation-adjusted) change in the exchange rate against the US dollar.
Source: Dimson, Marsh, and Staunton (2018).

Given the high risk levels associated with equity securities, it is reasonable to expect that investors' tolerance for risk will tend to differ across equity markets. This is illustrated in Exhibit 6, which shows the results of a series of studies conducted by the Australian Securities Exchange on international differences in equity ownership. During the 2004–2014 period, equity ownership as a percentage of the population was lowest in South Korea (averaging 9.0 percent), followed by Germany (14.5 percent) and Sweden (17.7 percent). In contrast, Australia and New Zealand had the highest equity ownership as a percentage of the population (averaging more than 20 percent). In addition, there has been a relative decline in share ownership in several countries over recent years, which is not surprising given the recent overall uncertainty in global economies and the volatility in equity markets that this uncertainty has created.

EXHIBIT 6   International Comparisons of Stock Ownership: 2004–2014[5]

	2004	2006	2008	2010	2012	2014
Australia – Direct/Indirect	55%	46%	41%	43%	38%	36%
South Korea – Shares	8	7	10	10	10	N/A
Germany – Shares/Funds	16	16	14	13	15	13
Sweden – Shares	22	20	18	17	15	14
United Kingdom – Shares/Funds	22	20	18	N/A	17	N/A
New Zealand – Direct	23	26	N/A	22	23	26

Source: Adapted from the *2014 Australian Share Ownership Study* conducted by the Australian Securities Exchange (see http://www.asx.com.au). For Australia and the United States, the data pertain to direct and indirect ownership in equity markets; for other countries, the data pertain to direct ownership in shares and share funds. Data not available in specific years are shown as "N/A."

An important implication from the above discussion is that equity securities represent a key asset class for global investors because of their unique return and risk characteristics. We next examine the various types of equity securities traded on global markets and their salient characteristics.

3. TYPES AND CHARACTERISTICS OF EQUITY SECURITIES

Companies finance their operations by issuing either debt or equity securities. A key difference between these securities is that debt is a liability of the issuing company, whereas equity is not. This means that when a company issues debt, it is contractually obligated to repay the amount it borrows (i.e., the principal or face value of the debt) at a specified future

---

[5]The percentages reported in the exhibit are based on samples of the adult population in each country who own equity securities either directly or indirectly through investment or retirement funds. For example, 36 percent of the adult population of Australia in 2014 (approximately 6.5 million people) owned equity securities either directly or indirectly. As noted in the study, it is not appropriate to make absolute comparisons across countries given the differences in methodology, sampling, timing, and definitions that have been used in different countries. However, trends across different countries can be identified.

date. The cost of using these funds is called interest, which the company is contractually obligated to pay until the debt matures or is retired.

When the company issues equity securities, it is not contractually obligated to repay the amount it receives from shareholders, nor is it contractually obligated to make periodic payments to shareholders for the use of their funds. Instead, shareholders have a claim on the company's assets after all liabilities have been paid. Because of this residual claim, equity shareholders are considered to be owners of the company. Investors who purchase equity securities are seeking total return (i.e., capital or price appreciation and dividend income), whereas investors who purchase debt securities (and hold until maturity) are seeking interest income. As a result, equity investors expect the company's management to act in their best interest by making operating decisions that will maximize the market price of their shares (i.e., shareholder wealth).

In addition to common shares (also known as ordinary shares or common stock), companies may also issue preference shares (also known as preferred stock), the other type of equity security. The following sections discuss the different types and characteristics of common and preference securities.

3.1. Common Shares

Common shares represent an ownership interest in a company and are the predominant type of equity security. As a result, investors share in the operating performance of the company, participate in the governance process through voting rights, and have a claim on the company's net assets in the case of liquidation. Companies may choose to pay out some, or all, of their net income in the form of cash dividends to common shareholders, but they are not contractually obligated to do so.[6]

Voting rights provide shareholders with the opportunity to participate in major corporate governance decisions, including the election of its board of directors, the decision to merge with or take over another company, and the selection of outside auditors. Shareholder voting generally takes place during a company's annual meeting. As a result of geographic limitations and the large number of shareholders, it is often not feasible for shareholders to attend the annual meeting in person. For this reason, shareholders may **vote by proxy**, which allows a designated party—such as another shareholder, a shareholder representative, or management—to vote on the shareholders' behalf.

Regular shareholder voting, where each share represents one vote, is referred to as **statutory voting**. Although it is the common method of voting, it is not always the most appropriate one to use to elect a board of directors. To better serve shareholders who own a small number of shares, **cumulative voting** is often used. Cumulative voting allows shareholders to direct their total voting rights to specific candidates, as opposed to having to allocate their voting rights evenly among all candidates. Total voting rights are based on the number of shares owned multiplied by the number of board directors being elected. For example, under cumulative voting, if four board directors are to be elected, a shareholder who owns 100 shares is entitled to 400 votes and can either cast all 400 votes in favor of a single candidate or spread them across the candidates in any proportion. In contrast, under

---

[6]It is also possible for companies to pay more than the current period's net income as dividends. Such payout policies are, however, generally not sustainable in the long run.

statutory voting, a shareholder would be able to cast only a maximum of 100 votes for each candidate.

The key benefit to cumulative voting is that it allows shareholders with a small number of shares to apply all of their votes to one candidate, thus providing the opportunity for a higher level of representation on the board than would be allowed under statutory voting.

Exhibit 7 describes the rights of Viacom Corporation's shareholders. In this case, a dual-share arrangement allows the founding chairman and his family to control more than 70 percent of the voting rights through the ownership of Class A shares. This arrangement gives them the ability to exert control over the board of director election process, corporate decision-making, and other important aspects of managing the company. A cumulative voting arrangement for any minority shareholders of Class A shares would improve their board representation.

EXHIBIT 7   Share Class Arrangements at Viacom Corporation[7]

Viacom has two classes of common stock: Class A, which is the voting stock, and Class B, which is the non-voting stock. There is no difference between the two classes except for voting rights; they generally trade within a close price range of each other. There are, however, far more shares of Class B outstanding, so most of the trading occurs in that class.

- **Voting Rights**—Holders of Class A common stock are entitled to one vote per share. Holders of Class B common stock do not have any voting rights, except as required by Delaware law. Generally, all matters to be voted on by Viacom stockholders must be approved by a majority of the aggregate voting power of the shares of Class A common stock present in person or represented by proxy, except as required by Delaware law.
- **Dividends**—Stockholders of Class A common stock and Class B common stock will share ratably in any cash dividend declared by the Board of Directors, subject to any preferential rights of any outstanding preferred stock. Viacom does not currently pay a cash dividend, and any decision to pay a cash dividend in the future will be at the discretion of the Board of Directors and will depend on many factors.
- **Conversion**—So long as there are 5,000 shares of Class A common stock outstanding, each share of Class A common stock will be convertible at the option of the holder of such share into one share of Class B common stock.
- **Liquidation Rights**—In the event of liquidation, dissolution, or winding-up of Viacom, all stockholders of common stock, regardless of class, will be entitled to share ratably in any assets available for distributions to stockholders of shares of Viacom common stock subject to the preferential rights of any outstanding preferred stock.

---

[7]This information has been adapted from Viacom's investor relations website and its 10-K filing with the US Securities and Exchange Commission; see www.viacom.com.

- **Split, Subdivision, or Combination**—In the event of a split, subdivision, or combination of the outstanding shares of Class A common stock or Class B common stock, the outstanding shares of the other class of common stock will be divided proportionally.
- **Preemptive Rights**—Shares of Class A common stock and Class B common stock do not entitle a stockholder to any preemptive rights enabling a stockholder to subscribe for or receive shares of stock of any class or any other securities convertible into shares of stock of any class of Viacom.

As seen in Exhibit 7, companies can issue different classes of common shares (Class A and Class B shares), with each class offering different ownership rights.[8] For example, as shown in Exhibit 8, the Ford Motor Company has Class A shares ("Common Stock"), which are owned by the investing public. It also has Class B shares, which are owned only by the Ford family. The exhibit contains an excerpt from Ford's *2017 Annual Report* (p. 144). Class A shareholders have 60 percent voting rights, whereas Class B shareholders have 40 percent. In the case of liquidation, however, Class B shareholders will not only receive the first US$0.50 per share that is available for distribution (as will Class A shareholders), but they will also receive the next US$1.00 per share that is available for distribution before Class A shareholders receive anything else. Thus, Class B shareholders have an opportunity to receive a larger proportion of distributions upon liquidation than do Class A shareholders.[9]

EXHIBIT 8   Share Class Arrangements at Ford Motor Company[10]

NOTE 21. CAPITAL STOCK AND AMOUNTS PER SHARE

All general voting power is vested in the holders of Common Stock and Class B Stock. Holders of our Common Stock have 60% of the general voting power and holders of our Class B Stock are entitled to such number of votes per share as will give them the remaining 40%. Shares of Common Stock and Class B Stock share equally in dividends when and as paid, with stock dividends payable in shares of stock of the class held.

---

[8]In some countries, including the United States, companies can issue different classes of shares, with Class A shares being the most common. The role and function of different classes of shares is described in more detail in Exhibit 8.

[9]For example, if US$2.00 per share is available for distribution, the Common Stock (Class A) shareholders will receive US$0.50 per share, while the Class B shareholders will receive US$1.50 per share. However, if there is US$3.50 per share available for distribution, the Common Stock shareholders will receive a total of US$1.50 per share and the Class B shareholders will receive a total of US$2.00 per share.

[10]Extracted from Ford Motor Company's *2017 Annual Report* (http://s22.q4cdn.com/857684434/files/doc_financials/2017/annual/Final-Annual-Report-2017.pdf).

If liquidated, each share of Common Stock is entitled to the first $0.50 available for distribution to holders of Common Stock and Class B Stock, each share of Class B Stock is entitled to the next $1.00 so available, each share of Common Stock is entitled to the next $0.50 so available, and each share of Common and Class B Stock is entitled to an equal amount thereafter.

3.2. Preference Shares

Preference shares (or preferred stock) rank above common shares with respect to the payment of dividends and the distribution of the company's net assets upon liquidation.[11] However, preference shareholders generally do not share in the operating performance of the company and do not have any voting rights, unless explicitly allowed for at issuance. Preference shares have characteristics of both debt securities and common shares. Similar to the interest payments on debt securities, the dividends on preference shares are fixed and are generally higher than the dividends on common shares. However, unlike interest payments, preference dividends are not contractual obligations of the company. Similar to common shares, preference shares can be perpetual (i.e., no fixed maturity date), can pay dividends indefinitely, and can be callable or putable.

Exhibit 9 provides an example of callable preference shares issued by the GDL Fund to raise capital to redeem the remaining outstanding Series B Preferred shares. In this case, the purchaser of the shares will receive an ongoing dividend from the GDL Fund. If the GDL Fund chooses to buy back the shares, it must do so at the $50 a share liquidation preference price. The purchasers of the shares also have the right to put back the shares to GDL at the $50 a share price.

EXHIBIT 9   Callable Stock offering by the GDL Fund[12]

RYE, NY—March 26, 2018—The GDL Fund (NYSE:GDL) (the "Fund") is pleased to announce the completion of a rights offering (the "Offering") in which the Fund issued 2,624,025 Series C Cumulative Puttable and Callable Preferred Shares (the "Series C Preferred"), totaling $131,201,250. Pursuant to the Offering, the Fund issued one non-transferable right (a "Right") for each outstanding Series B Cumulative Puttable and Callable Preferred Share (the "Series B Preferred") of the Fund to Series B Preferred shareholders of record as of February 14, 2018. Holders of Rights were entitled to purchase the Series C Preferred with any combination of cash or surrender of the Series B Preferred at

---

[11]Preference shares have a lower priority than debt in the case of liquidation. That is, debt holders have a higher claim on a firm's assets in the event of liquidation and will receive what is owed to them first, followed by preference shareholders and then common shareholders.

[12]https://www.businesswire.com/news/home/20180326005609/en/GDL-Fund-Successfully-Completes-Offering-Issues-131

liquidation preference. Therefore, one Right plus $50.00, or one Right plus one share of Series B Preferred with a liquidation value of $50.00 per share, was required to purchase each share of the Series C Preferred. The Offering expired at 5:00 PM Eastern Time on March 20, 2018.

Dividends on preference shares can be cumulative, non-cumulative, participating, non-participating, or some combination thereof (i.e., cumulative participating, cumulative non-participating, non-cumulative participating, non-cumulative non-participating).

Dividends on **cumulative preference shares** accrue so that if the company decides not to pay a dividend in one or more periods, the unpaid dividends accrue and must be paid in full before dividends on common shares can be paid. In contrast, **non-cumulative preference shares** have no such provision. This means that any dividends that are not paid in the current or subsequent periods are forfeited permanently and are not accrued over time to be paid at a later date. However, the company is still not permitted to pay any dividends to common shareholders in the current period unless preferred dividends have been paid first.

Participating preference shares entitle the shareholders to receive the standard preferred dividend plus the opportunity to receive an additional dividend if the company's profits exceed a pre-specified level. In addition, participating preference shares can also contain provisions that entitle shareholders to an additional distribution of the company's assets upon liquidation, above the par (or face) value of the preference shares. **Non-participating preference shares** do not allow shareholders to share in the profits of the company. Instead, shareholders are entitled to receive only a fixed dividend payment and the par value of the shares in the event of liquidation. The use of participating preference shares is much more common for smaller, riskier companies where the possibility of future liquidation is more of a concern to investors.

Preference shares can also be convertible. **Convertible preference shares** entitle shareholders to convert their shares into a specified number of common shares. This conversion ratio is determined at issuance. Convertible preference shares have the following advantages:

- They allow investors to earn a higher dividend than if they invested in the company's common shares.
- They allow investors the opportunity to share in the profits of the company.
- They allow investors to benefit from a rise in the price of the common shares through the conversion option.
- Their price is less volatile than the underlying common shares because the dividend payments are known and more stable.

As a result, the use of convertible preference shares is a popular financing option in venture capital and private equity transactions in which the issuing companies are considered to be of higher risk and when it may be years before the issuing company "goes public" (i.e., issues common shares to the public).

Exhibit 10 provides examples of the types and characteristics of preference shares as issued by Tsakos Energy Navigation Ltd (TNP.PRE).

EXHIBIT 10   Examples of Preference Shares Issued by TEN Ltd[13]

Athens, Greece, June 21, 2018—TEN Ltd. ("TEN") (NYSE: TNP), a leading diversified crude, product and LNG tanker operator, today announced the pricing of its public offering of its Series F Fixed-to-Floating Rate Cumulative Redeemable Perpetual Preferred Shares, par value $1.00 per share, liquidation preference $25.00 per share ("Series F Preferred Shares"). TEN will issue 5,400,000 Series F Preferred Shares at a price to the public of $25.00 per share. Dividends will be payable on the Series F Preferred Shares to July 30, 2028 at a fixed rate equal to 9.50% per annum and from July 30, 2028, if not redeemed, at a floating rate. In connection with the offering, TEN has granted the underwriters a 30-day option to purchase 810,000 additional Series F Preferred Shares, which, if exercised in full, would result in total gross proceeds of $155,250,000. TEN intends to use the net proceeds from the offering for general corporate purposes, which may include making vessel acquisitions and/or strategic investments and preferred share redemptions. Following the offering, TEN intends to file an application to list the Series F Preferred Shares on the New York Stock Exchange. The offering is expected to close on or about June 28, 2018.

4. PRIVATE VERSUS PUBLIC EQUITY SECURITIES

Our discussion so far has focused on equity securities that are issued and traded in public markets and on exchanges. Equity securities can also be issued and traded in private equity markets. **Private equity securities** are issued primarily to institutional investors via non-public offerings, such as private placements. Because they are not listed on public exchanges, there is no active secondary market for these securities. As a result, private equity securities do not have "market determined" quoted prices, are highly illiquid, and require negotiations between investors in order to be traded. In addition, financial statements and other important information needed to determine the fair value of private equity securities may be difficult to obtain because the issuing companies are typically not required by regulatory authorities to publish this information.

There are three primary types of private equity investments: venture capital, leveraged buyouts, and private investment in public equity (or PIPE). **Venture capital** investments provide "seed" or start-up capital, early-stage financing, or mezzanine financing to companies that are in the early stages of development and require additional capital for expansion. These funds are then used to finance the company's product development and growth. Venture capitalists range from family and friends to wealthy individuals and private equity funds. Because the equity securities issued to venture capitalists are not publicly traded, they generally require a commitment of funds for a relatively long period of time; the opportunity to "exit" the investment is typically within 3 to 10 years from the initial start-up. The exit return earned by these private equity investors is based on the price that the securities can be

---

[13]https://www.tenn.gr/wp-content/uploads/2018/06/tenn062118.pdf

sold for if and when the start-up company first goes public, either via an **initial public offering** (IPO) on the stock market or by being sold to other investors.

A **leveraged buyout** (LBO) occurs when a group of investors (such as the company's management or a private equity partnership) uses a large amount of debt to purchase all of the outstanding common shares of a publicly traded company. In cases where the group of investors acquiring the company is primarily comprised of the company's existing management, the transaction is referred to as a **management buyout** (MBO). After the shares are purchased, they cease to trade on an exchange and the investor group takes full control of the company. In other words, the company is taken "private" or has been privatized. Companies that are candidates for these types of transactions generally have large amounts of undervalued assets (which can be sold to reduce debt) and generate high levels of cash flows (which are used to make interest and principal payments on the debt). The ultimate objective of a buyout (LBO or MBO) is to restructure the acquired company and later take it "public" again by issuing new shares to the public in the primary market.

The third type of private investment is a **private investment in public equity**, or PIPE.[14] This type of investment is generally sought by a public company that is in need of additional capital quickly and is willing to sell a sizeable ownership position to a private investor or investor group. For example, a company may require a large investment of new equity funds in a short period of time because it has significant expansion opportunities, is facing high levels of indebtedness, or is experiencing a rapid deterioration in its operations. Depending on how urgent the need is and the size of the capital requirement, the private investor may be able to purchase shares in the company at a significant discount to the publicly-quoted market price. Exhibit 11 contains a recent PIPE transaction for the health care company TapImmune, which also included the proposed merger with Maker Therapeutics.

EXHIBIT 11   Example of a PIPE Transaction[15]

JACKSONVILLE, Florida, June 8, 2018—TapImmune Inc. (NASDAQ: TPIV), a clinical-stage immuno-oncology company, today announced that it has entered into security purchase agreements with certain institutional and accredited investors in connection with a private placement of its equity securities. The private placement will be led by New Enterprise Associates (NEA) with participation from Aisling Capital and Perceptive Advisors, among other new and existing investors. The private placement is expected to be completed concurrently with the closing of the proposed merger between TapImmune Inc. and Marker Therapeutics, Inc., which was previously announced on May 15, 2018.

Upon closing the private placement, TapImmune will issue 17,500,000 shares of its common stock at a price of $4.00 per share. The aggregate offering size, before deducting the placement agent fees and other offering expenses, is expected to be $70 million. Additionally, TapImmune will issue warrants to purchase 13,125,000 shares of TapImmune common stock at an exercise price of $5.00 per share that will be exercisable for a period of five years from the date of issuance. The closing of the

---

[14]The term PIPE is widely used in the United States and is also used internationally, including in emerging markets.

[15]https://tapimmune.com/2018/06/tapimmune-announces-pricing-of-70-million-private-placement/

transaction, which is subject to the closing of the merger with Marker, the approval by TapImmune's stockholders as required by NASDAQ Stock Market Rules, and other customary closing conditions, is anticipated to occur by the end of the third quarter of 2018.

While the global private equity market is relatively small in comparison to the global public equity market, it has experienced considerable growth over the past three decades. According to a study of the private equity market sponsored by the *World Economic Forum* and spanning the period 1970–2007, approximately US$3.6 trillion in debt and equity were acquired in leveraged buyouts. Of this amount, approximately 75 percent or US$2.7 trillion worth of transactions occurred during 2001–2007.[16] This pace continued with a further US$2.9 trillion in transactions occurring during 2008-2017.[17] While the US and the UK markets were the focus of most private equity investments during the 1980s and 1990s, private equity investments outside of these markets have grown substantially in recent years. In addition, the number of companies operating under private equity ownership has also grown. For example, during the mid-1990s, fewer than 2,000 companies were under LBO ownership compared to more than 20,000 companies that were under LBO ownership globally at the beginning of 2017. The holding period for private equity investments has also increased during this time period from 3 to 5 years (1980s and 1990s) to approximately 10 years.[18]

The move to longer holding periods has given private equity investors the opportunity to more effectively and patiently address any underlying operational issues facing the company and to better manage it for long-term value creation. Because of the longer holding periods, more private equity firms are issuing convertible preference shares because they provide investors with greater total return potential through their dividend payments and the ability to convert their shares into common shares during an IPO.

In operating a publicly traded company, management often feels pressured to focus on short-term results[19] (e.g., meeting quarterly sales and earnings targets from analysts biased toward near-term price performance) instead of operating the company to obtain long-term sustainable revenue and earnings growth. By "going private," management can adopt a more long-term focus and can eliminate certain costs that are necessary to operate a publicly traded company—such as the cost of meeting regulatory and stock exchange filing requirements, the cost of maintaining investor relations departments to communicate with shareholders and the media, and the cost of holding quarterly analyst conference calls.

As described above, public equity markets are much larger than private equity networks and allow companies more opportunities to raise capital that is subsequently actively traded in secondary markets. By operating under public scrutiny, companies are incentivized to be more open in terms of corporate governance and executive compensation to ensure that they are acting for the benefit of shareholders. In fact, some studies have shown that private equity firms score lower in terms of corporate governance effectiveness, which may be attributed to the fact that shareholders, analysts, and other stakeholders are able to influence management when corporate governance and other policies are public.

---

[16]Stromberg (2008).
[17]https://www.statista.com/statistics/270195/global-private-equity-deal-value/
[18]See, for example, Bailey, Wirth, and Zapol (2005).
[19]See, for example, Graham, Harvey, and Rajgopal (2005).

5. INVESTING IN NON-DOMESTIC EQUITY SECURITIES

Technological innovations and the growth of electronic information exchanges (electronic trading networks, the internet, etc.) have accelerated the integration and growth of global financial markets. As detailed previously, global capital markets have expanded at a much more rapid rate than global GDP in recent years; both primary and secondary international markets have benefited from the enhanced ability to rapidly and openly exchange information. Increased integration of equity markets has made it easier and less expensive for companies to raise capital and to expand their shareholder base beyond their local market. Integration has also made it easier for investors to invest in companies that are located outside of their domestic markets. This has enabled investors to further diversify and improve the risk and return characteristics of their portfolios by adding a class of assets with lower correlations to local country assets.

One barrier to investing globally is that many countries still impose "foreign restrictions" on individuals and companies from other countries that want to invest in their domestic companies. There are three primary reasons for these restrictions. The first is to limit the amount of control that foreign investors can exert on domestic companies. For example, some countries prevent foreign investors from acquiring a majority interest in domestic companies. The second is to give domestic investors the opportunity to own shares in the foreign companies that are conducting business in their country. For example, the Swedish home furnishings retailer IKEA abandoned efforts to invest in parts of the Asia/Pacific region because local governments did not want IKEA to maintain complete ownership of its stores. The third reason is to reduce the volatility of capital flows into and out of domestic equity markets. For example, one of the main consequences of the Asian Financial Crisis in 1997–98 was the large outflow of capital from such emerging market countries as Thailand, Indonesia, and South Korea. These outflows led to dramatic declines in the equity markets of these countries and significant currency devaluations and resulted in many governments placing restrictions on capital flows. Today, many of these same markets have built up currency reserves to better withstand capital outflows inherent in economic contractions and periods of financial market turmoil.

Studies have shown that reducing restrictions on foreign ownership has led to improved equity market performance over the long term.[20] Although restrictions vary widely, more countries are allowing increasing levels of foreign ownership. For example, Australia has sought tax reforms as a means to encourage international demand for its managed funds in order to increase its role as an international financial center.

Over the past two decades, three trends have emerged: a) an increasing number of companies have issued shares in markets outside of their home country; b) the number of companies whose shares are traded in markets outside of their home has increased; and c) an increasing number of companies are dual listed, which means that their shares are simultaneously issued and traded in two or more markets. Companies located in emerging markets have particularly benefited from these trends because they no longer have to be concerned with capital constraints or lack of liquidity in their domestic markets. These companies have found it easier to raise capital in the markets of developed countries because these markets generally have higher levels of liquidity and more stringent financial reporting requirements and accounting standards. Being listed on an international exchange has a

---

[20]See, for example, Henry and Chari (2004).

number of benefits. It can increase investor awareness about the company's products and services, enhance the liquidity of the company's shares, and increase corporate transparency because of the additional market exposure and the need to meet a greater number of filing requirements.

Technological advancements have made it easier for investors to trade shares in foreign markets. The German insurance company Allianz SE recently delisted its shares from the NYSE and certain European markets because international investors increasingly traded its shares on the Frankfurt Stock Exchange. Exhibit 12 illustrates the extent to which the institutional shareholder base at BASF, a large German chemical corporation, has become increasingly global in nature.

EXHIBIT 12   Example of Increased Globalization of Share Ownership[21]

BASF is one of the largest publicly owned companies with over 500,000 shareholders and a high free float. An analysis of the shareholder structure carried out in March 2018 showed that, at 21% of share capital, the United States and Canada made up the largest regional group of institutional investors. Institutional investors from Germany made up 12%. Shareholders from United Kingdom and Ireland held 12% of BASF shares, while a further 17% are held by institutional investors from the rest of Europe. Around 28% of the company's share capital is held by private investors, most of whom are resident in Germany.

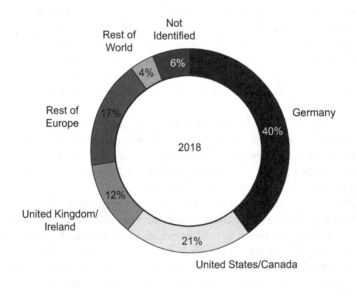

[21]Adapted from BASF's investor relations website (www.basf.com). **Free float** refers to the extent that shares are readily and freely tradable in the secondary market.

5.1. Direct Investing

Investors can use a variety of methods to invest in the equity of companies outside of their local market. The most obvious is to buy and sell securities directly in foreign markets. However, this means that all transactions—including the purchase and sale of shares, dividend payments, and capital gains—are in the company's, not the investor's, domestic currency. In addition, investors must be familiar with the trading, clearing, and settlement regulations and procedures of that market. Investing directly often results in less transparency and more volatility because audited financial information may not be provided on a regular basis and the market may be less liquid. Alternatively, investors can use such securities as depository receipts and global registered shares, which represent the equity of international companies and are traded on local exchanges and in the local currencies. With these securities, investors have to worry less about currency conversions (price quotations and dividend payments are in the investor's local currency), unfamiliar market practices, and differences in accounting standards. The sections that follow discuss various securities that investors can invest in outside of their home market.

5.2. Depository Receipts

A **depository receipt**[22] (DR) is a security that trades like an ordinary share on a local exchange and represents an economic interest in a foreign company. It allows the publicly listed shares of a foreign company to be traded on an exchange outside its domestic market. A depository receipt is created when the equity shares of a foreign company are deposited in a bank (i.e., the depository) in the country on whose exchange the shares will trade. The depository then issues receipts that represent the shares that were deposited. The number of receipts issued and the price of each DR is based on a ratio, which specifies the number of depository receipts to the underlying shares. Consequently, a DR may represent one share of the underlying stock, many shares of the underlying stock, or a fractional share of the underlying stock. The price of each DR will be affected by factors that affect the price of the underlying shares, such as company fundamentals, market conditions, analysts' recommendations, and exchange rate movements. In addition, any short-term valuation discrepancies between shares traded on multiple exchanges represent a quick arbitrage profit opportunity for astute traders to exploit. The responsibilities of the **depository bank** that issues the receipts include acting as custodian and as a registrar. This entails handling dividend payments, other taxable events, stock splits, and serving as the transfer agent for the foreign company whose securities the DR represents. The Bank of New York Mellon is the largest depository bank; however, Deutsche Bank, JPMorgan, and Citibank also offer depository services.[23]

A DR can be **sponsored** or **unsponsored**. A sponsored DR is when the foreign company whose shares are held by the depository has a direct involvement in the issuance of the receipts. Investors in sponsored DRs have the same rights as the direct owners of the common shares (e.g., the right to vote and the right to receive dividends). In contrast, with an unsponsored DR, the underlying foreign company has no involvement with the issuance of the receipts. Instead, the depository purchases the foreign company's shares in its domestic

---

[22]Note that the spellings *depositary* and *depository* are used interchangeably in financial markets. In this chapter, we use the spelling *depository* throughout.
[23]Boubakri, Cosset, and Samet (2010).

market and then issues the receipts through brokerage firms in the depository's local market. In this case, the depository bank, not the investors in the DR, retains the voting rights. Sponsored DRs are generally subject to greater reporting requirements than unsponsored DRs. In the United States, for example, sponsored DRs must be registered (meet the reporting requirements) with the US Securities and Exchange Commission (SEC). Exhibit 13 contains an example of a sponsored DR issued by Alibaba in September 2014.

EXHIBIT 13   Sponsored Depository Receipts[24]

NEW YORK—(BUSINESS WIRE)—Citi today announced that Alibaba Group Holding Limited ("Alibaba Group") has appointed Citi's Issuer Services business, acting through Citibank, N.A., as the depositary bank for its American Depositary Receipt ("ADR") program. Alibaba Group's ADRs, which began trading on September 19, 2014, represent the largest Depositary Receipt program in initial public offering market history.

Alibaba Group's ADR program was established through a $25.03 billion initial public offering of 368,122,000 American Depositary Shares ("ADSs"), representing ordinary shares of Alibaba Group, which was priced at $68 per ADS on September 18, 2014. The IPO ranks as the largest in history. The ADRs are listed on the New York Stock Exchange (the "NYSE") under the trading symbol BABA. Each ADS represents one ordinary share of the Company. In its role as depositary bank, Citibank will hold the underlying ordinary shares through its local custodian and issue ADSs representing such shares. Alibaba Group's ADSs trade on the NYSE in ADR form.

There are two types of depository receipts: Global depository receipts (GDRs) and American depository receipts (ADRs), which are described below.

5.2.1. Global Depository Receipts

A **global depository receipt** (GDR) is issued outside of the company's home country and outside of the United States. The depository bank that issues GDRs is generally located (or has branches) in the countries on whose exchanges the shares are traded. A key advantage of GDRs is that they are not subject to the foreign ownership and capital flow restrictions that may be imposed by the issuing company's home country because they are sold outside of that country. The issuing company selects the exchange where the GDR is to be traded based on such factors as investors' familiarity with the company or the existence of a large international investor base. The London and Luxembourg exchanges were the first ones to trade GDRs. Some other stock exchanges trading GDRs are the Dubai International Financial Exchange and the Singapore Stock Exchange. Currently, the London and Luxembourg exchanges are where most GDRs are traded because they can be issued in a more timely manner and at a lower cost. Regardless of the exchange they are traded on, the majority of GDRs are denominated in US dollars, although the number of GDRs denominated in pound sterling and euros is increasing. Note that although GDRs cannot be listed on US exchanges, they can be privately placed with institutional investors based in the United States.

---

[24]https://www.businesswire.com/news/home/20140924005984/en/Citi-Appointed-Depositary-Bank-Alibaba-Group-Holding

5.2.2. American Depository Receipts

An **American depository receipt** (ADR) is a US dollar-denominated security that trades like a common share on US exchanges. First created in 1927, ADRs are the oldest type of depository receipts and are currently the most commonly traded depository receipts. They enable foreign companies to raise capital from US investors. Note that an ADR is one form of a GDR; however, not all GDRs are ADRs because GDRs cannot be publicly traded in the United States. The term **American depository share** (ADS) is often used in tandem with the term ADR. A depository share is a security that is actually traded in the issuing company's domestic market. That is, while American depository receipts are the certificates that are traded on US markets, American depository shares are the underlying shares on which these receipts are based.

There are four primary types of ADRs, with each type having different levels of corporate governance and filing requirements. Level I Sponsored ADRs trade in the over-the-counter (OTC) market and do not require full registration with the Securities and Exchange Commission (SEC). Level II and Level III Sponsored ADRs can trade on the New York Stock Exchange (NYSE), NASDAQ, and American Stock Exchange (AMEX). Level II and III ADRs allow companies to raise capital and make acquisitions using these securities. However, the issuing companies must fulfill all SEC requirements.

The fourth type of ADR, an SEC Rule 144A or a Regulation S depository receipt, does not require SEC registration. Instead, foreign companies are able to raise capital by privately placing these depository receipts with qualified institutional investors or to offshore non-US investors. Exhibit 14 summarizes the main features of ADRs.

EXHIBIT 14   Summary of the Main Features of American Depository Receipts

	Level I (Unlisted)	**Level II** (Listed)	**Level III** (Listed)	**Rule 144A** (Unlisted)
Objectives	Develop and broaden US investor base with existing shares	Develop and broaden US investor base with existing shares	Develop and broaden US investor base with existing/new shares	Access qualified institutional buyers (QIBs)
Raising capital on US markets?	No	No	Yes, through public offerings	Yes, through private placements to QIBs
SEC registration	Form F-6	Form F-6	Forms F-1 and F-6	None
Trading	Over the counter (OTC)	NYSE, NASDAQ, or AMEX	NYSE, NASDAQ, or AMEX	Private offerings, resales, and trading through automated linkages such as PORTAL
Listing fees	Low	High	High	Low
Size and earnings requirements	None	Yes	Yes	None

Source: Adapted from Boubakri, Cosset, and Samet (2010): Table 1.

More than 2,000 DRs, from over 80 countries, currently trade on US exchanges. Based on current statistics, the total market value of DRs issued and traded is estimated at approximately US$2 trillion, or 15 percent of the total dollar value of equities traded in US markets.[25]

5.2.3. Global Registered Share

A **global registered share** (GRS) is a common share that is traded on different stock exchanges around the world in different currencies. Currency conversions are not needed to purchase or sell them, because identical shares are quoted and traded in different currencies. Thus, the same share purchased on the Swiss exchange in Swiss francs can be sold on the Tokyo exchange for Japanese yen. As a result, GRSs offer more flexibility than depository receipts because the shares represent an actual ownership interest in the company that can be traded anywhere and currency conversions are not needed to purchase or sell them. GRSs were created and issued by Daimler Chrysler in 1998 and by UBS AG in 2011.

5.2.4. Basket of Listed Depository Receipts

Another type of global security is a **basket of listed depository receipts** (BLDR), which is an exchange-traded fund (ETF) that represents a portfolio of depository receipts. An ETF is a security that tracks an index but trades like an individual share on an exchange. An equity-ETF is a security that contains a portfolio of equities that tracks an index. It trades throughout the day and can be bought, sold, or sold short, just like an individual share. Like ordinary shares, ETFs can also be purchased on margin and used in hedging or arbitrage strategies. The BLDR is a specific class of ETF security that consists of an underlying portfolio of DRs and is designed to track the price performance of an underlying DR index. For example, the Invesco BLDRS Asia 50 ADR Index Fund is a capitalization-weighted ETF designed to track the performance of 50 Asian market-based ADRs.

6. RISK AND RETURN CHARACTERISTICS OF EQUITY SECURITIES

Different types of equity securities have different ownership claims on a company's net assets. The type of equity security and its features affect its risk and return characteristics. The following sections discuss the different return and risk characteristics of equity securities.

6.1. Return Characteristics of Equity Securities

There are two main sources of equity securities' total return: price change (or capital gain) and dividend income. The price change represents the difference between the purchase price (P_{t-1}) and the sale price (P_t) of a share at the end of time $t-1$ and t, respectively. Cash or stock dividends (D_t) represent distributions that the company makes to its shareholders during period t. Therefore, an equity security's total return is calculated as:

$$\text{Total return, } R_t = (P_t - P_{t-1} + D_t)/P_{t-1} \tag{1}$$

For non-dividend-paying stocks, the total return consists of price appreciation only. Companies that are in the early stages of their life cycle generally do not pay dividends

---

[25] *JPMorgan Depositary Receipt Guide* (2005):4.

because earnings and cash flows are reinvested to finance the company's growth. In contrast, companies that are in the mature phase of their life cycle may not have as many profitable growth opportunities; therefore, excess cash flows are often returned to investors via the payment of regular dividends or through share repurchases.

For investors who purchase depository receipts or foreign shares directly, there is a third source of return: **foreign exchange gains (or losses)**. Foreign exchange gains arise because of the change in the exchange rate between the investor's currency and the currency that the foreign shares are denominated in. For example, US investors who purchase the ADRs of a Japanese company will earn an additional return if the yen appreciates relative to the US dollar. Conversely, these investors will earn a lower total return if the yen depreciates relative to the US dollar. For example, if the total return for a Japanese company was 10 percent in Japan and the yen depreciated by 10 percent against the US dollar, the total return of the ADR would be (approximately) 0 percent. If the yen had instead appreciated by 10 percent against the US dollar, the total return of the ADR would be (approximately) 20 percent.

Investors that only consider price appreciation overlook an important source of return: the compounding that results from reinvested dividends. Reinvested dividends are cash dividends that the investor receives and uses to purchase additional shares. As Exhibit 15 shows, in the long run total returns on equity securities are dramatically influenced by the compounding effect of reinvested dividends. Between 1900 and 2016, US$1 invested in US equities in 1900 would have grown in *real* terms to US$1,402 with dividends reinvested, but to just US$11.9 when taking only the price appreciation or capital gain into account. This corresponds to a real compounded return of 6.4 percent per year with dividends reinvested, versus only 2.1 percent per year without dividends reinvested. The comparable ending real wealth for bonds and bills are US$9.8 and US$2.60, respectively. These ending real wealth figures correspond to annualized real compounded returns of 2.0 percent on bonds and 0.8 percent on bills.

EXHIBIT 15   Impact of Reinvested Dividends on Cumulative Real Returns in the US and UK Equity Market: 1900–2016

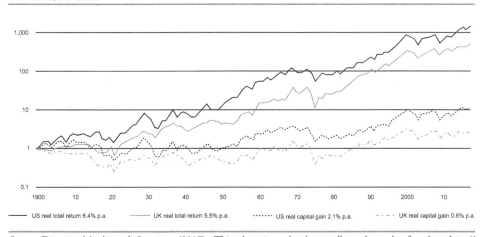

Source: Dimson, Marsh, and Staunton (2017). This chart is updated annually and can be found at http://publications.credit-suisse.com/index.cfm/publikationen-shop/research-institute/.

6.2. Risk of Equity Securities

The risk of any security is based on the uncertainty of its future cash flows. The greater the uncertainty of its future cash flows, the greater the risk and the more variable or volatile the security's price. As discussed above, an equity security's total return is determined by its price change and dividends. Therefore, the risk of an equity security can be defined as the uncertainty of its expected (or future) total return. Risk is most often measured by calculating the standard deviation of the equity's expected total return.

A variety of different methods can be used to estimate an equity's expected total return and risk. One method uses the equity's average historical return and the standard deviation of this return as proxies for its expected future return and risk. Another method involves estimating a range of future returns over a specified period of time, assigning probabilities to those returns, and then calculating an expected return and a standard deviation of return based on this information.

The type of equity security, as well as its characteristics, affects the uncertainty of its future cash flows and therefore its risk. In general, preference shares are less risky than common shares for three main reasons:

1. Dividends on preference shares are known and fixed, and they account for a large portion of the preference shares' total return. Therefore, there is less uncertainty about future cash flows.
2. Preference shareholders receive dividends and other distributions before common shareholders.
3. The amount preference shareholders will receive if the company is liquidated is known and fixed as the par (or face) value of their shares. However, there is no guarantee that investors will receive that amount if the company experiences financial difficulty.

With common shares, however, a larger portion of shareholders' total return (or all of their total return for non-dividend shares) is based on future price appreciation and future dividends are unknown. If the company is liquidated, common shareholders will receive whatever amount (if any) is remaining after the company's creditors and preference shareholders have been paid. In summary, because the uncertainty surrounding the total return of preference shares is less than common shares, preference shares have lower risk and lower expected return than common shares.

It is important to note that some preference shares and common shares can be riskier than others because of their associated characteristics. For example, from an investor's point of view, putable common or preference shares are less risky than their callable or non-callable counterparts because they give the investor the option to sell the shares to the issuer at a pre-determined price. This pre-determined price establishes a minimum price that investors will receive and reduces the uncertainty associated with the security's future cash flow. As a result, putable shares generally pay a lower dividend than non-putable shares.

Because the major source of total return for preference shares is dividend income, the primary risk affecting all preference shares is the uncertainty of future dividend payments. Regardless of the preference shares' features (callable, putable, cumulative, etc.), the greater the uncertainty surrounding the issuer's ability to pay dividends, the greater the risk. Because the ability of a company to pay dividends is based on its future cash flows and net income, investors try to estimate these amounts by examining past trends or forecasting future amounts. The more earnings and the greater amount of cash flow that the company has had, or is expected to have, the lower the uncertainty and risk associated with its ability to pay future dividends.

Callable common or preference shares are riskier than their non-callable counterparts because the issuer has the option to redeem the shares at a pre-determined price. Because the call price limits investors' potential future total return, callable shares generally pay a higher dividend to compensate investors for the risk that the shares could be called in the future. Similarly, putable preference shares have lower risk than non-putable preference shares. Cumulative preference shares have lower risk than non-cumulative preference shares because the cumulative feature gives investors the right to receive any unpaid dividends before any dividends can be paid to common shareholders.

7. EQUITY SECURITIES AND COMPANY VALUE

Companies issue equity securities on primary markets to raise capital and increase liquidity. This additional liquidity also provides the corporation an additional "currency" (its equity), which it can use to make acquisitions and provide stock option-based incentives to employees. The primary goal of raising capital is to finance the company's revenue-generating activities in order to increase its net income and maximize the wealth of its shareholders. In most cases, the capital that is raised is used to finance the purchase of long-lived assets, capital expansion projects, research and development, the entry into new product or geographic regions, and the acquisition of other companies. Alternatively, a company may be forced to raise capital to ensure that it continues to operate as a going concern. In these cases, capital is raised to fulfill regulatory requirements, improve capital adequacy ratios, or to ensure that debt covenants are met.

The ultimate goal of management is to increase the book value (shareholders' equity on a company's balance sheet) of the company and maximize the market value of its equity. Although management actions can directly affect the book value of the company (by increasing net income or by selling or purchasing its own shares), they can only indirectly affect the market value of its equity. The book value of a company's equity—the difference between its total assets and total liabilities—increases when the company retains its net income. The more net income that is earned and retained, the greater the company's book value of equity. Because management's decisions directly influence a company's net income, they also directly influence its book value of equity.

The market value of the company's equity, however, reflects the collective and differing expectations of investors concerning the amount, timing, and uncertainty of the company's future cash flows. Rarely will book value and market value be equal. Although management may be accomplishing its objective of increasing the company's book value, this increase may not be reflected in the market value of the company's equity because it does not affect investors' expectations about the company's future cash flows. A key measure that investors use to evaluate the effectiveness of management in increasing the company's book value is the accounting return on equity.

7.1. Accounting Return on Equity

Return on equity (ROE) is the primary measure that equity investors use to determine whether the management of a company is effectively and efficiently using the capital they have provided to generate profits. It measures the total amount of net income available to common shareholders generated by the total equity capital invested in the company. It is computed as net income available to ordinary shareholders (i.e., after preferred dividends have been deducted) divided by the average total book value of equity (BVE). That is:

$$\text{ROE}_t = \frac{\text{NI}_t}{\text{Average BVE}_t} = \frac{\text{NI}_t}{(\text{BVE}_t + \text{BVE}_{t-1})/2} \qquad (2)$$

where NI_t is the net income in year t and the average book value of equity is computed as the book values at the beginning and end of year t divided by 2. Return on equity assumes that the net income produced in the current year is generated by the equity existing at the beginning of the year and any new equity that was invested during the year. Note that some formulas only use shareholders' equity at the beginning of year t (that is, the end of year $t-1$) in the denominator. This assumes that only the equity existing at the beginning of the year was used to generate the company's net income during the year. That is:

$$\text{ROE}_t = \frac{\text{NI}_t}{\text{BVE}_{t-1}} \qquad (3)$$

Both formulas are appropriate to use as long as they are applied consistently. For example, using beginning of the year book value is appropriate when book values are relatively stable over time or when computing ROE for a company annually over a period of time. Average book value is more appropriate if a company experiences more volatile year-end book values or if the industry convention is to use average book values in calculating ROE.

One caveat to be aware of when computing and analyzing ROE is that net income and the book value of equity are directly affected by management's choice of accounting methods, such as those relating to depreciation (straight line versus accelerated methods) or inventories (first in, first out versus weighted average cost). Different accounting methods can make it difficult to compare the return on equity of companies even if they operate in the same industry. It may also be difficult to compare the ROE of the same company over time if its accounting methods have changed during that time.

Exhibit 16 contains information on the net income and total book value of shareholders' equity for three **blue chip** (widely held large market capitalization companies that are considered financially sound and are leaders in their respective industry or local stock market) pharmaceutical companies: Pfizer, Novartis AG, and GlaxoSmithKline. The data are for their financial years ending December 2015 through December 2017.[26]

EXHIBIT 16   Net Income and Book Value of Equity for Pfizer, Novartis AG, and GlaxoSmithKline (in Thousands of US Dollars)

	Financial Year Ending		
	31 Dec 2015	31 Dec 2016	31 Dec 2017
Pfizer			
Net income	$6,960,000	$7,215,000	$21,308,000
Total stockholders' equity	$64,998,000	$59,840,000	$71,287,000

[26]Pfizer uses US GAAP to prepare its financial statements; Novartis and GlaxoSmithKline use International Financial Reporting Standards. Therefore, it would be inappropriate to compare the ROE of Pfizer to that of Novartis or GlaxoSmithKline.

	Financial Year Ending		
	31 Dec 2015	**31 Dec 2016**	**31 Dec 2017**
Novartis AG			
Net income	$17,783,000	$6,712,000	$7,703,000
Total stockholders' equity	$77,122,000	$74,891,000	$74,227,000
GlaxoSmithKline			
Net income	$12,420,000	$1,126,000	$2,070,700
Total stockholders' equity	$113,092,500	$6,127,800	$4,715,800

Using the average book value of equity, the return on equity for Pfizer for the years ending December 2016 and 2017 can be calculated as:

Return on equity for the year ending December 2016

$$\text{ROE}_{2016} = \frac{\text{NI}_{2016}}{(\text{BVE}_{2015} + \text{BVE}_{2016})/2} = \frac{7,215,000}{(64,998,000 + 59,840,000)/2} = 11.6\%$$

Return on equity for the year ending December 2017

$$\text{ROE}_{2017} = \frac{\text{NI}_{2017}}{(\text{BVE}_{2016} + \text{BVE}_{2017})/2} = \frac{21,308,000}{(59,840,000 + 71,287,000)/2} = 32.5\%$$

Exhibit 17 summarizes the return on equity for Novartis and GlaxoSmithKline in addition to Pfizer for 2016 and 2017.

EXHIBIT 17   Return on Equity for Pfizer, Novartis AG, and GlaxoSmithKline

	31 Dec 2016 (%)	**31 Dec 2017 (%)**
Pfizer	11.6	32.5
Novartis AG	8.8	10.3
GlaxoSmithKline	11.7	38.2

In the case of Pfizer, the ROE of 32.5 percent in 2017 indicates that the company was able to generate a return (profit) of US$0.325 on every US$1.00 of capital invested by shareholders. GlaxoSmithKline almost tripled its return on equity over this period, from 11.7 percent to 38.2 percent. Novartis's ROE remained relatively unchanged.

ROE can increase if net income increases at a faster rate than shareholders' equity or if net income decreases at a slower rate than shareholders' equity. In the case of GlaxoSmithKline, ROE almost tripled between 2016 and 2017 due to its net income almost doubling during the period and due to its average shareholder's fund decreasing by almost 45 percent during the period. Stated differently, in 2017 compared to 2016, GlaxoSmithKline was significantly more effective in using its equity capital to generate profits. In the case of Pfizer, its ROE increased dramatically from 11.6 percent to 32.5 percent in 2017 versus 2016 even though its average shareholder equity increased by around 5 percent due to a nearly tripling of net income during the period.

An important question to ask is whether an increasing ROE is always good. The short answer is, "it depends." One reason ROE can increase is if net income decreases at a slower rate than shareholders' equity, which is not a positive sign. In addition, ROE can increase if the company issues debt and then uses the proceeds to repurchase some of its outstanding shares. This action will increase the company's leverage and make its equity riskier. Therefore, it is important to examine the source of changes in the company's net income *and* shareholders' equity over time. The DuPont formula, which is discussed in a separate chapter, can be used to analyze the sources of changes in a company's ROE.

The book value of a company's equity reflects the historical operating and financing decisions of its management. The market value of the company's equity reflects these decisions as well as investors' collective assessment and expectations about the company's future cash flows generated by its positive net present value investment opportunities. If investors believe that the company has a large number of these future cash flow-generating investment opportunities, the market value of the company's equity will exceed its book value. Exhibit 18 shows the market price per share, the total number of shares outstanding, and the total book value of shareholders' equity for Pfizer, Novartis AG, and GlaxoSmithKline at the end of December 2017. This exhibit also shows the total market value of equity (or market capitalization) computed as the number of shares outstanding multiplied by the market price per share.

EXHIBIT 18   Market Information for Pfizer, Novartis AG, and GlaxoSmithKline (in Thousands of US Dollars except market price)

	Pfizer	Novartis AG	GlaxoSmithKline
Market price	$35.74	$90.99	$18.39
Total shares outstanding	5,952,900	2,317,500	4,892,200
Total shareholders' equity	$71,287,000	$74,227,000	$4,715,800
Total market value of equity	$212,756,646	$210,869,325	$89,967,558

Note that in Exhibit 18, the total market value of equity for Pfizer is computed as:

$$\text{Market value of equity} = \text{Market price per share} \times \text{Shares outstanding}$$

$$\text{Market value of equity} = \text{US\$35.74} \times 5,952,900 = \text{US\$212,756,646}$$

The book value of equity per share for Pfizer can be computed as:

$$\text{Book value of equity per share} = \text{Total shareholders' equity/Shares outstanding}$$

$$\text{Book value of equity per share} = \text{US\$71,287,000/5,952,900} = \text{US\$11.98}$$

A useful ratio to compute is a company's price-to-book ratio, which is also referred to as the market-to-book ratio. This ratio provides an indication of investors' expectations about a company's future investment and cash flow-generating opportunities. The larger the price-to-book ratio (i.e., the greater the divergence between market value per share and book value per share), the more favorably investors will view the company's future investment opportunities. For Pfizer the price-to-book ratio is:

Price-to-book ratio = Market price per share/Book value of equity per share

Price-to-book ratio = US$35.74/US$11.98= 2.98

Exhibit 19 contains the market price per share, book value of equity per share, and price-to-book ratios for Novartis and GlaxoSmithKline in addition to Pfizer.

EXHIBIT 19   Pfizer, Novartis AG, and GlaxoSmithKline

	Pfizer	**Novartis AG**	**GlaxoSmithKline**
Market price per share	$35.74	$90.99	$18.39
Book value of equity per share	$11.98	$32.03	$0.96
Price-to-book ratio	2.98	2.84	19.16

The market price per share of all three companies exceeds their respective book values, so their price-to-book ratios are all greater than 1.00. However, there are significant differences in the sizes of their price-to-book ratios. GlaxoSmithKline has the largest price-to-book ratio, while the price-to-book ratios of Pfizer and Novartis are similar to each other. This suggests that investors believe that GlaxoSmithKline has substantially higher future growth opportunities than either Pfizer or Novartis.

It is not appropriate to compare the price-to-book ratios of companies in different industries because their price-to-book ratios also reflect investors' outlook for the industry. Companies in high growth industries, such as technology, will generally have higher price-to-book ratios than companies in slower growth (i.e., mature) industries, such as heavy equipment. Therefore, it is more appropriate to compare the price-to-book ratios of companies in the same industry. A company with relatively high growth opportunities compared to its industry peers would likely have a higher price-to-book ratio than the average price-to-book ratio of the industry.

Book value and return on equity are useful in helping analysts determine value but can be limited as a primary means to estimate a company's true or intrinsic value, which is the present value of its future projected cash flows. In Exhibit 20, Warren Buffett, one of the most successful investors in the world and CEO of Berkshire Hathaway, provides an explanation of the differences between the book value of a company and its intrinsic value in a letter to shareholders. As discussed above, market value reflects the collective and differing expectations of investors concerning the amount, timing, and uncertainty of a company's future cash flows. A company's intrinsic value can only be estimated because it is impossible to predict the amount and timing of its future cash flows. However, astute investors—such as Buffett—have been able to profit from discrepancies between their estimates of a company's intrinsic value and the market value of its equity.

EXHIBIT 20   Book Value versus Intrinsic Value[27]

We regularly report our per-share book value, an easily calculable number, though one of limited use. Just as regularly, we tell you that what counts is intrinsic value, a number that is impossible to pinpoint but essential to estimate.

For example, in 1964, we could state with certitude that Berkshire's per-share book value was $19.46. However, that figure considerably overstated the stock's intrinsic value since all of the company's resources were tied up in a sub-profitable textile business. Our textile assets had neither going-concern nor liquidation values equal to their carrying values. In 1964, then, anyone inquiring into the soundness of Berkshire's balance sheet might well have deserved the answer once offered up by a Hollywood mogul of dubious reputation: "Don't worry, the liabilities are solid."

Today, Berkshire's situation has reversed: Many of the businesses we control are worth far more than their carrying value. (Those we don't control, such as Coca-Cola or Gillette, are carried at current market values.) We continue to give you book value figures, however, because they serve as a rough, understated, tracking measure for Berkshire's intrinsic value.

We define intrinsic value as the discounted value of the cash that can be taken out of a business during its remaining life. Anyone calculating intrinsic value necessarily comes up with a highly subjective figure that will change both as estimates of future cash flows are revised and as interest rates move. Despite its fuzziness, however, intrinsic value is all-important and is the only logical way to evaluate the relative attractiveness of investments and businesses.

To see how historical input (book value) and future output (intrinsic value) can diverge, let's look at another form of investment, a college education. Think of the education's cost as its "book value." If it is to be accurate, the cost should include the earnings that were foregone by the student because he chose college rather than a job.

For this exercise, we will ignore the important non-economic benefits of an education and focus strictly on its economic value. First, we must estimate the earnings that the graduate will receive over his lifetime and subtract from that figure an estimate of what he would have earned had he lacked his education. That gives us an excess earnings figure, which must then be discounted, at an appropriate interest rate, back to graduation day. The dollar result equals the intrinsic economic value of the education.

7.2. The Cost of Equity and Investors' Required Rates of Return

When companies issue debt (or borrow from a bank) or equity securities, there is a cost associated with the capital that is raised. In order to maximize profitability and shareholder wealth, companies attempt to raise capital efficiently so as to minimize these costs.

When a company issues debt, the cost it incurs for the use of these funds is called the cost of debt. The cost of debt is relatively easy to estimate because it reflects the periodic interest (or coupon) rate that the company is contractually obligated to pay to its

---

[27]Extracts from Berkshire Hathaway's *2008 Annual Report* (www.berkshirehathaway.com).

bondholders (lenders). When a company raises capital by issuing equity, the cost it incurs is called the cost of equity. Unlike debt, however, the company is not contractually obligated to make any payments to its shareholders for the use of their funds. As a result, the cost of equity is more difficult to estimate.

Investors require a return on the funds they provide to the company. This return is called the investor's minimum required rate of return. When investors purchase the company's debt securities, their minimum required rate of return is the periodic rate of interest they charge the company for the use of their funds. Because all of the bondholders receive the same periodic rate of interest, their required rate of return is the same. Therefore, the company's cost of debt and the investors' minimum required rate of return on the debt are the same.

When investors purchase the company's equity securities, their minimum required rate of return is based on the future cash flows they expect to receive. Because these future cash flows are both uncertain and unknown, the investors' minimum required rate of return must be estimated. In addition, the minimum required return may differ across investors based on their expectations about the company's future cash flows. As a result, the company's cost of equity may be different from the investors' minimum required rate of return on equity.[28] Because companies try to raise capital at the lowest possible cost, the company's cost of equity is often used as a proxy for the investors' *minimum* required rate of return.

In other words, the cost of equity can be thought of as the minimum expected rate of return that a company must offer its investors to purchase its shares in the primary market and to maintain its share price in the secondary market. If this expected rate of return is not maintained in the secondary market, then the share price will adjust so that it meets the minimum required rate of return demanded by investors. For example, if investors require a higher rate of return on equity than the company's cost of equity, they would sell their shares and invest their funds elsewhere resulting in a decline in the company's share price. As the share price declined, the cost of equity would increase to reach the higher rate of return that investors require.

Two models commonly used to estimate a company's cost of equity (or investors' minimum required rate of return) are the dividend discount model (DDM) and the capital asset pricing model (CAPM). These models are discussed in detail in other curriculum chapters.

The cost of debt (after tax) and the cost of equity (i.e., the minimum required rates of return on debt and equity) are integral components of the capital budgeting process because they are used to estimate a company's weighted average cost of capital (WACC). Capital budgeting is the decision-making process that companies use to evaluate potential long-term investments. The WACC represents the minimum required rate of return that the company must earn on its long-term investments to satisfy all providers of capital. The company then chooses among those long-term investments with expected returns that are greater than its WACC.

SUMMARY

Equity securities play a fundamental role in investment analysis and portfolio management. The importance of this asset class continues to grow on a global scale because of the need for equity capital in developed and emerging markets, technological innovation, and the growing

---

[28]Another important factor that can cause a firm's cost of equity to differ from investors' required rate of return on equity is the flotation cost associated with equity

sophistication of electronic information exchange. Given their absolute return potential and ability to impact the risk and return characteristics of portfolios, equity securities are of importance to both individual and institutional investors.

This chapter introduces equity securities and provides an overview of global equity markets. A detailed analysis of their historical performance shows that equity securities have offered average real annual returns superior to government bills and bonds, which have provided average real annual returns that have only kept pace with inflation. The different types and characteristics of common and preference equity securities are examined, and the primary differences between public and private equity securities are outlined. An overview of the various types of equity securities listed and traded in global markets is provided, including a discussion of their risk and return characteristics. Finally, the role of equity securities in creating company value is examined as well as the relationship between a company's cost of equity, its accounting return on equity, investors' required rate of return, and the company's intrinsic value.

We conclude with a summary of the key components of this chapter:

- Common shares represent an ownership interest in a company and give investors a claim on its operating performance, the opportunity to participate in the corporate decision-making process, and a claim on the company's net assets in the case of liquidation.
- Callable common shares give the issuer the right to buy back the shares from shareholders at a price determined when the shares are originally issued.
- Putable common shares give shareholders the right to sell the shares back to the issuer at a price specified when the shares are originally issued.
- Preference shares are a form of equity in which payments made to preference shareholders take precedence over any payments made to common stockholders.
- Cumulative preference shares are preference shares on which dividend payments are accrued so that any payments omitted by the company must be paid before another dividend can be paid to common shareholders. Non-cumulative preference shares have no such provisions, implying that the dividend payments are at the company's discretion and are thus similar to payments made to common shareholders.
- Participating preference shares allow investors to receive the standard preferred dividend plus the opportunity to receive a share of corporate profits above a pre-specified amount. Non-participating preference shares allow investors to simply receive the initial investment plus any accrued dividends in the event of liquidation.
- Callable and putable preference shares provide issuers and investors with the same rights and obligations as their common share counterparts.
- Private equity securities are issued primarily to institutional investors in private placements and do not trade in secondary equity markets. There are three types of private equity investments: venture capital, leveraged buyouts, and private investments in public equity (PIPE).
- The objective of private equity investing is to increase the ability of the company's management to focus on its operating activities for long-term value creation. The strategy is to take the "private" company "public" after certain profit and other benchmarks have been met.
- Depository receipts are securities that trade like ordinary shares on a local exchange but which represent an economic interest in a foreign company. They allow the publicly listed shares of foreign companies to be traded on an exchange outside their domestic market.
- American depository receipts are US dollar-denominated securities trading much like standard US securities on US markets. Global depository receipts are similar to ADRs but contain certain restrictions in terms of their ability to be resold among investors.

- Underlying characteristics of equity securities can greatly affect their risk and return.
- A company's accounting return on equity is the total return that it earns on shareholders' book equity.
- A company's cost of equity is the minimum rate of return that stockholders require the company to pay them for investing in its equity.

REFERENCES

Bailey, Elizabeth, Meg Wirth, and David Zapol. 2005. "Venture Capital and Global Health." *Financing Global Health Ventures*, Discussion Paper (September 2005): http://www.commonscapital.com/downloads/Venture_Capital_and_Global_Health.pdf.

Boubakri, Narjess, Jean-Claude Cosset, and Anis Samet. 2010. "The Choice of ADRs." *Journal of Banking and Finance*, vol. 34, no. 9: 2077–2095.

Dimson, Elroy, Paul Marsh, and Mike Staunton. 2018. *Credit Suisse Global Investment Returns Sourcebook 2017*. Credit Suisse Research Institute.

Dimson, Elroy, Paul Marsh, and Mike Staunton. 2018. *Credit Suisse Global Investment Returns Yearbook 2018*. Credit Suisse Research Institute.

Graham, John R., Campbell R. Harvey, and Shiva Rajgopal. 2005. "The Economic Implications of Corporate Financial Reporting." *Journal of Accounting and Economics*, vol. 40, no. 1–3: 3–73.

Henry, Peter Blair, and Anusha Chari. 2004. "Risk Sharing and Asset Prices: Evidence from a Natural Experiment." *Journal of Finance*, vol. 59, no. 3: 1295–1324.

Strömberg, Per. 2008. "The New Demography of Private Equity." *The Global Economic Impact of Private Equity Report 2008*, World Economic Forum.

PRACTICE PROBLEMS

1. Which of the following is *not* a characteristic of common equity?
   A. It represents an ownership interest in the company.
   B. Shareholders participate in the decision-making process.
   C. The company is obligated to make periodic dividend payments.

2. The type of equity voting right that grants one vote for each share of equity owned is referred to as:
   A. proxy voting.
   B. statutory voting.
   C. cumulative voting.

3. All of the following are characteristics of preference shares *except*:
   A. They are either callable or putable.
   B. They generally do not have voting rights.
   C. They do not share in the operating performance of the company.

4. Participating preference shares entitle shareholders to:
   A. participate in the decision-making process of the company.
   B. convert their shares into a specified number of common shares.
   C. receive an additional dividend if the company's profits exceed a pre-determined level.

5. Which of the following statements about private equity securities is *incorrect*?
   A. They cannot be sold on secondary markets.
   B. They have market-determined quoted prices.
   C. They are primarily issued to institutional investors.

6. Venture capital investments:
   A. can be publicly traded.
   B. do not require a long-term commitment of funds.
   C. provide mezzanine financing to early-stage companies.

7. Which of the following statements *most accurately* describes one difference between private and public equity firms?
   A. Private equity firms are focused more on short-term results than public firms.
   B. Private equity firms' regulatory and investor relations operations are less costly than those of public firms.
   C. Private equity firms are incentivized to be more open with investors about governance and compensation than public firms.

8. Emerging markets have benefited from recent trends in international markets. Which of the following has *not* been a benefit of these trends?
   A. Emerging market companies do not have to worry about a lack of liquidity in their home equity markets.
   B. Emerging market companies have found it easier to raise capital in the markets of developed countries.
   C. Emerging market companies have benefited from the stability of foreign exchange markets.

9. When investing in unsponsored depository receipts, the voting rights to the shares in the trust belong to:
   A. the depository bank.
   B. the investors in the depository receipts.
   C. the issuer of the shares held in the trust.

10. With respect to Level III sponsored ADRs, which of the following is *least likely* to be accurate? They:
    A. have low listing fees.
    B. are traded on the NYSE, NASDAQ, and AMEX.
    C. are used to raise equity capital in US markets.

11. A basket of listed depository receipts, or an exchange-traded fund, would *most likely* be used for:
    A. gaining exposure to a single equity.
    B. hedging exposure to a single equity.
    C. gaining exposure to multiple equities.

12. Calculate the total return on a share of equity using the following data:
    Purchase price: $50
    Sale price: $42
    Dividend paid during holding period: $2
    A. −12.0%
    B. −14.3%
    C. −16.0%

13. If a US-based investor purchases a euro-denominated ETF and the euro subsequently depreciates in value relative to the dollar, the investor will have a total return that is:
    A. lower than the ETF's total return.
    B. higher than the ETF's total return.
    C. the same as the ETF's total return.

14. Which of the following is *incorrect* about the risk of an equity security? The risk of an equity security is:
    A. based on the uncertainty of its cash flows.
    B. based on the uncertainty of its future price.
    C. measured using the standard deviation of its dividends.

15. From an investor's point of view, which of the following equity securities is the *least* risky?
    A. Putable preference shares.
    B. Callable preference shares.
    C. Non-callable preference shares.

16. Which of the following is *least likely* to be a reason for a company to issue equity securities on the primary market?
    A. To raise capital.
    B. To increase liquidity.
    C. To increase return on equity.

17. Which of the following is *not* a primary goal of raising equity capital?
    A. To finance the purchase of long-lived assets.
    B. To finance the company's revenue-generating activities.
    C. To ensure that the company continues as a going concern.

18. Which of the following statements is *most accurate* in describing a company's book value?
    A. Book value increases when a company retains its net income.
    B. Book value is usually equal to the company's market value.
    C. The ultimate goal of management is to maximize book value.

19. Calculate the book value of a company using the following information:

Number of shares outstanding	100,000
Price per share	€52
Total assets	€12,000,000
Total liabilities	€7,500,000
Net Income	€2,000,000

    A. €4,500,000.
    B. €5,200,000.
    C. €6,500,000.

20. Which of the following statements is *least accurate* in describing a company's market value?
    A. Management's decisions do not influence the company's market value.
    B. Increases in book value may not be reflected in the company's market value.
    C. Market value reflects the collective and differing expectations of investors.

21. Calculate the return on equity (ROE) of a stable company using the following data:

Total sales	£2,500,000
Net income	£2,000,000
Beginning of year total assets	£50,000,000
Beginning of year total liabilities	£35,000,000
Number of shares outstanding at the end of the year	1,000,000
Price per share at the end of the year	£20

A. 10.0%.
B. 13.3%.
C. 16.7%.

22. Holding all other factors constant, which of the following situations will *most likely* lead to an increase in a company's return on equity?
A. The market price of the company's shares increases.
B. Net income increases at a slower rate than shareholders' equity.
C. The company issues debt to repurchase outstanding shares of equity.

23. Which of the following measures is the *most difficult* to estimate?
A. The cost of debt.
B. The cost of equity.
C. Investors' required rate of return on debt.

24. A company's cost of equity is often used as a proxy for investors':
A. average required rate of return.
B. minimum required rate of return.
C. maximum required rate of return.

CHAPTER 2

MARKET EFFICIENCY

Sean Cleary, PhD, CFA
Howard J. Atkinson, CIMA, ICD.D, CFA
Pamela Peterson Drake, PhD, CFA

LEARNING OUTCOMES

The candidate should be able to:

- describe market efficiency and related concepts, including their importance to investment practitioners;
- distinguish between market value and intrinsic value;
- explain factors that affect a market's efficiency;
- contrast weak-form, semi-strong-form, and strong-form market efficiency;
- explain the implications of each form of market efficiency for fundamental analysis, technical analysis, and the choice between active and passive portfolio management;
- describe market anomalies;
- describe behavioral finance and its potential relevance to understanding market anomalies.

1. INTRODUCTION

Market efficiency concerns the extent to which market prices incorporate available information. If market prices do not fully incorporate information, then opportunities may exist to make a profit from the gathering and processing of information. The subject of market efficiency is, therefore, of great interest to investment managers, as illustrated in Example 1.

EXAMPLE 1   Market Efficiency and Active Manager Selection

The chief investment officer (CIO) of a major university endowment fund has listed eight steps in the active manager selection process that can be applied both to traditional investments (e.g., common equity and fixed-income securities) and to alternative investments (e.g., private equity, hedge funds, and real assets). The first step specified is the evaluation of market opportunity:

> What is the opportunity and why is it there? To answer this question, we start by studying capital markets and the types of managers operating within those markets. We identify market inefficiencies and try to understand their causes, such as regulatory structures or behavioral biases. We can rule out many broad groups of managers and strategies by simply determining that the degree of market inefficiency necessary to support a strategy is implausible. Importantly, we consider the past history of active returns meaningless unless we understand why markets will allow those active returns to continue into the future.[1]

The CIO's description underscores the importance of not assuming that past active returns that might be found in a historical dataset will repeat themselves in the future. **Active returns** refer to returns earned by strategies that do *not* assume that all information is fully reflected in market prices.

Governments and market regulators also care about the extent to which market prices incorporate information. Efficient markets imply informative prices—prices that accurately reflect available information about fundamental values. In market-based economies, market prices help determine which companies (and which projects) obtain capital. If these prices do not efficiently incorporate information about a company's prospects, then it is possible that funds will be misdirected. By contrast, prices that are informative help direct scarce resources and funds available for investment to their highest-valued uses.[2] Informative prices thus promote economic growth. The efficiency of a country's capital markets (in which businesses raise financing) is an important characteristic of a well-functioning financial system.

The remainder of this chapter is organized as follows. Section 2 provides specifics on how the efficiency of an asset market is described and discusses the factors affecting (i.e., contributing to and impeding) market efficiency. Section 3 presents an influential three-way classification of the efficiency of security markets and discusses its implications for fundamental analysis, technical analysis, and portfolio management. Section 4 presents several market anomalies (apparent market inefficiencies that have received enough attention to be individually identified and named) and describes how these anomalies relate to investment strategies. Section 5 introduces behavioral finance and how that field of study relates to market efficiency. A summary concludes the chapter.

---

[1] The CIO is Christopher J. Brightman, CFA, of the University of Virginia Investment Management Company, as reported in Yau, Schneeweis, Robinson, and Weiss (2007, pp. 481–482).
[2] This concept is known as allocative efficiency.

2. THE CONCEPT OF MARKET EFFICIENCY

2.1. The Description of Efficient Markets

An **informationally efficient market** (an **efficient market**) is a market in which asset prices reflect new information quickly and rationally. An efficient market is thus a market in which asset prices reflect all past and present information.[3]

In this section we expand on this definition by clarifying the time frame required for an asset's price to incorporate information as well as describing the elements of information releases assumed under market efficiency. We discuss the difference between market value and intrinsic value and illustrate how inefficiencies or discrepancies between these values can provide profitable opportunities for active investment. As financial markets are generally not considered being either completely efficient or inefficient, but rather falling within a range between the two extremes, we describe a number of factors that contribute to and impede the degree of efficiency of a financial market. Finally, we conclude our overview of market efficiency by illustrating how the costs incurred by traders in identifying and exploiting possible market inefficiencies affect how we interpret market efficiency.

Investment managers and analysts, as noted, are interested in market efficiency because the extent to which a market is efficient affects how many profitable trading opportunities (market inefficiencies) exist. Consistent, superior, risk-adjusted returns (net of all expenses) are not achievable in an efficient market.[4] In an efficient market, a **passive investment** strategy (i.e., buying and holding a broad market portfolio) that does not seek superior risk-adjusted returns can be preferred to an **active investment** strategy because of lower costs (for example, transaction and information-seeking costs). By contrast, in a very inefficient market, opportunities may exist for an active investment strategy to achieve superior risk-adjusted returns (net of all expenses in executing the strategy) as compared with a passive investment strategy. In inefficient markets, an active investment strategy may outperform a passive investment strategy on a risk-adjusted basis. Understanding the characteristics of an efficient market and being able to evaluate the efficiency of a particular market are important topics for investment analysts and portfolio managers.

An efficient market is a market in which asset prices reflect information quickly. But what is the time frame of "quickly"? Trades are the mechanism by which information can be incorporated into asset transaction prices. The time needed to execute trades to exploit an inefficiency may provide a baseline for judging speed of adjustment.[5] The time frame for an asset's price to incorporate information must be at least as long as the shortest time a trader needs to execute a transaction in the asset. In certain markets, such as foreign exchange and developed equity markets, market efficiency relative to certain types of information has been studied using time frames as short as one minute or less. If the time frame of price adjustment allows many

---

[3]This definition is convenient for making several instructional points. The definition that most simply explains the sense of the word *efficient* in this context can be found in Fama (1976): "An efficient capital market is a market that is efficient in processing information" (p. 134).

[4]The technical term for *superior* in this context is *positive abnormal* in the sense of higher than expected given the asset's risk (as measured, according to capital market theory, by the asset's contribution to the risk of a well-diversified portfolio).

[5]Although the original theory of market efficiency does not quantify this speed, the basic idea is that it is sufficiently swift to make it impossible to consistently earn abnormal profits. Chordia, Roll, and Subrahmanyam (2005) suggest that the adjustment to information on the New York Stock Exchange (NYSE) is between 5 and 60 minutes.

traders to earn profits with little risk, then the market is relatively inefficient. These considerations lead to the observation that market efficiency can be viewed as falling on a continuum.

Finally, an important point is that in an efficient market, prices should be expected to react only to the elements of information releases that are not anticipated fully by investors— that is, to the "unexpected" or "surprise" element of such releases. Investors process the unexpected information and revise expectations (for example, about an asset's future cash flows, risk, or required rate of return) accordingly. The revised expectations enter or get incorporated in the asset price through trades in the asset. Market participants who process the news and believe that at the current market price an asset does not offer sufficient compensation for its perceived risk will tend to sell it or even sell it short. Market participants with opposite views should be buyers. In this way the market establishes the price that balances the various opinions after expectations are revised.

EXAMPLE 2   Price Reaction to the Default on a Bond Issue

Suppose that a speculative-grade bond issuer announces, just before bond markets open, that it will default on an upcoming interest payment. In the announcement, the issuer confirms various reports made in the financial media in the period leading up to the announcement. Prior to the issuer's announcement, the financial news media reported the following: 1) suppliers of the company were making deliveries only for cash payment, reducing the company's liquidity; 2) the issuer's financial condition had probably deteriorated to the point that it lacked the cash to meet an upcoming interest payment; and 3) although public capital markets were closed to the company, it was negotiating with a bank for a private loan that would permit it to meet its interest payment and continue operations for at least nine months. If the issuer defaults on the bond, the consensus opinion of analysts is that bondholders will recover approximately $0.36 to $0.38 per dollar face value.

1. If the market for the bond is efficient, the bond's market price is *most likely* to fully reflect the bond's value after default:
    A. in the period leading up to the announcement.
    B. in the first trade prices after the market opens on the announcement day.
    C. when the issuer actually misses the payment on the interest payment date.

2. If the market for the bond is efficient, the piece of information that bond investors *most likely* focus on in the issuer's announcement is that the issuer had:
    A. failed in its negotiations for a bank loan.
    B. lacked the cash to meet the upcoming interest payment.
    C. been required to make cash payments for supplier deliveries.

Solution to 1:   B is correct. The announcement removed any uncertainty about default. In the period leading up to the announcement, the bond's market price incorporated a probability of default, but the price would not have fully reflected the bond's value after default. The possibility that a bank loan might permit the company to avoid default was not eliminated until the announcement.

Solution to 2:   A is correct. The failure of the loan negotiations first becomes known in this announcement. The failure implies default.

2.2. Market Value versus Intrinsic Value

Market value is the price at which an asset can currently be bought or sold. **Intrinsic value** (sometimes called **fundamental value**) is, broadly speaking, the value that would be placed on it by investors if they had a complete understanding of the asset's investment characteristics.[6] For a bond, for example, such information would include its interest (coupon) rate, principal value, the timing of its interest and principal payments, the other terms of the bond contract (indenture), a precise understanding of its default risk, the liquidity of its market, and other issue-specific items. In addition, market variables such as the term structure of interest rates and the size of various market premiums applying to the issue (for default risk, etc.) would enter into a discounted cash flow estimate of the bond's intrinsic value (discounted cash flow models are often used for such estimates). The word *estimate* is used because in practice, intrinsic value can be estimated but is not known for certain.

If investors believe a market is highly *efficient*, they will usually accept market prices as accurately reflecting intrinsic values. Discrepancies between market price and intrinsic value are the basis for profitable active investment. Active investors seek to own assets selling below perceived intrinsic value in the marketplace and to sell or sell short assets selling above perceived intrinsic value.

If investors believe an asset market is relatively *inefficient*, they may try to develop an independent estimate of intrinsic value. The challenge for investors and analysts is estimating an asset's intrinsic value. Numerous theories and models, including the dividend discount model, can be used to estimate an asset's intrinsic value, but they all require some form of judgment regarding the size, timing, and riskiness of the future cash flows associated with the asset. The more complex an asset's future cash flows, the more difficult it is to estimate its intrinsic value. These complexities and the estimates of an asset's market value are reflected in the market through the buying and selling of assets. The market value of an asset represents the intersection of supply and demand—the point that is low enough to induce at least one investor to buy while being high enough to induce at least one investor to sell. Because information relevant to valuation flows continually to investors, estimates of intrinsic value change, and hence, market values change.

EXAMPLE 3   Intrinsic Value

1. An analyst estimates that a security's intrinsic value is lower than its market value. The security appears to be:
   A. undervalued.
   B. fairly valued.
   C. overvalued.

2. A market in which assets' market values are, on average, equal to or nearly equal to intrinsic values is *best described* as a market that is attractive for:
   A. active investment.
   B. passive investment.
   C. both active and passive investment.

---

[6]Intrinsic value is often defined as the present value of all expected future cash flows of the asset.

3. Suppose that the future cash flows of an asset are accurately estimated. The asset trades in a market that you believe is efficient based on most evidence, but your estimate of the asset's intrinsic value exceeds the asset's market value by a moderate amount. The *most likely* conclusion is that you have:
   A. overestimated the asset's risk.
   B. underestimated the asset's risk.
   C. identified a market inefficiency.

Solution to 1: C is correct. The market is valuing the asset at more than its true worth.

Solution to 2: B is correct because an active investment is not expected to earn superior risk-adjusted returns if the market is efficient. The additional costs of active investment are not justified in such a market.

Solution to 3: B is correct. If risk is underestimated, the discount rate being applied to find the present value of the expected cash flows (estimated intrinsic value) will be too low and the intrinsic value estimate will be too high.

2.3. Factors Contributing to and Impeding a Market's Efficiency

For markets to be efficient, prices should adjust quickly and rationally to the release of new information. In other words, prices of assets in an efficient market should "fully reflect" all information. Financial markets, however, are generally not classified at the two extremes as either completely inefficient or completely efficient but, rather, as exhibiting various degrees of efficiency. In other words, market efficiency should be viewed as falling on a continuum between extremes of completely efficient, at one end, and completely inefficient, at the other. Asset prices in a highly efficient market, by definition, reflect information more quickly and more accurately than in a less-efficient market. These degrees of efficiency also vary through time, across geographical markets, and by type of market. A number of factors contribute to and impede the degree of efficiency in a financial market.

2.3.1. Market Participants

One of the most critical factors contributing to the degree of efficiency in a market is the number of market participants. Consider the following example that illustrates the relationship between the number of market participants and market efficiency.

EXAMPLE 4   Illustration of Market Efficiency

Assume that the shares of a small market capitalization (cap) company trade on a public stock exchange. Because of its size, it is not considered "blue-chip" and not many professional investors follow the activities of the company.[7] A small-cap fund analyst

---

[7]A "blue-chip" share is one from a well-recognized company that is considered to be high quality but low risk. This term generally refers to a company that has a long history of earnings and paying dividends.

reports that the most recent annual operating performance of the company has been surprisingly good, considering the recent slump in its industry. The company's share price, however, has been slow to react to the positive financial results because the company is not being recommended by the majority of research analysts. This mispricing implies that the market for this company's shares is less than fully efficient. The small-cap fund analyst recognizes the opportunity and immediately recommends the purchase of the company's shares. The share price gradually increases as more investors purchase the shares once the news of the mispricing spreads through the market. As a result, it takes a few days for the share price to fully reflect the information.

Six months later, the company reports another solid set of interim financial results. But because the previous mispricing and subsequent profit opportunities have become known in the market, the number of analysts following the company's shares has increased substantially. As a result, as soon as unexpected information about the positive interim results are released to the public, a large number of buy orders quickly drive up the stock price, thereby making the market for these shares more efficient than before.

A large number of investors (individual and institutional) follow the major financial markets closely on a daily basis, and if mispricings exist in these markets, as illustrated by the example, investors will act so that these mispricings disappear quickly. Besides the number of investors, the number of financial analysts who follow or analyze a security or asset should be positively related to market efficiency. The number of market participants and resulting trading activity can vary significantly through time. A lack of trading activity can cause or accentuate other market imperfections that impede market efficiency. In fact, in many of these markets, trading in many of the listed stocks is restricted for foreigners. By nature, this limitation reduces the number of market participants, restricts the potential for trading activity, and hence reduces market efficiency.

EXAMPLE 5   Factors Affecting Market Efficiency

The expected effect on market efficiency of opening a securities market to trading by foreigners would *most likely* be to:

A. decrease market efficiency.
B. leave market efficiency unchanged.
C. increase market efficiency.

Solution: C is correct. The opening of markets as described should increase market efficiency by increasing the number of market participants.

2.3.2. Information Availability and Financial Disclosure

Information availability (e.g., an active financial news media) and financial disclosure should promote market efficiency. Information regarding trading activity and traded companies in such markets as the New York Stock Exchange, the London Stock Exchange, and the Tokyo Stock Exchange is readily available. Many investors and analysts participate in these markets, and analyst coverage of listed companies is typically substantial. As a result, these markets are quite efficient. In contrast, trading activity and material information availability may be lacking in smaller securities markets, such as those operating in some emerging markets.

Similarly, significant differences may exist in the efficiency of different types of markets. For example, many securities trade primarily or exclusively in dealer or over-the-counter (OTC) markets, including bonds, money market instruments, currencies, mortgage-backed securities, swaps, and forward contracts. The information provided by the dealers that serve as market makers for these markets can vary significantly in quality and quantity, both through time and across different product markets.

Treating all market participants fairly is critical for the integrity of the market and explains why regulators place such an emphasis on "fair, orderly, and efficient markets."[8] A key element of this fairness is that all investors have access to the information necessary to value securities that trade in the market. Rules and regulations that promote fairness and efficiency in a market include those pertaining to the disclosure of information and illegal insider trading.

For example, US Securities and Exchange Commission's (SEC's) Regulation FD (Fair Disclosure) requires that if security issuers provide nonpublic information to some market professionals or investors, they must also disclose this information to the public.[9] This requirement helps provide equal and fair opportunities, which is important in encouraging participation in the market. A related issue deals with illegal insider trading. The SEC's rules, along with court cases, define illegal insider trading as trading in securities by market participants who are considered insiders "while in possession of material, nonpublic information about the security."[10] Although these rules cannot guarantee that some participants will not have an advantage over others and that insiders will not trade on the basis of inside information, the civil and criminal penalties associated with breaking these rules are intended to discourage illegal insider trading and promote fairness. In the European Union, insider trading laws are generally enshrined in legislation and enforced by regulatory and judicial authorities.[11]

---

[8]"The Investor's Advocate: How the SEC Protects Investors, Maintains Market Integrity, and Facilitates Capital Formation," US Securities and Exchange Commission (www.sec.gov/about/whatwedo.shtml).

[9]Regulation FD, "Selective Disclosure and Insider Trading," 17 CFR Parts 240, 243, and 249, effective 23 October 2000.

[10]Although not the focus of this particular chapter, it is important to note that a party is considered an insider not only when the individual is a corporate insider, such as an officer or director, but also when the individual is aware that the information is nonpublic information [Securities and Exchange Commission, Rules 10b5-1 ("Trading on the Basis of Material Nonpublic Information in Insider Trading Cases") and Rule 10b5-2 "Duties of Trust or Confidence in Misappropriation Insider Trading Cases")].

[11]See the European Union's Market Abuse Regulation (Regulation (EU) no. 596/2014 of the European Parliament and of the Council of 16 April 2014 on market abuse) and Directive for Criminal Sanctions for Market Abuse (Directive 2014/57/EU of the European Parliament and of the Council of 16 April 2014 on criminal sanctions for market abuse).

2.3.3. Limits to Trading

Arbitrage is a set of transactions that produces riskless profits. Arbitrageurs are traders who engage in such trades to benefit from pricing discrepancies (inefficiencies) in markets. Such trading activity contributes to market efficiency. For example, if an asset is traded in two markets but at different prices, the actions of buying the asset in the market in which it is underpriced and selling the asset in the market in which it is overpriced will eventually bring these two prices together. The presence of these arbitrageurs helps pricing discrepancies disappear quickly. Obviously, market efficiency is impeded by any limitation on arbitrage resulting from operating inefficiencies, such as difficulties in executing trades in a timely manner, prohibitively high trading costs, and a lack of transparency in market prices.

Some market experts argue that restrictions on short selling limit arbitrage trading, which impedes market efficiency. **Short selling** is the transaction whereby an investor sells shares that he or she does not own by borrowing them from a broker and agreeing to replace them at a future date. Short selling allows investors to sell securities they believe to be overvalued, much in the same way they can buy those they believe to be undervalued. In theory, such activities promote more efficient pricing. Regulators and others, however, have argued that short selling may exaggerate downward market movements, leading to crashes in affected securities. In contrast, some researchers report evidence indicating that when investors are unable to borrow securities, that is to short the security, or when costs to borrow shares are high, market prices may deviate from intrinsic values.[12] Furthermore, research suggests that short selling is helpful in price discovery (that is, it facilitates supply and demand in determining prices).[13]

2.4. Transaction Costs and Information-Acquisition Costs

The costs incurred by traders in identifying and exploiting possible market inefficiencies affect the interpretation of market efficiency. The two types of costs to consider are transaction costs and information-acquisition costs.

- *Transaction costs*: Practically, transaction costs are incurred in trading to exploit any perceived market inefficiency. Thus, "efficient" should be viewed as efficient within the bounds of transaction costs. For example, consider a violation of the principle that two identical assets should sell for the same price in different markets. Such a violation can be considered to be a rather simple possible exception to market efficiency because prices appear to be inconsistently processing information. To exploit the violation, a trader could arbitrage by simultaneously shorting the asset in the higher-price market and buying the asset in the lower-price market. If the price discrepancy between the two markets is smaller than the transaction costs involved in the arbitrage for the lowest cost traders, the arbitrage will not occur, and both prices are in effect efficient within the bounds of arbitrage. These bounds of arbitrage are relatively narrow in highly liquid markets, such as the market for US Treasury bills, but could be wide in illiquid markets.
- *Information-acquisition costs:* Practically, expenses are always associated with gathering and analyzing information. New information is incorporated in transaction prices by traders placing trades based on their analysis of information. Active investors who place trades based on information they have gathered and analyzed play a key role in market prices

---

[12]See Deng, Mortal, and Gupta (2017) and references therein.
[13]See Bris, Goetzmann, and Zhu (2009).

adjusting to reflect new information. The classic view of market efficiency is that active investors incur information acquisition costs but that money is wasted because prices already reflect all relevant information. This view of efficiency is very strict in the sense of viewing a market as inefficient if active investing can recapture any part of the costs, such as research costs and active asset selection. Grossman and Stiglitz (1980) argue that prices must offer a return to information acquisition; in equilibrium, if markets are efficient, returns net of such expenses are just fair returns for the risk incurred. The modern perspective views a market as inefficient if, after deducting such costs, active investing can earn superior returns. Gross of expenses, a return should accrue to information acquisition in an efficient market.

In summary, a modern perspective calls for the investor to consider transaction costs and information-acquisition costs when evaluating the efficiency of a market. A price discrepancy must be sufficiently large to leave the investor with a profit (adjusted for risk) after taking account of the transaction costs and information-acquisition costs to reach the conclusion that the discrepancy may represent a market inefficiency. Prices may somewhat less than fully reflect available information without there being a true market opportunity for active investors.

3. FORMS OF MARKET EFFICIENCY

Eugene Fama developed a framework for describing the degree to which markets are efficient.[14] In his efficient market hypothesis, markets are efficient when prices reflect *all* relevant information at any point in time. This means that the market prices observed for securities, for example, reflect the information available at the time.

In his framework, Fama defines three forms of efficiency: weak, semi-strong, and strong. Each form is defined with respect to the available information that is reflected in prices.

	Market Prices Reflect:		
Forms of Market Efficiency	Past Market Data	Public Information	Private Information
Weak form of market efficiency	✓		
Semi-strong form of market efficiency	✓	✓	
Strong form of market efficiency	✓	✓	✓

A finding that investors can consistently earn **abnormal returns** by trading on the basis of information is evidence contrary to market efficiency. In general, abnormal returns are returns in excess of those expected given a security's risk and the market's return. In other words, abnormal return equals actual return less expected return.

3.1. Weak Form

In the **weak-form efficient market hypothesis**, security prices fully reflect *all past market data*, which refers to all historical price and trading volume information. If markets are weak-form

---

[14]Fama (1970).

efficient, past trading data are already reflected in current prices and investors cannot predict future price changes by extrapolating prices or patterns of prices from the past.[15]

Tests of whether securities markets are weak-form efficient require looking at patterns of prices. One approach is to see whether there is any serial correlation in security returns, which would imply a predictable pattern.[16] Although there is some weak correlation in daily security returns, there is not enough correlation to make this a profitable trading rule after considering transaction costs.

An alternative approach to test weak-form efficiency is to examine specific trading rules that attempt to exploit historical trading data. If any such trading rule consistently generates abnormal risk-adjusted returns after trading costs, this evidence will contradict weak-form efficiency. This approach is commonly associated with **technical analysis**, which involves the analysis of historical trading information (primarily pricing and volume data) in an attempt to identify recurring patterns in the trading data that can be used to guide investment decisions. Many technical analysts, also referred to as "technicians," argue that many movements in stock prices are based, in large part, on psychology. Many technicians attempt to predict how market participants will behave, based on analyses of past behavior, and then trade on those predictions. Technicians often argue that simple statistical tests of trading rules are not conclusive because they are not applied to the more sophisticated trading strategies that can be used and that the research excludes the technician's subjective judgment. Thus, it is difficult to definitively refute this assertion because there are an unlimited number of possible technical trading rules.

Can technical analysts profit from trading on past trends? Overall, the evidence indicates that investors cannot consistently earn abnormal profits using past prices or other technical analysis strategies in developed markets.[17] Some evidence suggests, however, that there are opportunities to profit on technical analysis in countries with developing markets, including Hungary, Bangladesh, and Turkey, among others.[18]

3.2. Semi-Strong Form

In a **semi-strong-form efficient market**, prices reflect all publicly known and available information. Publicly available information includes financial statement data (such as earnings, dividends, corporate investments, changes in management, etc.) and financial market data (such as closing prices, shares traded, etc.). Therefore, the semi-strong form of market efficiency encompasses the weak form. In other words, if a market is semi-strong efficient, then it must also be weak-form efficient. A market that quickly incorporates all publicly available information into its prices is semi-strong efficient.

In a semi-strong market, efforts to analyze publicly available information are futile. That is, analyzing earnings announcements of companies to identify underpriced or overpriced securities is pointless because the prices of these securities already reflect all publicly available information. If markets are semi-strong efficient, no single investor has access to information

---

[15]Market efficiency should not be confused with the random walk hypothesis, in which price changes over time are independent of one another. A random walk model is one of many alternative expected return generating models. Market efficiency does not require that returns follow a random walk.

[16]Serial correlation is a statistical measure of the degree to which the returns in one period are related to the returns in another period.

[17]Bessembinder and Chan (1998) and Fifield, Power, and Sinclair (2005).

[18]Fifield, Power, and Sinclair (2005), Chen and Li (2006), and Mobarek, Mollah, and Bhuyan (2008).

that is not already available to other market participants, and as a consequence, no single investor can gain an advantage in predicting future security prices. In a semi-strong efficient market, prices adjust quickly and accurately to new information. Suppose a company announces earnings that are higher than expected. In a semi-strong efficient market, investors would not be able to act on this announcement and earn abnormal returns.

A common empirical test of investors' reaction to information releases is the event study. Suppose a researcher wants to test whether investors react to the announcement that the company is paying a special dividend. The researcher identifies a sample period and then those companies that paid a special dividend in the period and the date of the announcement. Then, for each company's stock, the researcher calculates the expected return on the share for the event date. This expected return may be based on many different models, including the capital asset pricing model, a simple market model, or a market index return. The researcher calculates the excess return as the difference between the actual return and the expected return. Once the researcher has calculated the event's excess return for each share, statistical tests are conducted to see whether the abnormal returns are statistically different from zero. The process of an event study is outlined in Exhibit 1.

EXHIBIT 1   The Event Study Process

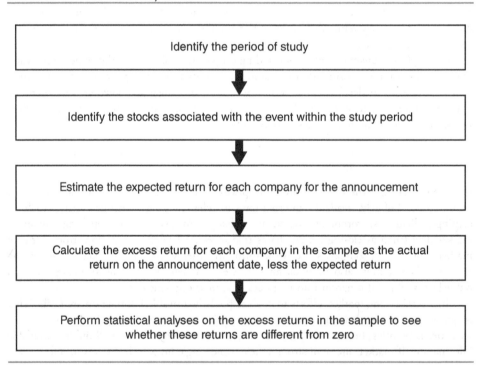

How do event studies relate to efficient markets? In a semi-strong efficient market, share prices react quickly and accurately to public information. Therefore, if the information is good news, such as better-than-expected earnings, one would expect the company's shares to increase immediately at the time of the announcement; if it is bad news, one would expect a swift, negative reaction. If actual returns exceed what is expected in absence of the announcement and these returns are confined to the announcement period, then they are consistent with the idea that market prices react quickly to new information. In other words, the finding of excess returns at the time of the announcement does not necessarily indicate market inefficiency. In contrast, the finding of consistent excess returns following the announcement would suggest a trading opportunity. Trading on the basis of the announcement—that is, once the announcement is made—would not, on average, yield abnormal returns.

EXAMPLE 6   Information Arrival and Market Reaction

Consider an example of a news item and its effect on a share's price. The following events related to Tesla, Inc. in August of 2018:

1 August 2018	After the market closes, Tesla, Inc., publicly reports that there was a smaller-than-expected cash burn for the most recent quarter.
2 August 2018	Elon Musk, chairman and CEO of Tesla, Inc., notifies Tesla's board of directors that he wants to take the company private. This is not public information at this point.
7 August 2018	Before the market opens, the *Financial Times* reports that a Saudi fund has a $2 billion investment in Tesla.
	During market trading, Musk announces on Twitter "Am considering taking Tesla private at $420. Funding secured." [Twitter, Elon Musk @elonmusk, 9:48 a.m., 7 August 2018]
24 August 2018	After the market closed, Musk announces that he no longer intends on taking Tesla private.

EXHIBIT 2   Price of Tesla, Inc. Stock: 31 July 2018–31 August 2018

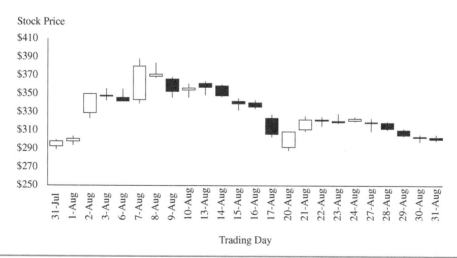

Note: Open-High-Low-Close graph of Tesla's stock price, with white rectangles indicating upward movement in the day and black rectangles indicating downward movement during the day.

Source of data: Yahoo! Finance.

Is the fact that the price of Tesla moves up immediately on the day after the Q2 earnings (the first day of trading with this information) indicative of efficiency regarding information? Most likely.

Does the fact that the price of Tesla moves up but does not reach $420 on the day the going-private Twitter announcement is made mean that investors underreacted? Not necessarily. There was confusion and uncertainty about the going-private transaction at the time, so the price did not close in on the proposed $420 per share for going private.

Does the fact that the market price of the stock declined well before the issue of going-private was laid to rest by Musk mean that the market is inefficient? Not necessarily. There were numerous analyses, discussions, and other news regarding the likelihood of the transaction, all of which was incorporated in the price of the stock before the going-private transaction was dismissed by Musk.

Researchers have examined many different company-specific information events, including stock splits, dividend changes, and merger announcements, as well as economy-wide events, such as regulation changes and tax rate changes. The results of most research are consistent with the view that developed securities markets might be semi-strong efficient. But some evidence suggests that the markets in developing countries may not be semi-strong efficient.[19]

3.3. Strong Form

In a **strong-form efficient market**, security prices fully reflect both public and private information. A market that is strong-form efficient is, by definition, also semi-strong- and weak-form efficient. In the case of a strong-form efficient market, insiders would not be able to earn abnormal returns from trading on the basis of private information. A strong-form efficient market also means that prices reflect all private information, which means that prices reflect everything that the management of a company knows about the financial condition of the company that has not been publicly released. However, this is not likely because of the strong prohibitions against insider trading that are found in most countries. If a market is strong-form efficient, those with insider information cannot earn abnormal returns.

Researchers test whether a market is strong-form efficient by testing whether investors can earn abnormal profits by trading on nonpublic information. The results of these tests are consistent with the view that securities markets are not strong-form efficient; many studies have found that abnormal profits can be earned when nonpublic information is used.[20]

3.4. Implications of the Efficient Market Hypothesis

The implications of efficient markets to investment managers and analysts are important because they affect the value of securities and how these securities are managed.

---

[19]See Gan, Lee, Hwa, and Zhang (2005) and Raja, Sudhahar, and Selvam (2009).
[20]Evidence that finds that markets are not strong-form efficient include Jaffe (1974) and Rozeff and Zaman (1988).

Several implications can be drawn from the evidence on efficient markets for developed markets:

- Securities markets are weak-form efficient, and therefore, investors cannot earn abnormal returns by trading on the basis of past trends in price.
- Securities markets are semi-strong efficient, and therefore, analysts who collect and analyze information must consider whether that information is already reflected in security prices and how any new information affects a security's value.[21]
- Securities markets are not strong-form efficient because securities laws are intended to prevent exploitation of private information.

3.4.1. Fundamental Analysis

Fundamental analysis is the examination of publicly available information and the formulation of forecasts to estimate the intrinsic value of assets. Fundamental analysis involves the estimation of an asset's value using company data, such as earnings and sales forecasts, and risk estimates as well as industry and economic data, such as economic growth, inflation, and interest rates. Buy and sell decisions depend on whether the current market price is less than or greater than the estimated intrinsic value.

The semi-strong form of market efficiency says that all available public information is reflected in current prices. So, what good is fundamental analysis? Fundamental analysis is necessary in a well-functioning market because this analysis helps the market participants understand the value implications of information. In other words, fundamental analysis facilitates a semi-strong efficient market by disseminating value-relevant information. And, although fundamental analysis requires costly information, this analysis can be profitable in terms of generating abnormal returns if the analyst creates a comparative advantage with respect to this information.[22]

3.4.2. Technical Analysis

Investors using **technical analysis** attempt to profit by looking at patterns of prices and trading volume. Although some price patterns persist, exploiting these patterns may be too costly and, hence, would not produce abnormal returns.

Consider a situation in which a pattern of prices exists. With so many investors examining prices, this pattern will be detected. If profitable, exploiting this pattern will eventually affect prices such that this pattern will no longer exist; it will be arbitraged away. In other words, by detecting and exploiting patterns in prices, technical analysts assist markets in maintaining weak-form efficiency. Does this mean that technical analysts cannot earn abnormal profits? Not necessarily, because there may be a possibility of earning abnormal profits from a pricing inefficiency. But would it be possible to earn abnormal returns on a consistent basis from exploiting such a pattern? No, because the actions of market participants will arbitrage this opportunity quickly, and the inefficiency will no longer exist.

---

[21]In the case of the Intel example, this implication would mean estimating how the actual filing of the lawsuit and the company's reaction to the lawsuit affect the value of Intel, while keeping in mind that the expectation of a lawsuit was already impounded in Intel's stock price.

[22]Brealey (1983).

3.4.3. Portfolio Management

If securities markets are weak-form and semi-strong-form efficient, the implication is that active trading, whether attempting to exploit price patterns or public information, is not likely to generate abnormal returns. In other words, portfolio managers cannot beat the market on a consistent basis, so therefore, passive portfolio management should outperform active portfolio management. Researchers have observed that mutual funds do not, on average, outperform the market on a risk-adjusted basis.[23] Mutual funds perform, on average, similar to the market before considering fees and expenses and perform worse than the market, on average, once fees and expenses are considered. Even if a mutual fund is not actively managed, there are costs to managing these funds, which reduces net returns.

So, what good are portfolio managers? The role of a portfolio manager is not necessarily to beat the market but, rather, to establish and manage a portfolio consistent with the portfolio's objectives, with appropriate diversification and asset allocation, while taking into consideration the risk preferences and tax situation of the investor.

4. MARKET PRICING ANOMALIES

Although considerable evidence shows that markets are efficient, researchers have identified a number of apparent market inefficiencies or anomalies. These market anomalies, if persistent, are exceptions to the notion of market efficiency. Researchers conclude that a **market anomaly** may be present if a change in the price of an asset or security cannot directly be linked to current relevant information known in the market or to the release of new information into the market.

The validity of any evidence supporting the potential existence of a market inefficiency or anomaly must be *consistent* over reasonably long periods. Otherwise, a detected market anomaly may largely be an artifact of the sample period chosen. In the widespread search for discovering profitable anomalies, many findings could simply be the product of a process called **data mining**, also known as **data snooping**. In generally accepted research practice, an initial hypothesis is developed which is based on economic rationale. Tests are then conducted on objectively selected data to either confirm or reject the original hypothesis. However, with data mining the process is typically reversed: data are examined with the intent to develop a hypothesis, instead of developing a hypothesis first. This is done by analyzing data in various manners, and even utilizing different empirical approaches until you find support for a desired result, in this case a profitable anomaly.

Can researchers look back on data and find a trading strategy that would have yielded abnormal returns? Absolutely. Enough data snooping often can detect a trading strategy that would have worked in the past by chance alone. But in an efficient market, such a strategy is unlikely to generate abnormal returns on a consistent basis in the future. Also, although identified anomalies may appear to produce excess returns, it is generally difficult to profitably exploit the anomalies after accounting for risk, trading costs, and so on.

Several well-known anomalies are listed in Exhibit 3. This list is by no means exhaustive, but it provides information on the breadth of the anomalies. A few of these anomalies are discussed in more detail in the following sections. The anomalies are placed into categories based on the research method that identified the anomaly. Time-series anomalies were

---

[23]See Malkiel (1995). One of the challenges to evaluating mutual fund performance is that the researcher must control for survivorship bias.

identified using time series of data. Cross-sectional anomalies were identified based on analyzing a cross section of companies that differ on some key characteristics. Other anomalies were identified by a variety of means, including event studies.

EXHIBIT 3   Sampling of Observed Pricing Anomalies

Time Series	Cross-Sectional	Other
January effect	Size effect	Closed-end fund discount
Day-of-the-week effect	Value effect	Earnings surprise
Weekend effect	Book-to-market ratios	Initial public offerings
Turn-of-the-month effect	P/E ratio effect	Distressed securities effect
Holiday effect	Value Line enigma	Stock splits
Time-of-day effect		Super Bowl
Momentum		
Overreaction		

4.1. Time-Series Anomalies

Two of the major categories of time-series anomalies that have been documented are 1) calendar anomalies and 2) momentum and overreaction anomalies.

4.1.1. Calendar Anomalies

In the 1980s, a number of researchers reported that stock market returns in January were significantly higher compared to the rest of the months of the year, with most of the abnormal returns reported during the first five trading days in January. Since its first documentation in the 1980s, this pattern, known as the **January effect**, has been observed in most equity markets around the world. This anomaly is also known as the **turn-of-the-year effect**, or even often referred to as the "small firm in January effect" because it is most frequently observed for the returns of small market capitalization stocks.[24]

The January effect contradicts the efficient market hypothesis because excess returns in January are not attributed to any new and relevant information or news. A number of reasons have been suggested for this anomaly, including tax-loss selling. Researchers have speculated that, in order to reduce their tax liabilities, investors sell their "loser" securities in December for the purpose of creating capital losses, which can then be used to offset any capital gains. A related explanation is that these losers tend to be small-cap stocks with high volatility.[25] This increased supply of equities in December depresses their prices, and then these shares are bought in early January at relatively attractive prices. This demand then drives their prices up again. Overall, the evidence indicates that tax-loss selling may account for a portion of January abnormal returns, but it does not explain all of it.

Another possible explanation for the anomaly is so-called "window dressing," a practice in which portfolio managers sell their riskier securities prior to 31 December. The explanation

---

[24]There is also evidence of a January effect in bond returns that is more prevalent in high-yield corporate bonds, similar to the small-company effect for stocks.

[25]See Roll (1983).

is as follows: many portfolio managers prepare the annual reports of their portfolio holdings as of 31 December. Selling riskier securities is an attempt to make their portfolios appear less risky. After 31 December, a portfolio manager would then simply purchase riskier securities in an attempt to earn higher returns. However, similar to the tax-loss selling hypothesis, the research evidence in support of the window dressing hypothesis explains some, but not all, of the anomaly.

Recent evidence for both stock and bond returns suggests that the January effect is not persistent and, therefore, is not a pricing anomaly. Once an appropriate adjustment for risk is made, the January "effect" does not produce abnormal returns.[26]

Several other calendar effects, including the day-of-the-week and the weekend effects,[27] have been found. These anomalies are summarized in Exhibit 4.[28] But like the size effect, which will be described later, most of these anomalies have been eliminated over time. One view is that the anomalies have been exploited such that the effect has been arbitraged away. Another view, however, is that increasingly sophisticated statistical methodologies fail to detect pricing inefficiencies.

EXHIBIT 4   Calendar-Based Anomalies

Anomaly	Observation
Turn-of-the-month effect	Returns tend to be higher on the last trading day of the month and the first three trading days of the next month.
Day-of-the-week effect	The average Monday return is negative and lower than the average returns for the other four days, which are all positive.
Weekend effect	Returns on weekends tend to be lower than returns on weekdays.
Holiday effect	Returns on stocks in the day prior to market holidays tend to be higher than other days.

4.1.2. Momentum and Overreaction Anomalies

Momentum anomalies relate to short-term share price patterns. One of the earliest studies to identify this type of anomaly was conducted by Werner DeBondt and Richard Thaler, who argued that investors overreact to the release of unexpected public information.[29] Therefore, stock prices will be inflated (depressed) for those companies releasing good (bad) information. This anomaly has become known as the overreaction effect. Using the overreaction effect, they proposed a strategy that involved buying "loser" portfolios and selling "winner" portfolios. They defined stocks as winners or losers based on their total returns over the previous three- to five-year period. They found that in a subsequent period, the loser portfolios outperformed the market, while the winner portfolios underperformed the market. Similar patterns have been documented in many, but not all, global stock markets as well as

---

[26]See, for example, Kim (2006).

[27]For a discussion of several of these anomalous patterns, see Jacobs and Levy (1988).

[28]The weekend effect consists of a pattern of returns around the weekend: abnormal positive returns on Fridays followed by abnormally negative returns on Mondays. This is a day-of-the-week effect that specifically links Friday and Monday returns. It is interesting to note that in 2009, the weekend effect in the United States was inverted, with 80 percent of the gains from March 2009 onward coming from the first trading day of the week.

[29]DeBondt and Thaler (1985).

in bond markets. One criticism is that the observed anomaly may be the result of statistical problems in the analysis.

A contradiction to weak-form efficiency occurs when securities that have experienced high returns in the short term tend to continue to generate higher returns in subsequent periods.[30] Empirical support for the existence of momentum in stock returns in most stock markets around the world is well documented. If investors can trade on the basis of momentum and earn abnormal profits, then this anomaly contradicts the weak form of the efficient market hypothesis because it represents a pattern in prices that can be exploited by simply using historical price information.[31]

Researchers have argued that the existence of momentum is rational and not contrary to market efficiency because it is plausible that there are shocks to the expected growth rates of cash flows to shareholders and that these shocks induce a serial correlation that is rational and short lived.[32] In other words, having stocks with some degree of momentum in their security returns may not imply irrationality but, rather, may reflect prices adjusting to a shock in growth rates.

4.2. Cross-Sectional Anomalies

Two of the most researched cross-sectional anomalies in financial markets are the size effect and the value effect.

4.2.1. Size Effect
The size effect results from the observation that equities of small-cap companies tend to outperform equities of large-cap companies on a risk-adjusted basis. Many researchers documented a small-company effect soon after the initial research was published in 1981. This effect, however, was not apparent in subsequent studies.[33] Part of the reason that the size effect was not confirmed by subsequent studies may be because of the fact that if it were truly an anomaly, investors acting on this effect would reduce any potential returns. But some of the explanation may simply be that the effect as originally observed was a chance outcome and, therefore, not actually an inefficiency.

4.2.2. Value Effect
A number of global empirical studies have shown that value stocks, which are generally referred to as stocks that have below-average price-to-earnings (P/E) and market-to-book

---

[30]Notice that this pattern lies in sharp contrast to DeBondt and Thaler's reversal pattern that is displayed over longer periods of time. In theory, the two patterns could be related. In other words, it is feasible that prices are bid up extremely high, perhaps too high, in the short term for companies that are doing well. In the longer term (three-to-five years), the prices of these short-term winners correct themselves and they do poorly.

[31]Jegadeesh and Titman (2001).

[32]Johnson (2002).

[33]Although a large number of studies documents a small-company effect, these studies are concentrated in a period similar to that of the original research and, therefore, use a similar data set. The key to whether something is a true anomaly is persistence in out-of-sample tests. Fama and French (2008) document that the size effect is apparent only in microcap stocks but not in small- and large-cap stocks and these microcap stocks may have a significant influence in studies that document a size effect.

(M/B) ratios, and above-average dividend yields, have consistently outperformed growth stocks over long periods of time.[34] If the effect persists, the value stock anomaly contradicts semi-strong market efficiency because all the information used to categorize stocks in this manner is publicly available.

Fama and French developed a three-factor model to predict stock returns.[35] In addition to the use of market returns as specified by the capital asset pricing model (CAPM), the Fama and French model also includes the size of the company as measured by the market value of its equity and the company's book value of equity divided by its market value of equity, which is a value measure. The Fama and French model captures risk dimensions related to stock returns that the CAPM model does not consider. Fama and French find that when they apply the three-factor model instead of the CAPM, the value stock anomaly disappears.

4.3. Other Anomalies

A number of additional anomalies has been documented in the financial markets, including the existence of closed-end investment fund discounts, price reactions to the release of earnings information, returns of initial public offerings, and the predictability of returns based on prior information.

4.3.1. Closed-End Investment Fund Discounts

A closed-end investment fund issues a fixed number of shares at inception and does not sell any additional shares after the initial offering. Therefore, the fund capitalization is fixed unless a secondary public offering is made. The shares of closed-end funds trade on stock markets like any other shares in the equity market (i.e., their prices are determined by supply and demand).

Theoretically, these shares should trade at a price approximately equal to their net asset value (NAV) per share, which is simply the total market value of the fund's security holdings less any liabilities divided by the number of shares outstanding. An abundance of research, however, has documented that, on average, closed-end funds trade at a discount from NAV. Most studies have documented average discounts in the 4–10 percent range, although individual funds have traded at discounts exceeding 50 percent and others have traded at large premiums.[36]

The closed-end fund discount presents a puzzle because conceptually, an investor could purchase all the shares in the fund, liquidate the fund, and end up making a profit. Some researchers have suggested that these discounts are attributed to management fees or expectations of the managers' performance, but these explanations are not supported by the evidence.[37] An alternative explanation for the discount is that tax liabilities are associated with unrealized capital gains and losses that exist prior to when the investor bought the shares, and hence, the investor does not have complete control over the timing of the realization of gains and losses.[38] Although the evidence supports this hypothesis to a certain extent, the tax effect

---

[34]For example, see Capaul, Rowley, and Sharpe (1993) and Fama and French (1998).

[35]Fama and French (1995).

[36]See Dimson and Minio-Kozerski (1999) for a review of this literature.

[37]See Lee, Sheifer, and Thaler (1990).

[38]The return to owners of closed-end fund shares has three parts: 1) the price appreciation or depreciation of the shares themselves, 2) the dividends earned and distributed to owners by the fund, and 3) the capital gains and losses earned by the fund that are distributed by the fund. The explanation of the anomalous pricing has to do with the timing of the distribution of capital gains.

is not large enough to explain the entire discount. Finally, it has often been argued that the discounts exist because of liquidity problems and errors in calculating NAV. The illiquidity explanation is plausible if shares are recorded at the same price as more liquid, publicly traded stocks; some evidence supports this assertion. But as with tax reasons, liquidity issues explain only a portion of the discount effect.

Can these discounts be exploited to earn abnormal returns if transaction costs are taken into account? No. First, the transaction costs involved in exploiting the discount—buying all the shares and liquidating the fund—would eliminate any profit.[39] Second, these discounts tend to revert to zero over time. Hence, a strategy to trade on the basis of these discounts would not likely be profitable.[40]

4.3.2. Earnings Surprise

Although most event studies have supported semi-strong market efficiency, some researchers have provided evidence that questions semi-strong market efficiency. One of these studies relates to the extensively examined adjustment of stock prices to earnings announcements.[41] The unexpected part of the earnings announcement, or **earnings surprise**, is the portion of earnings that is unanticipated by investors and, according to the efficient market hypothesis, merits a price adjustment. Positive (negative) surprises should cause appropriate and rapid price increases (decreases). Several studies have been conducted using data from numerous markets around the world. Most of the results indicate that earnings surprises are reflected quickly in stock prices, but the adjustment process is not always efficient. In particular, although a substantial adjustment occurs prior to and at the announcement date, an adjustment also occurs after the announcement.[42]

As a result of these slow price adjustments, companies that display the largest positive earnings surprises subsequently display superior stock return performance, whereas poor subsequent performance is displayed by companies with low or negative earnings surprises.[43] This finding implies that investors could earn abnormal returns using publicly available information by buying stocks of companies that had positive earnings surprises and selling those with negative surprises.

Although there is support for abnormal returns associated with earnings surprises, and some support for such returns beyond the announcement period, there is also evidence indicating that these observed abnormal returns are an artifact of studies that do not sufficiently control for transaction costs and risk.[44]

---

[39]See, for example, the study by Pontiff (1996), which shows how the cost of arbitraging these discounts eliminates the profit.

[40]See Pontiff (1995).

[41]See Jones, Rendleman, and Latané (1984).

[42]Not surprisingly, it is often argued that this slow reaction contributes to a momentum pattern.

[43]A similar pattern has been documented in the corporate bond market, where bond prices react too slowly to new company earnings announcements as well as to changes in company debt ratings.

[44]See Brown (1997) for a summary of evidence supporting the existence of this anomaly. See Zarowin (1989) for evidence regarding the role of size in explaining abnormal returns to surprises; Alexander, Goff, and Peterson (1989) for evidence regarding transaction costs and unexpected earnings strategies; and Kim and Kim (2003) for evidence indicating that the anomalous returns can be explained by risk factors.

4.3.3. Initial Public Offerings (IPOs)

When a company offers shares of its stock to the public for the first time, it does so through an initial public offering (or IPO). This offering involves working with an investment bank that helps price and market the newly issued shares. After the offering is complete, the new shares trade on a stock market for the first time. Given the risk that investment bankers face in trying to sell a new issue for which the true price is unknown, it is perhaps not surprising to find that, on average, the initial selling price is set too low and that the price increases dramatically on the first trading day. The percentage difference between the issue price and the closing price at the end of the first day of trading is often referred to as the degree of underpricing.

The evidence suggests that, on average, investors who are able to buy the shares of an IPO at their offering price may be able to earn abnormal profits. For example, during the internet bubble of 1995–2000, many IPOs ended their first day of trading up by more than 100 percent. Such performance, however, is not always the case. Sometimes the issues are priced too high, which means that share prices drop on their first day of trading. In addition, the evidence also suggests that investors buying after the initial offering are not able to earn abnormal profits because prices adjust quickly to the "true" values, which supports semi-strong market efficiency. In fact, the subsequent long-term performance of IPOs is generally found to be below average. Taken together, the IPO underpricing and the subsequent poor performance suggests that the markets are overly optimistic initially (i.e., investors overreact).

Some researchers have examined closely why IPOs may appear to have anomalous returns. Because of the small size of the IPO companies and the method of equally weighting the samples, what appears to be an anomaly may simply be an artifact of the methodology.[45]

4.3.4. Predictability of Returns Based on Prior Information

A number of researchers have documented that equity returns are related to prior information on such factors as interest rates, inflation rates, stock volatility, and dividend yields.[46] But finding that equity returns are affected by changes in economic fundamentals is not evidence of market inefficiency and would not result in abnormal trading returns.[47]

Furthermore, the relationship between stock returns and the prior information is not consistent over time. For example, in one study, the relationship between stock prices and dividend yields changed from positive to negative in different periods.[48] Hence, a trading strategy based on dividend yields would not yield consistent abnormal returns.

4.4. Implications for Investment Strategies

Although it is interesting to consider the anomalies just described, attempting to benefit from them in practice is not easy. In fact, most researchers conclude that observed anomalies are not violations of market efficiency but, rather, are the result of statistical methodologies used to detect the anomalies. As a result, if the methodologies are corrected, most of these anomalies disappear.[49] Another point to consider is that in an efficient market, overreactions

---

[45]See Brav, Geczy, and Gompers (1995).
[46]See, for example, Fama and Schwert (1977) and Fama and French (1988).
[47]See Fama and French (2008).
[48]Schwert (2003, Chapter 15).
[49]Fama (1998).

may occur, but then so do underreactions.[50] Therefore, on average, the markets are efficient. In other words, investors face challenges when they attempt to translate statistical anomalies into economic profits. Consider the following quote regarding anomalies from the *Economist* ("Frontiers of Finance Survey," 9 October 1993):

> Many can be explained away. When transactions costs are taken into account, the fact that stock prices tend to over-react to news, falling back the day after good news and bouncing up the day after bad news, proves unexploitable: price reversals are always within the bid-ask spread. Others such as the small-firm effect, work for a few years and then fail for a few years. Others prove to be merely proxies for the reward for risk taking. Many have disappeared since (and because) attention has been drawn to them.

It is difficult to envision entrusting your retirement savings to a manager whose strategy is based on buying securities on Mondays, which tends to have negative returns on average, and selling them on Fridays. For one thing, the negative Monday returns are merely an average, so on any given week, they could be positive. In addition, such a strategy would generate large trading costs. Even more importantly, investors would likely be uncomfortable investing their funds in a strategy that has no compelling underlying economic rationale.

5. BEHAVIORAL FINANCE

Behavioral finance examines investor behavior to understand how people make decisions, individually and collectively. Behavioral finance does not assume that people consider all available information in decision-making and act rationally by maximizing utility within budget constraints and updating expectations consistent with Bayes' formula. The resulting behaviors may affect what is observed in the financial markets.

In a broader sense, behavioral finance attempts to explain why individuals make the decisions that they do, whether these decisions are rational or irrational. The focus of much of the work in this area is on the behavioral biases that affect investment decisions. The behavior of individuals, in particular their behavioral biases, has been offered as a possible explanation for a number of pricing anomalies.

Most asset-pricing models assume that markets are rational and that the intrinsic value of a security reflects this rationality. But market efficiency and asset-pricing models do not require that each individual is rational—rather, only that the market is rational. If individuals deviate from rationality, other individuals are assumed to observe this deviation and respond accordingly. These responses move the market toward efficiency. If this does not occur in practice, it may be possible to explain some market anomalies referencing observed behaviors and behavioral biases.

5.1. Loss Aversion

In most financial models, the assumption is that investors are risk averse. **Risk aversion** refers to the tendency of people to dislike risk and to require higher expected returns to compensate for exposure to additional risk. Behavioral finance allows for the possibility that the

---

[50]This point is made by Fama (1998).

dissatisfaction resulting from a loss exceeds the satisfaction resulting from a gain of the same magnitude. **Loss aversion** refers to the tendency of people to dislike losses more than they like comparable gains. This results in a strong preference for avoiding losses as opposed to achieving gains.[51] Some argue that behavioral theories of loss aversion can explain observed overreaction in markets. If loss aversion is more important than risk aversion, researchers should observe that investors overreact.[52] Although loss aversion can explain the overreaction anomaly, evidence also suggests that underreaction is just as prevalent as overreaction, which counters these arguments.

5.2. Herding

Herding behavior has been advanced as a possible explanation of underreaction and overreaction in financial markets. **Herding** occurs when investors trade on the same side of the market in the same securities, or when investors ignore their own private information and/ or analysis and act as other investors do. Herding is clustered trading that may or may not be based on information.[53] Herding may result in under- or overreaction to information depending upon the direction of the herd.

5.3. Overconfidence

A behavioral bias offered to explain pricing anomalies is overconfidence. If investors are overconfident, they overestimate their ability to process and interpret information about a security. Overconfident investors may not process information appropriately, and if there is a sufficient number of these investors, stocks will be mispriced.[54] But most researchers argue that this mispricing is temporary, with prices correcting eventually. If it takes a sufficiently long time for prices to become correctly priced and the mispricing is predictable, it may be possible for investors to earn abnormal profits.

Evidence has suggested that overconfidence results in mispricing for US, UK, German, French, and Japanese markets.[55] This overconfidence, however, is predominantly in higher-growth companies, whose prices react slowly to new information.[56]

5.4. Information Cascades

An application of behavioral theories to markets and pricing focuses on the role of personal learning in markets. Personal learning is what investors learn by observing outcomes of trades and what they learn from "conversations"—ideas shared among investors about specific assets and the markets.[57] Social interaction and the resultant contagion is important in pricing and

---

[51]See DeBondt and Thaler (1985) and Tversky and Kahneman (1981).

[52]See Fama (1998).

[53]The term used when there is herding without information is "spurious herding."

[54]Another aspect to overconfidence is that investors who are overconfident in their ability to select investments and manage a portfolio tend to use less diversification, investing in what is most familiar. Therefore, investor behavior may affect investment results—returns and risk—without implications for the efficiency of markets.

[55]Scott, Stumpp, and Xu (2003) and Boujelbene Abbes, Boujelbene, and Bouri (2009).

[56]Scott, Stumpp, and Xu (2003).

[57]Hirshleifer and Teoh (2009).

may explain such phenomena as price changes without accompanying news and mistakes in valuation.

Biases that investors possess can lead to herding behavior or information cascades. Herding and information cascades are related but not identical concepts. An **information cascade** is the transmission of information from those participants who act first and whose decisions influence the decisions of others. Those who are acting on the choices of others may be ignoring their own preferences in favor of imitating the choices of others. In particular, information cascades may occur with respect to the release of accounting information because accounting information may be difficult to interpret and may be noisy. For example, the release of earnings is difficult to interpret because it is necessary to understand how the number was arrived at and noisy because it is uncertain what the current earnings imply about future earnings.

Information cascades may result in serial correlation of stock returns, which is consistent with overreaction anomalies. Do information cascades result in correct pricing? Some argue that if a cascade is leading toward an incorrect value, this cascade is "fragile" and will be corrected because investors will ultimately give more weight to public information or the trading of a recognized informed trader.[58] Information cascades, although documented in markets, do not necessarily mean that investors can exploit knowledge of them as profitable trading opportunities.

Are information cascades rational? If the informed traders act first and uninformed traders imitate the informed traders, this behavior is consistent with rationality. The imitation trading by the uninformed traders may help the market incorporate relevant information and improve market efficiency.[59] However, the imitation trading may lead to an overreaction to information. The empirical evidence indicates that information cascades are greater for a stock when the information quality regarding the company is poor.[60] Information cascades may enhance the information available to investors.

5.5. Other Behavioral Biases

Other behavioral biases that have been put forth to explain observed investor behavior include the following:

- **representativeness**—investors assess new information and probabilities of outcomes based on similarity to the current state or to a familiar classification;
- **mental accounting**—investors keep track of the gains and losses for different investments in separate mental accounts and treat those accounts differently;
- **conservatism**—investors tend to be slow to react to new information and continue to maintain their prior views or forecasts; and
- **narrow framing**—investors focus on issues in isolation and respond to the issues based on how the issues are posed.[61]

---

[58]Avery and Zemsky (1999).

[59]Another alternative is that the uninformed traders are the majority of the market participants and the imitators are imitating not because they agree with the actions of the majority but because they are looking to act on the actions of the uninformed traders.

[60]Avery and Zemsky (1999) and Bikhchandani, Hirshleifer, and Welch (1992).

[61]For a review of these behavioral issues, see Hirshleifer (2001).

The basic idea behind behavioral finance is that investors are humans and, therefore, imperfect. These observed, less-than-rational behaviors may help explain observed pricing anomalies. The beliefs investors have about a given asset's value may not be homogeneous. But an issue, which is controversial, is whether these insights can help someone identify and exploit any mispricing. In other words, can investors use knowledge of behavioral biases to predict how asset prices will be affected and act based on the predictions to earn abnormal profits?

5.6. Behavioral Finance and Investors

Behavior biases can affect all market participants, from the novice investor to the most experienced investment manager. An understanding of behavioral finance can help market participants recognize their own and others' behavioral biases. As a result of this recognition, they may be able to respond and make improved decisions, individually and collectively.

5.7. Behavioral Finance and Efficient Markets

The use of behavioral finance to explain observed pricing is an important part of the understanding of how markets function and how prices are determined. Whether there is a behavioral explanation for market anomalies remains a debate. Pricing anomalies are continually being uncovered, and then statistical and behavioral explanations are offered to explain these anomalies.

On the one hand, if investors must be rational for efficient markets to exist, then all the imperfections of human investors suggest that markets cannot be efficient. On the other hand, if all that is required for markets to be efficient is that investors cannot consistently beat the market on a risk-adjusted basis, then the evidence does support market efficiency.

SUMMARY

This chapter has provided an overview of the theory and evidence regarding market efficiency and has discussed the different forms of market efficiency as well as the implications for fundamental analysis, technical analysis, and portfolio management. The general conclusion drawn from the efficient market hypothesis is that it is not possible to beat the market on a consistent basis by generating returns in excess of those expected for the level of risk of the investment.

Additional key points include the following:

- The efficiency of a market is affected by the number of market participants and depth of analyst coverage, information availability, and limits to trading.
- There are three forms of efficient markets, each based on what is considered to be the information used in determining asset prices. In the weak form, asset prices fully reflect all market data, which refers to all past price and trading volume information. In the semi-strong form, asset prices reflect all publicly known and available information. In the strong form, asset prices fully reflect all information, which includes both public and private information.
- Intrinsic value refers to the true value of an asset, whereas market value refers to the price at which an asset can be bought or sold. When markets are efficient, the two should be the same or very close. But when markets are not efficient, the two can diverge significantly.

- Most empirical evidence supports the idea that securities markets in developed countries are semi-strong-form efficient; however, empirical evidence does not support the strong form of the efficient market hypothesis.
- A number of anomalies have been documented that contradict the notion of market efficiency, including the size anomaly, the January anomaly, and the winners–losers anomalies. In most cases, however, contradictory evidence both supports and refutes the anomaly.
- Behavioral finance uses human psychology, such as behavioral biases, in an attempt to explain investment decisions. Whereas behavioral finance is helpful in understanding observed decisions, a market can still be considered efficient even if market participants exhibit seemingly irrational behaviors, such as herding.

REFERENCES

Alexander, John C., Delbert Goff, and Pamela P. Peterson. 1989. "Profitability of a Trading Strategy Based on Unexpected Earnings." *Financial Analysts Journal*, vol. 45, no. 4: 65–71.

Avery, Christopher, and Peter Zemsky. 1998. "Multi-Dimensional Uncertainty and Herding in Financial Markets." *American Economic Review*, vol. 88, no. 4: 724–748.

Bessembinder, Hendrik, and Kalok Chan. 1998. "Market Efficiency and the Returns to Technical Analysis." *Financial Management*, vol. 27, no. 4: 5–17.

Bikhchandani, Sushil, David Hirshleifer, and Ivo Welch. 1992. "A Theory of Fads, Fashion, Custom, and Cultural Change as Informational Cascades." *Journal of Political Economy*, vol. 100, no. 5: 992–1026.

Bouljelbene Abbes, Mouna, Younes Boujelbene, and Abdelfettah Bouri. 2009. "Overconfidence Bias: Explanation of Market Anomalies French Market Case." *Journal of Applied Economic Sciences*, vol. 4, no. 1: 12–25.

Brav, Alon, Christopher Geczy, and Paul A. Gompers. 1995. "The Long-Run Underperformance of Seasoned Equity Offerings Revisited." Working paper, Harvard University.

Brealey, Richard. 1983. "Can Professional Investors Beat the Market?" *An Introduction to Risk and Return from Common Stocks*, 2nd edition. Cambridge, MA: MIT Press.

Bris, Arturo, William N. Goetzmann, and Ning Zhu. 2009. "Efficiency and the Bear: Short Sales and Markets around the World." *Journal of Finance*, vol. 62, no. 3: 1029–1079.

Brown, Laurence D. 1997. "Earning Surprise Research: Synthesis and Perspectives." *Financial Analysts Journal*, vol. 53, no. 2: 13–19.

Capaul, Carlo, Ian Rowley, and William Sharpe. 1993. "International Value and Growth Stock Returns." *Financial Analysts Journal*, vol. 49: 27–36.

Chen, Kong-Jun, and Xiao-Ming Li. 2006. "Is Technical Analysis Useful for Stock Traders in China? Evidence from the Szse Component A-Share Index." *Pacific Economic Review*, vol. 11, no. 4: 477–488.

Chordia, Tarun, Richard Roll, and Avanidhar Subrahmanyam. 2005. "Evidence on the Speed of Convergence to Market Efficiency." *Journal of Financial Economics*, vol. 76, no. 2: 271–292.

DeBondt, Werner, and Richard Thaler. 1985. "Does the Stock Market Overreact?" *Journal of Finance*, vol. 40, no. 3: 793–808.

Deng, Xiaohu, Sandra Mortal, and Vishal Gupta. 2017. "The Real Effects of Short Selling Constraints: Cross-Country Evidence." Working paper.

Dimson, Elroy, and Carolina Minio-Kozerski. 1999. "Closed-End Funds: A Survey." *Financial Markets, Institutions & Instruments*, vol. 8, no. 2: 1–41.

Fama, Eugene F. 1970. "Efficient Capital Markets: A Review of Theory and Empirical Work." *Journal of Finance*, vol. 25, no. 2: 383–417.

Fama, Eugene F. 1976. *Foundations of Finance*. New York: Basic Books.

Fama, Eugene F. 1998. "Market Efficiency, Long-Term Returns, and Behavioral Finance." *Journal of Financial Economics*, vol. 50, no. 3: 283–306.

Fama, Eugene F., and G. William Schwert. 1977. "Asset Returns and Inflation." *Journal of Financial Economics*, vol. 5, no. 2: 115–146.

Fama, Eugene F., and Kenneth R. French. 1988. "Dividend Yields and Expected Stock Returns." *Journal of Financial Economics*, vol. 22, no. 1: 3–25.

Fama, Eugene F., and Kenneth R. French. 1995. "Size and Book-to-Market Factors in Earnings and Returns." *Journal of Finance*, vol. 50, no. 1: 131–155.

Fama, Eugene F., and Kenneth R. French. 1998. "Value versus Growth: The International Evidence." *Journal of Finance*, vol. 53: 1975–1999.

Fama, Eugene F., and Kenneth R. French. 2008. "Dissecting Anomalies." *Journal of Finance*, vol. 63, no. 4: 1653–1678.

Fifield, Suzanne, David Power, and C. Donald Sinclair. 2005. "An Analysis of Trading Strategies in Eleven European Stock Markets." *European Journal of Finance*, vol. 11, no. 6: 531–548.

Gan, Christopher, Minsoo Lee, Au Yong Hue Hwa, and Jun Zhang. 2005. "Revisiting Share Market Efficiency: Evidence from the New Zealand, Australia, US and Japan Stock Indices." *American Journal of Applied Sciences*, vol. 2, no. 5: 996–1002.

Grossman, Sanford J., and Joseph E. Stiglitz. 1980. "On the Impossibility of Informationally Efficient Markets." *American Economic Review*, vol. 70, no. 3: 393–408.

Hirshleifer, David. 2001. "Investor Psychology and Asset Pricing." *Journal of Finance*, vol. 56, no. 4: 1533–1597.

Hirshleifer, David, and Siew Hong Teoh. 2009. "Thought and Behavior Contagion in Capital Markets." In *Handbook of Financial Markets: Dynamics and Evolution*. Edited by Klaus Reiner Schenk-Hoppe and Thorstein Hens. Amsterdam: North Holland.

Jacobs, Bruce I., and Kenneth N. Levy. 1988. "Calendar Anomalies: Abnormal Returns at Calendar Turning Points." *Financial Analysts Journal*, vol. 44, no. 6: 28–39.

Jaffe, Jeffrey. 1974. "Special Information and Insider Trading." *Journal of Business*, vol. 47, no. 3: 410–428.

Jegadeesh, Narayan, and Sheridan Titman. 2001. "Profitability of Momentum Strategies: An Evaluation of Alternative Explanations." *Journal of Finance*, vol. 56: 699–720.

Johnson, Timothy C. 2002. "Rational Momentum Effects." *Journal of Finance*, vol. 57, no. 2: 585–608.

Jones, Charles P., Richard J. Rendleman, and Henry. A. Latané. 1984. "Stock Returns and SUEs during the 1970's." *Journal of Portfolio Management*, vol. 10: 18–22.

Kim, Donchoi, and Myungsun Kim. 2003. "A Multifactor Explanation of Post-Earnings Announcement Drift." *Journal of Financial and Quantitative Analysis*, vol. 38, no. 2: 383–398.

Kim, Dongcheol. 2006. "On the Information Uncertainty Risk and the January Effect." *Journal of Business*, vol. 79, no. 4: 2127–2162.

Lee, Charles M.C., Andrei Sheifer, and Richard H. Thaler. 1990. "Anomalies: Closed-End Mutual Funds." *Journal of Economic Perspectives*, vol. 4, no. 4: 153–164.

Malkiel, Burton G. 1995. "Returns from Investing in Equity Mutual Funds 1971 to 1991." *Journal of Finance*, vol. 50: 549–572.

Mobarek, Asma, A. Sabur Mollah, and Rafiqul Bhuyan. 2008. "Market Efficiency in Emerging Stock Market." *Journal of Emerging Market Finance*, vol. 7, no. 1: 17–41.

Pontiff, Jeffrey. 1995. "Closed-End Fund Premia and Returns: Implications for Financial Market Equilibrium." *Journal of Financial Economics*, vol. 37: 341–370.

Pontiff, Jeffrey. 1996. "Costly Arbitrage: Evidence from Closed-End Funds." *Quarterly Journal of Economics*, vol. 111, no. 4: 1135–1151.

Raja, M., J. Clement Sudhahar, and M. Selvam. 2009. "Testing the Semi-Strong Form Efficiency of Indian Stock Market with Respect to Information Content of Stock Split Announcement—A Study of IT Industry." *International Research Journal of Finance and Economics*, vol. 25: 7–20.

Roll, Richard. 1983. "On Computing Mean Returns and the Small Firm Premium." *Journal of Financial Economics*, vol. 12: 371–386.

Rozeff, Michael S., and Mir A. Zaman. 1988. "Market Efficiency and Insider Trading: New Evidence."
    Journal of Business, vol. 61: 25–44.

Schwert, G. William. 2003. "Anomalies and Market Efficiency." *Handbook of the Economics of Finance.*
    Edited by George M. Constantinides, M. Harris, and Rene Stulz. Amsterdam: Elsevier Science, B. V.

Scott, James, Margaret Stumpp, and Peter Xu. 2003. "Overconfidence Bias in International Stock Prices."
    Journal of Portfolio Management, vol. 29, no. 2: 80–89.

Tversky, Amos, and Daniel Kahneman. 1981. "The Framing of Decisions and the Psychology of Choice."
    Science, vol. 211, no. 30: 453–458.

Yau, Jot, Thomas Schneeweis, Thomas Robinson, and Lisa Weiss. 2007. "Alternative Investments
    Portfolio Management." *Managing Investment Portfolios: A Dynamic Process*. Hoboken, NJ: John
    Wiley & Sons.

Zarowin, P. 1989. "Does the Stock Market Overreact to Corporate Earnings Information?" *Journal of
    Finance*, vol. 44: 1385–1399.

PRACTICE PROBLEMS

1. In an efficient market, the change in a company's share price is *most likely* the result of:
   A. insiders' private information.
   B. the previous day's change in stock price.
   C. new information coming into the market.

2. Regulation that restricts some investors from participating in a market will *most likely*:
   A. impede market efficiency.
   B. not affect market efficiency.
   C. contribute to market efficiency.

3. With respect to efficient market theory, when a market allows short selling, the efficiency of the market is *most likely* to:
   A. increase.
   B. decrease.
   C. remain the same.

4. Which of the following regulations will *most likely* contribute to market efficiency? Regulatory restrictions on:
   A. short selling.
   B. foreign traders.
   C. insiders trading with nonpublic information.

5. Which of the following market regulations will *most likely* impede market efficiency?
   A. Restricting traders' ability to short sell.
   B. Allowing unrestricted foreign investor trading.
   C. Penalizing investors who trade with nonpublic information.

6. If markets are efficient, the difference between the intrinsic value and market value of a company's security is:
   A. negative.
   B. zero.
   C. positive.

7. The intrinsic value of an undervalued asset is:
    A. less than the asset's market value.
    B. greater than the asset's market value.
    C. the value at which the asset can currently be bought or sold.

8. The market value of an undervalued asset is:
    A. greater than the asset's intrinsic value.
    B. the value at which the asset can currently be bought or sold.
    C. equal to the present value of all the asset's expected cash flows.

9. With respect to the efficient market hypothesis, if security prices reflect *only* past prices and trading volume information, then the market is:
    A. weak-form efficient.
    B. strong-form efficient.
    C. semi-strong-form efficient.

10. Which one of the following statements *best* describes the semi-strong form of market efficiency?
    A. Empirical tests examine the historical patterns in security prices.
    B. Security prices reflect all publicly known and available information.
    C. Semi-strong-form efficient markets are not necessarily weak-form efficient.

11. If markets are semi-strong efficient, standard fundamental analysis will yield abnormal trading profits that are:
    A. negative.
    B. equal to zero.
    C. positive.

12. If prices reflect all public and private information, the market is *best* described as:
    A. weak-form efficient.
    B. strong-form efficient.
    C. semi-strong-form efficient.

13. If markets are semi-strong-form efficient, then passive portfolio management strategies are *most likely* to:
    A. earn abnormal returns.
    B. outperform active trading strategies.
    C. underperform active trading strategies.

14. If a market is semi-strong-form efficient, the risk-adjusted returns of a passively managed portfolio relative to an actively managed portfolio are *most likely*:
    A. lower.
    B. higher.
    C. the same.

15. Technical analysts assume that markets are:
    A. weak-form efficient.
    B. weak-form inefficient.
    C. semi-strong-form efficient.

16. Fundamental analysts assume that markets are:
    A. weak-form inefficient.
    B. semi-strong-form efficient.
    C. semi-strong-form inefficient.

17. If a market is weak-form efficient but semi-strong-form inefficient, then which of the following types of portfolio management is *most likely* to produce abnormal returns?
    A. Passive portfolio management.
    B. Active portfolio management based on technical analysis.
    C. Active portfolio management based on fundamental analysis.

18. An increase in the time between when an order to trade a security is placed and when the order is executed *most likely* indicates that market efficiency has:
    A. decreased.
    B. remained the same.
    C. increased.

19. With respect to efficient markets, a company whose share price reacts gradually to the public release of its annual report *most likely* indicates that the market where the company trades is:
    A. semi-strong-form efficient.
    B. subject to behavioral biases.
    C. receiving additional information about the company.

20. Which of the following is *least likely* to explain the January effect anomaly?
    A. Tax-loss selling.
    B. Release of new information in January.
    C. Window dressing of portfolio holdings.

21. If a researcher conducting empirical tests of a trading strategy using time series of returns finds statistically significant abnormal returns, then the researcher has *most likely* found:
    A. a market anomaly.
    B. evidence of market inefficiency.
    C. a strategy to produce future abnormal returns.

22. Which of the following market anomalies is inconsistent with weak-form market efficiency?
    A. Earnings surprise.
    B. Momentum pattern.
    C. Closed-end fund discount.

23. Researchers have found that value stocks have consistently outperformed growth stocks. An investor wishing to exploit the value effect should purchase the stock of companies with above-average:
    A. dividend yields.
    B. market-to-book ratios.
    C. price-to-earnings ratios.

24. With respect to rational and irrational investment decisions, the efficient market hypothesis requires:
   A. only that the market is rational.
   B. that all investors make rational decisions.
   C. that some investors make irrational decisions.

25. Observed overreactions in markets can be explained by an investor's degree of:
   A. risk aversion.
   B. loss aversion.
   C. confidence in the market.

26. Like traditional finance models, the behavioral theory of loss aversion assumes that investors dislike risk; however, the dislike of risk in behavioral theory is assumed to be:
   A. leptokurtic.
   B. symmetrical.
   C. asymmetrical.

CHAPTER 3

OVERVIEW OF EQUITY PORTFOLIO MANAGEMENT

James Clunie, PhD, CFA
James Alan Finnegan, CAIA, RMA, CFA

LEARNING OUTCOMES

The candidate should be able to:

- describe the roles of equities in the overall portfolio;
- describe how an equity manager's investment universe can be segmented;
- describe the types of income and costs associated with owning and managing an equity portfolio and their potential effects on portfolio performance;
- describe the potential benefits of shareholder engagement and the role an equity manager might play in shareholder engagement;
- describe rationales for equity investment across the passive–active spectrum.

1. INTRODUCTION

Equities represent a sizable portion of the global investment universe and thus often represent a primary component of investors' portfolios. Rationales for investing in equities include potential participation in the growth and earnings prospects of an economy's corporate sector as well as an ownership interest in a range of business entities by size, economic activity, and geographical scope. Publicly traded equities are generally more liquid than other asset classes and thus may enable investors to more easily monitor price trends and purchase or sell securities with low transaction costs.

This chapter provides an overview of equity portfolio management. Section 2 discusses the roles of equities in a portfolio. Section 3 discusses the equity investment universe, including several ways the universe can be segmented. Section 4 covers the income and costs in an equity portfolio. Section 5 discusses shareholder engagement between equity investors

Portfolio Management, Second Edition, by James Clunie, PhD, CFA, and James Alan Finnegan, CAIA, RMA, CFA. Copyright © 2018 by CFA Institute.

and the companies in which they invest. Section 6 discusses equity investment across the passive–active investment spectrum. A summary of key points completes the chapter.

2. THE ROLES OF EQUITIES IN A PORTFOLIO

Equities provide several roles in (or benefits to) an overall portfolio, such as capital appreciation, dividend income, diversification with other asset classes, and a potential hedge against inflation. In addition to these benefits, client investment considerations play an important role for portfolio managers when deciding to include equities in portfolios.

2.1. Capital Appreciation

Long-term returns on equities, driven predominantly by capital appreciation, have historically been among the highest among major asset classes. Exhibit 1 demonstrates the average annual real returns on equities versus bonds and bills—both globally and within various countries—from 1967–2016. With a few exceptions, equities outperformed both bonds and bills, in particular, during this period across the world.

EXHIBIT 1   Real Returns on Equities (1967–2016)

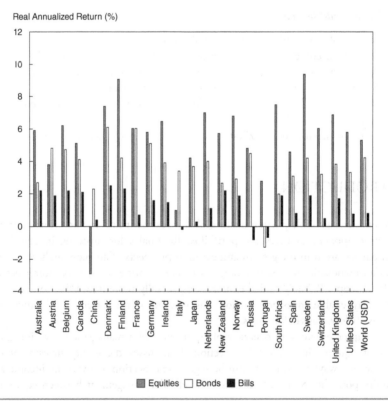

* China data are from 1993 to 2016.
** Russia data are from 1995 to 2016.
Source: Credit Suisse Global Investment Returns Yearbook 2017, Summary Edition.

Equities tend to outperform other asset classes during periods of strong economic growth, and they tend to underperform other asset classes during weaker economic periods. Capital (or price) appreciation of equities often occurs when investing in companies with growth in earnings, cash flows, and/or revenues—as well as in companies with competitive success. Capital appreciation can occur, for example, in such growth-oriented companies as small technology companies as well as in large, mature companies where management successfully reduces costs or engages in value-added acquisitions.

2.2. Dividend Income

The most common sources of income for an equity portfolio are dividends. Companies may choose to distribute internally generated cash flows as common dividends rather than reinvest the cash flows in projects, particularly when suitable projects do not exist or available projects have a high cost of equity or a low probability of future value creation. Large, well-established corporations often provide dividend payments that increase in value over time, although there are no assurances that common dividend payments from these corporations will grow or even be maintained. In addition to common dividends, preferred dividends can provide dividend income to those shareholders owning preferred shares.

Dividends have comprised a significant component of long-term total returns for equity investors. Over shorter periods of time, however, the proportion of equity returns from dividends (reflected as dividend yield) can vary considerably relative to capital gains or losses. Exhibit 2 illustrates this effect of dividend returns relative to annual total returns on the S&P 500 Index from 1936 through 2016. Since 1990, the dividend yield on the S&P 500 has been in the 1–3% range; thus, the effect of dividends can clearly be significant during periods of weak equity market performance. Also note that the dividend yield may vary considerably by sector within the S&P 500.

EXHIBIT 2   S&P 500 Dividend Contribution (1936–2016)

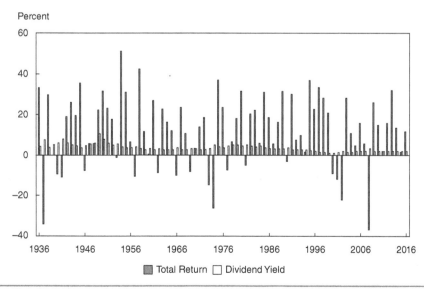

Source: Bloomberg.

2.3. Diversification with Other Asset Classes

Individual equities clearly have unique characteristics, although the correlation of returns among equities is often high. In a portfolio context, however, equities can provide meaningful diversification benefits when combined with other asset classes (assuming less than perfect correlation). Recall that a major reason why portfolios can effectively reduce risk (typically expressed as standard deviation of returns) is that combining securities whose returns are less than perfectly correlated reduces the standard deviation of the diversified portfolio below the weighted average of the standard deviations of the individual investments. The challenge in diversifying risk is to find assets that have a correlation that is much lower than +1.0.

Exhibit 3 provides a correlation matrix across various global equity indexes and other asset classes using total monthly returns from January 2001 to February 2017.[1] The correlation matrix shows that during this period, various broad equity indexes and, to a lesser extent, country equity indexes were highly correlated with each other. Conversely, both the broad and country equity indexes were considerably less correlated with indexes in other asset classes, notably global treasury bonds and gold. Overall, Exhibit 3 indicates that combining equities with other asset classes can result in portfolio diversification benefits.

It is important to note that correlations are not constant over time. During a long historical period, the correlation of returns between two asset classes may be low, but in any given period, the correlation can differ from the long term. Correlation estimates can vary based on the capital market dynamics during the period when the correlations are measured. During periods of market crisis, correlations across asset classes and among equities themselves often increase and reduce the benefit of diversification. As with correlations, volatility (standard deviation) of asset class returns may also vary over time.

EXHIBIT 3   Correlation Matrix, January 2001 to February 2017

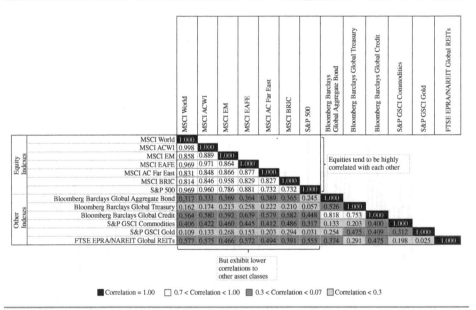

Source: Morningstar Direct.

---

[1]Monthly return data cover January 2001 to February 2017 for all indexes except the FTSE EPRA/ NAREIT Global Real Estate Index (whose inception date was November 2008).

2.4. Hedge Against Inflation

Some individual equities or sectors can provide some protection against inflation, although the ability to do so varies. For example, certain companies may be successful at passing along higher input costs (such as raw materials, energy, or wages) to customers. This ability to pass along costs to customers can protect a company's or industry's profit margin and cash flow and can be reflected in their stock prices. As another example, companies within sectors that produce broad-based commodities (e.g., oil or industrial metals producers) can more directly benefit from increases in commodity prices. Although individual equities or sectors can protect against inflation, the success of equities as an asset class in hedging inflation has been mixed. Certain empirical studies have indeed shown that real returns on equities and inflation have positive correlation over the long-term, thus in theory forming a hedge. However, the degree of correlation typically varies by country and is dependent on the time period assessed. In fact, for severe inflationary periods, some studies have shown that real returns on equities and inflation have been *negatively* correlated. When assessing the relationship between equity returns and inflation, investors should be aware that inflation is typically a lagging indicator of the business cycle, while equity prices are often a leading indicator.

2.5. Client Considerations for Equities in a Portfolio

The inclusion of equities in a portfolio can be driven by a client's goals or needs. A client's investment considerations are typically described in an investment policy statement (IPS), which establishes, among other things, a client's return objectives, risk tolerance, constraints, and unique circumstances. By understanding these client considerations, a financial adviser or wealth manager can determine whether—and how much—equities should be in a client's portfolio.

Equity investments are often characterized by such attributes as growth potential, income generation, risk and return volatility, and sensitivity to various macro-economic variables (e.g., energy prices, GDP growth, interest rates, and inflation). As a result, a portfolio manager can adapt such specific factors to an equity investor's investment goals and risk tolerance. For example, a risk-averse and conservative investor may prefer some exposure to well-established companies with strong and stable cash flow that pay meaningful dividends. Conversely, a growth-oriented investor with an aggressive risk tolerance may prefer small or large growth-oriented companies (e.g., those in the social media or alternative energy sectors).

Wealth managers and financial advisers often consider the following investment objectives and constraints when deciding to include equities (or asset classes in general, for that matter) in a client's portfolio:

- *Risk objective* addresses how risk is measured (e.g., in absolute or relative terms); the investor's willingness to take risk; the investor's ability to take risk; and the investor's specific risk objectives.
- *Return objective* addresses how returns are measured (e.g., in absolute or relative terms); stated return objectives.
- *Liquidity requirement* is a constraint in which cash is needed for anticipated or unanticipated events.
- *Time horizon* is the time period associated with an investment objective (e.g., short term, long term, or some combination of the two).

- *Tax concerns* include tax policies that can affect investor returns; for example, dividends may be taxed at a different rate than capital gains.
- *Legal and regulatory factors* are external factors imposed by governmental, regulatory, or oversight authorities.
- *Unique circumstances* are an investor's considerations other than liquidity requirements, time horizon, or tax concerns that may constrain portfolio choices. These considerations may include environmental, social, and governance (ESG) issues or religious preferences.

ESG considerations often occur at the request of clients because interest in sustainable investing has grown. With regard to equities, these considerations often determine the suitability of certain sectors or individual company stocks for designated investor portfolios. Historically, ESG approaches used by portfolio managers have largely represented **negative screening** (or exclusionary screening), which refers to the practice of excluding certain sectors or companies that deviate from accepted standards in such areas as human rights or environmental concerns. More recently, portfolio managers have increasingly focused on **positive screening** or **best-in-class** approaches, which attempt to identify companies or sectors that score most favorably with regard to ESG-related risks and/or opportunities. **Thematic investing** is another approach that focuses on investing in companies within a specific sector or following a specific theme, such as energy efficiency or climate change. **Impact investing** is a related approach that seeks to achieve targeted social or environmental objectives along with measurable financial returns through engagement with a company or by direct investment in projects or companies.

EXAMPLE 1   Roles of Equities

Alex Chang, Lin Choi, and Frank Huber manage separate equity portfolios for the same investment firm. Chang's portfolio objective is conservative in nature, with a regular stream of income as the primary investment objective. Choi's portfolio is more aggressive in nature, with a long-term horizon and with growth as the primary objective. Finally, Huber's portfolio consists of wealthy entrepreneurs who are concerned about rising inflation and wish to preserve the purchasing power of their wealth.

Discuss the investment approach that each portfolio manager would likely use to achieve his or her portfolio objectives.

Solution: Given that his portfolio is focused on a regular stream of income, Chang is likely to focus on companies with regular dividend income. More specifically, Chang is likely to invest in large, well-established companies with stable or growing dividend payments. With a long-term horizon, Choi is most interested in capital appreciation of her portfolio, so she is likely to focus on companies with earnings growth and competitive success. Finally, Huber's clients are concerned about the effects of inflation, so he will likely seek to invest in shares of companies that can provide an inflation hedge. Huber would likely seek companies that can successfully pass on higher input costs to their customers, and he may also seek commodity producers that may benefit from rising commodity prices.

3. EQUITY INVESTMENT UNIVERSE

Given the extensive range of companies in which an equity portfolio manager may invest, an important task for the manager is to segment companies or sectors according to similar characteristics. This segmentation enables portfolio managers to better evaluate and analyze their equity investment universe, and it can help with portfolio diversification. Several approaches to segmenting the equity investment universe are discussed in the following sections.

3.1. Segmentation by Size and Style

A popular approach to segmenting the equity universe incorporates two factors: (1) size and (2) style. Size is typically measured by market capitalization and often categorized by large cap, mid cap, and small cap. Style is typically classified as value, growth, or a combination of value and growth (typically termed "blend" or "core"). In addition, style is often determined through a "scoring" system that incorporates multiple metrics or ratios, such as price-to-book ratios, price-to-earnings ratios, earnings growth, dividend yield, and book value growth. These metrics are then typically "scored" individually for each company, assigned certain weights, and then aggregated. The result is a composite score that determines where the company's stock is positioned along the value–growth spectrum. A combination of growth and value style is not uncommon, particularly for large corporations that have both mature and higher growth business lines.

Exhibit 4 illustrates a common matrix that reflects size and style dimensions. Each category in the matrix can be represented by companies with considerably different business activities. For example, both a small, mature metal fabricating business and a small health care services provider may fall in the Small Cap Value category. In practice, individual stocks may not clearly fall into one of the size/style categories. As a result, the size/style matrix tends to be more of a scatter plot than a simple set of nine categories. An example of a scatter plot is demonstrated in Exhibit 5, which includes all listed equities on the New York Stock Exchange as of March 2017. Each company represents a single dot in Exhibit 5. This more granular representation enables the expansion of size and style categories, such as blue chip and micro-cap companies in size and deep value and high growth in style. It should be noted that Morningstar applies the term "core" for those stocks in which neither value nor growth characteristics dominate, and the term "blend" for those funds with a combination of both growth and value stocks or mostly core stocks.

EXHIBIT 4   Equity Size and Style Matrix

		Investment Style		
		Value	Core	Growth
Company Size (Market Cap)	Large Cap	Large Cap value	Large Cap core	Large Cap growth
	Mid Cap	Mid Cap value	Mid Cap core	Mid Cap growth
	Small Cap	Small Cap value	Small Cap core	Small Cap growth

Source: Morningstar.

EXHIBIT 5   Equity Size and Style Scatter Plot

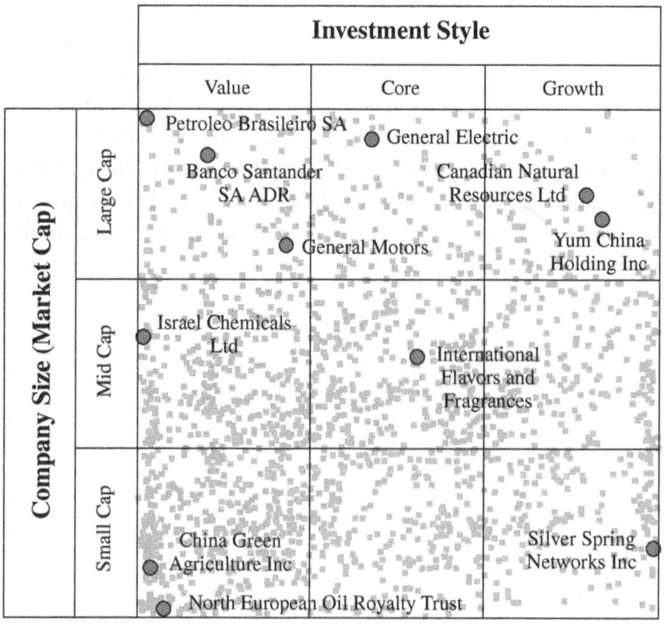

Source: Morningstar Direct.

Segmentation by size/style can provide several advantages for portfolio managers. First, portfolio managers can construct an overall equity portfolio that reflects desired risk, return, and income characteristics in a relatively straightforward and manageable way. Second, given the broad range of companies within each segment, segmentation by size/ style results in diversification across economic sectors or industries. Third, active equity managers—that is, those seeking to outperform a given benchmark portfolio—can construct performance benchmarks for specific size/style segments. Generally, large investment management firms may have sizable teams dedicated toward specific size/style categories, while small firms may specialize in a specific size/style category, particularly mid-cap and small-cap companies, seeking to outperform a standard benchmark or comparable peer group.

The final advantage of segmentation by size/style is that it allows a portfolio to reflect a company's maturity and potentially changing growth/value orientation. Specifically, many companies that undertake an IPO (initial public offering) are small and in a growth phase, and thus they may fall in the small-cap growth category. If these companies can successfully grow, their size may ultimately move to mid cap or even large cap, while their style may conceivably shift from high growth to value or a combination of growth and value (e.g., a growth and income stock). Accordingly, over the life cycle of companies, investor preferences for these companies may shift increasingly from capital appreciation to dividend income. In addition, segmentation also helps fund managers adjust holdings over time—for example, when stocks that were previously considered to be in the growth category mature and possibly become value stocks. The key disadvantages of segmentation by size/style are that the categories may change over time and may be defined differently among investors.

3.2. Segmentation by Geography

Another common approach to equity universe segmentation is by geography. This approach is typically based on the stage of markets' macroeconomic development and wealth. Common geographic categories are *developed markets*, *emerging markets*, and *frontier markets*. Exhibit 6 demonstrates the commonly used geographic segmentation of international equity indexes according to MSCI. Other major index providers—such as FTSE, Standard & Poor's, and Russell—also provide similar types of international equity indexes.

Geographic segmentation is useful to equity investors who have considerable exposure to their domestic market and want to diversify by investing in global equities. A key weakness of geographic segmentation is that investing in a specific market (e.g., market index) may provide lower-than-expected exposure to that market. As an example, many large companies domiciled in the United States, Europe, or Asia may be global in nature as opposed to considerable focus on their domicile. Another key weakness of geographic segmentation is potential currency risk when investing in different global equity markets.

EXHIBIT 6   MSCI International Equity Indexes (as of November 2016)

Developed Markets

Americas	Europe and Middle East	Pacific
Canada	Austria	Australia
United States	Belgium	Hong Kong SAR
	Denmark	Japan
	Finland	New Zealand
	France	Singapore
	Germany	
	Ireland	
	Israel	
	Italy	
	Netherlands	
	Norway	
	Portugal	
	Spain	
	Sweden	
	Switzerland	
	United Kingdom	

Emerging Markets

Americas	Europe, Middle East, and Africa	Asia Pacific
Brazil	Czech Republic	Chinese mainland
Chile	Egypt	India
Colombia	Greece	Indonesia
Mexico	Hungary	Korea
Peru	Poland	Malaysia
	Qatar	Philippines
	Russia	Taiwan Region
	South Africa	Thailand
	Turkey	Pakistan
	United Arab Emirates	

Frontier Markets

Americas	Europe and CIS	Africa	Middle East	Asia
Argentina	Croatia	Kenya	Bahrain	Bangladesh
	Estonia	Mauritius	Jordan	Sri Lanka
	Lithuania	Morocco	Kuwait	Vietnam
	Kazakhstan	Nigeria	Lebanon	
	Romania	Tunisia	Oman	
	Serbia			
	Slovenia			

Notes:

1. The following markets are not included in the developed, emerging, or frontier indexes but have their own market-specific indexes: Saudi Arabia, Jamaica, Trinidad & Tobago, Bosnia Herzegovina, Bulgaria, Ukraine, Botswana, Ghana, Zimbabwe, and Palestine.
2. Pakistan was reclassified from the frontier market to the emerging market category as of May 2017.
3. CIS: Commonwealth of Independent States (formerly the USSR).

3.3. Segmentation by Economic Activity

Economic activity is another approach that portfolio managers may use to segment the equity universe. Most commonly used equity classification systems group companies into industries/sectors using either a *production-oriented* approach or a *market-oriented* approach. The production-oriented approach groups companies that manufacture similar products or use similar inputs in their manufacturing processes. The market-oriented approach groups companies based on the markets they serve, the way revenue is earned, and the way customers use companies' products. For example, using a production-oriented approach, a coal company may be classified in the basic materials or mining sector. However, using a market-oriented approach, this same coal company may be classified in the energy sector given the primary market (heating) for the use of coal. As another example, a commercial airline carrier may be classified in the transportation sector using the production-oriented approach, while the same company may be classified in the travel and leisure sector using the market-oriented approach.

Four main global classification systems segment the equity universe by economic activity: (1) the Global Industry Classification Standard (GICS); (2) the Industrial Classification Benchmark (ICB); (3) the Thomson Reuters Business Classification (TRBC); and (4) the Russell Global Sectors Classification (RGS). The GICS uses a market-oriented approach, while the ICB, TRBC, and RGS all use a production-oriented approach. These classification systems help standardize industry definitions so that portfolio managers can compare and analyze companies and industries/sectors. In addition, the classification systems are useful in the creation of industry performance benchmarks.

Exhibit 7 compares the four primary classification systems mentioned. Each system is classified broadly and then increasingly more granular to compare companies and their underlying businesses.

EXHIBIT 7   Primary Sector Classification Systems

Level/ System	GICS	ICB	TRBC	RGS
1st	11 Sectors	10 Industries	10 Economic Sectors	9 Economic Sectors
2nd	24 Industry Groups	19 Super Sectors	28 Business Sectors	33 Sub-Sectors
3rd	68 Industries	41 Sectors	54 Industry Groups	157 Industries
4th	157 Sub-Industries	114 Sub-Sectors	136 Industries	Not Applicable

Sources: Thomson Reuters, S&P/MSCI, FTSE/Dow Jones.

To illustrate how segmentation of the classification systems may be used in practice, Exhibit 8 demonstrates how GICS, perhaps the most prominent classification system, subdivides selected sectors—in this case, Consumer Discretionary, Consumer Staples, and Information Technology—into certain industry group, industry, and sub-industry levels.

EXHIBIT 8   GICS Classification Examples

Sector	Consumer Discretionary	Consumer Staples	Information Technology
Industry Group Example	Automobiles & Components	Food, Beverage & Tobacco	Technology Hardware & Equipment
Industry Example	Automobiles	Beverages	Electronic Equipment, Instruments & Components
Sub-Industry Example	Motorcycle Manufacturers	Soft Drinks	Electronic Manufacturing Services

Source: MSCI.

As with other segmentation approaches mentioned previously, segmentation by economic activity enables equity portfolio managers to construct performance benchmarks for specific sectors or industries. Portfolio managers may also obtain better industry representation (diversification) by segmenting their equity universe according to economic activity. The key disadvantage of segmentation by economic activity is that the business activities of companies—particularly large ones—may include more than one industry or sub-industry.

EXAMPLE 2   Segmenting the Equity Investment Universe

A portfolio manager is initiating a new fund that seeks to invest in the Chinese robotics industry, which is experiencing rapidly accelerating earnings. To help identify appropriate company stocks, the portfolio manager wants to select an approach to segment the equity universe.

Recommend which segmentation approach would be most appropriate for the portfolio manager.

Solution: Based on his desired strategy to invest in companies with rapidly accelerating (growing) earnings, the portfolio manager would most likely segment his equity universe by size/style. The portfolio manager would most likely use an investment style that reflects growth, with size (large cap, mid cap, or small cap) depending on the company being analyzed. Other segmentation approaches, including those according to geography and economic activity, would be less appropriate for the portfolio manager given the similar geographic and industry composition of the Chinese robotics industry.

3.4. Segmentation of Equity Indexes and Benchmarks

Segmentation of equity indexes or benchmarks reflects some of or all the approaches previously discussed in this section. For example, the MSCI Europe Large Cap Growth Index, the MSCI World Small Cap Value Index, the MSCI Emerging Markets Large Cap

Growth Index, or the MSCI Latin America Midcap Index combine various geographic, size, and style dimensions. This combination of geography, size, and style also sometimes applies to individual countries—particularly those in large, developed markets.

A more focused approach to segmentation of equity indexes uses industries or sectors. Because many industries and sectors are global in scope, the most common types of these indexes are comprised of companies in different countries. A few examples include the following:

- Global Natural Resources—the *S&P Global Natural Resources Index* includes 90 of the largest publicly traded companies in natural resources and commodities businesses across three primary commodity-related sectors: agribusiness; energy; and metals and mining.
- Worldwide Oil and Natural Gas—the *MSCI World Energy Index* includes the large-cap and mid-cap segments of publicly traded oil and natural gas companies within the developed markets.
- Multinational Financials—the *Thomson Reuters Global Financials Index* includes the 100 largest publicly traded companies within the global financial services sector as defined by the TRBC classification system.

Finally, some indexes reflect specific investment approaches, such as ESG. Such ESG indexes are comprised of companies that reflect certain considerations, such as sustainability or impact investing.

4. INCOME AND COSTS IN AN EQUITY PORTFOLIO

Dividends are the primary source of income for equity portfolios. In addition, some portfolio managers may use securities lending or option-writing strategies to generate income. On the cost side, equity portfolios incur various fees and trading costs that adversely affect portfolio returns. The primary types of income and costs are discussed in this section.

4.1. Dividend Income

Investors requiring regular income may prefer to invest in stocks with large or frequent dividend payments, whereas growth-oriented investors may have little interest in dividends. Taxation is an important consideration for dividend income received, particularly for individuals. Depending on the country where the investor is domiciled, where dividends are issued, and the type of investor, dividends may be subject to withholding tax and/or income tax.

Beyond regular dividends, equity portfolios may receive **special dividends** from certain companies. Special dividends occur when companies decide to distribute excess cash to shareholders, but the payments may not be maintained over time. **Optional stock dividends** are another type of dividend in which shareholders may elect to receive either cash or new shares. When the share price used to calculate the number of stock dividend shares is established before the shareholder's election date, the choice between a cash or stock dividend may be important. This choice represents "optionality" for the shareholder, and the optionality has value. Some market participants, typically investment banks, may offer to purchase this "option," providing an additional, if modest, source of income to an equity investor.

4.2. Securities Lending Income

For some investors, **securities lending**—a form of collateralized lending—may be used to generate income for portfolios. Securities lending can facilitate short sales, which involve the sale of securities the seller does not own. When a securities lending transaction involves the transfer of equities, the transaction is generally known as **stock lending** and the securities are generally known as *stock loans*. Stock loans are collateralized with either cash or other high-quality securities to provide some financial protection to the lender. Stock loans are usually open-ended in duration, but the borrower must return the shares to the lender on demand.

Stock lenders generally receive a fee from the stock borrower as compensation for the loaned shares. Most stock loans in developed markets earn a modest fee, approximately 0.2–0.5% on an annualized basis. In emerging markets, fees are typically higher, often 1–2% annualized for large-cap stocks. In many equity markets, certain stocks—called "specials"—are in high demand for borrowing. These specials can earn fees that are substantially higher than average (typically 5–15% annualized), and in cases of extreme demand, they could be as high as 25–100% annually. However, such high fees do not normally persist for long periods of time.

In addition to fees earned, stock lenders can generate further income by reinvesting the cash collateral received (assuming a favorable interest rate environment). However, as with virtually any other investment, the collateral would be subject to market risk, credit risk, liquidity risk, and operational risk. The administrative costs of a securities lending program, in turn, will reduce the collateral income generated. Dividends on loaned stock are "manufactured" by the stock borrower for the stock lender—that is, the stock borrower ensures that the stock lender is compensated for any dividends that the lender would have received had the stock not been loaned.

Index funds are frequent stock lenders because of their large, long-term holdings in stocks. In addition, because index funds merely seek to replicate the performance of an index, portfolio managers of these funds are normally not concerned that borrowed stock used for short-selling purposes might decrease the prices of the corresponding equities. Large, actively managed pension funds, endowments, and institutional investors are also frequent stock lenders, although these investors are likely more concerned with the effect on their returns if the loaned shares are used to facilitate short-selling. The evidence on the impact of stock lending on asset prices has, however, been mixed (see, for example, Kaplan, Moskowitz, and Sensoy 2013).

4.3. Ancillary Investment Strategies

Additional income can be generated for an equity portfolio through a trading strategy known as **dividend capture**. Under this strategy, an equity portfolio manager purchases stocks just before their ex-dividend dates, holds these stocks through the ex-dividend date to earn the right to receive the dividend, and subsequently sells the shares. Once a stock goes ex-dividend, the share price should, in theory, decrease by the value of the dividend. In this way, capturing dividends would increase portfolio income, although the portfolio would, again in theory, experience capital losses of similar magnitude. However, the share price movement could vary from this theoretical assumption given income tax considerations, stock-specific supply/demand conditions, and general stock market moves around the ex-dividend date.

Selling (writing) options can also generate additional income for an equity portfolio. One such options strategy is writing a *covered call*, whereby the portfolio manager already owns the underlying stock and sells a call option on that stock. Another options strategy is writing a *cash-covered put* (also called a *cash-secured put*), whereby the portfolio manager writes a put option on a stock and simultaneously deposits money equal to the exercise price into a designated account. Under both covered calls and cash-covered puts, income is generated through the writing of options, but clearly the risk profile of the portfolio would be altered. For example, writing a covered call would limit the upside from share price appreciation of the underlying shares.

EXAMPLE 3   Equity Portfolio Income

Isabel Cordova is an equity portfolio manager for a large multinational investment firm. Her portfolio consists of several dividend-paying stocks, and she is interested in generating additional income to enhance the portfolio's total return. Describe potential sources of additional income for Cordova's equity portfolio.

Solution: Cordova's primary source of income for her portfolio would likely be "regular" and, in some cases, special dividends from those companies that pay them. Another potential source of income for Cordova is securities (stock) lending, whereby eligible equities in her portfolio can be loaned to other market participants, including those seeking to sell short securities. In this case, income would be generated from fees received from the stock borrower as well as from reinvesting the cash collateral received. Another potential income-generating strategy available to Cordova is dividend capture, which entails purchasing stocks just before their ex-dividend dates, holding the stocks through the ex-dividend date to earn the right to receive the dividend, and subsequently selling the shares. Selling (writing) options, including covered call and cash-covered put (cash-secured put) strategies, is another way Cordova can generate additional income for her equity portfolio.

4.4. Management Fees

Management fees are typically determined as a percentage of the funds under management (an *ad-valorem* fee) at regular intervals. For actively managed portfolios, the level of management fees involves a balance between fees that are high enough to fund investment research but low enough to avoid detracting too much from investor returns. Management fees for actively managed portfolios include direct costs of research (e.g., remuneration and expenses for investment analysts and portfolio managers) and the direct costs of portfolio management (e.g., software, trade processing costs, and compliance). For passively managed portfolios, management fees are typically low because of lower direct costs of research and portfolio management relative to actively managed portfolios.

4.5. Performance Fees

In addition to management fees, portfolio managers sometimes earn performance fees (also known as incentive fees) on their portfolios. Performance fees are generally associated with hedge funds and long/short equity portfolios, rather than long-only portfolios. These fees are an incentive for portfolio managers to achieve or outperform return objectives, to the benefit of both the manager and investors. As an example, a performance fee might represent

10–20% of any capital appreciation in a portfolio that exceeds some stated annual absolute return threshold (e.g., 8%). Several performance fee structures exist, although performance fees tend to be "upwards only"—that is, fees are earned by the manager when performance objectives are met, but fund investors are not reimbursed when performance is negative. However, performance fees could be reduced following a period of poor performance. Fee calculations also reflect high-water marks. A **high-water mark** is the highest value, net of fees, that the fund has reached. The use of high-water marks protects clients from paying twice for the same performance. For example, if a fund performed well in a given year, it might earn a performance fee. If the value of the same fund fell the following year, no performance fee would be payable. Then, if the fund's value increased in the third year to a point just below the value achieved at the end of the first year, no performance fee would be earned because the fund's value did not exceed the high-water mark. This basic fee structure is used by many alternative investment funds and partnerships, including hedge funds.

Investment managers typically present a standard schedule of fees to a prospective client, although actual fees can be negotiated between the manager and investors. For a fund, fees are established in the prospectus, although investors could negotiate special terms (e.g., a discount for being an early investor in a fund).

4.6. Administration Fees

Equity portfolios are subject to administration fees. These fees include the processing of corporate actions, such as rights issues; the measurement of performance and risk of a portfolio; and voting at company meetings. Generally, these functions are provided by an investment management firm itself and are included as part of the management fee.

Some functions, however, are provided by external parties, with the fees charged to the client in addition to management fees. These externally provided functions include:

- *Custody fees* paid for the safekeeping of assets by a custodian (often a subsidiary of a large bank) that is independent of the investment manager.
- *Depository fees* paid to help ensure that custodians segregate the assets of the portfolio and that the portfolio complies with any investment limits, leverage requirements, and limits on cash holdings.
- *Registration fees* that are associated with the registration of ownership of units in a mutual fund.

4.7. Marketing and Distribution Costs

Most investment management firms market and distribute their services to some degree. Marketing and distribution costs typically include the following:

- Costs of employing marketing, sales, and client servicing staff
- Advertising costs
- Sponsorship costs, including costs associated with sponsoring or presenting at conferences
- Costs of producing and distributing brochures or other communications to financial intermediaries or prospective clients
  - "Platform" fees, which are costs incurred when an intermediary offers an investment management firm fund services on the intermediary's platform of funds (e.g., a "funds supermarket")

- Sales commissions paid to such financial intermediaries as financial planners, independent financial advisers, and brokers to facilitate the distribution of funds or investment services

When marketing and distribution services are performed by an investment management firm, the costs are likely included as part of the management fee. However, those marketing and distribution services that are performed by external parties (e.g., consultants) typically incur additional costs to the investor.

4.8. Trading Costs

Buying and selling equities incurs a series of trading (or transaction) costs. Some of these trading costs are explicit, including brokerage commission costs, taxes, stamp duties, and stock exchange fees. In addition, many countries charge a modest regulatory fee for certain types of equity trading.

In contrast to explicit costs, some trading costs are implicit in nature. These implicit costs include the following:

- Bid–offer spread
- Market impact (also called price impact), which measures the effect of the trade on transaction prices
- Delay costs (also called slippage), which arise from the inability to complete desired trades immediately because of order size or lack of market liquidity

In an equity portfolio, total trading costs are a function of the size of trades, the frequency of trading, and the degree to which trades demand liquidity from the market. Unlike many other equity portfolio costs, such as management fees, the total cost of trading is generally not revealed to the investor. Rather, trading costs are incorporated into a portfolio's total return and presented as overall performance data. One final trading cost relates to stock lending transactions that were previously discussed. Equity portfolio managers who borrow shares in these transactions must pay fees on shares borrowed.

4.9. Investment Approaches and Effects on Costs

Equity portfolio costs tend to vary depending on their underlying strategy or approach. As mentioned previously, passively managed strategies tend to charge lower management fees than active strategies primarily because of lower research costs to manage the portfolios. Passively managed equity portfolios also tend to trade less frequently than actively managed equity portfolios, with trading in passive portfolios typically involving rebalancing or changes to index constituents. Index funds, however, do face a "hidden" cost from potential predatory trading. As an illustration, a predatory trader may purchase (or sell short) shares prior to their effective inclusion (or deletion) from an index, resulting in price movement and potential profit for a predatory trader. Such predatory trading strategies can be regarded as a cost to investors in index funds, albeit a cost that is not necessarily evident to a portfolio manager or investor.

Some active investing approaches "demand liquidity" from the market. For example, in a momentum strategy, the investor seeks to buy shares that are already rising in price (or sell those that are already falling). In contrast, some active investing approaches are more likely to "provide liquidity" to the market, such as deep value strategies (i.e., those involving stocks that are deemed to be significantly undervalued). Investment strategies that involve frequent trading and demand liquidity are, unsurprisingly, likely to have higher trading costs than long-term, buy-and-hold investment strategies.

5. SHAREHOLDER ENGAGEMENT

Shareholder engagement refers to the process whereby investors actively interact with companies. Shareholder engagement often includes voting on corporate matters at general meetings as well as other forms of communication (e.g., quarterly investor calls or in-person meetings) between shareholders and representatives of a company. Generally, shareholder engagement concerns issues that can affect the value of a company and, by extension, an investor's shares.

When shareholders engage with companies, several issues may be discussed. Some of these issues include the following:

- *Strategy*—a company's strategic goals, resources, plans for growth, and constraints. Also of interest may be a company's research, product development, culture, sustainability and corporate responsibility, and industry and competitor developments. Shareholders may ask the company how it balances short-term requirements and long-term goals and how it prioritizes the interests of its various stakeholders.
- *Allocation of capital*—a company's process for selecting new projects as well as its mergers and acquisitions strategy. Shareholders may be interested to learn about policies on dividends, financial leverage, equity raising, and capital expenditures.
- *Corporate governance* and regulatory and political risk—including internal controls and the operation of its audit and risk committees.
- *Remuneration*—compensation structures for directors and senior management, incentives for certain behaviors, and alignment of interests between directors and shareholders. In some cases, investors may be able to influence future remuneration structures. Such influence, especially regarding larger companies, often involves the use of remuneration consultants and an iterative process with large, long-term shareholders.
- *Composition of the board of directors*—succession planning, director expertise and competence, culture, diversity, and board effectiveness.

5.1. Benefits of Shareholder Engagement

Shareholder engagement can provide benefits for both shareholders and companies. From a company's perspective, shareholder engagement can assist in developing a more effective corporate governance culture. In turn, shareholder engagement may lead to better company performance to the benefit of shareholders (as well as other stakeholders).

Investors may also benefit from engagement because they will have more information about companies or the sectors in which companies operate. Such information may include a company's strategy, culture, and competitive environment within an industry. Shareholder engagement is particularly relevant for active portfolio managers given their objective to outperform a benchmark portfolio. By contrast, passive (or index) fund managers are primarily focused on tracking a given benchmark or index while minimizing costs to do so. Any process, such as shareholder engagement, that takes up management time (and adds to cost) would detract from the primary goal of a passive manager. This would be less of an issue for very large passively managed portfolios, where any engagement costs could be spread over a sizable asset base.

In theory, some investors could benefit from the shareholder engagement of others under the so-called "free rider problem." Specifically, assume that a portfolio manager using an active strategy actively engages with a company to improve its operations and was successful in increasing the company's stock price. The manager's actions in this case improved the value of his portfolio and also benefitted other investors who own the same stock in their portfolios. Investors who did not participate in shareholder engagement benefitted from improved performance but without the costs necessary for engagement.

In addition to shareholders, other stakeholders of a company may also have an interest in the process and outcomes of shareholder engagement. These stakeholders may include creditors, customers, employees, regulators, governmental bodies, and certain other members of society (e.g., community organizations and citizen groups). These other stakeholders can gain or lose influence with companies depending on the outcomes of shareholder engagement. For example, employees can be affected by cost reduction programs requested by shareholders. Another example is when creditors of a company are affected by a change in a company's vendor payment terms, which can impact the company's working capital and cash flow. Such external forces as the media, the academic community, corporate governance consultants, and proxy voting advisers can also influence the process of shareholder engagement.

Shareholders that also have non-financial interests, such as ESG considerations, may also benefit from shareholder engagement. However, these benefits are difficult to quantify. Empirical evidence relating shareholder returns to a company's adherence to corporate governance and ESG practices is mixed. This mixed evidence could be partly attributable to the fact that a company's management quality and effective ESG practices may be correlated with one another. As a result, it is often difficult to isolate non-financial factors and measure the direct effects of shareholder engagement.

5.2. Disadvantages of Shareholder Engagement

Shareholder engagement also has several disadvantages. First, shareholder engagement is time consuming and can be costly for both shareholders and companies. Second, pressure on company management to meet near-term share price or earnings targets could be made at the expense of long-term corporate decisions. Third, engagement can result in selective disclosure of important information to a certain subset of shareholders, which could lead to a breach of insider trading rules while in possession of specific, material, non-public information about a company. Finally, conflicts of interest can result for a company. For example, a portfolio manager could engage with a company that also happens to be an investor in the manager's portfolio. In such a situation, a portfolio manager may be unduly influenced to support the company's management so as not to jeopardize the company's investment mandate with the portfolio manager.

5.3. The Role of an Equity Manager in Shareholder Engagement

Active managers of equity portfolios typically engage, to some degree, with companies in which they currently (or potentially) invest. In fact, investment firms in some countries have legal or regulatory responsibilities to establish written policies on stewardship and/or shareholder engagement. Engagement activities for equity portfolio managers often include regular meetings with company management or investor relations teams. Such meetings can occur at any time but are often held after annual, semi-annual, or quarterly company results have been published.

For such non-financial issues as ESG, large investment firms, in particular, sometimes employ an analyst (or team of analysts) who focuses on ESG issues. These ESG-focused analysts normally work in conjunction with traditional fundamental investment analysts, with primary responsibility for shareholder voting decisions or environmental or social issues that affect equity investments. In lieu of—or in addition to—dedicated ESG analyst teams, some institutional investors have retained outside experts to assist with corporate governance monitoring and proxy voting. In response to this demand, an industry that provides corporate governance services, including governance ratings and proxy advice, has developed.

5.3.1. Activist Investing

A distinct and specialized version of engagement is known as activist investing. Activist investors (or activists) specialize in taking stakes in companies and creating change to generate a gain on the investment. Hedge funds are among the most common activists, possibly because of the potential for, in many cases, high performance fees. In addition, because hedge funds are subject to limited regulation, have fewer investment constraints, and can often leverage positions, these investors often have more flexibility as activists.

Engagement through activist investing can include meetings with management as well as shareholder resolutions, letters to management, presentations to other investors, and media campaigns. Activists may also seek representation on a company's board of directors as a way of exerting influence. Proxy contests are one method used to obtain board representation. These contests represent corporate takeover mechanisms in which shareholders are persuaded to vote for a group seeking a controlling position on a company's board of directors. Social media and other communication tools can help activists coordinate the actions of other shareholders.

5.3.2. Voting

The participation of shareholders in general meetings, also known as general assemblies, and the exercise of their voting rights are among the most influential tools available for shareholder engagement. General meetings enable shareholders to participate in discussions and to vote on major corporate matters and transactions that are not delegated to the board of directors. By engaging in general meetings, shareholders can exercise their voting rights on major corporate issues and better monitor the performance of the board and senior management.

Proxy voting enables shareholders who are unable to attend a meeting to authorize another individual (e.g., another shareholder or director) to vote on their behalf. Proxy voting is the most common form of investor participation in general meetings. Although most resolutions pass without controversy, sometimes minority shareholders attempt to strengthen their influence at companies via proxy voting. Occasionally, multiple shareholders may use this process to collectively vote their shares in favor of or in opposition to a certain resolution.

Some investors use external proxy advisory firms that provide voting recommendations and reduce research efforts by investors. Portfolio managers need not follow the recommendations of proxy advisory firms, but these external parties can highlight potential controversial issues. An investor's voting instructions are typically processed electronically via third-party proxy voting agents.

When an investor loans shares, the transaction is technically an assignment of title with a repurchase option; that is, the voting rights are transferred to the borrower. The transfer of voting rights with stock lending could potentially result in the borrower having different voting opinions from the lending investor. To mitigate this problem, some stock lenders recall shares ahead of voting resolutions to enable exercise of their voting rights. The downside of this action would be the loss of stock lending revenue during the period of stock loan recall and potential reputation risk as an attractive lender. Investors, in some cases, may borrow shares explicitly to exercise the voting rights attached. This process is called *empty voting*, whereby no capital is invested in the voted shares.

EXAMPLE 4   Shareholder Engagement

An investor manages a fund with a sizable concentration in the transportation sector and is interested in meeting with senior management of a small aircraft manufacturer. Discuss how the investor may benefit from his/her shareholder engagement activities, as well as from the shareholder engagement of other investors, with this manufacturer.

Solution: The investor may benefit from information obtained about the aircraft manufacturer, such as its strategy, allocation of capital, corporate governance, remuneration of directors and senior management, culture, and competitive environment within the aerospace industry. The investor may also benefit as a "free rider," whereby other investors may improve the manufacturer's operating performance through shareholder engagement—to the benefit of all shareholders. Finally, if the investor has non-financial interests, such as ESG, he or she may address these considerations as part of shareholder engagement.

---

6. EQUITY INVESTMENT ACROSS THE PASSIVE–ACTIVE SPECTRUM

The debate between passive management and active management of equity portfolios has been a longstanding one in the investment community. In reality, the decision between passive management and active management is not an "either/or" (binary) alternative. Instead, equity portfolios tend to exist across a passive–active spectrum, ranging from portfolios that closely track an equity market index or benchmark to unconstrained portfolios that are not subject to any benchmark or index. In some cases, portfolios may resemble a "closet index" in which the portfolio is advertised as actively managed but essentially resembles a passively managed fund. For an equity manager (or investment firm), several rationales exist for positioning a portfolio along the passive–active spectrum. Each of these rationales is discussed further.

6.1. Confidence to Outperform

An active investment manager typically needs to be confident that she can adequately outperform her benchmark. This determination requires an understanding of the manager's equity investment universe as well as a competitive analysis of other managers that have a similar investment universe.

6.2. Client Preference

For equity portfolio managers, client preference is a primary consideration when deciding between passive or active investing. Portfolio managers must assess whether their passive or active investment strategies will attract sufficient funds from clients to make the initiatives viable. Another consideration reflects investors' beliefs regarding the potential for active strategies to generate positive alpha. For example, in some equity market categories, such as large-cap/developed markets, companies are widely known and have considerable equity analyst coverage. For such categories as these, investors often believe that potential alpha is substantially reduced because all publicly available information is efficiently disseminated, analyzed, and reflected in stock prices.

A comparison of passive and active equities is illustrated in Exhibit 9. The exhibit demonstrates the relative proportion of investment passive and active equities in US open-ended mutual funds and exchange-traded funds (ETFs) by equity category. Nearly all equities in some categories, such as foreign small/mid-cap growth, are managed on an active basis. Conversely, equities in other categories, such as large-cap blend, are predominantly managed on a passive basis.

EXHIBIT 9   Passive versus Active Equities in US Open-Ended Mutual Funds and ETFs

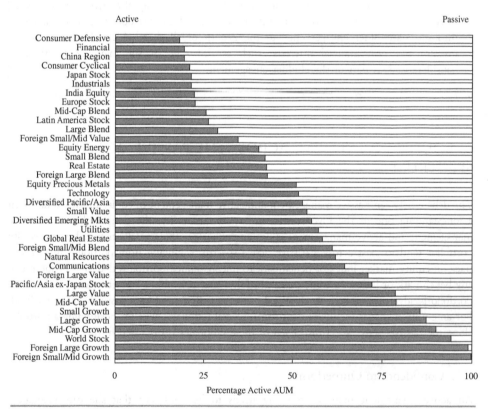

Source: Morningstar Direct. Data as of August 2016.

6.3. Suitable Benchmark

An investor or equity manager's choice of benchmark can play a meaningful role in the ability to attract new funds. This choice is particularly relevant in the institutional equity market, where asset owners (and their consultants) regularly screen new managers in desired equity segments. As part of the selection process in desired equity segments, active managers normally must have benchmarks with sufficient liquidity of underlying securities (thus maintaining a reasonable cost of trading). In addition, the number of securities underlying the benchmark typically must be broad enough to generate sufficient alpha. For this reason, many country or sector-specific investment strategies (e.g., consumer defensive companies) are managed passively rather than actively.

6.4. Client-Specific Mandates

Client-specific investment mandates, such as those related to ESG considerations, are typically managed actively rather than passively. This active approach occurs because passive management may not be particularly efficient or cost effective when managers must meet a client's desired holdings (or holdings to avoid). For example, a mandate to avoid investments in companies involved in certain "unacceptable" activities (e.g., the sale of military technology or weapons, tobacco/alcohol, or gambling) requires ongoing monitoring and management. As part of this *exclusionary (or negative) screening* process, managers need to determine those companies that are directly, as well as indirectly, involved in such "unacceptable" industries. Although ESG investing is typically more active than passive, several investment vehicles enable a portfolio manager to invest passively according to ESG-related considerations.

6.5. Risks/Costs of Active Management

As mentioned previously, active equity management is typically more expensive to implement than passive management. Another risk that active managers face—perhaps more so than with passive managers—is reputation risk from the potential violation of rules, regulations, client agreements, or ethical principles. Lastly, "key person" risk is relevant for active managers if the success of an investment manager's firm is dependent on one or a few individuals ("star managers") who may potentially leave the firm.

6.6. Taxes

Compared with active strategies, passive strategies generally have lower turnover and generate a higher percentage of long-term gains. An index fund that replicates its benchmark can have minimal rebalancing. In turn, active strategies can be designed to minimize tax consequences of gains/income at the expense of higher trading costs. One overall challenge is that tax legislation differs widely across countries.

EXAMPLE 5   Passive–Active Spectrum

James Drummond, an equity portfolio manager, is meeting with Marie Goudreaux, a wealthy client of his investment firm. Goudreaux is very cost conscious and believes that equity markets are highly efficient. Goudreaux also has a narrow investment focus, seeking stocks in specific country and industry sectors.

Discuss where Goudreaux's portfolio is likely to be positioned across the passive–active spectrum.

Solution: Goudreaux's portfolio is likely to be managed passively. Because she believes in market efficiency, Goudreaux likely believes that Drummond's ability to generate alpha is limited. Goudreaux's cost consciousness also supports passive management, which is typically less expensive to implement than active management. Finally, Goudreaux's stated desire to invest in specific countries and sectors would likely be better managed passively.

SUMMARY

This chapter provides an overview of the roles equity investments may play in the client's portfolio, how asset owners and investment managers segment the equity universe for purposes of defining an investment mandate, the costs and obligations of equity ownership (including shareholder engagement), and issues relevant to the decision to pursue active or passive management of an equity portfolio. Among the key points made in this chapter are the following:

- Equities can provide several roles or benefits to an overall portfolio, including capital appreciation, dividend income, diversification with other asset classes, and a potential hedge against inflation.
- The inclusion of equities in a portfolio can be driven by a client's goals or needs. Portfolio managers often consider the following investment objectives and constraints when deciding to include equities (or asset classes in general, for that matter) in a client's portfolio: *risk objective; return objective; liquidity requirement; time horizon; tax concerns; legal and regulatory factors*; and *unique circumstances.*
- Investors often segment the equity universe according to (1) size and style; (2) geography; and (3) economic activity.
- Sources of equity portfolio income include dividends; securities lending fees and interest; dividend capture; covered calls; and cash-covered puts (or cash-secured puts).
- Sources of equity portfolio costs include management fees; performance fees; administration fees; marketing/distribution fees; and trading costs.
- Shareholder engagement is the process whereby companies engage with their shareholders. The process typically includes voting on corporate matters at general meetings and other forms of communication, such as quarterly investor calls or in-person meetings.

- Shareholder engagement can provide benefits for both shareholders and companies. From a company's perspective, shareholder engagement can assist in developing a more effective corporate governance culture. In turn, shareholder engagement may lead to better company performance to the benefit of shareholders (as well as other stakeholders).
- Disadvantages of shareholder engagement include costs and time involved, pressure on a company to meet near-term share price or earnings targets, possible selective disclosure of information, and potential conflicts of interest.
- Activist investors (or activists) specialize in taking stakes in companies and creating change to generate a gain on the investment.
- The participation of shareholders in general meetings, also known as general assemblies, and the exercise of their voting rights are among the most influential tools available for shareholder engagement.
- The choice of using active management or passive management is not an "either/or" (binary) alternative but rather a decision involving a passive–active spectrum. Investors may decide to position their portfolios across the passive–active spectrum based on their confidence to outperform, client preference, suitable benchmarks, client-specific mandates, risks/costs of active management, and taxes.

REFERENCES

Chincarini, Ludwig, and Kim Daehwan. 2006. *Quantitative Equity Portfolio Management.* New York, NY: McGraw-Hill.

Kaplan, Steven, Tobias Moskowitz, and Berk Sensoy. 2013. "The Effects of Stock Lending on Security Prices: An Experiment." *Journal of Finance*, vol. 68, no. 5: 1891–1936.

McMillan, Michael, Jerald Pinto, Wendy Pirie, and Gerhard Van de Venter. 2011. *Investments: Principles of Portfolio and Equity Analysis.* CFA Institute Investment Series. Hoboken, NJ: John Wiley & Sons.

Weigand, Robert. 2014. *Applied Equity Analysis and Portfolio Management.* Hoboken, NJ: John Wiley & Sons.

Zhou, Xinfeng, and Sameer Jain. 2014. *Active Equity Management.* 1st ed. Cambridge, MA: MIT University Press.

PRACTICE PROBLEMS

The following information relates to questions 1–8

Three years ago, the Albright Investment Management Company (Albright) added four new funds—the Barboa Fund, the Caribou Fund, the DoGood Fund, and the Elmer Fund—to its existing fund offering. Albright's new funds are described in Exhibit 1.

EXHIBIT 1   Albright Investment Management Company New Funds

Fund	Fund Description
Barboa Fund	Invests solely in the equity of companies in oil production and transportation industries in many countries.
Caribou Fund	Uses an aggressive strategy focusing on relatively new, fast-growing companies in emerging industries.
DoGood Fund	Investment universe includes all US companies and sectors that have favorable environmental, social, and governance (ESG) ratings and specifically excludes companies with products or services related to aerospace and defense.
Elmer Fund	Investments selected to track the S&P 500 Index. Minimizes trading based on the assumption that markets are efficient.

Hans Smith, an Albright portfolio manager, makes the following notes after examining these funds:

Note 1.   The fee on the Caribou Fund is a 15% share of any capital appreciation above a 7% threshold and the use of a high-water mark.

Note 2.   The DoGood Fund invests in Fleeker Corporation stock, which is rated high in the ESG space, and Fleeker's pension fund has a significant investment in the DoGood Fund. This dynamic has the potential for a conflict of interest on the part of Fleeker Corporation but not for the DoGood Fund.

Note 3.   The DoGood Fund's portfolio manager has written policies stating that the fund does not engage in shareholder activism. Therefore, the DoGood Fund may be a free-rider on the activism by these shareholders.

Note 4.   Of the four funds, the Elmer Fund is most likely to appeal to investors who want to minimize fees and believe that the market is efficient.

Note 5.   Adding investment-grade bonds to the Elmer Fund will decrease the portfolio's short-term risk.

Smith discusses means of enhancing income for the three funds with the junior analyst, Kolton Frey, including engaging in securities lending or writing covered calls. Frey tells Smith the following:

Statement 1.   Securities lending would increase income through reinvestment of the cash collateral but would require the fund to miss out on dividend income from the lent securities.

Statement 2.   Writing covered calls would generate income, but doing so would limit the upside share price appreciation for the underlying shares.

1. The Barboa Fund can be *best* described as a fund segmented by:
   A. size/style.
   B. geography.
   C. economic activity.

2. The Caribou Fund is *most likely* classified as a:
   A. large-cap value fund.
   B. small-cap value fund.
   C. small-cap growth fund.

3. The DoGood Fund's approach to the aerospace and defense industry is *best* described as:
   A. positive screening.
   B. negative screening.
   C. thematic investing.

4. The Elmer Fund's management strategy is:
   A. active.
   B. passive.
   C. blended.

5. Based on Note 1, the fee on the Caribou Fund is *best* described as a:
   A. performance fee.
   B. management fee.
   C. administrative fee.

6. Which of the following notes about the DoGood Fund is *correct*?
   A. Only Note 2
   B. Only Note 3
   C. Both Note 2 and Note 3

7. Which of the notes regarding the Elmer Fund is *correct*?
   A. Only Note 4
   B. Only Note 5
   C. Both Note 4 and Note 5

8. Which of Frey's statements about securities lending and covered call writing is *correct*?
   A. Only Statement 1
   B. Only Statement 2
   C. Both Statement 1 and Statement 2

CHAPTER 4

PASSIVE EQUITY INVESTING

David M. Smith, PhD, CFA
Kevin K. Yousif, CFA

LEARNING OUTCOMES

The candidate should be able to:

- discuss considerations in choosing a benchmark for a passively managed equity portfolio;
- compare passive factor-based strategies to market-capitalization-weighted indexing;
- compare different approaches to passive equity investing;
- compare the full replication, stratified sampling, and optimization approaches for the construction of passively managed equity portfolios;
- discuss potential causes of tracking error and methods to control tracking error for passively managed equity portfolios;
- explain sources of return and risk to a passively managed equity portfolio.

1. INTRODUCTION

This chapter provides a broad overview of passive equity investing, including index selection, portfolio management techniques, and the analysis of investment results.

Although they mean different things, passive equity investing and indexing have become nearly synonymous in the investment industry. Indexing refers to strategies intended to replicate the performance of benchmark indexes, such as the S&P 500 Index, the Topix 100, the FTSE 100, and the MSCI All-Country World Index. The main advantages of indexing include low costs, broad diversification, and tax efficiency. Indexing is the purest form of a more general idea: passive investing. Passive investing refers to any rules-based, transparent, and investable strategy that does not involve identifying mispriced individual securities. Unlike indexing, however, passive investing can include investing in a changing set of market segments that are selected by the portfolio manager.

Studies over the years have reported support for passive investing. Renshaw and Feldstein (1960) observe that the returns of professionally managed portfolios trailed the returns on the principal index of that time, the Dow Jones Industrial Average. They also conclude that the index would be a good basis for what they termed an "unmanaged investment company." French (2008) indicates that the cost of passive investing is lower than the cost of active management.

Further motivation for passive investing comes from studies that examine the return and risk consequences of stock selection, which involves identifying mispriced securities. This differs from asset allocation, which involves selecting asset class investments that are, themselves, essentially passive indexed-based portfolios. Brinson, Hood, and Beebower (1986) find a dominant role for asset allocation rather than security selection in explaining return variability. With passive investing, portfolio managers eschew the idea of security selection, concluding that the benefits do not justify the costs.

The efficient market hypothesis gave credence to investors' interest in indexes by theorizing that stock prices incorporate all relevant information—implying that after costs, the majority of active investors could not consistently outperform the market. With this backdrop, investment managers began to offer strategies to replicate the returns of stock market indexes as early as 1971.

In comparison with passive investing strategies, active management of an investment portfolio requires a substantial commitment of personnel, technological resources, and time spent on analysis and management that can involve significant costs. Consequently, passive portfolio fees charged to investors are generally much lower than fees charged by their active managers. This fee differential represents the most significant and enduring advantage of passive management.

Another advantage is that passive managers seeking to track an index can generally achieve their objective. Passive managers model their clients' portfolios to the benchmark's constituent securities and weights as reported by the index provider, thereby replicating the benchmark. The skill of a passive manager is apparent in the ability to trade, report, and explain the performance of a client's portfolio. Gross-of-fees performance among passive managers tends to be similar, so much of the industry views passive managers as undifferentiated apart from their scope of offerings and client-servicing capabilities.

Investors of passively managed funds may seek market return, otherwise known as beta exposure, and do not seek outperformance, known as alpha. A focus on beta is based on a single-factor model: the capital asset pricing model.

Since the turn of the millennium, passive factor-based strategies, which are based on more than a single factor, have become more prevalent as investors gain a different understanding of what drives investment returns. These strategies maintain the low-cost advantage of index funds and provide a different expected return stream based on exposure to such factors as style, capitalization, volatility, and quality.

This chapter contains the following sections. Section 2 focuses on how to choose a passive benchmark, including weighting considerations. Section 3 looks at how to gain exposure to the desired index, whether through a pooled investment, a derivatives-based approach, or a separately managed account. Section 4 describes passive portfolio construction techniques. Section 5 discusses how a portfolio manager can control tracking error against the benchmark, including the sources of tracking error. Section 6 introduces methods a portfolio manager can use to attribute the sources of return in the portfolio, including country returns, currency returns, sector returns, and security returns. This section also describes sources of portfolio risk. A summary of key points concludes the chapter.

2. CHOOSING A BENCHMARK

Investors initially used benchmark indexes solely to compare the performance of an active portfolio manager against the performance of an unmanaged market portfolio. Indexes are now used as a basis for investment strategies. Many investment vehicles try to replicate index performance, which has contributed to a proliferation of indexes. Indeed, many indexes are developed specifically as a basis for new investment securities.

Successful investors choose their performance benchmarks with care. It is surprising that investors who spend countless hours analyzing the investment process and past performance of an active management strategy may accept a strategy based on a benchmark index without question. A comprehensive analysis of the creation methodology and performance of an index is just as important to investors as the analysis of an active strategy.

2.1. Indexes as a Basis for Investment

For an index to become the basis for an equity investment strategy, it must meet three initial requirements. It must be rules-based, transparent, and investable.

Examples of rules include criteria for including a constituent stock and the frequency with which weights are rebalanced. An active manager may use rules and guidelines, but it is often impossible for others to replicate the active manager's decision process. Index rules, on the other hand, must be objective, consistent, and predictable.

Transparency may be the most important requirement because passive investors expect to understand the rules underlying their investment choices. Benchmark providers disclose the rules used and constituents in creating their indexes without any black-box methodologies, which assures investors that indexes will continue to represent the intended strategy.

Equity index benchmarks are investable when their performance can be replicated in the market. For example, the FTSE 100 Index is an investable index because its constituent securities can be purchased easily on the London Stock Exchange. In contrast, most investors cannot track hedge fund-of-funds indexes, such as the HFRI series of indexes, because of the difficulty of buying the constituent hedge funds. Another example of a non-investable index is the Value Line Geometric Index, which is a multiplicative average price. In other words, the value of the index is obtained by multiplying the prices and taking a root corresponding to the number of stocks. This index is not useful for investing purposes because it cannot be replicated.

Certain features of individual securities make them non-investable as index constituents. Many stock indexes "free-float adjust" their shares outstanding, which means that they count only shares available for trade by the public, excluding those shares that are held by founders, governments, or other companies. When a company's shares that are floated in the market are a small fraction of the total shares outstanding, trading can result in disproportionate effects. Similarly, stocks for which trading volume is a small fraction of the total shares outstanding are likely to have low liquidity and commensurately high trading costs. Many indexes consequently require that stocks have float and average shares traded above a certain percent of shares outstanding.

Equity index providers include CRSP, FTSE Russell, Morningstar, MSCI, and S&P Dow Jones. These index providers publicize the rules underlying their indexes, communicate changes in the constituent securities, and report performance. For a fee, they may also provide data to investors who want to replicate the underlying basket of securities.

Index providers have taken steps to make their indexes more investable. One key decision concerns when individual stocks will migrate from one index to another. As a stock increases in market capitalization (market cap) over time, it might move from small-cap to mid-cap to large-cap status. Some index providers have adopted policies intended to limit stock migration problems and keep trading costs low for investors who replicate indexes. Among these policies are buffering and packeting. **Buffering** involves establishing ranges around breakpoints that define whether a stock belongs in one index or another. As long as stocks remain within the buffer zone, they stay in their current index. For example, the MSCI USA Large Cap Index contains the 300 largest companies in the US equity market. But a company currently in the MSCI USA Mid Cap Index must achieve a rank as the 200th largest stock to move up to the Large Cap Index. Similarly, a large-cap constituent must shrink and be the 451st largest stock to move down to the Mid Cap Index. Size rankings may change almost every day with market price movements, so buffering makes index transitions a more gradual and orderly process.

The effect of buffering is demonstrated with the MSCI USA Large Cap Index during the regularly scheduled May 2016 reconstitution. The MSCI USA Large Cap Index consists of stocks of US-based companies that meet the criterion to be considered for large cap. Further, the MSCI USA Large Cap Index is intended to represent the largest 70% of the market capitalization of the US equity market.

At each rebalance date, MSCI sets a cutoff value for the smallest company in the index and then sets the buffer value at 67% of the cutoff value. During the May 2016 rebalance, the cutoff market capitalization (market cap) of the smallest company in the index was USD 15,707 million; so, the buffer value was USD 10,524 million or approximately USD 10.5 billion.

Whole Foods Market, a grocery store operating primarily in the United States, had experienced a drop in market value from USD 15.3 billion in May of 2015 to USD 10.4 billion in May of 2016. The drop in value put the market cap of Whole Foods Market at a lower value than the acceptable buffer. That is, Whole Foods Market was valued at USD 10.4 billion, which was below the buffer point of USD 10.5 billion. Per the stated rules, Whole Foods Market was removed from the MSCI USA Large Cap Index and was added to the MSCI USA Mid Cap Index.

Packeting involves splitting stock positions into multiple parts. Let us say that a stock is currently in a mid-cap index. If its capitalization increases and breaches the breakpoint between mid-cap and large-cap indexes, a portion of the total holding is transferred to the large-cap index but the rest stays in the mid-cap index. On the next reconstitution date, if the stock value remains large-cap and all other qualifications are met, the remainder of the shares are moved out of the mid-cap and into the large-cap index. A policy of packeting can keep portfolio turnover and trading costs low. The Center for Research in Security Prices (CRSP) uses packeting in the creation of the CRSP family of indexes.

2.2. Considerations When Choosing a Benchmark Index

The first consideration when choosing a benchmark index is the desired *market exposure*, which is driven by the objectives and constraints in the investor's investment policy statement (IPS). For equity portfolios, the choices to be made include the market segment (broad versus sectors; domestic versus international), equity capitalization (large, mid, or small), style (value, growth, or blend/core), exposure, and other constituent characteristics (e.g., high or low momentum, low volatility, and quality) that are considered risk factors.

The choice of market depends on the investor's perspective. The investor's domicile, risk tolerance, liquidity needs, and legal considerations all influence the decision. For example, the decision will proceed differently for an Indian institutional investor than for a US-based individual investor. In India, the domestic equity universe is much smaller than in the United States, making the Indian investor more likely to invest globally. But a domestic investment does not carry with it the complexities of cross-border transactions.

A common way to implement the domestic/international investment decision is to use country indexes. Some indexes cover individual countries, and others encompass multiple country markets. For example, the global equity market can also be broken into geographic regions or based on development status (developed, emerging, or frontier markets). The US market is frequently treated as distinct from other developed markets because of its large size.

Another decision element is the *risk-factor exposure* that the index provides. As described later, equity risk factors can arise from several sources, including the holdings' market capitalization (the Size factor), investment style (growth vs. value, or the Value factor), price momentum (the Momentum factor), and liquidity (the Liquidity factor).

The Size factor is perhaps the best known of these. Market history and empirical studies show that small-cap stocks tend to be riskier and provide a higher long-term return than large-cap stocks. This return difference is considered a risk factor. To the extent that a benchmark's return is correlated with this risk factor, the benchmark has exposure to the Size factor. A similar argument applies to the Value factor, which is calculated as the return on value stocks less the return on growth stocks.

Practically speaking, some investors consider certain size ranges (e.g., small cap) to be more amenable to alpha generation using active management and others (e.g., large cap) amenable to lower-cost passive management. Size classifications range from mega cap to micro cap. Classifications are not limited to individual size categories. For example, many indexes seek to provide equity exposure to both small- and mid-cap companies ("smid-cap" indexes). Investors who desire exposure across the capitalization spectrum may use an "all-cap" index. Such indexes do not necessarily contain all stocks in the market; they usually just combine representative stocks from each of the size ranges. Note that a large-cap stock in an emerging market may have the same capitalization as a small-cap stock in a developed country. Accordingly, index providers usually classify company capitalizations in the context of the local market environment.

Equity benchmark selection also involves the investor's preference for exposure on the growth vs. value style spectrum. Growth stocks exhibit such characteristics as high price momentum, high P/Es, and high EPS growth. Value stocks, however, may exhibit high dividend yields, low P/Es, and low price-to-book value ratios. Depending on their basic philosophy and market outlook, investors may have a strong preference for growth or value.

Exhibit 1 shows the number of available total-return equity indexes[1] in various classifications available worldwide. Broad market exposure is provided by nearly two-thirds of all indexes, while the others track industry sectors. Developed market indexes are about twice as common as emerging-market indexes. The majority of broad market indexes cover the all-cap space or are otherwise focused on large-cap and mid-cap stocks.

---

[1]Total-return indexes account for both price and income (e.g., from cash dividends) returns to the constituent securities. The value of price-return indexes changes only because of return from the constituents' price changes.

EXHIBIT 1   Characteristics of Equity Indexes

Equity indexes	9,165
Broad market indexes	5,658
Sector indexes	3,479
Not classified	28
Of the 5,658 broad market indexes:	
Developed markets	2,903
Emerging markets	1,701
Developed & emerging markets	1,050
Not classified	4
Of the 5,658 broad market indexes:	
All-cap stocks	1,892
Large-cap stocks	121
Large-cap and mid-cap stocks	2,100
Mid-cap stocks	657
Mid- and small-cap stocks	39
Small-cap stocks	846
Not classified	3

Source: Morningstar Direct, May 2017.

Once the investor has settled on the market, capitalization, and style of benchmark, the next step is to explore the method used in constructing and maintaining the benchmark index.

2.3. Index Construction Methodologies

Equity index providers differ in their stock inclusion methods, ranging from **exhaustive** to **selective** in their investment universes. Exhaustive stock inclusion strategies are those that select every constituent of a universe, while selective approaches target only those securities with certain characteristics. The CRSP US Total Market Index has perhaps the most exhaustive set of constituents in the US market. This market-cap-weighted index includes approximately 4,000 publicly traded stocks from across the market-cap spectrum. In contrast, the S&P 500 Index embodies a selective approach and aims to provide exposure to US large-cap stocks. Its constituent securities are selected using a committee process and are based on both size and broad industry affiliation.

The weighting method used in constructing an index influences its performance. One of the most common weighting methods is market-cap weighting. The equity market cap of a constituent company is its stock price multiplied by the number of shares outstanding. Each constituent company's weight in the index is calculated as its market capitalization divided by the total market capitalization of all constituents of the index. In the development of the capital asset pricing model, the capitalization-weighted market portfolio is mean–variance efficient, meaning that it offers the highest return for a given level of risk. To the extent a capitalization-weighted equity index is a reasonable proxy for the market portfolio, the tracking portfolio may be close to mean–variance efficient.

A further advantage of the capitalization-weighted approach is that it reflects a strategy's investment capacity. A cap-weighted index can be thought of as a liquidity-weighted index because the largest-cap stocks tend to have the highest liquidity and the greatest capacity to handle investor flows at a manageable cost. Many investor portfolios tend to be biased toward large-cap stocks and use benchmarks that reflect that bias.

The most common form of market-cap weighting is free-float weighting, which adjusts each constituent's shares outstanding for closely held shares that are not generally available to the investing public. The process to determine the free-float-adjusted shares outstanding relies on publicly available information to determine the holders of the shares and whether those shares would be available for purchase in the marketplace. One reason to adjust a company's share count may include strategic holdings by governments, affiliated companies, founders, and employees. Another less common reason is to account for limitations on foreign ownership of a company; these limitations typically represent rules that are generally set up by a governmental entity through regulation.

Adjusting a company's shares outstanding for float can be a complex task and often requires an index provider to reach out to the company's shareholder services unit or to rely on analytical judgments. Although all data used in determining a company's free-float-adjusted shares outstanding are public information, the various index providers often report a different number of shares outstanding for the same security. This variation in reported shares outstanding can often be attributed to small differences in their methodologies.

In a *price-weighted* index, the weight of each stock is its price per share divided by the sum of all share prices in the index. A price-weighted index can be interpreted as a portfolio that consists of one share of each constituent company. Although some price-weighted indexes, such as the Dow Jones Industrial Average and the Nikkei 225, have high visibility as indicators of day-to-day market movements, price-weighted investment approaches are not commonly used by portfolio managers. A stock split for any constituent of the index complicates the index calculation. The weight in the index of the stock that split decreases, and the index divisor decreases as well. With its divisor changed, the index ceases to be a simple average of the constituent stocks' prices. For price-weighted indexes, the assumption that the same number of shares is held in each component stock is a shortcoming, because very few market participants invest in that way.

Equally weighted indexes produce the least-concentrated portfolios. Such indexes have constituent weights of $1/n$, where n represents the number of stocks in the index. Equal weighting of stocks within an index is considered a naive strategy because it does not show preference toward any single stock. The reduction of single stock concentration risk and slow changing sector exposures make equal weighting attractive to many investors.

As noted by Zeng and Luo (2013), broad market equally weighted indexes are factor-indifferent and the weighting randomizes factor mispricing. Equal weighting also produces higher volatility than cap weighting, one reason being that it imparts a small-cap bias to the portfolio. Equal weights deviate from market weights most dramatically for large-cap indexes, which contain mega-cap stocks. Constrained market-cap ranges such as mid-cap indexes, even if market weighted, tend to have relatively uniform weights.

Equally weighted indexes require regular rebalancing because immediately after trading in the constituent stocks begins, the weights are no longer equal. Most investors use a regular reweighting schedule. Standard & Poor's offers its S&P 500 Index in an equally weighted format and rebalances the index to equal weights once each quarter. Therein would appear to lie a misleading aspect of equally weighted indexes. For a 91-day quarter, the index is not equally weighted for 90/91 = 99% of the time.

Another drawback of equal weighting is its limited investment capacity. The smallest-cap constituents of an equally weighted index may have low liquidity, which means that investors cannot purchase a large number of shares without causing price changes. Zeng and Luo (2013) address this issue by assuming that 10% of shares in the cap-weighted S&P 100 and 500 and 5% of shares in the cap-weighted S&P 400 and 600 indexes are currently held in cap-weighted indexing strategies without any appreciable liquidity problems. They then focus on the smallest-cap constituent of each index as of December 2012, and they determine the value that 10% (5%) of its market capitalization represents. Finally, they multiply this amount by the number of stocks in the index to estimate the total investment capacity for tracking each of the S&P equally weighted equity indexes. Zeng's and Luo's estimates are shown in Exhibit 2.

EXHIBIT 2   Estimated Investment Capacity of Equally Weighted (EW) Equity Indexes

Index	Capitalization Category	Estimated Capacity
S&P 100 EW	Mega cap	USD 176 billion
S&P 500 EW	Large cap	USD 82 billion
S&P 400 EW	Mid cap	USD 8 billion
S&P 600 EW	Small cap	USD 2 billion

Source: Zeng and Luo (2013).

Qin and Singal (2015) show that equally weighted portfolios have a natural advantage over cap-weighted portfolios. To the extent that any of the constituent stocks are mispriced, equally weighted portfolios will experience return superiority as the stock prices move up or down toward their correct intrinsic value. Because of the aforementioned need to rebalance back to equal weights, Qin and Singal find that the advantage largely vanishes when taxes and transaction costs are considered. However, based on their results, tax-exempt institutional investors could experience superior returns from equal weighting.

Other non-cap-weighted indexes are weighted based on such attributes as a company or stock's fundamental characteristics (e.g., sales, income, or dividends). Discussed in more detail later, fundamental weighting delinks a constituent stock's portfolio weight from its market value. The philosophy behind fundamental weighting is that although stock prices may become over- or undervalued, the market price will eventually converge to a level implied by the fundamental attributes.

Market-cap-weighted indexes and fundamentally weighted indexes share attractive characteristics, including low cost, rules-based construction, transparency, and investability. Their philosophies, however, are different. Market-cap-weighted portfolios are based on the efficient market hypothesis, while fundamentally weighted indexes look to exploit possible inefficiencies in market pricing.

An important concern in benchmark selection relates to how concentrated the index is. In this case, the concept of the effective number of stocks, which is an indication of portfolio concentration, can provide important information. An index that has a high degree of stock concentration or a low effective number of stocks may be relatively undiversified. Woerheide and Persson (1993) show that the Herfindahl–Hirschman Index (HHI) is a valid measure of stock-concentration risk in a portfolio, and Hannam and Jamet (2017) demonstrate its use by practitioners. The HHI is calculated as the sum of the constituent weightings squared, as shown in Equation 1:

$$\text{HHI} = \sum_{i=1}^{n} w_i^2 \qquad (1)$$

where w_i is the weight of stock i in the portfolio.

The HHI can range in value from $1/n$, where n is equal to the number of securities held, to 1.0. An HHI of $1/n$ would signify an equally weighted portfolio, and a value of 1.0 would signify portfolio concentration in a single security.

Using the HHI, one can estimate the effective (or equivalent) number of stocks, held in equal weights, that would mimic the concentration level of the chosen index. The effective number of stocks for a portfolio is calculated as the reciprocal of the HHI, as shown in Equation 2.

$$\text{Effective number of stocks} = \frac{1}{\sum_{i=1}^{n} w_i^2} = 1/\text{HHI} \qquad (2)$$

Malevergne, Santa-Clara, and Sornette (2009) demonstrate that cap-weighted indexes have a surprisingly low effective number of stocks. Consider the NASDAQ 100, a US-based market-cap-weighted index consisting of 100 stocks. If the index were weighted uniformly, each stock's weight would be 0.01 (1%). In May 2017, the constituent weights ranged from 0.123 for Apple, Inc., to 0.0016 for Liberty Global plc, a ratio of 77:1. Weights for the top five stocks totaled almost 0.38 (38%), a significant allocation to those securities. Across all stocks in the index, the median weight was 0.0039 (that is, 0.39%). The effective number of stocks can be estimated by squaring the weights for the stocks, summing the results, and calculating the reciprocal of that figure. The squared weights for the NASDAQ 100 stocks summed to 0.0404, the reciprocal of which is $1/0.0404 = 24.75$, the effective number of stocks. Thus, the 100 stocks in the index had a concentration level that can be thought of as being equivalent to approximately 25 stocks held in equal weights.

EXAMPLE 1   Effective Number of Stocks

A market-cap-weighted index contains 50 stocks. The five largest-cap stocks have weights of 0.089, 0.080, 0.065, 0.059, and 0.053. The bottom 45 stocks represent the remaining weight of 0.654, and the sum of the squares of those weights is 0.01405. What are the portfolio's Herfindahl–Hirschman Index and effective number of stocks held?

Solution: The stocks, their weights, and their squared weights are shown in Exhibit 3.

EXHIBIT 3   Calculations for Effective Number of Stocks

Stock	Weight	Squared Weight
1	0.089	0.00792
2	0.080	0.00640
3	0.065	0.00423
4	0.059	0.00348
5	0.053	0.00281
Stocks 6–50	0.654	Sum of squared weights for stocks 6–50: 0.01405
Total for stocks 1–50	1.000	0.03889

The HHI is shown in the final row: 0.03889. The reciprocal of the HHI is $1/0.03889 = 25.71$. Thus, the effective number of stocks is approximately 26. The fact that the portfolio weights are far from being a uniform 2% across the 50 stocks makes the effective number of stocks held in equal weights less than 26.

The stock market crises of 2000 and 2008 brought heightened attention to investment strategies that are defensive or volatility reducing. For example, some income-oriented investors are drawn to strategies that weight benchmark constituents based on the dividend yield of each stock. Volatility weighting calculates the volatility of each constituent stock and weights the index based on the inverse of each stock's relative volatility. A related method produces a minimum-variance index using mean–variance optimization.

Exhibit 4 shows the various methods for weighting the constituent securities of broad-based, non-industry-sector, total-return equity indexes.

EXHIBIT 4   Equity Index Constituent Weighting Methods

Weighting Method	Number of Indexes
Market-cap, free-float adjusted	5,182
Market-cap-weighted	169
Multi-factor-weighted	143
Equal-weighted	63
Dividend-weighted	36

Source: Morningstar Direct, May 2017.

Another consideration in how an index is constructed involves its periodic rebalancing and reconstitution schedule. Reconstitution of an index frequently involves the addition and deletion of index constituents, while rebalancing refers to the periodic reweighting of those constituents. Index reconstitution and rebalancing create turnover. The turnover for developed-market, large-cap indexes that are infrequently reconstituted tends to be low, while benchmarks constructed using stock selection rather than exhaustive inclusion have higher turnover. As seen in Exhibit 5, both rebalancing and reconstitution occur with varied frequency, although the former is slightly more frequent.

EXHIBIT 5   Index Rebalancing/Reconstitution Frequency for Broad Equity Market Total-Return Indexes

Frequency	Rebalancing	Reconstitution
Daily	3	2
Monthly	4	3
Quarterly	2,481	1,379
Semi-annually	2,743	3,855
Annually	260	308
As needed	74	13

Note: The totals for the Rebalancing and Reconstitution columns differ slightly, as does the index total in Exhibit 4.
Source: Morningstar Direct, May 2017.

The method of reconstitution may produce additional effects. When reconstitution occurs, index-tracking portfolios, mutual funds, and ETFs will want to hold the newly included names and sell the deleted names. The demand created by investors seeking to track an index can push up the stock prices of added companies while depressing the prices of the deleted ones. Research shows that this produces a significant price effect in each case. Depending on the reconstitution method used by index publishers, arbitrageurs may be able to anticipate the changes and front-run the trades that will be made by passive investors. In some cases, the index rules are written so that the decision to add or remove an index constituent is voted on by a committee maintained by the index provider. Where a committee makes the final decision, the changes become difficult to guess ahead of time. In other cases, investors know the precise method used for reconstitution so guessing is often successful.

Chen, Noronha, and Singal (2004) find that constituent changes for indexes that reconstitute using subjective criteria are often more difficult for arbitrageurs to predict than indexes that use objective criteria. Even indexes that use objective criteria for reconstitution often announce the changes several weeks before they are implemented. Stocks near the breakpoint between small-cap and large-cap indexes are especially vulnerable to reconstitution-induced price changes. The smallest-cap stocks in the Russell 1000 Large-Cap Index have a low weight in that cap-weighted index. After any of those stocks are demoted to the Russell 2000 Small-Cap Index, they are likely to have some of the highest weights. Petajisto (2010) shows that the process of moving in that direction tends to be associated with increases in stock prices, while movements into the large-cap index tend to have negative effects. He also concludes that transparency in reconstitution is a virtue rather than a drawback.

A final consideration is investability. As stated in a prior section, an effective benchmark must be investable in that its constituent stocks are available for timely purchase in a liquid trading environment. Indexes that represent the performance of a market segment that is not available for direct ownership by investors must be replicated through derivatives strategies, which for reasons explained later may be sub-optimal for many investors.

2.4. Factor-Based Strategies

Traditional indexing generally involves tracking the returns to a market-cap-weighted benchmark index. Yet most benchmark returns are driven by factors, which are risk exposures that can be identified and isolated. An investor who wants access only to specific aspects of an index's return stream can invest in a subset of constituent securities that best reflect the investor's preferred risk factors, such as Size, Value, Quality, and Momentum. The goal of being exposed to one or more specific risk factors will also drive the choice of a benchmark index.

Factor-based strategies are an increasingly popular variation on traditional indexing, and they have important implications for benchmark selection. Some elaboration on the topic is warranted. The origin of passive factor-based strategies dates to at least the observation by Banz (1981) that small-cap stocks tend to outperform large-cap stocks. Work by Fama and French (2015) shows that at least five risk factors explain US equity market returns. Their asset pricing model incorporates the market risk premium from the CAPM plus factors for a company's size, book-to-market (value or growth style classification), operating profitability, and investment intensity. Consistent with prior research, they find a positive risk premium for small companies and value stocks over large companies and growth stocks. They measure operating profitability as the previous year's gross profit minus selling, general, and administrative expenses as well as interest expense—all divided by the beginning book value of equity. Investment intensity is measured as the growth rate in total assets in the previous year.

Although the concepts underlying passive factor investing, sometimes marketed as "smart beta," have been known for a long time, investors' use of the technique increased dramatically over time. There presently exist many passive investment vehicles and indexes that allow access to such factors as Value, Size, Momentum, Volatility, and Quality, which are described in Exhibit 6. Many investors use their beliefs about market conditions to apply factor tilts to their portfolios. This is the process of intentionally overweighting and underweighting certain risk factors. Passive factor-based strategies can be used in place of or to complement a market-cap-weighted indexed portfolio.

EXHIBIT 6   Common Equity Risk Factors

Factor	Description
Growth	Growth stocks are generally associated with high-performing companies with an above-average net income growth rate and high P/Es.
Value	Value stocks are generally associated with mature companies that have stable net incomes or are experiencing a cyclical downturn. Value stocks frequently have low price-to-book and price-to-earnings ratios as well as high dividend yields.
Size	A tilt toward smaller size involves buying stocks with low float-adjusted market capitalization.
Yield	Yield is identified as dividend yield relative to other stocks. High dividend-yielding stocks may provide excess returns in low interest rate environments.
Momentum	Momentum attempts to capture further returns from stocks that have experienced an above-average increase in price during the prior period.
Quality	Quality stocks might include those with consistent earnings and dividend growth, high cash flow to earnings, and low debt-to-equity ratios.
Volatility	Low volatility is generally desired by investors seeking to lower their downside risk. Volatility is often measured as the standard deviation of stock returns.

Passive factor-based equity strategies use passive rules, but they frequently involve active decision-making: Decisions on the timing and degree of factor exposure are being made. As Jacobs and Levy (2014) note, the difference between passive factor investing and conventional active management is that with the former, active management takes place up front rather than continuously. Relative to broad-market-cap-weighting, passive factor-based strategies tend to concentrate risk exposures, leaving investors exposed during periods when a chosen risk factor is out of favor. The observation that even strong risk factors experience periods of underperformance has led many investors toward multi-factor approaches. Passive factor-based strategies tend to be transparent in terms of factor selection, weighting, and rebalancing. Possible risks include ease of replication by other investors, which can produce overcrowding and reduce the realized advantages of a strategy.

Fundamental Factor Indexing

Capitalization weighting of indexes and index-tracking portfolios involve treating each constituent stock as if investors were buying all the available shares. Arnott, Hsu, and Moore (2005) developed an alternative weighting method based on the notion that if stock market prices deviate from their intrinsic value, larger-cap stocks will exhibit this tendency more than smaller-cap stocks. Thus, traditional cap weighting is likely to overweight overpriced stocks and underweight underpriced stocks. The combination is intended to make cap-weighting inferior to a method that does not use market prices as a basis for weighting.

The idea advanced by Arnott, Hsu, and Moore is to use a cluster of company fundamentals—book value, cash flow, revenue, sales, dividends, and employee count—as a basis for weighting each company. A separate weighting is developed for each fundamental measure. In the case of a large company, its sales might be 1.3% of the total sales for all companies in the index, so its weight for this criterion would be 0.013. For each company, the weightings are averaged across all of the fundamental measures, and those average values represent the weight of each stock in a "composite fundamentals" index.

The authors show that over a 43-year period, a fundamental index would have outperformed a related cap-weighted index by an average of almost 200 basis points per year. They hasten to add that the result should not necessarily be considered alpha, because the fundamental portfolio provides heightened exposure to the Value and Size factors.

Since the time of the seminal article's publication, fundamental-weighted indexing strategies for country markets as well as market segments have gained in popularity and attracted a large amount of investor funds.

No matter the style of a passive factor-based strategy, its ultimate goal is to improve upon the risk or return performance of the market-cap-weighted strategy. Passive factor-based approaches gain exposure to many of the same risk factors that active managers seek to exploit. The strategies can be return oriented, risk oriented, or diversification oriented.

Return-oriented factor-based strategies include dividend yield strategies, momentum strategies, and fundamentally weighted strategies. Dividend yield strategies can include dividend growth as well as absolute dividend yield. The low interest rate environment, which followed the 2008–2009 global financial crisis, led to an increase in dividend yield strategies as investors sought reliable income streams. An example index is the S&P 1500 High Yield Dividend Aristocrats Index. This index selects securities within the S&P 1500 that increased dividends in each of the past 20 years and then weights those securities by their dividend yield, with the highest dividend-yielding stocks receiving the highest weight.

Another return-oriented strategy is momentum, which is generally defined by the amount of a stock's excess price return relative to the market over a specified time period. Momentum can be determined in various ways. One example is MSCI's Momentum Index family, in which a stock's most recent 12-month and 6-month price performance are determined and then used to weight the securities in the index.[2]

Risk-oriented strategies take several forms, seeking to reduce downside volatility and overall portfolio risk. For example, risk-oriented factor strategies include volatility weighting, where all of an index's constituents are held and then weighted by the inverse of their relative price volatility. Price volatility is defined differently by each index provider, but two common methods include using standard deviation of price returns for the past 252 trading days (approximately one calendar year) or the weekly standard deviation of price returns for the past 156 weeks (approximately three calendar years).

Volatility weighting can take other forms as well. Minimum variance investing is another risk reducing strategy, and it requires access to a mean–variance optimizer. Minimum variance weights are those that minimize the volatility of the portfolio's returns based on historical price returns, subject to certain constraints on the index's construction. Constraints can include limitations on sector over/under weights, country selection limits, and limits on single stock concentration levels. Mean–variance optimizer programs can be accessed from such vendors as Axioma, BARRA, and Northfield.

Risk weighting has the advantages of being simple to understand and providing a way to reduce absolute volatility and downside returns. However, the development of these strategies is based on past return data, which may not reflect future returns. Thus, investors will not always achieve their objectives despite the strategy's stated goal.

Diversification-oriented strategies include equally weighted indexes and maximum-diversification strategies. Equal weighting is intuitive and is discussed elsewhere in the chapter as having a low amount of single-stock risk. The low single-stock risk comes by way of the weighting structure of $1/n$, where n is equal to the number of securities held. Choueifaty and Coignard (2008) define maximum diversification by calculating a "diversification ratio" as the ratio of the weighted average volatilities divided by the portfolio volatility. Diversification strategies then can attempt to maximize future diversification by determining portfolio weights using past price return volatilities.

Portfolio managers who pursue factor-based strategies often use multiple benchmark indexes, including a factor-based index and a broad market-cap-weighted index. This mismatch in benchmarks can also produce an unintended mismatch in returns, known as tracking error, from the perspective of the end investor who has modeled a portfolio against a broad market-cap-weighted index. Tracking error indicates how closely the portfolio behaves like its benchmark and is measured as the standard deviation of the differences between a portfolio's returns and its benchmark returns. The concept of tracking error is discussed in detail later.

---

[2]The indexes are rebalanced semi-annually. More information can be found at www.msci.com/eqb/methodology/meth_docs/MSCI_Momentum_Indices_Methodology.pdf.

Finally, passive factor-based strategies can involve higher management fees and trading commissions than broad-market indexing. Factor-based index providers and managers demand a premium price for the creation and management of these strategies, and those fees decrease performance. Also, commission costs can be higher in factor-based strategies than they are in market-cap-weighted strategies. All else equal, higher costs will lead to lower net performance.

Passive factor-based approaches may offer an advantage for those investors who believe it is prudent to seek out groups of stocks that are poised to have desirable return patterns. Active managers also believe in seeking those stocks, but active management brings the burden of higher fees that can eat into any outperformance. Active managers may also own stocks that are outside the benchmark and are, thus, incompatible with the investment strategy. In contrast, passive factor-based strategies can provide nearly pure exposure to specific market segments, and there are numerous benchmarks against which to measure performance. Fees are restricted because factor-based strategies are rules based and thus do not require constant monitoring. An investor's process of changing exposures to specific risk factors as market conditions change is known as factor rotation. With factor rotation, investors can use passive vehicles to make active bets on future market conditions.

3. APPROACHES TO PASSIVE EQUITY INVESTING

Passive equity investment strategies may be implemented using several approaches, from the do-it-yourself method of buying stocks to hiring a subadviser to create and maintain the investment strategy. Passively managed investment strategies can be replicated by any internal or external portfolio manager who has the index data, trading tools, and necessary skills. In contrast, actively managed funds each, in theory, have a unique investment strategy developed by the active portfolio manager.

This section discusses different approaches to gain access to an investment strategy's desired performance stream: pooled investments (e.g., mutual funds and exchange-traded funds), derivatives-based portfolios (using options, futures, and swaps contracts), and direct investment in the stocks underlying the strategy.

Some passive investments are managed to establish a target beta, and managers are judged on how closely they meet that target. Portfolio managers commonly use futures and open-end mutual funds to transform a position (in cash, for example) and obtain the desired equity exposure. This process is known as "equitizing." The choice of which method to use is largely determined by the financing costs of rolling the futures contracts over time.[3] With multinational indexes, it can be expedient to buy a set of complementary exchange-traded funds to replicate market returns for the various countries.

---

[3]Rolling a futures contract involves closing out a contract prior to its last trading day before expiration while taking a similar position in the next month's contract. Contracts that are cash-settled are marked to market, and any resulting funds in the account are available as margin that is used to initiate a position in the next month's contract.

3.1. Pooled Investments

Pooled investments are the most convenient approach for the average investor because they are easy to purchase, hold, and sell. This section covers conventional open-end mutual funds and exchange-traded funds (ETFs).

The Qualidex Fund, started in 1970, was the first open-end index mutual fund available to retail investors. It was designed to track the Dow Jones Industrial Average. The Vanguard S&P 500 Index Fund, started in 1975, was the first retail fund to attract investors on a large scale. The primary advantage provided by a mutual fund purchase is its ease of investing and record keeping.

Investors who want to invest in a passively managed mutual fund must take the same steps as those investing in actively managed ones. First, a needs analysis must be undertaken to decide on the investor's return and risk objectives as well as investment constraints, and then to find a corresponding strategy. For example, risk-averse equity investors may seek a low volatility strategy, while investors looking to match the broad market may prefer an all-cap market-cap-weighted strategy. Once the need has been identified, it is likely that a mutual fund-based strategy can be built to match that need.

Traditional mutual fund shares can be purchased directly from the adviser who manages the fund, through a fund marketplace, or through an individual financial adviser. The process is the same for any mutual fund whether passively or actively managed. Investment companies generally have websites and call centers to help their prospective investors transact shares.

A fund marketplace is a brokerage company that offers funds from different providers. The advantage of buying a mutual fund from a fund marketplace is the ease of purchasing a mutual fund from different providers while maintaining a single account for streamlined record keeping

A financial adviser can also help in purchasing a fund by offering the guidance needed to identify the strategy, providing the single account to house the fund shares, and gaining access to lower-cost share classes that may not be available to all investors.

No matter how mutual fund shares are purchased, the primary benefits of investing passively using mutual funds are low costs and the convenience of the fund structure. The manager of the passively managed fund handles all of the needed rebalancing, reconstitution, and other changes that are required to keep the investment portfolio in line with the index. Passively managed strategies require constant maintenance and care to reinvest cash from dividends and to execute the buys and sells required to match the additions and deletions of securities to the index. The portfolio manager of a passively managed mutual fund also has most of the same responsibilities as a direct investor. These include trading securities, managing cash, deciding how to proceed with corporate actions, voting proxies, and reporting performance. Moreover, index-replicating mutual funds bear costs in such areas as registration, custodial, and audit, which are similar to those for actively managed mutual funds.

Record keeping functions for a mutual fund include maintaining a record of who owns the shares and when and at what price those shares were purchased. Record keepers work closely with both the custodian of the fund shares to ensure that the security is safely held in the name of the investor and the mutual fund sponsor who communicates those trades.

In the United States, mutual funds are governed by provisions of the Investment Company Act of 1940. In Europe, Undertakings for Collective Investment in Transferable Securities (UCITS) is an agreement among countries in the European Union that governs the management and sale of collective investment funds (mutual funds) across European borders.

ETFs are another form of pooled investment vehicle. The first ETF was launched in the Canadian market in 1990 to track the return of 35 large stocks listed on the Toronto Stock Exchange. ETFs were introduced in the US market in 1993. They are registered funds that can be bought and sold throughout the trading day and change hands like stocks. Advantages of the ETF structure include ease of trading, low management fees, and tax efficiency. Unlike with traditional open-end mutual funds, ETF shares can be bought by investors using margin borrowing; moreover, investors can take short positions in an ETF. ETFs offer flexibility in that they track a wide array of indexes.

ETFs have a unique structure that requires a fund manager as well as an authorized participant who can deliver the assets to the manager. The role of the authorized participant is to be the market maker for the ETF and the intermediary between investors and the ETF fund manager when shares are created or redeemed. To create shares of the ETF, the authorized participant delivers a basket of the underlying stocks to the fund manager and, in exchange, receives shares of the ETF that can be sold to the public. When an authorized participant needs to redeem shares, the process is reversed so that the authorized participant delivers shares of the ETF in exchange for a basket of the underlying stocks that can then be sold in the market.

The creation/redemption process is used when the authorized participant is either called upon to deliver new shares of the ETF to meet investor needs or when large redemptions are requested. The redemption process occurs when an authorized participant needs to reduce its exposure to the ETF holding and accepts shares of the underlying securities in exchange for shares of the ETF.

All else equal, taxable investors in an ETF will have a smaller taxable event than those in a similarly managed mutual fund. Managers of mutual funds must sell their portfolio holdings to fulfill shareholder redemptions, creating a taxable event where gains and losses are realized. ETFs have the advantage of accommodating those redemptions through an in-kind delivery of stock, which is the redemption process. Capital gains are not recorded when a redemption is fulfilled through an in-kind delivery of securities, so the taxable gain/loss passed to the investor becomes smaller.

Disadvantages of the ETF structure include the need to buy at the offer and sell at the bid price, commission costs, and the risk of an illiquid market when the investor needs to buy or sell the actual ETF shares.

ETFs that track indexes are used to an increasing degree by financial advisers to provide targeted exposure to different sectors of the investable market. Large investors find it more cost effective to build their own portfolios through replication, stratified sampling, and optimization, concepts to be introduced later. Other investors find ETFs to be a relatively low-cost method of tracking major indexes. Importantly, like traditional open-end mutual funds, ETFs are an integrated approach in that portfolio management and accounting are conducted by the fund adviser itself. A limitation is that there are far more benchmark indexes than ETFs, so not all indexes have an exchange-traded security that tracks them, although new ETFs are constantly being created. Exhibit 7 depicts the strong global trend in investor net flows into index-tracking equity ETFs since 1998. The exhibit does not reflect changes in value caused by market fluctuations, but rather purely investments and redemptions.

Exhibit 7 also shows that, over time, factor-based ETFs have become a large segment of the market. Factor-based ETFs provide exposure to such single factors as Size, Value, Momentum, Quality, Volatility, and Yield. Among the most important innovations are ETFs that track multiple factors simultaneously. For example, the iShares Edge MSCI Multifactor USA ETF emphasizes exposure to Size, Value, Momentum, and Quality factors. Meanwhile, the ETF attempts to maintain characteristics that are similar to the underlying MSCI USA Diversified Multiple-Factor Index, including industry sector exposure. As of 2017, the fund's expense ratio is 0.20% and it holds all 139 of the stocks in the index.

EXHIBIT 7 Cumulative Monthly Flows (USD millions) into Index-Tracking Equity ETF Shares Listed in 33 Markets, January 1997–April 2017

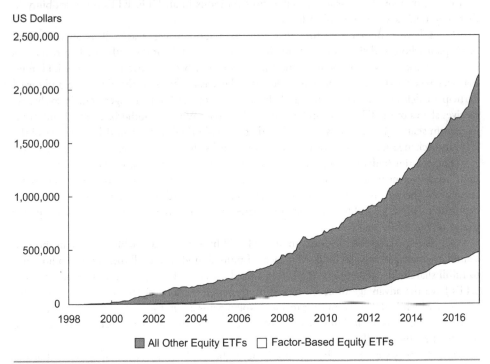

Source: Morningstar Direct, May 2017.

Exhibit 8 shows that, among 33 major exchange locations, the market value of equity ETFs that track indexes approaches USD 3 trillion. US exchanges have about one-third of the individual ETFs and more than 75% of the total market value as of May 2017. Japan, the United Kingdom, and Switzerland have more than half of the remaining market value. These numbers reflect purely passive ETFs, including factor-based securities.

EXHIBIT 8 Number of Index-Tracking Equity ETFs and Their Market Values (in USD millions) May 2017

Exchange Location	ETFs	Market Value
United States	1,104	2,236,166
Japan	99	200,965
United Kingdom	365	139,900
Switzerland	272	104,025
Germany	205	81,047
France	260	66,680

Exchange Location	ETFs	Market Value
Canada	252	47,625
Netherlands	24	22,350
South Korea	177	12,162
Hong Kong SAR	63	9,605
Italy	22	3,724
Singapore	41	3,451
Australia	55	2,873
Mexico	12	2,319
Sweden	4	1,922
Spain	6	1,654
Brazil	13	1,411
South Africa	27	1,347
New Zealand	11	566
Finland	1	234
Next 13 Locations	52	794
Total for 33 Locations	3,166	2,940,818

Source: Morningstar Direct, May 2017.

The decision of whether to use a conventional open-end mutual fund versus an ETF often comes down to cost and flexibility. Investors who seek to mimic an index must identify a suitable tracking security. According to Morningstar, in the United States, ETFs track 1,354 distinct equity indexes while conventional open-end mutual funds track only 184. Of the ETFs, 38 benchmarks are for price-only returns and the remainder are for total returns, which also include the return from reinvested dividends. Long-term investors benefit from the slightly lower expense ratios of ETFs than otherwise equivalent conventional open-end mutual funds. However, the brokerage fees associated with frequent investor trades into ETF shares can negate the expense ratio advantage and thus make ETFs less economical.

3.2. Derivatives-Based Approaches

Beyond purchasing a third-party-sponsored pooled investment and building it themselves, investors can access index performance through such derivatives as options, swaps, or futures contracts. Derivative strategies are advantageous in that they can be low cost, easy to implement, and provide leverage. However, they also present a new set of risks, including counterparty default risk for derivatives that are not traded on exchanges or cleared through a clearing house. Derivatives can also be relatively difficult to access for individual investors.

Options, swaps, and futures contracts can be found on many of the major indexes, such as the MSCI EAFE Index (EAFE stands for Europe, Australasia, and the Far East) and the S&P 500 Index. Options and futures are traded on exchanges and so are processed through a clearing house. This is important because a clearing house eliminates virtually all of the default risk present in having a contract with a single counterparty. Equity swaps, on the other hand, are generally executed with a single counterparty and so add the risk of default by that counterparty.

Derivatives allow for leverage through their notional value amounts. Notional value of the contracts can be many times greater than the initial cash outlay. However, derivatives expire, whereas stocks can be held indefinitely. The risk of an expiring options contract is a complete loss of the relatively small premium paid to acquire the exposure. Futures and swaps can be extended by "rolling" the contract forward, which means selling the expiring contract and buying a longer dated one.

Futures positions must be initiated with a futures commission merchant (FCM), a clearing house member assigned to trade on behalf of the investor. The FCM posts the initial margin required to open the position and then settles on a daily basis to comply with the maintenance margin required by the clearing house. The FCM also helps close the position upon expiration. However, futures accounts are not free of effort on the client's part. Having a futures account requires the management of daily cash flows, sometimes committing additional money and sometimes drawing it down.

It is uncommon for passive portfolio managers to use derivatives in the long term to synthetically mimic the return from physical securities. Derivatives are typically used to adjust a pre-existing portfolio to move closer to meeting its objectives. These derivative positions are often referred to as an **overlay**. A **completion overlay** addresses an indexed portfolio that has diverged from its proper exposure. A common example is a portfolio that has built up a surplus of cash from investor flows or dividends, causing the portfolio's beta to be significantly less than that of the benchmark. Using derivatives can efficiently restore the overall portfolio beta to its target. A **rebalancing overlay** addresses a portfolio's need to sell certain constituent securities and buy others. Particularly in the context of a mixed stock and bond portfolio, using equity index derivatives to rebalance toward investment policy target weights can be efficient and cost-effective. A **currency overlay** assists a portfolio manager in hedging the returns of securities that are held in a foreign currency back to the home country's currency.

Equity index derivatives offer several advantages over cash-based portfolio construction approaches. A passive portfolio manager can increase or decrease exposure to the entire index portfolio in a single transaction. Managers who want to make tactical adjustments to portfolio exposure often find derivatives to be a more efficient tool than cash-market transactions for achieving their goals. Many derivatives contracts are highly liquid, sometimes more so than the underlying cash assets. Especially in this case, portfolio exposures can be tactically adjusted quickly and at low cost.

For the longer term, strategic changes to portfolios are usually best made using cash instruments, which have indefinite expirations and do not necessitate rolling over expiring positions. Futures markets, for example, can impose position limits on such instruments that constrain the scale of use. Derivatives usage is also sometimes restricted by regulatory bodies or investment policy statement stipulations, so in this case cash could be a preferred approach. Finally, depending on the index that is being tracked by the passive portfolio manager, a suitable exchange-traded futures contract may not be available.

In addition to options, which have nonlinear payoffs,[4] the two primary types of equity index derivatives contracts are futures and swaps. Equity index futures provide exposure to a

---

[4]The nonlinearity of option payoffs arises because all prices of the underlying that cause the option to be out-of-the-money at expiration produce zero payoff for the investor who holds the option. When an option is in the money, the investor holding it experiences a linearly increasing payoff at all prices of the underlying in that range. In the case of futures and swaps, the payoffs are two-sided and linear for price changes in the underlying that are in the investor's favor as well as those that are against the investor.

specific index. Unlike many commodity futures contracts, index futures are cash-settled, which means the counterparties exchange cash rather than the underlying shares.

The buyer of an equity index futures contract obtains the right to buy the underlying (in this case, an index) on the expiration date of the contract at the futures price prevailing at the time the derivative was purchased. For exchange-traded futures, the buyer is required to post margin (collateral) in the account to decrease the credit risk to the exchange, which is the effective counterparty. For S&P 500 Index futures contracts as traded on the Chicago Mercantile Exchange, every USD change in the futures price produces a USD 250 change in the contract value (thus a "multiplier" of 250). On 4 August 2016, the September S&P 500 futures contract settled at a price of 2,159.30, after settling at 2,157 the day before. The change in contract value was thus $250 \times USD (2,159.30 - 2,157) = USD 575$.

Equity index futures contracts for various global markets are shown in Exhibit 9.

EXHIBIT 9   Representative Equity-Index Futures Contracts

Index Futures Contract	Market	Contract Currency and Multiplier
Americas		
Dow Jones mini	United States	USD 5
S&P 500	United States	USD 250
S&P 500 mini	United States	USD 50
NASDAQ 100 mini	United States	USD 20
Mexican IPC	Mexico	MXN 10
S&P/TSX Composite mini	Canada	CAD 5
S&P/TSX 60	Canada	CAD 200
Ibovespa	Brazil	BRL 1
Europe, Middle East, and Africa		
Euro STOXX 50	Europe	EUR 10
FTSE 100	United Kingdom	GBP 10
DAX 30	Germany	EUR 25
CAC 40	France	EUR 10
FTSE/Athens 20	Greece	EUR 5
OMX Stockholm 30	Sweden	SEK 100
Swiss Market	Switzerland	CHF 10
OMX Copenhagen 20	Denmark	DKK 100
PSI-20	Portugal	EUR 1
IBEX 35	Spain	EUR 10
WIG20	Poland	PLN 10
BIST 30	Turkey	TRY 100
FTSE/JSE Top 40	South Africa	ZAR 10

Index Futures Contract	Market	Contract Currency and Multiplier
Asia Pacific		
S&P/ASX 200	Australia	AUD 25
CSI 300	Chinese mainland	CNY 300
Hang Seng	Hong Kong SAR	HKD 50
H-Shares	Hong Kong SAR	HKD 50
Nifty 50	India	INR 50
Nikkei 225	Japan	JPY 1,000
Topix	Japan	JPY 10,000
KOSPI 200	Korea	KRW 500,000

Source: Please see www.investing.com/indices/indices-futures, May 2017.

Given that futures can be traded using only a small amount of margin, it is clear that futures provide a significant degree of potential leverage to a portfolio. Leverage can be considered either a positive or negative characteristic, depending on the manner with which the derivative instrument is used. Unlike some institutional investors' short-sale constraints on stock positions, many investors do not face constraints on opening a futures position with a sale of the contracts. Among other benefits of futures is the high degree of liquidity in the market, as evidenced by low bid–ask spreads. Both commission and execution costs also tend to be low relative to the exposure achieved. The low cost of transacting makes it easy for portfolio managers to use futures contracts to modify the equity risk exposure of their portfolios.

Equity index futures do come with some disadvantages. Futures are used by index fund managers because the instruments are expected to move in line with the underlying index. To the extent that the futures and spot prices do not move in concert, the portfolio may not track the benchmark perfectly. The extent to which futures prices do not move with spot prices is known as basis risk. Basis risk results from using a hedging instrument that is imperfectly matched to the investment being hedged. Basis risk can arise when the underlying securities pay dividends, while the futures contract tracks only the price of the underlying index. The difference can be partially mitigated when futures holders combine that position with interest-bearing securities.

As noted, futures account holders also must post margin. The margin amount varies by trading exchange. In the case of an ASX-200 futures contract, the initial margin required by the Sydney Futures Exchange in January 2017 for an overnight position is AUD 6,700. The minimum maintenance margin for one contract is AUD 5,300.

By way of example, assume an investor buys an ASX-200 futures contract priced at AUD 5,700, and the futures contract has a multiplier of 25. The investor controls AUD 142,500 [= 25 × AUD 5,700] in value. This currency amount is known as the contract unit value. With the initial margin of AUD 6,700 and a maintenance margin of AUD 5,300, a margin call will be triggered if the contract unit value decreases by more than AUD 1,400. A decrease of AUD 1,400 in the margin is associated with a contract unit value of AUD 142,500 – AUD 1,400 = AUD 141,100. This corresponds to an ASX-200 futures price of AUD 5,644 [= AUD 141,100/25]. Thus, a futures price decrease of 0.98% [= (AUD 5,644 – AUD 5,700)/ AUD 5,700] is associated with a decrease in the margin account balance of 20%.

This example demonstrates how even a small change in the index value can result in a margin call once the mark-to-market process occurs.

Another derivatives-based approach is the use of equity index swaps. Equity index swaps are negotiated arrangements in which two counterparties agree to exchange cash flows in the future. For example, consider an investor who has a EUR 20 million notional amount and wants to be paid the return on her benchmark index, the Euro STOXX 50, during the coming year. In exchange, the investor agrees to pay a floating rate of return of Libor + 0.20% per year, with settlement occurring semi-annually. Assuming a six-month stock index return of 2.3% and annualized Libor of 0.18% per year, the first payment on the swap agreement would be calculated as follows. The investor would receive EUR 20 million × 0.023 = EUR 460,000. The investor would be liable to the counterparty for EUR 20 million × (0.0018 + 0.0020) × (180/360) = EUR 38,000; so, when the first settlement occurs the investor would receive EUR 460,000 − EUR 38,000 = EUR 422,000. In this case, the payment received by the passive portfolio manager is from the first leg of the swap, and the payment made by that manager is from the second leg. Libor is used in this example, but the second leg can also involve the return on a different index, stock, or other asset, or even a fixed currency amount per period.

Disadvantages of swaps include counterparty, liquidity, interest rate, and tax policy risks. Relatively frequent settlement decreases counterparty risk and reduces the potential loss from a counterparty's failure to perform. Equity swaps tend to be non-marketable instruments, so once the agreement is made there is not a highly liquid market that allows them to be sold to another party (though it is usually possible to go back to the dealer and enter into an offsetting position). Although the equity index payment recipient is an equity investor, this investor must deliver an amount linked to Libor; the investor bears interest rate risk. One prime motivation for initiating equity swaps is to avoid paying high taxes on the full return amount from an equity investment. This advantage is dependent on tax laws remaining favorable, which means that equity swaps carry tax policy risk.

There are a number of advantages to using an equity swap to gain synthetic exposure to index returns. Exchange-traded futures contracts are available only on a limited number of equity indexes. Yet as long as there is a willing counterparty, a swap can be initiated on virtually any index. So swaps can be customized with respect to the underlying as well as to settlement frequency and maturity. Although most swap agreements are one year or shorter in maturity, they can be negotiated for as long a tenor as the counterparties are willing. If a swap is used, it is not necessary for an investor to pay transaction costs associated with buying all of the index constituents. Like futures, a swap can help a portfolio manager add leverage or hedge a portfolio, which is usually done on a tactical or short-term basis.

3.3. Separately Managed Equity Index-Based Portfolios

Building an index-based equity portfolio as a separately managed portfolio requires a certain set of capabilities and tools. An equity investor who builds an indexed portfolio will need to subscribe to certain data on the index and its constituents. The investor also requires a robust trading and accounting system to manage the portfolio, broker relationships to trade efficiently and cheaply, and compliance systems to meet applicable laws and regulations.

The data subscription can generally be acquired directly from the index provider and may be offered on a daily or less-frequent basis. Generally, the data are provided for analysis only and a separate license must be purchased for index replication strategies. The index subscription data should include company and security identifiers, weights, cash dividend, return, and corporate action information. Corporate actions can include stock dividends and splits, mergers and acquisitions, liquidations, and other reasons for index constituent inclusion and exclusion. These data are generally provided in electronic format and can be delivered via file downloads or fed through a portfolio manager's analytical systems, such as Bloomberg or FactSet. The data are then used as the basis for the indexed portfolio.

Certain trading systems, such as those provided by Charles River Investment Management Solution, SS&C Advent (through Moxy), and Eze Castle Integration, allow the manager to see her portfolio and compare it to the chosen benchmark. Common features of trading systems include electronic communication with multiple brokers and exchanges, an ability to record required information on holdings for taxable investors, and modeling tools so that a portfolio can be traded to match its benchmark.

Accounting systems should be able to report daily performance, record historical transactions, and produce statements. Portfolio managers rely heavily on their accounting systems and teams to help them understand the drivers of portfolio performance.

Broker relationships are an often-overlooked advantage of portfolio managers that are able to negotiate better commission rates. Commissions are a negative drag on a portfolio's returns. The commission rates quoted to a manager can differ on the basis of the type of securities being traded, the size of the trade, and the magnitude of the relationship between the manager and broker.

Finally, compliance tools and teams are necessary. Investors must adhere to a myriad of rules and regulations, which can come from client agreements and regulatory bodies. Sanctions for violating compliance-related rules can range from losing a client to losing the registration to participate in the investment industry; thus, a robust compliance system is essential to the success of an investment manager.

Compliance rules can be company-wide or specific to an investor's account. Company-wide rules take such forms as restricting trades in stocks of affiliated companies. Rules specific to an account involve such matters as dealing with a directed broker or steps to prevent cash overdrafts. Compliance rules should also be written to prohibit manager misconduct, such as front-running in a personal account prior to executing client trades.

To ensure that their portfolios closely match the return stream of the chosen index, indexed portfolio managers must review their holdings and their weightings versus the index each day. Although a perfect match is a near impossibility because of rounding errors and trading costs, the manager must always weigh the benefits and costs of maintaining a close match.

To establish the portfolio, the manager creates a trading file and transmits the file to an executing broker, who buys the securities using a program trade. **Program trading** is a strategy of buying or selling many stocks simultaneously. Index portfolio managers may trade thousands of positions in a single trade file and are required to deliver the orders and execute the trades quickly. The creation of trades may be done on something as rudimentary as an Excel spreadsheet, but it is more likely to be created on an order management system (OMS), such as Charles River

Portfolio managers use their OMS to model their portfolios against the index, decide which trades to execute, and transmit the orders. Transmitting an order in the United States is generally done on a secure communication line, such as through FIX Protocol. FIX Protocol is an electronic communication protocol to transmit the orders from the portfolio manager to the broker or directly to the executing market place. The orders are first transmitted via FIX Protocol to a broker who executes the trade and then delivers back pricing and settlement instructions to the OMS. International trading is usually communicated using a similar protocol through SWIFT. SWIFT stands for "Society for Worldwide Interbank Financial Telecommunication," and is a service that is used to securely transmit trade instructions.

Index-based strategies seek to replicate an index that is priced at the close of business each day. Therefore, most index-based trade executions take place at the close of the business day using market-on-close (MOC) orders. Matching the trade execution to the benchmark price helps the manager more closely match the performance of the index.

Beyond the portfolio's initial construction, managers maintain the portfolio by trading any index changes, such as adds/deletes, rebalances, and reinvesting cash dividend payments. These responsibilities require the manager to commit time each day to oversee the portfolio and create the necessary trades. Best practice would be to review the portfolio's performance each day and its composition at least once a month.

Dividends paid over time can accumulate to significant amounts that must be reinvested into the securities in the index. Index fund managers must determine when the cash paid out by dividends should be reinvested and then create trades to purchase the required securities.

4. PORTFOLIO CONSTRUCTION

This section discusses the principal approaches that equity portfolio managers use when building a passive-indexed portfolio by transacting in individual securities. The three approaches are full replication, stratified sampling, and optimization. According to Morningstar, among index-tracking equity ETF portfolios globally:

- 38% of funds (representing 42% of July 2016 assets) use full replication,
- 41% of funds (representing 54% of assets) use stratified sampling or optimization techniques, and
- 21% of funds (representing only about 4% of assets) use synthetic replication, using over-the-counter derivatives).

4.1. Full Replication

Full replication in index investing occurs when a manager holds all securities represented by the index in weightings that closely match the actual index weightings. Advantages of full replication include the fact that it usually accomplishes the primary goal of matching the index performance, and it is easy to comprehend. Full replication, however, requires that the asset size of the mandate is sufficient and that the index constituents are available for trading.

Not all indexes lend themselves to full replication. For example, the MSCI ACWI Investable Markets Index consists of over 8,000 constituents,[5] but not all securities need be held to closely match the characteristics and performance of that index. Other indexes, such as the S&P 500, have constituents that are readily available for trading and can be applied to portfolios as small as USD 10 million.

---

[5]The MSCI ACWI Investable Markets Index captures large, mid-, and small-cap stocks across developed and emerging market countries and represents 8,609 securities as of April 2016.

With respect to the choice between index replication versus sampling, as the number of securities held increases, tracking error decreases because the passive portfolio gets closer to replicating the index perfectly. Yet as the portfolio manager adds index constituent stocks that are smaller and more thinly traded than average, trading costs increase. The trading costs can take the form of brokerage fees and upward price pressure as a result of the portfolio's purchases. These transaction costs can depress performance and start to impose a small negative effect on tracking effectiveness. As the portfolio manager moves to the least liquid stocks in the index, transaction costs begin to dominate and tracking error increases again. Thus, for an index that has some constituent securities that are relatively illiquid, the conceptual relationship between tracking error and the number of securities held is U-shaped. The relation can be depicted as shown in Exhibit 10.

EXHIBIT 10   Relation Between Tracking Error and Transaction Costs versus Number of Benchmark Index Constituent Stocks Held

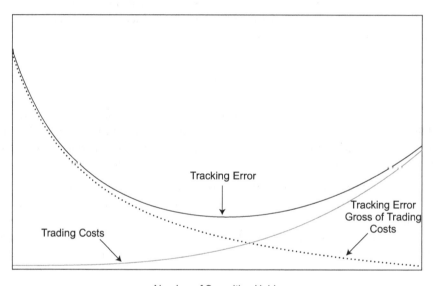

Source: Author team.

Many managers attempt to match an index's characteristics and performance through a full replication technique, but how does a manager create the portfolio? As mentioned in a prior section, the passive equity manager needs data from the index provider to construct the portfolio. This includes the constituent stocks, their relevant identifiers (ticker, CUSIP, SEDOL, or ISIN), shares outstanding, and price. Additional data, such as constituents' dividends paid and total return, facilitate management of the portfolio.

The manager then uses the index data to create the portfolio by replicating as closely as possible the index constituents and weights. The portfolio construction method may vary by investor, but the most common method is to import the provided data into a data compiler such as Charles River, Moxy, or some other external or internally created OMS. The imported data show the manager the trades that are needed to match the index. Exhibit 11 contains an example for a portfolio that has an initial investment of USD 10 million.

EXHIBIT 11   Sample Index Portfolio Positions and Transactions

Security Identifier	Description	Current Price	Model Weight	Current Weight	Current Weight – Model Weight = Variance	Current Shares	New Shares	Shares to Trade
Cash	Cash	1	50%	0%	50%	5,000,000	0	−5,000,000
SECA	Security 1	100	50%	50%	0%	50,000	50,000	0
SECB	Security 2	50	0%	50%	−50%	0	100,000	100,000

Exhibit 11 shows a current portfolio made up of one security and a cash holding that needs to be traded to match a two-security index. The index becomes the model for the portfolio, and that model is used to match the portfolio. This type of modeling can easily and cheaply be conducted using spreadsheet and database programs, such as Excel and Access. However, the modeling is only a part of the portfolio management process.

The OMS should also be programmed to provide the investor with pre-trade compliance to check for client-specific restrictions, front-running issues, and other compliance rules. The OMS is also used to deliver the buy and sell orders for execution using FIX or SWIFT Protocol, as described previously.

After initial creation of the indexed portfolio, the manager must maintain the portfolio according to any changes in the index. The changes are announced publicly by the index provider. Index fund managers use those details to update their models in the OMS and to determine the number of shares to buy or sell. A fully replicated portfolio must make those changes in a timely manner to maintain its performance tracking with the index. Again, a perfectly replicated index portfolio must trade at the market-on-close price where available to match the price used by the index provider in calculating the index performance.

4.2. Stratified Sampling

Despite their preference to realize the benefits of pure replication of an index, portfolio managers often find it impractical to hold all the constituent securities. Some equity indexes have a large number of constituents, and not all constituents offer high trading liquidity. This can make trading expensive, especially if a portfolio manager needs to scale up the portfolio. Brokerage fees can also become excessive if the number of constituents is large.

Holding a limited sample of the index constituents can produce results that track the index return and risk characteristics closely. But such sampling is not done randomly. Rather, portfolio managers use stratified sampling. To stratify is to arrange a population into distinct strata or subgroupings. Arranged correctly, the various strata will be mutually exclusive and also exhaustive (a complete set), and they should closely match the characteristics and performance of the index. Common stratification approaches include using industry membership and equity style characteristics. Investors who use stratified sampling to track the S&P 500 commonly assign each stock to one of the eleven sectors designated by the Global Industry Classification Standard (GICS). For multinational indexes, stratification is often done first on the basis of country affiliation. Indexes can be stratified along multiple dimensions (e.g., country affiliation and then industry affiliation) within each country. An advantage of stratifying along multiple dimensions is closer index tracking.

In equity indexing, stratified sampling is most frequently used when the portfolio manager wants to track indexes that have many constituents or when dealing with a relatively low level of assets under management. Indexes with many constituents are usually multi-country or multi-cap indexes, such as the S&P Global Broad Market Index that consists of more than 11,000 constituents. Most investors are reluctant to trade and maintain 11,000 securities when a significantly smaller number of constituents would achieve most portfolios' tracking objectives. Regardless of the stratified sampling approach used, passive equity managers tend to weight portfolio holdings proportionately to each stratum's weight in the index.

EXAMPLE 2   Stratified Sampling

A portfolio manager responsible for accounts of high-net-worth individuals is asked to build an index portfolio that tracks the S&P 500 Value Index, which has more than 300 constituents. The manager and the client agree that the minimum account size will be USD 750,000, but the manager explains to the client that full replication is not feasible at a reasonable cost because of the mandate size. How can the manager use stratified sampling to achieve her goal of tracking the S&P 500 Value Index?

Solution: The manager recommends that the client set a maximum number of constituents (for example, 200) to limit the average lot size and to reduce commission costs. Next, the manager seeks to identify the constituents to hold based on their market capitalization. That is, the manager selects the 200 securities with the largest market capitalizations. Then the manager seeks to more closely match the performance of the index by matching the sector weightings of the sampled portfolio to the sector weightings of the index. After comparing sector weights, the manager reweights the sampled portfolio. Using this method of stratified sampling meets the manager's stated goal of closely tracking the performance of the index at a reasonable cost.

4.3. Optimization

Optimization approaches for index portfolio construction, such as full replication and stratified sampling, have index-tracking goals. Optimization typically involves maximizing a desirable characteristic or minimizing an undesirable characteristic, subject to one or more constraints. For an indexed portfolio, optimization could involve minimizing index tracking error, subject to the constraint that the portfolio holds 50 constituent securities or fewer. The desired output from the optimization process is identification of the 50 securities and their weights that results in the lowest possible tracking error. The number of security holdings is not the only possible constraint. Other common constraints include limiting portfolio membership to stocks that have a market capitalization above a certain specified level, style characteristics that mimic those of the benchmark, restricting trades to round lots, and using only stocks that will keep rebalancing costs low.

Roll (1992) and Jorion (2003) demonstrate that running an optimization to minimize tracking error can lead to portfolios that are mean–variance inefficient versus the benchmark.

That is, the optimized portfolio may exhibit higher risk than the benchmark it is being optimized against. They show that a useful way to address this problem is to add a constraint on total portfolio volatility. Accordingly, the manager of an optimized passive fund would aim to make its total volatility equal to that of the benchmark index.

Fabozzi, Focardi, and Kolm (2010) note that in practice, passive portfolio managers often conduct a mean–variance optimization using all the index constituents, the output from which shows highly diverse weightings for the stocks. Given that investing in the lowest-weight stocks may involve marginal transaction costs that exceed marginal diversification benefits, in a second, post-optimization stage, the managers may then delete the lowest-weighted stocks.

Optimization can be conducted in conjunction with stratified sampling or alone. Optimization programs, when run without constraints, do not consider country or industry affiliation but rather use security level data. Optimization requires an analyst who has a high level of technical sophistication, including familiarity with computerized optimization software or algorithms, and a good understanding of the output.

Advantages of optimization involve a lower amount of tracking error than stratified sampling. Also, the optimization process accounts explicitly for the covariances among the portfolio constituents. Although two securities from different industry sectors may be included in a passive portfolio under stratified sampling, if their returns move strongly together, one will likely be excluded from an optimized portfolio.

Usually the constituents and weights of an optimized portfolio are determined based on past market data; however, returns, variances, and correlations between securities tend to vary over time. Thus, the output from an optimization program may apply only to the period from which the data are drawn and not to a future period. Even if current results apply to the future, they might not be applicable for long. This means that optimization would need to be run frequently and adjustments made to the portfolio, which can be costly.

4.4. Blended Approach

For indexes that have few constituent securities or for which the constituents are homogeneous, full replication is typically advisable. When the reverse is true, sampling or optimization are likely to be the preferred methods. But such indexes as the Russell 3000, the S&P 1500, and the Wilshire 5000 span the capitalization spectrum from large to small. For these indexes, the 1,000 or so largest constituents are quite liquid, which means that brokerage fees, bid–ask spreads, and trading costs are low. For the largest-cap portion of an indexed portfolio, full replication is a sensible and desirable approach. For the index constituents that have smaller market capitalizations or less liquidity, however, a stratified sampling or optimization approach can be useful for all the reasons mentioned previously in this section. Thus, an indexed portfolio can actually be managed using a blended approach consisting of full replication for more-liquid issues and one of the other methods for less-liquid issues.

5. TRACKING ERROR MANAGEMENT

As discussed previously, managers of passive strategies use a variety of approaches to track indexes in cost-efficient ways. To the extent the portfolio manager's skills are ineffective, tracking error results. This section discusses the measurement and management of tracking error.

5.1. Tracking Error and Excess Return

Tracking error and excess return are two measures that enable investors to differentiate performance among passive portfolio managers. Tracking error indicates how closely the portfolio behaves like its benchmark and measures a manager's ability to replicate the benchmark return. Tracking error is calculated as the standard deviation of the difference between the portfolio return and its benchmark index return. Excess return measures the difference between the portfolio returns and benchmark returns. Tracking error for portfolio p then can be expressed by Equation 3.

$$\text{Tracking error}_p = \sqrt{\text{Variance}_{(R_p - R_b)}} \qquad (3)$$

where R_p is the return on the portfolio and R_b is the return on the benchmark index. Excess return for portfolio p is calculated as in Equation 4.

$$\text{Excess return}_p = R_p - R_b \qquad (4)$$

Tracking error and excess return are distinct measures; the terms should not be used interchangeably. Tracking error measures the manager's ability to closely track the benchmark over time. In principle, a manager whose return is identical to that of the index could have arrived at that point by lagging and subsequently leading the index, producing a net difference of zero. But being a standard deviation, tracking error cannot be zero in cases such as the one described. Excess returns can be positive or negative and tell the investor how the manager performed relative to the benchmark. Tracking error, which is a standard deviation, is always presented as a non-negative number.

Index fund managers endeavor to have low tracking error and excess returns that are not negative. Low tracking error is important in measuring the skill of the index fund manager because the investor's goal is to mimic the return stream of the index. Avoiding negative excess returns versus the benchmark is also important because the manager will want to avoid underperforming the stated index.

Tracking error varies according to the manager's approach to tracking the index. An index that contains a large number of constituents will tend to create higher tracking error than those with fewer constituents. This is because a large number of constituents may prevent the manager from fully replicating the index.

For an index fund, the degree of tracking error fluctuates over time. Also, the value will differ depending on whether the data frequency is daily or less frequent.

EXAMPLE 3   Tracking Error and Excess Return

Exhibit 12 illustrates key portfolio metrics for three of the older and larger conventional open-end funds in the Australian and South Korean markets. Based on the levels of tracking error and excess return figures provided in the exhibit, explain whether the funds are likely replicating or sampling.

EXHIBIT 12   Major Conventional Index Mutual Funds in Australia and South Korea

Fund Name (Holdings)	Holdings	Annual Management Fee (bps)	3-Year Annualized Tracking Error	3-Year Annualized Excess Return
Australian market benchmark for the following funds is the S&P/ASX 300 Index. Number of securities in the index: 300.				
BlackRock Indexed Australian Equity Fund	296	20	0.0347%	−0.1684%
Macquarie True Index Australian Shares	259	0	0.0167%	0.0111%
Vanguard Australian Shares Index	293	18	0.1084%	−0.1814%
South Korean market benchmark for the funds below is the KRX KOSPI 200 Korea Index. Number of securities in the index: 200.				
KB Star Korea Index Equity CE	190	36	1.2671%	0.3356%
KIM Cruise Index F2.8 Equity-Deriv A	178	9	1.5019%	1.7381%
Samsung Index Premium Equity-Deriv A	204	40	1.3325%	1.1097%

Solution: Based on the number of stocks in the fund compared to the index constituent number, it appears most funds are attempting to replicate. Two of the funds (Macquarie True Index and KIM Cruise Index) have 80% to 90% of the stocks in the index, which indicates they are more likely to be using sampling. One fund (Samsung Index Premium) actually holds more than the index, which can happen if buffering is used. No fund contains the same number of stocks as constituents in the index. Thus, it is not surprising that the funds failed to track their respective indexes perfectly. On an annualized basis, tracking error for the Australian funds is less than one-tenth the level of the Korean funds. However, the Korean funds' excess return—which is fund return less the benchmark index return—is positive in all three cases. The negative excess returns for two of the Australian funds are relatively close and possibly attributable to their management fees of 18–20 basis points.

5.2. Potential Causes of Tracking Error and Excess Return

Tracking error in an indexed equity fund can arise for several reasons. A major reason involves the fees charged. Although tracking error is expressed as an absolute value, fees are always negative because they represent a cost and drive down the excess return. Therefore, higher fees will contribute to lower excess returns and higher tracking error.

A second issue to consider is the number of securities held by the portfolio versus the benchmark index. Stock indexes that are liquid and investable may be fully replicated, while indexes with hard-to-find securities or a great number of securities are sampled. Sampled portfolios typically report greater tracking error than those that are fully replicated.

The intra-day trading of the constituent stocks of an indexed portfolio also presents an important issue to consider when attributing tracking error. The effect of intra-day trading can be positive or negative for a portfolio's returns compared to its benchmark index. The price levels used to report index returns are struck at the close of the trading day, so any securities that are bought or sold at a different price than that of the index will contribute to portfolio tracking error. Index fund managers can minimize this type of tracking error by transacting at the market-on-close price or as near to the closing time as feasible.

A secondary component of trading costs that contributes to tracking error is the trading commission paid to brokers. Commission costs make excess returns more negative and also affect tracking error. According to Perold and Salomon (1991), the trading cost for passive portfolio managers is likely to be lower than the trading cost for active managers who are suspected by their counterparties to possess an information advantage.

Another issue to consider is the cash holding of the portfolio. Equity indexes do not have a cash allocation, so any cash balance creates tracking error for the index fund manager. Cash can be accumulated in the portfolio from a variety of sources, such as dividends received, sale proceeds, investor contributions, and other sources of income. Cash flows from investors and from the constituent companies may not be invested immediately, and investing them often entails a commission cost. Both may affect tracking error. The tracking error caused by temporarily uninvested cash is known as **cash drag**. The effect of cash drag on portfolio value is negative when the market is rising and positive when it is falling.

Hill and Cheong (1996) discuss how to equitize a portfolio that would otherwise suffer from cash drag. One method is to use futures contracts. ETFs have been used widely for this purpose. Some portfolio managers establish a futures commission merchant relationship to offset their cash positions with a futures contract that represents the replicated index. When a manager does this, she will calculate the accrued dividends as well to hedge the dividend drag, which is cash drag attributable to accrued cash dividends paid to shareholders.

5.3. Controlling Tracking Error

The process of controlling tracking error involves trade-offs between the benefits and costs of maintaining complete faithfulness to the benchmark index, as illustrated in Exhibit 10. Portfolio managers who are unconstrained would keep the number of constituent securities and their weights as closely aligned to the benchmark index as possible. Even so, trading costs and other fees cause actual investment performance to deviate from index performance. Passive investing does not mean that the fund does not trade. Managers trade to accommodate inflows and outflows of cash from investors, to reinvest dividends, and to reflect changes in constituents of the underlying index.

As discussed in Section 5.2, most passive portfolio managers attempt to minimize cash held because a cash position generally creates undesirable tracking error. To keep tracking error low, portfolio managers need to invest cash flows received at the same valuations used by the benchmark index provider. Of course, because this is not always feasible, portfolio managers aim to maintain a beta of 1.0 relative to the benchmark index, while keeping other risk factor exposures similar to those of the index.

6. SOURCES OF RETURN AND RISK IN PASSIVE EQUITY PORTFOLIOS

Indexed portfolios began as a representation of market performance, and some investors accept the returns of the indexed portfolio without judgment. However, understanding both positive and negative sources of return through attribution analysis is an important step in the passive equity investment process.

6.1. Attribution Analysis

An investor has many choices across the investable spectrum of assets. An investor must first choose between stocks, bonds, and other asset classes and then partition each asset class by its sub-categories. In partitioning stocks, the process begins with choosing what countries to invest in, what market-cap sizes and investment style to use, and whether to weight the constituents using market cap or an alternative weighting method.

The return on an indexed portfolio can come from any of the aforementioned criteria. Return analyses are conducted ex-post, which means that the returns of the portfolio are studied after they have been experienced.

The sources of return for an equity index replication portfolio are the same as for any actively managed fund and include company-specific returns, sector returns, country returns, and currency returns. Beyond the traditional methods of grouping the risk and returns of the indexed portfolio, portfolio managers can group their indexed portfolios according to the stated portfolio objective. For example, a high dividend yield indexed portfolio may be grouped against the broad market benchmark by dividend yield. A low volatility portfolio could be grouped by volatility buckets to show how the lowest volatility stocks performed in the indexed portfolio as well as the broad market.

Most portfolio managers will rely on their portfolio attribution system to help them in understanding the sources of return. Index fund managers who track a broad market index need to understand what factors are driving the returns of that portfolio and its underlying index. Index fund managers of passive factor-based strategies should understand both the sources of return for their indexed portfolios and how those returns relate to the broad market index from which the constituents were chosen. In this way, passive factor-based strategies are very similar to actively managed funds in the sense that they are actively chosen.

Exhibit 13 shows an example of a portfolio attribution analysis using annual returns. Portfolio X is an index fund that seeks to replicate the performance of its benchmark. The manager of Portfolio X confirms that the portfolio, which has a return of 5.62%, is closely replicating the performance of the benchmark, which has a return of 5.65%.

Using Exhibit 13, the manager analyzes the relative sector weights and sources of the three basis points of return difference. A portfolio that is within three basis points of its benchmark index is undoubtedly tracking the index closely. Beyond seeking the source of the tracking error, the portfolio manager will also seek to understand the source of the positive returns.

EXHIBIT 13   Example of Sector Attribution Analysis (All figures in %)

Sector	Sector Return (A)	Sector Weight (B)	Contribution to Return (C) = (A) × (B)	Sector Weight (D)	Contribution to Return (E) = (A) × (D)	Difference (F) = (C) − (E)
	Portfolio X			**Benchmark for Portfolio X**		**Attribution Analysis**
Total	5.62	100.00	5.62	100.00	5.65	−0.03
Telecom. Services	16.94	2.25	0.38	2.34	0.40	−0.02

| Sector | Sector Return (A) | Portfolio X | | Benchmark for Portfolio X | | Attribution Analysis |
		Sector Weight (B)	Contribution to Return (C) = (A) × (B)	Sector Weight (D)	Contribution to Return (E) = (A) × (D)	Difference (F) = (C) – (E)
Utilities	15.45	12.99	2.01	13.03	2.01	−0.01
Consumer Discretionary	12.09	3.89	0.47	3.90	0.47	0.00
Materials	9.61	2.08	0.20	2.08	0.20	0.00
Information Technology	7.03	2.82	0.20	2.85	0.20	0.00
Consumer Staples	6.82	15.07	1.03	15.09	1.03	0.00
Industrials	3.93	16.08	0.63	16.15	0.63	0.00
Financials	0.50	19.85	0.10	19.32	0.10	0.00
Health Care	0.31	12.70	0.04	12.77	0.04	0.00
Real Estate	0.80	5.04	0.04	5.23	0.04	0.00
Energy	7.21	7.23	0.52	7.24	0.52	0.00
[Cash]	0.00	0.00	0.00	0.00	0.00	0.00

Attribution analyses like the one in Exhibit 13 can be structured in many ways. This analysis is grouped by economic sector. Sector attribution can help an investor develop expectations about how a portfolio might perform in different market conditions. For example, during an era of low interest rates, high-dividend stocks such as utilities are likely to outperform while financial stocks such as banks are likely to underperform, other things held equal. To the extent the portfolio holds financial stocks in a lower concentration than the benchmark, the portfolio will likely outperform if interest rates stay low.

Column A in Exhibit 13 shows the total return for each sector. For example, the Telecommunications sector posted a return of 16.94% over this period.

Column B shows Portfolio's X's sector weight. The portfolio is heavily invested in Financials, because this is the largest sector in the benchmark index.

Column C shows each sector's contribution to the overall return of Portfolio X, obtained by multiplying each sector weight in Portfolio X by the sector's total return. The sum of the eleven sectors' contributions to return is equal to the total return of the portfolio.

Column D shows the benchmark's sector weights.

Column E shows the contribution to return of each sector held by the benchmark, obtained by multiplying each sector's weight in the benchmark by the sector's total return. The sum of the eleven sectors' contributions to return is equal to the total return of the benchmark.

Finally, column F shows the difference in contribution to returns between Portfolio X and the benchmark. Column F is the difference between columns C and E.

Portfolio X has 15.07% invested in Consumer Staples, which compares to the benchmark index's 15.09% weight in that sector. The negligible underweighting combined with a sector return of 6.82% enabled the portfolio to closely match the contribution to return of the portfolio to that of the index.

The Telecommunications and Utilities sectors were the best-performing sectors over the period. Telecommunications and Utilities holdings made up 15.24% of the portfolio's holdings and contributed 2.39 percentage points (or 239 basis points) of the 5.62% total return.

Companies in the Telecommunications and Utilities sectors are high-dividend payers and are positively affected by falling interest rates. Given this information, the manager could then connect the positive performance of the sectors to the prevailing interest rate environment. The manager would also note in the attribution analysis that the same interest rate environment, in part, caused the Financials sector to underperform the market. These opposing forces act as a good hedge against interest rate movements in either direction and are part of a robust portfolio structure.

The portfolio manager of the strategy may use the attribution analysis to determine the sources of tracking error. In this case, the analysis confirmed that the portfolio is meeting its goal of closely tracking the composition and performance of its benchmark. Further, the portfolio manager is able to determine the sources of return, which in this case are in large part from the high-dividend-yielding Telecommunications and Utilities sectors.

6.2. Securities Lending

Investors who hold long equity positions usually keep the shares in their brokerage accounts, so they are ready to sell when the time arises. But there is a demand for those shares independent of fellow investors who may wish to buy them. Investors who want to sell short may need to borrow the shares, and they are willing to pay for the right to borrow. The securities-lending income received by long portfolio managers can be a valuable addition to portfolio returns. At the very least, the proceeds can help offset the other costs of managing the portfolio. In the case of low-cost indexed portfolios, securities lending income can actually make net expenses negative—meaning that in addition to tracking the benchmark index, the portfolio earns a return in excess of the index.

An investor who wants to lend securities often uses a lending agent. In the case of institutional investors (e.g., mutual funds, pension funds, and hedge funds), the custodian (i.e., custody bank) is frequently used. Occasionally, the asset management firm will offer securities lending services. Two legal documents are usually put in place, including a securities lending authorization agreement between the lender and the agent and a master securities lending agreement between the agent and borrowers.

The lending agent identifies a borrower who posts collateral (typically 102–105% of the value of the securities). When the collateral is in securities rather than cash, the lending agent holds them as a guarantee. The lending agent evaluates the collateral daily to ensure that it is sufficient. When the collateral is in the form of cash, the lending agent invests it in money market instruments and receives interest income. In this case, the borrower sometimes receives a rebate that partially defrays its lost interest income. Regardless, the borrower pays a fee to the lender when borrowing the securities, and the lender typically splits part of this fee with the lending agent.

According to the International Securities Lending Association (2016), the 30 June 2016 global value of securities made available for lending by institutional investors was EUR 14 trillion. Of this, EUR 1.9 trillion in value was actually loaned, 53% of which was in equity securities. Of global securities on loan, US and Canadian lenders represented 67% of value. Mutual funds and pension funds accounted for 66% of the total value of equity securities loaned. In North America, cash represents approximately 70% of all collateral; in Europe, noncash collateral is more than 80% of the total. ISLA reports that over 60 countries have issued formal legal opinions on the responsibilities of securities lending counterparties.

Securities lending carries risks that can offset the benefits. The main risks are the credit quality of the borrower (credit risk) and the value of the posted collateral (market risk), although liquidity risk and operational risk are additional considerations. Lenders are permitted to sell loaned securities at any time under the normal course of the portfolio management mandate, and the borrowed shares must be returned in time for normal settlement of that sale. However, there is no guarantee that the borrower can deliver on a timely basis.

An additional risk is that lenders can invest cash held as collateral; and if a lender elects to invest the cash in long-term or risky securities, the collateral value is at risk of erosion. As long as the cash is invested in low-risk securities, risk is kept low. Typically, an agreed return on the invested cash is rebated by the lender to the borrower. Similarly, borrowers must pay cash to lenders in lieu of any cash dividends received because the dividends paid by the issuers of the shares will go to the holders. According to Duffie, Gârleanu, and Pedersen (2002), institutional investors such as index mutual funds and pension funds are viewed as preferred lenders because they are long-term holders of shares and unlikely to claim their shares back abruptly from borrowers.

The example of Sigma Finance Company illustrates collateral investment risk. Sigma Finance was a structured investment vehicle that primarily held long-term debt financed by short-term borrowings, and profit came from the interest differential. During the credit 2008–2009 global financial crisis, Sigma was downgraded by the rating agencies and lost its ability to borrow in the short-term markets, which led to default. Investors in Sigma's credit offerings, many of them security lenders, suffered substantial losses because of the default.

Borrowers take formal legal title to the securities, receive all cash flows and voting rights, and pay an annualized cost of borrowing (typically 2–10%). The borrowing cost depends on the borrower's credit quality and how difficult it is to borrow the security in question. Some securities are widely recognized as "easy to borrow" (ETB).

A popular exchange-traded fund (ETF) represents a good example of how securities lending revenue can provide a benefit to investment beneficiaries. As of 31 March 2016, the USD 25.344 billion iShares Russell 2000 ETF had loaned out USD 4.273 billion in securities to 19 counterparties. This amount was 100% collateralized with cash. An affiliated party, BlackRock Institutional Trust Company, served as the securities lending agent in exchange for 4 basis points of collateral investment fees annually, totaling USD 29 million for the year ending 31 March 2016. IWM's net securities lending income for the year was slightly above USD 10 million, which nearly offset the approximately USD 14 million in investment advisory fees charged by the portfolio managers.

6.3. Investor Activism and Engagement by Passive Managers

Institutional investors, especially index fund managers, are among the largest shareholders of many companies. The shares that they vote can have a large influence on corporate elections and outcomes of the proxy process. Their status as large shareholders often gives such investors access to private meetings with corporate management to discuss their concerns and preferences regarding corporate policies on board structure and composition, management compensation, operational risk management, the integrity of accounting statements, and other matters. Goldstein (2014) reports that in a survey, about two-thirds of public companies indicate investor engagement in 2014 was higher than it had been three years earlier. The typical points of contact were investor relations specialists, general counsel/ corporate secretary, the board chair, and the CEO or CFO of the company. The respondents also reported that engagement is now covering more topics, but the subject matter is not principally financial. Governance policies, executive compensation, and social, environmental, and strategy issues are dominant.

Ferguson (2010) argues that institutional investors—who are themselves required to act in a fiduciary capacity—have a key responsibility to carry out their duties as voting shareholders. Lambiotte, Gibney, and Hartley (2014) assert that if done in an enlightened way, voting and engagement with company management by passive investors can be a return-enhancing activity. Many hedge funds and other large investors even specialize in activism to align governance in their invested companies with shareholder interests.

Activist investors are usually associated with active portfolio management. If their activism efforts do not produce the desired result, they can express their dissatisfaction by selling their shares. In contrast, passive investors hold index-constituent stocks directly or indirectly. If they are attempting to match an index's performance, they do not have the flexibility to sell. Yet both types of investors usually have the opportunity to vote their shares and participate in governance improvements.

Why should governance matter for passive investors in broadly diversified portfolios? Across such portfolios, governance quality is broadly diversified; moreover, by definition, passive investors do not try to select the best-performing companies or avoid the worst. However, corporate governance improvements are aimed at improving the effectiveness of the operations, management, and board oversight of the business. If the resulting efficiency improvements are evidenced in higher returns to index-constituent stocks, the index performance rises and so does the performance of an index-tracking portfolio. Thus, a goal of activism is to increase returns.

Passive investors may even have a higher duty than more-transient active managers to use their influence to improve governance. As long as a stock has membership in the benchmark index, passive managers can be considered permanent shareholders. Such investors might benefit from engaging with company management and boards, even outside the usual proxy season. Reinforcing the concept of permanence, some companies even give greater voting rights to long-term shareholders. Dallas and Barry (2016) examine 12 US companies with voting rights that increase to four, five, or even ten votes per share if the holding period is greater than three and sometimes four years.

Most passive managers have a fiduciary duty to their clients that includes the obligation to vote proxy ballots on behalf of investors. Although shareholder return can be enhanced by engagement, the costs of these measures must also be considered. Among the more significant costs are staff resources required to become familiar with key issues and to engage management, regulators, and other investors. Researching and voting thousands of proxy ballots becomes problematic for many managers. They frequently hire a proxy voting service, such as Institutional Shareholder Services or Broadridge Financial Services, to achieve their goal of voting the proxy ballots in their clients' favor.

Although a strong argument can be made in favor of even passive managers voting their shares in an informed way and pursuing governance changes when warranted, potential conflicts of interest may limit investors' propensity to challenge company management. Consider the hypothetical case of a large financial firm that earns substantial fees from its business of administering corporate retirement plans, including the pension plan of Millheim Corp. Let us say that the financial firm also manages index funds, and Millheim's stock is one of many index constituents. If Millheim becomes the target of shareholder activism, the financial firm's incentives are structured to support Millheim's management on any controversial issue.

Some may question the probable effectiveness of activist efforts by passive investors. Management of the company targeted by activist investors is likely to see active portfolio managers as skillful and willing users of the proxy process to effect changes and accordingly will respond seriously. In contrast, passive investors are required to hold the company's shares to fulfill their tracking mandate (without the flexibility to sell or take a short position), and management may be aware of this constrained position and thus take passive investors' activist activities less seriously.

SUMMARY

This chapter explains the rationale for passive investing as well as the construction of equity market indexes and the various methods by which investors can track the indexes. Passive portfolio managers must understand benchmark index construction and the advantages and disadvantages of the various methods used to track index performance.

Among the key points made in this chapter are the following:

- Active equity portfolio managers who focus on individual security selection have long been unsuccessful at beating benchmarks and have charged high management fees to their end investors. Consequently, passive investing has increased in popularity.
- Passive equity investors seek to track the return of benchmark indexes and construct their portfolios to reflect the characteristics of the chosen benchmarks.
- Selection of a benchmark is driven by the equity investor's objectives and constraints as presented in the investment policy statement. The benchmark index must be rules-based, transparent, and investable. Specific important characteristics include the domestic or foreign market covered, the market capitalization of the constituent stocks, where the index falls in the value–growth spectrum, and other risk factors.
- The equity benchmark index weighting scheme is another important consideration for investors. Weighting methods include market-cap weighting, price weighting, equal weighting, and fundamental weighting. Market cap-weighting has several advantages, including the fact that weights adjust automatically.
- Index rebalancing and reconstitution policies are important features. Rebalancing involves adjusting the portfolio's constituent weights after price changes, mergers, or other corporate events have caused those weights to deviate from the benchmark index. Reconstitution involves deleting names that are no longer in the index and adding names that have been approved as new index members.

- Increasingly, passive investors use index-based strategies to gain exposure to individual risk factors. Examples of known equity risk factors include Capitalization, Style, Yield, Momentum, Volatility, and Quality.
- For passive investors, portfolio tracking error is the standard deviation of the portfolio return net of the benchmark return.
- Indexing involves the goal of minimizing tracking error subject to realistic portfolio constraints.
- Methods of pursuing passive investing include the use of such pooled investments as mutual funds and exchange-traded funds (ETFs), a do-it-yourself approach of building the portfolio stock-by-stock, and using derivatives to obtain exposure.
- Conventional open-end index mutual funds generally maintain low fees. Their expense ratios are slightly higher than for ETFs, but a brokerage fee is usually required for investor purchases and sales of ETF shares.
- Index exposure can also be obtained through the use of derivatives, such as futures and swaps.
- Building a passive portfolio by full replication, meaning to hold all the index constituents, requires a large-scale portfolio and high-quality information about the constituent characteristics. Most equity index portfolios are managed using either a full replication strategy to keep tracking error low, are sampled to keep trading costs low, or use optimization techniques to match as closely as possible the characteristics and performance of the underlying index.
- The principal sources of passive portfolio tracking error are fees, trading costs, and cash drag. Cash drag refers to the dilution of the return on the equity assets because of cash held. Cash drag can be exacerbated by the receipt of dividends from constituent stocks and the delay in getting them converted into shares.
- Portfolio managers control tracking error by minimizing trading costs, netting investor cash inflows and redemptions, and using equitization tools like derivatives to compensate for cash drag.
- Many index fund managers offer the constituent securities held in their portfolios for lending to short sellers and other market participants. The income earned from lending those securities helps offset portfolio management costs, often resulting in lower net fees to investors.
- Investor activism is engagement with portfolio companies and recognizing the primacy of end investors. Forms of activism can include expressing views to company boards or management on executive compensation, operational risk, board governance, and other value-relevant matters.
- Successful passive equity investment requires an understanding of the investor's needs, benchmark index construction, and methods available to track the index.

REFERENCES

Arnott, Robert, Jason Hsu, and Philip Moore. 2005. "Fundamental Indexation." *Financial Analysts Journal*, vol. 61, no. 2: 83–99.

Banz, Rolf W. 1981. "The Relationship between Return and Market Value of Common Stocks." *Journal of Financial Economics*, vol. 9, no. 1: 3–18.

Brinson, Gary P., L. Randolph Hood, and Gilbert L. Beebower. 1986. "Determinants of Portfolio Performance." *Financial Analysts Journal*, vol. 42, no. 4: 39–44.

Chen, Honghui, Gregory Noronha, and Vijay Singal. 2004. "The Price Response to S&P 500 Index Additions and Deletions: Evidence of Asymmetry and a New Explanation." *Journal of Finance*, vol. 63, no. 4: 1537–1573.

Choueifaty, Yves, and Yves Coignard. 2008. "Toward Maximum Diversification." *Journal of Portfolio Management*, vol. 35, no. 1: 40–51.

Dallas, Lynne, and Jordan M. Barry. 2016. "Long-Term Shareholders and Time-Phased Voting." *Delaware Journal of Corporate Law*, vol. 40, no. 2: 541–646.

Duffie, Darrell, Nicolae Gârleanu, and Lasse Heje Pedersen. 2002. "Securities Lending, Shorting, and Pricing." *Journal of Financial Economics*, vol. 66, no. 2–3: 307–339.

Fabozzi, Frank J., Sergio M. Focardi, and Petter N. Kolm. 2010. *Quantitative Equity Investing: Techniques and Strategies*. Hoboken, NJ: John Wiley & Sons.

Fama, Eugene F., and Kenneth R. French. 2015. "A Five-Factor Asset Pricing Model." *Journal of Financial Economics*, vol. 116, no. 1: 1–22.

Ferguson, Roger W. Jr. 2010. "Riding Herd on Company Management." *Wall Street Journal* (27 April).

French, Kenneth R. 2008. "The Cost of Active Investing." *Journal of Finance*, vol. 63, no. 4: 1537–1573.

Goldstein, Marc. 2014. "Defining Engagement: An Update on the Evolving Relationship between Shareholders, Directors, and Executives." Institutional Shareholder Services for the Investor Responsibility Research Center Institute: 1–48.

Hannam, Richard, and Frédéric Jamet. 2017. "IQ Insights: Equal Weighting and Other Forms of Size Tilting." SSGA white paper (January).

Hill, Joanne M., and Rebecca K. Cheong. 1996. "Minimizing Cash Drag with S&P 500 Index Tools." Goldman Sachs New York working paper.

International Securities Lending Association. 2015. "Establishing an Agency Securities Lending Program." ISLA white paper available at www.isla.co.uk.

International Securities Lending Association. 2016. "ISLA Securities Lending Market Report" (September) http://www.isla.co.uk/wp-content/uploads/2016/10/ISLA-SL-REPORT-9-16-final.pdf.

Jacobs, Bruce I., and Kenneth N. Levy. 2014. "Smart Beta versus Smart Alpha." *Journal of Portfolio Management*, vol. 40, no. 4: 4–7.

Jorion, Philippe. 2003. "Portfolio Optimization with Tracking-Error Constraints." *Financial Analysts Journal*, vol. 59, no. 5: 70–82.

Lambiotte, Clay, Paul Gibney, and Joel Hartley. 2014. "Activist Equity Investing: Unlocking Value by Acting as a Catalyst for Corporate Change." LCP: Insight-Clarity-Advice. Lane, Clark, and Peacock LLP (August): 1–2.

Malevergne, Yannick, Pedro Santa-Clara, and Didier Sornette. 2009. "Professor Zipf Goes to Wall Street." NBER Working Paper 15295 (August).

MSCI. 2017. "MSCI US Equity Indexes Methodology": www.msci.com/eqb/methodology/meth_docs/MSCI_Feb17_USEI_Methodology.pdf.

Perold, André, and Robert S. Salomon Jr. 1991. "The Right Amount of Assets under Management." *Financial Analysts Journal*, vol. 47, no. 3: 31–39.

Petajisto, Antti. 2010. "The Index Premium and Its Hidden Cost for Index Funds." NYU Stern working paper.

Podkaminer, Gene. 2015. "The Education of Beta—Revisited." Callan Investments Institute white paper.

Qin, Nan, and Vijay Singal. 2015. "Investor Portfolios When Stocks Are Mispriced: Equally-Weighted or Value-Weighted?" Virginia Tech working paper.

Renshaw, Edward F., and Paul J. Feldstein. 1960. "The Case for an Unmanaged Investment Company." *Financial Analysts Journal*, vol. 16, no. 1: 43–46.

Roll, Richard. 1992. "A Mean/Variance Analysis of Tracking Error." *Journal of Portfolio Management*, vol. 18, no. 4: 13–22.

Soe, Aye M., and Ryan Poirier. 2016. "SPIVA U.S. Scorecard." S&P Dow Jones Indices Report.

Woerheide, Walt, and Don Persson. 1993. "An Index of Portfolio Diversification." *Financial Services Review*, vol. 2, no. 2: 73–85.

Zeng, Liu, and Frank Luo. 2013. "10 Years Later: Where in the World Is Equal Weight Indexing Now?" Standard & Poor's white paper.

PRACTICE PROBLEMS

The following information relates to questions 1–8

Evan Winthrop, a senior officer of a US-based corporation, meets with Rebecca Tong, a portfolio manager at Cobalt Wealth Management. Winthrop recently moved his investments to Cobalt in response to his previous manager's benchmark-relative underperformance and high expenses.

Winthrop resides in Canada and plans to retire there. His annual salary covers his current spending needs, and his vested defined benefit pension plan is sufficient to meet retirement income goals. Winthrop prefers passive exposure to global equity markets with a focus on low management costs and minimal tracking error to any index benchmarks. The fixed-income portion of the portfolio may consist of laddered maturities with a home-country bias.

Tong proposes using an equity index as a basis for an investment strategy and reviews the most important requirements for an appropriate benchmark. With regard to investable indexes, Tong tells Winthrop the following:

Statement 1.   A free-float adjustment to a market-capitalization weighted index lowers its liquidity.

Statement 2.   An index provider that incorporates a buffering policy makes the index more investable.

Winthrop asks Tong to select a benchmark for the domestic stock allocation that holds all sectors of the Canadian equity market and to focus the portfolio on highly liquid, well-known companies. In addition, Winthrop specifies that any stock purchased should have a relatively low beta, a high dividend yield, a low P/E, and a low price-to-book ratio (P/B).

Winthrop and Tong agree that only the existing equity investments need to be liquidated. Tong suggests that, as an alternative to direct equity investments, the new equity portfolio be composed of the exchange-traded funds (ETFs) shown in Exhibit 1.

EXHIBIT 1   Available Equity ETFs

Equity Benchmark	ETF Ticker	Number of Constituents	P/B	P/E	Fund Expense Ratio
S&P/TSX 60	XIU	60	2.02	17.44	0.18%
S&P 500	SPY	506	1.88	15.65	0.10%
MSCI EAFE	EFA	933	2.13	18.12	0.33%

Winthrop asks Tong about the techniques wealth managers and fund companies use to create index-tracking equity portfolios that minimize tracking error and costs. In response, Tong outlines two frequently used methods:

Method 1.   One process requires that all index constituents are available for trading and liquid, but significant brokerage commissions can occur when the index is large.

Method 2.   When tracking an index with a large number of constituents and/or managing a relatively low level of assets, a relatively straightforward and technically unsophisticated method can be used to build a passive portfolio that requires fewer individual securities than the index and reduces brokerage commission costs.

Tong adds that portfolio stocks may be used to generate incremental revenue, thereby partially offsetting administrative costs but potentially creating undesirable counterparty and collateral risks.

After determining Winthrop's objectives and constraints, the CAD147 million portfolio's new strategic policy is to target long-term market returns while being fully invested at all times. Tong recommends quarterly rebalancing, currency hedging, and a composite benchmark composed of equity and fixed-income indexes. Currently the USD is worth CAD1.2930, and this exchange rate is expected to remain stable during the next month. Exhibit 2 presents the strategic asset allocation and benchmark weights.

EXHIBIT 2   Composite Benchmark and Policy Weights

Asset Class	Benchmark Index	Policy Weight
Canadian equity	S&P/TSX 60	40.0%
US equity	S&P 500	15.0%
International developed markets equity	MSCI EAFE	15.0%
Canadian bonds	DEX Universe	30.0%
Total portfolio		100.0%

In one month, Winthrop will receive a performance bonus of USD5,750,000. He believes that the US equity market is likely to increase during this timeframe. To take advantage of Winthrop's market outlook, he instructs Tong to immediately initiate an equity transaction using the S&P 500 futures contract with a current price of 2,464.29 while respecting the policy weights in Exhibit 2. The S&P 500 futures contract multiplier is 250, and the S&P 500 E-mini multiplier is 50.

Tong cautions Winthrop that there is a potential pitfall with the proposed request when it comes time to analyze performance. She discloses to Winthrop that equity index futures returns can differ from the underlying index, primarily because of corporate actions such as the declaration of dividends and stock splits.

1. Which of Tong's statements regarding equity index benchmarks is *correct*?
    A. Only Statement 1
    B. Only Statement 2
    C. Both Statement 1 and Statement 2

2. To satisfy Winthrop's benchmark and security selection specifications, the Canadian equity index benchmark Tong selects should be:
    A. small-capitalization with a core tilt.
    B. large-capitalization with a value tilt.
    C. mid-capitalization with a growth tilt.

3. Based on Exhibit 1 and assuming a full-replication indexing approach, the tracking error is expected to be highest for:
   A. XIU.
   B. SPY.
   C. EFA.

4. Method 1's portfolio construction process is *most likely*:
   A. optimization.
   B. full replication.
   C. stratified sampling.

5. Method 2's portfolio construction process is *most likely*:
   A. optimization.
   B. full replication.
   C. stratified sampling.

6. The method that Tong suggests to add incremental revenue is:
   A. program trading.
   B. securities lending.
   C. attribution analysis.

7. In preparation for receipt of the performance bonus, Tong should immediately:
   A. buy two US E-mini equity futures contracts.
   B. sell nine US E-mini equity futures contracts.
   C. buy seven US E-mini equity futures contracts.

8. The risk that Tong discloses regarding the equity futures strategy is *most likely*:
   A. basis risk.
   B. currency risk.
   C. counterparty risk.

The following information relates to questions 9–14

The Mackenzie Education Foundation funds educational projects in a four-state region of the United States. Because of the investment portfolio's poor benchmark-relative returns, the foundation's board of directors hired a consultant, Stacy McMahon, to analyze performance and provide recommendations.

McMahon meets with Autumn Laubach, the foundation's executive director, to review the existing asset allocation strategy. Laubach believes the portfolio's underperformance is attributable to the equity holdings, which are allocated 55% to a US large-capitalization index fund, 30% to an actively managed US small-cap fund, and 15% to an actively managed developed international fund.

Laubach states that the board is interested in following a passive approach for some or all of the equity allocation. In addition, the board is open to approaches that could generate returns in excess of the benchmark for part of the equity allocation. McMahon suggests that the board consider following a passive factor-based momentum strategy for the allocation to international stocks.

McMahon observes that the benchmark used for the US large-cap equity component is a price-weighted index containing 150 stocks. The benchmark's Herfindahl–Hirschman Index (HHI) is 0.0286.

McMahon performs a sector attribution analysis based on Exhibit 1 to explain the large-cap portfolio's underperformance relative to the benchmark.

EXHIBIT 1   Trailing 12-Month US Large-Cap Returns and Foundation/Benchmark Weights

Sector	Sector Returns	Foundation Sector Weights	Benchmark Sector Weights
Information technology	10.75%	18.71%	19.06%
Consumer staples	12.31%	16.52%	16.10%
Energy	8.63%	9.38%	9.53%
Utilities	−3.92%	8.76%	8.25%
Financials	7.05%	6.89%	6.62%

The board decides to consider adding a mid-cap manager. McMahon presents candidates for the mid-cap portfolio. Exhibit 2 provides fees and cash holdings for three portfolios and an index fund.

EXHIBIT 2   Characteristics of US Mid-Cap Portfolios and Index Fund

	Portfolio 1	Portfolio 2	Portfolio 3	Index Fund
Fees	0.10%	0.09%	0.07%	0.03%
Cash holdings	6.95%	3.42%	2.13%	0.51%

9. Compared with broad-market-cap weighting, the international equity strategy suggested by McMahon is *most likely* to:
   A. concentrate risk exposure.
   B. be based on the efficient market hypothesis.
   C. overweight stocks that recently experienced large price decreases.

10. The international strategy suggested by McMahon is *most likely* characterized as:
    A. risk based.
    B. return oriented.
    C. diversification oriented.

11. The initial benchmark used for the US large-cap allocation:
    A. is unaffected by stocks splits.
    B. is essentially a liquidity-weighted index.
    C. holds the same number of shares in each component stock.

12. Based on its HHI, the initial US large-cap benchmark *most likely* has:
    A. a concentration level of 4.29.
    B. an effective number of stocks of approximately 35.
    C. individual stocks held in approximately equal weights.

13. Using a sector attribution analysis based on Exhibit 1, which US large-cap sector is the primary contributor to the portfolio's underperformance relative to the benchmark?
    A. Utilities
    B. Consumer staples
    C. Information technology

14. Based on Exhibit 2, which portfolio will *most likely* have the lowest tracking error?
    A. Portfolio 1
    B. Portfolio 2
    C. Portfolio 3

CHAPTER 5

ANALYSIS OF ACTIVE PORTFOLIO MANAGEMENT

Roger G. Clarke, PhD
Harindra de Silva, PhD, CFA
Steven Thorley, PhD, CFA

LEARNING OUTCOMES

The candidate should be able to:

- describe how value added by active management is measured;
- calculate and interpret the information ratio (*ex post* and *ex ante*) and contrast it to the Sharpe ratio;
- state and interpret the fundamental law of active portfolio management, including its component terms—transfer coefficient, information coefficient, breadth, and active risk (aggressiveness);
- explain how the information ratio may be useful in investment manager selection and choosing the level of active portfolio risk;
- compare active management strategies, including market timing and security selection, and evaluate strategy changes in terms of the fundamental law of active management;
- describe the practical strengths and limitations of the fundamental law of active management.

1. INTRODUCTION

The Markowitz (1952) framework of what was originally called modern portfolio theory (MPT) has now become the prominent paradigm for communicating and applying principles of risk and return in portfolio management. Much of the mathematics and terminology of mean–variance portfolio theory was subsequently combined with the notion of informational efficiency by Sharpe (1964) and other financial economists to develop equilibrium models, such as the traditional capital asset pricing model. Separately, the tools of MPT were applied by Treynor and Black (1973) to guide investors in their selection of securities when prices differ from their equilibrium values. The application of portfolio theory to active management was further developed by Grinold (1989) in "The Fundamental Law of Active Management" and by Black and Litterman (1992).

We summarize the principles of active portfolio management using the terminology and mathematics of the fundamental law introduced by Grinold (1989) and further developed by Clarke, de Silva, and Thorley (2002). Active management theory deals with how an investor should construct a portfolio given an assumed competitive advantage or skill in predicting returns. Thus, active management relies on the assumption that financial markets are not perfectly efficient. Although investors might ultimately care about total risk and return, when asset management is delegated to professional investors in institutional settings (e.g., pension funds) the appropriate perspective is risk and return relative to a benchmark portfolio. In addition to the principal–agent problem in delegated asset management, the availability of passively managed portfolios requires a focus on value added above and beyond the alternative of a low-cost index fund.

We assume an understanding of basic portfolio theory, including the mathematics of expected values, variances, and correlation coefficients, as well as some familiarity with the related disciplines of mean–variance optimization and multi-factor risk models. The following sections introduce the mathematics of value added through active portfolio management, including the concepts of active weights, relative returns, and performance attribution systems. The subsequent section compares the well-known Sharpe ratio for measuring the total risk-adjusted value added with the information ratio for measuring relative risk-adjusted value added. This section also makes a distinction between *ex ante*, or expected, risk and return versus *ex post*, or realized, risk and return and explains that the information ratio is the best criterion for evaluating active investors. We then introduce the fundamental law that describes how relative skill, breadth of application, active management aggressiveness, and the constraints in portfolio construction combine to affect value added. The remaining sections provide examples of active portfolio management strategies in both the equity and fixed-income markets, describe some of the practical limitations of the fundamental law, and provide a summary of the concepts and principles.

2. ACTIVE MANAGEMENT AND VALUE ADDED

The objective of active management is to add value in the investment process by doing better than a benchmark portfolio. Value added is a relative performance comparison to investing in the benchmark portfolio, often called passive investing. If the investor outperforms the benchmark portfolio, value added is positive. If the investor underperforms the benchmark portfolio, value added is negative. In the latter case, the investor would have been better off during the measurement period by simply holding the benchmark portfolio, particularly net of fees and expenses. Examples of indexes that are used as benchmark portfolios include the MSCI All Country World Index and the Bloomberg Barclays Global Aggregate Bond Index, which represent the performance of global equities and global bonds, respectively.

2.1. Choice of Benchmark

A benchmark or passive portfolio should have a number of qualities to serve as a relevant comparison for active management:

- The benchmark is representative of the assets from which the investor will select.
- Positions in the benchmark portfolio can actually be replicated at low cost.
- Benchmark weights are verifiable *ex ante*, and return data are timely *ex post*.

An available security market index is often used as the benchmark portfolio. The most common market indexes weight the individual assets by their market capitalization. Capitalization weighting has played a prominent role in the development of capital market theory because such indexes are generally self-rebalancing and can be simultaneously held by many investors. Float-adjusted market capitalization-weighted indexes represent an incremental improvement over non-float-adjusted indexes by accounting for the percentage of a security or asset that is not privately held and thus available to the general investing public. One important consequence of using a float-adjusted capitalization-weighted market index as the benchmark is that when all relevant assets are included in the market, the value added from active management becomes a zero-sum game with respect to the market. Because the market portfolio represents the average performance across all investors that own securities before costs, active investors as a group cannot outperform the market (i.e., active management is a zero-sum game). For benchmarks that have a narrower definition than the total market, active management is not a zero-sum game because investors can select assets outside the benchmark.

The return on the benchmark portfolio, R_B, is based on the returns to the individual securities and the weights of each security in the portfolio:

$$R_B = \sum_{i=1}^{N} w_{B,i} R_i \tag{1}$$

where R_i is the return on security i, $w_{B,i}$ is the benchmark weight of security i, and N is the number of securities. Similarly, the return on an actively managed portfolio, R_P, is a function of the weights of the securities, i, held in the portfolio, $w_{P,i}$, and the returns to the individual securities:

$$R_P = \sum_{i=1}^{N} w_{P,i} R_i \tag{2}$$

The benchmark might include securities that are not part of the actively managed portfolio and thus would have a weight of zero by definition or simply be left out of the calculation in Equation 2. Similarly, an investor could include securities in the active portfolio that are not in the benchmark, and those would have a benchmark weight of zero in Equation 1. Please note that for simplicity, the same notation, N, is used in the summation in the expression for the managed portfolio return and the benchmark return, although fewer or more securities may be in the managed portfolio than in the benchmark.

2.2. Measuring Value Added

The value added or "active return" of an actively managed portfolio is typically calculated as the simple difference between the return on that portfolio and the return on the benchmark portfolio,

$$R_A = R_P - R_B$$

and can thus be either positive or negative. A risk-adjusted calculation of value added, which we will refer to as the managed portfolio's alpha, incorporates some estimate of the managed portfolio's risk relative to the benchmark, often captured by the portfolio's beta, $\alpha_P = R_P - \beta_P R_B$. Unfortunately, the term *alpha* in practice is often used to refer to active return as well, which implicitly assumes that the beta of the managed portfolio relative to the benchmark is 1.

Equations 1 and 2 can be combined to illustrate the important principle that value added is ultimately driven by the differences in managed portfolio weights and benchmark weights: $\Delta w_i = w_{P,i} - w_{B,i}$. These values are called the active weights of the managed portfolio, and the symbol Δ (Greek letter delta) is used to indicate the difference from the benchmark weights. Combining Equations 1 and 2 and employing this definition for active weights yields the conceptually important result that value added is the sum product of the active weights and asset returns:

$$R_A = \sum_{i=1}^{N} \Delta w_i R_i$$

Given that the sum of the active weights is zero, we can also write the value added as the sum product of active weights and active security returns:

$$R_A = \sum_{i=1}^{N} \Delta w_i R_{Ai} \tag{3}$$

where $R_{Ai} = R_i - R_B$. Equation 3 indicates that positive value added is generated when securities that have returns greater than the benchmark are overweighted and securities that have returns less than the benchmark are underweighted.

Whereas many applications of value added focus on individual securities as the assets, we first illustrate the concept with a simple numerical example of a composite portfolio that has just two assets—a stock portfolio and a bond portfolio. Suppose the benchmark is a 60/40 weighted composite portfolio of stocks and bonds. The investor believes that over the next year stocks will outperform bonds, so the investor holds a portfolio that is weighted 70% stocks and 30% bonds. The managed portfolio is said to be *overweight* stocks by 10 percentage points and *underweight* bonds by 10 percentage points—in other words, an active weight of −10 percentage points on bonds. Assume that *ex post* (i.e., "after the fact"), the return on the stock market turned out to be 14.0% and the return on the bond market turned out to be just 2.0%. In this case, the return on the managed portfolio is 0.70(14.0) + 0.30(2.0) = 10.4% and the return on the benchmark is 0.60(14.0) + 0.40(2.0) = 9.2%.

From these final numbers, one could directly calculate the value added as 10.4 − 9.2 = 1.2%. But using Equation 3, a more informative calculation of value added showing the contributions from each segment is $R_A = 0.10(14.0 - 9.2) - 0.10(2.0 - 9.2) = 0.5 + 0.7 = 1.2\%$. This breakout suggests that a 0.5% return relative to the benchmark was generated by being overweight stocks, and a 0.7% return was generated simultaneously by being underweight bonds—for a total of 1.2%. Of course, the actual returns might have been different—with the stock market return being lower than the bond market return, resulting in negative value added in the managed portfolio. For example, if the stock market had a return of −14.0% instead of +14.0%, the portfolio return and benchmark return would have been −9.2% and −7.6%, respectively. Then the value added from this single overweight/underweight decision would have been $R_A = 0.10(-14.0) - 0.10(2.0) = -1.4\% - 0.2\% = -1.6\%$.

EXAMPLE 1   Value Added and Country Equity Markets

Consider the MSCI EAFE Index as the benchmark for an actively managed portfolio that includes allocations to individual countries, as given in the following exhibit. The portfolio (both benchmark and managed) weights are for the beginning of 2018. The portfolio manager actively changes country allocations but does not engage in security selection.

Country	Benchmark Weight	Portfolio Weight	2018 Return
United Kingdom	17%	16%	−7.6%
Japan	25%	14%	−9.0%
France	11%	8%	−3.5%
Germany	9%	24%	−15.8%
Other Countries	38%	38%	−0.1%

Source: Data from MSCI.

1. Which countries have the largest overweight and largest underweight in the managed portfolio compared with the benchmark portfolio? What are the active weights for these two countries?
2. Using active weights and total returns, what was the value added of the managed portfolio over the benchmark portfolio in the calendar year 2018?

Solution to 1: Germany has the largest overweight at $24 - 9 = +15\%$, and Japan has the largest underweight at $14 - 25 = -11\%$.

Solution to 2: The value added is $-0.01(-7.6) - 0.11(-9.0) - 0.03(-3.5) + 0.15(-15.8) = -1.2\%$. Note that the "Other Countries" active weight is zero, so this asset does not contribute anything to the portfolio's active return. The value added can also be calculated using relative returns in Equation 3 with the same net result.

2.3. Decomposition of Value Added

In contrast to the previous simple example, performance attribution systems often attempt to decompose the value added into *multiple* sources. The most common decomposition is between value added due to asset allocation and value added due to security selection. Consider a composite portfolio of stocks and bonds where the asset allocation weights differ from a composite benchmark *and* each asset class is actively managed by selecting individual securities. The total value added is the difference between the actual portfolio return and the benchmark return:

$$R_A = \sum_{j=1}^{M} w_{P,j} R_{P,j} - \sum_{j=1}^{M} w_{B,j} R_{B,j}$$

The first summation has both portfolio weights and the returns on actively managed portfolios, designated by the "P" subscript. The second summation has both benchmark weights and benchmark returns, designated by the "B" subscript. The subscript $j = 1$ to M counts the number of asset classes, leaving the notation subscript $i = 1$ to N for use elsewhere to count the securities within each asset class.

We can rewrite the total value added as the sum of the active asset allocation decisions and the weighted sum of the value added from security selection, $R_{A,j} = R_{P,j} - R_{B,j}$, within each asset class:

$$R_A = \sum_{j=1}^{M} \Delta w_j R_{B,j} + \sum_{j=1}^{M} w_{P,j} R_{A,j} \qquad (4)$$

although this formulation arbitrarily assigns an interactive effect to security selection. The performance attribution system in Equation 4 may be easier to conceptualize with just two asset classes, stocks and bonds (in other words, with $M = 2$). Using *stocks* and *bonds* as the subscripts, Equation 4 becomes:

$$R_A = (\Delta w_{stocks} R_{B,stocks} + \Delta w_{bonds} R_{B,bonds}) + (w_{P,stocks} R_{A,stocks} + w_{P,bonds} R_{A,bonds})$$

The first (parenthetical) term is the value added from the asset allocation decision. The second term is the value added from security selection within the stock and bond portfolios. The active weights in the first term refer to differences from the policy portfolio. For example, the long-term policy portfolio might be 60/40 stocks versus bonds, and the investor deviates from this policy portfolio from year to year based on beliefs about the returns to each asset class.

To give a numerical example, consider the fund returns for the calendar year 2018 in the following table.

Fund	Fund Return (%)	Benchmark Return (%)	Value Added (%)
Fidelity Magellan	−5.6	−4.5	−1.1
PIMCO Total Return	−0.3	0.0	−0.3
Portfolio Return	−3.9	−2.7	−1.2

Specifically, the Fidelity Magellan mutual fund had a return of −5.6%, compared with a −4.5% return for its benchmark, the S&P 500 Index. In the same year, the PIMCO Total Return Fund had a return of −0.3%, compared with a 0.0% return for its benchmark, the Bloomberg Barclays US Aggregate Index. Consider an investor who invested in both actively managed funds, with 68% of the total portfolio in Fidelity and 32% in PIMCO. Assume that the investor's policy portfolio (strategic asset allocation) specifies weights of 60% for equities and 40% for bonds.

- As shown in the table, Fidelity Magellan added value of $R_A = R_P - R_B = -5.6\% - (-4.5)\% = -1.1\%$, and PIMCO Total Return added value of $R_A = R_P - R_B = -0.3\% - (0.0\%) = -0.3\%$. These value added numbers represent the skill in security selection within each individual fund.
- Using the actual weights of 68% and 32% in the Fidelity and PIMCO funds, the combined value added from security selection was $0.68(-1.1\%) + 0.32(-0.3\%) = -0.8\%$.
- The active asset allocation weights in 2018 were $68\% - 60\% = +8\%$ for equities and 8% for bonds, so the value added by the active asset allocation decision was $0.08(-4.5\%) - 0.08(0.0\%) = -0.4\%$. The total value added by the investor's active asset allocation decision *and* by the mutual funds through security selection was $-0.8\% - 0.4\% = -1.2\%$. To confirm this total value added, note that the return on the investor's portfolio was $0.68(-5.6\%) + 0.32(-0.3\%) = -3.9\%$ and the return on the policy portfolio was $0.60(-4.5\%) + 0.40(0.0\%) = -2.7\%$, for a difference of $-3.9\% - (-2.7) = -1.2\%$.

Performance attribution systems can be expanded to include several asset classes—for example, stocks, bonds, real estate, and cash (in other words, with $M = 4$ in Equation 4). For a given asset class, the performance attribution system might also include value added from the selection of industries or sectors relative to the benchmark. For example, an equity portfolio might measure value added from over- and underweighting different industry sectors, as well as individual stock selection within those sectors, and a fixed-income portfolio might decompose value added from the mix of sovereign government bonds versus corporate bonds, as well as individual bond selection.

In summary, deviations from portfolio benchmark weights drive the value added by active portfolio management. If every asset in the managed portfolio is held at its benchmark weight, there would be no value added relative to the benchmark. The total value added can be decomposed into various sources that capture the contribution from different decisions, such as asset allocation and security selection.

3. COMPARING RISK AND RETURN

The risk–return trade-off of a portfolio can be represented in either *absolute* or *relative* terms. The Sharpe ratio provides an absolute expected (*ex ante*) or realized (*ex post*) reward-to-risk measure. As we have noted, however, value added is a relative return comparison. The information ratio provides a benchmark relative expected (*ex ante*) or realized (*ex post*) reward-to-risk measure.

3.1. The Sharpe Ratio

The Sharpe ratio is used to compare the portfolio return in excess of a riskless rate with the volatility of the portfolio return. The ratio provides a measure of how much the investor is receiving in excess of a riskless rate for assuming the risk of the portfolio. The Sharpe ratio, SR_P, is calculated for any portfolio, either actively managed or a benchmark, using the formula

$$SR_P = \frac{R_P - R_F}{\sigma_P} \tag{5}$$

where R_P is the portfolio return, R_F is the risk-free rate, and σ_P is the standard deviation of the portfolio return. In this context, the standard deviation of the portfolio return is often called either volatility or total risk. The Sharpe ratio can be used as an *ex ante* measure of *expected* return and risk, in which case the general formula in Equation 5 would have the expected portfolio return, $E(R_P)$, minus the risk-free rate in the numerator and a forecast of volatility in the denominator. As subjective forecasts, the expected return and standard deviation of return will likely vary among different investors.

The Sharpe ratio can also be used to measure the *ex post* or *realized* performance of a portfolio over some time period. In that case, when applied to multiple time periods, the numerator in Equation 5 is the difference between the average realized portfolio return, $\overline{R_P}$, and the average risk-free rate, $\overline{R_F}$, and the denominator in Equation 5 is the sample standard deviation. The convention for Sharpe ratios is to annualize both the portfolio average return and the portfolio risk. For example, if the past return data are measured monthly, the average monthly return can be multiplied by 12 and the monthly return volatility can be multiplied by the square root of 12. The logic for multiplying the standard deviation by the *square root* of 12 is that variance (i.e., standard deviation squared), under certain assumptions, increases proportionally with time.

Although this scaling convention is common in practice, multiplying monthly returns by a factor of 12 for averages and the square root of 12 for standard deviations ignores the multiplicative (i.e., compound) nature of returns over time. Simple multiplication factors (e.g., 250 and the square root of 250 for annualizing trading-day returns) are only technically correct if the underlying returns are independent and continuously compounded or logarithmic. Similarly, annualized compound returns for the two values in the numerator of the Sharpe ratio (i.e., the portfolio return and the riskless rate) may be used instead of the annualized difference of arithmetic returns. The various methodologies produce slightly different results but should not be a serious problem as long as comparisons between different portfolios use the same approach.

EXHIBIT 1   Benchmark Sharpe Ratios for 1994–2018 (based on a risk-free rate of 2.3%)

	MSCI World	S&P 500	Russell 2000	MSCI EAFE	Bloomberg Barclays US Aggregate
Average annual return	7.9%	9.9%	10.3%	6.3%	5.0%
Return standard dev.	14.5%	14.4%	19.1%	15.8%	3.5%
Sharpe ratio	0.38	0.53	0.41	0.25	0.77

Exhibit 1 reports the annualized monthly historical return data (not compounded) in US dollars for several different benchmark portfolios for the 25-year period from 1994 to 2018. Long-term *ex post* Sharpe ratios for equity benchmarks have typically fallen within a range of 0.20–0.60, although over a shorter horizon they will vary over a wider range and can be either negative or positive. The Sharpe ratio for the Bloomberg Barclays US Aggregate fixed-income benchmark in Exhibit 1 is particularly high because of the secular decline in interest rates over this 25-year period that boosted the average return for fixed income. Exhibit 2 reports historical return data and Sharpe ratios from 1994 to 2018 for some well-known actively managed mutual funds over the same period. The Sharpe ratios in both exhibits are based on a risk-free rate of 2.3%, the average annualized US Treasury bill return during this 25-year period. The comparison of Sharpe ratios between funds intentionally uses data from the same measurement period. One should not compare the Sharpe ratio of one fund over one period with that of another fund over a different period.

EXHIBIT 2   Active Fund Sharpe Ratios for 1994–2018 (based on a risk-free rate of 2.3%)

	Fidelity Magellan	Growth Fund of America	Templeton World	T. Rowe Price Small Cap	JPMorgan Bond
Average annual return	8.5%	11.1%	7.9%	11.6%	5.2%
Return standard dev.	16.5%	15.7%	15.2%	16.7%	3.6%
Sharpe ratio	0.38	0.56	0.37	0.56	0.80

Note: The selection of funds for illustration was made without any intended implication, positive or negative, concerning their performance relative to other possible choices.

An important property is that the Sharpe ratio is unaffected by the addition of cash or leverage in a portfolio. Consider a combined portfolio with a weight of w_P on the actively managed portfolio and a weight of $(1 - w_P)$ on risk-free cash. The return on the combined portfolio is $R_C = w_P R_P + (1 - w_P) R_F$, and the volatility of the combined portfolio is just $\sigma_C = w_P \sigma_P$ because the $(1 - w_P) R_F$ portion is risk free. Applying these two relationships in Equation 5 gives the Sharpe ratio for the combined portfolio as

$$SR_C = \frac{R_C - R_F}{\sigma_C} = \frac{w_P(R_P - R_F)}{w_P \sigma_P} = SR_P$$

which is the same as the Sharpe ratio of the actively managed portfolio. Note that the weight in the combined portfolio, w_P, could be greater than 1, so $(1 - w_P)$ could be negative, indicating that leverage created by *borrowing* risk-free cash and investing in risky assets also does not affect the portfolio's Sharpe ratio.

The proposition that independent of preferences investors should form portfolios using two funds—one of which is the risk-free asset and the other the risky asset portfolio with the highest Sharpe ratio—is known as two-fund separation. On the one hand, if the expected volatility of the risky asset portfolio is higher than the investor prefers, the volatility can be reduced by holding more cash and less of the risky portfolio. On the other hand, if the expected volatility of the risky portfolio is lower than the investor allows, the volatility and expected return can be increased by leverage. For example, suppose an investor believes the performance of the Growth Fund of America shown in Exhibit 2 will repeat going forward but only allows a volatility of 10%. The investor might invest 64% of assets in the Growth Fund of America and 36% in cash to reduce overall portfolio risk. The expected return of the combined portfolio is 0.64(11.1%) + 0.36(2.3%) = 7.9%. The volatility of the combined portfolio is 0.64(15.7%) = 10.0%. The Sharpe ratio of the combined portfolio is (7.9% − 2.3%)/10.0% = 0.56, the same as the 0.56 Sharpe ratio of the Growth Fund of America shown in Exhibit 2.

EXAMPLE 2   Adjusting Risk and Return Using the Sharpe Ratio

Consider an investor choosing between two risky portfolios: a large-cap stock portfolio and a small-cap stock portfolio. Although forecasts about the future are subjective, suppose for simplicity that the investor expects that the future statistics will be those in the following table, with a risk-free rate of 2.3%. The forecasted 0.42 Sharpe ratio of the small-cap portfolio is higher than the 0.40 ratio of the large-cap portfolio, but suppose the investor does not want the high 19.2% volatility associated with the small-cap stocks.

	Large Cap	Small Cap
Expected return	8.2%	10.3%
Expected volatility	14.6%	19.2%
Sharpe ratio	0.40	0.42

1. What percentage of the portfolio would an investor need to hold in cash to reduce the risk of a portfolio invested in the small-cap portfolio and cash to the same risk level as that of the large-cap portfolio?
2. Based on your answer to 1, calculate the Sharpe ratio of the small-cap plus cash portfolio.
3. Compare the expected return of the small-cap plus cash portfolio with the expected return of the large-cap portfolio.

Solution to 1: We want to reduce the 19.2% volatility to 14.6% by adding cash. The weight of small-cap stocks in the combined portfolio must therefore be 14.6/19.2 = 76%, leaving a 24% weight in risk-free cash. With that amount of cash, the volatility of the combined portfolio will be 0.76(19.2%) = 14.6%, the same as the large-cap portfolio.

Solution to 2: The Sharpe ratio of the combined portfolio is unaffected by the amount in cash, so it remains 0.42.

Solution to 3: The expected return of the combined portfolio is 0.76(10.3%) + 0.24(2.3%) = 8.4%, 20 basis points (bps) higher than the 8.2% expected return on the large-cap portfolio, but with the same risk as the large-cap portfolio. To reconfirm, the Sharpe ratio of the combined portfolio is (84% − 2.3%)/14.6% = 0.42, the same as the original 0.42 value.

3.2. The Information Ratio

The simplest definition of the information ratio compares the active return from a portfolio relative to a benchmark with the volatility of the active return, called "active risk" or "benchmark tracking risk." The information ratio can be thought of as a way to measure the consistency of active return, as most investors would prefer a more evenly generated value added (low active risk) rather than a lumpy active return pattern. Like the more formal distinction between active portfolio return and alpha, active risk has a more exact beta-adjusted counterpart, which Grinold and Kahn (1999) called "residual risk." In this discussion, the information ratio is based on the implicit assumption that the beta of the managed portfolio relative to the benchmark is exactly 1.0, although in practice that assumption can be relaxed. For example, Fischer and Wermers (2013) present the information ratio that does not assume beta is 1.

The information ratio tells the investor how much active return has been earned, or is expected to be earned, for incurring the level of active risk. Active return, R_A, is the difference between the managed portfolio return, R_P, and the benchmark portfolio return, R_B. The information ratio of an actively managed portfolio, IR, is calculated by dividing the active return by active risk:

$$IR = \frac{R_P - R_B}{\sigma(R_P - R_B)} = \frac{R_A}{\sigma_A} \tag{6}$$

where $\sigma(\cdot)$ is the standard deviation function—in this case, the standard deviation of the excess return of the portfolio (R_P) over the return of the benchmark (R_B). As with the Sharpe ratio, the typical convention is to annualize both the active return and the active risk. The information ratio can refer to the investor's *ex ante*, or forecasted, active return. Thus, the numerator in Equation 6 would be replaced by the expected returns—that is, $E(R_A) = E(R_P) - E(R_B)$—and the denominator would be the expected active risk. Alternatively, the calculation of an *ex post*, or historical, information ratio would use realized average active returns and the realized sample standard deviation of the active return.

Two investment strategies and associated terminology can help reinforce the conceptual distinction between the Sharpe ratio and the information ratio. First, a "closet index fund" (a fund that advertises itself as being actively managed but is actually close to being an index fund) will have a Sharpe ratio that is close to the benchmark because the excess return and volatility will be similar to the benchmark. However, the closet index fund will have a small amount of active risk, although positive by definition like any volatility estimate. While there may be little active risk, the information ratio of a closet index fund will likely be close to zero or slightly negative if value added cannot overcome the management fees. If one has the actual holdings of the fund, closet indexing is easy to detect on the basis of a measurement called "active share," a measure of how similar a portfolio is to its benchmark. [Cremers and Petajisto (2009) defined active share as half the sum of the absolute values of the active weights.] As a second example, the Sharpe ratio and the information ratio for a market-neutral long–short equity fund (a fund with offsetting long and short positions that has a beta of zero with respect to the market) would be identical if we consider the benchmark to be the riskless rate because the excess return and active return would be the same calculation, as would be total risk and active risk.

Exhibit 3 shows historical information ratios for the mutual funds in Exhibit 2, with the benchmark portfolio for each calculation shown at the bottom of Exhibit 3. The average active return in the first row of Exhibit 3 can be calculated by subtracting the specified benchmark average return in Exhibit 1 from the average fund return in Exhibit 2. The active risk is the annualized standard deviation of the return differences from 1994 to 2018, which cannot be verified with just the summary data in Exhibits 1 and 2.

As shown in Exhibit 3, *ex post* information ratios will be negative if the active return is negative. In fact, under the zero-sum property of active management, the average realized information ratio across investment funds with the same benchmark should be about zero. The realized information ratios in Exhibit 3 are within a range of about −0.30 to +0.30, although the range would be much wider over shorter periods. Of course, *ex ante*, or before the fact, if an investor did not expect the information ratio to be positive, he or she would simply invest in the benchmark. Note that ranking by active risk, a relative measure, does not necessarily equate to ranking by total risk, an absolute measure. For example, the relative risk of Fidelity Magellan in Exhibit 3 is slightly lower than the relative risk of the Growth Fund of America; however, the absolute risk of Fidelity Magellan in Exhibit 2 is slightly higher.

EXHIBIT 3   Active Fund Information Ratios for 2014–2018

	Fidelity Magellan	Growth Fund of America	Templeton World	T. Rowe Price Small Cap	JPMorgan Bond
Active return	−1.4%	1.2%	0.0%	1.4%	0.2%
Active risk	5.1%	6.2%	5.0%	4.7%	1.0%
Information ratio	−0.27	0.20	0.00	0.29	0.19
Benchmark	S&P 500	S&P 500	MSCI World	Russell 2000	Bloomberg Barclays US Aggregate

Unlike the Sharpe ratio, the information ratio is affected by the addition of cash or the use of leverage. For example, if the investor adds cash to a portfolio of risky assets, the information ratio for the combined portfolio will generally shrink. However, the information ratio of an unconstrained portfolio is unaffected by the aggressiveness of active weights. Specifically, if the active security weights, Δw_i, defined as deviations from the benchmark portfolio weights, are all multiplied by some constant, c, the information ratio of an actively managed portfolio will remain unchanged.

Recall the expression for the active return of a managed portfolio in Equation 3. If each active weight in Equation 3 is multiplied by some constant, c, then the active return on the altered portfolio, R_C, is

$$R_C = \sum_{i=1}^{N} c\Delta w_i R_{Ai} = c\sum_{i=1}^{N} \Delta w_i R_{Ai} = cR_A$$

Similarly, the active risk of the altered portfolio is $c\sigma_A$, so the information ratio of the altered portfolio is

$$\mathrm{IR}_C = \frac{cR_A}{c\sigma_A} = \mathrm{IR}$$

the same as that of the actively managed portfolio with no proportional increase in the active weights. Specifically, if the active weights in a managed portfolio are all doubled, the expected active return (or realized average active return) would be doubled, along with the expected or realized active risk, leaving the information ratio unchanged.

Of course, an outside investor would not be able to adjust the active risk of an existing fund by changing the individual asset active weight positions, but the same objective can be met by taking positions in the benchmark portfolio. For example, if the active risk of a fund is

5.0%, combining that fund in an 80/20 mix with the benchmark portfolio (i.e., a benchmark portfolio weight of 20%) will result in an active risk of the combined portfolio of 0.80(5.0%) = 4.0%, with a proportional reduction in the active return. Similarly, the investor can short sell the benchmark portfolio and use the proceeds to invest in the actively managed fund to increase the active risk and return. Note that in practice, institutional investors might simply reduce the amount they would have otherwise invested in the benchmark portfolio—or, if possible, another actively managed fund—rather than employ an explicit short sell.

3.3. Constructing Optimal Portfolios

An important concept from basic portfolio theory is that with a risk-free asset, the portfolio on the efficient frontier of risky assets that is tangent to a ray extended from the risk-free rate is optimal because it has the highest possible Sharpe ratio. Thus, given the opportunity to adjust absolute risk and return with cash or leverage, the overriding objective is to find the single risky asset portfolio with the maximum Sharpe ratio, whatever the investor's risk aversion. A similarly important property in active management theory is that given the opportunity to adjust active risk and return by investing in both the actively managed and benchmark portfolios, the squared Sharpe ratio of an actively managed portfolio is equal to the squared Sharpe ratio of the benchmark plus the information ratio squared:

$$SR_P^2 = SR_B^2 + IR^2 \tag{7}$$

Equation 7 implies that the active portfolio with the highest (squared) information ratio will also have the highest (squared) Sharpe ratio. (Note that Equation 7 is not practical for comparisons of investment skill involving negative IR because the sign is lost in squaring.) As a consequence, according to mean–variance theory, the expected information ratio is the single best criterion for assessing active performance among various actively managed funds with the same benchmark (Grinold 1989). For any given asset class, an investor should choose the manager with the highest expected skill as measured by the information ratio, because investing with the highest information-ratio manager will produce the highest Sharpe ratio for the investor's portfolio.

The preceding discussion on adjusting active risk raises the issue of determining the *optimal* amount of active risk, without resorting to utility functions that measure risk aversion. For unconstrained portfolios, the level of active risk that leads to the optimal result in Equation 7 is

$$\sigma(R_A) = \frac{IR}{SR_B} \sigma_B \tag{8}$$

where σ_B is the standard deviation of the benchmark return. (Note that the right-hand side of the equation should be multiplied by the benchmark beta of the actively managed portfolio if that value is different from 1.) This Sharpe ratio-maximizing level of active risk or "aggressiveness" comes from the general mean–variance optimality condition that the ratio of expected active return to active return variance of the managed portfolio be set equal to the ratio of expected benchmark excess return to benchmark return variance:

$$\frac{E(R_A)}{\sigma_A^2} = \frac{E(R_B - R_F)}{\sigma_B^2}$$

For example, if the actively managed portfolio has an information ratio of 0.30 and active risk of 8.0% and the benchmark portfolio has an expected excess return of 6.4% and total risk of 16.0% resulting in a Sharpe ratio of 0.40, then according to Equation 8, the optimal amount of aggressiveness in the actively managed portfolio is $(0.30/0.40)16.0\% = 12.0\%$. If the actively managed portfolio is constructed with this amount of active risk, the Sharpe ratio will be $(0.40^2 + 0.30^2)^{1/2} = 0.50$, as shown in Equation 7. To verify this Sharpe ratio, note that the more aggressively managed portfolio in this example has an expected active return of $(0.30)12.0\% = 3.6\%$ over the benchmark, or a total expected excess return of $6.4\% + 3.6\% = 10.0\%$. By definition, the total risk of the actively managed portfolio is the sum of the benchmark return variance and active return variance,

$$\sigma_P^2 = \sigma_B^2 + \sigma_A^2$$

At the optimal active risk of 12.0%, the total portfolio risk is $(16.0^2 + 12.0^2)^{1/2} = 20.0\%$, verifying the maximum possible Sharpe ratio of $10.0/20.0 = 0.50$.

The initial actively managed portfolio has active risk of only 8.0%, whereas the optimal amount required under the assumed information ratio needed to maximize the Sharpe ratio is 12.0%. The actively managed portfolio would thus need to be managed more aggressively to increase the active risk while preserving the same information ratio; alternatively, the investor could short the benchmark and use the proceeds to increase the amount invested in the actively managed fund. The proportion required to be invested in the actively managed fund would be 12.0/8.0 − 1.5 times; shorting the benchmark by 0.5 times would fund the increase.

For readers familiar with risk–return charts in basic portfolio theory, Exhibit 4 will help illustrate these concepts.

EXHIBIT 4   Portfolio Risk and Return

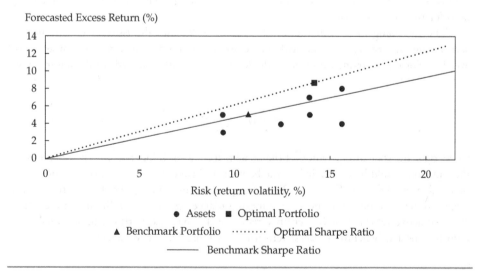

Several individual risky assets are plotted in Exhibit 4 in terms of their forecasted return in excess of the risk-free rate ("excess return") on the vertical axis and risk on the horizontal axis. The values for the individual assets are based on subjective assessments supplied by the investor. The theory described here explains how to optimally employ those expectations assuming they are based on reasonable judgment. Using the benchmark portfolio weights (not shown), the risks and expected returns of the individual assets combine into the benchmark portfolio risk and expected return shown in Exhibit 4. Because the expected returns plotted along the vertical axis are in excess of the risk-free rate, the slope of a line that emanates from the origin (zero risk and zero excess return) is the Sharpe ratio of the benchmark portfolio. Specifically, the Sharpe ratio of the benchmark portfolio (i.e., slope of the dark line) in Exhibit 4 is the expected excess return of 5.0% divided by return volatility of 10.8%, or 5.0%/10.8% = 0.46.

Because of diversification, the Sharpe ratio of the benchmark portfolio is higher than those of most of the individual assets; however, the benchmark portfolio does not have the highest possible Sharpe ratio of all portfolios that can be constructed from these assets. In fact, the optimal portfolio (i.e., mean–variance efficient frontier portfolio with the highest possible Sharpe ratio) shown in Exhibit 4 has an expected excess return of 8.7% and return volatility of 14.2%, resulting in a Sharpe ratio of 8.7%/14.2% = 0.61 (i.e., slope of the dotted line). This higher Sharpe ratio could be retained in the portfolio while adjusting the level of risk through the use of cash or leverage. For example, the risk of the optimal portfolio could be reduced along the dotted line to the benchmark portfolio risk of 10.8% with an expected excess return of 0.61(10.8%) = 6.6%, compared with the benchmark expected excess return of 5.0%.

EXHIBIT 5   Portfolio Active Risk and Return

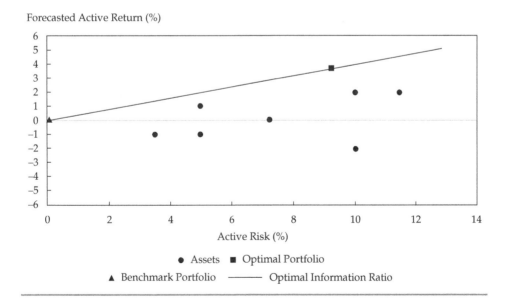

Exhibit 5 plots the same individual assets, the benchmark portfolio, and the optimal portfolio from Exhibit 4 in terms of their expected *active* return on the vertical axis and *active* risk on the horizontal axis. By definition, the benchmark portfolio is plotted at the origin in

Exhibit 5 with zero active return and zero active risk. The individual assets have both positive and negative expected active returns compared with the benchmark portfolio return, whereas the optimal portfolio has a positive active return of 3.8% and active risk of 9.4%. The information ratio of the optimal portfolio is therefore 3.8%/9.4% = 0.40, the slope of the dark line in Exhibit 5. The information ratio of the optimal portfolio is higher than that of any of the individual assets; in fact, it can be shown to be the square root of the sum of the squared values of the individual assets' information ratios, similar to Equation 7, including those assets with negative information ratios. The asset weights required for the construction of this optimal portfolio are the subject of the next section, but here we note they might be negative for negative-IR assets—that is, short sells of individual assets may be required.

Although the information ratio will remain constant at 0.40, various levels of aggressiveness can be applied to the actively managed portfolio in Exhibit 5 by scaling the optimal active weights or, alternatively, taking a position in the benchmark portfolio—leading to portfolios that plot along the dark line. But to construct the *optimal* actively managed portfolio given the assumed information ratio, the active risk must be adjusted to a level of (0.40/0.46)10.8% = 9.4% in accordance with Equation 8. Specifically, this level of aggressiveness is required to construct the optimal portfolio in Exhibit 4, and according to Equation 7, the Sharpe ratio of this optimal portfolio is $(0.46^2 + 0.40^2)^{1/2} = 0.61$.

As we will see later, optimal levels of active risk in equity management practice are typically lower than those shown in this numerical example because the underlying portfolios are constrained to be long only, leading to information ratios that are substantially lower. As the information ratio gets close to zero, either because of constraints or because the manager is judged to be less skilled, the optimal amount of active risk in Equation 8 goes to zero (i.e., the optimal portfolio becomes the passive benchmark portfolio).

EXAMPLE 3   Expected Value Added Based on the Information Ratio

Suppose that the historical performance of the Fidelity Magellan and Growth Fund of America mutual funds from Exhibits 2 and 3 are indicative of the future performance of hypothetical funds, "Fund I" and "Fund II." In addition, suppose that the historical performance of the S&P 500 benchmark portfolio shown in Exhibit 1 is indicative of expected returns and risk going forward, as shown in the following excerpts. We use historical values in this problem for convenience, but in practice the forecasted, or expected, values for both the benchmark portfolio and the active funds would be subjectively determined by the investor.

Excerpted from Exhibits 1 and 2 (based on a risk-free rate of 2.3%)

	S&P 500	Fidelity Magellan (Fund I)	Growth Fund of America (Fund II)
Average annual return	9.9%	8.5%	11.1%
Return standard dev.	14.4%	16.5%	15.7%
Sharpe ratio	0.53	0.38	0.56

Excerpted from Exhibit 3

	Fidelity Magellan (Fund I)	Growth Fund of America (Fund II)
Active return	−1.4%	1.2%
Active risk	5.1%	6.2%
Information ratio	−0.27	0.20
Benchmark	S&P 500	S&P 500

1. State which of the two actively managed funds, Fund I or Fund II, would be better to combine with the passive benchmark portfolio and why.
2. Calculate the possible improvement over the S&P 500 Sharpe ratio from the optimal deployment of Fund II, which has an expected information ratio of 0.20.
3. Fund I comes with an active (i.e., benchmark relative) risk of 5.1%, but the investor wants to adjust the active risk to 5.4%. Describe how that adjustment would be made. (No calculations are required; give a qualitative description.)
4. Fund II comes with an active risk of 6.2%. Determine the weight of the benchmark portfolio required to create a combined portfolio with the highest possible expected Sharpe ratio.

Solution to 1: Fund II is better, as measured by the combined Sharpe ratio, because Fund II has the higher expected information ratio: 0.20 compared with −0.27 in Fund I.

Solution to 2: Properly combined with the S&P 500 benchmark portfolio, Fund II has the potential to increase the expected Sharpe ratio from 0.53 for the passive benchmark portfolio to an expected Sharpe ratio of $(0.53^2 + 0.20^2)^{1/2} = 0.57$.

Solution to 3: To increase the active risk of Fund I, the investor would need to be more aggressive in managing the portfolio, take a short (i.e., negative) position in the benchmark, or, more simply, invest less than he or she otherwise would have in the benchmark or another actively managed fund.

Solution to 4: According to Equation 8, the optimal amount of active risk is (0.20/0.53)14.4% = 5.4%. A positive position in the benchmark is needed to adjust the active weight down from 6.2%. Specifically, the benchmark portfolio weight needed to adjust the active risk in Fund II is 1 − 5.4%/6.2% = 13%.

Note that at the 5.4% optimal level of active risk, Fund II has an expected active return of 0.20(5.4%) = 1.1%, a total expected excess return of 7.6% + 1.1% = 8.7%, and a total risk of $(14.4^2 + 5.4^2)^{1/2} = 15.4\%$. The result is an expected Sharpe ratio of 8.7/15.4 = 0.57, the same as the value calculated for Question 2.

In summary, the information ratio is active return over active risk (in contrast to the excess return-to-risk measure known as the Sharpe ratio). Information ratios help investors focus on the relative valued added by active management. The information ratio is unaffected by the aggressiveness of the active weights (i.e., deviations from benchmark weights) in the managed portfolio because both the active return and the active risk increase proportionally. The potential improvement in an active portfolio's expected Sharpe ratio compared with the benchmark's Sharpe ratio is a function of the squared information ratio. Thus, the expected information ratio becomes the single best criterion for constructing an actively managed portfolio, and the *ex post* information ratio is the best criterion for evaluating the past performance of various actively managed funds.

4. THE FUNDAMENTAL LAW OF ACTIVE MANAGEMENT

The fundamental law is a framework for thinking about the potential value added through active portfolio management. The framework can be used to size individual asset active weights, estimate the expected value added of an active management strategy, or measure the realized value added after the fact; however, the most common use is the description and evaluation of active management strategies. The law itself is a mathematical relationship that relates the expected information ratio of an actively managed portfolio to a few key parameters.

4.1. Active Security Returns

On the basis of the prior section, we assume that the investor is concerned about maximizing the managed portfolio's active return subject to a limit on active risk (also called "benchmark tracking risk"). To this end, the investor uses forecasts for each security of the active return, R_{Ai}, or thus the benchmark relative return,

$$R_{Ai} = R_i - R_B \tag{9}$$

for the N individual assets that might be included in the portfolio. Our notation for the investor's forecasts of the active security returns is μ_i (Greek letter mu). The term μ_i can be thought of as the security's expected active return, $\mu_i = E(R_{Ai})$, referring to the investor's subjective expectation, in contrast to an expectation based on a formal equilibrium model.

Although we focus on the simple definition of active security return in Equation 9, there are several possible choices depending on the assumed risk model (i.e., statistical model of returns) and the desired trade-off between a conceptual treatment and more complex but implementable formulas. For example, Equation 9 can be modified to define the active security return as the residual return in a single-factor model, $R_{Ai} = R_i - \beta_i R_B$, where β_i is the sensitivity of the security return to the benchmark return. Although this expression may appear to be related to the CAPM, the benchmark return may or may not be the market return. Moreover, the fundamental law does not require the empirical validity of the CAPM, the multi-factor APT (arbitrage pricing theory), or any other equilibrium theory of required returns. The individual security active return can also be defined as the residual return in a multi-factor model:

$$R_{Ai} = R_i - \sum_{j=1}^{K} \beta_{j,i} R_j$$

with K market-wide factor returns, R_j, and security sensitivities, $\beta_{j,i}$, to those factors.

Exhibit 6 provides a conceptual diagram in which to think about the various parameters in the fundamental law of active management. At the three corners of the triangle are the sets of forecasted active returns, μ_i, active portfolio weights, Δw_i, and realized active returns, R_{Ai}. The base of the triangle reflects the realized value added through active management, defined as the difference between the realized returns on the actively managed portfolio and the benchmark portfolio. Value added is the sum of the products of active weights and active returns for the $i = 1$ to N securities in the portfolio, as shown in Equation 3. The value of this sum is ultimately a function of the correlation coefficient between the active weights, Δw_i, and realized active returns, R_{Ai}.

EXHIBIT 6   The Correlation Triangle

To understand the role of the correlation coefficient, consider the following algebraic expansion of Equation 3 that uses COV, STD (σ), and COR (ρ) to designate the covariance, standard deviation, and correlation coefficient functions, respectively:

$$R_A = \sum_{i=1}^{N} \Delta w_i R_{Ai}$$

$$= \rho(\Delta w_i, R_{Ai}) N$$

$$= \rho(\Delta w_i, R_{Ai}) \sigma(\Delta w_i) \sigma(R_{Ai}) N$$

The exact equalities in this expansion depend on the fact that the cross-sectional means of active weights and active returns are zero. Specifically, the population covariance between two variables, X and Y, is calculated as $COV(X,Y) = \frac{1}{N} \sum_{i=1}^{N} (X_i - \overline{X})(Y_i - \overline{Y})$, or simply $COV(X,Y) = \frac{1}{N} \sum_{i=1}^{N} X_i Y_i$. Similarly, the population variance for a single variable is $VAR(X) = \frac{1}{N} \sum_{i=1}^{N} X_i^2$ if the mean is zero.

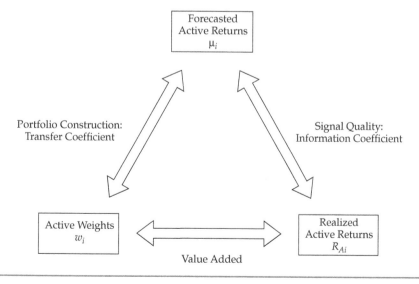

In Exhibit 6, the arrows in the legs of the triangle represent the correlation between the quantities at the corners of the triangle to which the arrows point. While the arrow at the base of the triangle reflects value added, a better understanding of the sources and limitations of value added can be obtained by examining the correlations on the two vertical legs. First, there is little hope of adding value if the investor's forecasts of active returns do not correspond at least loosely to the realized active returns. Signal quality is measured by the correlation between the forecasted active returns, μ_i, at the top of the triangle, and the realized active returns, R_{Ai}, at the right corner, commonly called the information coefficient (IC). Investors with higher IC, or ability to forecast returns, will add more value over time but only to the extent that those forecasts are exploited in the construction of the managed portfolio. The correlation between any set of active weights—Δw_i, in the left corner, and forecasted active returns, μ_i, at the top of the triangle—measures the degree to which the investor's forecasts are translated into active weights, called the transfer coefficient (TC).

The mathematics of the fundamental law were introduced by Grinold (1989) and further developed by Clarke, de Silva, and Thorley (2002). The mean–variance-optimal active security weights for uncorrelated active returns, subject to a limit on active portfolio risk, are given by

$$\Delta w_i^* = \frac{\mu_i}{\sigma_i^2} \frac{\sigma_A}{\sqrt{\sum_{i=1}^{N} \frac{\mu_i^2}{\sigma_i^2}}}$$

where σ_A represents active portfolio risk and σ_i is the forecasted volatility of the active return on security i. This formula for active weights makes intuitive sense. The deviation (positive or negative) from the benchmark weight for security i are higher for larger values of the forecasted active return, μ_i, but are reduced by forecasted volatility, σ_i. In addition, the active weights are scaled by the active risk of the portfolio, σ_A, so that the desire for more active portfolio risk requires larger individual active weights.

In addition to employing mean–variance optimization, proofs of the fundamental law generally assume that active return forecasts are scaled prior to optimization using the Grinold (1994) rule:

$$\mu_i = IC\sigma_i S_i \tag{10}$$

where IC is the expected information coefficient and S_i represents a set of standardized forecasts of expected returns across securities, sometimes called "scores." Scores with a cross-sectional variance of 1 are used in Equation 10 to ensure that the scaling process using the multipliers σ_i (separate values for individual securities) and IC (one value for all securities) result in expected active returns of the correct magnitude. Specifically, if the assumed IC value is low, then the cross-sectional variation of the expected active returns in Equation 10 will be low. However, the exact process for calculating expected active returns may be more involved than the simple rule indicated in Equation 10 depending on how the investor's views on individual asset returns are originally formulated.

Using the Grinold rule shown in Equation 10, the mean–variance optimal active weights are

$$\Delta w_i^* = \frac{\mu_i}{\sigma_i^2} \frac{\sigma_A}{IC\sqrt{BR}} \tag{11}$$

where IC stands for information coefficient and BR, which has replaced the symbol N, stands for breadth. We discuss these two key fundamental law parameters next.

As previously stated, IC is the *ex ante* (i.e., anticipated) cross-sectional correlation between the N forecasted active returns, μ_i, and the N realized active returns, R_{Ai}. To be more accurate, IC is the *ex ante risk-weighted* correlation

$$IC = \rho\left(\frac{R_{Ai}}{\sigma_i}, \frac{\mu_i}{\sigma_i}\right) \tag{12}$$

where $\rho(\cdot)$ indicates correlation. As a correlation coefficient, IC can take on values anywhere from -1.00 to $+1.00$, although small positive values less than 0.20 are often the norm. The *ex ante*, or anticipated, IC must be positive or the investor would not pursue active management but simply invest in the passive benchmark. Later, we will discuss the realized, or *ex post*, information coefficient in terms of measuring active management performance after the fact—where the realized information coefficient might be either positive or negative, leading to positive or negative value added.

The other important fundamental law parameter in Equation 11 is BR, or breadth, conceptually equal to the number of independent decisions made per year by the investor in constructing the portfolio. The simplest case for the calculation of breadth is a single-factor risk model, where the only source of correlation between the securities is the common market factor and decisions about the active return for any given security are independent from one year to the next. In this case, breadth is equal to the number of securities: Each active return is independent from the other active return forecasts for that period and independent from the forecast for that security in subsequent periods.

However, most risk models will incorporate other factors—for example, economic sectors or industries. If the risk model includes the assumption that all the securities within a given industry are positively correlated, then part of the forecast that the active returns for securities in that industry will be higher or lower is based on just one perspective the investor has about the industry. In this case, breadth is intuitively lower than the number of securities. Alternatively, breadth can be higher than the number of securities if factors in the risk model suggest that their active returns are negatively correlated. For these more complicated cases, breadth will be a non-integer number, as noted in Clarke, de Silva, and Thorley (2006).

Similarly, if some aspect of a security is fairly constant over time and the investor makes decisions about expected active return based on that characteristic, then breadth over time is lower. Alternatively, if the investor makes quarterly or monthly forecasts about a security that are truly independent over time, then breadth can be as high as the number of securities times the number of rebalancing periods per year.

EXAMPLE 4   Scaling Active Return Forecasts and Sizing Active Weights

Consider the simple case of four individual securities whose active returns are assumed to be uncorrelated with each other and have active return volatilities of 25.0% and 50.0%. After some analysis, an active investor believes the first two securities will outperform the other two over the next year and thus assigns scores of $+1$ and -1 to the first and second groups, respectively. The scenario is depicted in the following exhibit:

Security	Score	Volatility
#1	1.0	25.0%
#2	1.0	50.0%
#3	1.0	25.0%
#4	1.0	50.0%

1. Assume that the anticipated accuracy of the investor's ranking of securities is measured by an information coefficient of IC $= 0.20$. What are the forecasted active returns for each of the four securities using the scaling rule $\mu_i = IC\sigma_i S_i$?
2. Given the assumptions that the four securities' active returns are uncorrelated with each other and forecasts are independent from year to year, what is the breadth of the investor's forecasts?
3. Suppose the investor wants to maximize the expected active return of the portfolio subject to an active risk constraint of 9.0%. Calculate the active weights that should be assigned to each of these securities using the formula $\Delta w_i^* = \frac{\mu_i}{\sigma_i^2} \frac{\sigma_A}{IC\sqrt{BR}}$.

Solution to 1: The forecasted active return to Security #1 is $0.20(25.0\%)(1.0) = 5.0\%$. Similar calculations for the other three securities are shown in the following exhibit.

Security	Score	Active Return Volatility	Expected Active Return
#1	1.0	25.0%	5.0%
#2	1.0	50.0%	10.0%
#3	−1.0	25.0%	−5.0%
#4	−1.0	50.0%	−10.0%

Solution to 2: If the active returns are uncorrelated with each other and the forecasts are independent from year to year, then the investor has made four separate decisions and breadth is BR $= 4$, the number of securities.

Solution to 3: The size of the active weight for Security #1 is $\Delta w_i^* = \frac{0.05}{0.25^2} \frac{0.09}{0.20\sqrt{4}} = 18\%$. Similar calculations for the other four securities are shown in the following exhibit.

Security	Expected Active Return	Active Return Volatility	Active Weight
#1	5.0%	25.0%	18.0%
#2	10.0%	50.0%	9.0%
#3	−5.0%	25.0%	−18.0%
#4	−10.0%	50.0%	−9.0%

4.2. The Basic Fundamental Law

On the basis of Equation 3, the anticipated value added for an actively managed portfolio, or expected active portfolio return, is the sum product of active security weights and forecasted active security returns:

$$E(R_A) = \sum_{i=1}^{N} \Delta w_i \mu_i$$

Using the optimal active weights in Equation 11 and forecasted active security returns in Equation 10, the expected active portfolio return is

$$E(R_A)^* = IC\sqrt{BR}\sigma_A \tag{13}$$

where the * indicates that the actively managed portfolio is constructed from *optimal* active security weights, Δw_i^*. Remember that the algebra for this result assumes that breadth is the number of securities: $BR = N$. A more general proof where breadth is different from the number of securities is provided in Clarke, de Silva, and Thorley (2006).

    The basic fundamental law of active management in Equation 13 states that the optimal expected active return, $E(R_A)^*$, is the product of three key parameters: the assumed information coefficient, IC, the square root of breadth, BR, and portfolio active risk, σ_A. Using Equation 13, we can also express the information ratio of the unconstrained optimal portfolio, $E(R_A)^*/\sigma_A$, as the product of just two terms: $IR^* = IC\sqrt{BR}$.

EXAMPLE 5   The Basic Fundamental Law

Consider the simple case of four individual securities whose active returns are uncorrelated with each other and forecasts are independent from year to year. The active return forecasts, active risks, and the active weights for each security are shown in the following exhibit.

Security	Expected Active Return	Active Return Volatility	Active Weight
#1	5.0%	25.0%	18%
#2	10.0%	50.0%	9%
#3	−5.0%	25.0%	−18%
#4	−10.0%	50.0%	−9%

1. Suppose that the benchmark portfolio for these four securities is equally weighted (i.e., $w_{B,i} = 25\%$ for each security) and that the forecasted return on the benchmark portfolio is 10.0%. What are the portfolio weights and the total expected returns for each of the four securities?
2. Calculate the forecasted total return and active return of the managed portfolio.
3. Calculate the active risk of the managed portfolio.
4. Verify the basic fundamental law of active management using the expected active return and active risk of the managed portfolio. The individual security active

return forecasts and active weights were sized using an information coefficient of IC = 0.20, breadth of BR = 4, and active risk of σ_A = 9.0%.

Solution to 1: The portfolio weight for Security #1 is the benchmark weight plus the active weight, 25% + 18% = 43%. The total expected return for Security #1 is the expected benchmark return plus the expected active return, 10.0% + 5.0% = 15.0%. Similar calculations for the other three securities are shown in the following exhibit.

Security	Total Weight	Total Return Forecast
#1	43%	15.0%
#2	34%	20.0%
#3	7%	5.0%
#4	16%	0.0%
	100%	

Solution to 2: The forecasted total return of the portfolio is the sum of portfolio weights times total returns for each security: 0.43(15.0) + 0.34(20.0) + 0.07(5.0) + 0.16(0.0) = 13.6%. The expected active return of the portfolio is the managed portfolio return minus the benchmark return: 13.6 − 10.0 = 3.6%. Alternatively, the calculation is the sum of active weights times active returns for each security: 0.18 (5.0%) + 0.09(10.0%) − 0.18(−5.0%) − 0.09(−10.0%) = 3.6%.

Solution to 3: The active risk of the managed portfolio is the square root of the sum of active weights squared times the active volatility squared for each security, which gives $[0.18^2 \times 25.0^2 + 0.09^2 \times 50.0^2 + (-0.18)^2 \times 25.0^2 + (-0.09)^2 \times 50.0^2]^{1/2}$ = 9.0%.

Solution to 4: The basic fundamental law states that the expected active portfolio return is $IC\sqrt{BR}\sigma_A$ = 0.20 × $4^{1/2}$ × 9.0 = 3.6%, which is consistent with the calculation in the Solution to 2. Alternatively, the information ratio of 3.6/9.0 = 0.40 confirms the basic fundamental law that IR^* = $IC\sqrt{BR}$ = 0.20 × $4^{1/2}$ = 0.40.

4.3. The Expanded Fundamental Law

Although we were able to derive an analytic (i.e., formula-based) solution for the set of unconstrained optimal active weights in Equation 11, a number of practical or strategic constraints are often imposed in practice. For example, if the unconstrained active weight of a particular security is negative and large, that might lead to a negative absolute weight or short sell of the security. Many investors are constrained to be long only, either by regulation or by preference because of the extra complexity and costs of short selling. For quantitatively oriented investors, optimal solutions for active weights under long-only constraints, limits on turnover, ESG screens, or other constraints generally require the use of a numerical optimizer. Alternatively, one can use the fundamental law framework to better analyze the active weights that are subjectively determined by less quantitative techniques.

Let w_i (without an *) represent the *actual* active security weights for a constrained portfolio—in contrast to the optimal active weights, w_i^*, specified in Equation 11.

As explained previously, the transfer coefficient, TC, is essentially the cross-sectional correlation between the forecasted active security returns and actual active weights. To be more precise, for a single-factor risk model, TC is the following *risk-weighted* correlation:

$$TC = \rho(\mu_i/\sigma_i, \Delta w_i \sigma_i)$$

Based on the correspondence between optimal active weights and forecasted active returns in Equation 11, the transfer coefficient can also be expressed as the risk-weighted correlation between the optimal active weights and the actual active weights, $TC = \rho(\Delta w_i^* \sigma_i, \Delta w_i \sigma_i)$.

As a correlation coefficient, TC can take on values anywhere from -1.00 to $+1.00$, although TC values are typically positive and range from about 0.20 to 0.90. A low TC results from the formal or informal constraints imposed on the structure of the portfolio. In fact, at TC = 0.00, there would be no correspondence between the active return forecasts and active weights taken and thus no expectation of value added from active management. In contrast, TC = 1.00 (no binding constraints) represents a perfect correspondence between active weights taken and forecasted active returns, allowing the full expected value added to be reflected in the portfolio structure. The portfolio TC could even conceivably be negative if relative weights are negatively correlated with current expected returns because the portfolio needs rebalancing.

Including the impact of the transfer coefficient, the expanded fundamental law is expressed in the following equation:

$$E(R_A) = (TC)(IC)\sqrt{BR}\sigma_A \qquad (14)$$

where an * is not used because the managed portfolio is constructed from *constrained* active security weights, Δw_i. The expanded fundamental law of active management shown in Equation 14, which we will refer to simply as the *fundamental law* henceforward, states that the expected active return, $E(R_A)$, is the product of four key parameters: the transfer coefficient, TC, the assumed information coefficient, IC, the square root of breadth, BR, and portfolio active risk, σ_A. Using Equation 14, we can also express the portfolio's information ratio, $E(R_A)/\sigma_A$, as the product of just three terms: $IR = (TC)(IC)\sqrt{BR}$.

The fundamental law as stated in Equation 14, although more practical than Equation 13, is still based on a simple risk model for the individual securities. Specifically, the equations in this section are based on the simplifying assumption of a single-index model; so, the active security returns are residual returns and are uncorrelated with each other. If we go even further in terms of simplicity and assume that the individual securities all have the same residual volatility, then the correlation formulas for IC and TC do not need to be risk weighted. Alternatively, we could move in the direction of more complexity by using the single-factor risk model with factor sensitivity: $R_{Ai} = R_i - \beta_i R_B$. In quantitative portfolio management practice, even more sophisticated multi-factor risk models are used with correspondingly more complex fundamental law parameter values, although the basic form of Equation 14 is preserved.

EXAMPLE 6   The Expanded Fundamental Law

Consider the simple case of four individual securities whose active returns are uncorrelated with each other and forecasts are independent from year to year. The securities have a range of active return forecasts, risks, optimal active weights, and actual active weights as given in the following exhibit. The optimal active weights are based on a formula for maximizing the active return of a managed portfolio for a given level of active risk. The actual active weights are the result of a numerical optimizer with a number of constraints, in addition to the active risk constraint of 9.0%.

Security	Expected Active Return	Active Return Volatility	Optimal Active Weight	Actual Active Weight
#1	5.0%	25.0%	18%	6%
#2	10.0%	50.0%	9%	4%
#3	−5.0%	25.0%	−18%	7%
#4	−10.0%	50.0%	−9%	−17%

1. Calculate the transfer coefficient (TC) as the risk-weighted correlation coefficient between the four active return forecasts and the four actual active weights. Compare this number with the transfer coefficient for the optimal active weights.
2. The forecasted active return of the optimal portfolio is the sum of the active weights times active returns for each security: $0.18(5.0) + 0.09(10.0) + (-0.18)(-5.0) + (-0.09)(-10.0) = 3.6\%$. The active risk of the optimal portfolio is the square root of the sum of active weights squared times the active volatility squared for each security: $[(0.18)^2(25.0)^2 + (0.09)^2 (50.0)^2 + (-0.18)^2 (25.0)^2 + (-0.09)^2 (50.0)^2]^{1/2} = 9.0\%$. Calculate the forecasted active return and active risk of the managed portfolio using the *actual* rather than unconstrained optimal active weights.
3. Verify the expanded fundamental law of active management using the active portfolio return, active portfolio risk, and transfer coefficient calculations in Parts 1 and 2. The individual active return forecasts and optimal active weights were sized using an information coefficient of IC = 0.20 and breadth of BR = 4.

Solution to 1: The transfer coefficient is the correlation between the risk-weighted expected active returns and actual active weights: $TC = \rho(\Delta w_i \sigma_i, \mu_i / \sigma_i)$, where ρ denotes correlation (you can use the Microsoft Excel function CORREL) with four pairs of numbers. The risk-weighted values for Security #1 are $\Delta w_1 \sigma_1 = 0.06(25.0) = 1.5\%$ and $\mu_1 / \sigma_1 = 5.0/25.0 = 20.0\%$. The correlation coefficient across all four securities (calculated in Excel) is TC = 0.58. The transfer coefficient for the optimal active weights is by definition 1.0 but can be verified by the calculated correlation coefficient. The risk-weighted values for Security #1 are then $\Delta w_1 \sigma_1 = 0.18(25.0) = 4.5\%$ and $\mu_1 / \sigma_1 = 5.0/25.0 = 20.0\%$.

Solution to 2: The forecasted active return of the managed portfolio is $0.06(5.0) + 0.04(10.0) + 0.07(-5.0) + (-0.17)(-10.0) = 2.1\%$. The active risk of the managed portfolio is the square root of the sum of actual active weights squared times the active volatility squared for each security, $[(0.06)^2(25.0)^2 + (0.04)^2 (50.0)^2 + (0.07)^2 (25.0)^2 + (-0.17)^2 (50.0)^2]^{1/2} = 9.0\%$, as specified by the active risk constraint.

Solution to 3: The expanded fundamental law states that the expected portfolio active return will be $E(R_A) = (TC)(IC)\sqrt{BR}\sigma_A = 0.58 \times 0.20 \times (4)^{1/2} \times 9.0 = 2.1\%$, consistent with the direct calculation in the Solution to 2.

We close this sub-section by noting that the transfer coefficient, TC, also comes into play when calculating the optimal amount of active risk for an actively managed portfolio with constraints. Specifically, with constraints and using notation consistent with expressions in the fundamental law, Equation 8 becomes

$$\sigma_A = TC\frac{IR^*}{SR_B}\sigma_B$$

where IR* is the information ratio of an otherwise unconstrained portfolio. Employing this optimal level of aggressiveness leads to a maximum possible value of the constrained portfolio's squared Sharpe ratio:

$$SR_P^2 = SR_B^2 + (TC)^2(IR^*)^2$$

As noted previously, the active risk of an actively managed fund can be adjusted to its optimal level while preserving the information ratio by adding long or short positions in the benchmark portfolio. For further insight, note that with a transfer coefficient of 0.00, the optimal amount of active risk calculated is zero. In other words, the investor should just invest in the benchmark portfolio.

We now illustrate the impact of the transfer coefficient with the following example. If the actively managed portfolio has a transfer coefficient of 0.50 and an unconstrained information ratio of 0.30 and the benchmark portfolio has a Sharpe ratio of 0.40 and risk of 16.0%, then the optimal amount of aggressiveness in the actively managed portfolio is 0.50(0.30/ 0.40)16.0 = 6.0%. If the actively managed portfolio is constructed with this amount of active risk, the Sharpe ratio will be $(0.40^2 + 0.50^2 \times 0.30^2)^{1/2} = 0.43$. If the constrained portfolio has an active risk of 8.0%, the active risk can be lowered to the optimal level of 6.0% by mixing $1 - 6.0/8.0 = 25\%$ in the benchmark and 75.0% in the actively managed fund.

4.4. *Ex Post* Performance Measurement

Most of the fundamental law perspectives discussed up to this point relate to the expected value added through active portfolio management. Actual performance in any given period will vary from its expected value in a range determined by the benchmark tracking risk. We now turn our attention to examining actual performance, the *ex post* analysis of the realized value added.

The key determinant of the sign and magnitude of the realized value added in Equation 3 is the degree to which the portfolio has positive active weights on securities that realize positive relative returns and negative active weights on securities that realize negative relative returns. In other words, actual performance is measured by the relationship between relative weights and realized relative returns. Knowing how actual returns match up with realized returns (the *realized* information coefficient, IC_R) allows the investor to examine what realized return to expect given the transfer coefficient. Specifically, expected value added conditional on the realized information coefficient, IC_R, is

$$E(R_A|IC_R) = (TC)(IC_R)\sqrt{BR}\sigma_A \tag{15}$$

Equation 15 is similar to the fundamental law, shown in Equation 14, but in Equation 15 the realized information coefficient, IC_R, replaces the *expected* information coefficient, IC.

We can represent any difference between the actual active return of the portfolio and the conditional expected active return with a noise term:

$$R_A = E(R_A \mid IC_R) + \text{Noise} \tag{16}$$

Equation 16 states that the realized value added of an actively managed portfolio can be divided into two parts. The first part comes from the expected value added given the realized skill of the investor that period. The second part represents any noise that results from constraints that impinge on the optimal portfolio structure.

Equation 15 also leads to an *ex post* (i.e., realized) decomposition of the portfolio's active return variance into two parts: variation due to the realized information coefficient and variation due to constraint-induced noise. Clarke, de Silva, and Thorley (2005) showed that the two parts of the realized variance are proportional to TC^2 and $1 - TC^2$. For example, with a TC value of, say, 0.60, only $TC^2 = 36\%$ of the realized variation in performance is attributed to variation in the realized information coefficient, and $1 - TC^2 = 64\%$ comes from constraint-induced noise. Low-TC investors will frequently experience periods when the forecasting process succeeds but actual performance is poor or when actual performance is good even though the return forecasting process fails.

EXAMPLE 7   *Ex Post* Performance

Consider an active management strategy that includes BR = 100 investment decisions (e.g., 100 individual stocks, whose active returns are uncorrelated, and annual rebalancing), an expected information coefficient of IC = 0.05, a transfer coefficient of TC = 0.80, and annualized active risk of σ_A = 4.0%. Thus, the expected value added according to the fundamental law is

$$E(R_A) = (TC)(IC)\sqrt{BR}\sigma_A = 0.80 \times 0.05 \times \sqrt{100} \times 4.0\% = 1.6\%$$

1. Suppose that the *realized* information coefficient in a given period is −0.10, instead of the expected value of IC = 0.05. In the absence of constraint-induced noise, what would be the value added that period?
2. Suppose that the actual return on the active portfolio was −2.6%. Given the −0.10 realized information coefficient, how much of the forecasted active return was offset by the noise component?
3. What percentage of the performance variance (i.e., tracking risk squared) in this strategy over time is attributed to variation in the realized information coefficient (i.e., forecasting success), and what percentage of performance variance is attributed to constraint-induced noise?

Solution to 1: The value added, without including constraint-induced noise (which has an expected value of zero) is

$$E(R_A | IC_R) = (TC)(IC_R)\sqrt{BR}\sigma_A = 0.80 \times (-0.10) \times \sqrt{100} \times 4.0\% = -3.2\%$$

In other words, conditional on the actual information coefficient, the investor should expect an active return that is negative because the realized information coefficient is negative.

Solution to 2: The noise portion of the active return is the difference between the actual active return and the forecasted active return: $-2.6 - (-3.2) = 0.6\%$. In other words, the noise component helped offset the negative value added from poor return forecasting. Of course, the constraint-induced noise component could just as easily have gone the other way, exacerbating the negative value added. Note that the negative realized active return of -2.6% is well within the range associated with the tracking error (active risk) of 4.0% per period.

Solution to 3: Given the transfer coefficient of $TC = 0.80$, $TC^2 = 64\%$ of the variation in performance over time is attributed to the success of the forecasting process, leaving 36% due to constraint-induced noise.

5. APPLICATIONS OF THE FUNDAMENTAL LAW

In this section, we discuss three specific applications of active portfolio management: one application to a global equity strategy with different sets of active return forecasts and constraints and two applications to US fixed income. These applications will further illustrate how the fundamental law is used to evaluate active portfolio strategies, including security selection and market timing.

5.1. Global Equity Strategy

In our first example, we show how the fundamental law can be used to calculate the expected active return for an actively managed portfolio benchmarked to the MSCI All Country World Index (ACWI). This global equity example focuses on the cross-sectional characteristics of the fundamental law, whereas the US fixed-income examples that follow also include time-series implications of the law. The investable assets in this example are the individual MSCI market indexes—including the 21 EAFE (Europe, Australasia, and Far East) markets, the United States, Canada, and the Emerging Markets Index—for a total of 24 assets. "Now" is the beginning of the calendar year 2019. For purposes of illustration, we will assume that the future will be like the past in terms of active risk, and thus we will base our estimates on the US dollar return to the MSCI market indexes from 2009 to 2018. In practice, managerial judgment or a commercial model would be used to forecast risk. The various rankings of the markets' forecasted active returns for the calendar year 2019 are hypothetical.

The *ex ante* expected active risk of each asset is equal to the annualized historical standard deviation of beta-adjusted differences between the individual market return and the ACWI return, as shown in the third column of Exhibit 7. For example, the active risk of the United

Kingdom is 6.4% and the active risk of Japan is 9.1%. Note that the risk estimates are for active returns (i.e., the difference between the individual asset and benchmark returns). The total risk of each market would be higher based on the estimated risk of the benchmark and the benchmark beta.

EXHIBIT 7   Long–Short Global Equity Fund for 2019 (risk statistics based on MSCI returns from 2009 to 2018)

Market	Score	Active Return Volatility	Expected Active Return	Active Weight	ACWI Benchmark Weight	Portfolio Weight
United Kingdom	2.0	6.4%	1.3%	15.7%	5.2%	20.9%
Japan	0.0	9.1%	0.0%	−2.0%	7.6%	5.7%
France	−2.0	8.5%	−1.7%	−12.0%	3.4%	−8.5%
Germany	0.0	8.4%	0.0%	2.8%	2.7%	5.6%
Switzerland	2.0	7.8%	1.6%	9.7%	2.7%	12.3%
Australia	0.0	11.1%	0.0%	−1.0%	2.1%	1.1%
Spain	−2.0	16.0%	−3.2%	−5.3%	1.0%	−4.3%
Sweden	0.0	10.1%	0.0%	−1.2%	0.8%	−0.4%
Hong Kong SAR	1.0	12.0%	1.2%	2.3%	1.2%	3.5%
Netherlands	0.0	7.9%	0.0%	1.8%	1.1%	2.9%
Italy	−1.0	15.1%	−1.5%	−0.8%	0.7%	−0.1%
Singapore	0.0	11.8%	0.0%	−1.8%	0.4%	−1.3%
Belgium	1.0	10.2%	1.0%	4.4%	0.3%	4.7%
Denmark	0.0	12.3%	0.0%	−1.2%	0.5%	−0.7%
Finland	−1.0	13.7%	−1.4%	−2.5%	0.3%	−2.2%
Norway	0.0	13.7%	0.0%	0.1%	0.2%	0.3%
Israel	1.0	15.3%	1.5%	1.4%	0.2%	1.6%
Ireland	0.0	14.9%	0.0%	0.3%	0.2%	0.5%
Austria	−1.0	14.6%	−1.5%	−1.6%	0.1%	−1.6%
Portugal	0.0	15.2%	0.0%	0.9%	0.0%	0.9%
New Zealand	1.0	14.2%	1.4%	1.8%	0.1%	1.8%
United States	0.0	3.8%	0.0%	−5.3%	54.3%	48.9%
Canada	−1.0	9.2%	−0.9%	−6.7%	3.0%	−3.7%
Emerging	0.0	9.0%	0.0%	0.1%	11.9%	12.0%
Total	0.0			0.0%	100.0%	100.0%

Transfer Coefficient	Information Coefficient	Breadth
0.995	0.099	24.5
Active Return	Active Risk	Information Ratio
0.98%	2.00%	0.49

The 24 individual assets in Exhibit 7 are listed approximately by size in the EAFE benchmark, followed by the United States, Canada, and the emerging markets. For example, the United Kingdom has a benchmark weight of 5.2% and Canada has a benchmark weight of 3.0%. Scores representing an active investor's forecasts of the relative performance of each asset during 2019 are assigned to each market. The scores are one of five numerical values that represent a managerial forecast of strong outperformance (2.0), weak outperformance (1.0), neutral performance (0.0), weak underperformance (−1.0), and strong underperformance (−2.0). The number of scores in each of these five categories is based on the requirement that the scores sum to zero and have a cross-sectional standard deviation of 1.

The active return forecasts in the fourth column of Exhibit 7 are based on the Grinold rule in Equation 10 of "IC times volatility times score," where IC is the *ex ante* information coefficient that measures the assumed accuracy of the investor's relative rankings, as illustrated by the right leg of the correlation triangle in Exhibit 6. In this example, we use an assumed information coefficient of 0.10; thus, forecasted and realized active security returns are expected to have a cross-sectional correlation coefficient of 0.10. For example, the active return forecast for the United Kingdom, which has a score of 2.0, is 0.10(6.4)(2.0) = 1.3%. Alternatively, the active return forecast for Japan is 0.0% because the score is 0. As explained later, the information coefficient used in fundamental law accounting will be adjusted down to 0.095, as shown at the bottom of Exhibit 7, to account for the assignment of scores in this particular example.

The active weights for each market are based on the active return forecast and a numerical optimizer (i.e., Excel Solver) with the objective to maximize the expected active return of the portfolio, subject to a 2.00% constraint on active risk. Note that while the active weights for each market are generally correlated with the forecasted active returns in Exhibit 7, they are not perfectly proportional for two reasons. First, the optimizer also takes into account the estimated correlations between each market's active return, based on the MSCI monthly return data from 2009 to 2018. Exhibit 8 reports the estimated active return correlations for the eight largest EAFE countries; the full correlation matrix is not reported to conserve space. For example, the correlation coefficient between the United Kingdom (GB) and Japan (JP) is fairly low at −0.02, while the correlation coefficient between France (FR) and Germany (DE) is higher at 0.30. Note that these correlation coefficients are for *active* returns (i.e., the differences between the individual market and ACWI benchmark returns). The correlations for *total* market returns would all be positive and much higher—for example, values that range from 0.4 to 0.9.

EXHIBIT 8   Active Return Correlation Coefficients for Eight Countries (based on MSCI returns from 2009 to 2018)

Country	GB	JP	FR	DE	CH	AU	ES	SE	
GB	1.000	−0.02	0.21	0.08	0.13	0.00	0.18	0.14	…
JP	−0.02	1.000	−0.08	−0.03	0.04	−0.08	0.01	−0.07	…
FR	0.21	−0.08	1.000	0.30	0.16	−0.03	0.34	0.15	…
DE	0.08	−0.03	0.30	1.000	0.10	−0.07	0.19	0.15	…
CH	0.13	0.04	0.16	0.10	1.000	0.06	0.11	0.10	…
AU	0.00	−0.08	−0.03	−0.07	0.06	1.000	0.01	0.06	…
ES	0.18	0.01	0.34	0.19	0.11	0.01	1.000	0.11	…
SE	0.14	−0.07	0.15	0.15	0.10	0.06	0.11	1.000	…
	…	…	…	…	…	…	…	…	…

The second reason that the active weights in Exhibit 7 are not perfectly proportional to the forecasted active returns is that the active weights are constrained by the optimizer to sum to zero. For example, the highest active weight in Exhibit 7 is for the United Kingdom, at 15.7%, and the lowest active weight is for France, at −12.0%. These active weights are added to the benchmark weights to give the total portfolio weights in the last column of Exhibit 7. For example, the total weight for the United States is 48.9%, even though the active weight is −5.3%, because the US benchmark weight in the ACWI is 54.3%. In fact, the optimization in Exhibit 7 is for a relatively unconstrained long–short portfolio where the sum of the positive total weights is about 120% and the sum of the negative total weights is about −20%, what might be called a "120/20 long–short" strategy in practice.

Because the optimization is basically unconstrained, the transfer coefficient or risk-weighted correlation between active return forecasts and active weights shown at the bottom of Exhibit 7 is 0.995, almost perfect. The transfer coefficient in this example takes into account all the risk statistics (i.e., forecasted active volatilities *and* forecasted correlations), but it is not exactly 1.0 because of the budget constraint that the active weights sum to zero. Alternatively, if the sum of active weights were allowed to be non-zero, effectively allowing for risk-free cash or leverage in the equity portfolio to meet the budget constraint, the transfer coefficient would be exactly 1.0. The breadth of the strategy shown at the bottom of Exhibit 7 is 24.5, slightly higher than the number of individual assets, 24.0, because the risk model includes active return correlation coefficients that are different from zero. If all the off-diagonal correlations in the extended table in Exhibit 8 were exactly zero, then breadth would be exactly 24.0, instead of 24.5.

The fundamental law in Equation 14 states that the expected active return on the portfolio is $E(R_A) = (TC)(IC)\sqrt{BR}\sigma_A = 0.995 \times 0.099 \times (24.5)^{1/2} \times 2.00 = 0.98\%$. Alternatively, the expected active return of 0.98%, shown at the bottom of Exhibit 7, is calculated as the sum of the active weights times active returns. Thus, the accuracy of the fundamental law is quite high. The fundamental law is often expressed in terms of the information ratio, or forecasted active return over active risk. Using this framework, the validation of the fundamental law is $IR = (TC)(IC)\sqrt{BR} = 0.995 \times 0.099 \times (24.5)^{1/2} = 0.49$, equal to actual forecasted active return divided by active risk, $0.98/2.00 = 0.490$. Because the information ratio in this relatively unconstrained portfolio is unaffected by the aggressiveness of the strategy, we would get the same IR value if the active risk were allowed to be higher. For example, if the active risk specified to the optimizer were increased to 3.00%, the forecasted active return would increase to 1.47%, an information ratio of, again, 1.47/3.00 = 0.49.

Exhibit 9 continues examining the global equity strategy but uses a slightly different assignment of scores than Exhibit 7 to illustrate how this change affects the values in the fundamental law. Specifically, the scores for Germany (DE) and the United Kingdom (UK) have been switched as well as the scores for Switzerland (CH) and Australia (AU). While the breadth in Exhibit 9 is unchanged at 24.5, the information coefficient has increased slightly to 0.105, compared with 0.099 in Exhibit 7. Even though the assumed IC used to create the expected active returns in Exhibit 9 is still 0.10, the IC used in fundamental law accounting has increased because the new assignment of scores represents a slightly more ambitious forecast. For example, the active (i.e., benchmark relative) returns for France and Germany in Exhibit 9 are now forecasted to go strongly in opposite directions, even though they are positively correlated according to the risk model in Exhibit 8. Given the increase in IC and slight change in TC, the fundamental law calculation for Exhibit 9 is now $\mathrm{IR} = (\mathrm{TC})(\mathrm{IC})\sqrt{\mathrm{BR}} = 0.997 \times 0.105 \times (24.5)^{1/2} = 0.532$, equal to the actual value of 0.52.

EXHIBIT 9   Long–Short Global Equity Fund with Different Scores for 2019 (risk statistics based on MSCI returns from 2009 to 2018)

Market	Score	Active Return Volatility	Expected Active Return	Active Weight	ACWI Benchmark Weight	Portfolio Weight
United Kingdom	0.0	6.4%	0.0%	1.7%	5.2%	6.9%
Japan	0.0	9.1%	0.0%	−0.3%	7.6%	7.3%
France	−2.0	8.5%	−1.7%	−11.4%	3.4%	−8.0%
Germany	2.0	8.4%	1.7%	14.5%	2.7%	17.2%
Switzerland	0.0	7.8%	0.0%	−2.0%	2.7%	0.6%
Australia	2.0	11.1%	2.2%	7.7%	2.1%	9.9%
Spain	−2.0	16.0%	−3.2%	−4.9%	1.0%	−4.0%
Sweden	0.0	10.1%	0.0%	−1.2%	0.8%	−0.4%
Hong Kong SAR	1.0	12.0%	1.2%	2.8%	1.2%	4.0%
Netherlands	0.0	7.9%	0.0%	3.0%	1.1%	4.1%
Italy	−1.0	15.1%	−1.5%	−0.9%	0.7%	−0.2%
Singapore	0.0	11.8%	0.0%	−1.4%	0.4%	−1.0%
Belgium	1.0	10.2%	1.0%	5.8%	0.3%	6.1%
Denmark	0.0	12.3%	0.0%	−0.7%	0.5%	−0.1%
Finland	−1.0	13.7%	−1.4%	−3.2%	0.3%	−2.9%
Norway	0.0	13.7%	0.0%	1.3%	0.2%	1.5%
Israel	1.0	15.3%	1.5%	1.5%	0.2%	1.7%
Ireland	0.0	14.9%	0.0%	0.2%	0.2%	0.4%
Austria	−1.0	14.6%	−1.5%	−1.8%	0.1%	−1.7%
Portugal	0.0	15.2%	0.0%	1.4%	0.0%	1.4%
New Zealand	1.0	14.2%	1.4%	1.4%	0.1%	1.4%
United States	0.0	3.8%	0.0%	−5.0%	54.3%	49.2%
Canada	−1.0	9.2%	−0.9%	−5.3%	3.0%	−2.3%
Emerging	0.0	9.0%	0.0%	−2.9%	11.9%	9.0%
Total	0.0			0.0%	100.0%	100.0%

Transfer Coefficient	Information Coefficient	Breadth
0.997	0.105	24.5

Active Return	Active Risk	Information Ratio
1.04%	2.00%	0.52

We now apply constraints to the global equity strategy to focus on the transfer coefficient. Specifically, Exhibit 10 shows two *constrained* portfolio optimizations using the same score assignments and thus active return forecasts as in Exhibit 7. The first optimization, shown on the left-hand side of Exhibit 10, has two constraints. First, the portfolio is constrained to be long only (i.e., a negative active weight for any given market cannot be bigger than the benchmark weight). For example, France has an active weight of −3.4%, bounded by the benchmark weight of 3.4%, so that the total weight for France in the managed portfolio is zero. Second, the portfolio weights are constrained to not be more than 10.0% over or under the benchmark weight (i.e., the absolute value of any given market active weight cannot be greater than 10.0%). For example, the active weights for the United Kingdom and Switzerland are limited to 10.0% and the active weight for the United States is limited to −10.0%.

EXHIBIT 10   Constrained Global Equity Funds for 2019 (risk statistics based on MSCI returns from 2009 to 2018)

Market	Active Weight	ACWI Benchmark Weight	Portfolio Weight	Active Weight	ACWI Benchmark Weight	Portfolio Weight
United Kingdom	10.0%	5.2%	15.2%	8.6%	5.2%	15.2%
Japan	−6.6%	7.6%	1.0%	−7.8%	7.76%	0.0%
France	−3.4%	3.4%	0.0%	−3.7%	3.4%	0.0%
Germany	−2.7%	2.7%	0.0%	−3.5%	2.7%	0.0%
Switzerland	10.0%	2.7%	12.7%	10.0%	2.7%	12.7%
Australia	−2.1%	2.1%	0.0%	−2.8%	2.1%	0.0%
Spain	−1.0%	1.0%	0.0%	−1.2%	1.0%	0.0%
Sweden	−0.8%	0.8%	0.0%	−1.2%	0.8%	0.0%
Hong Kong SAR	5.9%	1.2%	7.1%	9.5%	1.2%	5.7%
Netherlands	−1.1%	1.1%	0.0%	−1.0%	1.1%	0.0%
Italy	−0.7%	0.7%	0.0%	−0.8%	0.7%	0.0%
Singapore	−0.4%	0.4%	0.0%	−0.5%	0.4%	0.0%
Belgium	6.1%	0.3%	6.4%	−0.4%	0.3%	0.0%
Denmark	−0.5%	0.5%	0.0%	−0.4%	0.5%	0.0%
Finland	−0.3%	0.3%	0.0%	−0.3%	0.3%	0.0%
Norway	−0.2%	0.2%	0.0%	−0.3%	0.2%	0.0%
Israel	4.2%	0.2%	4.4%	10.0%	0.2%	10.2%
Ireland	−0.2%	0.2%	0.0%	−0.1%	0.2%	0.0%
Austria	−0.1%	0.1%	0.0%	−0.1%	0.1%	0.0%
Portugal	0.0%	0.0%	0.0%	−0.1%	0.0%	0.0%
New Zealand	4.7%	0.1%	4.8%	10.0%	0.1%	10.1%
United States	−10.0%	54.3%	44.3%	−10.0%	54.3%	44.3%

Market	Active Weight	ACWI Benchmark Weight	Portfolio Weight	Active Weight	ACWI Benchmark Weight	Portfolio Weight
Canada	−3.0%	3.0%	0.0%	−3.7%	3.0%	0.0%
Emerging	−7.7%	11.9%	4.2%	−10.0%	11.9%	1.9%
Total	0.0%	100.0%	100.0%	0.0%	100.0%	100.0%

Transfer Coefficient	Information Coefficient	Breadth	Transfer Coefficient	Information Coefficient	Breadth
0.694	0.099	24.5	0.567	0.099	24.5

Active Return	Active Risk	Information Ratio	Active Return	Active Risk	Information Ratio
0.68%	2.00%	0.34	0.76%	2.74%	0.28

The long-only and maximum over- or underweight constraints substantially reduce the transfer of active return forecasts into active weights, as shown by the transfer coefficient of 0.694 at the bottom of the left side of Exhibit 10, compared with 0.995 for the same scores and active return forecasts in Exhibit 7. The impact of this transfer coefficient on expected active return according to the fundamental law is $E(R_A) = (TC)(IC)\sqrt{BR}\sigma_A = 0.694 \times 0.099 \times (24.5)^{1/2} \times 2.00 = 0.68\%$, compared with 0.98% for the unconstrained portfolio in Exhibit 7. Similarly, the impact of this transfer coefficient measured by the information ratio is $IR = (TC)(IC)\sqrt{BR} = 0.694 \times 0.099 \times (24.5)^{1/2} = 0.34$, compared with 0.49 for the unconstrained portfolio. In other words, the expected active return and information ratio are reduced by almost a third because of the constraints imposed in portfolio construction.

As previously mentioned, an increase in the allowed active risk from 2.00% to 3.00% in the unconstrained portfolio in Exhibit 7 proportionally increases the active return, leaving the information ratio at about 0.49. However, an increase in allowed active risk to 3.00% does *not* preserve the information ratio of the constrained portfolio, as shown by the optimization on the right-hand side of Exhibit 10. Specifically, the higher active risk leads to more variation in unconstrained active weights, as shown in Equation 11; thus, the constraints become more binding. For example, the active weight for New Zealand, which is 4.7% on the left-hand side of Exhibit 10, is capped at the maximum possible value of 10.0% on the right-hand side of Exhibit 10. The result is a further reduction in the transfer coefficient from 0.694 to 0.567, leading to a reduction in the information ratio to $IR = (TC)(IC)\sqrt{BR} = 0.567 \times 0.099 \times (24.5)^{1/2} = 0.28$, compared with 0.34 at the lower active portfolio risk of 2.0%.

The key concept is that although an unconstrained IR is invariant to the level of active risk, as shown by the dark line in Exhibit 5, the IR for a *constrained* portfolio generally decreases with the aggressiveness of the strategy. Specifically, the dark line in Exhibit 5 for a constrained portfolio would curve downward from left to right in accordance with an increasingly lower transfer coefficient. Thus, the constraints that are imposed on the portfolio should inform the decision of how aggressively to apply an active management strategy.

EXAMPLE 8   Compare and Contrast Active Management Strategies

Consider two active management strategies: individual stock selection, with a benchmark composed of 100 securities, and industrial sector selection, with a benchmark of nine sectors. The active security returns are defined as residuals in a risk model and thus are essentially uncorrelated, and forecasts are independent from year to year. Suppose the individual stock investor is expected to exhibit skill as measured by an information coefficient of 0.05, while the industrial sector investor has a higher information coefficient of 0.15.

1. Conceptually, what is the breadth (i.e., number of independent decisions per year) of each active management strategy?
2. Calculate the expected information ratio for each strategy under the assumption that each investor's forecasts can be implemented without constraints, such as the long-only constraint or a limit on turnover each year.
3. Suppose the aggressiveness of each active management strategy is established by a portfolio active risk target of 3.0% per year. What is the expected active return to each strategy?
4. Under the more realistic assumption that the individual security selection strategy is constrained to be long only and has turnover limits, the transfer coefficient has a value of 0.60. Calculate the constrained information ratio and expected active return of the security selection strategy.
5. Suppose the aggressiveness of the constrained individual security selection strategy is increased to a portfolio active risk target of 4.0% per year. Conceptually, what is likely to happen to the information ratio, and why?

Solution to 1: Given that the active asset returns in each strategy are uncorrelated and forecasts are independent from year to year, the breadth of the security selection strategy is $BR = 100$ and of the sector selection strategy is $BR = 9$.

Solution to 2: The expected information ratio of the unconstrained security selection strategy is calculated as $IR = (IC)\sqrt{BR} = 0.05 \times \sqrt{100} = 0.50$, while the information ratio of the industrial sector selection strategy is $IR = (IC)\sqrt{BR} = 0.15 \times \sqrt{9} = 0.45$.

Solution to 3: The expected active return to the unconstrained security selection strategy is $0.50(3.0) = 1.50\%$, while the expected active return of the industrial sector selection strategy is $0.45(3.0) = 1.35\%$.

Solution to 4: The information ratio of the constrained security selection strategy is $IR = (TC)(IC)\sqrt{BR} = 0.60 \times 0.05 \times \sqrt{100} = 0.30$, rather than 0.50, and the expected active return is $0.30(3.0) = 0.90\%$, rather than 1.50%.

Solution to 5: A more aggressive implementation of the constrained security selection strategy will likely result in larger deviations of constrained weights from unconstrained weights and thus a lower transfer coefficient. For example, the transfer coefficient might drop from 0.60 to 0.50, leading to an information ratio of only $IR = (TC)(IC)\sqrt{BR} = 0.50 \times 0.05 \times \sqrt{100} = 0.25$. Thus, instead of a proportional increase in the expected active return associated with an increase in the active portfolio risk from 3.0% to 4.0%, the expected active return would only increase from 0.9% to $0.25(4.0) = 1.0\%$.

5.2. Fixed-Income Strategies

Two additional examples of the fundamental law in practice are based on the Bloomberg Barclays US fixed-income index returns. Consider first an active management strategy of over- and underweighting credit exposure once a quarter using corporate investment-grade and high-yield bond portfolios as assets. Let the benchmark portfolio be composed of 70% investment-grade bonds and 30% high-yield bonds. Each quarter, the active investor makes a single dichotomous decision either to overweight the investment-grade asset (and thus underweight the high-yield asset) or to overweight the high-yield asset (and thus underweight the investment-grade asset). In addition to switching to a fixed-income example, we are also now moving into a time-series application of the fundamental law instead of the purely cross-sectional application.

For example, consider two bond portfolios, an investment-grade portfolio and a high-yield portfolio. The quarterly return volatility of the IG (investment-grade) asset is 2.84%, and the quarterly return volatility of the HY (high-yield) asset is 4.64%, with an estimated correlation between the two of 0.575. The *active* risk of this decision is the volatility of the differential returns between the two bond portfolios, $[(2.84)^2 - 2(2.84)(4.64)(0.575) + (4.64)^2]^{1/2} = 3.80\%$. In effect, the active investor assigns a "score" of either $+1.0$ or -1.0 on credit exposure each quarter, with an *annualized* active risk of $3.80 \times (4)^{1/2} = 7.60\%$. Suppose the fixed-income investor expects to call the market correctly 55% of the time (i.e., 11 out of 20 quarters). If the investor makes the correct decision 55% of the time and an incorrect decision 45% of the time, then the time-series information coefficient is $0.55 - 0.45 = 0.10$.

If a time series of T predicted dichotomous (i.e., plus or minus 1.0) scores, $S_{P,t}$, and a time series of T realized dichotomous scores, $S_{R,t}$, both have zero means, then the time-series covariance between the two is $\text{COV}(S_P, S_R) = \frac{1}{T}\sum_{t=1}^{T} S_{P,t} S_{R,t}$. The product of the two scores at time period t is 1.0 if the scores have the same sign (i.e., the decision is correct) and -1.0 if the scores have different signs (i.e., the decision is incorrect). Because the scores have unit variances, the correlation coefficient is equal to the covariance. Thus, the time-series correlation is equal to the number of correct decisions minus the number of incorrect decisions all over total decisions, or, in other words, the percentage correct minus the percentage incorrect.

Without a limit on active risk, the expected active return can be calculated using a simple probability-weighted average: $0.55(3.80) + 0.45(-3.80) = 38$ bps per quarter. But to illustrate the fundamental law, we use the Grinold rule in Equation 10 of "alpha equals IC times volatility times score": $0.10(3.80)(1.0) = 38$ bps.

The investor decides to limit the annual active risk to 2.00% and thus sets the active weight (i.e., deviation from the 70/30 benchmark weights) at $2.00/7.60 = 26.3\%$. Under the assumption that active returns are uncorrelated over time, the breadth of this strategy is 4.0, the four quarterly rebalancing decisions made each year. Thus, in quarters when the investor believes credit risk will pay off, the managed portfolio is invested $70.0\% - 26.3\% = 43.7\%$ in investment-grade bonds and $30\% + 26.3\% = 56.3\%$ in high-yield bonds. Alternatively, in quarters where the investor believes credit risk will not pay off, the active portfolio has $70.0\% + 26.3\% = 96.3\%$ in investment-grade bonds and only $30\% - 26.3\% = 3.7\%$ in high-yield bonds. According to the simple form of the fundamental law, the expected annualized active return to this strategy is $E(R_A) = (IC)\sqrt{BR}\sigma_A = 0.10 \times (4.0)^{1/2} \times 2.00 = 40$ bps a year, or 10 bps per quarter. Alternatively, given the active weight of 26.3% motivated by the desire to limit active risk, the expected quarterly return can be calculated more directly as $0.263 \times 38 = 10$ bps. Given the small breadth of this strategy, the annual information ratio is only $IR = (IC)\sqrt{BR} = 0.10 \times (4.0)^{1/2} = 0.20$.

The key concept in this illustration is that the breadth of the strategy is only 4, meaning four active management decisions per year. The same small-breadth problem also applies to quarterly tactical asset allocation decisions in a simple strategy that switches between equity and cash. There are so few opportunities to make an active decision in these "market-timing" strategies that the investor's accuracy as measured by the information coefficient must be quite high to achieve even a modest information ratio. A full description of the breadth calculation requires relatively complex matrix formulas that take into account the correlations between security returns. However, one "rule of thumb" is that breadth is approximately $BR = N/[1 + (N - 1)\rho]$, where N is the number of securities and ρ is the average correlation between the active security returns. In this fixed-income example, $\rho = 0.0$, so breadth is $BR = 4.0$.

A natural question is whether the expected information ratio can be increased by switching more frequently—say, monthly. Although it is somewhat more complicated to show, the basic answer is yes—*if* the information coefficient of 0.10 can be maintained and *if* the credit exposure decisions in this example are truly independent over time. For example, making monthly decisions that do not change during the quarter (i.e., signals of $+1.0, +1.0$, and $+1.0$ in January, February, and March) will *not* increase the information ratio of 0.20. However, if the monthly signals are truly uncorrelated with each other, then the information ratio in this example would be $IR = (IC)\sqrt{BR} = 0.10 \times \sqrt{12} = 0.35$. Although somewhat implausible, if an investor made daily decisions (250 trading days a year) that were truly independent and were *still* correct 55% of the time, the expected information ratio could potentially increase to $IR = (IC)\sqrt{BR} = 0.10 \times \sqrt{250} = 1.58$.

The high 1.58 information ratio indicates that the investor could earn an expected active return of 3.16% with active risk of only 2.00%. With such a high information ratio, the investor might be inclined to increase the aggressiveness of the credit risk strategy—for example, doubling to an expected return of $2 \times 3.16\% = 6.32\%$ and active risk of $2 \times 2.00\% = 4.00\%$. Besides the issue of transaction costs, this more aggressive strategy would likely bump up against various constraints. For example, at the higher 4.00% active risk, the required active weights would be plus and minus $4.00/7.60 = 52.6\%$. In other words, a tilt against credit risk would require a total portfolio weight of $70\% + 52.6\% = 122.6\%$ in investment-grade bonds funded by a -22.6% *short* position in high-yield bonds.

The essential logic of this example is not confined to a dichotomous decision; the same general perspectives would hold if the single credit risk signal were continuous—for example, numbers like -0.57 or 1.32. Then under the more aggressively applied active risk target of 4.0%, a signal of -0.57 would require an active weight of $-0.57(4.0)/7.6 = -30.0\%$. With a benchmark portfolio of 70.0% investment-grade and 30.0% high-yield bonds, this active weight translates into a 100% position in investment-grade bonds and no position in high-yield bonds. Alternatively, for a positive credit risk signal of 1.32, the required active weight would be 1.32(4.00)/7.60 = 69.5% (i.e., 100% in high-yield bonds and almost no position in investment-grade bonds). In other words, for this more aggressive strategy under a long-only constraint, the transfer coefficient would be less than 1 and the expanded fundamental law, $IR = (TC)(IC)\sqrt{BR}$, would come into play. Under a normal distribution for scores, the transfer coefficient of this strategy is 0.62, so the expected information ratio is only $IR = 0.62 \times 0.10 \times \sqrt{250} = 0.98$, not 1.58. For an active risk of 4.00%, the expected active return is thus only 0.98 × 4.00% = 3.92%, not 6.32%. Please note that the transfer coefficient in this example is based on the calculation $\Phi(1.32) - \Phi(-0.57) = 0.62$, where $\Phi(S)$ is the cumulative standard normal distribution function. Given long-only limits on positions, the actual active risk of the constrained portfolio would be lower than 4.0%. In other words, the actual active weights (determined by a numerical optimizer) would need to be larger than the simple formula (S)4.0/7.6 to get back up to an actual active risk of 4.0%.

For our second fixed-income example, consider an active management strategy using the five US Treasury bond portfolios in Exhibit 11 as the individual assets. Let the neutral benchmark be an equally weighted composite portfolio of the five, or 20% invested in each asset, but with annual rebalancing. In other words, we are now moving back into a purely cross-sectional application of the fundamental law.

EXHIBIT 11   Bloomberg Barclays US Treasury Bond Average Returns and Risk (return statistics from 2009 to 2018)

	Treas. 0–1	Treas. 1–3	Treas. 3–7	Treas. 7–10	Treas. 10–20
Avg. Ret.	0.40%	0.90%	2.21%	3.15%	3.89%
Volatility	0.17%	0.85%	3.20%	5.86%	7.95%

Exhibit 12 shows the volatility of the historical return differences between each asset and the equally weighted benchmark. Note that while the absolute volatility of each asset return goes up with maturity in Exhibit 11, the *active* volatility with respect to the benchmark is highest for the assets with the shortest maturity, at 3.45%, and the longest maturity, at 4.57%. Exhibit 12 also shows the estimated active (i.e., benchmark relative) return correlation matrix, which has both positive and negative values, in contrast to the absolute return correlation matrix (not shown), which would only have large positive values. For example, the correlation between the 0–1-year T-bond active return and the 1–3-year T-bond active return in Exhibit 12 is *positive* 0.49, showing that these shorter-maturity active returns tend to move together. However, the correlation between the 0–1-year active return and the 7–10-year active return is *negative*, at −0.49, showing that these two diverse maturity active returns tend to move apart.

EXHIBIT 12   US Treasury Bond Estimated Active Return Risk and Correlations (return statistics from 2009 to 2018)

	Treas. 0–1	Treas. 1–3	Treas. 3–7	Treas. 7–10	Treas. 10–20
Active Vol.	3.45%	2.85%	1.05%	2.40%	4.57%
Active Corr.	**Treas. 0–1**	**Treas. 1–3**	**Treas. 3–7**	**Treas. 7–10**	**Treas. 10–20**
Treas. 0–1	1.000	0.49	0.21	−0.49	−0.47
Treas. 1–3	0.49	1.000	0.26	−0.49	−0.49
Treas. 3–7	0.21	0.26	1.000	−0.19	−0.33
Treas. 7–10	−0.49	−0.49	−0.19	1.000	0.46
Treas. 10–20	−0.47	−0.49	−0.33	0.46	1.000

The breadth associated with the risk estimates in Exhibit 12 is 9.4, even though there are only 5 assets. The breadth is different from the number of assets because the off-diagonal values in the correlation matrix are substantially different from zero. Exhibit 13 shows the fundamental law calculations for two sets of scores given an active portfolio risk target of 1.0% per year. The first set of scores has positive values for the shorter-maturity bonds and negative scores for the longer-maturity bonds. The associated active returns are calculated using the Grinold rule in Equation 10 and an assumed information coefficient of 0.20; for example, the active return for 10–20-year T-bonds is $0.20 \times 4.57\% \times -1.76 = -1.61\%$. The active weights in Exhibit 13 are calculated by an optimizer given the constraint on active risk of 1.00%. For example, the active weight for the 10–20-year T-bonds is −19.1%, shown in the upper half of Exhibit 13. Given the benchmark weights of 20% for each asset, this results in a total weight of only $20 - 19.1 = 0.9\%$ in the managed portfolio.

Although the information coefficient used to scale the active returns was 0.20, the first set of scores in Exhibit 13 does not represent a very ambitious forecast, so the information coefficient used in the fundamental law calculation is 0.12. The intuition for the large downward adjustment in the information coefficient is that the positive scores for the shorter-maturity bonds and the negative scores for the longer-maturity bonds are all based on essentially one active decision that interest rates will rise. Specifically, the expected active (i.e., benchmark relative) return for the managed fixed-income portfolio is $E(R_A) = (IC)\sqrt{BR}\sigma_A = 0.12 \times (9.4)^{1/2} \times 1.00 = 37$ bps a year.

EXHIBIT 13   Signals and Weights for a Fixed-Income Portfolio with Breadth of 9.4 and Active Risk of 1.00% (return statistics from 2009 to 2018)

	Treas. 0–1	Treas. 1–3	Treas. 3–7	Treas. 7–10	Treas. 10–20	IC	Active Ret.
Score	0.63	0.67	0.92	−0.46	−1.76	0.12	0.37%
Active Ret.	0.43%	0.38%	0.19%	−0.22%	−1.61%		
Active Wgt.	−1.6%	−2.1%	15.4%	7.4%	−19.1%		
Total Wgt.	18.4%	17.9%	35.4%	27.4%	0.9%		

	Treas. 0–1	Treas. 1–3	Treas. 3–7	Treas. 7–10	Treas. 10–20	IC	Active Ret.
Score	−0.22	1.20	0.23	0.57	−1.77	0.18	0.55%
Active Ret.	−0.15%	0.68%	0.05%	0.27%	−1.62%		
Active Wgt.	−11.3%	17.0%	−12.8%	24.3%	−17.2%		
Total Wgt.	8.7%	37.0%	7.2%	44.3%	2.8%		

In contrast, the second set of scores in Exhibit 13 is a more ambitious set of active forecasts that specify a modification in the shape of the yield curve. As a result, the information coefficient is 0.18, not much lower than the 0.20 value used to scale the active returns, and the expected active return for the portfolio using the fundamental law is $E(R_A) = (\text{IC})\sqrt{\text{BR}}\sigma_A = 0.18 \times (9.4)^{1/2} \times 1.00 = 55$ bps a year. The fundamental law in terms of the expected information ratio for the second set of scores in Exhibit 13 is $\text{IR} = (\text{IC})\sqrt{\text{BR}} = 0.18 \times (9.4)^{1/2} = 0.55$, alternatively calculated as the expected active return over active risk, $55/100 = 0.55$.

At this relatively high information ratio, the investor may be inclined to increase the active risk to, say, 2.00% instead of 1.00%. However, given that the longest-maturity asset has a total weight that is approaching zero (i.e., 2.8%, as shown in the lower right-hand corner of Exhibit 13), such a strategy would likely require shorting; if short sells are not allowed, the transfer coefficient would likely end up being less than 1.00.

EXAMPLE 9   Breadth and Rebalancing in Active Management Strategies

Consider an active portfolio management strategy that involves decisions on overweighting or underweighting four individual assets. For example, the assets might be ETFs for four country equity markets or four different fixed-income ETFs. The active returns to Assets #1 and #2 are positively correlated, as are the active returns to Assets #3 and #4. However, the assumed risk model for active returns has no other non-zero correlations. The correlation structure in this risk model is shown in the following 4-by-4 correlation matrix, and the breadth calculation is BR = 3.2. For simplicity, we will assume that the portfolio management decisions are dichotomous; thus, each year the investor forecasts two of the assets to outperform the benchmark and the other two assets to underperform.

Correlations	#1	#2	#3	#4
#1	1.00	0.25	0.00	0.00
#2	0.25	1.00	0.00	0.00
#3	0.00	0.00	1.00	0.25
#4	0.00	0.00	0.25	1.00

1. Conceptually speaking (i.e., exact numbers are not necessary), why is the breadth less than the number of assets for this strategy?

2. Suppose the investor predicts that Assets #1 and #2 will outperform and that Assets #3 and #4 will underperform. Conceptually speaking (i.e., exact numbers are not necessary), how will these scores affect the information coefficient in the fundamental law compared with a prediction that Assets #1 and #3 will outperform and Assets #2 and #4 will underperform?
3. Suppose the active investor rebalances monthly instead of just once a year. Explain how this would affect the information ratio of this strategy, clearly stating your assumptions.

Solution to 1: According to the risk model, the active returns to Assets #1 and #2 tend to move together, with a correlation coefficient of 0.25, as do the active returns for Assets #3 and #4. As a result, the 3.2 breadth of this strategy is lower than the number of assets, $N = 4$.

Solution to 2: According to the risk model, the active returns to Assets #1 and #2 tend to move together, so a forecast that both will outperform is not as ambitious as a forecast that one will outperform while the other underperforms. As a result, the information coefficient will be adjusted downward by more under the first set of forecasts than under the second set of forecasts.

Solution to 3: Rebalancing monthly instead of annually could increase the breadth by a factor of 12 but only if the active management decisions for each asset are truly uncorrelated over time. For example, the breadth could increase to as much as $12 \times 3.2 = 38.4$. However, to increase the information ratio, one would have to assume that the information coefficient remains at the same level and that there are no constraints to fully implementing the active management decisions (i.e., a transfer coefficient of 1.00). For example, turnover constraints might limit the degree to which the monthly active management decisions could be fully implemented into new active positions, resulting in a lower transfer coefficient.

In summary, these examples illustrate how the information coefficient, IC, measures the strength of the return-forecasting process, or signal. The information coefficient is the correlation between the forecasted and realized security active returns and is anticipated to be positive or active management is not justified. Breadth, BR, measures the number of independent decisions made by the investor each year and is equal to the number of securities if the active returns are cross-sectionally uncorrelated. Similarly, breadth increases with the number of rebalancing periods but only if the active returns are uncorrelated over time.

Like the information coefficient, the transfer coefficient, TC, is a simple multiplicative factor in the fundamental law. It measures the extent to which constraints reduce the expected value added of the investor's forecasting ability. In the absence of constraints, the transfer coefficient is approximately 1.00, resulting in the basic form of the fundamental law. However, in practice, investors often work under constraints that result in TC values between 0.20 and 0.80. The lower transfer coefficient suggests that average performance in practice is only a fraction (20%–80%) of what would otherwise be predicted by the basic form of the fundamental law.

6. PRACTICAL LIMITATIONS

The limitations of the fundamental law include both practical considerations, such as ignoring transaction costs and taxes, and more conceptual issues, such as dynamic implementation over time. In this section, we focus on two limitations: the *ex ante* measurement of skill using the information coefficient and assumptions of independence in forecasts across assets and over time. The fundamental law extends the mean–variance-optimization approach to relative performance and hence has many of the same limitations of mean–variance optimization. In our discussion, we do not deal with the shortcomings of mean–variance optimization in general (e.g., assumptions of normality in return distributions or the degree of risk aversion) or the technical problems associated with the estimation and use of a risk model (e.g., the correct set of risk factors, nonlinearities, and non-stationary returns). The fundamental law takes as given that mean–variance optimization to balance risk and return against a benchmark is the correct objective function and that the investor has a way to adequately model risk.

6.1. *Ex Ante* Measurement of Skill

A core element of the fundamental law is the information coefficient, generally defined as the correlation between the portfolio investor's forecasts and actual outcomes. Active investors assume that the financial market they are trading in is not perfectly efficient in terms of public information and that they have some differential skill in competing with other active investors; otherwise, active management is generally not justified. Behaviorally, one might argue that investors tend to overestimate their own skills as embedded in the assumed IC, but even if that bias did not exist, questions about assessing an accurate level of skill remain. Furthermore, forecasting ability probably differs among different asset segments and varies over time.

For example, Qian and Hua (2004) expanded the basic form of the fundamental law by including the uncertainty about the level of skill, or the reality that the realized information coefficient can vary over time. Specifically, they showed that realized active portfolio risk, σ_A, is a product of both the benchmark tracking risk predicted by the risk model, denoted σ_{RM}, and the additional risk induced by the uncertainty of the information coefficient, denoted σ_{IC}:

$$\sigma_A = \sigma_{IC}\sqrt{N}\sigma_{RM} \tag{17}$$

Their insight about "strategy risk" is derived under the simplifying assumptions that portfolio positions are unconstrained, TC = 1.00, and that breadth is the number of securities, BR = N, but can be expanded to include both refinements. In other words, they suggest that a more accurate representation of the basic fundamental law using the expression in Equation 17 is

$$E(R_A) = \frac{IC}{\sigma_{IC}}\sigma_A \tag{18}$$

The key impact of accounting for the uncertainty of skill is that actual information ratios are substantially lower than predicted by an objective application of the original form of the fundamental law. Specifically, security (i.e., individual stock) selection strategies can be analytically and empirically confirmed to be 45%–91% of original estimates using the fundamental law. Like the refinement for implementation issues associated with constraints as measured by the transfer coefficient, strategy risk reduces expected and average realized information ratios. The higher the uncertainty about forecasting ability, the smaller the likely expected value added.

6.2. Independence of Investment Decisions

As we have discussed, the number of individual assets, N, is not an adequate measure of strategy breadth, BR, when the active returns between individual assets are correlated, as defined by the risk model, and forecasts are not independent from period to period. Specifically, decisions to overweight all the stocks in a given industry or all the countries in a given region because they are responding to similar influences cannot be counted as completely independent decisions, so breadth in these contexts is lower than the number of assets. Similarly, when fundamental law concepts are applied to hedging strategies using derivatives or other forms of arbitrage, breadth can increase well beyond the number of securities.

For example, arbitrage of just two securities—say, a country equity market ETF traded on two different exchanges—can have extremely high breadth (i.e., the expected active return on the strategy is large compared with the active risk). To illustrate, Clarke, de Silva, and Thorley (2006) showed that a practical measure of breadth is

$$\text{BR} = \frac{N}{1 + (N-1)\rho} \tag{19}$$

where ρ is the same correlation coefficient in all the off-diagonal elements of the risk model. For just two securities, $N = 2$, and a correlation coefficient associated with near-arbitrage opportunities, $\rho = -0.8$, breadth could be BR $= 2/[1 - (2 - 1)0.8] = 10.0$ so that information ratios are quite high for even modest values of IC or forecasting skill.

Another example of the limitation of the fundamental law due to the lack of decision independence is the active management of fixed-income portfolios. Most descriptions of the fundamental law are based on individual stock selection strategies where the risk of equity securities is decomposed into systematic and idiosyncratic factors by a risk model. Once the systematic risk factors are removed, the active asset returns (defined as the idiosyncratic returns) are essentially independent, so breadth can be more easily determined. In contrast, almost all bonds represent some form of duration risk, as well as credit risk and optionality, so returns are highly correlated in more subtle ways. In addition, the implicit assumption of normality in the realized return distribution of bonds with default risk and embedded options is clearly unwarranted.

The limitation of independent decisions within the fundamental law also affects time-series implementation. In particular, increasing the rebalancing frequency may increase the realized information ratio but only to the extent that sequential active return forecasts are independent from period to period. Refinements on the concept of breadth—for example, Buckle (2004)—have improved the cross-sectional operationalization of the fundamental law, but more work is needed to provide conceptually useful modifications of the fundamental law in a multi-period, multi-asset setting.

In summary, the fundamental law is a useful conceptual framework in many active management applications and can even produce operational measurements of the essential elements of an active management strategy. But an understanding of the limitations of the law is warranted—particularly the issues of uncertainty in the level of assumed skill and the measurement of breadth in the face of time-dependent rebalancing policies and multi-period optimization.

EXAMPLE 10   Limitations of the Fundamental Law

Consider an active portfolio management strategy of selecting individual stocks in the S&P 500 on a monthly basis. The investor does a quick calculation of the fundamental law based on an information coefficient of $IC = 0.05$ and $BR = 12 \times 500 = 6,000$, giving an astounding information ratio of $IR = 3.87$. In other words, at an active portfolio risk of 3.0%, the expected active return would be $3.87(3.0) = 11.6\%$.

Provide at least two different explanations of *why* the information ratio in this example could be too high based on practical limitations of the fundamental law.

Solution: Potential answers include the following:

1. Cross-sectional dependence: The active returns on the 500 stocks in the S&P 500 are probably correlated, so the number of independent monthly decisions is lower than 500. For example, the investor could be forecasting outperformance of all the stocks in a given industrial sector and underperformance of all the stocks in another sector.
2. Time-series dependence: The decisions on any particular stock may be correlated from month to month. For example, the forecasting process might be based on the earnings yield (reported EPS over price), which changes slowly over time. A stock that is forecasted to outperform in one month is likely to retain the outperformance forecast for several months in a row.
3. Uncertainty: Although an information coefficient of 0.05 appears to be modest, the basic form of the fundamental law does not account for uncertainty in the information coefficient or the likelihood that the information coefficient changes over time and could be different for different sets of stocks.
4. Constraints: An answer that involves accounting for such constraints as long only or turnover limits using a transfer coefficient is a weaker answer because the impact of constraints and the transfer coefficient is a well-known refinement of the fundamental law, even though it does not appear to be used in this example.

---

7. SUMMARY

We have covered a number of key concepts and principles associated with active portfolio management. Active management is based on the mathematics and principles of risk and return from basic mean–variance portfolio theory but with a focus on value added compared with a benchmark portfolio. Critical concepts include the following:

- Value added is defined as the difference between the return on the managed portfolio and the return on a passive benchmark portfolio. This difference in returns might be positive or negative after the fact but would be expected to be positive before the fact or active management would not be justified.

- Value added is related to active weights in the portfolio, defined as differences between the various asset weights in the managed portfolio and their weights in the benchmark portfolio. Individual assets can be overweighted (have positive active weights) or underweighted (have negative active weights), but the complete set of active weights sums to zero.

- Positive value added is generated when positive-active-weight assets have larger returns than negative-active-weight assets. By defining individual asset active returns as the difference between the asset total return and the benchmark return, value added is shown to be positive if and only if end-of-period realized active asset returns are positively correlated with the active asset weights established at the beginning of the period.

- Value added can come from a variety of active portfolio management decisions, including security selection, asset class allocation, and even further decompositions into economic sector weightings and geographic or country weights.

- The Sharpe ratio measures reward per unit of risk in absolute returns, whereas the information ratio measures reward per unit of risk in benchmark relative returns. Either ratio can be applied *ex ante* to expected returns or *ex post* to realized returns. The information ratio is a key criterion on which to evaluate actively managed portfolios.

- Higher information ratio portfolios can be used to create higher Sharpe ratio portfolios. The optimal amount of active management that maximizes a portfolio's Sharpe ratio is positively related to the assumed forecasting accuracy or *ex ante* information coefficient of the active strategy.

- The active risk of an actively managed strategy can be adjusted to its desired level by combining it with a position in the benchmark. Furthermore, once an investor has identified the maximum Sharpe ratio portfolio, the total volatility of a portfolio can be adjusted to its desired level by combining it with cash (two-fund separation concept).

- The fundamental law of active portfolio management began as a conceptual framework for evaluating the potential value added of various investment strategies, but it has also emerged as an operational system for measuring the essential components of those active strategies.

- Although the fundamental law provides a framework for analyzing investment strategies, the essential inputs of forecasted asset returns and risks still require judgment in formulating the expected returns.

- The fundamental law separates the expected value added, or portfolio return relative to the benchmark return, into the basic elements of the strategy:
  - *skill* as measured by the information coefficient,
  - *structuring* of the portfolio as measured by the transfer coefficient,
  - *breadth* of the strategy measured by the number of independent decisions per year, and
  - *aggressiveness* measured by the benchmark tracking risk.
  The last three of these four elements may be beyond the control of the investor if they are specified by investment policy or constrained by regulation.

- The fundamental law has been applied in settings that include the selection of country equity markets in a global equity fund and the timing of credit and duration exposures in a fixed-income fund.

- The fundamental law of active management has limitations, including uncertainty about the *ex ante* information coefficient and the conceptual definition of breadth as the number of independent decisions by the investor.

REFERENCES

Black, Fischer, and Robert Litterman. 1992. "Global Portfolio Optimization." *Financial Analysts Journal* 48 (5): 28–43.

Buckle, David. 2004. "How to Calculate Breadth: An Evolution of the Fundamental Law of Active Portfolio Management." *Journal of Asset Management* 4 (6): 393–405.

Clarke, Roger, Harindra de Silva, and Steven Thorley. 2002. "Portfolio Constraints and the Fundamental Law of Active Management." *Financial Analysts Journal* 58 (5): 48–66.

Clarke, Roger, Harindra de Silva, and Steven Thorley. 2005. "Performance Attribution and the Fundamental Law." *Financial Analysts Journal* 61 (5): 70–83.

Clarke, Roger, Harindra de Silva, and Steven Thorley. 2006. "The Fundamental Law of Active Portfolio Management." *Journal of Investment Management* 4 (3): 54–72.

Cremers, K.J. Martijn, and Antti Petajisto. 2009. "How Active Is Your Fund Manager?" *Review of Financial Studies* 22 (9): 3329–65.

Elton, Edward, and Martin Gruber. 1973. "Estimating the Dependence Structure of Share Prices." *Journal of Finance* 28 (5): 1203–32.

Fischer, Bernd, and Russell Wermers. 2013. *Performance Evaluation and Attribution of Security Portfolios.* Oxford, UK: Elsevier Inc.

Grinold, Richard C. 1989. "The Fundamental Law of Active Management." *Journal of Portfolio Management* 15 (3): 30–37.

Grinold, Richard C. 1994. "Alpha Is Volatility Times IC Times Score, or Real Alphas Don't Get Eaten." *Journal of Portfolio Management* 20 (4): 9–16.

Grinold, Richard C., and Ronald N. Kahn. 1999. *Active Portfolio Management: A Quantitative Approach for Providing Superior Returns and Controlling Risk.* 2nd ed. New York: McGraw-Hill.

Markowitz, Harry M. 1952. "Portfolio Selection." *Journal of Finance* 7 (1): 77–91.

Qian, Edward, and Ronald Hua. 2004. "Active Risk and Information Ratio." *Journal of Investment Management* 2 (3): 20–34.

Sharpe, William F. 1964. "Capital Asset Prices: A Theory of Market Equilibrium under Conditions of Risk." *Journal of Finance* 19 (3): 425–42.

Treynor, J., and Fischer Black. 1973. "How to Use Security Analysis to Improve Portfolio Selection." *Journal of Business* 46: 66–86.

PRACTICE PROBLEMS

1. Wei Liu makes two statements about active portfolio management:

   Statement 1. The "active return" of an actively managed portfolio is the difference between the portfolio's return and the return on the benchmark portfolio, and it is equal to the managed portfolio's alpha.

   Statement 2. The active weights are the differences in the managed portfolio's weights and the benchmark's weights.

   Are Liu's statements correct?

   A. Only Statement 1 is correct.

   B. Only Statement 2 is correct.

   C. Both statements are correct.

2. The benchmark weights and returns for each of the five stocks in the Capitol Index are given in the following table. The Tukol Fund uses the Capitol Index as its benchmark, and the fund's portfolio weights are also shown in the table.

Stock	Portfolio Weight (%)	Benchmark Weight (%)	20X2 Return (%)
1	30	24	14
2	30	20	15
3	20	20	12
4	10	18	8
5	10	18	10

What is the value added (active return) for the Tukol Fund?
A. 0.00%
B. 0.90%
C. 1.92%

3. Consider the following asset class returns for calendar year 20X2:

Asset Class	Portfolio Weight (%)	Benchmark Weight (%)	Portfolio Return (%)	Benchmark Return (%)
Domestic equities	55	40	10	8
International equities	20	30	10	9
Bonds	25	30	5	6

What is the value added (or active return) for the managed portfolio?
A. 0.25%
B. 0.35%
C. 1.05%

4. Gertrude Fischer mentions two properties of the Sharpe ratio and the information ratio that she says are very useful.

Property 1. The Sharpe ratio is unaffected by the addition of cash or leverage in a portfolio.

Property 2. The information ratio for an unconstrained portfolio is unaffected by the aggressiveness of the active weights.

Are Fischer's two properties correct?
A. Yes.
B. No. Only Property 1 is correct.
C. No. Only Property 2 is correct.

The following information relates to Questions 5 and 6

	S&P 500	Indigo Fund
Expected annual return	9.0%	10.5%
Return standard deviation	18.0%	25.0%
Sharpe ratio	0.333	0.30
Active return		1.2%
Active risk		8.0%
Information ratio		0.15

Note: Data are based on a risk-free rate of 2.3%.

5. What is the maximum Sharpe ratio that a manager can achieve by combining the S&P 500 benchmark portfolio and the Indigo Fund?
   A. 0.333
   B. 0.365
   C. 0.448

6. Which of the following pairs of weights would be used to achieve the highest Sharpe ratio and optimal amount of active risk through combining the Indigo Fund and benchmark portfolio, respectively?
   A. 1.014 on Indigo and −0.014 on the benchmark
   B. 1.450 on Indigo and −0.450 on the benchmark
   C. 1.500 on Indigo and −0.500 on the benchmark

7. The benchmark portfolio is the S&P 500. Which of the following three portfolios can be combined with the benchmark portfolio to produce the highest combined Sharpe ratio?

	S&P 500	Portfolio A	Portfolio B	Portfolio C
Expected annual return	9.0%	10.0%	9.5%	9.0%
Return standard deviation	18.0%	20.0%	20.0%	18.0%
Sharpe ratio	0.333	0.350	0.325	0.333
Active return	0	1.0%	0.5%	0
Active risk	0	10.0%	3.0%	2.0%

Note: Data are based on a risk-free rate of 2.3%.
   A. Portfolio A
   B. Portfolio B
   C. Portfolio C

8. Based on the fundamental law of active management, if a portfolio manager has an information ratio of 0.75, an information coefficient of 0.1819, and a transfer coefficient of 1.0, how many securities are in the portfolio manager's fund, making the assumption that the active returns are uncorrelated.
   A. About 2
   B. About 4
   C. About 17

9. Two analysts make the following statements about the transfer coefficient in the expanded fundamental law of active management:

Analyst One says, "The transfer coefficient measures how well the realized returns correlate with the anticipated returns, adjusted for risk."

Analyst Two says, "The transfer coefficient measures how well the realized returns correlate with the active weights, adjusted for risk."

Which, if either, analyst is correct?
   A. Only Analyst One is correct.
   B. Only Analyst Two is correct.
   C. Neither analyst is correct.

10. The expanded fundamental law of active management is stated as follows:

$$E(R_A) = (TC)(IC)\sqrt{BR}\sigma_A$$

Which component on the righthand side represents the extent to which the portfolio manager's expectations are realized? The
   A. transfer coefficient, TC.
   B. information coefficient, IC.
   C. breadth, BR.

11. An analyst is given the following information about a portfolio and its benchmark. In particular, the analyst is concerned that the portfolio is a closet index fund. The T-bill return chosen to represent the risk-free rate is 0.50%.

	Benchmark	Portfolio
Return	8.75%	8.90%
Risk	17.50%	17.60%
Active return	0.00%	0.15%
Active risk	0.00%	0.79%
Sharpe ratio	0.4714	0.4773
Information ratio	N/A	0.1896

Which of the following three statements *does not* justify your belief that the portfolio is a closet index?
   I. The Sharpe ratio of the portfolio is close to the Sharpe ratio of the benchmark.
   II. The information ratio of the portfolio is relatively small.
   III. The active risk of the portfolio is very low.
   A. Statement I
   B. Statement II
   C. Statement III

12. You are considering three managers for a small-cap growth mandate. After careful analysis, you produce the following forward-looking expectations about the managers' active risk and active return:

	Manager A	Manager B	Manager C
Active return	0.7%	0.6%	1.2%
Active risk	3.2%	3.1%	6.3%

    If you intend to rely on the information ratio to make your decision, which manager should you choose?
    A. Manager A
    B. Manager B
    C. Manager C

13. You have a portfolio 100% allocated to a manager with an *ex post*, active risk at 8.0%. You choose to allocate a 75% position to the active manager and 25% to the benchmark to bring the portfolio back to your target active risk of 6.0%. If the manager's information ratio is 0.50, what happens to the information ratio of the portfolio after the reallocation?
    A. The information ratio increases because the lower active risk reduces the denominator of the ratio.
    B. The information ratio remains unchanged because allocations between the active portfolio and the benchmark don't affect the information ratio.
    C. The information ratio decreases because allocating some of the portfolio to the benchmark means that the external manager generates less active return.

The following information relates to Questions 14 and 15

You are analyzing three investment managers for a new mandate. The following table provides the managers' ex-ante active return expectations and portfolio weights. The last two columns include the risk and the *ex post*, realized active returns for the four stocks. Use the following data for the following two questions:

	Manager 1		Manager 2		Manager 3		Risk	Realized R_A
	Δw	$E(R_A)$	Δw	$E(R_A)$	Δw	$E(R_A)$		
Security 1	−0.125	0.03	0.2	0.04	−0.05	0.025	0.17	0.06
Security 2	0.025	0.04	0	0.01	0.05	0.015	0.10	0.07
Security 3	0.075	0.05	−0.1	0	0.05	0.005	0.12	0.04
Security 4	0.025	0.06	−0.1	0.02	−0.05	0.015	0.25	0.02

14. Suppose all three managers claim to be good at forecasting returns. According to the expanded fundamental law of active management, which manager is the best at efficiently building portfolios by anticipating future returns?
    A. Manager 1
    B. Manager 2
    C. Manager 3

15. Suppose all three managers claim to be efficient in portfolio construction. According to the expanded fundamental law of active management, which manager is the best at building portfolios to make full use of their ability to correctly anticipate returns?
    A. Manager 1
    B. Manager 2
    C. Manager 3

16. Manager 1 has an information coefficient of 0.15, a transfer coefficient of 1.0, and invests in 50 securities. Manager 2 has a different strategy, investing in more securities; however, he is subject to investment constraints that reduce his transfer coefficient. Manager 2 has an information coefficient of 0.10, a transfer coefficient of 0.8, and invests in 100 securities. The investment selections of each manager are independent decisions. If both managers target an active risk of 5.0%, which manager will have the greater expected active return?
    A. Manager 1
    B. Manager 2
    C. Both managers will have the same active return.

17. Nick Young is concerned that Goudon Partners, one of his money managers, overestimates its expected active return because Goudon overstates its strategy breadth. Young makes two notes about his concern:
    Note 1.   Although Goudon claims that the number of independent asset decisions is high because it uses 200 stocks, many of these stocks cluster in industries where the same general analysis applies to several stocks.
    Note 2.   Goudon claims that each stock is independent and evaluated each month, or 12 times per year. These analyses are not independent because some of their strategies, such as favoring a particular industry or favoring value stocks, persist beyond one month. For example, a strategy of favoring low-P/E stocks will persist for several months and the investment decisions are not independent.
    If his judgments are correct, are Young's notes about the overstatement of breadth correct?
    A. Only Note 1 is correct.
    B. Only Note 2 is correct.
    C. Both Notes 1 and 2 are correct.

18. Caramel Associates uses the fundamental law to estimate its expected active returns. Two things have changed. First, Caramel will lower its estimate of the information coefficient because they felt their prior estimates reflected overconfidence. Second, their major clients have relaxed several constraints on their portfolios—including social screens, prohibitions on short selling, and constraints on turnover. Which of these changes will increase the expected active return?
    A. Only the lower information coefficient.
    B. Only the relaxation of several portfolio constraints.
    C. Both the lower information coefficient and the relaxation of portfolio constraints.

The following information relates to Questions 19–25

James Frazee is chief investment officer at H&F Capital Investors. Frazee hires a third-party adviser to develop a custom benchmark for three actively managed balanced funds he oversees: Fund X, Fund Y, and Fund Z. (Balanced funds are funds invested in equities and bonds.) The benchmark needs to be composed of 60% global equities and 40% global bonds. The third-party adviser submits the proposed benchmark to Frazee, who rejects the benchmark based on the following concerns:

Concern 1. Many securities he wants to purchase are not included in the benchmark portfolio.
Concern 2. One position in the benchmark portfolio will be somewhat costly to replicate.
Concern 3. The benchmark portfolio is a float-adjusted, capitalization-weighted portfolio.

After the third-party adviser makes adjustments to the benchmark to alleviate Frazee's concerns, Frazee accepts the benchmark portfolio. He then asks his research staff to develop risk and expected return forecasts for Funds X, Y, and Z as well as for the benchmark. The forecasts are presented in Exhibit 1.

EXHIBIT 1   Forecasted Portfolio Statistics for Funds X, Y, and Z and the Benchmark

	Fund X	Fund Y	Fund Z	Benchmark
Portfolio weights:				
Global equities (%)	60.0	65.0	68.0	60.0
Global bonds (%)	40.0	35.0	32.0	40.0
Expected return (%)	10.0	11.6	13.2	9.4
Expected volatility (%)	17.1	18.7	22.2	16.3
Active risk (%)	5.2	9.2	15.1	N/A
Sharpe ratio (SR)	0.45	0.50	0.49	0.44

Note: Data are based on a risk-free rate of 2.3%.

Frazee decides to add a fourth offering to his group of funds, Fund W, which will use the same benchmark as in Exhibit 1. Frazee estimates Fund W's information ratio to be 0.35. He is considering adding the following constraint to his portfolio construction model: Fund W would now have maximum over- and underweight constraints of 7% on single-country positions.

Frazee conducts a search to hire a manager for the global equity portion of Fund W and identifies three candidates. He asks the candidates to prepare risk and return forecasts relative to Fund W's benchmark based on their investment strategy, with the only constraint being no short selling. Each candidate develops independent annual forecasts with active return projections that are uncorrelated and constructs a portfolio made up of stocks that are diverse both geographically and across economic sectors. Selected data for the three candidates' portfolios are presented in Exhibit 2.

EXHIBIT 2   Forecasted Portfolio Data for Equity Portion of Fund W

	Candidate A	Candidate B	Candidate C
Rebalancing	Annually	Annually	Annually
Number of securities	100	64	36
Information ratio (IR)	0.582	0.746	0.723
Transfer coefficient (TC)	0.832	0.777	0.548
Information coefficient*	0.07	0.12	0.22

* Information coefficient based on previously managed funds.

Frazee asks Candidate C to re-evaluate portfolio data given the following changes:

Change 1: Fix the number of securities to 50.
Change 2: Rebalance on a semi-annual basis.
Change 3: Add maximum over- or underweight constraints on sector weightings.

19. Which of Frazee's concerns *best* justifies his decision to reject the proposed benchmark?
    A. Concern 1
    B. Concern 2
    C. Concern 3

20. Based on Exhibit 1, the expected active return from asset allocation for Fund X is:
    A. negative.
    B. zero.
    C. positive.

21. Based on Exhibit 1, which fund is expected to produce the greatest consistency of active return?
    A. Fund X
    B. Fund Y
    C. Fund Z

22. Based on Exhibit 1, combining Fund W with a fund that replicates the benchmark would produce a Sharpe ratio *closest* to:
    A. 0.44.
    B. 0.56.
    C. 0.89.

23. If Frazee added the assumption he is considering in Fund W's portfolio construction, it would *most likely* result in:
    A. a decrease in the optimal aggressiveness of the active strategy.
    B. the information ratio becoming invariant to the level of active risk.
    C. an increase in the transfer of active return forecasts into active weights.

24. Based on the data presented in Exhibit 2, the candidate with the greatest skill at achieving active returns appears to be:
    A. Candidate A.
    B. Candidate B.
    C. Candidate C.

25. Which proposed change to Fund W would *most likely* decrease Candidate C's information ratio?
    A. Change 1
    B. Change 2
    C. Change 3

The following information relates to Questions 26–29

John Martinez is assessing the performance of the actively managed diversified asset portfolio. The diversified asset portfolio is invested in equities, bonds, and real estate, and allocations to these asset classes and to the holdings within them are unconstrained.

Selected return and financial data for the portfolio for 2019 are presented in Exhibit 1.

EXHIBIT 1   Diversified Asset Portfolio 2019 Portfolio Performance

	Sub-Portfolio Return (%)	Benchmark Return (%)	Portfolio Allocation (%)	Strategic Asset Allocation (%)
Equities sub-portfolio	36.9	31.6	63	60
Bond sub-portfolio	−2.4	−2.6	28	35
Real estate sub-portfolio	33.4	28.3	9	5

Martinez uses several risk-adjusted return metrics to assess the performance of the diversified asset portfolio, including the information ratio and the Sharpe ratio. Selected risk, return, and statistical data for the portfolio are presented in Exhibit 2.

EXHIBIT 2   Diversified Asset Portfolio Data, 2000-2019

	Transfer Coefficient (TC)	Information Coefficient (IC)	Breadth (BR)
Equities sub-portfolio	0.90	0.091	21
Bond sub-portfolio	0.79	0.087	23
Real estate sub-portfolio	0.86	0.093	19

Martinez has recently hired Kenneth Singh to help him evaluate portfolios. Martinez asks Singh about the possible effects on the portfolio's information ratio if cash were added to the diversified asset portfolio or if the aggressiveness of the portfolio's active weights were increased. Singh responds with two statements:

Statement 1.   Adding cash to the portfolio would change the portfolio's information ratio.
Statement 2.   Increasing the aggressiveness of active weights would not change the portfolio's information ratio.

26. Based on Exhibit 1, the value added to the diversified asset portfolio attributable to the security selection decision in 2019 was *closest* to:
    A. 2.3%.
    B. 3.9%.
    C. 6.1%.

27. Based on Exhibit 1, the value added of the diversified asset portfolio attributable to the asset allocation decision in 2019 was *closest* to:
    A. 2.3%.
    B. 3.9%.
    C. 6.1%.

28. Based on data in Exhibit 2 and using the information ratio as the criterion for evaluating performance, which sub-portfolio had the best performance in the period 2000–2019?
    A. The bond sub-portfolio.
    B. The equities sub-portfolio.
    C. The real estate sub-portfolio.

29. Which of Singh's statements regarding the information ratio is correct?
    A. Only Statement 1
    B. Only Statement 2
    C. Both Statement 1 and Statement 2

CHAPTER 6

ACTIVE EQUITY INVESTING: STRATEGIES

Bing Li, PhD, CFA
Yin Luo, CPA, PStat, CFA
Pranay Gupta, CFA

LEARNING OUTCOMES

The candidate should be able to:

- compare fundamental and quantitative approaches to active management;
- analyze bottom-up active strategies, including their rationale and associated processes;
- analyze top-down active strategies, including their rationale and associated processes;
- analyze factor-based active strategies, including their rationale and associated processes;
- analyze activist strategies, including their rationale and associated processes;
- describe active strategies based on statistical arbitrage and market microstructure;
- describe how fundamental active investment strategies are created;
- describe how quantitative active investment strategies are created;
- discuss equity investment style classifications.

1. INTRODUCTION

This chapter provides an overview of active equity investing and the major types of active equity strategies. The chapter is organized around a classification of active equity strategies into two broad approaches: fundamental and quantitative. Both approaches aim at outperforming a passive benchmark (for example, a broad equity market index), but they tend to make investment decisions differently. Fundamental approaches stress the use of human judgment in processing information and making investment decisions, whereas quantitative approaches tend to rely more heavily on rules-based quantitative models. As a

Portfolio Management, Second Edition, by Bing Li, PhD, CFA, Yin Luo, CPA, PStat, CFA, and Pranay Gupta, CFA. Copyright © 2018 by CFA Institute.

result, some practitioners and academics refer to the fundamental, judgment-based approaches as "discretionary" and to the rules-based, quantitative approaches as "systematic."

This chapter is organized as follows. Section 2 introduces fundamental and quantitative approaches to active management. Section 3 discusses bottom-up, top-down, factor-based, and activist investing strategies. Section 4 describes the process of creating fundamental active investment strategies, including the parameters to consider as well as some of the pitfalls. Section 5 describes the steps required to create quantitative active investment strategies, as well as the pitfalls in a quantitative investment process. Section 6 discusses style classifications of active strategies and the uses and limitations of such classifications. A summary of key points completes the chapter.

2. APPROACHES TO ACTIVE MANAGEMENT

Active equity investing may reflect a variety of ideas about profitable investment opportunities. However, with regard to how these investment ideas are implemented—for example, how securities are selected—active strategies can be divided into two broad categories: fundamental and quantitative. Fundamental approaches are based on research into companies, sectors, or markets and involve the application of analyst discretion and judgment. In contrast, quantitative approaches are based on quantitative models of security returns that are applied systematically with limited involvement of human judgment or discretion. The labels *fundamental* and *quantitative* in this context are an imperfect shorthand that should not be misunderstood. The contrast with quantitative approaches does not mean that fundamental approaches do not use quantitative tools. Fundamental approaches often make use of valuation models (such as the free cash flow model), quantitative screening tools, and statistical techniques (e.g., regression analysis). Furthermore, quantitative approaches often make use of variables that relate to company fundamentals. Some investment disciplines may be viewed as hybrids in that they combine elements of both fundamental and quantitative disciplines. In the next sections, we examine these two approaches more closely.

Fundamental research forms the basis of the fundamental approach to investing. Although it can be organized in many ways, fundamental research consistently involves and often begins with the analysis of a company's financial statements. Through such an analysis, this approach seeks to obtain a detailed understanding of the company's current and past profitability, financial position, and cash flows. Along with insights into a company's business model, management team, product lines, and economic outlook, this analysis provides a view on the company's future business prospects and includes a valuation of its shares. Estimates are typically made of the stock's intrinsic value and/or its relative value compared to the shares of a peer group or the stock's own history of market valuations. Based on this valuation and other factors (including overall portfolio considerations), the portfolio manager may conclude that the stock should be bought (or a position increased) or sold (or a position reduced). The decision can also be stated in terms of overweighting, market weighting, or underweighting relative to the portfolio's benchmark.

In the search for investment opportunities, fundamental strategies may have various starting points. Some strategies start at a top or macro level—with analyses of markets, economies, or industries—to narrow the search for likely areas for profitable active investment. These are called top-down strategies. Other strategies, often referred to as bottom-up strategies, make little or no use of macro analysis and instead rely on individual stock analysis to identify areas of opportunity. Research distributed by investment banks and reports produced by internal analysts, organized by industry or economic sector, are also potential sources of investment ideas. The vetting of such ideas may be done by portfolio managers, who may themselves be involved in fundamental research, or by an investment committee.

Quantitative strategies, on the other hand, involve analyst judgment at the design stage, but they largely replace the ongoing reliance on human judgment and discretion with systematic processes that are often dependent on computer programming for execution. These systematic processes search for security and market characteristics and patterns that have predictive power in order to identify securities or trades that will earn superior investment returns. ("Superior" in the sense of expected added value relative to risk or expected return relative to a benchmark—for example, an index benchmark or peer benchmark.) Variables that might be considered include valuation metrics (e.g., earnings yield), size (e.g., market capitalization), profitability metrics (e.g., return on equity), financial strength metrics (e.g., debt-to-equity ratio), market sentiment (e.g., analyst consensus on companies' long-term earnings growth), industry membership (e.g., stocks' GICS classification), and price-related attributes (e.g., price momentum).

Once a pattern or relationship between a given variable (or set of variables) and security prices has been established by analysis of past data, a quantitative model is used to predict future expected returns of securities or baskets of securities. Security selection then flows from expected returns, which reflect securities' exposures to the selected variables with predictive power.[1] From a quantitative perspective, investment success depends not on individual company insights but on model quality.

Exhibit 1 presents typical differences between the main characteristics of fundamental and quantitative methodologies.

EXHIBIT 1   Differences between Fundamental and Quantitative Approaches

	Fundamental	**Quantitative**
Style	Subjective	Objective
Decision-making process	Discretionary	Systematic, non-discretionary
Primary resources	Human skill, experience, judgment	Expertise in statistical modeling
Information used	Research (company/industry/economy)	Data and statistics
Analysis focus	Conviction (high depth) in stock-, sector-, or region-based selection	A selection of variables, subsequently applied broadly over a large number of securities
Orientation to data	Forecast future corporate parameters and establish views on companies	Attempt to draw conclusions from a variety of historical data
Portfolio construction	Use judgment and conviction within permissible risk parameters	Use optimizers

[1]A wide range of security characteristics have been used to define "factors." Some factors (most commonly, size, value, momentum, and quality) have been shown to be positively associated with a long-term return premium. These we call *rewarded* factors. Many other factors are used in portfolio construction but have not been empirically proven to offer a persistent return premium. Some call these *unrewarded* factors. The average investor doesn't typically distinguish between rewarded and unrewarded factors, but it is important to draw that distinction for the sake of clarity across curriculum chapters.

In the following section, we take a closer look at some of the distinguishing characteristics listed in Exhibit 1 and how they are evolving with the advent of new technologies available to investors.

2.1. Differences in the Nature of the Information Used

To contrast the information used in fundamental and quantitative strategies, we can start by describing typical activities for fundamental investors with a bottom-up investment discipline. Bottom-up fundamental analysts research and analyze a company, using data from company financial statements and disclosures to assess attributes such as profitability, leverage, and absolute or peer-relative valuation. They typically also assess how those metrics compare to their historical values to identify trends and scrutinize such characteristics as the company's management competence, its future prospects, and the competitive position of its product lines. Such analysts usually focus on the more recent financial statements (which include current and previous years' accounting data), notes to the financial statements and assumptions in the accounts, and management discussion and analysis disclosures. Corporate governance is often taken into consideration as well as wider environmental, social, and governance (ESG) characteristics.

Top-down fundamental investors' research focuses first on region, country, or sector information (e.g., economic growth, money supply, and market valuations). Some of the data used by fundamental managers can be measured or expressed numerically and therefore "quantified." Other items, such as management quality and reputation, cannot.

Quantitative approaches often use large amounts of historical data from companies' financial reports (in addition to other information, such as return data) but process those data in a systematic rather than a judgmental way. Judgment is used in model building, particularly in deciding which variables and signals are relevant. Typically, quantitative approaches use historical stock data and statistical techniques to identify variables that may have a statistically significant relationship with stock returns; then these relationships are used to predict individual security returns. In contrast to the fundamental approach, the quantitative approach does not normally consider information or characteristics that cannot be quantified. In order to minimize survivorship and look-ahead biases, historical data used in quantitative research should include stocks that are no longer listed, and accounting data used should be the original, un-restated numbers that were available to the market at that point in time.

Investment Process: Fundamental vs. Quantitative

The goal of the investment process is to construct a portfolio that best reflects the stated investment objective and risk tolerance, with an optimal balance between expected return and risk exposure, subject to the constraints imposed by the investment policy. The investment processes under both fundamental and quantitative approaches involve a number of considerations, such as the methodology and valuation process, which are the subject of this chapter. Other considerations, such as portfolio construction and risk management, trade execution, and ongoing performance monitoring, are the subjects of subsequent curriculum chapters.

	Fundamental	**Quantitative**
Methodology	Determine methodology to evaluate stocks (bottom-up or top-down, value or growth, income or deep value, intrinsic or relative value, etc.)	Define model to estimate expected stock returns (choose time-series macro-level factors or cross-sectional stock-level factors, identify factors that have a stable positive information coefficient IC, use a factor combination algorithm, etc.)
Valuation process	• Prescreen to identify potential investment candidates with stringent financial and market criteria • Perform in-depth analysis of companies to derive their intrinsic values • Determine buy or sell candidates trading at a discount or premium to their intrinsic values	• Construct factor exposures across all shares in the same industry • Forecast IC and/or its volatility for each factor by using algorithms (such as artificial intelligence or time-series analysis) or fundamental research • Combine factor exposures to estimate expected returns
Portfolio construction and rebalancing	• Allocate assets by determining industry and country/region exposures • Set limits on maximum sector, country, and individual stock positions • Determine buy-and-sell list • Monitor portfolio holdings continuously	• Determine which factors to underweight or overweight • Use risk model to measure *ex ante* active risk • Run portfolio optimization with risk model, investment, and risk constraints, as well as the structure of transaction costs • Rebalance at regular intervals

2.2. Differences in the Focus of the Analysis

Fundamental investors usually focus their attention on a relatively small group of stocks and perform in-depth analysis on each one of them. This practice has characteristically given fundamental (or "discretionary") investors an edge of depth in understanding individual companies' businesses over quantitative (or "systematic") investors, who do not focus on individual stocks. Quantitative investors instead usually focus on factors across a potentially very large group of stocks. Therefore, fundamental investors tend to take larger positions in their selected stocks, while quantitative investors tend to focus their analysis on a selection of factors but spread their selected factor bets across a substantially larger group of holdings.[2]

---

[2]The implications for portfolio risk of using individual stocks or factors will be considered in the chapter on portfolio construction.

2.3. Difference in Orientation to the Data: Forecasting the Future vs. Analyzing the Past

Fundamental analysis places an emphasis on forecasting future prospects, including the future earnings and cash flows of a company. Fundamental investors use judgment and in-depth analysis to formulate a view of the company's outlook and to identify the catalysts that will generate future growth. They rely on knowledge, experience, and their ability to predict future conditions in a company to make investment decisions. Conceptually, the fundamental approach aims at forecasting forward parameters in order to make investment decisions.

In contrast, quantitative analysis uses a company's history to arrive at investment decisions. Quantitative investors construct models by backtesting past data, using what is known about or has been reported by a company, including future earnings estimates that have been published by analysts, to search for the best company characteristics for purposes of stock selection. Once a model based on historical data has been finalized, it is applied to the latest available data to determine investment decisions. Conceptually, the quantitative approach aims to predict future returns using conclusions derived from analyzing historical data.

Forestalling Look-Ahead Bias

Satyam Computers is an India-based company that provides IT consulting and solutions to its global customers. In the eight years preceding 2009, Satyam overstated its revenues and profits and reported a cash holdings total of approximately $1.04 billion that did not exist. The falsification of the accounts came to light in early 2009, and Satyam was removed from the S&P CNX Nifty 50 index on 12 January.

If a quantitative analyst runs a simulation benchmarked against the S&P CNX Nifty 50 index on 31 December 2008, he or she should include the 50 stocks that were in the index on 31 December 2008 and use only the data for the included stocks that were available to investors as of that date. The analyst should therefore include Satyam as an index constituent and use the original accounting data that were published by the company at that time. While it was subsequently proved that these accounting data were fraudulent, this fact was not known to analysts and investors on 31 December 2008. As a result, it would not have been possible for any analyst to incorporate the true accounting data for Satyam on that date.

2.4. Differences in Portfolio Construction: Judgment vs. Optimization

Fundamental investors typically select stocks by performing extensive research on individual companies, which results in a list of high-conviction stocks. Thus, fundamental investors see risk at the company level. There is a risk that the assessment of the company's fair value is inaccurate, that the business's performance will differ from the analyst's expectations, or that the market will fail to recognize the identified reason for under- or overvaluation. Construction of a fundamental portfolio therefore often depends on judgment, whereby the absolute or index-relative sizes of positions in stocks, sectors, or countries are based on the manager's conviction of his or her forecasts. The portfolio must, of course, still comply with the risk parameters set out in the investment agreements with clients or in the fund prospectus.

In quantitative analysis, on the other hand, the risk is that factor returns will not perform as expected. Because the quantitative approach invests in baskets of stocks, the risks lie at the portfolio level rather than at the level of specific stocks. Construction of a quantitative portfolio is therefore generally done using a portfolio optimizer, which controls for risk at the portfolio level in arriving at individual stock weights.

The two approaches also differ in the way that portfolio changes or rebalancings are performed. Managers using a fundamental approach usually monitor the portfolio's holdings continuously and may increase, decrease, or eliminate positions at any time. Portfolios managed using a quantitative approach are usually rebalanced at regular intervals, such as monthly or quarterly. At each interval, the program or algorithm, using pre-determined rules, automatically selects positions to be sold, reduced, added, or increased.

EXAMPLE 1   Fundamental vs. Quantitative Approach

Consider two equity portfolios with the same benchmark index, the MSCI Asia ex Japan. The index contains 627 stocks as of December 2016. One portfolio is managed using a fundamental approach, while the other is managed using a quantitative approach. The fundamental approach–based portfolio is made up of 50 individually selected stocks, which are reviewed for potential sale or trimming on an ongoing basis. In the fundamental approach, the investment universe is first pre-screened by valuation and by the fundamental metrics of earnings yield, dividend yield, earnings growth, and financial leverage. The quantitative approach–based portfolio makes active bets on 400 stocks with monthly rebalancing. The particular approach used is based on a five-factor model of equity returns.

Contrast fundamental and quantitative investment processes with respect to the following:

1. Constructing the portfolio
2. Rebalancing the portfolio

Solution to 1: Fundamental: Construct the portfolio by overweighting stocks that are expected to outperform their peers or the market as a whole. Where necessary for risk reduction, underweight some benchmark stocks that are expected to underperform. The stocks that fell out in the pre-screening process do not have explicit forecasts and will not be included in the portfolio.

Quantitative: Construct the portfolio by maximizing the objective function (such as portfolio alpha or information ratio) with risk models.

Solution to 2: Fundamental: The manager monitors each stock continuously and sells stocks when their market prices surpass the target prices (either through appreciation of the stock price or through reduction of the target price due to changes in expectations).

Quantitative: Portfolios are usually rebalanced at regular intervals, such as monthly.

3. TYPES OF ACTIVE MANAGEMENT STRATEGIES

Equity investors have developed many different techniques for processing all the information necessary to arrive at an investment decision. Multiple approaches may be taken into account in formulating an overall opinion of a stock; however, each analyst will have his or her own set of favorite techniques based on his or her experience and judgment. Depending on the specifics of the investment discipline, most fundamental and quantitative strategies can be characterized as either bottom-up or top-down.

3.1. Bottom-Up Strategies

Bottom-up strategies begin the asset selection process with data at the individual asset and company level, such as price momentum and profitability. Bottom-up quantitative investors harness computer power to apply their models to this asset- and company-level information (with the added requirement that the information be quantifiable). The balance of this section illustrates the bottom-up process as used by fundamental investors. These investors typically begin their analysis at the company level before forming an opinion on the wider sector or market. The ability to identify companies with strong or weak fundamentals depends on the analyst's in-depth knowledge of each company's industry, product lines, business plan, management abilities, and financial strength. After identifying individual companies, the bottom-up approach uses economic and financial analysis to assess the intrinsic value of a company and compares that value with the current market price to determine which stocks are undervalued or overvalued. The analyst may also find companies operating efficiently with good prospects even though the industry they belong to is deteriorating. Similarly, companies with poor prospects may be found in otherwise healthy and prosperous industries.

Fundamental investors often focus on one or more of the following parameters for a company, either individually or in relation to its peers:

- business model and branding
- competitive advantages
- company management and corporate governance

Valuation is based on either a discounted cash flow model or a preferred market multiple, often earnings-related. We address each of these parameters and valuation approaches in turn.

Business Model and Branding.
The business model of a company refers to its overall strategy for running the business and generating profit. The business model details how a company converts its resources into products or services and how it delivers those products or services to customers. Companies with a superior business model compete successfully, have scalability, and generate significant earnings. Further, companies with a robust and adaptive business model tend to outperform their peers in terms of return on shareholder equity. The business model gives investors insight into a company's value proposition, its operational flow, the structure of its value chain, its branding strategy, its market segment, and the resulting revenue generation and profit margins. This insight helps investors evaluate the sustainability of the company's competitive advantages and make informed investment decisions.

Corporate branding is a way of defining the company's business for the market in general and retail customers in particular and can be understood as the company's identity as well as its promise to its customers. Strong brand names convey product quality and can give the company an edge over its competitors in both market share and profit margin. It is widely recognized that brand equity plays an important role in the determination of product price, allowing companies to command price premiums after controlling for observed product differentiation. Apple in consumer technology and BMW in motor vehicles, for example, charge more for their products, but customers are willing to pay the premium because of brand loyalty.

Competitive Advantages.
A competitive advantage typically allows a company to outperform its peers in terms of the return it generates on its capital. There are many types of competitive advantage, such as access to natural resources, superior technology, innovation, skilled personnel, corporate reputation, brand strength, high entry barriers, exclusive distribution rights, and superior product or customer support.

For value investors, who search for companies that appear to be trading below their intrinsic value (often following earnings disappointments), it is important to understand the sustainability of the company's competitive position when assessing the prospects for recovery.

Company Management.
A good management team is crucial to a company's success. Management's role is to allocate resources and capital to maximize the growth of enterprise value for the company's shareholders. A management team that has a long-term rather than a short-term focus is more likely to add value to an enterprise over the long term.

To evaluate management effectiveness, one can begin with the financial statements. Return on assets, equity, or invested capital (compared either to industry peers or to historical rates achieved by the company) and earnings growth over a reasonable time period are examples of indicators used to gauge the value added by management.

Qualitative analysis of the company's management and governance structures requires attention to (1) the alignment of management's interests with those of shareholders to minimize agency problems; (2) the competence of management in achieving the company's objectives (as described in the mission statement) and long-term plans; (3) the stability of the management team and the company's ability to attract and retain high-performing executives; and (4) increasingly, risk considerations and opportunities related to a company's ESG attributes. Analysts also monitor management insider purchases and sales of the company's shares for potential indications of the confidence of management in the company's future.

The above qualitative considerations and financial statement analysis will help in making earnings estimates, cash flow estimates, and evaluations of risk, providing inputs to company valuation. Fundamental strategies within the bottom-up category may use a combination of approaches to stock valuation. Some investors rely on discounted cash flow or dividend models. Others focus on relative valuation, often based on earnings-related valuation metrics such as a P/E, price to book (P/B), and enterprise value (EV)/EBITDA. A conclusion that a security's intrinsic value is different from its current market price means the valuation is using estimates that are different from those reflected in current market prices. Conviction that the analyst's forecasts are, over a particular time period, more accurate than the market's is therefore important, as is the belief that the market will reflect the more accurate estimates within a time frame that is consistent with the strategy's investment horizon.

Bottom-up strategies are often broadly categorized as either value-based (or value-oriented) or growth-based (or growth-oriented), as the following section explains.

3.1.1. Value-Based Approaches

Benjamin Graham is regarded as the father of value investing. Along with David Dodd, he wrote the book *Security Analysis* (1934), which laid the basic framework for value investing. Graham posited that buying earnings and assets relatively inexpensively afforded a "margin of safety" necessary for prudent investing. Consistent with that idea, value-based approaches aim to buy stocks that are trading at a significant discount to their estimated intrinsic value. Value investors typically focus on companies with attractive valuation metrics, reflected in low earnings (or asset) multiples. In their view, investors' sometimes irrational behavior can make stocks trade below the intrinsic value based on company fundamentals. Such opportunities may arise due to a variety of behavioral biases and often reflect investors' overreaction to negative news. Various styles of value-based investing are sometimes distinguished; for example, "relative value" investors purchase stocks on valuation multiples that are high relative to historical levels but that compare favorably to those of the peer group.

3.1.1.1. Relative Value

Investors who pursue a relative value strategy evaluate companies by comparing their value indicators (e.g., P/E or P/B multiples) to the average valuation of companies in the same industry sector with the aim of identifying stocks that offer value relative to their sector peers. As different sectors face different market structures and different competitive and regulatory conditions, average sector multiples vary.

Exhibit 2 lists the key financial ratios for sectors in the Hang Seng Index on the last trading day of 2016. The average P/E for companies in the energy sector is almost five times the average P/E for those in real estate. A consumer staples company trading on a P/E of 12 would appear undervalued relative to its sector, while a real estate company trading on the same P/E multiple of 12 would appear overvalued relative to its sector.

EXHIBIT 2   Key Financial Ratios of Hang Seng Index (30 December 2016)

	Weight	Dividend Yield	Price-to-Earnings Ratio (P/E)	Price-to-Cash-Flow Ratio (P/CF)	Price-to-Book Ratio (P/B)	Total Debt to Common Equity (%)	Current Ratio
Hang Seng Index	**100.0**	**3.5**	**12.2**	**6.1**	**1.1**	**128.4**	**1.3**
Consumer discretionary	2.9	4.1	21.3	12.5	3.0	26.3	1.4
Consumer staples	1.6	2.6	16.8	14.3	3.3	62.1	1.4
Energy	7.0	2.6	39.5	3.7	0.9	38.5	1.0
Financials	47.5	4.3	10.1	5.0	1.1	199.8	1.1
Industrials	5.5	3.8	11.8	6.0	0.9	158.7	1.2
Information technology	11.4	0.6	32.7	19.9	8.2	60.2	1.0
Real estate	10.6	3.9	8.3	8.0	0.7	30.3	2.5
Telecommunication services	7.8	3.2	13.3	4.6	1.4	11.5	0.7
Utilities	5.6	3.7	14.2	10.8	1.7	47.0	1.3

Source: Bloomberg.

Investors usually recognize that in addition to the simple comparison of a company's multiple to that of the sector, one needs a good understanding of why the valuation is what it is. A premium or discount to the industry may well be justified by the company's fundamentals.

3.1.1.2. Contrarian Investing
Contrarian investors purchase and sell shares against prevailing market sentiment. Their investment strategy is to go against the crowd by buying poorly performing stocks at valuations they find attractive and then selling them at a later time, following what they expect to be a recovery in the share price. Companies in which contrarian managers invest are frequently depressed cyclical stocks with low or even negative earnings or low dividend payments. Contrarians expect these stocks to rebound once the company's earnings have turned around, resulting in substantial price appreciation.

Contrarian investors often point to research in behavioral finance suggesting that investors tend to overweight recent trends and to follow the crowd in making investment decisions. A contrarian investor attempts to determine whether the valuation of an individual company, industry, or entire market is irrational—that is, undervalued or overvalued at any time—and whether that irrationality represents an exploitable mispricing of shares. Accordingly, contrarian investors tend to go against the crowd.

Both contrarian investors and value investors who do not describe their style as contrarian aim to buy shares at a discount to their intrinsic value. The primary difference between the two is that non-contrarian value investors rely on fundamental metrics to make their assessments, while contrarian investors rely more on market sentiment and sharp price movements (such as 52-week high and low prices as sell and buy prices) to make their decisions.

3.1.1.3. High-Quality Value
Some value-based strategies give valuation close attention but place at least equal emphasis on financial strength and demonstrated profitability. For example, one such investment discipline requires a record of consistent earnings power, above-average return on equity, financial strength, and exemplary management. There is no widely accepted label for this value style, the refinement of which is often associated with investor Warren Buffett.[3]

3.1.1.4. Income Investing
The income investing approach focuses on shares that offer relatively high dividend yields and positive dividend growth rates. Several rationales for this approach have been offered. One argument is that a secure, high dividend yield tends to put a floor under the share price in the case of companies that are expected to maintain such a dividend. Another argument points to empirical studies that demonstrate the higher returns to equities with these characteristics and their greater ability to withstand market declines.

---

[3]See Greenwald, Kahn, Sonkin, and Biema (2001).

3.1.1.5. Deep-Value Investing

A value investor with a deep-value orientation focuses on undervalued companies that are available at extremely low valuation relative to their assets (e.g., low P/B). Such companies are often those in financial distress. The rationale is that market interest in such securities may be limited, increasing the chance of informational inefficiencies. The deep-value investor's special area of expertise may lie in reorganizations or related legislation, providing a better position from which to assess the likelihood of company recovery.

3.1.1.6. Restructuring and Distressed Investing

While the restructuring and distressed investment strategies are more commonly observed in the distressed-debt space, some equity investors specialize in these disciplines. Opportunities in restructuring and distressed investing are generally countercyclical relative to the overall economy or to the business cycle of a particular sector. A weak economy generates increased incidence of companies facing financial distress. When a company is having difficulty meeting its short-term liabilities, it will often propose to restructure its financial obligations or change its capital structure.

Restructuring investors seek to purchase the debt or equity of companies in distress. A distressed company that goes through restructuring may still have valuable assets, distribution channels, or patents that make it an attractive acquisition target. Restructuring investing is often done before an expected bankruptcy or during the bankruptcy process. The goal of restructuring investing is to gain control or substantial influence over a company in distress at a large discount and then restructure it to restore a large part of its intrinsic value.

Effective investment in a distressed company depends on skill and expertise in identifying companies whose situation is better than the market believes it to be. Distressed investors assume that either the company will survive or there will be sufficient assets remaining upon liquidation to generate an appropriate return on investment.

3.1.1.7. Special Situations

The "special situations" investment style focuses on the identification and exploitation of mispricings that may arise as a result of corporate events such as divestitures or spinoffs of assets or divisions or mergers with other entities. In the opinion of many investors, such situations represent short-term opportunities to exploit mispricing that result from such special situations. According to Greenblatt (2010), investors often overlook companies that are in such special situations as restructuring (involving asset disposals or spinoffs) and mergers, which may create opportunities to add value through active investing. To take advantage of such opportunities, this type of investing requires specific knowledge of the industry and the company, as well as legal expertise.

3.1.2. Growth-Based Approaches

Growth-based investment approaches focus on companies that are expected to grow faster than their industry or faster than the overall market, as measured by revenues, earnings, or cash flow. Growth investors usually look for high-quality companies with consistent growth or companies with strong earnings momentum. Characteristics usually examined by growth investors include historical and estimated future growth of earnings or cash flows, underpinned by attributes such as a solid business model, cost control, and exemplary management able to execute long-term plans to achieve higher growth. Such companies typically feature above-average return on equity, a large part of which they retain and reinvest in funding future growth. Because growth companies may also have volatile earnings and cash flows going forward, the intrinsic values calculated by discounting expected future cash flows are subject to relatively high uncertainty. Compared to value-focused investors, growth-focused investors have a higher tolerance for above-average valuation multiples.

GARP (growth at a reasonable price) is a sub-discipline within growth investing. This approach is used by investors who seek out companies with above-average growth that trade at reasonable valuation multiples, and is often referred to as a hybrid of growth and value investing. Many investors who use GARP rely on the P/E-to-growth (PEG) ratio—calculated as the stock's P/E divided by the expected earnings growth rate (in percentage terms)—while also paying attention to variations in risk and duration of growth.

EXAMPLE 2   Characteristic Securities for Bottom-Up Investment Disciplines

The following table provides information on four stocks.

Company	Price	12-Month Forward EPS	3-Year EPS Growth Forecast	Dividend Yield	Industry Sector	Sector Average P/E
A	50	5	20%	1%	Industrial	10
B	56	2	2%	0%	Information technology	35
C	22	10	−5%	2%	Consumer staples	15
D	32	2	2%	8%	Utilities	16

Using only the information given in the table above, for each stock, determine which fundamental investment discipline would most likely select it.

Solution:

- Company A's forward P/E is 50/5 = 10, and its P/E-to-growth ratio (PEG) is 10/20 = 0.5, which is lower than the PEGs for the other companies (28/2 = 14 for Company B, negative for Company C, and 16/2 = 8 for Company D). Given the favorable valuation relative to growth, the company is a good candidate for investors who use GARP.
- Company B's forward P/E is 56/2 = 28, which is lower than the average P/E of 35 for its sector peers. The company is a good candidate for the relative value approach.
- Company C's forward P/E is 22/10 = 2.2, which is considered very low in both absolute and relative terms. Assuming the investor pays attention to company circumstances, the stock could be a good candidate for the deep-value approach.
- Company D's forward P/E is 32/2 = 16, which is the same as its industry average. Company D's earnings are growing slowly at 2%, but the dividend yield of 8% appears high. This combination makes the company a good candidate for income investing.

EXAMPLE 3   Growth vs. Value

Tencent Holdings Limited is a leading provider of value-added internet services in China. The company's services include social networks, web portals, e-commerce, and multiplayer online games.

Exhibit 3 shows an excerpt from an analyst report on Tencent published following the release of the company's Q3 2016 results on 16 November 2016.

EXHIBIT 3   Financial Summary and Valuation for Tencent Holdings Limited

Market Data: 16 November 2016			2014	2015	2016E	2017E	2018E
Closing price	196.9	Revenue (RMB millions)	78,932	102,863	150,996	212,471	276,538
Price target	251.5	YOY (%)	30.60	30.32	46.79	40.71	30.15
HSCEI	9,380	Net income (RMB millions)	23,810	28,806	42,292	56,533	68,994
HSCCI	3,669	YOY (%)	53.49	21.85	46.76	32.87	22.04
52-Week high/low	132.10/ 220.8	EPS (RMB)	2.58	3.10	4.56	6.05	7.39
Market cap (USD millions)	240,311	Diluted EPS (RMB)	2.55	3.06	4.51	5.99	7.31
Market cap (HKD millions)	1,864,045	ROE (%)	29.09	23.84	26.11	26.18	24.71
Shares outstanding (millions)	9,467	Debt/Assets (%)	52.02	60.20	61.33	61.26	60.37
Exchange rate (RMB/HKD)	0.8857	Dividend yield (%)	0.20	0.20	0.28	0.38	0.46
		P/E	54.78	55.17	38.27	28.80	23.60
		P/B	22.31	19.35	13.39	9.99	7.54
		EV/EBITDA	40.79	35.88	28.06	20.09	15.39

Notes: Market data are quoted in HKD; the company's filing is in RMB. Diluted EPS is calculated as if all outstanding convertible securities (such as convertible preferred shares, convertible debentures, stock options, and warrants) were exercised. P/E is calculated as closing price divided by each year's EPS.
Source: SWS Research.

From the perspective of the date of Exhibit 3:

1. Which metrics would support a decision to invest by a growth investor?
2. Which characteristics would a growth investor tend to weigh less heavily than a high-quality value investor?

Solution to 1: A growth investor would focus on the following:

- The year-over-year change in revenue exceeded 30% in 2014 and 2015 and is expected to accelerate over 2016–2018.
- Past and expected net income growth rates are also high.

Solution to 2: A growth investor would tend to be less concerned about the relatively high valuation levels (high P/E, P/B, and EV/EBITDA) and low dividend yield.

3.2. Top-Down Strategies

As the name suggests, in contrast to bottom-up strategies, top-down strategies use an investment process that begins at a top or macro level. Instead of focusing on individual company- and asset-level variables in making investment decisions, top-down portfolio managers study variables affecting many companies, such as the macroeconomic environment, demographic trends, and government policies. These managers often use instruments such as futures contracts, ETFs, swaps, and custom baskets of individual stocks to capture macro dynamics and generate portfolio return. Some bottom-up stock pickers also incorporate top-down analysis as part of their process for arriving at investment decisions. A typical method of incorporating both top-down macroeconomic and bottom-up fundamental processes is to have the portfolio strategist set the target country and sector weights. Portfolio managers then construct stock portfolios that are consistent with these preset weights.

3.2.1. Country and Geographic Allocation to Equities

Investors using country allocation strategies form their portfolios by investing in different geographic regions depending on their assessment of the regions' prospects. For example, the manager may have a preference for a particular region and may establish a position in that region while limiting exposure to others. Managers of global equity funds may, for example, make a decision based on a tradeoff between the US equity market and the European equity market, or they may allocate among all investable country equity markets using futures or ETFs. Such strategies may also seek to track the overall supply and demand for equities in regions or countries by analyzing the aggregate volumes of share buybacks, investment fund flows, the volumes of initial public offerings, and secondary share issuance.

The country or geographic allocation decision itself can be based on both top-down macroeconomic and bottom-up fundamental analysis. For example, just as economic data for a given country are available, the market valuation of a country can be calculated by aggregating all company earnings and market capitalization.

3.2.2. Sector and Industry Rotation

Just as one can formulate a strategy that allocates to different countries or regions in an investment universe, one can also have a view on the expected returns of various sectors and industries across borders. Industries that are more integrated on a global basis—and therefore subject to global supply and demand dynamics—are more suitable to global sector allocation decisions. Examples of such industries include information technology and energy. On the other hand, sectors and industries that are more local in nature to individual countries are more suitable to sector allocation within a country. Examples of these industries are real estate and consumer staples. The availability of sector and industry ETFs greatly facilitates the implementation of sector and industry rotation strategies for those portfolio managers who cannot or do not wish to implement such strategies by investing in individual stocks.

As with country and geographic allocation, both top-down macroeconomic and bottom-up fundamental variables can be used to predict sector/industry returns. Many bottom-up portfolio managers also add a top-down sector overlay to their portfolios.

3.2.3. Volatility-Based Strategies

Another category of top-down equity strategies is based on investors' view on volatility and is usually implemented using derivative instruments. Those managers who believe they have the skill to predict future market volatility better than option-implied volatility (reflected, for example, in the VIX Index) can trade the VIX futures listed on the CBOE Futures Exchange (CFE), trade instruments such as index options, or enter into volatility swaps (or variance swaps).

Let's assume that an investor predicts a major market move, not anticipated by others, in the near term. The investor does not have an opinion on the direction of the move and only expects the index volatility to be high. The investor can use an index straddle strategy to capitalize on his or her view. Entering into an index straddle position involves the purchase of call and put options (on the same underlying index) with the same strike price and expiry date. The success of this long straddle strategy depends on whether or not volatility turns out to be higher than anticipated by the market; the strategy incurs losses when the market stays broadly flat. Exhibit 4 shows the payoff of such an index straddle strategy. The maximum loss of the long straddle is limited to the total call and put premiums paid.

EXHIBIT 4   Payoff Pattern of a Classic Long Straddle Strategy

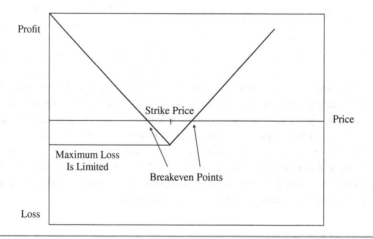

3.2.4. Thematic Investment Strategies

Thematic investing is another broad category of strategies. Thematic strategies can use broad macroeconomic, demographic, or political drivers, or bottom-up ideas on industries and sectors, to identify investment opportunities. Disruptive technologies, processes, and regulations; innovations; and economic cycles present investment opportunities and also pose challenges to existing companies. Investors constantly search for new and promising ideas or themes that will drive the market in the future.

It is also important to determine whether any new trend is structural (and hence long-term) or short-term in nature. Structural changes can have long-lasting impacts on the way people behave or a market operates. For example, the development of smartphones and tablets and the move toward cloud computing are probably structural changes. On the other hand, a manager might attempt to identify companies with significant sales exposure to foreign countries as a way to benefit from short-term views on currency movements. The success of a structural thematic investment depends equally on the ability to take advantage of future trends and the ability to avoid what will turn out to be merely fashionable for a limited time, unless the strategy specifically focuses on short-term trends. Further examples of thematic investment drivers include new technologies, mobile communication and computing devices, clean energy, fintech, and advances in medicine.

Implementation of Top-Down Investment Strategies

A global equity portfolio manager with special insights into particular countries or regions can tactically choose to overweight or underweight those countries or regions on a short-term basis. Once the country or region weights are determined by a top-down process, the portfolio can be constructed by selecting stocks in the relevant countries or regions.

A portfolio manager with expertise in identifying drivers of sector or industry returns will establish a view on those drivers and will set weights for those sectors in a portfolio. For example, the performance of the energy sector is typically driven by the price of crude oil. The returns of the materials sector rest on forecasts for commodity prices. The consumer and industrials sectors require in-depth knowledge of the customer–supplier chains and a range of other dynamics. Once a view is established on the return and risk of each sector, a manager can then decide which industries to invest in and what weightings to assign to those industries relative to the benchmark.

The significant growth of passive factor investing—sometimes marketed as "smart beta" products—has given portfolio managers more tools and flexibility for investing in different equity styles. One can exploit the fact, for example, that high-quality stocks tend to perform well in recessions, or that cyclical deep-value companies are more likely to deliver superior returns in a more "risk-on" environment, in which the market becomes less risk-averse. For example, where the investment mandate permits, top-down managers can choose among different equity style ETFs and structured products to obtain risk exposures that are consistent with their views on different stages of the economic cycle or their views on market sentiment.

Portfolio Overlays

Bottom-up fundamental strategies often lead to unintended macro (e.g., sector or country) risk exposures. However, bottom-up fundamental investors can incorporate some of the risk control benefits of top-down investment strategies via portfolio overlays. (A **portfolio overlay** is an array of derivative positions managed separately from the securities portfolio to achieve overall portfolio characteristics that are desired by the portfolio manager.) The fundamental investor's sector weights, for example, may vary from the benchmark's weights as a result of the stock selection process even though the investor did not intend to make sector bets. In that case, the investor may be able to adjust the sector weights to align with the benchmark's weights via long and short positions in derivatives. In this way, top-down strategies can be effective in controlling risk exposures. Overlays can also be used to attempt to add active returns that are not correlated with those generated by the underlying portfolio strategy.

3.3. Factor-Based Strategies

A factor is a variable or characteristic with which individual asset returns are correlated. It can be broadly defined as any variable that is believed to be valuable in ranking stocks for investment and in predicting future returns or risks. A wide range of security characteristics have been used to define "factors." Some factors (most commonly, size, value, momentum, and quality) have been shown to be positively associated with a long-term return premium and are often referred to as *rewarded* factors. In fact, hundreds of factors have been identified and used in portfolio construction, but a large number have not been empirically proven to offer a persistent return premium (some call these *unrewarded* factors).

Broadly defined, a factor-based strategy aims to identify significant factors that can predict future stock returns and to construct a portfolio that tilts toward such factors. Some strategies rely on a single factor, are transparent, and maintain a relatively stable exposure to that factor with regular rebalancing (as is explained in the curriculum chapter on passive equity investing). Other strategies rely on a selection of factors. Yet other strategies may attempt to time the exposure to factors, recognizing that factor performance varies over time.

For new factor ideas, analysts and managers of portfolios that use factor strategies often rely on academic research, working papers, in-house research, and external research performed by entities such as investment banks. The following exhibits illustrate how some of the traditional style factors performed in recent decades, showing the varying nature of returns. Exhibit 5 shows the cumulative performance of large-cap versus small-cap US equities, using the S&P 500 and Russell 2000 total return indexes. Exhibit 6 presents the total returns of value (Russell 1000 Value Index) versus growth (Russell 1000 Growth Index) styles. Over the 28 years from January 1988 to April 2016, small-cap stocks earned marginally higher returns than large-cap stocks, but with significantly higher risk. Value and growth styles produce about the same return, but growth equities seem to be slightly more volatile (see Exhibit 7).

Equity style rotation strategies, a subcategory of factor investing, are based on the belief that different factors—such as size, value, momentum, and quality—work well during some time periods but less well during other time periods. These strategies use an investment process that allocates to stock baskets representing each of these styles when a particular style is expected to offer a positive excess return compared to the benchmark. While style rotation as a strategy can be used in both fundamental and quantitative investment processes, it is generally more in the domain of quantitative investing. Unlike sector or country allocation, discussed earlier, the classification of securities into style categories is less standardized.

EXHIBIT 5   Large-Cap vs. Small-Cap Equities

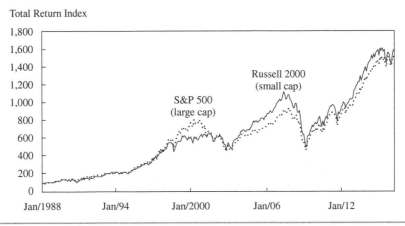

Sources: S&P, FTSE Russell.

EXHIBIT 6   Value vs. Growth Equities

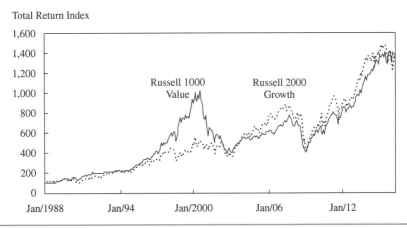

Sources: S&P, FTSE Russell.

EXHIBIT 7   Summary Statistics

	S&P 500	Russell 2000	Russell 1000 Value	Russell 1000 Growth
Annual return (%)	10.7	11.1	10.9	10.7
Annual volatility (%)	14.4	18.7	14.2	16.4
Sharpe Ratio	0.74	0.59	0.77	0.65

Sources: S&P, FTSE Russell.

The most important test, however, is the "smell" test: Does the factor make intuitive sense? A factor can often pass statistical backtesting, but if it does not make common sense—if justification for the factor's efficacy is lacking—then the manager may be data-mining. Investors should always remember that impressive performance in backtesting does not necessarily imply that the factor will continue to add value in the future.

An important step is choosing the appropriate investment universe. Practitioners mostly define their investment universe in terms of well-known broad market indexes—for the United States, for example, the S&P 500, Russell 3000, and MSCI World Index. Using a well-defined index has several benefits: Such indexes are free from look-ahead and survivorship biases, the stocks in the indexes are investable with sufficient liquidity, and the indexes are also generally free from foreign ownership restrictions.

The most traditional and widely used method for implementing factor-based portfolios is the hedged portfolio approach, pioneered and formulated by Fama and French (1993). In this approach, after choosing the factor to be scrutinized and ranking the investable stock universe by that factor, investors divide the universe into groups referred to as *quantiles* (typically quintiles or deciles) to form quantile portfolios. Stocks are either equally weighted or capitalization weighted within each quantile. A long/short hedged portfolio is typically formed by going long the best quantile and shorting the worst quantile. The performance of the hedged long/short portfolio is then tracked over time.

There are a few drawbacks to this "hedged portfolio" approach. First, the information contained in the middle quantiles is not utilized, as only the top and bottom quantiles are used in forming the hedged portfolio. Second, it is implicitly assumed that the relationship between the factor and future stock returns is linear (or at least monotonic), which may not be the case.[4] Third, portfolios built using this approach tend to be concentrated, and if many managers use similar factors, the resulting portfolios will be concentrated in specific stocks. Fourth, the hedged portfolio requires managers to short stocks. Shorting may not be possible in some markets and may be overly expensive in others. Fifth, and most important, the hedged portfolio is not a "pure" factor portfolio because it has significant exposures to other risk factors.

---

[4]The payoff patterns between factor exposures and future stock returns are becoming increasingly non-linear, especially in the United States and Japan.

Exhibit 8 shows the performance of a factor called "year-over-year change in debt outstanding." The factor is calculated by taking the year-over-year percentage change in the per share long-term debt outstanding on the balance sheet, using all stocks in the Russell 3000 universe. The portfolio is constructed by buying the top 10% of companies that reduce their debt and shorting the bottom 10% of companies that issue the most debt. Stocks in both the long and short portfolios are equally weighted.[5] The bars in the chart indicate the monthly portfolio returns. The average monthly return of the strategy is about 0.22% (or 2.7% per year), and the Sharpe ratio is 0.53 over the test period. All cumulative performance is computed on an initial investment in the factor of $100, with monthly rebalancing and excluding transaction costs.

EXHIBIT 8   Hedged Portfolio Return, "Year-over-Year Change in Debt Outstanding" Strategy

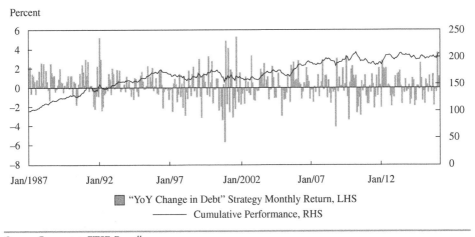

Sources: Compustat, FTSE Russell.

Exhibit 9 shows the average monthly returns of the 10 decile portfolios. It shows that companies with the highest year-over-year increase in debt financing (D10 category) marginally underperform companies with the lowest year-over-year increase in debt financing (average monthly return of 0.6% versus average monthly return of 0.8%). However, it can also be seen that the best-performing companies are the ones with reasonable financial leverage in Deciles 3 to 6. A long/short hedged portfolio approach based on the 1st and 10th deciles (as illustrated in Exhibit 9) would not take advantage of this information, as stocks in these deciles would not be used in such a portfolio. Portfolio managers observing this pattern concerning the different deciles could change the deciles used in the strategy if they believed the pattern would continue into the future.

---

[5]Stocks can also be weighted based on their market capitalization.

EXHIBIT 9   Average Decile Portfolio Return Based on Year-over-Year Change in Debt Outstanding

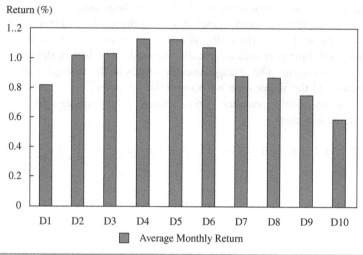

Sources: Compustat, FTSE Russell.

For investors who desire a long-only factor portfolio, a commonly used approach is to construct a factor-tilting portfolio, where a long-only portfolio with exposures to a given factor can be built with controlled tracking error. The factor-tilting portfolio tracks a benchmark index closely but also provides exposures to the chosen factor. In this way, it is similar to an enhanced indexing strategy.

A "factor-mimicking portfolio," or FMP, is a theoretical implementation of a pure factor portfolio. An FMP is a theoretical long/short portfolio that is dollar neutral with a unit exposure to a chosen factor and no exposure to other factors. Because FMPs invest in almost every single stock, entering into long or short positions without taking into account short availability issues or transaction costs, they are very expensive to trade. Managers typically construct the pure factor portfolio by following the FMP theory but adding trading liquidity and short availability constraints.

3.3.1. Style Factors

Factors are the raw ingredients of quantitative investing and are often referred to as signals. Quantitative managers spend a large amount of time studying factors. Traditionally, factors have been based on fundamental characteristics of underlying companies. However, many investors have recently shifted their attention to unconventional and unstructured data sources in an effort to gain an edge in creating strategies.

3.3.1.1. Value

Value is based on Graham and Dodd's (1934) concept and can be measured in a number of ways. The academic literature has a long history of documenting the value phenomenon. Basu (1977) found that stocks with low P/E or high earnings yield tend to provide higher returns. Fama and French (1993) formally outlined value investing by proposing the book-to-market ratio as a way to measure value and growth.

Although many academics and practitioners believe that value stocks tend to deliver superior returns, there has been considerable disagreement over the explanation of this effect. Fama and French (1992, 1993, 1996) suggested that the value premium exists to compensate investors for the greater likelihood that these companies will experience financial distress. Lakonishok, Shleifer, and Vishny (1994) cited behavioral arguments, suggesting that the effect is a result of behavioral biases on the part of the typical investor rather than compensation for higher risk.

Value factors can also be based on other fundamental performance metrics of a company, such as dividends, earnings, cash flow, EBIT, EBITDA, and sales. Investors often add two more variations on most value factors by adjusting for industry (and/or country) and historical differences. Most valuation ratios can be computed using either historical (also called *trailing*) or forward metrics. Exhibit 10 shows the performance of the price-to-earnings multiple factor implemented as a long/short decile portfolio.

EXHIBIT 10   Performance of the P/E Factor (Long/Short Decile Portfolio)

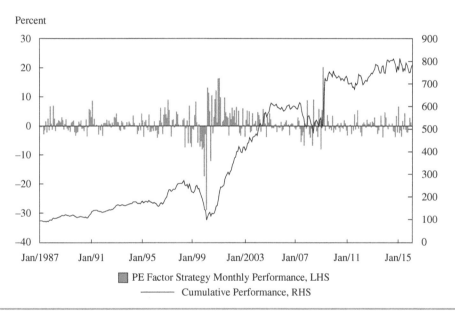

Sources: Compustat, FTSE Russell.

3.3.1.2. Price Momentum

Researchers have also found a strong price momentum effect in almost all asset classes in most countries. In fact, value and price momentum have long been the two cornerstones of quantitative investing.

Jegadeesh and Titman (1993) first documented that stocks that are "winners" over the previous 12 months tend to outperform past "losers" (those that have done poorly over the previous 12 months) and that such outperformance persists over the following 2 to 12 months. The study focused on the US market during the 1965–1989 period. The authors also found a short-term reversal effect, whereby stocks that have high price momentum in the previous month tend to underperform over the next 2 to 12 months. This price momentum anomaly is commonly attributed to behavioral biases, such as overreaction to information.[6] It is interesting to note that since the academic publication of these findings, the performance of the price momentum factor has become much more volatile (see Exhibit 11). Price momentum is, however, subject to extreme tail risk. Over the three-month March–May 2009 time period, the simple price momentum strategy (as measured by the long/short decile portfolio) lost 56%. For this data period, some reduction in downside risk can be achieved by removing the effect of sector exposure from momentum factor returns: We will call this modified version the "sector-neutralized price momentum factor."[7] The results are shown in Exhibits 12 and 13 for US, European, and Japanese markets.

EXHIBIT 11   Performance of the Price Momentum Factor (Long/Short Decile Portfolio)

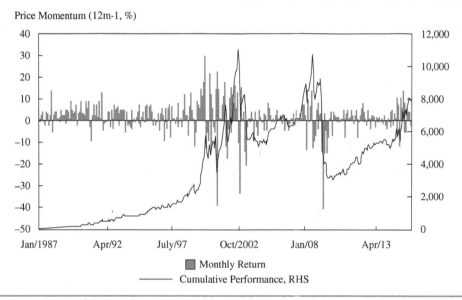

Price Momentum (12m-1, %)

Sources: Compustat, FTSE Russell.

---

[6]Behavioral biases are covered in the Level III chapters on behavioral finance.

[7]The methods for removing sector exposure are beyond the scope of this chapter.

EXHIBIT 12   Performance of the Sector-Neutralized Price Momentum Factor (Long/Short Decile Portfolio)

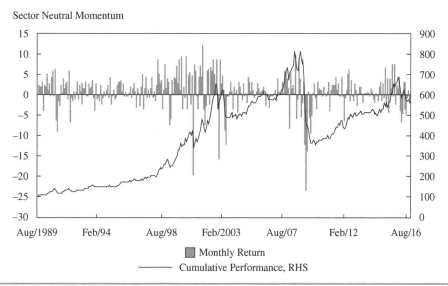

Sources: Compustat, FTSE Russell.

Exhibit 13 extends the analysis to include European and Japanese markets, where a similar effect on downside risk can be shown to have been operative over the period.

EXHIBIT 13   Performance of the Sector-Neutralized Price Momentum Factor in US, European, and Japanese Markets (Long/Short Decile Portfolio)

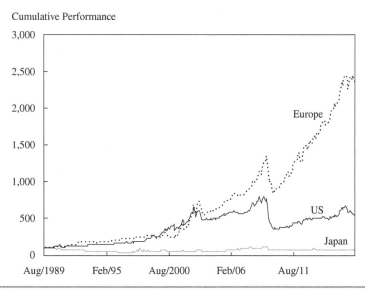

Sources: Compustat, FTSE Russell.

EXAMPLE 4   Factor Investing

A quantitative manager wants to expand his current strategy from US equities into international equity markets. His current strategy uses a price momentum factor. Based on Exhibit 13:

1. State whether momentum has been a factor in European and Japanese equity returns overall in the time period examined.
2. Discuss the potential reasons why neutralizing sectors reduces downside risk.

Solution to 1: As shown in Exhibit 13, price momentum has performed substantially better in Europe than in the United States. On the other hand, there does not appear to be any meaningful pattern of price momentum in Japan. Exhibit 13 suggests that the price momentum factor could be used for a European portfolio but not for a Japanese portfolio. However, managers need to perform rigorous backtesting before they can confidently implement a factor model in a market that they are not familiar with. Managers should be aware that what appears to be impressive performance in backtests does not necessarily imply that the factor will continue to add value in the future.

Solution to 2: Using the simple price momentum factor means that a portfolio buys past winners and shorts past losers. The resulting portfolio could have exposure to potentially significant industry bets. Sector-neutral price momentum focuses on stock selection without such risk exposures and thus tends to reduce downside risk.

3.3.1.3. Growth

Growth is another investment approach used by some style investors. Growth factors aim to measure a company's growth potential and can be calculated using the company's historical growth rates or projected forward growth rates. Growth factors can also be classified as short-term growth (last quarter's, last year's, next quarter's, or next year's growth) and long-term growth (last five years' or next five years' growth). While higher-than-market or higher-than-sector growth is generally considered to be a possible indicator for strong future stock price performance, the growth of some metrics, such as assets, results in weaker future stock price performance.

Exhibit 14 shows the performance of the year-over-year earnings growth factor. The exhibit is based on a strategy that invests in the top 10% of companies with the highest year-over-year growth in earnings per share and shorts all the stocks in the bottom 10%.

EXHIBIT 14   Performance of Year-over-Year Earnings Growth Factor (Long/Short Decile Portfolio)

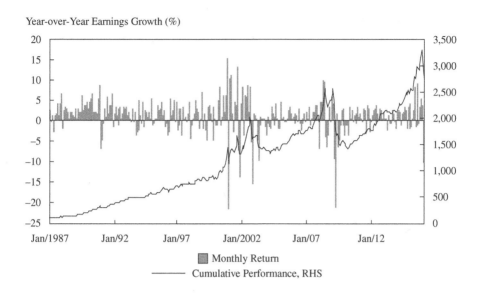

Year-over-Year Earnings Growth (%)

Sources: Compustat, FTSE Russell.

3.3.1.4. Quality
In addition to using accounting ratios and share price data as fundamental style factors, investors have continued to create more complex factors based on the variety of accounting information available for companies. One of the best-known examples of how in-depth accounting knowledge can impact investment performance is Richard Sloan's (1996) seminal paper on earnings quality, with its proposition of the accruals factor. Sloan suggests that stock prices fail to reflect fully the information contained in the accrual and cash flow components of current earnings.[8] The performance of the accruals anomaly factor, however, appears to be quite cyclical.

---

[8]Sloan (1996) argues that in the long term, cash flows from operations and net income (under accruals-based accounting) should converge and be consistent. In the short term, they could diverge. Management has more discretion in accruals-based accounting; therefore, the temporary divergence between cash flows and net income reflects how conservative a company chooses to be in reporting its net income.

EXHIBIT 15   Performance of Earnings Quality Factor

Accruals (Sloan 1996, %)

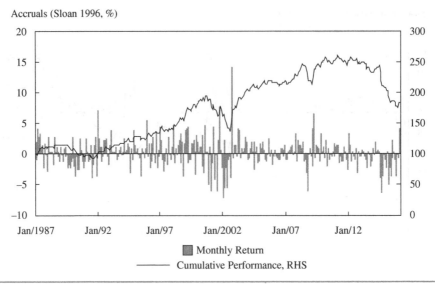

Monthly Return
——— Cumulative Performance, RHS

Sources: Compustat, FTSE Russell.

In addition to the accruals anomaly, there are many other potential factors based on a company's fundamental data, such as profitability, balance sheet and solvency risk, earnings quality, stability, sustainability of dividend payout, capital utilization, and management efficiency measures. Yet another, analyst sentiment, refers to the phenomenon of sell-side analysts revising their forecasts of corporate earnings estimates, which is called *earnings revision*. More recently, with the availability of more data, analysts have started to include cash flow revisions, sales revisions, ROE revisions, sell-side analyst stock recommendations, and target price changes as variables in the "analyst sentiment" category.

A new and exciting area of research involves news sentiment. Rather than just relying on the output of sell-side analysts, investors could use natural language processing (NLP) algorithms to analyze the large volume of news stories and quantify the news sentiment on stocks.

3.3.2. Unconventional Factors Based on Unstructured Data

With the rapid growth in technology and computational algorithms, investors have been embracing big data. "Big data" is a broad term referring to extremely large datasets that may include structured data—such as traditional financial statements and market data—as well as unstructured or "alternative" data that has previously not been widely used in the investment industry because it lacks recognizable structure. Examples of such alternative data include satellite images, textual information, credit card payment information, and the number of online mentions of a particular product or brand.

Exhibit 16 shows the performance (as measured by the long/short quintile portfolio) of a factor based on customer–supplier chain data.[9] The signal is based on the trailing one-month

---

[9]These data can be obtained from FactSet Revere's historical point-in-time supply chain dataset.

stock price return of a company's largest customer. Stocks are ranked by largest customer performance, and the portfolio goes long the top quintile and shorts the lowest quintile. The positions are held until the following month's stock ranking and rebalancing. The intuition is that the positive performance of customers is likely to benefit the supplier company in subsequent periods. Indeed, compared to many traditional factors, the supply-chain signal seems to have shown more consistent returns, especially in recent years.

EXHIBIT 16   Performance of Customer–Supplier-Chain Factor

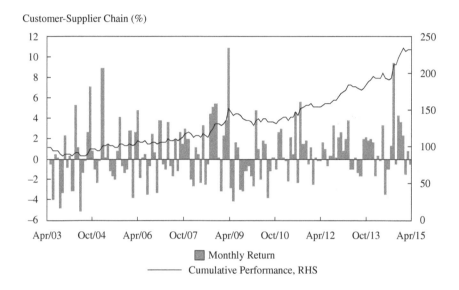

Customer-Supplier Chain (%)

■ Monthly Return
—— Cumulative Performance, RHS

Sources: Compustat, FactSet Revere, FTSE Russell.

Portfolio construction is covered in the curriculum chapter titled "Active Equity Portfolio Construction."

EXAMPLE 5   Researching Factor Timing

An analyst is exploring the relationship between interest rates and style factor returns for the purpose of developing equity style rotation strategies for the US equity market. The analysis takes place in early 2017. The first problem the analyst addresses is how to model the interest rate variable. The data in Exhibit 17 show an apparent trend of declining US government bond yields over the last 30 years. Trends may or may not continue into the future. The analyst decides to normalize the yield data so that they do not incorporate a prediction on continuation of the trend and makes a simple transformation by subtracting the yield's own 12-month moving average:

$$\text{Normalized yield}_t = \text{Nominal yield}_t - \frac{1}{12}\sum_{\tau=1}^{12}\text{Nominal yield}_{t-\tau+1}$$

The normalized yield data are shown in Exhibit 18. Yields calculated are as of the beginning of the month. Do the fluctuations in yield have any relationship with style factor returns? The analyst explores possible contemporaneous (current) and lagged relationships by performing two regressions (using the current month's and the next month's factor returns, respectively) against the normalized long-term bond yield:

$$f_{i,t} = \beta_{i,0} + \beta_{i,1}\text{Normalized yield}_t + \varepsilon_{i,t}$$

and

$$f_{i,t+1} = \beta_{i,0} + \beta_{i,1}\text{Normalized yield}_t + \varepsilon_{i,t}$$

where $f_{i,t}$ is the return of style factor i at time t and $f_{i,t+1}$ is the subsequent (next) month's return to style factor i. The first regression reveals the contemporaneous relationship between interest rate and factor performance—that is, how well the current interest rate relates to the current factor performance. The second equation states whether the current interest rate can predict the next month's factor return. Exhibit 19 shows the findings.

EXHIBIT 17   Current and Expected Bond Yield, US

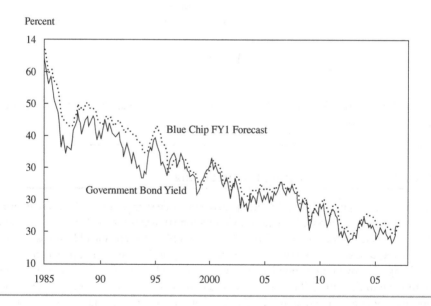

EXHIBIT 18   Normalized 10-Year Treasury Bond Yield, US

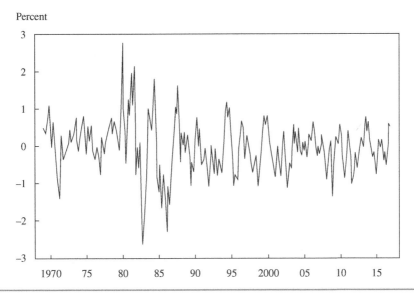

Source: Haver Analytics.

EXHIBIT 19   Normalized Bond Yield and Style Factor Returns

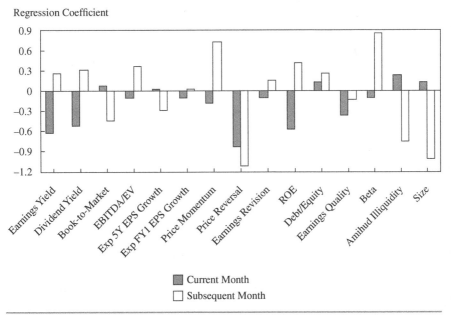

Source: Haver Analytics.

Using only the information given, address the following:

1. Interpret Exhibit 19.
2. Discuss the relevance of contemporaneous and forward relationships in an equity factor rotation strategy.
3. What concerns could the analyst have in relation to an equity factor rotation strategy, and what possible next steps could the analyst take to address those concerns?

Solution to 1: Exhibit 19 suggests an inverse relationship between concurrent bond yields and returns to the dividend yield, price reversal, and ROE factors. For some factors (such as earnings quality), the relationship between bond yields and forward (next month's) factor returns is in the same direction as the contemporaneous relationship.

Solution to 2: Attention needs to be given to the timing relationship of variables to address this question. A contemporaneous style factor return becomes known as of the end of the month. If the known value of bond yields at the beginning of the month is correlated with factor returns, the investor may be able to gain some edge relative to investors who do not use that information. The same conclusion holds concerning the forward relationship. If the contemporaneous variable were defined so that it is realized at the same time as the variable we want to predict, the forward but not the contemporaneous variable would be relevant.

Solution to 3: The major concern is the validity of the relationships between normalized interest rates and the style variables. Among the steps the analyst can take to increase his or her conviction in the relationships' validity are the following:

- Establish whether the relationships have predictive value out of sample (that is, based on data not used to model the relationship).
- Investigate whether or not there are economic rationales for the relationships such that those relationships could be expected to persist into the future.

Exhibit 19 shows both weak relationships (e.g., for earnings revision) and strong relationships (e.g., for size and beta) in relation to the subsequent month's returns. This fact suggests some priorities in examining this question.

3.4. Activist Strategies

Activist investors specialize in taking stakes in listed companies and advocating changes for the purpose of producing a gain on the investment. The investor may wish to obtain representation on the company's board of directors or use other measures in an effort to initiate strategic, operational, or financial structure changes. In some cases, activist investors may support activities such as asset sales, cost-cutting measures, changes to management, changes to the capital structure, dividend increases, or share buybacks. Activists—including hedge funds, public pension funds, private investors, and others—vary greatly in their approaches, expertise, and investment horizons. They may also seek different outcomes. What they have in common is that they advocate for change in their target companies.

Shareholder activism typically follows a period of screening and analysis of opportunities in the market. The investor usually reviews a number of companies based on a range of parameters and carries out in-depth analysis of the business and the opportunities for unlocking value. Activism itself starts when an investor buys an equity stake in the company and starts advocating for change (i.e., pursuing an activist campaign). These equity stakes are generally made public. Stakes above a certain threshold must be made public in most jurisdictions. Exhibit 20 shows a typical activist investing process. The goal of activist investing could be either financial gain (increased shareholder value) or a non-financial cause (e.g., environmental, social, and governance issues). Rather than pursuing a full takeover bid, activist investors aim to achieve their goals with smaller stakes, typically of less than 10%. Activist investors' time horizon is often shorter than that of buy-and-hold investors, but the whole process can last for a number of years.

EXHIBIT 20   A Typical Shareholder Activist Investing Process

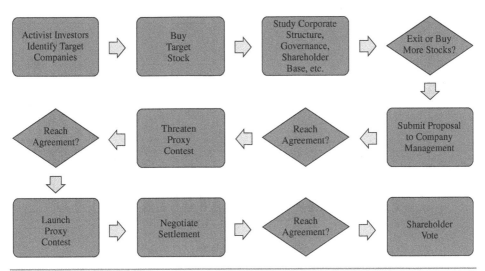

Source: Deutsche Bank.

3.4.1. The Popularity of Shareholder Activism

Shareholder (or investor) activism is by no means a new investment strategy. Its foundations go back to the 1970s and 1980s, when investors known as corporate raiders took substantial stakes in companies in order to influence their operations, unlock value in the target companies, and thereby raise the value of their shares. Proponents of activism argue that it is an important and necessary activity that helps monitor and discipline corporate management to the benefit of all shareholders. Opponents argue that such interventionist tactics can cause distraction and negatively impact management performance.

Activist hedge funds—among the most prominent activist investors—saw growing popularity for a number of years, with assets under management (AUM) reaching $50 billion in 2007[10] before falling sharply during the global financial crisis. Activist hedge fund investing has since strongly recovered, with AUM close to $120 billion in 2015.[11] The activity of such investors can be tracked by following the activists' announcements that they are launching a campaign seeking to influence companies. Exhibit 21 shows the number of

---

[10]Hedge Fund Research.
[11]See "Activist Funds: An Investor Calls," *Economist* (7 February 2015).

activist events reported by the industry. Hedge funds that specialize in activism benefit from lighter regulation than other types of funds, and their fee structure, offering greater rewards, justifies concerted campaigns for change at the companies they hold. The popularity and viability of investor activism are influenced by the legal frameworks in different jurisdictions, shareholder structures, and cultural considerations. The United States has seen the greatest amount of activist activity initiated by hedge funds, individuals, and pension funds, but there have been a number of activist events in Europe too. Other regions have so far seen more limited activity on the part of activist investors. Cultural reasons and more concentrated shareholder ownership of companies are two frequently cited explanations.

EXHIBIT 21   Number of Global Activist Events

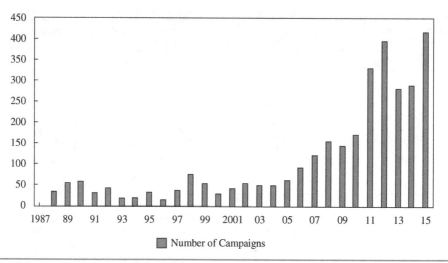

Number of Campaigns

Source: Thomson Reuters Activism database.

3.4.2. Tactics Used by Activist Investors

Activists use a range of tactics on target companies in order to boost shareholder value. These tactics include the following:

- Seeking board representation and nominations
- Engaging with management by writing letters to management calling for and explaining suggested changes, participating in management discussions with analysts or meeting the management team privately, or launching proxy contests whereby activists encourage other shareholders to use their proxy votes to effect change in the organization
- Proposing significant corporate changes during the annual general meeting (AGM)
- Proposing restructuring of the balance sheet to better utilize capital and potentially initiate share buybacks or increase dividends
- Reducing management compensation or realigning management compensation with share price performance
- Launching legal proceedings against existing management for breach of fiduciary duties
- Reaching out to other shareholders of the company to coordinate action
- Launching a media campaign against existing management practices
- Breaking up a large conglomerate to unlock value

The effectiveness of shareholder activism depends on the response of the existing management team and the tools at that team's disposal. In many countries, defense mechanisms can be employed by management or a dominant shareholder to hinder activist intervention. These techniques include multi-class share structures whereby a company founder's shares are typically entitled to multiple votes per share; "poison pill" plans allowing the issuance of shares at a deep discount, which causes significant economic and voting dilution; staggered board provisions whereby a portion of the board members are not elected at annual shareholders meetings and hence cannot all be replaced simultaneously; and charter and bylaw provisions and amendments.

3.4.3. Typical Activist Targets

Activist investors look for specific characteristics in deciding which companies to target. Exhibit 22 shows the characteristics of target companies relative to the market as a whole. The exhibit provides a measure of these characteristics on the event day as well as a year before the announcement, giving a flavor of the dynamics of these attributes. It shows that, on average,[12] target companies feature slower revenue and earnings growth than the market, suffer negative share price momentum, and have weaker-than-average corporate governance.[13] By building stakes and initiating change in underperforming companies, activists hope to unlock value. In addition, by targeting such companies, activist investors are more likely to win support for their actions from other shareholders and the wider public. Traditionally, the target companies have been small and medium-sized listed stocks. This has changed as a number of larger companies have become subject to activism.[14]

EXHIBIT 22   Fundamental Characteristics of Target Companies

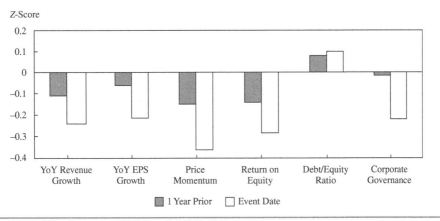

Sources: Capital IQ, Compustat, FTSE Russell, MSCI, S&P.

---

[12]The fundamental characteristics of all companies in the investment universe (i.e., the Russell 3000) are standardized using z-scores (by subtracting the mean and dividing by the standard deviation) every month from 1988 until 2015. Thus, we can compare the average exposure to each fundamental characteristic over time.

[13]We normalize all target and non-target companies' factor exposures using z-scores (i.e., subtracting the sample mean and dividing by the sample standard deviation).

[14]Trian Fund Management proposed splitting PepsiCo into standalone public companies; Third Point called for leadership change at Yahoo!.

Do Activists Really Improve Company Performance?

Exhibit 23 shows that, on average, fundamental characteristics of targeted companies do improve in subsequent years following activists' efforts, with evidence that revenue and earnings growth increase, profitability improves, and corporate governance indicators become more robust. There is evidence, however, that the financial leverage of such companies increases significantly.

EXHIBIT 23   Fundamentals of Target Companies Improve

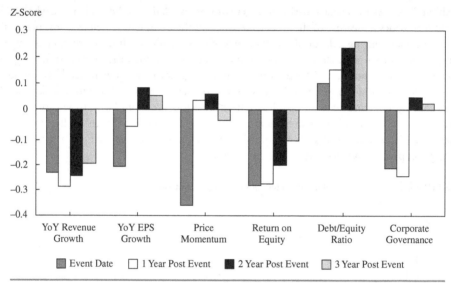

Note: Data are for US companies, 1988–2015.
Sources: Capital IQ, Compustat, FTSE Russell, MSCI, S&P.

Do Activist Investors Generate Alpha?

Activist hedge funds are among the major activist investors. Based on the HFRX Activist Index, in the aggregate, activist hedge funds have delivered an average annual return of 7.7% with annual volatility of 13.7% and therefore a Sharpe ratio of 0.56—slightly higher than the Sharpe ratio of the S&P 500 Index of 0.54 (see Exhibit 24). However, it is difficult to conclude how much value activist investors add because the HFRX index does not include a large enough number of managers. Furthermore, managers themselves vary in their approaches and the risks they take.

EXHIBIT 24   Performance of HFRX Activist Index vs. S&P 500

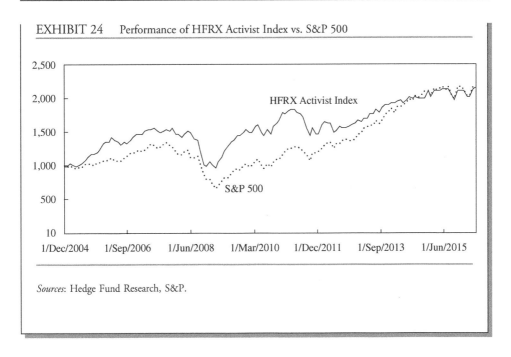

Sources: Hedge Fund Research, S&P.

How Does the Market React to Activist Events?

Investors have generally reacted positively to activism announcements: On average, target company stocks go up by 2% on the announcement day (based on all activist events in the Thomson Reuters Corporate Governance Intelligence database from 1987 to 2016).[15] Interestingly, the positive reaction comes on top of stock appreciation prior to activism announcements (see Exhibit 25). According to the model of Maug (1998), activist investors trade in a stock prior to the announcement to build up a stake, assert control, and profit from the value creation. It may also be argued that there must be information leakage about the activists' involvement, driving the stock higher even before the first public announcement. There is a modest post-announcement drift: In the month after the activist announcement date, target share prices move up by 0.6%, on average, relative to the market.

---

[15]All returns are excess returns, adjusted for the market and sector. For details, see Jussa, Webster, Zhao, and Luo (2016).

EXHIBIT 25   Market Reactions to Activist Events

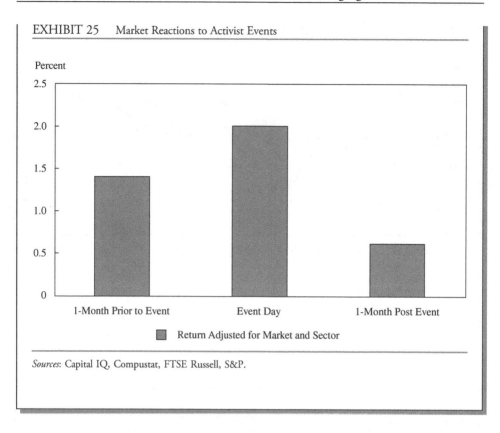

Percent

Sources: Capital IQ, Compustat, FTSE Russell, S&P.

EXAMPLE 6   Activist Investing

Kendra Cho is an analyst at an investment firm that specializes in activist investing and manages a concentrated portfolio of stocks invested in listed European companies. Cho and her colleagues hope to identify and buy stakes in companies with the potential to increase their value through strategic, operational, or financial change. Cho is considering the following three companies:

- Company A is a well-established, medium-sized food producer. Its profitability, measured by operating margins and return on assets, is ahead of industry peers. The company is recognized for its high corporate governance standards and effective communication with existing and potential investors. Cho's firm has invested in companies in this sector in the past and made gains on those positions.
- Company B is a medium-sized engineering business that has experienced a significant deterioration in profitability in recent years. More recently, the company has been unable to pay interest on its debt, and its new management team has recognized the need to restructure the business and negotiate with its creditors. Due to the company's losses, Cho cannot use earnings-based price multiples to assess

upside potential, but based on sales and asset multiples, she believes there is significant upside potential in the stock if the company's current difficulties can be overcome and the debt can be restructured.

- Company C is also a medium-sized engineering business, but its operating performance, particularly when measured by the return on assets, is below that of the rest of the industry. Cho has identified a number of company assets that are underutilized. She believes that the management has significant potential to reduce fixed-asset investments, concentrate production in fewer facilities, and dispose of assets, in line with what the company's peers have been doing. Such steps could improve asset turnover and make it possible to return capital to shareholders through special dividends.

Identify the company that is most appropriate for Cho to recommend to the fund managers:

Solution: Company C is the most appropriate choice. The company offers upside potential because of its ability to improve operating performance and cash payout using asset disposals, a strategy being implemented by other companies in its sector. Neither Company A nor Company B offers an attractive opportunity for activist investing: Company A is already operating efficiently, while Company B is more suitable for investors that focus on restructuring and distressed investing.

3.5. Other Strategies

There are many other strategies that active portfolio managers employ in an attempt to beat the market benchmark. In this section, we explain two other categories of active strategies that do not fit neatly into our previous categorizations—namely, statistical arbitrage and event-driven strategies. Both rely on extensive use of quantitative data and are usually implemented in a systematic, rules-based way but can also incorporate the fund manager's judgment in making investment decisions.

3.5.1. Strategies Based on Statistical Arbitrage and Market Microstructure

Statistical arbitrage (or "stat arb") strategies use statistical and technical analysis to exploit pricing anomalies. Statistical arbitrage makes extensive use of data such as stock price, dividend, trading volume, and the limit order book for this purpose. The analytical tools used include (1) traditional technical analysis, (2) sophisticated time-series analysis and econometric models, and (3) machine-learning techniques. Portfolio managers typically take advantage of either mean reversion in share prices or opportunities created by market microstructure issues.

Pairs trading is an example of a popular and simple statistical arbitrage strategy. Pairs trading uses statistical techniques to identify two securities that are historically highly correlated with each other. When the price relationship of these two securities deviates from its long-term average, managers that expect the deviation to be temporary go long the underperforming stock and simultaneously short the outperforming stock. If the prices do converge to the long-term average as forecast, the investors close the trade and realize a profit. This kind of pairs trading therefore bets on a mean-reversion pattern in stock prices. The biggest risk in pairs trading and most other mean-reversion strategies is that the observed price divergence is not temporary; rather, it might be due to structural reasons.[16] Because risk management is critical for the success of such strategies, investors often employ stop-loss rules to exit trades when a loss limit is reached.

The most difficult aspect of a pairs-trading strategy is the identification of the pairs of stocks. This can be done either by using a quantitative approach and creating models of stock prices or by using a fundamental approach to judge the two stocks whose prices should move together for qualitative reasons.

Consider Canadian National Railway (CNR) and Canadian Pacific Railway (CP). These are the two dominant railways in Canada. Their business models are fairly similar, as both operate railway networks and transport goods throughout the country. Exhibit 26 shows that the prices of the two stocks have been highly correlated.[17] The y-axis shows the log price differential, referred to as the spread.[18] The exhibit also shows the moving average of the spread computed on a rolling 130-day window and bands at two standard deviations above and two standard deviations below the moving average. A simple pairs-trading strategy would be to enter into a trade when the spread is more than (or less than) two standard deviations from the moving average. The trade would be closed when the spread reaches the moving average again. Exhibit 26 shows the three trades based on our decision rules. The first trade was opened on 2 October 2014, when the spread between CNR and CP crossed the −2 standard deviation mark.[19] This trade was closed on 18 November 2014, when the spread reached the moving average. The first trade was profitable, and the position was maintained for slightly more than a month. The second trade was also profitable but lasted much longer. After the third trade was entered on 21 July 2015, however, there was a structural break, in that CP's decline further intensified while CNR stayed relatively flat; therefore, the spread continued to widen. The loss on the third trade could have been significantly greater than the profits made from the first two transactions if the positions had been closed prior to mean reversion in the spring of 2016. This example highlights the risk inherent in mean-reversion strategies.

---

[16]For example, the outperformance of one stock might be due to the fact that the company has developed a new technology or product that cannot be easily replicated by competitors.

[17]The correlation coefficient between the two stocks was 69% based on daily returns from 2 January 2014 to 26 May 2016.

[18]ln(Price of CNR/Price of CP).

[19]The position is long CNR and short CP.

EXHIBIT 26   Pairs Trade between CNR and CP

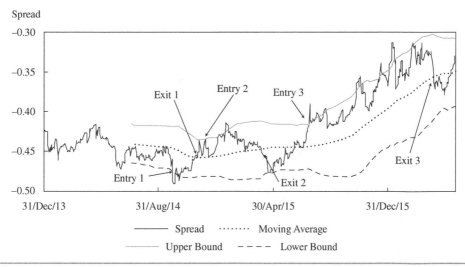

Sources: Bloomberg, Wolfe Research

In the United States, many market microstructure–based arbitrage strategies take advantage of the NYSE Trade and Quote (TAQ) database and often involve extensive analysis of the limit order book to identify very short-term mispricing opportunities. For example, a temporary imbalance between buy and sell orders may trigger a spike in share price that lasts for only a few milliseconds. Only those investors with the analytical tools and trading capabilities for high-frequency trading are in a position to capture such opportunities, usually within a portfolio of many stocks designed to take advantage of very short-term discrepancies.

EXAMPLE 7

An analyst is asked to recommend a pair of stocks to be added to a statistical arbitrage fund. She considers the following three pairs of stocks:

- Pair 1 consists of two food-producing companies. Both are mature companies with comparable future earnings prospects. Both typically trade on similar valuation multiples. The ratio of their share prices shows mean reversion over the last two decades. The ratio is currently more than one standard deviation above its moving average.
- Pair 2 consists of two consumer stocks: One is a food retailer, and the other is a car manufacturer. Although the two companies operate in different markets and have different business models, statistical analysis performed by the analyst shows strong correlation between their share prices that has persisted for more than a decade. The stock prices have moved significantly in opposite directions in recent days. The analyst, expecting mean reversion, believes this discrepancy represents an investment opportunity.

- Pair 3 consists of two well-established financial services companies with a traditional focus on retail banking. One of the companies recently saw the arrival of a new management team and an increase in acquisition activity in corporate and investment banking—both new business areas for the company. The share price fell sharply on news of these changes. The price ratio of the two banks now deviates significantly from the moving average.

Based on the information provided, select the pair that would be most suitable for the fund.

Solution: Pair 1 is the most suitable for the fund. The companies' share prices have been correlated in the past, with the share price ratio reverting to the moving average. They have similar businesses, and there is no indication of a change in either company's strategies, as there is for Pair 3. By contrast with the price ratio for Pair 1, the past correlation of share prices for Pair 2 may have been spurious and is not described as exhibiting mean reversion.

3.5.2. Event-Driven Strategies

Event-driven strategies exploit market inefficiencies that may occur around corporate events such as mergers and acquisitions, earnings or restructuring announcements, share buybacks, special dividends, and spinoffs.

Risk arbitrage associated with merger and acquisition (M&A) activity is one of the most common examples of an event-driven strategy.

In a cash-only transaction, the acquirer proposes to purchase the shares of the target company for a given price. The stock price of the target company typically remains below the offered price until the transaction is completed. Therefore, an arbitrageur could buy the stock of the target company and earn a profit if and when the acquisition closes.

In a share-for-share exchange transaction, the acquirer uses its own shares to purchase the target company at a given exchange ratio. A risk arbitrage trader normally purchases the target share and simultaneously short-sells the acquirer's stock at the same exchange ratio. Once the acquisition is closed, the arbitrageur uses his or her long positions in the target company to exchange for the acquirer's stocks, which are further used to cover the arbitrageur's short positions.

The first challenge in managing risk arbitrage positions is to accurately estimate the risk of the deal failing. An M&A transaction, for example, may not go through for numerous reasons. A regulator may block the deal because of antitrust concerns, or the acquirer may not be able to secure the approval from the target company's shareholders. If a deal fails, the price of the target stock typically falls sharply, generating significant loss for the arbitrageur. Hence, this strategy has the label "risk arbitrage."

Another important consideration that an arbitrageur has to take into account is the deal duration. At any given point in time, there are many M&A transactions outstanding, and the arbitrageur has to decide which ones to participate in and how to weight each position, based on the predicted premium and risk. The predicted premium has to be annualized to enable the arbitrageur to compare different opportunities. Therefore, estimating deal duration is important for accurately estimating the deal premium.

4. CREATING A FUNDAMENTAL ACTIVE INVESTMENT STRATEGY

Fundamental (or discretionary) investing remains one of the prevailing philosophies of active management. In the following sections, we discuss how fundamental investors organize their investment processes.

4.1. The Fundamental Active Investment Process

The broad goal of active management is to outperform a selected benchmark on a risk-adjusted basis, net of fees and transaction costs. Value can be added at different stages of the investment process. For example, added value may come from the use of proprietary data, from special skill in security analysis and valuation, or from insight into industry/sector allocation.

Many fundamental investors use processes that include the following steps:

1. Define the investment universe and the market opportunity—the perceived opportunity to earn a positive risk-adjusted return to active investing, net of costs—in accordance with the investment mandate. The market opportunity is also known as the investment thesis.
2. Prescreen the investment universe to obtain a manageable set of securities for further, more detailed analysis.
3. Understand the industry and business for this screened set by performing:
    *   industry and competitive analysis and
    *   analysis of financial reports.
4. Forecast company performance, most commonly in terms of cash flows or earnings.
5. Convert forecasts to valuations and identify *ex ante* profitable investments.
6. Construct a portfolio of these investments with the desired risk profile.
7. Rebalance the portfolio with buy and sell disciplines.

The investment universe is mainly determined by the mandate agreed on by the fund manager and the client. The mandate defines the market segments, regions, and/or countries in which the manager will seek to add value. For example, if an investment mandate specifies Hong Kong's Hang Seng Index as the performance benchmark, the manager's investment universe will be primarily restricted to the 50 stocks in that index. However, an active manager may also include non-index stocks that trade on the same exchange or whose business activities significantly relate to this region. It is important for investors who seek to hold a diversified and well-constructed portfolio to understand the markets in which components of the portfolio will be invested. In addition, a clear picture of the market opportunity to earn positive active returns is important for active equity investment. The basic question is, what is the opportunity and why is it there? The answer to this two-part question can be called the investment thesis. The "why" part involves understanding the economic, financial, behavioral, or other rationale for a strategy's profitability in the future.

Practically, the investment thesis will suggest a set of characteristics that tend to be associated with potentially profitable investments. The investor may prescreen the investment universe with quantitative and/or qualitative criteria to obtain a manageable subset that will be analyzed in greater detail. Prescreening criteria can often be associated with a particular investment style. A value style manager, for example, may first exclude those stocks with high P/E multiples and high debt-to-equity ratios. Growth style managers may first rule out stocks that do not have high enough historical or forecast EPS growth. Steps 3 to 5 cover processes of in-depth analysis described in the Level II CFA Program chapters on industry and company analysis and equity valuation. Finally, a portfolio is constructed in which stocks that have high upside potential are overweighted relative to the benchmark and stocks that are expected to underperform the benchmark are underweighted, not held at all, or (where relevant) shorted.[20]

As part of the portfolio construction process (step 6), the portfolio manager needs to decide whether to take active exposures to particular industry groups or economic sectors or to remain sector neutral relative to the benchmark. Portfolio managers may have top-down views on the business trends in some industries. For example, innovations in medical technology may cause an increase in earnings in the health care sector as a whole, while a potential central bank interest rate hike may increase the profitability of the banking sector. With these views, assuming the changed circumstances are not already priced in by the market, a manager could add extra value to the portfolio by overweighting the health care and financial services sectors. If the manager doesn't have views on individual sectors, he or she should, in theory, establish a neutral industry position relative to the benchmark in constructing the portfolio. However, a manager who has very strong convictions on the individual names in a specific industry may still want to overweight the industry that those names belong to. The potential high excess return from overweighting individual stocks can justify the risk the portfolio takes on the active exposure to that industry.

In addition to the regular portfolio rebalancing that ensures that the investment mandate and the desired risk exposures are maintained, a stock sell discipline needs to be incorporated into the investment process. The stock sell discipline will enable the portfolio to take profit from a successful investment and to exit from an unsuccessful investment at a prudent time.

In fundamental analysis, each stock is typically assigned a target price that the analyst believes to be the fair market value of the stock. The stock will be reclassified from undervalued to overvalued if the stock price surpasses this target price. Once this happens, the upside of the stock is expected to be limited, and holding that stock may not be justified, given the potential downside risk. The sell discipline embedded within an investment process requires the portfolio manager to sell the stock at this point. In practice, recognizing that valuation is an imprecise exercise, managers may continue to hold the stock or may simply reduce the size of the position rather than sell outright. This flexibility is particularly relevant when, in relative valuation frameworks where the company is being valued against a peer group, the valuations of industry peers are also changing. The target price of a stock need not be a constant but can be updated by the analyst with the arrival of new information. Adjusting the target price downward until it is lower than the current market price would also trigger a sale or a reduction in the position size.

Other situations could arise in which a stock's price has fallen and continues to fall for what the analyst considers to be poorly understood reasons. If the analyst remains positive on the stock, he or she should carefully consider the rationale for maintaining the position; if the company fundamentals indeed worsened, the analyst must also consider his or her own

---

[20]A portfolio that is benchmarked against an index that contains hundreds or thousands of constituents will most likely have zero weighting in most of them.

possible behavioral biases. The portfolio manager needs to have the discipline to take a loss by selling the stock if, for example, the price touches some pre-defined stop-loss trigger point. The stop-loss point is intended to set the maximum loss for each asset, under any conditions, and limit such behavioral biases.

EXAMPLE 8   Fundamental Investing

A portfolio manager uses the following criteria to prescreen his investment universe:

1. The year-over-year growth rate in earnings per share from continuing operations has increased over each of the last four fiscal years.
2. Growth in earnings per share from continuing operations over the last 12 months has been positive.
3. The percentage difference between the actual announced earnings and the consensus earnings estimate for the most recent quarter is greater than or equal to 10%.
4. The percentage change in stock price over the last four weeks is positive.
5. The 26-week relative price strength is greater than or equal to the industry's 26-week relative price strength.
6. The average daily volume for the last 10 days is in the top 50% of the market.

   Describe the manager's investment mandate.

Solution: The portfolio manager has a growth orientation with a focus on companies that have delivered EPS growth in recent years and that have maintained their earnings and price growth momentum. Criterion 1 specifies accelerating EPS growth rates over recent fiscal years, while criterion 2 discards companies for which recent earnings growth has been negative. Criterion 3 further screens for companies that have beaten consensus earnings expectations—have had a positive earnings surprise—in the most recent quarter. A positive earnings surprise suggests that past earnings growth is continuing. Criteria 4 and 5 screen for positive recent stock price momentum. Criterion 6 retains only stocks with at least average market liquidity. Note the absence of any valuation multiples among the screening criteria: A value investor's screening criteria would typically include a rule to screen out issues that are expensively valued relative to earnings or assets.

4.2. Pitfalls in Fundamental Investing

Pitfalls in fundamental investing include behavioral biases, the value trap, and the growth trap.

4.2.1. Behavioral Bias
Fundamental, discretionary investing in general and stock selection in particular depend on subjective judgments by portfolio managers based on their research and analysis.

However, human judgment, though potentially more insightful than a purely quantitative method, can be less rational and is often susceptible to human biases. The CFA Program curriculum chapters on behavioral finance divide behavioral biases into two broad groups: cognitive errors and emotional biases. Cognitive errors are basic statistical, information-processing, or memory errors that cause a decision to deviate from the rational decisions of traditional finance, while emotional biases arise spontaneously as a result of attitudes and feelings that can cause a decision to deviate from the rational decisions of traditional finance. Several biases that are relevant to active fundamental equity management are discussed here.

4.2.1.1. Confirmation Bias

A cognitive error, confirmation bias—sometimes referred to as "stock love bias"—is the tendency of analysts and investors to look for information that confirms their existing beliefs about their favorite companies and to ignore or undervalue any information that contradicts their existing beliefs. This behavior creates selective exposure, perception, and retention and may be thought of as a selection bias. Some of the consequences are a poorly diversified portfolio, excessive risk exposure, and holdings in poorly performing securities. Actively seeking out the opinions of other investors or team members and looking for information from a range of sources to challenge existing beliefs may reduce the risk of confirmation bias.

4.2.1.2. Illusion of Control

The basic philosophy behind active equity management is that investors believe they can control or at least influence outcomes. Skilled investors have a healthy confidence in their own ability to select stocks and influence outcomes, and they expect to outperform the market. The illusion of control bias refers to the human tendency to overestimate these abilities. Langer (1983) defines the illusion of control bias as "an expectancy of a personal success probability inappropriately higher than the objective probability would warrant." The illusion of control is a cognitive error.

Having an illusion of control could lead to excessive trading and/or heavy weighting on a few stocks. Investors should seek contrary viewpoints and set and enforce proper trading and portfolio diversification rules to try to avoid this problem.

4.2.1.3. Availability Bias

Availability bias is an information-processing bias whereby individuals take a mental shortcut in estimating the probability of an outcome based on the availability of the information and how easily the outcome comes to mind. Easily recalled outcomes are often perceived as being more likely than those that are harder to recall or understand. Availability bias falls in the cognitive error category. In fundamental equity investing, this bias may reduce the investment opportunity set and result in insufficient diversification as the portfolio manager relies on familiar stocks that reflect a narrow range of experience. Setting an appropriate investment strategy in line with the investment horizon, as well as conducting a disciplined portfolio analysis with a long-term focus, will help eliminate any short-term over-emphasis caused by this bias.

4.2.1.4. Loss Aversion

Loss aversion is an emotional bias whereby investors tend to prefer avoiding losses over achieving gains. A number of studies on loss aversion suggest that, psychologically, losses are significantly more powerful than gains. In absolute value terms, the utility derived from a gain is much lower than the utility given up in an equivalent loss.

Loss aversion can cause investors to hold unbalanced portfolios in which poorly performing positions are maintained in the hope of potential recovery and successful investments are sold (and the gains realized) prematurely in order to avoid further risk. A disciplined trading strategy with firmly established stop-loss rules is essential to prevent fundamental investors from falling into this trap.

4.2.1.5. Overconfidence Bias

Overconfidence bias is an emotional bias whereby investors demonstrate unwarranted faith in their own intuitive reasoning, judgment, and/or cognitive abilities. This overconfidence may be the result of overestimating knowledge levels, abilities, and access to information. Unlike the illusion of control bias, which is a cognitive error, overconfidence bias is an illusion of exaggerated knowledge and abilities. Investors may, for example, attribute success to their own ability rather than to luck. Such bias means that the portfolio manager underestimates risks and overestimates expected returns. Regularly reviewing actual investment records and seeking constructive feedback from other professionals can help investors gain awareness of such self-attribution bias.

4.2.1.6. Regret Aversion Bias

An emotional bias, regret aversion bias causes investors to avoid making decisions that they fear will turn out poorly. Simply put, investors try to avoid the pain of regret associated with bad decisions. This bias may actually prevent investors from making decisions. They may instead hold on to positions for too long and, in the meantime, lose out on profitable investment opportunities.

A carefully defined portfolio review process can help mitigate the effects of regret aversion bias. Such a process might, for example, require investors to periodically review and justify existing positions or to substantiate the decision not to have exposure to other stocks in the universe.

4.2.2. Value and Growth Traps

Value- and growth-oriented investors face certain distinctive risks, often described as "traps."

4.2.2.1. The Value Trap

A value trap is a stock that appears to be attractively valued—with a low P/E multiple (and/or low price-to-book-value or price-to-cash-flow multiples)—because of a significant price fall but that may still be overpriced given its worsening future prospects. For example, the fact that a company is trading at a low price relative to earnings or book value might indicate that the company or the entire sector is facing deteriorating future prospects and that stock prices may stay low for an extended period of time or decline even further. Often, a value trap appears to be such an attractive investment that investors struggle to understand why the stock fails to perform. Value investors should conduct thorough research before investing in any company that appears to be cheap so that they fully understand the reasons for what appears to be an attractive valuation. Stock prices generally need catalysts or a change in perceptions in order to advance. If a company doesn't have any catalysts to trigger a reevaluation of its prospects, there is less of a chance that the stock price will adjust to reflect its fair value. In such a case, although the stock may appear to be an attractive investment because of a low multiple, it could lead the investor into a value trap.

HSBC Holdings is a multinational banking and financial services holding company headquartered in London. It has a dual primary listing on the Hong Kong Stock Exchange (HKSE) and the London Stock Exchange (LSE) and is a constituent of both the Hang Seng Index (HSI) and the FTSE 100 Index (UKX).

The stock traded on the HKSE at a price of over $80 at the end of 2013 and dropped below $50 in mid-June 2016. It declined by 43.7% in two and a half years, while the industry index (the Hang Seng Financial Index) lost only 5.4% over the same period. At the start of the period, HSBC Holdings looked cheap compared to peers and its own history, with average P/E and P/B multiples of 10.9x and 0.9x, respectively. Despite appearing undervalued, the stock performed poorly over the subsequent two-and-a-half-year period (see Exhibit 27) for reasons that included the need for extensive cost cutting. The above scenario is an illustration of a value trap.

EXHIBIT 27   Performance of HSBC vs. Its Value Indicators

Panel A

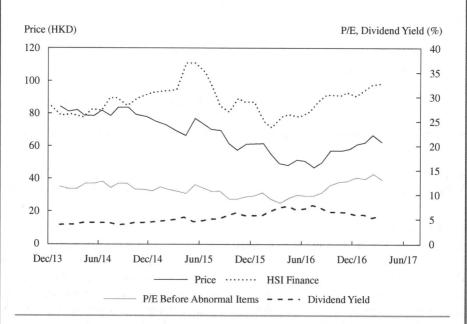

Price (HKD)   P/E, Dividend Yield (%)

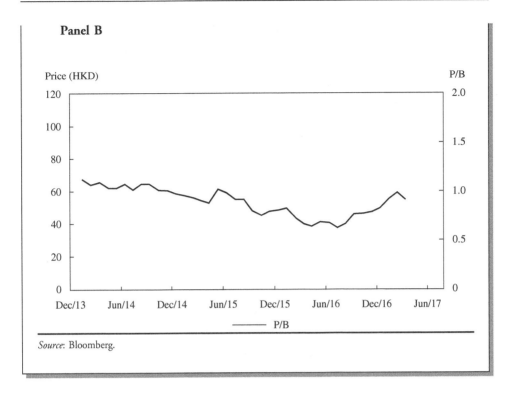

Panel B

Source: Bloomberg.

4.2.2.2. *The Growth Trap*

Investors in growth stocks do so with the expectation that the share price will appreciate when the company experiences above-average earnings (or cash flow) growth in the future. However, if the company's results fall short of these expectations, stock performance is affected negatively. The stock may also turn out to have been overpriced at the time of the purchase. The company may deliver above-average earnings or cash flow growth, in line with expectations, but the share price may not move any higher due to its already high starting level. The above circumstances are known as a growth trap. As with the value trap in the case of value stocks, the possibility of a growth trap should be considered when investing in what are perceived to be growth stocks.

Investors are often willing to justify paying high multiples for growth stocks in the belief that the current earnings are sustainable and that earnings are likely to grow fast in the future. However, neither of these assumptions may turn out to be true: The company's superior market position may be unsustainable and may last only until its competitors respond. Industry-specific variables often determine the pace at which new entrants or existing competitors respond and compete away any supernormal profits. It is also not uncommon to see earnings grow quickly from a very low base only to undergo a marked slowdown after that initial expansion.

5. CREATING A QUANTITATIVE ACTIVE INVESTMENT STRATEGY

Quantitative active equity investing began in the 1970s and became a mainstream investment approach in the subsequent decades. Many quantitative equity funds suffered significant losses in August 2007, an event that became known as the "quant meltdown." The subsequent global financial crisis contributed to growing suspicions about the sustainability of quantitative investing. However, both the performance and the perception of quantitative investing have recovered significantly since 2012 as this approach has regained popularity.

5.1. Creating a Quantitative Investment Process

Quantitative (systematic, or rules-based) investing generally has a structured and well-defined investment process. It starts with a belief or hypothesis. Investors collect data from a wide range of sources. Data science and management are also critical for dealing with missing values and outliers. Investors then create quantitative models to test their hypothesis. Once they are comfortable with their models' investment value, quantitative investors combine their return-predicting models with risk controls to construct their portfolios.

5.1.1. Defining the Market Opportunity (Investment Thesis)

Like fundamental active investing, quantitative active investing is based on a belief that the market is competitive but not necessarily efficient. Fund managers use publicly available information to predict future returns of stocks, using factors to build their return-forecasting models.

5.1.2. Acquiring and Processing Data

Data management is probably the least glamorous part of the quantitative investing process. However, investors often spend most of their time building databases, mapping data from different sources, understanding the data availability, cleaning up the data, and reshaping the data into a usable format. The most commonly used data in quantitative investing typically fall into the following categories:

- **Company mapping** is used to track many companies over time and across data vendors. Each company may also have multiple classes of shares. New companies go public, while some existing companies disappear due to bankruptcies, mergers, or takeovers. Company names, ticker symbols, and other identifiers can also change over time. Different data vendors have their own unique identifiers.
- **Company fundamentals** include company demographics, financial statements, and other market data (e.g., price, dividends, stock splits, trading volume). Quantitative portfolio managers almost never collect company fundamental data themselves. Instead, they rely on data vendors, such as Capital IQ, Compustat, Worldscope, Reuters, FactSet, and Bloomberg.
- **Survey data** include details of corporate earnings, forecasts, and estimates by various market participants, macroeconomic variables, sentiment indicators, and information on funds flow.

- **Unconventional data,** or unstructured data, include satellite images, measures of news sentiment, customer–supplier chain metrics, and corporate events, among many other types of information.

Data are almost never in the format that is required for quantitative investment analysis. Hence, investors spend a significant amount of time checking data for consistency, cleaning up errors and outliers, and transforming the data into a usable format.

5.1.3. Backtesting the Strategy

Once the required data are available in the appropriate form, strategy backtesting is undertaken. Backtesting is a simulation of real-life investing. For example, in a standard monthly backtest, one can build a portfolio based on a value factor as of a given month-end—perhaps 10 years ago—and then track the return of this portfolio over the subsequent month. Investors normally repeat this process (i.e., rebalance the portfolio) according to a predefined frequency or rule for multiple years to evaluate how such a portfolio would perform and assess the effectiveness of a given strategy over time.

5.1.3.1. Information Coefficient

Under the assumption that expected returns are linearly related to factor exposures, the correlation between factor exposures and their holding period returns for a cross section of securities has been used as a measure of factor performance in quantitative backtests. This correlation for a factor is known in this context as the factor's information coefficient (IC). An advantage of the IC is that it aggregates information about factors from all securities in the investment universe, in contrast to an approach that uses only the best and worst deciles (a quantile-based approach), which captures only the top and bottom extremes.

The Pearson IC is the simple correlation coefficient between the factor scores (essentially standardized exposures) for the current period's and the next period's stock returns. As it is a correlation coefficient, its value is always between –1 and +1 (or, expressed in percentage terms, between –100% and +100%). The higher the IC, the higher the predictive power of the factor for subsequent returns. As a simple rule of thumb, in relation to US equities, any factor with an average monthly IC of 5%–6% is considered very strong. The coefficient is sensitive to outliers, as is illustrated below.

A similar but more robust measure is the Spearman rank IC, which is often preferred by practitioners. The Spearman rank IC is essentially the Pearson correlation coefficient between the ranked factor scores and ranked forward returns.

In the example shown in Exhibit 28 for earnings yield, the Pearson IC is negative at –0.8%, suggesting that the signal did not perform well and was negatively correlated with the subsequent month's returns. Looking more carefully, however, we can see that the sample factor is generally in line with the subsequent stock returns, with the exception of Stock I, for which the factor predicts the highest return but which turns out to be the worst performer. A single outlier can therefore turn what may actually be a good factor into a bad one, as the Pearson IC is sensitive to outliers. In contrast, the Spearman rank IC is at 40%, suggesting that the factor has strong predictive power for subsequent returns. If three equally weighted portfolios had been constructed, the long basket (Stocks G, H, and I) would have outperformed the short basket (Stocks A, B, and C) by 56 bps in this period.

EXHIBIT 28   Pearson Correlation Coefficient IC and Spearman Rank IC

Stock	Factor Score	Subsequent Month Return (%)	Rank of Factor Score	Rank of Return
A	−1.45	−3.00%	9	8
B	−1.16	−0.60%	8	7
C	−0.60	−0.50%	7	6
D	−0.40	−0.48%	6	5
E	0.00	1.20%	5	4
F	0.40	3.00%	4	3
G	0.60	3.02%	3	2
H	1.16	3.05%	2	1
I	1.45	−8.50%	1	9
Mean	0.00	−0.31%		
Standard deviation	1.00	3.71%		
Pearson IC		−0.80%		
Spearman rank IC				40.00%
Long/short tercile portfolio return				0.56%

Note: The portfolio is split into terciles, with each tercile containing one-third of the stocks.
Source: QES (Wolfe Research).

5.1.3.2. Creating a Multifactor Model

After studying the efficacy of single factors, managers need to decide which factors to include in a multifactor model. Factor selection and weighting is a fairly complex subject. Managers can select and weight each factor using either qualitative or systematic processes. For example, Qian, Hua, and Sorensen (2007) propose treating each factor as an asset; therefore, factor weighting becomes an asset allocation decision. A standard mean–variance optimization can also be used to weight factors. Deciding on which factors to include and their weight is a critical piece of the strategy. Investors should bear in mind that factors may be effective individually but not add material value to a factor model because they are correlated with other factors.

5.1.4. Evaluating the Strategy

Once backtesting is complete, the performance of the strategy can be evaluated. An out-of-sample backtest, in which a different set of data is used to evaluate the model's performance, is generally done to confirm model robustness. However, even strategies with great out-of-sample performance may perform poorly in live trading. Managers generally compute various statistics—such as the *t*-statistic, Sharpe ratio, Sortino ratio, VaR, conditional VaR, and drawdown characteristics—to form an opinion on the outcome of their out-of-sample backtest.

5.1.5. Portfolio Construction Issues in Quantitative Investment

Most quantitative managers spend the bulk of their time searching for and exploring models that can predict stock returns, and may overlook the importance of portfolio construction to the quantitative investment process. While portfolio construction is covered in greater detail in other chapters, the following aspects are particularly relevant to quantitative investing:

- **Risk models:** Risk models estimate the variance–covariance matrix of stock returns—that is, the risk of every stock and the correlation among stocks. Directly estimating the variance–covariance matrix using sample return data typically is infeasible and suffers from significant estimation errors.[21] Managers generally rely on commercial risk model vendors[22] for these data.
- **Trading costs:** There are two kinds of trading costs—explicit (e.g., commissions, fees, and taxes) and implicit (e.g., bid–ask spread and market impact). When two stocks have similar expected returns and risks, normally the one with lower execution costs is preferred.[23]

Unconventional Big Data and Machine-Learning Techniques

Rohal, Jussa, Luo, Wang, Zhao, Alvarez, Wang, and Elledge (2016) discuss the implications and applications of big data and machine-learning techniques in investment management. The rapid advancement in computing power today allows for the collection and processing of data from sources that were traditionally impossible or overly expensive to access, such as satellite images, social media, and payment-processing systems.

Investors now have access to data that go far beyond the traditional company fundamentals metrics. There are also many data vendors providing increasingly specialized or unique data content. Processing and incorporating unconventional data into existing investment frameworks, however, remains a challenge. With the improvements in computing speed and algorithms, significant successes in machine-learning techniques have been achieved. Despite concerns about data mining, machine learning has led to significant improvement in strategy performance.

5.2. Pitfalls in Quantitative Investment Processes

All active investment strategies have their pros and cons. There are many pitfalls that investors need to be aware of when they assess any quantitative strategy. Wang, Wang, Luo, Jussa, Rohal, and Alvarez (2014) discuss some of the common issues in quantitative investing in detail.

---

[21]One problem with a sample covariance matrix is the curse of dimensionality. For a portfolio of N assets, we need to estimate $N \times (N+1)/2$ parameters—that is, $N \times (N-1)/2$ covariance parameters and N estimates of stock-specific risk. For a universe of 3,000 stocks, we would have to estimate about 4.5 million parameters.

[22]MSCI Barra and Axioma are examples of data providers.

[23]Trading costs are covered in depth in separate curriculum chapters.

5.2.1. Survivorship Bias, Look-Ahead Bias, Data Mining, and Overfitting

Survivorship bias is one of the most common issues affecting quantitative decision-making. While investors are generally aware of the problem, they often underestimate its significance. When backtests use only those companies that are currently in business today, they ignore the stocks that have left the investment universe due to bankruptcy,[24] delisting, or acquisition. This approach creates a bias whereby only companies that have survived are tested and it is assumed that the strategy would never have invested in companies that have failed. Survivorship bias often leads to overly optimistic results and sometimes even causes investors to draw wrong conclusions.

The second major issue in backtesting is look-ahead bias. This bias results from using information that was unknown or unavailable at the time an investment decision was made. An example of this bias is the use of financial accounting data for a company at a point in time before the data were actually released by the company.

In computer science, data mining refers to automated computational processes for discovering patterns in large datasets, often involving sophisticated statistical techniques, computation algorithms, and large-scale database systems. In finance, data mining can refer to such a process and can introduce a bias that results in model overfitting. It can be described as excessive search analysis of past financial data to uncover patterns and to conform to a pre-determined model for potential use in investing.

5.2.2. Turnover, Transaction Costs, and Short Availability

Backtesting is often conducted in an ideal, but unrealistic world without transaction costs, constraints on turnover, or limits on the availability of long and short positions. In reality, managers may face numerous constraints, such as limits on turnover and difficulties in establishing short positions in certain markets. Depending on how fast their signal decays, they may or may not be able to capture their model's expected excess return in a live trading process.

More importantly, trading is not free. Transaction costs can easily erode returns significantly. An example is the use of short-term reversal as a factor: Stocks that have performed well recently (say, in the last month) are more likely to revert (underperform) in the subsequent month. This reversal factor has been found to be a good stock selection signal in the Japanese equity market (before transaction costs). As shown in Exhibit 29, in a theoretical world with no transaction costs, a simple long/short strategy (buying the top 20% dividend-paying stocks in Japan with the worst performance in the previous month and shorting the bottom 20% stocks with the highest returns in the previous month) has generated an annual return of 12%, beating the classic value factor of price to book. However, if the transaction cost assumption is changed from 0 bps to 30 bps per trade, the return of the reversal strategy drops sharply, while the return of the price-to-book value strategy drops only modestly.

---

[24]In the United States, companies may continue to trade after filing for bankruptcy as long as they continue to meet listing requirements. However, their stocks are normally removed from most equity indexes.

EXHIBIT 29   Annualized Returns with Different Transaction Cost Assumptions

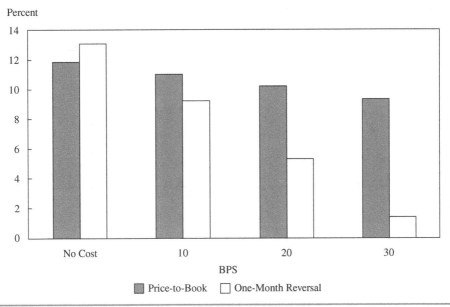

Sources: Compustat, Capital IQ, Thomson Reuters.

Quant Crowding

In the first half of 2007, despite some early signs of the US subprime crisis, the global equity market was relatively calm. Then, in August 2007, many of the standard factors used by quantitative managers suffered significant losses,[25] and quantitative equity managers' performance suffered. These losses have been attributed to crowding among quantitative managers following similar trades (see Khandani and Lo 2008). Many of these managers headed for the exit at the same time, exacerbating the losses.

How can it be concluded that the August 2007 quant crisis was due to crowding? More importantly, how can crowding be measured so that the next crowded trade can be avoided? Jussa et al (2016a) used daily short interest data from Markit's securities finance database to measure crowding. They proposed that if stocks with poor price momentum are heavily shorted[26] relative to outperforming stocks, it indicates that many investors are following a momentum style. Hence, momentum as an investment strategy might get crowded. A measure of crowding that may be called a "crowding coefficient" can be estimated by regressing short interest on price momentum.

---

[25]The average performance of many common factors was strong and relatively stable in 2003–2007. Actually, value and momentum factors suffered more severe losses in late 2002 and around March 2009.
[26]Short interest can be defined as the ratio of the number of stocks shorted to the number of stocks in the available inventory for lending.

Details of such regression analysis are beyond the scope of this chapter.[27] As shown in Exhibit 30, the level of crowding for momentum reached a local peak in mid-2007. In the exhibit, increasing values of the crowding coefficient indicate greater crowding in momentum strategies.

EXHIBIT 30   Crowding in Momentum Strategies

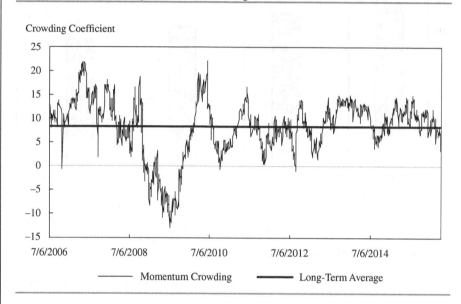

Sources: Compustat, FTSE Russell, Markit.

EXAMPLE 9   How to Start a Quantitative Investment Process

An asset management firm that traditionally follows primarily a fundamental value investing approach wants to diversify its investment process by incorporating a quantitative element. Discuss the potential benefits and hurdles involved in adding quantitative models to a fundamental investment approach.

Solution: Quantitative investing is based on building models from attributes of thousands of stocks. The performance of quantitative strategies is generally not highly correlated with that of fundamental approaches. Therefore, in theory, adding a quantitative overlay may provide some diversification benefit to the firm.

---

[27]For more on this subject, see Jussa, Rohal, Wang, Zhao, Luo, Alvarez, Wang, and Elledge (2016) and Cahan and Luo (2013).

In practice, however, because the processes behind quantitative and fundamental investing tend to be quite different, combining these two approaches is not always straightforward. Quantitative investing requires a large upfront investment in data, technology, and model development. It is generally desirable to use factors and models that are different from those used by most other investors to avoid potential crowded trades.

Managers need to be particularly careful with their backtesting so that the results do not suffer from look-ahead and survivorship biases. Transaction costs and short availability (if the fund involves shorting) should be incorporated into the backtesting.

6. EQUITY INVESTMENT STYLE CLASSIFICATION

An investment style classification process generally splits the stock universe into two or three groups, such that each group contains stocks with similar characteristics. The returns of stocks within a style group should therefore be correlated with one another, and the returns of stocks in different style groups should have less correlation. The common style characteristics used in active management include value, growth, blend (or core), size, price momentum, volatility, income (high dividend), and earnings quality. Stock membership in an industry, sector, or country group—for example, the financial sector or emerging markets—is also used to classify the investment style. Exhibit 31 lists a few mainstream categories of investment styles in use today.

EXHIBIT 31   Examples of Investment Styles

Characteristics based	Value, Growth or Blend/Core
	Capitalization
	Volatility
Membership based	Sector
	Country
	Market (developed or emerging)
Position based	Long/short (net long, short, or neutral)

Investment style classification is important for asset owners who seek to select active strategies. It allows active equity managers with similar styles to be compared with one another. Further, comparing the active returns or positions of a manager with those of the right style index can provide more information about the manager's active strategy and approach. A manager's portfolio may appear to have active positions when compared with the general market benchmark index; however, that manager may actually follow a style index and do so passively. Identifying the actual investment style of equity managers is important for asset owners in their decision-making process.

6.1. Different Approaches to Style Classification

Equity styles are defined by pairs of common attributes, such as value and growth, large cap and small cap, high volatility and low volatility, high dividend and low dividend, or developed markets and emerging markets. Style pairs need not be mutually exclusive. Each pair interprets the stock performance from a different perspective. A combination of several style pairs may often give a more complete picture of the sources of stock returns.

Identifying the investment styles of active managers helps to reveal the sources of added value in the portfolio. Modern portfolio theory advocates the use of efficient portfolio management of a diversified portfolio of stocks and bonds. Gupta, Skallsjö, and Li (2016) detail how the concept of diversification, when extended to different strategies and investment processes, can have a significant impact on the risk and reward of an investor's portfolio. A portfolio's risk–return profile is improved not only by including multiple asset classes but also by employing managers with different investment styles. An understanding of the investment style of a manager helps in evaluating the manager and confirming whether he or she sticks with the claimed investment style or deviates from it.

Two main approaches are often used in style analysis: a holdings-based approach and a returns-based approach. Each approach has its own strengths and weaknesses.

6.1.1. Holdings-Based Approaches

An equity investment style is actually the aggregation of attributes from individual stocks in the portfolio. Holdings-based approaches to style analysis are done bottom-up, but they are executed differently by the various commercial investment information providers. Using different criteria or different sources of underlying value and growth numbers may lead to slightly different classifications for stocks and therefore may result in different style characterizations for the same portfolio. In the style classification process followed by Morningstar and Thomson Reuters Lipper, the styles of individual stocks are clearly defined in that a stock's attribute for a specific style is 1 if it is included in that style index; otherwise, it is 0. The methodology used by MSCI and FTSE Russell, on the other hand, assumes that a stock can have characteristics of two styles, such as value and growth, at the same time. This methodology uses a multifactor approach to assign style inclusion factors to each stock. So a particular stock can belong to both value and growth styles by a pre-determined fraction. A portfolio's active exposure to a certain style equals the sum of the style attributes from all the individual stocks, weighted by their active positions.

The Morningstar Style Box

The Morningstar Style Box first appeared in 1992 to help investors and advisers determine the investment style of a fund. In a style box, each style pair splits the stock universe into two to three groups, such as value, core (or "blend"), and growth. The same universe can be split by another style definition—for example, large cap, mid cap, and small cap. The Morningstar Style Box splits the stock universe along both style dimensions, creating a grid of nine squares. It uses holdings-based style analysis and classifies about the same number of stocks in each of the value, core, and growth styles. Morningstar determines the value and growth scores by using five stock attributes (see Exhibit 33). The current Morningstar Style Box, as shown in Exhibit 32, is a nine-square grid featuring three stock investment styles for each of three size categories: large, mid, and small. Two of the three style categories are "value" and "growth," common to both stocks and funds. However, the third, central column is labeled "core" for stocks (i.e., those stocks for which neither value nor growth characteristics dominate) and "blend" for funds (meaning that the fund holds a mixture of growth and value stocks).

EXHIBIT 32   Morningstar Fund Style Classification

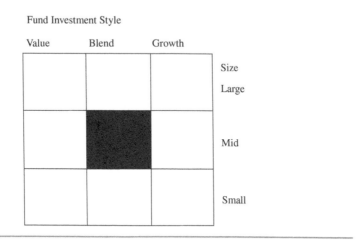

Source: Morningstar.

6.1.1.1. Large-Cap, Mid-Cap, and Small-Cap Classifications

The size classification is determined by the company's market capitalization. There is no consensus on what the size thresholds for the different categories should be, and indeed, different data and research providers use different criteria for size classification purposes. Large-cap companies tend to be well-established companies with a strong market presence, good levels of information disclosure, and extensive scrutiny by the investor community and the media. While these attributes may not apply universally across different parts of the world, large-cap companies are recognized as being lower risk than smaller companies and offering more limited future growth potential. Small-cap companies, on the other hand, tend to be less mature companies with potentially greater room for future growth, higher risk of failure, and a lower degree of analyst and public scrutiny.

Mid-cap companies tend to rank between the two other groups on many important parameters, such as size, revenues, employee count, and client base. In general, they are in a more advanced stage of development than small-cap companies but provide greater growth potential than large-cap companies.

There is no consensus on the boundaries that separate large-, mid-, and small-cap companies. One practice is to define large-cap stocks as those that account for the top ~70% of the capitalization of all stocks in the universe, with mid-cap stocks representing the next ~20% and small-cap stocks accounting for the balance.

6.1.1.2. Measuring Growth, Value, and Core Characteristics

Equity style analysis starts with assigning a style score to each individual stock. Taking the value/growth style pair as an example, each stock is assigned a value score based on the combination of several value and growth characteristics or factors of that stock. The simplest value scoring model uses one factor, price-to-book ratio, to rank the stock. The bottom half of the stocks in this ranking (smaller P/Bs) constitute the value index, while the stocks ranked in the top half (higher P/Bs) constitute the growth index. Weighting the stocks by their market capitalization thus creates both a value index and a growth index, with the condition that each style index must represent 50% of the market capitalization of all stocks in the target universe. A comprehensive value scoring model may use more factors in addition to price to book, such as price to earnings, price to sales, price to cash flow, return on equity, dividend yield, and so on. The combination of these factors through a predefined process, such as assigning a fixed weight to each selected factor, generates the value score. The value score is usually a number between 0 and 1, corresponding to 0% and 100% contribution to the value index. Depending on the methodologies employed by the vendors, the value score may be a fraction. A security with a value score of 0.6 will have 60% of its market capitalization allocated to the value index and the remaining 40% to the growth index.

Morningstar's Classification Criteria for Value Stocks

For each stock, Morningstar assigns a growth score and a value score, each based on five components that are combined with pre-determined weights, as shown in Exhibit 33.

EXHIBIT 33   Morningstar Value and Growth Scoring Scheme

Value Score Components and Weights		Growth Score Components and Weights	
Forward-looking measures	**50.0%**	*Forward-looking measures*	**50.0%**
*Price to projected earnings		*Long-term projected earnings growth	
Historical measures	**50.0%**	*Historical measures*	**50.0%**
*Price to book	12.5%	*Historical earnings growth	12.5%
*Price to sales	12.5%	*Sales growth	12.5%
*Price to cash flow	12.5%	*Cash flow growth	12.5%
*Dividend yield	12.5%	*Book value growth	12.5%

The scores are scaled to a range of 0 to 100, and the difference between the stock's growth and value scores is called the net style score. If this net style score is strongly negative, approaching −100, the stock's style is classified as value. If the result is strongly positive, the stock is classified as growth. If the scores for value and growth are similar in strength, the net style score will be close to zero and the stock will be classified as core. On average, value, core, and growth stocks each account for approximately one-third of the total capitalization in a given row of the Morningstar Style Box.

MSCI World Value and Growth Indexes

MSCI provides a range of indexes that include value and growth. In order to construct those indexes, the firm needs to establish the individual stocks' characteristics. The following (simplified) process is used to establish how much of each stock's market capitalization should be included in the respective indexes.

The value investment style characteristics for index construction are defined using three variables: book-value-to-price ratio, 12-month forward-earnings-to-price ratio, and dividend yield. The growth investment style characteristics for index construction are defined using five variables: long-term forward EPS growth rate, short-term forward EPS growth rate, current internal growth rate, long-term historical EPS growth trend, and long-term historical sales-per-share growth trend. Z-scores for each variable are calculated and aggregated for each security to determine the security's overall style characteristics. For example, a stock is assigned a so-called "value inclusion factor" of 0.6, which means that the stock could have both value and growth characteristics and contributes to the performance of the value and growth indexes by 60% and 40%, respectively. Exhibit 34 shows the cumulative return of the MSCI World Value and MSCI World Growth indexes since 1975.

EXHIBIT 34   Cumulative Return of MSCI World Value and Growth Indexes since 1975

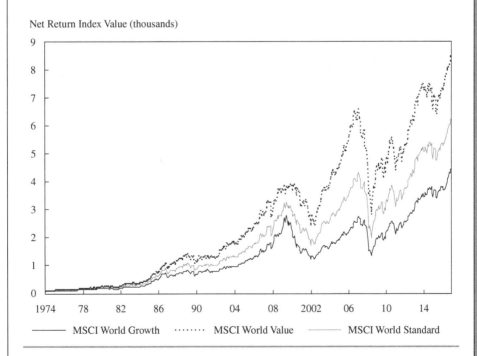

Net Return Index Value (thousands)

——— MSCI World Growth   ⋯⋯⋯ MSCI World Value   ——— MSCI World Standard

Source: MSCI.

6.1.2. Returns-Based Style Analysis

Many investment managers do not disclose the full details of their portfolios, and therefore a holdings-based approach cannot be used to assess their strategies. The investment style of these portfolio managers is therefore analyzed by using a returns-based approach to compare the returns of the employed strategy to those of a set of style indexes.

The objective of a returns-based style analysis is to find the style concentration of underlying holdings by identifying the style indexes that provide significant contributions to fund returns with the help of statistical tools. Such an analysis attributes fund returns to selected investment styles by running a constrained multivariate regression:[28]

$$r_t = \alpha + \sum_{s=1}^{m} \beta^s R_t^s + \varepsilon_t$$

where

r_t = the fund return within the period ending at time t

R_t^s = the return of style index s in the same period

β^s = the fund exposure to style s (with constraints $\sum_{s=1}^{m} \beta^s = 1$ and $\beta^s > 0$ for a long-only portfolio)

α = a constant often interpreted as the value added by the fund manager

ε_t = the residual return that cannot be explained by the styles used in the analysis

The key inputs to a returns-based style analysis are the historical returns for the portfolio and the returns for the style indexes. The critical part, however, is the selection of the styles used, as stock returns can be highly correlated within the same sector, across sectors, and even across global markets. If available, the manager's own description of his or her style is a good starting point for determining the investment styles that can be used.

Commercial investment information providers, such as Thomson Reuters Lipper and Morningstar, perform the role of collecting and analyzing fund data and classifying the funds into style groups.

Data Sources

The success of a returns-based style analysis depends, to some extent, on the choice of style indexes. The component-based style indexes provided by investment information providers enable analysts to identify the style that is closest to the investment strategy employed by the fund manager.

Thomson Reuters Lipper provides mutual and hedge fund data as well as analytical and reporting tools to institutional and retail investors. All funds covered by Lipper are given a classification based on statements in the funds' prospectuses. Funds that are considered "diversified," because they invest across economic sectors and/or countries, also have a portfolio-based classification. Exhibit 35 shows the Lipper fund classifications for US-listed open-end equity funds.

[28]Sharpe (1992).

EXHIBIT 35   Lipper's Style Classification

	OPEN-END EQUITY FUNDS		
	General Domestic Equity	**World Equity**	**Sector Equity**
Prospectus-Based Classifications	**All** prospectus-based classifications in this group are considered diversified.	**Some** prospectus-based classifications in this group are considered diversified (global and international types only).	**No** prospectus-based classifications in this group are considered diversified.
	Capital Appreciation	Gold	Health/Biotech
	Growth	European Region	Natural
	Micro Cap	Pacific Region	Resources
	Mid Cap	Japan	Technology
	Small Cap	Pacific ex-Japan	Telecom
	Growth & Income	China	Utilities
	S&P 500	Emerging Markets	Financial
	Equity	Latin America	Services
	Income	Global	Real Estate
		Global Small Cap	Specialty &
		International	Miscellaneous
		International Small Cap	
Portfolio-Based Classifications	Large-Cap Growth	Global Large-Cap Growth	
	Large-Cap Core	Global Large-Cap Core	
	Large-Cap Value	Global Large-Cap Value	
	Multi-Cap Growth	Global Multi-Cap Growth	
	Multi-Cap Core	Global Multi-Cap Core	
	Multi-Cap Value	Global Multi-Cap Value	
	Mid-Cap Growth	Global Small-/Mid-Cap Growth	
	Mid-Cap Core	Global Small-/Mid-Cap Core	
	Mid-Cap Value	Global Small-/Mid-Cap Value	
	Small-Cap Growth	International	
	Small-Cap Core	Large-Cap Growth	
	Small-Cap Value	International Large-Cap Core	
	S&P 500	International Large-Cap Value	
	Equity Income	International	
		Multi-Cap Growth	
		International Multi-Cap Core	
		International Multi-Cap Value	
		International Small-/Mid-Cap Growth	
		International Small-/Mid-Cap Core	
		International Small-/Mid-Cap Value	

Source: Thomson Reuters Lipper.

6.1.3. Manager Self-Identification

Equity strategy investment styles result from the active equity manager's employment of a particular strategy to manage the fund. The fund's investment strategy is usually described in the fund prospectus and can be used to identify the fund's investment objective. This objective can be regarded as the manager's self-identification of the investment style.

Returns-based or holdings-based style analysis is commonly used to identify the investment style—such as value/growth or large cap/small cap—and to determine whether it corresponds to the manager's self-identified style. Some other styles, however, cannot be easily identified by such methods. For example, the styles of equity hedge funds, equity income funds, and special sector funds can be more efficiently identified using a combination of manager self-identification and holdings- or returns-based analysis.

Some equity hedge fund styles are non-standard and do not fit into any of the established style categories. Examples include long/short equity, equity market neutral, and dedicated short bias. For such funds, the investment objective is often laid out in the prospectus, which explains the fund's investment strategy. The prospectus becomes the key source of information for those assigning styles to such funds.

6.2. Strengths and Limitations of Style Analysis

Holdings-based style analysis is generally more accurate than returns-based analysis because it uses the actual portfolio holdings. Portfolio managers (and those who assess their strategies and performance) can see how each portfolio holding contributes to the portfolio's style, verify that the style is in line with the stated investment philosophy, and take action if they wish to prevent the portfolio's style from moving away from its intended target. Unlike returns-based style analysis, holdings-based style analysis is able to show the styles that any portfolio is exposed to, thus providing input for style allocation decisions.

Holdings-based style analysis requires the availability of all the portfolio constituents as well as the style attributes of each stock in the portfolio. While this information may be accessible for current portfolios, an analyst who wants to track the historical change in investment styles may face some difficulty. In this case, point-in-time databases are required for both the constituents of the fund and the stocks' style definitions.

As investment style research uses statistical and empirical methods to arrive at conclusions, it can produce inaccurate results due to limitations of the data or flaws in the application design. Kaplan (2011) argued that most returns-based style analysis models impose unnecessary constraints that limit the results within certain boundaries, making it difficult to detect more aggressive positions, such as deep value or micro cap. Furthermore, the limited availability of data on derivatives often makes holdings-based style analysis less effective for funds with substantial positions in derivatives. It is therefore important to understand the strengths and limitations of style analysis models in order to interpret the results correctly. Morningstar studies have concluded that holdings-based style analysis generally produces more accurate results than returns-based style analysis, although there may be exceptions. Ideally, practitioners should use both approaches: Returns-based models can often be more widely applied, while holdings-based models allow deeper style analysis.

Variation of Fund Characteristics within a Style Classification

Consider the Morningstar Style Box, in which funds are classified along two dimensions: value/growth and size (market capitalization). Within the same value style box, funds can be classified as large cap or small cap. To keep the classification map simple and concise, Morningstar omits other styles and characteristics, such as performance volatility and sector or market/region exposure. It is important to note that style classification provides only a reference to the key investment styles that may contribute to performance. The funds within the same style classification can be quite different in other characteristics, which may also contribute to fund returns and lead to differences in performance.

EXAMPLE 10   Equity Investment Styles

Consider an actively managed equity fund that has a five-year track record. An analyst performed both holdings-based and returns-based style analysis on the portfolio. She used the current portfolio holdings to perform the holdings-based style analysis and five-year historical monthly returns to carry out the returns-based analysis. The analyst found the following:

- Holdings-based style analysis on the current portfolio shows that the fund has value and growth exposures of 0.85 and 0.15, respectively.
- Returns-based style analysis with 60 months' historical returns shows that the value and growth exposures of the fund are equal to 0.4 and 0.6, respectively.

   Explain possible reason(s) for the inconsistency between the holdings-based and returns-based style analyses.

Solution: Some active equity managers may maintain one investment style over time in the belief that that particular style will outperform the general market. Others may rotate or switch between styles to accommodate the then-prevailing investment thesis. Returns-based style analysis regresses the portfolio's historical returns against the returns of the corresponding style indexes (over 60 months in this example). Its output indicates the average effect of investment styles employed during the period. While the holdings-based analysis suggests that the current investment style of the equity fund is value oriented, the returns-based analysis indicates that the style actually employed was likely in the growth category for a period of time within the past five years.

7. SUMMARY

This chapter discusses the different approaches to active equity management and describes how the various strategies are created. It also addresses the style classification of active approaches.

- Active equity management approaches can be generally divided into two groups: fundamental (also referred to as discretionary) and quantitative (also known as systematic or rules-based). Fundamental approaches stress the use of human judgment in arriving at an investment decision, whereas quantitative approaches stress the use of rules-based, quantitative models to arrive at a decision.
- The main differences between fundamental and quantitative approaches include the following characteristics: approach to the decision-making process (subjective versus objective); forecast focus (stock returns versus factor returns); information used (research versus data); focus of the analysis (depth versus breadth); orientation to the data (forward looking versus backward looking); and approach to portfolio risk (emphasis on judgment versus emphasis on optimization techniques).
- The main types of active management strategies include bottom-up, top-down, factor-based, and activist.
- Bottom-up strategies begin at the company level, and use company and industry analyses to assess the intrinsic value of the company and determine whether the stock is undervalued or overvalued relative to its market price.
- Fundamental managers often focus on one or more of the following company and industry characteristics: business model and branding, competitive advantages, and management and corporate governance.
- Bottom-up strategies are often divided into value-based approaches and growth-based approaches.
- Top-down strategies focus on the macroeconomic environment, demographic trends, and government policies to arrive at investment decisions.
- Top-down strategies are used in several investment decision processes, including the following: country and geographic allocation, sector and industry rotation, equity style rotation, volatility-based strategies, and thematic investment strategies.
- Quantitative equity investment strategies often use factor-based models. A factor-based strategy aims to identify significant factors that drive stock prices and to construct a portfolio with a positive bias toward such factors.
- Factors can be grouped based on fundamental characteristics—such as value, growth, and price momentum—or on unconventional data.
- Activist investors specialize in taking meaningful stakes in listed companies and influencing those companies to make changes to their management, strategy, or capital structures for the purpose of increasing the stock's value and realizing a gain on their investment.
- Statistical arbitrage (or "stat arb") strategies use statistical and technical analysis to exploit pricing anomalies and achieve superior returns. Pairs trading is an example of a popular and simple statistical arbitrage strategy.
- Event-driven strategies exploit market inefficiencies that may occur around corporate events such as mergers and acquisitions, earnings announcements, bankruptcies, share buybacks, special dividends, and spinoffs.
- The fundamental active investment process includes the following steps: define the investment universe; prescreen the universe; understand the industry and business; forecast

the company's financial performance; convert forecasts into a target price; construct the portfolio with the desired risk profile; and rebalance the portfolio according to a buy and sell discipline.

- Pitfalls in fundamental investing include behavioral biases, the value trap, and the growth trap.
- Behavioral biases can be divided into two groups: cognitive errors and emotional biases. Typical biases that are relevant to active equity management include confirmation bias, illusion of control, availability bias, loss aversion, overconfidence, and regret aversion.
- The quantitative active investment process includes the following steps: define the investment thesis; acquire, clean, and process the data; backtest the strategy; evaluate the strategy; and construct an efficient portfolio using risk and trading cost models.
- The pitfalls in quantitative investing include look-ahead and survivorship biases, overfitting, data mining, unrealistic turnover assumptions, transaction costs, and short availability.
- An investment style generally splits the stock universe into two or three groups, such that each group contains stocks with similar characteristics. The common style characteristics used in active management include value, size, price momentum, volatility, high dividend, and earnings quality. A stock's membership in an industry, sector, or country group is also used to classify the investment style.
- Two main approaches are often used in style analysis: a returns-based approach and a holdings-based approach. Holdings-based approaches aggregate the style scores of individual holdings, while returns-based approaches analyze the investment style of portfolio managers by comparing the returns of the strategy to those of a set of style indexes.

REFERENCES

Basu, S. 1977. "Investment Performance of Common Stocks in Relation to Their Price-Earnings Ratios: A Test of the Efficient Market Hypothesis." *Journal of Finance* 32 (3): 663–82.

Cahan, R., and Y. Luo. 2013. "Standing Out From the Crowd: Measuring Crowding in Quantitative Strategies." *Journal of Portfolio Management* 39 (4): 14–23.

Fama, E., and K.R. French. 1992. "The Cross-Section of Expected Stock Returns." *Journal of Finance* 47 (2): 427–65.

Fama, E., and K.R. French. 1993. "Common Risk Factors in the Returns on Stocks and Bonds." *Journal of Financial Economics* 33 (1): 3–56.

Fama, E., and K.R. French. 1996. "Multifactor Explanations of Asset Pricing Anomalies." *Journal of Finance* 51 (1): 55–84.

Graham, B., and D.L. Dodd. 1934. *Security Analysis*. New York: McGraw-Hill.

Greenblatt, J. 2010. *The Little Book That Still Beats the Market*. Hoboken, NJ: John Wiley & Sons.

Greenwald, B., J. Kahn, P. Sonkin, and M. Biema. 2001. *Value Investing: From Graham to Buffett and Beyond*. Hoboken, NJ: John Wiley & Sons.

Gupta, P., S. Skallsjö, and B. Li. 2016. *Multi-Asset Investing: A Practitioner's Framework*. Chichester, UK: John Wiley & Sons.

Jegadeesh, N., and S. Titman. 1993. "Returns to Buying Winners and Selling Losers: Implications for Stock Market Efficiency." *Journal of Finance* 48 (1): 65–91.

Jussa, J., G. Rohal, S. Wang, G. Zhao, Y. Luo, M. Alvarez, A. Wang, and D. Elledge. 2016a. "Strategy Crowding." Deutsche Bank (16 May).

Jussa, J., K. Webster, G. Zhao, and Y. Luo. 2016b. "Activism, Alpha and Action Heroes." Deutsche Bank (6 January).

Kaplan, P. 2011. *Frontiers of Modern Asset Allocation*. Hoboken, NJ: John Wiley & Sons.

Khandani, A., and A. Lo. 2008. "What Happened to the Quants in August 2007? Evidence from Factors and Transactions Data." NBER Working Paper 14465.

Lakonishok, J., A. Shleifer, and R.W. Vishny. 1994. "Contrarian Investment, Extrapolation, and Risk." *Journal of Finance* 49 (5): 1541–78.

Langer, E.J. 1983. *The Psychology of Control*. Beverly Hills, CA: Sage Publications.

Maug, E. 1998. "Large Shareholders as Monitors: Is There a Trade-Off between Liquidity and Control?" *Journal of Finance* 53 (1): 65–98.

Qian, E.E., R.H. Hua, and E.H. Sorensen. 2007. *Quantitative Equity Portfolio Management: Modern Techniques and Applications*. Boca Raton, FL: Chapman & Hall/CRC.

Rohal, G., J. Jussa, Y. Luo, S. Wang, G. Zhao, M. Alvarez, A. Wang, and D. Elledge. 2016. "Big Data in Investment Management." Deutsche Bank (17 February).

Sharpe, W.F. 1992. "Asset Allocation, Management Style, and Performance Measurement." *Journal of Portfolio Management* 18 (2): 7–19.

Sloan, R.G. 1996. "Do Stock Prices Fully Reflect Information in Accruals and Cash Flows about Future Earnings?" *Accounting Review* 71 (3): 289–315.

Wang, S., A. Wang, Y. Luo, J. Jussa, G. Rohal, and M. Alvarez. 2014. "Seven Sins of Quantitative Investing." Deutsche Bank Market Research (September).

PRACTICE PROBLEMS

The following information relates to questions 1–6

James Leonard is a fund-of-funds manager with Future Generation, a large sovereign fund. He is considering whether to pursue more in-depth due diligence processes with three large-cap long-only funds proposed by his analysts. Although the funds emphasize different financial metrics and use different implementation methodologies, they operate in the same market segment and are evaluated against the same benchmark. The analysts prepared a short description of each fund, presented in Exhibit 1.

EXHIBIT 1   Description of Each Candidate Fund

Fund	Description
Furlings	Furlings Investment Partners combines sector views and security selection. The firm's head manager uses several industry and economic indicators identified from his own experience during the last two decades, as well as his personal views on market flow dynamics, to determine how to position the fund on a sector basis. Sector deviations from the benchmark of 10% or more are common and are usually maintained for 12 to 24 months. At the same time, sector managers at Furlings use their expertise in dissecting financial statements and their understanding of the corporate branding and competitive landscape within sectors to build equally weighted baskets of securities within sectors. Each basket contains their 7 to 10 highest-conviction securities, favoring firms that have good governance, strong growth potential, competitive advantages such as branding, and attractive relative valuations. The Furlings master fund holds approximately 90 securities.

Fund	Description
Asgard	Asgard Investment Partners is a very large asset manager. It believes in investing in firms that have a strong business model and governance, reasonable valuations, solid capital structures with limited financial leverage, and above-average expected earnings growth for the next three years. Although the Asgard master fund invests in fewer than 125 securities, each sector analyst builds financial models that track as many as 50 firms. To support them in their task, analysts benefit from software developed by the Asgard research and technology group that provides access to detailed market and accounting information on 5,000 global firms, allowing for the calculation of many valuation and growth metrics and precise modeling of sources of cash-flow strengths and weaknesses within each business. Asgard analysts can also use the application to backtest strategies and build their own models to rank securities' attractiveness according to their preferred characteristics. Security allocation is determined by a management team but depends heavily on a quantitative risk model developed by Asgard. Asgard has a low portfolio turnover.
Tokra	Tokra Capital uses a factor-based strategy to rank securities from most attractive to least attractive. Each security is scored based on three metrics: price to book value (P/B), 12-month increase in stock price, and return on assets. Tokra's managers have a strong risk management background. Their objective is to maximize their exposure to the most attractive securities using a total scoring approach subject to limiting single-security concentration below 2%, sector deviations below 3%, active risk below 4%, and annual turnover less than 40%, while having a market beta close to 1. The master fund holds approximately 400 positions out of a possible universe of more than 2,000 securities evaluated.

When Leonard's analysts met with Asgard, they inquired whether its managers engage in activist investing because Asgard's portfolio frequently holds significant positions, because of their large asset size, and because of their emphasis on strong governance and their ability to model sources of cash-flow strengths and weaknesses within each business. The manager indicated that Asgard engages with companies from a long-term shareholder's perspective, which is consistent with the firm's low portfolio turnover, and uses its voice, and its vote, on matters that can influence companies' long-term value.

Leonard wants to confirm that each manager's portfolios are consistent with its declared style. To this end, Exhibit 2 presents key financial information associated with each manager's portfolio and also with the index that all three managers use.

EXHIBIT 2   Key Financial Data

Fund	Index	Furlings	Asgard	Tokra
Dividend/price (trailing 12-month)	2.3%	2.2%	2.2%	2.6%
P/E (trailing 12-month)	26.5	24.7	26.6	27.3
Price/cash flows (12-month forward)	12.5	13.8	12.5	11.6
P/B	4.8	4.30	4.35	5.4
Average EPS growth (three to five years forward)	11.9%	11.0%	13.1%	10.8%
Net income/assets	2.8%	4.5%	4.3%	3.2%
Average price momentum (trailing 12 months)	10.5%	14.0%	10.0%	12.0%

1. Which fund manager's investing approach is *most consistent* with fundamental management?
   A. Furlings
   B. Asgard
   C. Tokra

2. Which of the following statements about the approaches and styles of either Furlings, Asgard, or Tokra is *incorrect*?
   A. Furlings is a top-down sector rotator with a value orientation within sectors.
   B. Asgard is a bottom-up manager with a GARP (growth at a reasonable price) style.
   C. Tokra is a factor-based manager using value, growth, and profitability metrics.

3. Which manager is *most likely* to get caught in a value trap?
   A. Furlings
   B. Asgard
   C. Tokra

4. Which activist investing tactic is Asgard *least likely* to use?
   A. Engaging with management by writing letters to management, calling for and explaining suggested changes, and participating in management discussions with analysts or meeting the management team privately
   B. Launching legal proceedings against existing management for breach of fiduciary duties
   C. Proposing restructuring of the balance sheet to better utilize capital and potentially initiate share buybacks or increase dividends

5. Based on the information provided in Exhibits 1 and 2, which manager's portfolio characteristics is *most likely* at odds with its declared style?
   A. Furlings
   B. Asgard
   C. Tokra

6. Leonard is looking at the style classification from Asgard as reported by Morningstar and Thomson Reuters Lipper. He is surprised to find that Asgard is classified as a blend fund by Morningstar and a value fund by Lipper. Which of the following statements is *correct*?
   A. Although the Morningstar methodology classifies securities as either value, growth, or core, the Lipper methodology assumes a stock can have the characteristics of many styles. This approach can result in a different classification for the same portfolio.
   B. The Lipper methodology can only lead to a value or growth classification. It does not offer a core/blend component.
   C. The Morningstar methodology classifies securities as either value, growth, or core by looking at the difference between their respective growth and value scores. It is possible that the Asgard funds hold a balanced exposure to both value and growth and/or core stocks.

The following information relates to questions 7–14

Aleksy Nowacki is a new portfolio manager at Heydon Investments. The firm currently offers a single equity fund, which uses a top-down investment strategy based on fundamentals. Vicky Knight, a junior analyst at Heydon, assists with managing the fund.

Nowacki has been hired to start a second fund, the Heydon Quant Fund, which will use quantitative active equity strategies. Nowacki and Knight meet to discuss distinct characteristics of the quantitative approach to active management, and Knight suggests three such characteristics:

Characteristic 1.   The focus is on factors across a potentially large group of stocks.
Characteristic 2.   The decision-making process is systematic and non-discretionary.
Characteristic 3.   The approach places an emphasis on forecasting the future prospects of underlying companies.

Nowacki states that quantitative investing generally follows a structured and well-defined process. Knight asks Nowacki:

"What is the starting point for the quantitative investment process?"

The new Heydon Quant Fund will use a factor-based strategy. Nowacki assembles a large dataset with monthly standardized scores and monthly returns for the strategy to back-test a new investment strategy and calculates the information coefficient. $FS(t)$ is the factor score for the current month, and $FS(t + 1)$ is the score for the next month. $SR(t)$ is the strategy's holding period return for the current month, and $SR(t + 1)$ is the strategy's holding period return for the next month.

As an additional step in backtesting of the strategy, Nowacki computes historical price/book ratios (P/Bs) and price/earnings ratios (P/Es) using calendar year-end (31 December) stock prices and companies' financial statement data for the same calendar year. He notes that the financial statement data for a given calendar year are not typically published until weeks after the end of that year.

Because the Heydon Quant Fund occasionally performs pairs trading using statistical arbitrage, Nowacki creates three examples of pairs trading candidates, presented in Exhibit 1. Nowacki asks Knight to recommend a suitable pair trade.

EXHIBIT 1   Possible Pairs Trades Based on Statistical Arbitrage

Stock Pair	Current Price Ratio Compared with Long-Term Average	Historical Price Ratio Relationship	Historical Correlation between Returns
1 and 2	Not significantly different	Mean reverting	High
3 and 4	Significantly different	Mean reverting	High
5 and 6	Significantly different	Not mean reverting	Low

Knight foresees a possible scenario in which the investment universe for the Heydon Quant Fund is unchanged but a new factor is added to its multifactor model. Knight asks Nowacki whether this scenario could affect the fund's investment-style classifications using either the returns-based or holdings-based approaches.

7. Which of the following asset allocation methods would *not likely* be used by Nowacki and Knight to select investments for the existing equity fund?
    A. Sector and industry rotation
    B. Growth at a reasonable price
    C. Country and geographic allocation

8. Relative to Heydon's existing fund, the new fund will *most likely*:
    A. hold a smaller number of stocks.
    B. rebalance at more regular intervals.
    C. see risk at the company level rather than the portfolio level.

9. Which characteristic suggested by Knight to describe the quantitative approach to active management is *incorrect*?
    A. Characteristic 1
    B. Characteristic 2
    C. Characteristic 3

10. Nowacki's *most appropriate* response to Knight's question about the quantitative investment process is to:
    A. backtest the new strategy.
    B. define the market opportunity.
    C. identify the factors to include and their weights.

11. In Nowacki's backtesting of the factor-based strategy for the new fund, the calculated information coefficient should be based on:
    A. $FS(t)$ and $SR(t)$.
    B. $FS(t)$ and $SR(t + 1)$.
    C. $SR(t)$ and $FS(t + 1)$.

12. Nowacki's calculated price/book ratios (P/Bs) and price/earnings ratios (P/Es), in his backtesting of the new strategy, are a problem because of:
    A. data mining.
    B. look-ahead bias.
    C. survivorship bias.

13. Based on Exhibit 1, which stock pair should Knight recommend as the *best* candidate for statistical arbitrage?
    A. Stock 1 and Stock 2
    B. Stock 3 and Stock 4
    C. Stock 5 and Stock 6

14. The *most appropriate* response to Knight's question regarding the potential future scenario for the Heydon Quant Fund is:
    A. only the returns-based approach.
    B. only the holdings-based approach.
    C. both the returns-based approach and the holdings-based approach.

The following information relates to questions 15–19

Jack Dewey is managing partner of DC&H, an investment management firm, and Supriya Sardar is an equity analyst with the firm. Dewey recently took over management of the firm's Purity Fund. He is developing a fundamental active investment process for managing this fund that emphasizes financial strength and demonstrated profitability of portfolio companies. At his previous employer, Dewey managed a fund for which his investment process involved taking active exposures in sectors based on the macroeconomic environment and demographic trends.

Dewey and Sardar meet to discuss developing a fundamental active investment process for the Purity Fund. They start by defining the investment universe and market opportunity for the fund, and then they pre-screen the universe to obtain a manageable set of securities for further, more detailed analysis. Next, Dewey notes that industry and competitive analysis of the list of securities must be performed. He then asks Sardar to recommend the next step in development of the fundamental active management process.

During the next few months, Dewey rebalances the Purity Fund to reflect his fundamental active investment process. Dewey and Sardar meet again to discuss potential new investment opportunities for the fund. Sardar recommends the purchase of AZ Industrial, which she believes is trading below its intrinsic value, despite its high price-to-book value (P/B) relative to the industry average.

Dewey asks Sardar to perform a bottom-up style analysis of the Purity Fund based on the aggregation of attributes from individual stocks in the portfolio. Dewey plans to include the results of this style analysis in a profile he is preparing for the fund.

15. In managing the fund at his previous employer, Dewey's investment process can be *best* described as:
    A. an activist strategy.
    B. a top-down strategy.
    C. a bottom-up strategy.

16. Sardar's recommendation for the next step should be to:
    A. review results from backtesting the strategy.
    B. make recommendations for rebalancing the portfolio.
    C. forecast companies' performances and convert those forecasts into valuations.

17. Based upon Dewey's chosen investment process for the management of the Purity Fund, rebalancing of the fund will *most likely* occur:
    A. at regular intervals.
    B. in response to changes in company-specific information.
    C. in response to updated output from optimization models.

18. Which investment approach is the *most likely* basis for Sardar's buy recommendation for AZ Industrial?
    A. Relative value
    B. High-quality value
    C. Deep-value investing

19. The analysis performed by Sardar on the Purity Fund can be *best* described as being based on:
    A. a holdings-based approach.
    B. manager self-identification.
    C. a returns-based style analysis.

CHAPTER 7

ACTIVE EQUITY INVESTING: PORTFOLIO CONSTRUCTION

Jacques Lussier, PhD, CFA
Marc R. Reinganum, PhD

LEARNING OUTCOMES

The candidate should be able to:

- describe elements of a manager's investment philosophy that influence the portfolio construction process;
- discuss approaches for constructing actively managed equity portfolios;
- distinguish between Active Share and active risk and discuss how each measure relates to a manager's investment strategy;
- discuss the application of risk budgeting concepts in portfolio construction;
- discuss risk measures that are incorporated in equity portfolio construction and describe how limits set on these measures affect portfolio construction;
- discuss how assets under management, position size, market liquidity, and portfolio turnover affect equity portfolio construction decisions;
- evaluate the efficiency of a portfolio structure given its investment mandate;
- discuss the long-only, long extension, long/short, and equitized market-neutral approaches to equity portfolio construction, including their risks, costs, and effects on potential alphas.

1. INTRODUCTION

Active equity investing is based on the concept that a skilled portfolio manager can both identify and differentiate between the most attractive securities and the least attractive securities—typically relative to a pre-specified benchmark. If this is the case, why is a portfolio—a collection of securities—even necessary? Why shouldn't the portfolio manager

Portfolio Management, Second Edition, by Jacques Lussier, PhD, CFA, and Marc R. Reinganum, PhD. Copyright © 2018 by CFA Institute.

just identify the most attractive security and invest all assets in this one security? Or in a long/short context, why not buy the "best" security and sell the "worst" one? Although very simple, this one-stock approach is not likely to be optimal or even feasible. No manager has perfect foresight, and his predictions will likely differ from realized returns. What he predicted would be the "best security" may quite likely turn out *not* to be the best. Active equity portfolio managers, even those with great skill, cannot avoid this risk. Security analysis is the process for ranking the relative attractiveness of securities, whereas portfolio construction is about selecting the securities to be included and carefully determining what percentage of the portfolio is to be held in each security—balancing superior insights regarding predicted returns against some likelihood that these insights will be derailed by events unknown or simply prove to be inaccurate.

Active managers rely on a wide array of investment strategies and methodologies to build portfolios of securities that they expect to outperform the benchmark. The challenges faced by active managers are similar whether they manage long-only traditional strategies, systematic/quantitative strategies, or long/short opportunistic strategies. Managers may differ in their investment style, operational complexity, flexibility of investment policy, ability to use leverage and short positions, and implementation methodologies, but predictions about returns and risk are essential to most active equity management styles.

In Section 2, we introduce the "building blocks" of portfolio construction, and in Section 3, we discuss the different approaches to portfolio construction. In Sections 4 and 5, we discuss risk budgeting concepts relevant to portfolio construction and the measures used to evaluate portfolio risk. Section 6 looks at how issues of scale may affect portfolio construction. Section 7 addresses the attributes of a well-constructed portfolio. Section 8 looks at certain specialized equity strategies and how their approaches to portfolio construction may differ from a long-only equity strategy. The chapter concludes with a summary.

2. BUILDING BLOCKS OF ACTIVE EQUITY PORTFOLIO CONSTRUCTION

Investors who pursue active management are looking to generate portfolio returns in excess of benchmark returns (adjusted for all costs) for an appropriate level of risk. The excess return—also called **active return** (R_A)—of an actively managed portfolio is driven by the difference in weights between the active portfolio and the benchmark. It can be mathematically expressed as

$$R_A = \sum_{i=1}^{N} \Delta W_i R_i \tag{1}$$

where
R_i = the return on security i and
ΔW_i = the difference between the portfolio weights W_{Pi} and the benchmark weights W_{Bi}. ΔW_i is also referred to as the active weight.
An active manager will generate positive active returns if:

The gains generated by	are,	The losses generated by
• overweighting the securities that outperform the benchmark and	on average, >	• underweighting the securities that outperform the benchmark and
• underweighting the securities that underperform the benchmark.		• overweighting the securities that underperform the benchmark.

2.1. Fundamentals of Portfolio Construction

Conceptually, a manager can generate active returns by

- strategically adjusting the active weights of the securities to create long-term exposures to rewarded risks that are different from those of his benchmark;
- tactically adjusting the active weights of the securities using his skills/expertise in identifying mispricing in securities, sectors, rewarded risks, and so on, to generate alpha that cannot be explained by long-term exposure to rewarded risks; and
- assuming excessive idiosyncratic risk that may result in lucky or unlucky returns.

Historically, any excess return over the benchmark was often termed "alpha." More sophisticated investors then moved to evaluating managers on the basis of excess *risk-adjusted* returns, where risk was assessed relative to a cap-weighted index. The information ratio became an important measure of the manager's value-added. Today, research supports the argument that much of what was historically viewed as alpha is, in fact, "alternative beta"— exposure to rewarded risks (often referred to as "priced factors" or "rewarded factors") that can be obtained at much lower cost.[1] In this chapter, we use "rewarded factors" as a generic term that refers specifically to investment risks for which investors expect to be compensated through a long-run return premium, such as exposure to market risk and liquidity risk. The existence of numerous rewarded factors is well documented in the literature and supported by strong empirical evidence. The recognition of this phenomenon is fundamentally altering the investment management industry, with large asset owners negotiating fee structures that compensate active managers for returns above and beyond those that can be generated by simple exposure to rewarded factors.[2]

These three sources of active return remain the same whether a manager follows a fundamental/discretionary or quantitative/systematic approach, a bottom-up or top-down strategy, or a style such as value or growth at a reasonable price. Of course, the proportion of return sourced from exposure to rewarded factors, alpha, and luck will vary among managers and portfolio management approaches. Equation 2 expresses the decomposition of *ex post* active returns in terms of these components:

---

[1]Kahn and Lemmon (2016); Bender, Hammond, and Mok (2014).

[2]Rewarded factors were discussed in the Level II chapter "An Introduction to Multifactor Models." For example, Fama and French (1992) introduced a three-factor model that includes Market, Size, and Value, which was complemented with Momentum by Carhart (1997). However, there are potentially many more factors, such as liquidity, low beta, and credit. There are also factors related to surprises in macroeconomic variables, such as interest rates, inflation, and business cycles, although academicians have had much more difficulty identifying reliable return premiums to these types of macroeconomic factors.

$$R_A = \sum (\beta_{pk} - \beta_{bk}) \times F_k + (\alpha + \varepsilon) \tag{2}$$

where

β_{pk} = the sensitivity of the portfolio (p) to each rewarded factor (k)

β_{bk} = the sensitivity of the benchmark to each rewarded factor[3]

F_k = the return of each rewarded factor

$(\alpha + \varepsilon)$ = the part of the return that cannot be explained by exposure to rewarded factors

The volatility of this component is very much dependent on how a manager sizes individual positions in his portfolio. The alpha (α) is the active return of the portfolio that can be attributed to the specific skills/strategies of the manager—skills such as security selection and factor timing. ε is the idiosyncratic return, often resulting from a random shock, such as a company announcing unexpected earnings. It could also be called noise or luck (good or bad). Although managers generate returns above or below those that can be explained by the exposure to rewarded factors, it is very difficult to isolate how much of this return differential can be attributed to alpha/skill or to noise/luck.[4]

Although not all active managers expressly employ a factor methodology in creating active returns, the growth of exchange-traded funds, coupled with the disappointing after-fee performance of many active managers, is expanding the factor-based view of the investment landscape. It is important to understand the components of active returns (exposure to rewarded risks, alpha, and luck) and how Equation 2 explicitly or implicitly relates to various management styles and approaches.

To illustrate, let's consider two hypothetical managers: a systematic manager (Quanto) and a discretionary manager (Evolo). Each claims to have a "Value" orientation.

Quanto estimates the "Value" characteristics of each security in his investment universe using such proxies as the ratios of price to book and forward earnings to price. He then uses a systematic allocation methodology that determines the specific active weights that can be expected to deliver the desired exposure to the Value factor. Quanto holds a large number of securities to limit the impact of idiosyncratic risks on performance. Quanto attempts to outperform the benchmark by choosing factor exposures that differ from those of the benchmark.

Evolo has developed a comprehensive measure of value using a forward-looking free cash flow model. This allows Evolo to compare her own estimates of security valuation to the current market price for each security covered by the firm. The manager uses her judgment to determine the appropriate active weights based on her own level of confidence in each estimate. She runs a concentrated portfolio because she believes she has an edge in setting the appropriate active weights.

Although Evolo is not using a systematic approach to determine the active security weights and the overall portfolio exposure to the Value factor, she is driven by a Value philosophy and is exposed to the Value factor. Her returns will be driven in part by this factor exposure, even if she has never seen Equation 2. Indeed, if her portfolio is not exposed to the Value factor, clients

---

[3]Because the investable universe as a whole (the market) is usually much larger than the investment universe defined by any single benchmark, most benchmarks have an inherent exposure to the Market factor different from one and some net exposure (different from zero) to other rewarded factors.

[4]If one observes only a small number of active returns, it may be difficult to infer whether the active return is zero or significantly different from zero given the likely volatility of realized active returns.

and consultants may question her claim to run a value-oriented portfolio. If Evolo has developed a better Value proxy than her competitors and if she is skilled at identifying the best and worst securities and setting appropriate active weights, part of her active return will be attributed to her alpha skills. Because Evolo runs a more concentrated portfolio, the portion of her active performance attributed to idiosyncratic risk will likely be greater.

2.2. Building Blocks Used in Portfolio Construction

This section introduces the three main building blocks of portfolio construction—*rewarded factor weightings, alpha skills,* and *position sizing* (shown in Exhibit 1)—and explains how each relates to the three broad sources of active returns. A fourth critical component of portfolio construction, *breadth of expertise*, is necessary to assemble these three building blocks into a successful portfolio construction process.

EXHIBIT 1   Building Blocks Used in Portfolio Construction

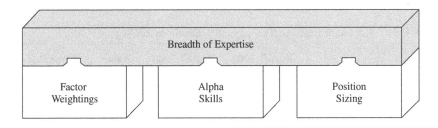

2.2.1. First Building Block: Overweight or Underweight Rewarded Factors

Let's begin by considering the market portfolio as our benchmark. The market portfolio encompasses all securities, and the weight of each security is proportional to its market capitalization. Our benchmark would have an exposure (or beta, β) of 1 to the Market factor and no net exposure to other rewarded factors, such as Size, Value, and Momentum.[5]

However, most individual securities have a β less than or greater than 1 to the Market factor and most will also have a non-zero exposure to the other factors. Indeed, one way an active manager can try to add value over and above the market portfolio is to choose, explicitly or implicitly, exposures to rewarded risks that differ from those of the market.

Practically speaking, most investors use narrower market proxies as a benchmark: the S&P 500 Index for a US mandate, the FTSE 100 Index for a UK mandate, or the MSCI All Country World Index (ACWI)[6] for a global mandate, for example. These indexes, although quite broad, do not include all securities that are publicly traded. Thus, these well-known indexes may not have a β of exactly 1 to the Market factor and could very well have a net exposure to other rewarded factors. For example, although most large-cap indexes usually have a β close to 1 to the Market factor, they usually have a negative sensitivity to the Size factor, indicating their large-cap tilt.

---

[5]Market is a long-only factor, whereas other factors, such as Size and Value, are defined as long/short factors. Hence, the exposure of the market portfolio to the Market factor should be 1, whereas the exposure of the market portfolio to other factors should be 0.

[6]The MSCI ACWI is a cap-weighted index that represents sources of equity returns from 23 developed and 24 emerging markets.

When a manager is creating an exposure to a rewarded risk, the exposure must be established relative to that of his benchmark to achieve an expected excess return.

The growing understanding of rewarded factors is profoundly changing the view of active and passive investing. There are many investment products that allow investors to directly access such factors as Value, Size, Momentum, and Quality, and the bar for active managers is rising: An active value manager not only needs to outperform a passive value benchmark but may also need to outperform a rules-based value-tilted product. In the following discussion, we illustrate the concept of returns to factors and the application of this concept to portfolio management.

Exhibit 2 illustrates the factor exposures of the Russell 1000 Index, the Russell 1000 Value Index, and a discretionary mid-cap value fund (using the four Fama–French and Carhart factors). The performance of the actively managed fund is presented before the deduction of fees to make the comparison with benchmark returns fair.

The average monthly performance of each factor from February 1990 to December 2016 is specified in the last column.[7] All four factors showed positive returns over the period. Most regression coefficients are statistically significant at the 5% level (not shown); the momentum coefficients of the Russell 1000 and the Russell 1000 Value are the exceptions.

EXHIBIT 2   Risk Factor Exposure (February 1990–December 2016)

	Russell 1000 Index	Russell 1000 Value Index	Value Fund	Factor Performance US Market
Monthly performance in excess of the risk-free rate	0.64%	0.66%	0.40%	—
β to specified factor:				
Market*	0.99	0.92	0.90	0.64%
Size	−0.16	−0.23	0.13	0.16%
Value	0.02	0.41	0.59	0.18%
Momentum	−0.01	0.13	0.09	0.61%
"Alpha" (monthly)	0.05%	−0.05%	−0.35%	—
R^2	0.99	0.95	0.74	

* As mentioned in footnote 3, the Market factor is built from a much larger universe of securities than are traditional benchmarks, such as the Russell 1000. Therefore, we should not expect the β of indexes to the Market factor to be necessarily equal to one.
Note: All data are measured in US dollars.
Sources: Factor data for the United States are from AQR Capital Management, market data are from Bloomberg, and calculations are from the authors.

The Russell 1000 Index has a Market β close to 1, a negative exposure to the Size factor (indicating it has a large-cap tilt), and almost no sensitivity to the Value and Momentum factors. This is what we would expect for a capitalization-weighted large-cap index. In comparison, the Russell 1000 Value Index has a lower Market β and a significant exposure to the Value factor, also in line with expectations. Finally, the mid-cap value fund has positive exposure to the Size factor (consistent with its mid-cap tilt) and a very significant exposure to the Value factor.

---

[7]Pricing and accounting data used by AQR are from the union of the CRSP tape and the Compustat/Xpressfeed Global database. The data include all available common stocks in the merged CRSP/Xpressfeed data.

In these regression specifications, there is still a component of return that cannot be explained by the rewarded factors alone. It is often labeled "alpha." This may be true alpha, or it may be simply noise/luck. The two indexes have a relatively small alpha, whereas the value fund has a significantly negative alpha of −0.35% per month. An alpha of this magnitude is unlikely to be explained by a small misspecification in the factor model. An investor considering this fund would need to investigate the causes of this negative alpha.

In Exhibit 3, we show the sources of performance of each product in terms of its exposure to each of the four factors and its respective alpha. In all cases, the Market factor is the dominant source of performance. The Value and Momentum factors did contribute positively to performance for the Russell 1000 Value, but much of this performance was lost because of the large-cap tilt and the negative alpha. The value fund did get a significant performance boost from the Value tilt, but much of it was lost to the very poor alpha in this period.

EXHIBIT 3   Sources of Performance (February 1990–December 2016)

Source of Performance	Russell 1000	Russell 1000 Value	Value Fund
Market	0.63%	0.59%	0.57%
Size	−0.03%	−0.04%	0.02%
Value	0.00%	0.08%	0.11%
Momentum	−0.01%	0.08%	0.05%
Alpha	0.05%	−0.05%	−0.35%
Total monthly performance	0.64%	0.66%	0.40%

Source: Calculations by authors.

These examples illustrate the components of Equation 2. Irrespective of the manager's investment approach—whether she explicitly targets factors or focuses only on securities she believes to be attractively priced—her portfolio performance can be analyzed in terms of factors. Some portion of returns will not be explained by factors, which may be attributable to

- the unique skills and strategies of the manager (alpha),
- an incomplete factor model that ignores relevant factors, or
- exposure to idiosyncratic risks that either helped or hurt performance.

The next section discusses the alpha skills building block.

2.2.2. Second Building Block: Alpha Skills
In principle, there are many approaches that can be used to generate alpha, but in practice, generating positive alpha in a zero-sum game environment (before fees) is a challenge.[8]

---

[8]Investing is often considered a zero-sum game (before fees) because all investors in aggregate own the market. Assuming all investors in a specific market (such as US equity) have a similar and appropriate benchmark, for each investor that outperforms the benchmark by $1, there would be another investor or group of investors that underperforms the benchmark by $1. Hence, in a zero-sum game, we can outperform only at the expense of someone else. The average level of expertise of market participants in that market does not change this observation. Although beyond the scope of this chapter, if different investors use different benchmarks, the zero-sum game analogy may not be appropriate.

Furthermore, the alpha generated by active managers must be sufficient to cover the higher fees usually associated with active management.

Let's initially consider rewarded factors. With exposures to rewarded factors increasingly accessible via rule-based indexes, simple static exposure to known rewarded factors is no longer widely considered a source of alpha. However, successfully timing that exposure *would* be a source of alpha. For example, some managers believe part of their skill emanates from an understanding of when rewarded factor returns might be greater than or less than their average returns (factor timing). Hence, in periods when the market return is negative, a manager with an exposure (β) to the Market factor substantially less than 1 will outperform the market and will probably also outperform many other managers. Similarly, a beta greater than 1 in a rising market would drive strong portfolio performance relative to the market. Exposure to the Market factor can be adjusted by investing in securities having, on average, Market betas less than or greater than 1.

The same can be said for the other rewarded factors. Exhibit 4 shows the cumulative value of $100 invested in both the Russell 1000 Growth Index and the Russell 1000 Value Index over a 10-year period ending in 2006. The Value index produced superior performance over the full 10-year time span, although it underperformed the growth index in 1998 and 1999. A manager skilled at timing his exposure to the Value factor would have owned the Growth index until the late 1990s and the Value index afterward, outperforming a manager with static exposure to the Value factor. However, as we have indicated, factor timing is difficult, and there is no consensus on the ability to generate alpha from factor timing.[9]

EXHIBIT 4   Cumulative Value—Russell 1000 Growth and Russell 1000 Value

Value of 100 Invested on 31 December 1996 (US $)

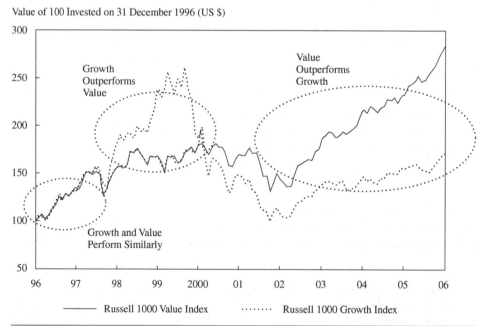

Source: Langlois and Lussier (2017, p. 44).

---

[9]See Asness (2017).

In principle, alpha can also be generated from timing exposure to *unrewarded* factors, such as regional exposure, sector exposure, the price of commodities, or even security selection. For example, there is no theoretical basis supporting an expectation that a portfolio with greater-than-benchmark sensitivity to oil prices will be rewarded in the long term. Oil price fluctuations are certainly a risk, but oil price is not a rewarded factor. However, a manager who held a very specific view about the future of oil prices and correctly anticipated the decline in the price of oil that started in June 2014 and ended in March 2016 would have had a strong incentive to reduce his exposure to the energy sector and especially to smaller, less integrated, and more indebted energy companies, which performed poorly as a result of the price movement. A discretionary manager might refer to these as *thematic exposures.* Although oil prices are not a rewarded "factor," his skill in timing that exposure would have been amply rewarded. The literature thus far has found little evidence of an ability to consistently time rewarded factors, but it is conceivable that a skillful manager could have identified a factor that has yet to be recognized by the academic or investment community.

In summary, active returns arising from skillful timing of exposure to rewarded factors, unrewarded factors, or even other asset classes (such as cash) constitute a manager's alpha—the second building block.

2.2.3. Third Building Block: Sizing Positions

Position sizing is about balancing managers' confidence in their alpha and factor insights while mitigating idiosyncratic risks. Although position sizing influences all three components of Equation 2, its most dramatic impact is often on idiosyncratic risk. For example, consider a manager seeking to create a greater exposure to the Value and Size factors. She could achieve the same average exposure (beta) to these factors by allocating her portfolio to 20 securities or 200 securities. However, the level of idiosyncratic risk and the potential impact of luck on performance will be much greater in the concentrated portfolio. In concentrated portfolios, the volatility of the active return (σ_{R_A}) attributed to idiosyncratic risks (σ_ε) will likely be more significant. In other words, there may be greater deviations between realized portfolio returns and expected returns.

A manager's choices with respect to portfolio concentration are a function of his beliefs regarding the nature of his investment skill. The factor-oriented manager believes that she is skilled at properly setting and balancing her exposure to rewarded factors. She targets specific exposure to factors (the $\sum(\beta_{pk} - \beta_{bk}) \times F_k$ part of Equation 2) and maintains a diversified portfolio to minimize the impact of idiosyncratic risk. The stock picker believes that he is skilled at forecasting security-specific performance over a specific horizon and expresses his forward-looking views using a concentrated portfolio, assuming a higher degree of idiosyncratic risk (the $\alpha + \varepsilon$ part of Equation 2).

Diversification, Volatility, and Idiosyncratic risk

The stock picker must carefully consider influences that can substantially alter the absolute or relative risk profile of his portfolio. Consider, for example, the absolute volatility of the Russell 1000 Index and its underlying securities over the 12 months ending in October 2016. During this period:

- the index had an annualized daily volatility of 15.7%;

- the weighted average volatility of all securities in the index was substantially higher, about 26.7%;
- the average volatility of the 100 smallest securities in the index was approximately 41%;
- the average volatility of the 100 largest securities in the index was approximately 24%.

This disparity in individual stock volatility illustrates the potential of diversification. A concentrated portfolio is unlikely to achieve the low volatility of the Russell 1000 unless the manager specifically emphasizes investing in stocks that have a lower average volatility than that of the average security in the index.

Exhibit 5 illustrates the effect of diversification on total portfolio risk at two different levels of average individual stock volatility. (We use the standard deviation of returns as our measure of risk here.) Total portfolio volatility is a function of the average individual stock volatility and the number of securities in the portfolio. The calculations assume an average cross correlation of 0.24, consistent with the historical average correlation for Russell 1000 securities since 1979.

EXHIBIT 5   Total Portfolio Volatility as a Function of Concentration and Single Stock Volatility[10]

	Single Stock Volatility	
	25%	30%
Number of Securities	**Portfolio Volatility**	
10	14.1%	16.9%
30	12.9%	15.5%
50	12.6%	15.2%
100	12.4%	14.9%
500	12.3%	14.7%

Examining this table closely, we can see that diversification is a powerful tool but that it has its limitations. Even the most diversified portfolio of high-volatility stocks (the 500-stock portfolio with an average single-stock volatility of 30%) cannot achieve the same level of volatility inherent in the portfolios of lower-volatility stocks. Even the most concentrated portfolio of lower-volatility stocks displays a portfolio volatility lower than that of the highly diversified portfolio of higher-volatility stocks.

The concentrated portfolio, however, bears higher idiosyncratic risk, which can substantially influence portfolio performance. The manager's choices with respect to the magnitude of his active weights and the volatility of the securities with the highest active weights will be significant determinants of the portfolio's active return and active risk.

Active risk is a measure of the volatility of portfolio returns relative to the volatility of benchmark returns. It is expressed as follows:

---

[10]This is a simplified example of Markowitz portfolio diversification where securities are equally weighted and all securities have the same volatility and cross correlation:

$$\sigma_p = \sqrt{\frac{1}{n}\sigma^2 + \frac{(n-1)}{n}\sigma^2 C},$$

where n is the number of securities, σ^2 is the equal variance of all securities, and C is the cross correlation between them.

$$\text{Active risk } (\sigma_{R_A}) = \sqrt{\frac{\sum_{t=1}^{T}(R_{At})^2}{T-1}} \tag{3}$$

where R_{At} represents the active return at time t and T equals the number of return periods. Active risk is often referred to as "tracking error."

All else being equal, a 1.0% allocation to a security that has a 0.2% weighting in the benchmark (Security A) will have a greater effect on the active risk of the portfolio than a 2.0% allocation to a security that has a 2.5% weighting in the benchmark (Security B). Despite the overall smaller position size of Security A, the active decision the manager made with respect to the weighting of Security A (an 80 bp difference from the benchmark weight) is significantly larger than the active decision with respect to the weight of Security B (a 50 bp difference). If Security A also has a higher volatility than Security B, the effect of the active decision will be magnified.

Similarly, all else equal, an active weight of 1.0% on a single security will have a greater impact on active risk than will an active weight of 0.2% on five separate securities. The imperfect cross correlations of active returns of the basket of five stocks would contribute to lowering the level of active risk.

To summarize, a manager's choice with respect to position sizing is influenced by her investment approach and the level of confidence she places on her analytic work. On the one hand, the stock picker with high confidence in her analysis of individual securities may be willing to assume high levels of idiosyncratic risk. This is consistent with her emphasis on the "$\alpha + \varepsilon$" part of Equation 2. On the other hand, a manager focused on creating balanced exposures to rewarded factors is unlikely to assume a high level of idiosyncratic risk and is, therefore, quite likely to construct a highly diversified portfolio of individual securities.

2.2.4. Integrating the Building Blocks: Breadth of Expertise

The three foregoing building blocks encompass all of Equation 2, which we used to describe the sources of a manager's active returns:

- exposure to rewarded risks,
- timing of exposures to rewarded and unrewarded risks, and
- position sizing and its implications for idiosyncratic risk.

A manager may be more or less successful at combining these three sources of return into a portfolio. Success is a function of a manager's breadth of expertise. Broader expertise may increase the manager's likelihood of generating consistent, positive active returns.

The importance of breadth of expertise is implicit in the fundamental law of active management (covered extensively in the Level II chapter "Analysis of Active Portfolio Management"), which implies that confidence in a manager's ability to outperform his benchmark increases when that performance can be attributed to a larger sample of independent decisions. Independent decisions are not the same thing as individual securities. Independent decisions are uncorrelated decisions, much like two uncorrelated stocks are diversifying. Thus, overweighting both General Motors and Toyota, two auto companies, relative to their benchmark weights are not fully independent decisions because much of their respective returns are driven by common influences—the strength of consumer spending, the price of gasoline, and the price of steel and aluminum, for example. In evaluating portfolio construction, one must distinguish between the nominal number of decisions a manager makes about his active weights and the effective number of independent decisions. Without truly independent decisions, performance may be influenced more significantly by common exposures to specific factors.[11] According to the fundamental law, the expected active portfolio return $E(R_A)$ is determined by the following:[12]

$$E(R_A) = IC\sqrt{BR}\sigma_{R_A}TC \tag{4}$$

where

IC = Expected **information coefficient** of the manager—the extent to which a manager's forecasted active returns correspond to the managers realized active returns

BR = **Breadth**—the number of truly independent decisions made each year

TC = **Transfer coefficient**, or the ability to translate portfolio insights into investment decisions without constraint (a truly unconstrained portfolio would have a transfer coefficient of 1)

σ_{R_A} = the manager's active risk

For example, assuming an active risk of 6% (which many institutional investors would consider to be high), a transfer coefficient of 0.25 (representative of a constrained long-only investor), and an information coefficient of 0.10, the manager could expect to generate an active return of 15 bps yearly, on average, if she makes a single independent decision. If the manager wanted to achieve excess return of 1%, she would need to make approximately 40 fully independent decisions. Even if a manager does have positive information and transfer coefficients, it does not necessarily follow that excess return will be positive every year. A horizon of many years is required to have a reasonable probability of generating the expected excess return. However, a larger number of independent decisions will increase the probability of outperforming over a shorter horizon.

What is the implication of making multiple independent decisions? Assume two managers hold similarly diversified portfolios in terms of the number of securities and that both managers have outperformed the market over a specific period. Manager A has a pure value style and favors securities that have a low price-to-book ratio (a single valuation metric), whereas Manager B has a multidimensional, factor-based approach. Manager B's approach includes considerations related to valuation, price momentum, growth, balance sheet sustainability, quality of management, and so on, and considers a much larger set of metrics

---

[11]Although the fundamental law is an interesting concept for illustrating the main drivers of positive expected active returns, investment decisions are rarely truly independent. When using specific metrics to determine how to allocate to securities, managers emphasize securities that have common characteristics they deem to be relevant. The process by which managers determine their allocation to securities will affect the degree of independence of investment decisions. In other words, investing in the 100 securities among 1,000 that have the lowest price-to-book ratio does not lead to 100 independent decisions. Furthermore, we should not assume that the information coefficient of the manager is insensitive to the number of securities in his portfolio.

[12]The basic fundamental law was initially introduced by Grinold (1989) but was further expanded into the full fundamental law with the addition of the transfer coefficient by Clarke, de Silva, and Thorley (2002).

for each dimension (such as several metrics for valuation). Manager A's performance is largely attributed to a single dimension: his narrowly defined value bias. Although he holds 100 securities, he did not make 100 independent decisions.[13]

Manager B may not have 100 independent decisions embedded in her portfolio, but she likely has more than Manager A. Thus, the historical performance of Manager B may be a more reliable indicator of her ability to outperform in the future because her portfolio construction process integrates several dimensions and metrics, as well as their interactions. Her performance is less likely to be explained by how the market has recently favored a specific management style.

Let's take this example a bit further. Suppose Manager A makes 20 independent decisions and Manager B makes 40 independent decisions. Assume they both have the same information coefficient (0.2), the same active risk (4%), and the same transfer coefficient (0.6). What would be the expected active return of each manager? Using Equation 4:

Manager A: $0.2 \times \sqrt{20} \times 4\% \times 0.6 = 2.15\%$
Manager B: $0.2 \times \sqrt{40} \times 4\% \times 0.6 = 3.04\%$

What if Manager A's information coefficient was only 0.1? How many independent decisions would the manager need to make to generate the same 2.15% expected active return?

$$\text{Manager A: } 0.1 \times \sqrt{x} \times 4\% \times 0.6 = 2.15\%$$

$$x \approx 80$$

Assuming Manager A maintains a concentrated portfolio of twenty securities, what information coefficient would be required for Manager A to match the expected performance of Manager B?

$$\text{Manager A: } x \times \sqrt{20} \times 4\% \times 0.6 = 3.04\%$$

$$x \approx 0.28$$

Equation 4 illustrates the importance of breadth of expertise. As a practical matter, long-term success is not achieved by being right all the time but, rather, by being right often through small victories achieved consistently over long periods.

EXAMPLE 1   The Building Blocks of Asset Management

Proteus was launched as an asset management firm 20 years ago, after receiving assets of $100 million from a seed investor. Today, the firm has grown into a large organization with more than $30 billion in assets. Although the investment process has evolved, the

---

[13]Consider an active manager who has a value and momentum style. Value is measured by the price-to-book ratio, and momentum is measured over a single historical period, such as $P_{t-1\,month}/P_{t-12months}$. Assume that his exposure to these two factors explains more than 60% of his excess return (consistent with a study by Bender, Hammond, and Mok, 2014). The portfolio exposure to these two risk factors has, therefore, had greater bearing on excess returns than have the security selection skills of the manager.

firm has remained true to its core philosophy. It has also delivered strong risk-adjusted performance to its investors.

Proteus's emphasis has always been to invest in quality companies, appropriately priced, which are benefiting from positive and sustained price momentum. Although fairly agnostic in terms of portfolio weights compared with benchmark weights, the managers of Proteus believe in avoiding extreme views. For example, sector deviations are limited to between 80% and 120% of benchmark weights plus or minus 500 bps; for example, a sector with a 20% weight in the index could have a weight in the portfolio ranging from 11% [(0.8 × 20%) − 5%] to 29% [(1.2 × 20%) + 5%]. An individual security position can be no more than the lesser of (1) 10 times its weight in the index or (2) its weight in the index + 1%. On average, Proteus's portfolios hold between 120 and 150 securities. The active risk is above 5%.

As the firm grew in experience, research, and resources, the process of defining and measuring what is a quality company, appropriately priced, and benefiting from positive momentum evolved. Initially, the firm avoided companies that were the most indebted within their sector and favored those that generated strong cash flows to sales. It also favored companies that had a lower price-to-book value and had positive price momentum in the last 12 months.

Today, Proteus still emphasizes quality, valuation, and price momentum but has considerably improved how those characteristics are measured and weighed. It now evaluates 45 metrics related to the financial health of the companies, the quality of its financial reporting, its valuation within its sector, and its short- and medium-term price momentum. It also developed its own weighting mechanism to appropriately weight each metric. The managers at Proteus believe their competitive advantage is the effort they invest in identifying, measuring, and weighing these metrics.

Discuss the contributions of rewarded factors, alpha skills, position sizing, and breadth of expertise for Proteus.

Solution: Overall, Proteus has integrated all the primary dimensions of the investment process.

- Rewarded factors: Proteus recognizes the existence of rewarded factors, and it has significantly enhanced its measures of Quality, Value, and Momentum over time.
- Alpha skills: Given the commercial success of Proteus as a firm, we might safely assume that there is an alpha component in the process.
- Position sizing: Position size limits are integrated into the investment process to ensure diversification limits idiosyncratic risks.
- Breadth of expertise: Proteus has 20 years of experience refining and improving an investment process based on a consistent investment philosophy.

3. APPROACHES TO PORTFOLIO CONSTRUCTION

Portfolio construction is part art and part science. It is about investment philosophy and the implementation of that philosophy. It requires an understanding of the technical principles of portfolio construction, filtered through a manager's core beliefs regarding her ability to add value using the building blocks discussed earlier:

- *Factor exposures:* How does she create her factor exposures? Does the manager believe she is skilled at extracting return premiums from rewarded factors? Or are her exposures to rewarded factors a residual of her in-depth research into the securities' fundamentals?
- *Timing:* Does she believe that she has skill in generating alpha through timing of portfolio exposures to rewarded and unrewarded factors or to security selection uncorrelated with exposures to either rewarded or unrewarded factors?
- *Position sizing:* How does she size portfolio positions? Is she confident about her expected return forecasts, and therefore runs a high-conviction portfolio? Or does she seek to reduce idiosyncratic risk by running a highly diversified portfolio?
- *Breadth or depth:* Does she rely on a specialized but narrower skill set or on a greater breadth of expertise?

A manager's portfolio construction process should reflect her beliefs with respect to the nature of her skills in each of these areas. The majority of investment approaches can be classified as either

- *systematic or discretionary* (the degree to which a portfolio construction process is subject to a set of predetermined rules or is left to the discretionary views of the manager)

and

- *bottom-up or top-down* (the degree to which security-specific factors, rather than macroeconomic factors, drive portfolio construction).

In addition, these approaches can vary in the extent to which they are *benchmark aware* versus *benchmark agnostic*. Each manager's investment approach is implemented within a framework that specifies the acceptable levels of active risk and **Active Share** relative to a clearly articulated benchmark. (Active Share is a measure of how similar a portfolio is to its benchmark.) A manager may emphasize these dimensions to varying degrees as he attempts to differentiate his portfolio from the benchmark.

3.1. The Implementation Process: The Choice of Portfolio Management Approaches

We previously identified three primary building blocks that managers can use in constructing a portfolio that reflects their core beliefs. Let's look at these in a little more detail, beginning with the systematic–discretionary continuum.

3.1.1. Systematic vs. Discretionary

How are a manager's beliefs regarding rewarded factor exposures, timing of factor exposures, exposure to unrewarded factors, and willingness to assume idiosyncratic risk reflected in a systematic investment process and in a discretionary investment process?

- Systematic strategies are more likely to be designed around the construction of portfolios seeking to extract return premiums from a balanced exposure to known, rewarded factors.
- Discretionary strategies search for active returns by building a greater depth of understanding of a firm's governance, business model, and competitive landscape, through the development of better factor proxies (e.g., a better definition of Quality), or through

successful timing strategies. Factor timing is a challenging endeavor, and few factor-based systematic strategies have integrated a factor timing approach.

- Systematic strategies typically incorporate research-based rules across a broad universe of securities. For example, a simple systematic value methodology could filter out the 50% of securities that have the highest price-to-book ratio and then equally weight the remaining securities, leading to small individual portfolio positions. A more comprehensive approach might integrate a much larger number of considerations and balance total portfolio risk equally across them.

- Discretionary strategies integrate the judgment of the manager, usually on a smaller subset of securities. While a discretionary value manager might also rely on financial metrics to estimate the value characteristics of each security, she is likely to use her judgment to evaluate the relative importance of this information and assign appropriate weights to each security. A discretionary manager is also likely to integrate nonfinancial variables to the equation, such as the quality of management, the competitive landscape, and the pricing power of the firm. (Systematic strategies also integrate judgment, but their judgment is largely expressed up front through the design of the strategy and the learning process that comes with its implementation.)

- Systematic strategies seek to reduce exposure to idiosyncratic risk and often use broadly diversified portfolios to achieve the desired factor exposure while minimizing security-specific risk.

- Discretionary strategies are generally more concentrated portfolios, reflecting the depth of the manager's insights on company characteristics and the competitive landscape.

- Systematic strategies are typically more adaptable to a formal portfolio optimization process. The systematic manager must, however, carefully consider the parameters of that optimization. What objective function is he seeking to maximize (information ratio, Sharpe ratio, index or factor exposure, etc.) or minimize (volatility, downside risk, etc.)? Will elements of his investment style (such as performance and valuation metrics) be incorporated into the objective function or into the constraints?

- Discretionary portfolio managers typically use a less formal approach to portfolio construction, building a portfolio of securities deemed attractive, subject to a set of agreed-upon risk constraints.

Bridging the Divide

The philosophical divide between systematic and discretionary managers seems to be shrinking. Systematic and discretionary strategies were commonly differentiated in terms of their breadth and depth (discretionary managers conducting more in-depth research on a sub-set of the securities universe) and systematic managers having more breadth (less in-depth research across the entire universe of securities). Although this remains generally true today, research and technology have been narrowing the gap. Advancements in and the accessibility of technology, together with the greater range of quality data available, are allowing discretionary managers to extend their in-depth analyses across a broader universe of securities. Technology also allows systematic managers to design strategies that can capture risk premiums in rewarded factors, a source of active returns that was previously considered to be part of the alpha of discretionary managers.

3.1.2. Bottom-Up vs. Top-Down

A top-down approach seeks to understand the overall geo-political, economic, financial, social, and public policy environment and then project how the expected environment will affect countries, asset classes, sectors, and then securities. An investment manager who projects that growth companies will outperform value companies, that financials will outperform industrials, that the US market will outperform the European market, that oil prices will increase, or that cash will outperform equity and then targets individual securities and/or a cash/stock allocation to reflect these views is following a top-down approach.

A manager following a bottom-up approach develops his understanding of the environment by first evaluating the risk and return characteristics of individual securities. The aggregate of these risk and return expectations implies expectations for the overall economic and market environment. An investment manager who expects Ford to outperform GM, AstraZeneca (a bio-pharmaceutical company) to outperform Ford, and Sony to outperform AstraZeneca and builds a portfolio based on these stock-specific forecasts is following a bottom-up approach. Although the resulting portfolio will contain an implicit expectation for sector, style, and country performance, this is nonetheless a bottom-up approach.

- Both top-down and bottom-up strategies typically rely on returns from factors. However, top-down managers are more likely to emphasize macro factors, whereas bottom-up managers emphasize security-specific factors.
- A top-down investment process contains an important element of factor timing. A manager who opportunistically shifts the portfolio to capture returns from rewarded or unrewarded factors, such as country, sectors, and styles, is following a top-down investment process. They may also embrace the same security characteristics sought by bottom-up managers as they translate their macro views into security-specific positions. A top-down investment process is also more likely to raise cash opportunistically when the overall view of the Market factor is unfavorable.
- Bottom-up managers may embrace such styles as Value, Growth at Reasonable Price, Momentum, and Quality. These strategies are often built around documented rewarded factors, whether explicitly or implicitly.
- A top-down manager is likely to run a portfolio concentrated with respect to macro factor exposures. Bottom-up managers and top-down managers can run portfolios that are either diversified or concentrated in terms of securities. Both a bottom-up stock picker and a top-down sector rotator can run concentrated portfolios. Both a bottom-up value manager and a top-down risk allocator can run diversified portfolios.

Some managers will incorporate elements of both top-down and bottom-up investment approaches.

3.1.3. A Summary of the Different Approaches

While most managers make some use of all the building blocks, we can make some general assertions about the relative importance and use of these building blocks to each of the implementation choices. They are summarized in the four quadrants of Exhibit 6.

EXHIBIT 6   Approaches and Their Use of Building Blocks

	Top-Down	
Systematic	• Emphasizes macro factors • Factor timing • Diversified	• Emphasizes macro factors • Factor timing • Diversified or concentrated depending on strategy and style
	• Emphasizes security specific factors • No factor timing • Diversified	• Emphasizes firm specific characteristics or factors • Potential factor timing • Diversified or concentrated depending on strategy and style
	Bottom-Up	**Discretionary**

- Exposure to rewarded factors can be achieved with either a systematic or discretionary approach.
- Bottom-up managers first emphasize security-specific factors, whereas top-down managers first emphasize macro factors.
- Factor timing is more likely to be implemented among discretionary managers, especially those with a top-down approach.
- Systematic managers are unlikely to run concentrated portfolios. Discretionary managers can have either concentrated or diversified portfolios, depending on their strategy and portfolio management style.
- In principle, a systematic top-down manager would emphasize macro factors and factor timing and would have diversified portfolios. However, there are few managers in this category.

3.1.4. Active Share and Active Risk

Managers have very specific beliefs about the level of security concentration and the absolute or relative risk that they (and their investors) are willing to tolerate. Relative risk is measured with respect to the benchmark that the manager has adopted as representative of his investment universe. We know that a manager must have active weights different from zero in order to outperform his benchmark. How do we measure these weights?

There are two measures of benchmark-relative risk used to evaluate a manager's success—Active Share and active risk—and they do not always move in tandem. A manager can pursue a higher Active Share without necessarily increasing active risk (and vice versa).

Active Share is easier to calculate than active risk; one only needs to know the weight of each security in the portfolio and the weight of the security in the benchmark. The formula for Active Share is shown in Equation 5. It measures the extent to which the number and sizing positions in a manager's portfolio differ from the benchmark.

$$\text{Active Share} = \frac{1}{2} \sum_{i=1}^{n} \left| \text{Weight}_{portfolio,i} - \text{Weight}_{benchmark,i} \right| \tag{5}$$

where n represents the total number of securities that are in either the portfolio or the benchmark.

The Active Share calculation involves no statistical analysis or estimation; it is simple arithmetic. If a portfolio has an Active Share of 0.5, we can conclude that 50% of the allocation positions of this portfolio are identical to that of the benchmark and 50% are not. There are only two sources of Active Share:

- Including securities in the portfolio that are not in the benchmark
- Holding securities in the portfolio that are in the benchmark but at weights different than the benchmark weights

If two portfolios are managed against the same benchmark (and if they invest only in securities that are part of the benchmark), the portfolio with fewer securities will have a higher level of Active Share than the highly diversified portfolio. A portfolio manager has complete control over his Active Share because he determines the weights of the securities in his portfolio.

Active risk is a more complicated calculation. Like Active Share, active risk depends on the differences between the security weights in the portfolio and the security weights in the benchmark. There are two different measures of active risk. One is realized active risk, which is the actual, historical standard deviation between the portfolio return and the benchmark return as described in Equation 3. This number relies on historical returns and is easy to calculate. But portfolio construction is a forward-looking exercise, and in this context, the relevant measure is predicted active risk, which requires a forward-looking estimate of correlations and variances.[14] As the accuracy of the forward-looking estimates of correlations and variances improves, the likelihood of better portfolio outcomes also improves.

The variance–covariance matrix of returns is very important in the calculation of active risk. Although portfolios that have higher active risk tend to have higher Active Share (and vice versa), this is not always the case. For example, underweighting one bank stock to overweight another bank stock will likely have less effect on active risk than underweighting one bank stock and overweighting an information technology stock. Active risk is affected by the degree of cross correlation, but Active Share is not. Active Share is not concerned with the

---

[14]To generate estimates of future volatility and correlations, different levels of sophistication can be considered. Although several methodologies are available, two dominant methodologies are exponentially weighted moving average (EWMA) and generalized autoregressive conditional heteroskedasticity (GARCH). EWMA applies greater weights to recent return observations, allowing for a more accurate representation of the near-term volatility environment. However, EWMA does not allow for regression to the mean to occur. More specifically, abnormally high or low levels of volatility in financial markets are expected to eventually normalize toward a long-term mean. The family of GARCH models integrates the benefits of EWMA and regression to the mean. The efficiency of risk forecasting and its implementation are illustrated in Langlois and Lussier (2017, pp. 82–85).

efficiency of diversification.[15] If the extent of underweighting and overweighting is the same in the bank/bank over-/underweight and in the bank/technology over-/underweight, the effect on Active Share would be identical. The effect on active risk would be different, however, because the correlation of the bank/technology pair is most likely lower than the correlation of the bank/bank pair. This highlights an important difference in Active Share versus active risk. A portfolio manager can completely control Active Share, but she cannot completely control active risk because active risk depends on the correlations and variances of securities that are beyond her control. Recall that in Equation 2, we decomposed active return into returns to factors, alpha, and idiosyncratic risk.

$$\sigma_{R_A} = \sqrt{\sigma^2 \left(\sum (\beta_{pk} - \beta_{bk}) \times F_k \right) + \sigma_e^2} \tag{6}$$

Here, we show that the active *risk* of a portfolio (σ_{R_A}) is a function of the *variance* attributed to the factor exposure $\sigma^2 \left(\sum (\beta_{pk} - \beta_{bk}) \times F_k \right)$ and of the *variance* attributed to the idiosyncratic risk (σ_e^2).[16] Although realized active risk will almost never be identical to predicted active risk, existing risk forecasting methodologies allow the manager to predict active risk over a short horizon with a high level of accuracy. Managers can then control the level of active risk through portfolio structure.

Sapra and Hunjan (2013) derived a relationship between active risk, Active Share, and factor exposure for an unconstrained investor, assuming a single-factor model. They found that

- high net exposure to a risk factor will lead to a high level of active risk, irrespective of the level of idiosyncratic risk;
- if the factor exposure is fully neutralized, the active risk will be entirely attributed to Active Share;
- the active risk attributed to Active Share will be smaller if the number of securities is large and/or average idiosyncratic risk is small; and
- the level of active risk will rise with an increase in factor and idiosyncratic volatility (such as occurred in 2008).[17]

These observations are very intuitive: Active risk increases when a portfolio becomes more uncorrelated with its benchmark. As discussed previously, although overweighting or underweighting GM relative to Ford will generate some Active Share, it will typically not generate much active risk. However, overweighting or underweighting energy firms versus

---

[15]Active Share is often used to determine how much fees an investor is paying for active management. For example, if two managers charge asset management fees of 0.5%, the manager with an Active Share of 0.80 offers twice as much "active" management per unit of fees as a manager with an Active Share of 0.40.

[16]The variance attributed to alpha returns is embedded in the variance of idiosyncratic risks.

[17]In 2008, markets were faced with the worst crisis of confidence and liquidity since the Great Depression. This situation triggered a deep global recession and rising unemployment and debt levels. The Market factor performed poorly, but the onset of the economic decline, the Lehman Brothers' bankruptcy on 15 September 2008, and the exposure of financial firms to weak mortgage and leveraged credit led to poor performance of value stocks and, consequently, of the Value factor. Furthermore, the forced deleveraging of many trades/strategies led to the biggest decline of the Momentum factor in more than 70 years.

financial firms, small-cap firms versus large-cap firms, or growth firms versus value firms will certainly contribute more to active risk.

So how do we use these two measures to discriminate between different portfolio management approaches and management styles? Using the observations from Sapra and Hunjan (2013), we could characterize a manager as

- factor neutral, factor diversified, or factor concentrated and as
- diversified (with low security concentration and low idiosyncratic risk) or concentrated (with high security concentration and high idiosyncratic risk).[18]

Exhibit 7 illustrates how various combinations of factor exposure and idiosyncratic risk affect Active Share and active risk.[19]

EXHIBIT 7   Investment Styles, Active Share, and Active Risk

*A **closet indexer** is defined as a fund that advertises itself as being actively managed but is substantially similar to an index fund in its exposures.

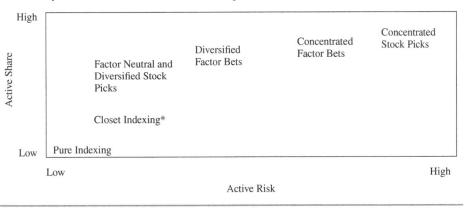

Using this framework, we can classify most equity strategies in terms of active risk and Active Share by analyzing the specific management style of the manager. For example, most multi-factor products have a low concentration among securities, often holding more than 250 positions (the purpose of these products is to achieve a balanced exposure to risk factors and minimize idiosyncratic risks). They are diversified across factors and securities. Thus, they typically have a high Active Share, such as 0.70, but they have reasonably low active risk (tracking error), often in the range of ±3%.

The concentrated stock picker, in contrast, has both a high Active Share (typically above 0.90) and a high active risk (such as 8%–12% or higher).[20] (The average active manager owns about 100 stocks, and fewer than 20% of managers own more than 200 stocks.) It follows, then, that the level of idiosyncratic risk in the average active discretionary portfolio is greater than that of the average multi-factor fund, with its 250+ positions. Therefore, on average, we could expect the portfolio of a typical discretionary manager to display higher active risk.

---

[18]See Ceria (2015).

[19]Factor portfolios usually have low security concentration.

[20]See Yeung, Pellizzari, Bird, and Abidin (2012).

Consequently, a manager can increase his degree of control over the level of Active Share and/or active risk in his portfolio by decreasing his security concentration. For example, it would not be uncommon for a sector rotator—typically a high-active-risk strategy—to have an active risk above 8%. If he chooses to run a concentrated portfolio, he might also have high Active Share. Or he can diversify his portfolio and reduce his Active Share.[21]

Petajisto (2013) provided examples of funds of different styles and their corresponding active risk and Active Share; see Exhibit 8A. The risk tolerance and portfolio construction approach of each manager is partially revealed by his Active Share and active risk. Exhibit 8B presents the same information but plots it in the Active Share/active risk dimension using the format of Exhibit 7.

EXHIBIT 8A   Active Risk, Active Share, and Portfolio Styles, 2009

Name of Fund	Style/Comments	Active Risk	Active Share
Vanguard Index Fund	Indexed	0.0%	0.00
RiverSource Disciplined Equity Fund	Large-Cap Growth (Small active weight, limited factor timing)	4.4%	0.54
T. Rowe Price Mid-Cap Value Fund	Mid-Cap Value (Limited active weights on sectors but significant stock picking)	5.4%	0.93
AIM Constellation Fund	Large-Cap Growth (Significant sector bets)	9.7%	0.66
GMO Quality Fund	Mega-Cap Core (Timing on a number of factors and cash)	12.9%	0.65
Sequoia	Stock Picker (Highly concentrated positions)	14.1%	0.97

Source: Petajisto (2013).

---

[21]It is important to use an appropriate index when calculating the level of Active Share. A manager whose investment universe is the S&P 500 could see her Active Share increase by approximately 12% if the Russell 1000 index was used to compute the Active Share. By default, a portfolio of 500 stocks will have high Active Share if Active Share is measured against the Russell 1000 Index.

EXHIBIT 8B   Active Risk, Active Share, and Portfolio Styles

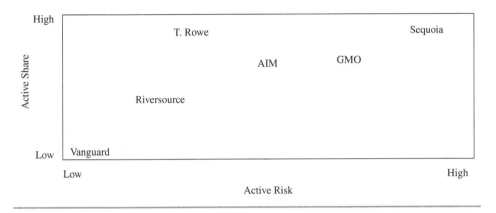

Active risk and Active Share provide information about the level of managers' activism against their benchmark, but there is little research on the relative efficiency of different asset management styles translating higher active risk or Active Share into higher active returns. However, many investors are using Active Share to assess the fees that they pay per unit of active management. For example, a fund with an Active Share of 0.25 (a closet indexer) would be considered expensive relative to a fund with an Active Share of 0.75 if both funds were charging the same fees.

Not all investment products neatly fall into the categorization we have just presented. Niche equity strategies, such as statistical arbitrage, event-driven investing, and activist investing, focus on generating alpha returns generally without regard to factor exposures or factor timing. These strategies do, however, typically assume a high level of idiosyncratic risk.

EXAMPLE 2   Portfolio Construction—Approaches and Return Drivers

1. You are evaluating two equity managers. Explain how Manager A, with his high level of Active Share, is able to achieve such a low active risk. What are the implications for Manager B's performance relative to that of Manager A?

	Manager A	Manager B
Active Share	0.73	0.71
Active risk	2.8%	6.0%
Number of positions	120	125

2. Discuss the drivers of return for Managers A and B.

	Manager A	Manager B	Factor Returns
Monthly performance in excess of the risk-free rate	0.65%	0.65%	
"Alpha" (monthly)	0.00%	0.20%	
Beta to:			
Market*	0.99	1.05	0.45%
Size	0	–0.2	0.20%
Value	0.15	0.05	0.35%
Momentum	0.25	0	0.60%
R-squared	0.99	0.78	

*Market factor is built from a much larger universe of securities than traditional benchmarks such as the Russell 1000. Therefore, we should not expect the β of indexes to the Market factor to be necessarily equal to one.

3. Based on the information provided below regarding four managers benchmarked against the MSCI World Index, identify the manager most likely to be a:
    a. closet indexer.
    b. concentrated stock picker.
    c. diversified multi-factor investor.
    d. sector rotator.
        Justify your response.

Manager Constraints:	**A**	**B**	**C**	**D**
Target active risk	10%	1%	4%	7%
Max. sector deviations	0%	3%	10%	15%
Max. risk contribution, single security	5%	1%	1%	3%

4. Discuss the main differences between top-down and bottom-up portfolio management approaches and how they relate to two of the building blocks: exposure to rewarded factors and alpha.

Solution to 1: Managers A and B have a similar number of positions and similar Active Share. Manager B has much higher active risk. A high Active Share says only that a manager's security-level weights are quite different from those of the index. A 0.5% underallocation to one security and a 0.5% over-allocation to another security will have the same impact on Active Share whether these two securities are in the same sector or in different sectors. Given similar levels of Active Share, it is likely that Manager B's active risk is driven by active decisions at the sector level rather than at the security level. Clearly, they implement very different investment strategies. Although we cannot draw a direct conclusion about the ability of Manager B to outperform Manager A, we can assume that the realized outcomes of Manager B are likely to be much more dispersed about the benchmark (both in positive and negative directions) given the higher level of active risk.

Solution to 2: Both managers generated the same absolute return, but they achieved their performance in very different ways. All of Manager A's performance can be explained from exposure to rewarded factors. There is no alpha, and the high R^2 shows that the four factors explain much of the monthly variability in returns. Manager A did outperform the Market factor by 20 bps (0.65% − 0.45%). The excess return can be attributed to the significant exposure (0.25) to the strong-performing Momentum factor (0.60%). Exposure to the Value factor explains the balance.

Manager B generated significant alpha (20 bps per month). The relatively low R^2 indicates that much of the variability of returns is unexplained by the factors. Manager B's performance must, therefore, be attributed to either her alpha skills or idiosyncratic risks that favored the manager's investment approach during the period.

Solution to 3: Manager B is a closet indexer. The low targeted active risk combined with the narrow sector deviation constraint indicates that the manager is making very few active bets.

Manager A is likely a concentrated stock picker. The 10% active risk target indicates a willingness to tolerate significant performance deviations from the market. The 5% limit on a single security's contribution to portfolio risk indicates he is willing to run a concentrated portfolio. The unwillingness to take sector deviations combined with the high tolerance for idiosyncratic risk indicates that the manager likely focuses on stock selection and is, therefore, a stock picker.

Manager C limits single-security risk contribution to no more than 1%, which implies a highly diversified portfolio. The significant sector deviations despite this high diversification are often indicative of a multi-factor manager. The relatively low tracking error further supports the argument that Manager C is a multi-factor manager.

Manager D has characteristics consistent with a sector rotator. The significant active risk and high tolerance for sector deviations and security concentration are what one would expect to find with a sector rotator.

Solution to 4:

Factor exposure.
Bottom-up managers look at characteristics of securities to build their portfolios. The factor exposure inherent in their portfolios may be intentional, or it may be a by-product of their security selection process. Top-down managers articulate a macro view of the investment universe and build a portfolio emphasizing the macro factors that reflect those views. Although their macro views could then be translated into security views using a bottom-up approach, their performance will likely be dominated by their macro-level factor exposures.

Alpha.
In the context of Equation 2, the alpha of bottom-up managers is most likely attributable to their security selection skills. Some portion of their active return can also be explained through exposure to rewarded factors. Top-down managers' alphas are largely derived from factor timing.

3.2. The Implementation Process: The Objectives and Constraints

The simplest conceptual way to think about portfolio construction is to view it as an optimization problem. A standard optimization problem has an objective function and a set of constraints. The objective function defines the desired goal while the constraints limit the actions one can take to achieve that goal. Portfolio managers are trying to achieve desirable outcomes within the bounds of permissible actions. The nature of the objective function and the nature and specifics of the constraints can be indicative of an investment manager's philosophy and style.

A common objective function in portfolio management is to maximize a risk-adjusted return. If risk is being measured by predicted active risk, then the objective function is seeking to maximize the information ratio (the ratio of active return to active risk). If risk is being measured by predicted portfolio volatility, then the objective function is seeking to maximize the Sharpe ratio (the ratio of return in excess of the risk-free rate to portfolio volatility). Ideally, these objective functions would specify *net* returns—adjusted for the costs associated with implementation.

Typical constraints in the portfolio optimization problem may include limits on geographic, sector, industry, and single-security exposures and may also specify limits on transaction costs (to limit turnover and/or help manage liquidity issues). They may also include limits on exposure to specific factors; for example, the investment process may specify a required minimum market capitalization for any single security or a minimum weighted average capitalization for the portfolio as a whole. Or it may specify a maximum price-to-book ratio for any single security or a maximum weighted average price-to-book ratio for the portfolio. Constraints can be defined relative to the benchmark or without regard to it. Setting constraints that properly express the risk dimensions being monitored, the desired level of risk taking, and the preferred portfolio structure while still allowing sufficient flexibility to achieve the risk and return goals is a challenging task. In principle, the active equity manager's portfolio is the final blend that maximizes the objective function subject to the portfolio constraints.

Not all portfolio managers engage in such a formalistic, scientific approach to portfolio construction. The objectives and constraints of systematic managers are explicitly specified, whereas those of discretionary managers are less explicitly specified. However, most managers at least conceptually optimize their portfolios using the expected returns for each security, their own view of risk, and constraints imposed by the stated portfolio construction process or by the client. For our purposes, it is useful to frame the problem in this technical manner to provide a framework for discussion of the portfolio construction process.

Objectives and constraints may be stated in absolute terms or relative to a benchmark. Exhibit 9 illustrates two generic objective functions—one that is absolute and one that is relative. Each is subject to a few specific constraints.

EXHIBIT 9   Objective Functions and Constraints

	Absolute Framework	**Relative Framework**
Objective Function:	*Maximize Sharpe Ratio*	*Maximize Information Ratio*
Constraint		
Individual security weights (w)	$w_i \leq 2\%$	$|w_{ip} - w_{ib}| \leq 2\%$
Sectors weights (S)	$S_i \leq 20\%$	$|S_{ip} - S_{ib}| \leq 10\%$
Portfolio volatility (σ)	$\sigma_p < 0.9\,\sigma_b$	—
Active risk (TE)	—	$TE \leq 5\%$
Weighted average capitalization (Z)	$Z \geq 20\text{bn}$	$Z \geq 20\text{bn}$

- The absolute approach seeks to maximize the Sharpe ratio; the relative approach seeks to maximize the information ratio.
- The absolute approach limits any single security position to no more than 2% of the portfolio and any single sector to no more than 20% of the portfolio; the relative approach imposes a constraint that a security must remain within ±2% of its index weight and sector weights must remain within ±10% of the index weights.
- The absolute approach imposes a portfolio volatility limit equal to 90% of the estimated benchmark volatility and imposes a minimum weighted average security capitalization of $20 billion; the relative approach imposes a 5% active risk limit and the same capitalization constraint.
- Managers can also combine relative and absolute constraints in the same framework, such as limiting sector deviations against a benchmark while imposing absolute limits on security positions.

Other optimization approaches specify their objectives in terms of the risk metrics, such as portfolio volatility, downside risk, maximum diversification, and drawdowns. These approaches do not integrate an explicit expected return component. However, they do implicitly create an exposure to risk factors. For example, products built using a risk-based objective function (such as minimum variance or maximum diversification)[22] often exhibit a Market beta below 1.0 and have a statistically significant exposure to the Value factor and to the low-minus-high-β factor.[23] This occurs because an objective function that seeks to manage or minimize risk will tend to favor value and low-beta securities.

Finally, not all objective functions are explicitly concerned with risk or returns. For example, Equation 7 shows an explicit objective function that might be specified by a quantitative manager seeking to maximize exposure to rewarded factors:

---

[22]The maximum diversification concept seeks to maximize the ratio of the average volatility of securities within a portfolio to portfolio volatility. It does not seek to achieve the lowest volatility, but rather, it seeks to maximize the benefits that diversification can bring.

[23]The low-minus-high-β factor compensation is justified as a structural impediment. Frazzini and Pederson (2014) expanded on an idea raised by Fischer Black (1972). They made the argument that investors looking for higher returns but who are constrained by borrowing limits bid up the prices of high-β securities.

$$\text{MAX} \left(\sum_{i=1}^{N} \frac{1}{3} \text{Size}_i + \frac{1}{3} \text{Value}_i + \frac{1}{3} \text{Momentum}_i \right) \qquad (7)$$

where Size_i, Value_i, and Momentum_i are standardized[24] proxy measures of Size, Value, and Momentum for security i.[25] The portfolio may also be subject to additional constraints similar to those in Exhibit 9.

Of course, articulating an explicit objective of maximizing the Sharpe ratio or the information ratio or minimizing a given risk measure implies that we have information about expected returns and expected risk. Some managers—typically discretionary managers—do not make explicit return and risk forecasts and instead seek to "maximize" their exposure to securities having specific characteristics. Embedded in their investment process is an implicit return-to-risk objective.

For example, the objective function of a discretionary manager may be expressed in a mission statement such as: "We are a deep value manager in large-cap US equity with a concentrated, best ideas style." They then identify securities possessing deep value characteristics (as they define value). The portfolio construction process will balance security concentration and sector exposure as the manager seeks to maximize the return at an acceptable level of risk. The allocation may be driven by the manager's judgment about the risk and return trade-offs, or a formal risk management protocol may be used to drive the allocation process, or a feedback mechanism may be put in place to ensure that constraints are being respected as the portfolio is being assembled or rebalanced by the manager.

When an explicit objective function is not used, many heuristic methodologies can be considered to determine security weighting in a portfolio. We list a few examples below.

- Identify securities that have the desired characteristics and weight them relative to their scoring on these characteristics. For example, a security with a price-to-book ratio of 8 would have half the weight of a security with a price-to-book ratio of 4.
- Identify securities that have the desired characteristics and weight them per their ranking or risk on these characteristics. For example, if there are five securities ranked on their price-to-book ratios, the security with the lowest price-to-book ratio would constitute 33% of the portfolio value [5/(5 + 4 + 3 + 2 + 1)] and the security with the highest price-to-book ratio would constitute 6.7% of the portfolio value [1/(5 + 4 + 3 + 2 + 1)].
- Identify stocks that have the desired characteristics, rank them according to how strongly they adhere to these characteristics, select the top x% of these stocks, and assign them portfolio weights based on one of several methodologies, such as equal weight, equal risk, scoring, or ranking on these characteristics. For example, if there are 1,000 securities in an index, the 500 securities with the lowest price-to-book ratios could be selected. Each security would then be weighted using the chosen methodology.

---

[24]Because it can be unwise to compare securities of different size, price-to-book ratio, and other metrics across sectors or countries, proxies of factors are often standardized by sectors or countries.

[25]For example, a manager could rank securities per these three measures and determine a score for each security. For example, a small firm with a high book-to-price ratio and positive price momentum would score higher than a large firm with a low book-to-price ratio and negative price momentum. Other approaches could be used to attribute scores on each factor.

Although these alternative methodologies may be intuitively appealing, they may not allocate active risk as efficiently as a formal optimization framework would. The constraints and objective function will be strongly reflective of the philosophy and style of a manager. For example, a stock picker is likely to have fewer and more permissive constraints on security weights than a multi-factor manager seeking to minimize idiosyncratic risks. A manager specializing in sector rotation will have more permissive constraints with respect to sector concentration than a value manager.

EXAMPLE 3   Approaches to Portfolio Construction

Marc Cohen is a portfolio manager whose primary skill is based on having a good understanding of rewarded sources of risk. He does not believe in factor timing. Sophie Palmer is a portfolio manager who believes she has skill in anticipating shifts in sector performance. She does not profess to have skill in individual security selection but tolerates significant deviations in sector exposure. Sean Christopher is a stock picker running a high-turnover strategy based on recent movements in market price among the Russell 1000 stock universe. He is highly sector and size agnostic and has significant active risk. Discuss the expected profile of each manager in terms of

- the sensitivity of their performance to risk factors,
- the level of security concentration, and
- the contribution of idiosyncratic risk to the total active risk of their portfolios.

Solution: We should be able to explain a large part of Cohen's excess return using the performance of rewarded factors. We would not expect alpha to be a significant component of his performance. His exposure to risk factors would be relatively stable across time periods because he does not believe in factor timing. Because his primary emphasis is on long-term exposure to risk factors, he would hold a highly diversified portfolio to minimize idiosyncratic risk. As a multi-factor manager running a diversified portfolio, his active risk should be relatively low.

Palmer's performance is likely to be explained by tactical exposures to sectors, which we have said are unrewarded risks, rather than static exposures to known rewarded factor returns. Her excess performance against her benchmark will likely be attributed to alpha. With no professed skill in security selection, she is likely to hold a large number of securities in each sector to minimize idiosyncratic risk. The active risk arising from her sector weightings will overshadow the active risk from security weightings. Her active risk is likely to be higher than that of Marc Cohen.

Christopher's portfolio is more difficult to assess. His focus on recent price movements indicates a sensitivity to the Momentum factor, although the sensitivity to this factor may depend on the time horizons and methodologies he uses to measure price momentum. He is size agnostic and may at times have exposure to the Size factor, a smaller-cap bias. With the information given, we cannot make an inference regarding the diversification of his portfolio. As a discretionary manager, he is to run a concentrated portfolio in order to more closely monitor his positions. However, if he makes extensive use of quantitative tools in monitoring his portfolio, he may be able to hold a more diversified portfolio. His active risk will be high, and his performance is likely to have a significant alpha component, whether positive or negative.

EXAMPLE 4   Approaches to Portfolio Construction

Manager A uses a scoring process and seeks to maximize the portfolio score based on the factor characteristics of individual securities. His purpose is not to time factor exposure but to achieve an appropriate diversification of factor risks. His approach is fully systematic, and he has a tracking error constraint of less than 4%. No one position can be greater than 2%, irrespective of its benchmark weight.

Manager B has a strong fundamental process based on a comprehensive understanding of the business model and competitive advantages of each firm. However, Manager B also uses sophisticated models to make explicit three-year forecasts of the growth of free cash flow to determine the attractiveness of each security's current valuation. A committee of portfolio managers meets once a month to debate the portfolio allocation. The manager has a large staff of portfolio managers and analysts and thus can maintain wide coverage of companies within each industry. Individual positions are constrained to the lower of (1) benchmark weight + 2% or (2) five times the benchmark weight.

Manager C specializes in timing sector exposure and has little appetite for idiosyncratic risks within sectors. Using technical analyses and econometric methodologies, she produces several types of forecasts. The manager uses this information to determine appropriate sector weights. The risk contribution from any single sector is limited to 30% of total portfolio risk. The final decision on sector allocations rests with the manager.

Discuss each manager's implementation approach, security selection approach, portfolio concentration, objective function, and constraints.

Solution: Manager A is best characterized as a systematic, bottom-up manager.

- *Implementation approach.* An implementation approach that is fully quantitative (allocations are unaffected by a portfolio manager's judgment) is systematic.
- *Security selection approach.* A scoring process that ranks individual securities based on their factor characteristics is a bottom-up approach.
- *Concentration.* Although the limit of no more than 2% of the portfolio in any single position means the portfolio could hold as few as 50 securities, the tracking error constraint of 4% indicates that the portfolio is likely diversified.
- *Objective function.* A process that aims to maximize the portfolio's score based on the factor characteristics of single securities is an example of an explicit objective function.
- *Constraints.* The tracking error constraint of less than 4% is a relative constraint function. The limit on any single position to no more than 2% of the portfolio is an absolute—not a relative—constraint. It does not depend on benchmark weights.

The following table summarizes this information for all three managers:

	Manager A	**Manager B**	**Manager C**
Implementation approach	Systematic	Discretionary	Discretionary
Security selection approach	Bottom-up	Bottom-up	Top-down
Portfolio concentration	Diversified	Diversified	Security diversified
			Factor concentrated
Objective function	Explicit	Explicit	Explicit
Constraints	Relative and absolute	Relative	Absolute

4. ALLOCATING THE RISK BUDGET

Risk budgeting is a process by which the total risk appetite of the portfolio is allocated among the various components of portfolio choice. As an example, if the portfolio manager has an *ex ante* active risk budget explicitly provided by the client, with risk budgeting, she seeks to optimize the portfolio's exposures relative to the benchmark to ensure that the choices she makes among stocks, sectors, or countries make efficient use of the active risk budget. But *ex ante* active risk is just one possible measure of risk. An effective risk management process requires that the portfolio manager do the following:

- Determine which type of risk measure is most appropriate to her strategy.
  - For example, a long/short equity manager benchmarked against a cash plus target will usually prefer an absolute risk measure (such as total volatility of portfolio returns), whereas a long-only equity manager benchmarked against a capitalization-weighted index may prefer a relative risk measure (such as active risk).

- Understand how each aspect of the strategy contributes to its overall risk.
  - Total portfolio variance may be dominated by exposure to rewarded risk factors or by allocations to countries, sectors, or securities. If these exposures are dynamic, the timing of portfolio exposures also introduces risk. An important step in risk budgeting is to understand what drives a portfolio's risk and to ensure the portfolio has the right kinds of specific risks.

- Determine what level of risk budget is appropriate.
  - Targeted levels of risk vary widely among managers and strategies. Although there are general principles that limit the level of advisable risk in a specific strategy, it is also very much a policy issue.

- Properly allocate risk among individual positions/factors.
  - Whether the risk measure is absolute or relative, managers must efficiently allocate their targeted risk budget.

4.1. Absolute vs. Relative Measures of Risk

The choice between an absolute and a relative risk portfolio management orientation is driven by the mandate of the manager and the goals of investors. If the mandate is to outperform a market index over a horizon, such as three years, then the manager will focus on active risk. If the investment objective is expressed in terms of total returns, then the manager will likely focus on the volatility of portfolio returns.

Managers' beliefs about how they add value can influence the choice between an absolute and a relative risk measure. Some managers may believe that the benchmark-relative constraints so common in the world of investment management today inhibit the ability of their investment approach to realize its full potential. To address this issue, they may prefer either an absolute risk measure or a relative risk measure with a wide range of allowed deviations. An absolute risk measure is just that: Whatever the risk threshold, the portfolio risk must remain at or below that level. The manager is free to construct his portfolio without regard to the characteristics of the benchmark. A relative risk measure with wide bands around a central target implies a benchmark-relative approach with significant degrees of freedom to diverge from the characteristics of the benchmark. Ultimately, however, risk and reward will be measured relative to that benchmark. Although some large institutional investors have adopted investment strategies in recent years that are agnostic to the benchmark (an absolute/total return approach) or have had a very high active risk target in a benchmark-relative framework, most assets under management are managed under benchmark-relative mandates. Irrespective of whether a manager focuses on absolute risk or relative risk, the risks he chooses to take should be related to his perceived skills. All other risk should be diversified or minimized. For example,

- market timers should be concerned with timing their factor exposure,
- sector rotators should be concerned with timing their sector exposure, and
- multi-factor managers should be concerned with balancing their factor exposure.

The first step in determining how risk should be allocated is understanding the generic drivers of absolute and relative portfolio risk.

4.1.1. Causes and Sources of Absolute Risk
We start with the following fundamental principles:

- If a manager adds a new asset (such as a security) to his portfolio that has a higher covariance with the portfolio than most current securities, total portfolio risk will rise. (A high covariance with the existing portfolio can be driven by a high variance or a higher correlation of the new security with the portfolio.)
- If a manager replaces an existing security with another security that has a higher covariance with the portfolio than that of the security being replaced, total portfolio risk will rise.

These principles also work in reverse. Consider the three-asset portfolio in Exhibit 10.

EXHIBIT 10   Absolute Risk Attribution

	Portfolio Weight	Standard Deviation	Correlation			Portfolio Risk Attribution — Contribution to Portfolio Variance	
			Asset A	Asset B	Asset C	Absolute	%
Asset A	40%	20%	1	0.40	0.20	0.008416	59.22%
Asset B	50%	12%	0.40	1	0.20	0.005592	39.35%
Asset C	10%	6%	0.20	0.20	1	0.000204	1.44%
Portfolio	100%	11.92%	0.88	0.78	0.20	0.014212	100%

	Covariance		
	Asset A	Asset B	Asset C
Asset A	0.040000	0.009600	0.002400
Asset B	0.009600	0.014400	0.001440
Asset C	0.002400	0.001440	0.003600
Portfolio	0.020926	0.011129	0.001427

Portfolio variance is a function of the individual asset returns and the covariance of returns between assets. In this example, the total variance is 0.014212, which equates to a portfolio standard deviation of 11.92%. Equation 8a expresses the calculation of total portfolio variance (V_p), and Equation 8b determines the contribution of each asset to portfolio variance (CV_i).

$$V_p = \sum_{i=1}^{n} \sum_{j=1}^{n} x_i x_j C_{ij} \tag{8a}$$

$$CV_i = \sum_{j=1}^{n} x_i x_j C_{ij} = x_i C_{ip} \tag{8b}$$

where
   x_j = the asset's weight in the portfolio
   C_{ij} = the covariance of returns between asset i and asset j
   C_{ip} = the covariance of returns between asset i and the portfolio

In other words, the contribution of an asset to total portfolio variance is equal to the product of the weight of the asset and its covariance with the entire portfolio. For example, Asset A's contribution to total portfolio variance is calculated as follows:

Weight of Asset A × Weight of Asset A × Covariance of Asset A with Asset A	$0.40 \times 0.40 \times 0.04$
+ Weight of Asset A × Weight of Asset B × Covariance of Asset B with Asset A	$+ 0.40 \times 0.50 \times 0.0096$
+ Weight of Asset A × Weight of Asset C × Covariance of Asset C with Asset A	$+ 0.40 \times 0.10 \times 0.0024$
= Asset A's contribution to total portfolio variance	$= 0.008416$

The proportion of total portfolio variance contributed by Asset A is, therefore, 0.008416/ 0.014212 = 59.22%. Asset A, which has an allocation of 40%, accounts for nearly 60% of total portfolio variance. This is not surprising, because the correlation of Asset A with the portfolio is 0.88. Asset B contributes 39.35% of total portfolio variance, and Asset C contributes 1.44%.

As you read the foregoing discussion, you naturally thought of Assets A, B, and C as securities, but the "assets" might also be sectors, countries, or pools of assets representing risk factors (Value versus Growth, Small versus Large). Hence, if a manager specializes in sector rotation and replaces an allocation to one sector with an allocation to another sector having a higher covariance with the portfolio, total portfolio risk will increase.

We have explained risk by looking at how a single asset contributes to total portfolio variance, but a manager might also seek to understand how his portfolio variance can be attributed to factor exposures versus that which is unexplained by these factors. As we noted earlier, the risks a manager chooses to take should be related to his perceived skills. If the manager's skills can be attributed to certain factors, then he would want to minimize the level of portfolio risk not explained by those factors. The segmentation of absolute portfolio variance into these two components—variance attributed to factor exposure and variance unexplained—is expressed by Equation 9:[26]

$$V_p = \text{Var}\left(\sum_{i=1}^{K}(\beta_{ip} \times F_i)\right) + \text{Var}(\varepsilon_p) \tag{9}$$

If the manager's portfolio were the market portfolio, all the variance of the portfolio returns would be explained by a beta of 1 to the Market factor. Idiosyncratic risks would be fully diversified. However, as we move away from the market portfolio, total portfolio variance will be influenced by other factor exposures and other risks unexplained by factors.[27]

Exhibit 11 presents the risk factor attribution (as measured by the variance of returns) of the three products presented earlier in Exhibit 2: the Russell 1000 Index, the Russell 1000

---

[26]Equation 9 is the same general formulation as Equation 6. However, Equation 6 was concerned with active risk.

[27]There are two ways of determining the portion of the variance of returns attributed to factors versus idiosyncratic risk. One approach consists of simply calculating each period's returns attributed to factors (the sum of the product of factor coefficients and the factor returns, which is the first term of Equation 9) and then calculating the variance of the calculated return series. This is variance attributed to factors. It can then be compared with the actual portfolio variance. A second approach identifies the variance contribution of each individual factor. However, it requires the variance–covariance matrix of factors and the vector of factor coefficients.

Value Index, and a Value fund. Exhibit 11 shows that more than 100% of the absolute risk of the Russell 1000 Index is explained by the Market factor. The size exposure (the large-cap tilt of the Russell 1000 relative to the market) has a slight negative contribution to total risk.

The risk of the Russell 1000 Value Index is also dominated by the Market factor, and unsurprisingly, the Value factor explains 12.5% of total risk.

The Value fund appears to have much idiosyncratic risk. Its sensitivity to the Market factor is only 57.7%, whereas the Value factor accounts for 18.1% of total risk. Overall, the four factors account for slightly more than 74% of total portfolio risk, and almost 26% remains unexplained. The percentage of total variance that is explained corresponds to the R^2 of the regressions as reported in Exhibit 2.

EXHIBIT 11   Absolute Risk Factor Attribution, February 1990–December 2016[28]

	Russell 1000 Index	Russell 1000 Value Index	Value Fund
Market	100.4%	88.9%	57.7%
Size	−1.8%	−1.6%	1.8%
Value	0.2%	12.5%	18.1%
Momentum	0.5%	−5.2%	−3.5%
Total explained risk	99.3%	94.6%	74.1%
Total unexplained risk	0.7%	5.4%	25.9%
Total absolute risk (standard deviation annualized)	14.5%	14.2%	18.0%

Source: Calculations by authors.

4.1.2. Causes and Sources of Relative/Active Risk

Relative risk becomes an appropriate measure when the manager is concerned with her performance relative to a benchmark. One measure of relative risk is the variance of the portfolio's active return (AV_p):

$$AV_p = \sum_{i=1}^{n} \sum_{j=1}^{n} (x_i - b_i)(x_j - b_j)RC_{ij} \tag{10a}$$

where
  x_i = the asset's weight in the portfolio
  b_i = the benchmark weight in asset i
  RC_{ij} = the covariance of relative returns between asset i and asset j

---

[28]The Market factor is built from a much larger universe of securities than traditional benchmarks, such as the Russell 1000. Therefore, we should not expect the β of indexes to the Market factor to necessarily equal one.

The contribution of each asset to the portfolio active variance (CAV_i) is

$$CAV_i = (x_i - b_i)RC_{ip} \tag{10b}$$

where RC_{ip} is the covariance of relative returns between asset i and the portfolio.

If you are assessing risk using a relative risk construct, you can no longer assume that a lower-risk asset reduces active risk or that a higher-risk asset increases it. In fact, depending on the composition of the benchmark, a lower-risk asset could increase active risk whereas a higher-risk asset might reduce it.

Let's consider a simple example. Assume a benchmark is composed of a 50/50 allocation to two equity indexes. The portfolio is composed of allocations to these two indexes and to a third asset—cash. What happens to the active risk of the portfolio if, instead of a 50/50 allocation to the two indexes, the portfolio allocation is 40/40 and 20% in cash? The benchmark is still 50/50. Let's look at the contribution of the active weights to the active variance of the portfolio. Exhibit 12 presents the relevant information and the results.

EXHIBIT 12   Relative Risk Attribution

	Benchmark Weight	Portfolio Weight	Standard Deviation	Active Risk	Correlation of Active Returns			Variance of Active Returns Attributed to Each Asset
					Index A	Index B	Cash	
Index A	50%	40%	16%	5.0%	1.00	−1.00	−0.69	14.3%
Index B	50%	40%	10%	5.0%	−1.00	1.00	0.69	−14.3%
Cash	0%	20%	0.5%	12.0%	−0.69	0.69	1.00	100%
Total	100%	100%		2.4%	−0.69	0.69	1.00	100%

Index A and Index B have absolute volatilities of 16% and 10%, respectively, whereas cash has a very low volatility. The manager is concerned with active risk, however, not portfolio volatility. Both Index A and Index B have an active risk of 5% against the 50/50 benchmark. Cash has higher active risk because it has a low correlation with the equity benchmark.

Exhibit 12 shows that the correlations of active returns between the benchmark and Index A and between the benchmark and Index B are both −1.0. This is not a coincidence; it must be so. Because the benchmark comprises just these two indexes, any outperformance of one index relative to the benchmark must be offset by underperformance of the other index. Similarly, cash has a positive correlation of relative returns with one index and a negative relative correlation with the other.

This example illustrates that this portfolio's risk (defined here as variance of active returns) can be attributed entirely to the allocation to cash, which is a low-risk asset—in an absolute sense. Hence, in the context of relative measures of risk, what matters is not the volatility of an asset but its relative (active) volatility. Introducing a low-volatility asset within a portfolio benchmarked against a high-volatility index would increase the active risk. Similarly, introducing a high-volatility asset to a portfolio might lower the active risk if the asset has a high covariance with the benchmark. These principles hold whether allocating among countries, sectors, securities, or other factors.

Exhibit 13 is similar to Exhibit 11, but it considers the attribution of active risk rather than absolute risk. It shows how much of the active risk of each product can be attributed to the four factors and how much remains unexplained. The Russell 1000 Index has some active risk (though very low, at 2% annualized). The active risk of the Russell 1000 Value Index and the Value fund are higher, at 6.0% and 11.4%, respectively.[29]

The Market factor does not explain much of the active risk; the very action of building a portfolio that is structurally different from the market creates the active risk. The two indexes have a significant portion of their active risk explained by the four rewarded factors. More than half of the active risk of the Russell 1000 Index is generated from the larger-cap tilt of the index. About 37% of the active risk remains unexplained. More than half of the active risk of the Russell 1000 Value Index is generated from the value tilt of the index. About 31% of the active risk remains unexplained. Finally, the Value fund has significant active risk (11.4%). Virtually all of this risk can be attributed the Value factor. In this case, though, nearly two-thirds of the active risk remains unexplained. An investor would want to investigate more carefully what is driving the active risk of the value manager.

EXHIBIT 13   Active Risk Factor Attribution, February 1990–December 2016

	Russell 1000	**Russell 1000 Value**	**Value Fund**
Total active risk	2.0%	6.0%	11.4%
Risk Factor Contribution to Active Risk			
Market	3.0%	6.0%	1.2%
Size	56.4%	15.4%	0.8%
Value	3.0%	53.9%	38.4%
Momentum	0.5%	–5.4%	–4.1%
Total explained risk	62.8%	69.9%	36.4%
Total unexplained risk	37.2%	31.1%	63.6%

Source: Calculations by authors.

4.2. Determining the Appropriate Level of Risk

Listed below are representative examples of risk targets for different mandates:

- a market-neutral hedge fund targeting an absolute risk of 10%,
- a long-only equity manager targeting an active risk of something less than 2% (a closet indexer),
- a long-only manager targeting active risk of 6%–10% (benchmark agnostic), and
- a benchmark-agnostic equity manager targeting an absolute risk equal to 85% of the index risk.

Establishing the appropriate level of absolute or relative risk is a subjective exercise, highly sensitive to managers' investment style and their conviction in their ability to add value

---

[29]For a detailed explanation of risk decomposition, see MacQueen (2007).

using the various levers at their disposal. Managers with similar investment approaches may have very different risk appetites. This has implications for portfolio structure, portfolio turnover, and other facets of portfolio implementation. Managers must clearly communicate to investors their overall risk orientation, and investors must understand the implications of this risk orientation. This does not mean that a strategy can or should be executed at any level of risk. Here are three scenarios that give some insights into practical risk limits:

- portfolios may face implementation constraints that degrade the information ratio if active risk increases beyond a specific level;
- portfolios with high absolute risk targets face limited diversification opportunities, which may lead to a decrease in the Sharpe ratio; and
- there is a level of leverage beyond which volatility reduces expected compounded returns.

4.2.1. Implementation constraints

Consider two managers (A and B), each with a relative risk focus. Irrespective of the targeted level of active risk, the managers seek to use that risk efficiently. They are concerned with the ratio of active return to active risk—the information ratio. Assume that their portfolios have the same information ratio but different levels of active risk. If the investor is willing to tolerate the higher level of active risk, Manager A might proportionately scale up his active risk to match the active risk level of Manager B. He would accomplish this by scaling up his active weights, which would increase Manager A's excess returns while maintaining the same information ratio. This scenario is illustrated in Exhibit 14.

EXHIBIT 14   Active Returns and Active Risk

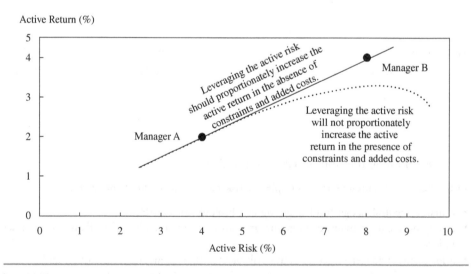

However, there may be constraints that prevent Manager A from scaling his active weights. For example, if the investment policy does not allow short positions, he may be unable to increase underweights. If the policy does not allow leverage, he may be unable to increase overweights. If some of the security positions have poor liquidity, leveraging these positions may be imprudent and may also have a trading cost impact. If the policy restricts maximum position sizes, Manager A may be unable to proportionately scale his active risk.[30]

4.2.2. Limited diversification opportunities

Consider a manager with a high absolute risk target. Despite his higher risk tolerance, he still strives to use risk efficiently. We know, though, that twice the absolute risk will not lead to twice the return: The mathematics of the Markowitz efficient investment frontier clearly shows that the relationship between return and risk is concave. Expected returns increase with risk but at a declining pace. Portfolios with higher risk/return targets eventually run out of high-return investment opportunities and lose the ability to diversify efficiently, thereby reducing the Sharpe ratio.

4.2.3. Leverage and its implications for risk

Sharpe demonstrated that if there is a risk-free rate at which investors can borrow or lend, there is a linear relationship between absolute risk and return in a one-period setting. Managers can scale expected returns and absolute risk up or down proportionately and maintain a constant, optimal Sharpe ratio. A manager could choose to leverage her portfolio to extend the implementation limits of a strategy. However, as we show below, leverage eventually leads to a reduction of expected compounded return in a multi-period setting.

We know that the expected compounded/geometric return of an asset (R_g) is approximately related to its expected arithmetic/periodic return (R_a) and its expected volatility (σ):[31]

$$R_g = R_a - \sigma^2/2 \tag{11}$$

For example, let's consider again the performance of the Russell 1000 between February 1990 and December 2016. The average monthly compounded return was 0.789%, the monthly arithmetic return was 0.878%, and the volatility, as measured by the standard deviation of return, was 4.199%. Applying Equation 11, we obtain the compounded return as follows:

$$R_g = 0.878\% - \frac{4.199\%^2}{2} = 0.790\%$$

which is very close to the realized compounded return. Now, what happens to the relationship between the arithmetic return and the compounded return when leverage is used? Let's consider an asset with a 20% standard deviation and a 10% expected arithmetic return. This asset has an expected compounded return of 8%:

$$10\% - 20\%^2/2 = 8\%$$

Ignoring the cost of funding, if we leverage the asset by a factor of 2, the expected compounded return increases to 12%:

---

[30]This constraint is also implicit in the full fundamental law of active management, which expresses the main sources of active returns. The transfer coefficient represents the ability to translate portfolio insights into investment decisions without constraint. If a manager is limited in his ability to implement his strategy, the transfer coefficient will decline. If he attempts to maintain the same level of active risk, his information ratio will also decline. In this case, there is an optimal/maximum level of active risk.

[31]The arithmetic return and the geometric returns are the same only when there is no volatility.

$$2 \times 10\% - (2 \times 20\%)^2/2 = 12\%$$

If we leverage the asset by a factor of 3, however, there is no additional improvement in return:

$$3 \times 10\% - (3 \times 20\%)^2/2 = 12\%$$

If we incorporate the cost of funding leverage, the active return is reduced while the volatility remains proportional to the amount of leverage. The Sharpe ratio will decline even faster. For example, using the same example, we could show that a portfolio with a leverage of $3\times$ would have the same expected return as an unlevered portfolio if the cost of funding leverage were 2%:

$$(3 \times 10\% - 2 \times 2\%) - (3 \times 20\%)^2/2 = 8\%$$

Furthermore, if the realized volatility is significantly greater than expected, such as in crisis time, the combined impact of volatility and leverage on compounded return could be dramatic.

The information ratio and the Sharpe ratio will not always be degraded by a reasonable rise in active or absolute risk, and a reasonable level of leverage can increase expected compounded return. The appropriate tactics must be evaluated by the manager in the context of his investment approach and investors' expectations.

4.3. Allocating the Risk Budget

We have explained how absolute and relative risk are determined by the position sizing of assets/factors (absolute or relative) and by the covariance of assets/factors with the portfolio (absolute or relative). By understanding both components (position sizing and covariance), a manager can determine the contribution of each position (whether a factor, country, sector, or security) to the portfolio's variance or active variance.

Let's consider a benchmark-agnostic US sector rotator. Although he himself is benchmark agnostic, his client is going to evaluate his performance relative to *some* benchmark—one that represents the universe of securities he typically draws from. The nature of his strategy indicates that he will likely exhibit a high level of active risk. In assessing whether he has effectively used this risk budget, the client will look to decompose the sources of realized risk: How much is attributable to market risk and other risk factors? How much is attributable to other decisions, such as sector and security allocation? If the manager runs a concentrated portfolio, we should expect sector and security allocation to be the main source of active risk. Although all these aspects may not be explicit elements of his portfolio construction process, because his effectiveness will be evaluated using these metrics, he would be well served to understand their contributions to his risk and return.

A fund's style and strategy will also dictate much of the structure of its risk budget. We explore this further with an examination of the three US equity managers presented in Exhibit 15A. All managers draw their securities from a universe of large-cap and mid-cap securities defined by the Russell 1000, which has a weighted average market capitalization of approximately \$133 billion. The first two managers believe their skill is their ability to create balanced exposures to rewarded risk factors. The third specializes in sector timing, but he also makes significant use of cash positions. The first two managers have many securities in their portfolios, which suggests that their active risk is unlikely to be driven by idiosyncratic risks related to security concentration. Their low level of security concentration is consistent with their respective investment style.

The third manager runs a highly concentrated portfolio. As a sector rotator, he is exposed to significant unrewarded risk related to his sector views and to idiosyncratic risk related to his security views. A sector rotator could choose to run either a diversified portfolio or a highly concentrated portfolio within sectors. Manager C chose the latter. A greater concentration of risk implicitly leads to a greater sensitivity to unrewarded factors and idiosyncratic risks.

EXHIBIT 15A   Comparative Sources of Risk, Drivers of Return

	Manager A	Manager B	Manager C
Investment Approach:	**Factor Diversified**	**Factor Diversified**	**Sector Rotator**
Number of securities	251	835	21
Weight of top 5 securities	6.54%	3.7%	25.1%
Cash and bond position	0.8%	0.0%	21.3%
Weighted average capitalization ($ billions)	33.7	21.3	164.0
Market beta	0.90	0.97	1.28
Absolute risk	10.89%	10.87%	11.69%
Active risk	3.4%	3.6%%	4.5%
Active Share	0.76	0.63	0.87
Average sector deviation	3.6%	3.9%	5.6%
Source of risk: Market	98.0%	99.2%	69.2%
Source of risk: Sectors	−0.8%	−3.8%	11.6%
Source of risk: Styles	1.8%	4.2%	9.7%
Unexplained	1.0%	0.4%	9.5%

Note: Manager C owns 49 positions, but several of these positions are cash and bond related.
Source: Bloomberg.

None of the managers is tightly tracking the benchmark; active risk exceeds 3% for all three. Somewhat surprisingly, the active risk of the sector rotator (4.5%) is only slightly greater than that for the other managers, especially given that the rotator has 25.1% of his portfolio invested in the top five positions and holds 21.3% in cash and bonds.[32] The large position in cash and bonds may also explain why the absolute volatility is not higher. We can see, however, that the sector rotator is taking less of a size bet: The weighted average capitalization of his portfolio is close to that of the index, whereas the weighted average capitalization of the two factor managers is quite low. This smaller size bet is likely what has constrained the active risk of the sector rotator.

Although managers may view their investment process and evaluation of securities as benchmark agnostic, the outcomes may, in fact, be similar to the benchmark along critical dimensions, such as active risk. The portfolio construction process of multi-factor managers often leads to a balanced exposure to risk factors, constraining active risk. The sector rotator

---

[32]The active risk is calculated from daily data over a one-year horizon. This calculation usually leads to a lower active risk than would be obtained from monthly data over a longer period.

has a higher level of active risk, but not dramatically so. The returns of the sector rotator are more driven by concentrated sector and style exposures than are the returns of the multi-factor managers. These differences are likely to influence returns over shorter horizons. Two strategies with similar active risk may have very different patterns of realized returns. When evaluating an investment manager, the asset owner needs to understand the drivers of active risk that can lead to differences in realized portfolio returns over time.

The strategy and portfolio structure of Manager C is also revealed by the sources of absolute risk. The risk attribution in Exhibit 15 not only considers the Market factor but also adds a sector factor and a style factor.

The exposures of Managers A and B are dominated by the Market factor. Manager B's active risk, however, can be explained in part by the sector and style factors: The sector exposure reduces risk by 3.8%, and the style exposure increases it by 4.2%.

Let's look more closely at the risk profile of Manager C in Exhibit 15B.

EXHIBIT 15B

		Manager C
Investment Approach:	Sector Rotator	Risk Positioning Relative to Managers A and B
Number of securities	21	Very concentrated; high levels of security-specific risk
Weight of top 5 securities	25.1%	
Cash and bond position	21.3%	Large cash position dampens overall portfolio volatility
Weighted average capitalization ($ billions)	164.0	Much closer to the capitalization of the index
Market beta	1.28	Significantly higher, consistent with the absolute risk measures
Absolute risk	11.69%	Absolute risk only slightly higher, likely dampened by the large cash position
Active risk	4.5%	Higher
Active Share	0.87	High, consistent with the level of security concentration
Average sector deviation	5.6%	Higher, consistent with willingness to take sector bets
Source of risk: Market	69.2%	Significantly less exposure to the Market factor, consistent with a concentrated, high-Active-Share manager
Source of risk: Sectors	11.6%	Significantly more Sector risk
Source of risk: Styles	9.7%	Significantly more Style risk
Unexplained	9.5%	Significantly higher proportion of risk is unexplained

Taken together, these measures indicate a benchmark-agnostic strategy with significant and concentrated security, sector, and style exposures.

EXAMPLE 5   Application of Risk Budgeting Concepts

1. Using the information in Exhibit 15, discuss key differences in the risk profiles of Manager A and Manager C.
2. The table below presents the risk factor coefficients of a four-factor model and the factor variance–covariance matrix of a manager running a low-risk strategy. All data are monthly. The monthly standard deviation of the manager's return is 3.07%. What portion of the total portfolio risk is explained by the Market factor?

	Coefficients	Variance/Covariance of Returns			
		Market	**Size**	**Value**	**Momentum**
Market	0.733	0.00178	0.00042	0.00066	−0.00062
Size	−0.328	0.00042	0.00048	0.00033	−0.00035
Value	0.045	0.00066	0.00033	0.00127	−0.00140
Momentum	0.042	−0.00062	−0.00035	−0.00140	0.00214

3. If a manager benchmarked against the FTSE 100 makes a significant allocation to cash, how will that allocation affect the portfolio's absolute risk and active risk?
4. Manager A has been running a successful strategy achieving a high information ratio with a relatively low active risk of 3.4%. The manager is considering offering a product with twice the active risk. What are the obstacles that may make it difficult for the manager to maintain the same information ratio?

Solution to 1: Manager C holds significantly fewer positions than Manager A, and the weight of his top five securities is nearly four times that of Manager B. This indicates a willingness to assume a much higher level of idiosyncratic risk. This observation is reinforced by Manager C's higher Active Share and higher proportion of unexplained risk. The Market beta of Manager C is significantly greater, and the risk decomposition indicates that Manager C appears more willing to make sector and style bets. Finally, the absolute risk of Manager's C portfolio is higher, even though it appears that he makes greater use of lower-risk bond and cash positions.

Solution to 2: 91% of total portfolio risk is explained by the Market factor. From Equation 8b (repeated below), the contribution of an asset to total portfolio variance is equal to the product of the weight of the asset and its covariance with the entire portfolio. To calculate the variance attributed to the Market factor,

$$CV_i = \sum_{j=1}^{n} x_i x_j C_{ij} = x_i C_{ip} \qquad (8b)$$

where
   x_j = the asset's weight in the portfolio
   C_{ij} = the covariance of returns between asset i and asset j
   C_{ip} = the covariance of returns between asset i and the portfolio
   Therefore, the variance attributed to the Market factor is

$$(0.733 \times 0.00178 \times 0.733) + (0.733 \times 0.00042 \times -0.328) + (0.733 \times 0.00066$$
$$\times 0.045) + (0.733 \times -0.00062 \times 0.042) = 0.000858$$

Divide this result by the portfolio variance of returns:

$$0.000858/3.07\%^2 = 0.000858/0.000942 = 91\% \text{ of total portfolio variance is}$$
explained by the Market factor.

Solution to 3: Cash has a low volatility and a low correlation of returns with any asset. Therefore, it will contribute to a reduction in absolute risk. However, because cash has a low correlation with other assets, it will contribute to an increase in active risk.

Solution to 4: If the manager is running a long-only portfolio without leverage, she is likely able to increase her exposure to securities she wants to overweight, but she may be limited in her ability to reduce exposure to securities she wishes to avoid or underweight. Increased exposure to the most desirable securities (in her view) will lead to increased security concentration and may substantially increase active risk. The manager risks a degradation of her information ratio if there is not a corresponding increase in her active return. If the manager can short, she will be able to increase underweighting when desired (assuming the securities can be easily borrowed). Although leverage can increase total exposure and reduce concentration issues, its impact on volatility may be substantial, and the additional return enabled by leverage may be eroded by the impact of the increased volatility on compounded returns and the other associated costs.

5. ADDITIONAL RISK MEASURES USED IN PORTFOLIO CONSTRUCTION AND MONITORING

5.1. Heuristic Constraints

Risk constraints imposed as part of the portfolio construction process may be either formal or heuristic. Heuristic constraints appear as controls imposed on the permissible portfolio composition through some exogenous classification structure. Such constraints are often based on experience or practice, rather than empirical evidence of their effectiveness. These risk controls may be used to limit

- exposure concentrations by security, sector, industry, or geography;
- net exposures to risk factors, such as beta, size, value, and momentum;
- net exposures to currencies;
- degree of leverage;
- degree of illiquidity;
- turnover/trading-related costs;
- exposures to reputational and environmental risks, such as actual or potential carbon emissions; and
- other attributes related to an investor's core concerns.

A major concern of any portfolio manager is a risk that is unknown or unexpected. Risk constraints are one way that managers try to limit the portfolio losses from unexpected events. Listed below are sample heuristic constraints that may be used by a portfolio manager:

- Any single position is limited to the lesser of
  - five times the weight of the security in the benchmark or
  - 2%.

- The portfolio must have a weighted average capitalization of no less than 75% of that of the index.
- The portfolio may not size any position such that it exceeds two times the average daily trading volume of the past three months.
- The portfolio's carbon footprint must be limited to no more than 75% of the benchmark's exposure.

Such heuristic constraints as these may limit active managers' ability to fully exploit their insights into expected returns, but they might also be viewed as safeguarding against overconfidence and hubris.

Managing risk through portfolio characteristics is a "bottom-up" risk management process. Managers that rely on such an approach express their risk objectives through the heuristic characteristics of their portfolios. The resulting statistical risk measures of such portfolios do not drive the portfolio construction process but are an outcome of those heuristic characteristics. For example, if a manager imposes maximum sector deviations of $\pm 3\%$ and limits security concentration to no more than the index weight $+ 1\%$ or twice the weight of any security in the index, then we could expect the active risk of that portfolio to be small even if no constraint on active risk is explicitly imposed. The portfolio construction process ensures that the desired heuristic risk is achieved. Continuous monitoring is necessary to determine whether the evolution of market prices causes a heuristic constraint to be breached or nearly breached.

Managers will often impose constraints on the heuristic characteristics of their portfolios even if they also use more formal statistical measures of risk. The investment policy of most equity products, for example, will usually specify constraints on allocations to individual securities and to sectors or, for international mandates, regions. Some may also have constraints related to liquidity and capitalization. Even managers with a low-volatility mandate will have security and sector constraints to avoid unbalanced and concentrated portfolio solutions that may have significant idiosyncratic risk or allocations that are unduly influenced by estimation error.

5.2. Formal Constraints

Formal risk measures are distinct from these heuristic controls. They are often statistical in nature and directly linked to the distribution of returns for the portfolio.

Formal measures of risk include the following:

- Volatility
- Active risk
- Skewness
- Drawdowns
- Value at risk (VaR)

- Conditional Value at risk (CVaR)
- Incremental Value at risk (IVaR)
- Marginal Value at risk (MVaR)

A major difference between formal and heuristic risk measures is that formal measures require a manager to estimate or predict risk. For example, a formal risk measure might be that predicted active risk be no more than, say, 5%. With the benefit of hindsight, one can always calculate the historical active risk, but in portfolio construction, the forward-looking view of risk and active risk is what matters: Portfolio decisions are based on these forward-looking estimates. If predicted risk deviates substantially from realized risk, it is likely that portfolio performance will be quite different than expected. In times of crisis or financial stress, predicted and realized risks could diverge very significantly.

Exhibit 16 presents five different risk measures for the same three products discussed in Exhibit 15. Four one-day VaR measures are presented: VaR and CVaR at two different levels of probability (1% and 5%).

EXHIBIT 16   Risk Measures

| | Manager A | Manager B | Manager C |
Risk Measure	Factor Diversified	Factor Diversified	Sector Rotator
Absolute risk	10.89%	10.87%	11.69%
Active risk	3.4%	3.6%%	4.5%
VaR (5%)	1.08%	1.11%	1.20%
VaR (1%)	1.77%	1.77%	1.87%
CVaR (5%)	1.50%	1.53%	1.65%
CVaR (1%)	2.21%	2.24%	2.41%

Source: Bloomberg.

In this example, Manager A has a 5% probability of realizing a one-day loss greater than 1.08% and a 1% probability of a loss greater than 1.77%. If we look at the distribution of losses beyond the 5% and 1% probability levels, the averages of the tail losses (CVaR) are 1.50% and 2.21%, respectively. Despite the high security concentration, the loss estimates of Manager C are not much higher than those of Managers A and B, most likely because of the large position in cash and bonds.

Risk Measures

- Volatility is the standard deviation of portfolio returns.
- Active risk is the standard deviation of the differences between a portfolio's returns and its benchmark's returns. It is also called *tracking error* or *tracking risk*.
- Skewness is a measure of the degree to which return expectations are non-normally distributed. If a distribution is positively skewed, the mean of the distribution is greater than its median (more than half of the deviations from the mean are negative and less than half are positive) and the average magnitude of positive deviations is larger than the average magnitude of negative deviations. Negative skew indicates

that the mean of the distribution lies below its median and the average magnitude of negative deviations is larger than the average magnitude of positive deviations.

- Drawdown measures the portfolio loss from its high point until it begins to recover.
- VaR is the minimum loss that would be expected a certain percentage of the time over a specific period of time (e.g., a day, a week, a month) given the modeled market conditions. It is typically expressed as the minimum loss that can be expected to occur 5% of the time.
- CVaR is the average loss that would be incurred if the VaR cutoff is exceeded. It is also sometimes referred to as the **expected tail loss** or **expected shortfall**. It is not technically a VaR measure.
- IVaR is the change in portfolio VaR when adding a new position to a portfolio, thereby reducing the position size of current positions.
- MVaR reflects the effect of a very small change in the position size. In a diversified portfolio, marginal VaR may be used to determine the contribution of each asset to the overall VaR.

Formal risk constraints may be applied as part of a portfolio optimization process (as is common with systematic strategies) or using an iterative feedback mechanism to determine whether the portfolio would remain within the risk tolerance limits given the proposed change (an approach more common among discretionary managers).

All risk measures, whether formal or heuristic, can be expressed on an absolute basis or relative to a benchmark. For example, a benchmark-aware long-only equity manager may limit sector deviations to 5%, whereas a long/short hedge fund manager concerned with the overall diversification of his portfolio may limit any given sector exposure to no more than 30% of his gross exposure. Similarly, a long-only equity manager may limit active risk to 5%, whereas a long/short equity manager may limit overall portfolio volatility to 10%. In many cases, the investment policy imposes both formal and heuristic constraints on a portfolio. Exhibit 17 illustrates a product for which the investment policy statement considers constraints on both types of risk measures.

EXHIBIT 17   Sample Investment Policy Risk Constraints

The MSCI Diversified Multi-Factor Index

This index uses an optimization process to maximize the exposure score to several risk factors. The index seeks to achieve this objective while controlling for several portfolio and risk characteristics, such as the following:

- Weight of index constituents: maximum of weight in the parent (capitalization-weighted) index + 2% or 10 times weight in the parent index
- Sector weights: restricted to a 5% deviation against the parent index
- Exposure to style factors, such as growth and liquidity: restricted to a 0.25 standard deviation from the parent index
- Limit on volatility: restricted to a 0.25 standard deviation from the parent index

5.3. The Risks of Being Wrong

The consequences of being wrong about risk expectations can be significant but even more so when a strategy is leveraged. In 2008, for example, a hedge fund owned a two-times levered portfolio of highly rated mortgage-related securities. Although the specific securities were not materially exposed to subprime mortgages, concerns about the economy and poor market liquidity led to a steep decline in the prices of these securities. Prices quickly recovered, but the presence of the 2× leverage combined with an unprecedented price decline led to a forced liquidation of the assets just a few days before prices recovered. The manager and his investors lost all capital.

Similarly, a pension fund created an indexed equity position by combining an investment of short-term highly rated (AAA) commercial paper with an equivalent notional position in equity derivatives (a receiver swap on a large-cap equity index), creating a synthetic indexed equity position. In principle, this pension fund believed it owned the equivalent of an index equity position. However, as the liquidity crisis worsened in 2008 and early 2009, the pension fund was faced with a substantial decline in equity markets *and* a simultaneous spike in the perceived riskiness of the short-term commercial paper. The equity derivatives position and the commercial paper each lost 50% of their value, creating a paper loss equivalent to 100% of the invested capital. Although both components eventually recovered, such unexpected losses can lead to a forced liquidation of all or part of the portfolio in an unfavorable market environment, crystalizing the losses.

Exhibit 18 illustrates the time-varying volatility of the S&P 500. Although volatility remains in a range of 10%–20% most of the time, periods of much higher volatility are observed: in 1973–1974 during the first oil shock, in 1987 during the October crisis, in 2000–2002 when technology stocks collapsed, and during the 2008 liquidity crisis. Effective risk management requires the manager to account for the fact that unexpected volatility can derail the investment strategy. Furthermore, spikes in volatility can also be sector specific—the technology sector in the early 2000s and the energy sector in 2014 and 2015. Therefore, what may seem to be an acceptable sector deviation limit in normal times may be the source of significant active losses in a different environment. Some managers may tighten risk constraints in more volatile periods to protect the portfolio against excessive variability.

Despite these "tail events," risk can usually be managed efficiently. The dotted line in Exhibit 18[33] shows the realized volatility of a portfolio dynamically allocated between the S&P 500 Index and short-term bonds. The portfolio targets a 10% annualized volatility.[34] The realized volatility stayed very close to the target.

---

[33]Langlois and Lussier (2017).

[34]The management of this portfolio required forecasts of volatility and correlation for both assets. The same general techniques described in footnote 15 were used.

EXHIBIT 18   Volatility of the S&P 500, 1950–2015

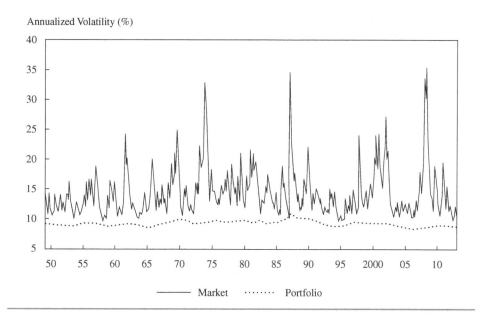

The statistical risk measures used in equity portfolio construction often depend on the style of management. A benchmark-agnostic manager with an absolute return philosophy is less likely to be concerned with active risk but is much more likely to be concerned with drawdowns. A long/short equity manager who neutralizes market risk but is exposed to other risk premiums is likely to target a volatility within a specific range.

Portfolios with a very limited number of securities may be more difficult to manage using formal risk measures because estimation errors in portfolio risk parameters are likely to be higher: The dispersion in possible outcomes may be wide, and the distributions may not easily conform to standard assumptions underlying many of the formal risk measures.

This does not mean, however, that these measures cannot be used on an *ex ante* basis. It merely suggests that they should be used with an understanding of their limitations. For example, VaR is particularly useful to a pension plan sponsor that has a multi-asset-class portfolio and needs to measure its exposure to a variety of risk factors (Simons, 2000). However, this information may be less useful to an equity manager holding only 40 equity positions. Measures of risk and their efficacy must be appropriate to the nature and objective of the portfolio mandate.

Formal, statistical measures of risk are often not outlined in investment policy statements even if the manager is actively tracking such risks and using such measures to adjust security weights. One reason may be the difficulty in measuring and forecasting such measures as volatility and value at risk. The resultant answers are likely to be different depending on what methodology is used. Even if the historical measures were in alignment with one another, what happened in the past will not necessarily be indicative of what is to come. When formal, statistical measures of risk are used by managers, they are typically expressed as a soft target, such as, "We are targeting a 10%–12% annualized volatility."

Calibrating risk is as much an art as it is a science. If an active manager imposes restrictions that are too tightly anchored to her investment benchmark (or perhaps these restrictions are imposed by the investor), the resulting portfolio may have performance that too closely mirrors that of the benchmark.

EXAMPLE 6   Risk Measures in Portfolio Construction

Matthew Rice runs a discretionary equity strategy benchmarked on the Russell 1000 Index. His fund contains approximately 80 securities and has recently passed $2 billion in assets. His strategy emphasizes quality companies that are attractively priced within their sector. This determination is based on careful analyses of the balance sheet, free cash flows, and quality of management of the companies they invest in. Rice is not benchmark agnostic, but his strategy does require the ability to tolerate some sector deviations because attractive positions are sometimes concentrated in three or four sectors. Rice is supported by a team of six analysts but makes all final allocation decisions. Historically, no single position or bet has dominated the performance of the fund. However, Rice believes there is no point in holding a position so small that it will barely affect excess returns even if it is successful. Rice does not believe in taking aggressive views. His investors do not expect him to have the active risk of a sector rotator. The portfolio has lower turnover than that of most of his peers. Single positions can easily remain in the portfolio for two or three years.

1.   What heuristic constraints could be appropriate for such a fund?
2.   What role might such statistical measures as VaR or active risk play in the management of Rice's fund?

Solution to 1: Because no single position or bet has dominated historical returns, a heuristic constraint on maximum position size is a logical one. Given that his portfolio is built around a relatively small number of positions (80), single positions might be constrained to no more than 3%. Given his view on small position sizes, a minimum position size of 0.5% might also be appropriate.

Rice's strategy requires some active risk, but he could not tolerate the sector deviations taken by a sector rotator. A sector constraint in the range of ±5%–7.5% relative to the index is appropriate for his strategy.

The fund's benchmark incorporates many mid-cap securities. With $2 billion in assets, a single position can be as small as $10 million (0.5%) but as high as perhaps $60 million (3%). Positions on the higher end of this range could represent a large portion of the average daily trading of some mid-cap securities, which range in size from $2 billion to $10 billion. The fund's long investment horizon means that trading into and out of a position can be stretched over days or even weeks. Nevertheless, it could make sense to consider a constraint that accounts for the size (capitalization) of individual securities and their trading volume, such as not owning more than five times the capitalization weight in the index of any security.

Solution to 2: Discretionary managers usually do not use statistical measures as hard constraints, but they can be used as guidelines in the portfolio management process. A fund that contains only 80 positions out of a universe of 1,000 possible securities and takes views across capitalization and sectors is likely to see significant variability in its active risk or VaR over time. Although Rice is not very sensitive to what happens in the short run (he is a long-term investor), statistical measures can be used to monitor changes in the risks within his portfolio. If these risk exposures deviate from his typical risk exposures, it might signal a need to investigate the sources of such changes and initiate some portfolio changes if those exposures are unwanted.

6. IMPLICIT COST-RELATED CONSIDERATIONS IN PORTFOLIO CONSTRUCTION

There are numerous costs that can affect the net performance of an investment product. The same investment strategy can easily cost twice as much to manage if a manager is not careful with her implementation approach. Assets under management (AUM) will affect position size. Position size and the liquidity of the securities in the portfolio will affect the level of turnover that can be sustained at an acceptable level of costs.[35] Although smaller-AUM funds may pay more in explicit costs (such as broker commissions), these funds may incur lower implicit costs (such as delay and market impact) than large-AUM funds. Overall, smaller funds may be able to sustain greater turnover and still deliver superior performance. A manager needs to carefully weigh both explicit and implicit costs in his implementation approach.

Thoughtful portfolio management requires a manager to balance the potential benefits of turnover against the costs of turnover. When considering a rebalancing or restructuring of the portfolio, the benefits of the post-trade risk/return position must justify the costs of getting there.

This section concerns the implicit costs of implementing an active strategy and implementation issues related to asset under management, position sizing, turnover, and market liquidity. Explicit costs, such as broker commissions, financial transaction taxes, custody/safekeeping fees, and transaction processing, are covered in other parts of the CFA Program curriculum.

6.1. Implicit Costs—Market Impact and the Relevance of Position Size, Assets under Management, and Turnover

The price movement (or market impact) resulting from a manager's purchase or sale of a security can materially erode a manager's alpha. Market impact is a function of the liquidity and trade size of the security. A manager's investment approach and style will influence the extent to which he is exposed to market impact costs. A manager whose strategy demands immediacy in execution or requires a higher portfolio turnover is likely to incur higher market impact costs relative to a manager who patiently trades into a position. A manager who believes her investment insights will be rewarded over a longer-term investment horizon may be able to mitigate market impact costs by slowly building up positions as liquidity becomes

---

[35]The portfolio turnover ratio is a measure of the fund's trading activity. It is computed by taking the lesser of purchases or sales and dividing by average monthly net assets.

available. A manager whose trades contain "information" is more vulnerable to market impact costs. A trade contains information when the manager's decision to buy or sell the security signals to the market that something has changed. If a discretionary manager with sizable assets under management begins to buy a stock, the trade signals to other market participants that there is likely to be upward pressure on the stock price as the manager builds the position. Some market participants may try to "front-run" the manager, buying up known supply to sell it to the manager at a higher price. If that same manager begins to sell his position following a company "event," it signals to the market that the manager's view on the stock has changed and he is likely to be selling off his position, putting downward pressure on the price. Assets under management, portfolio turnover, and the liquidity of the underlying assets all affect the potential market impact costs.

Consider the relationship between the size of a security, as measured by its capitalization, and a manager's ability to trade in this security, as measured by its average daily trading volume. Exhibit 19 presents the capitalization and average daily trading volume of the Russell 1000 companies in declining order of their capitalization. The figure is built using a moving average of the capitalization of groups of 20 companies. The first point on the graph shows the average capitalization and trading volume of the largest 20 companies by capitalization. The next point on the graph presents the same information for the averages of the companies ranking 2nd to 21st in terms of capitalization, and so on.

EXHIBIT 19   Capitalization and Trading Volume (in $) of the Russell 1000 Companies in Declining Order of Capitalization

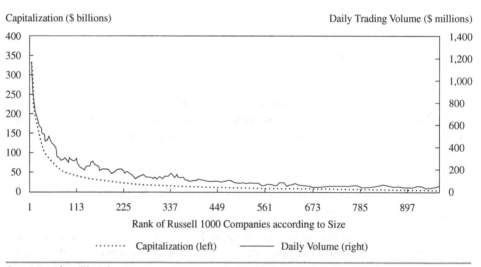

Source: Data from Bloomberg.

Two observations are warranted. First, the distribution of market cap is skewed: The average capitalization declines quickly. The combined capitalization of the top 500 companies is more than seven times that of the bottom 500 companies. Second, smaller-capitalization companies have lower daily trading volume (in dollars). However, smaller-cap companies trade a greater percentage of their capitalization. The smallest 900 companies within the index trade nearly two times more volume—as a percentage of their market capitalization—than the

100 largest companies (e.g., the 900 smallest companies on average trade 1% of their market cap daily, whereas the 100 largest companies trade 0.5% of their market cap daily). Nevertheless, the lower absolute level of average trading volume of the smaller securities can be a significant implementation hurdle for a manager running a strategy with significant assets under management and significant positive active weights on smaller companies.

For example, let's assume the smallest company within an index has a capitalization of $2 billion and that 1% of its capitalization trades each day on average—about $20 million. Let's also assume that a manager has a policy not to own a position that constitutes more than 10% of the average trading volume of a security and that no position in the portfolio can be larger than 2% of total assets. If this manager has $200 million under management, the allocation constraint indicates that he could own as much as $4 million of that security ($200 million × 2% = $4 million), but the liquidity constraint limits the position to $2 million ($20 million × 10%). Thus, the position size is limited to about 1.0% of the fund's assets. A $1 billion fund with similar constraints would be limited to the same $2 million position, a much smaller position size relative to his total portfolio.

A $100 million fund can typically implement its strategy with very few obstacles arising from trading volume and position size constraints. However, the manager of a $5 billion fund could not effectively operate with the same constraints. A 2% position in a $5 billion fund is $100 million, yet only approximately 35% of the securities in the Russell 1000 have an average daily trading volume greater than $100 million. The trading volume constraint significantly limits the manager's opportunity set. A large-AUM fund can address this issue in several ways:

- It may establish position limits on individual securities that consider their respective market-cap weights on both an absolute and relative basis. For example, it may limit the allocation to the lesser of market-cap weight + 1% (100 bps) or 10 times the market-cap weight allocation of the security within the index. In other words, the position limit would be related to the market cap of each security.
- It may establish position limits based on the average daily trading volume of a security. For example, it may limit the position size to, say, no more than 10 days of average trading volume.
- It may build a rebalancing strategy into the investment process that anticipates a longer rebalancing period or that gradually and consistently rebalances over time, assuming the performance of the strategy is not affected by the implementation delay.

The challenges are even greater for small-cap funds. The weighted average capitalization of the Russell 2000 Index is only $2.2 billion, and nearly 60% of the companies in the index have a market capitalization below $1 billion (as of March 2017). The average market cap of companies over this $1 billion market-cap threshold is only $1.2 billion. The average daily volume of these "larger" companies is approximately 2% of their market capitalization—less than $25 million. Approximately 75% of securities within the index have a lower average daily trading volume.

A small-cap manager with the same limits on position size relative to trading volume as the manager above would have an average position size of no more than $2.5 million, based on average daily trading volume. A strategy rooted in a smaller number of securities—say, 40—may find it difficult to run a $100 million fund and may have to concentrate its allocation among the 25% largest securities in the index or accept a lower turnover. Although a strategy with a larger number of securities—say, 200—would be able to support a substantially higher level of AUM, it may still be constrained to concentrate its exposure among the larger and more liquid securities. Small-cap funds with capacities of $1 billion or greater may very well need to hold 400 securities or more.

The strategy of the manager must be consistent with the feasibility of implementing it. A high-turnover strategy with a significant allocation to smaller securities will at some point reach a level of AUM at which the strategy becomes difficult to implement successfully. The level of idiosyncratic risk inherent in the strategy will also play a role in the suitable level of AUM. A manager targeting low levels of idiosyncratic risk in his portfolio is likely to have more securities and smaller position sizes and could, therefore, conceivably support a higher level of AUM.

6.2. Estimating the Cost of Slippage

Slippage is often measured as the difference between the execution price and the midpoint of the bid and ask quotes at the time the trade was first entered.[36] It incorporates both the effect of volatility/trend costs and market impact. (Volatility/trend costs are the costs associated with buying in a rising market and selling in a declining market.) This measure provides an estimate of the cost to execute a transaction when the order is executed in a single trade.

When a larger trade is executed in increments over multiple days, the estimate of market impact costs for later trades does not account for the impact of earlier trades on subsequent execution prices. Depending on the size of the trade, the manager's own sell (buy) orders may put downward (upward) pressure on the security's price, thereby increasing the effective cost of implementation. Large institutional investors today will often try to camouflage the potential size of their trade by breaking a trade into many smaller trades or by trading in "unlit" venues. Unlit venues allow buyers and sellers to trade anonymously with one another. Dark pools and crossing networks are examples of unlit venues.[37]

Studies have shown that small-cap stocks have consistently had higher effective trading costs than large-cap stocks and that illiquidity can be very cyclical, increasing prior to the beginning of a recession and decreasing prior to the end of a recession.[38] It is difficult to quantify this cost, but we know intuitively that a given trading volume causes a larger price move for a less liquid asset.[39] The larger a trade size relative to a stock's average daily volume is, the more likely it is that the trade will affect prices. Thus, a fund with a focus on large-cap stocks can support a higher level of AUM than can a similar-strategy fund focused on small-cap stocks. A fund focused on small-cap stocks must either limit its AUM, hold a more diversified portfolio, limit turnover, or devise a trading strategy to mitigate market impact costs.

Exhibit 20 provides estimates of the average slippage for several markets in 2016 and for the last two quarters of 2009. The table also presents the information per capitalization segment for the US market alone. There are four conclusions we can draw:

---

[36] See Taleb (1997).

[37] If a large institution wants to sell a big block of stock but doesn't want to alert other market participants about the pending activity, it may choose to trade anonymously. Unlit venues—private trading venues where transactions are completed "in the dark" (without full transparency)—have become a powerful force in financial markets.

[38] Hasbrouck (2009) and Amihud (2002).

[39] Ilmanen (2011).

- Slippage costs are usually more important than commission costs.
- Slippage costs are greater for smaller-cap securities than for large-cap securities.
- Slippage costs are not necessarily greater in emerging markets.
- Slippage costs can vary substantially over time, especially when market volatility is higher.

EXHIBIT 20   Average Slippage by Cap Size and Country

A. US Market by Cap Size

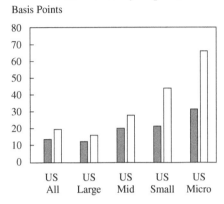

B. By Country

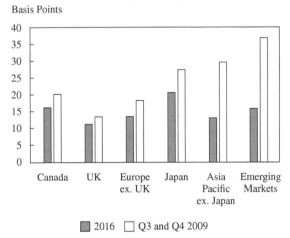

■ 2016 □ Q3 and Q4 2009

Source: ITG, "Global Cost Review Q4/2016" (2017).

Slippage cost can be managed with a strategic approach to implementation. Smaller-AUM managers have an advantage in this respect. For example, two hypothetical $100 million trades were sent to an execution platform that provides estimates of trading costs. The first trade mirrored the Russell 1000. The second trade bought just 250 securities in the same Russell 1000 universe, but the weighted average capitalization was only $26 billion (versus $133 billion for the index). Assuming the trading was accomplished in the course of a single day, the first trade had an estimated implementation cost of just 1 bp, whereas the second trade incurred implementation costs of 3%.

For some strategies, the true cost of slippage may be the opportunity cost of not being able to implement the strategy as assets grow. Investors choose a given fund based on the manager's stated strategy and implementation approach. If this approach is modified as the manager's level of AUM grows, it may have unanticipated consequences for expected risks and returns to investors. In these situations, the manager must either inform investors of changes being made to the strategy and its implementation or they must limit the size of the fund assets—that is, close the fund to new investors or new contributions from existing investors. Managers need to very carefully think about capacity as a new product is launched; although historical results based on a lower level of AUM may attract attention and clients, if the strategy cannot be scaled for the larger AUM, the product delivered to clients may be different from the strategy they thought they were investing in.

A study by Frazzini, Israel, and Moskowitz (2012) examined the scalability of well-known factor-based strategies, such as Size, Value, Momentum, and Short-Term Reversal, and considered the price impact of implementing such strategies. The study covered 19 developed markets over the period 1998–2001. It concluded that strategies based on Value could support significant scale. However, scaling up Size and especially Short-Term Reversal led to a steeper decline in performance and an increase in tracking error. Clearly, investors need to monitor a strategy's capacity by observing the evolution of portfolio turnover and portfolio characteristics, such as an increasing allocation to larger-cap stocks.[40]

EXAMPLE 7   Issues of Scale

1. Stephen Lo has been the sole portfolio manager of the Top Asia Fund since its inception 20 years ago. He is supported by a group of analysts. The fund has been highly successful as it grew from assets of less than $30 million in his first year to more than $7 billion. As a potential investor in the Top Asia Fund, you have been asked to determine how Lo has been able to generate his performance and whether his style has evolved over the years. You prepared the following analysis of the return and risk characteristics of the fund for its first five years and last five years of existence.

   Discuss the evolution of the fund's characteristics and its implications for Lo's success as a manager.

Top Asia Fund Characteristics	First Five Years	Last Five Years
Average assets ($ millions)	200	5,000
Average number of positions	80	300
Market Beta	0.90	0.91
Size coefficient	−0.30	0.10
Value coefficient	0.25	0.24

---

[40]Peter Lynch, while managing the highly successful Magellan Fund, generated a 2% gross *monthly* alpha on average (less than $1 million per year) assets under management of $40 million during his first five years of tenure and a 0.20% alpha per month during his last five years on assets of about $10 billion (more than $20 million per year). It is likely that the portfolio management approach evolved as the asset base grew.

Top Asia Fund Characteristics	First Five Years	Last Five Years
Momentum coefficient	0.20	0.10
Portfolio turnover	100%	30%
Alpha (gross of fees)	2.5%	0.40%

2. Andrew Isaac runs a $100 million diversified equity portfolio (about 200 positions) using the the Russell 1000 as his investable universe. The total capitalization of the index is approximately $20 trillion. Isaac's strategy is very much size agnostic. He consistently owns securities along the entire size spectrum of permissible securities. The strategy was designed with the following constraints:
    - No investment in any security whose index weight is less than 0.015% (approximately 15% of the securities in the index)
    - Maximum position size equal to the lesser of 10× the index weight or the index weight plus 150 bps
    - No position size that represents more than 5% of the security's average daily trading volume (ADV) over the trailing three months

    The smaller securities in Isaac's permissible universe trade about 1% of shares outstanding daily. At what level of AUM is Isaac's strategy likely to be affected by the liquidity and concentration constraints?

Solution to 1: AUM grew rapidly over the past 20 years. The number of positions in the portfolio nearly quadrupled while assets grew by a factor of 25. Still, there are aspects of his style that have not changed: He is still very much a value manager investing in lower-beta securities. However, the portfolio no longer has a small-cap tilt, and the exposure to the momentum factor has also declined. It is likely that these are both byproducts of the increase in AUM; for example, a large fund has greater difficulty executing in small-cap securities. This last point is supported by the decline in portfolio turnover. The decline in alpha indicates that the growth in AUM has altered the implementation of the investment approach.

Solution to 2: Based on the index capitalization of $20 trillion, the size constraint indicates that the smallest stocks in his portfolio will have a minimum market cap of about $3 billion (0.015% × $20 trillion). The ADV of the stocks at the lower end of his capitalization constraint would be about $30 million (1% × $3 billion). Because Isaac does not want to represent more than 5% of any security's ADV, the maximum position size for these smaller-cap stocks is about $1.5 million (5% × $30 million). It appears that Isaac's strategy will not be constrained until the portfolio reaches about $1 billion in size ($1.5 million ÷ 0.15% = $1 billion). If the level of AUM exceeds $1 billion, his position size constraints will require the portfolio to hold a larger number of smaller-cap positions. There is room to grow this strategy.

7. THE WELL-CONSTRUCTED PORTFOLIO

A well-constructed portfolio should deliver results consistent with investors' risk and return expectations. It will not guarantee excess return relative to the appropriate benchmark, especially over a shorter horizon, but it will be designed to deliver the risk characteristics desired by the manager and promised to investors. The well-constructed portfolio possesses

- a clear investment philosophy and a consistent investment process,
- risk and structural characteristics as promised to investors,
- a risk-efficient delivery methodology, and
- reasonably low operating costs given the strategy.

Investors and managers may have different requirements with respect to the characteristics they seek in a well-structured portfolio. For some managers, substantial diversification is required, whereas others seek a high-conviction, less diversified strategy. Some investors require formal and heuristic risk metrics that are tightly constrained, and others tolerate more permissive risk limits. A well-structured portfolio must, at the very least, deliver the promised characteristics in a cost- and risk-efficient way.

Consider the following large-cap US equity products, Product A and Product B. Between January 1999 and September 2016, the two products had similar annualized absolute volatility, 15.1% and 15.2%, and similar active risk, 4.9% and 4.8%. However, they differ on other dimensions. Exhibit 21 presents the factor exposure of each product using a six-factor model. The factors are Market, Size, Value, Momentum, Betting against Beta (BAB), and Quality. The exhibit also shows the volatility of each factor. Exhibit 22 illustrates the contribution to the total variance of each product originating from these factors, as well as the portion of total variance that remains unexplained. Other characteristics are also presented.[41]

EXHIBIT 21   Factor Exposure, January 1999–September 2016

Factor	Product A	Product B	Factor Volatility
Market	0.92	1.08	15.8%
Size	−0.29	0.04	9.7%
Value	0.33	0.06	14.7%
Momentum	0.04	0.06	19.2%
BAB	0.02	0.09	14.4%
Quality	0.03	0.23	11.4%

Sources: Data are from Bloomberg and AQR.

---

[41]The style of a particular product may evolve over time because of changes in investment philosophy and even changes in the product management team. Although the two products presented in Exhibits 21 and 22 were selected for the consistency of their respective approaches over time, when the period covers several decades, it would be prudent to do factor analyses over several sub-periods to determine whether changes in management style did, in fact, occur.

EXHIBIT 22   Risk Characteristics

Factor	Factor Risk Contribution	
	Product A	**Product B**
Market	87.4%	105.9%
Size	−2.3%	0.6%
Value	14.0%	1.2%
Momentum	−2.7%	−2.0%
BAB	−0.4%	−2.0%
Quality	−1.6%	−10.5%
Unexplained	5.5%	6.8%
Total	100%	100%
	Other Characteristics	
Number of securities	≈320	≈120
Annualized active risk	4.9%	4.8%
Active Share	0.43	0.80
Annualized volatility	15.1%	15.2%
Maximum drawdown	54.6%	51.8%

Since the two products have similar volatility and active risk, what opinion can we form about the risk efficiency of each product?

Product A exhibits the following relevant characteristics:

- A Market β slightly less than 1
- A large-cap bias (a negative coefficient on the Size factor)
- A very large exposure to the Value factor
- Greater security-level diversification than Product B
- Market risk representing only 87.4% of the total portfolio risk
- A significant portion of the absolute risk attributed to the Value factor

The relevant characteristics for Product B are:

- A Market β slightly more than 1
- A more balanced exposure to all factors
- A large exposure to the Quality factor (although the factor itself has a relatively low volatility)
- Active Share nearly double that of Product A
- Modestly lower drawdowns
- More than 100% of its absolute risk attributed to the Market factor

Thus, Product B's emphasis on quality companies having a high return on equity, a low debt-to-equity ratio, and a low earnings variability is a likely explanation for absolute and relative risk measures that are not significantly different from those of Manager A. That Product B can achieve this level of risk efficiency with less than half the number of securities held by Product A indicates that risk management is an important component of the portfolio construction process of Product B. Although there is no guarantee that a more efficiently risk-structured portfolio will outperform, Product B outperformed Product A by more than 3.1% annually over the period.

In a well-constructed portfolio, we would be looking for risk exposures that are aligned with investor expectations and constraints and low idiosyncratic risk (unexplained) relative to total risk. If two products have comparable factor exposures, the product with a lower absolute volatility and lower active risk will likely be preferred (assuming similar costs). If two products have similar active and absolute risks, the portfolios have similar costs, and the alpha skills of the managers are similar, the product having a higher Active Share is preferable, because it leverages the alpha skills of the manager and will have higher expected returns.

Finally, the "risk efficiency" of any given portfolio approach should be judged in the context of the investor's total portfolio. The active risk of a concentrated stock picker should be higher than that of a diversified factor investor, and the concentrated stock picker may have a lower information ratio. Yet both managers could be building a well-structured portfolio relative to their mandate. It is important to consider the diversification effect of a manager's portfolio on the total portfolio of the investor to arrive at an appropriate solution.

EXAMPLE 8   The Well-Structured Portfolio

David Larrabee is CIO of a pension fund with $5 billion in assets. The fund has 60% of its assets invested in equities with more than 10 managers. Larrabee is considering creating a core equity position that would represent 65% of all equity assets. The remaining 35% would then be allocated to approximately five active satellite (non-core) managers. The core position would be invested in a customized passive portfolio designed specifically for the pension fund using a well-documented construction and rebalancing process. The portfolio would be implemented by a known counterparty at a low cost (less than 10 bps). The main specifications for the custom portfolio were the following:

- Investable universe composed of securities within the MSCI World Index
- Low volatility achieved through an optimization process
- High payout yield (dividend and share repurchase)
- No fewer than 250 securities
- No position greater than 2%
- Average portfolio turnover less than 50% annually

Larrabee understands that a low-volatility objective usually leads to portfolios with large-cap, Value, and Quality biases.

Exhibits 23 and 24 present the results of a pro forma analysis of the custom portfolio. The portfolio was simulated over a period of 12 years. Exhibit 23 presents some key risk and structural characteristics, as well as the average active sector exposure. Exhibit 24 presents the results of factor analyses for both the MSCI World and the custom portfolio.

EXHIBIT 23.

	MSCI World	Custom Portfolio
Return annualized	7.0%	8.45%
Volatility annualized	11.3%	9.0%
Active risk	—	6.0%
Number of securities	1,700	325
Turnover	2.4%	35%
Dividend yield	2.6%	3.6%
Average Active Sector Exposure		
Energy	—	−2.00%
Materials	—	−1.50%
Industrials	—	−1.50%
Consumer discretionary	—	3.00%
Consumer staples	—	4.20%
Health care	—	2.40%
Financials	—	−1.00%
Information technology	—	−10.00%
Telecommunication services	—	3.20%
Utilities	—	3.20%

EXHIBIT 24.

	Factor Exposure		Factor Relative Risk Attribution	
	MSCI World	Custom Portfolio	MSCI World	Custom Portfolio
Alpha (annualized)	−1.0%	−3.1%	—	—
Market	1.00	0.84	103%	105%
Size	−0.13	−0.26	−1%	−1%
Value	0.06	0.30	2%	10%
Momentum	0.02	0.02	−1%	−3%
BAB	0.01	0.32	0%	2%
Quality	0.10	0.54	−4%	−22%
Unexplained	—	—	1%	9%

Larrabee has hired you to advise him on the proposed core product. Considering the information provided,

1. Does the pro forma custom portfolio meet the specifications of a well-structured portfolio, and are there any characteristics of this product that concern you?
2. If the custom portfolio were implemented, what recommendations would you make to Larrabee in terms of the style of the satellite managers or in general?

Solution to 1: The proposed solution is aligned with many of the characteristics of a well-constructed portfolio. It is based on a consistent investment process, and it appears to meet the requirements of the investor: It has significantly lower volatility than the MSCI World and a significantly higher dividend yield (although we do not have the information on the payout yield), the portfolio has a low security concentration, and the estimated turnover is lower than the required limit. It can also be implemented at a low cost. The factor analysis also confirms what we could expect from a high-payout/low-volatility portfolio. The Market beta is significantly below 1, the negative Size coefficient indicates a larger-capitalization bias, and finally, the portfolio has a Value and Quality bias. The risk attribution analysis indicates that the exposure to Quality companies is largely responsible for reducing the total risk of the portfolio.

However, there are some aspects of the portfolio that create some concerns. Although the custom portfolio meets all of Larrabee's specified objectives, the portfolio construction process leads to a high tracking error (active risk). Given the size of this allocation relative to the total equity portfolio, this poses a problem. Some of this tracking error may be attributed to a significant under-allocation to the information technology sector. Finally, although the portfolio would have generated an excess return on average over the past 12 years, the alpha is negative. Understanding the source of this negative alpha is essential. In this instance, the excess return was achieved largely through a very high and intentional exposure to rewarded factors, such as Value, BAB, and Quality, which may not have been rewarded over the simulated period.

Solution to 2: The first recommendation would be to investigate further the source of the significant negative alpha. Because the excess performance is so strongly explained by exposure to specific factors, we should be concerned about how the portfolio would perform if factor returns were to decline. Is there a systemic reason that can explain this observation? Secondly, if tracking error is a concern, it is important to identify satellite managers whose active returns have a low correlation with the core mandate, perhaps even a lower active risk. Finally, considering the importance of the information technology sector, it could be prudent to hire a manager that has a strong technology orientation. The objective is not necessarily to maintain a technology exposure equal to that of the MSCI World Index but perhaps to lower the consistent underexposure to a more reasonable level. At the very least, these structural biases should be continuously monitored.

8. LONG/SHORT, LONG EXTENSION, AND MARKET-NEUTRAL PORTFOLIO CONSTRUCTION

Long/short, long extension, and market-neutral portfolio approaches are all variations on a theme: Each is predicated on the belief that research insights can be exploited not only in the pursuit of stocks that are expected to perform well but also to profit from the negative insights gathered during the research process. "Long/short" is the most encompassing term and can include long extension and market-neutral products. Most commonly, the term "long/short" refers to strategies that are relatively unconstrained in the extent to which they can lever both positive and negative insights.

Long extension strategies are constrained long/short strategies. The capital committed by the client is invested similarly to a manager's long-only strategy but levered to some extent to exploit the manager's insights on projected losers as well as winners. A typical long-extension strategy is constrained to have a net exposure of 100%; for example, 130% of the capital is invested long and 30% of the capital is invested short, for a net exposure of 100%—the same as it would be in a long-only portfolio. There may or may not be a relationship between the long and the short portfolios.

Market-neutral strategies are long/short portfolios constructed in a manner to ensure that the portfolio's exposures to a wide variety of risk factors is zero. In addition, these portfolios may be neutralized against a wide variety of other risk factors.

8.1. The Merits of Long-Only Investing

An investor's choice of whether to pursue a long-only strategy or some variation of a long/ short strategy is likely to be influenced by several considerations:

• Long-term risk premiums
• Capacity and scale (the ability to invest assets)
• Limited legal liability and risk appetite
• Regulatory constraints
• Transactional complexity
• Management costs
• Personal ideology

8.1.1. Long-term risk premiums

A major motivation for investors to be long only is the generally accepted belief that there is a positive long-run premium to be earned from bearing market risk. Investors may also believe that risk premiums can be earned from other sources of risk, such as Size, Value, or Momentum. To capture these risk premiums, investors must over time own (go net "long") the underlying securities that are exposed to these risks. Although risk premiums have been shown to earn a return in the long run, realized risk premium returns can be negative in the short run; the market can and does experience returns less than the risk-free rate, and recall the earlier discussion regarding the cyclicality of the Size, Value, and Momentum factors. For investors with shorter-term investment horizons, the potential benefits of a positive expected risk premium over the long run may not offset the potential risk of market declines or other reversals. These investors may pursue an approach other than strictly long-only investing and may prefer to short-sell some securities.

8.1.2. Capacity and scalability

Long-only investing, particularly strategies that focus on large-cap stocks, generally offers greater investment capacity than other approaches. For example, the MSCI ACWI has a total market cap of nearly $37 trillion, and the 10 largest companies are worth $3.4 trillion.[42] For large institutional investors, such as pension plans, there are no effective capacity constraints in terms of the total market cap available for long-only large-cap investing. Long-only strategies may face capacity constraints, however, if they focus on smaller and illiquid stocks or employ a strategy reliant on a high level of portfolio turnover. Unlike long-only strategies, the capacity of short-selling strategies is limited by the availability of securities to borrow.

---

[42]Market cap is not necessarily the same as shares available for general investors, because some shares may be closely held and not traded. Most index providers now calculate "float," which represents shares the public can trade.

8.1.3. Limited legal liability

Common stocks are limited liability financial instruments. The lowest a stock price can fall to is zero, so the maximum amount that a long-only investor in a common stock can lose is the amount of money that she invested in the stock. Thus, long-only investing puts a firm floor on how much an investor can lose. In contrast, a short-seller's potential losses are unlimited in principle. The short-seller loses money as the stock price rises, and there is no ceiling limiting the price increase. This type of "naked" short-selling is quite risky. To offset this risk, investors often combine a short-selling strategy with a long-only strategy. Indeed, long/short strategies are often less risky than long-only or short-only strategies.

8.1.4. Regulatory

Some countries ban short-selling activities. Others have temporarily restricted or banned short-selling. For example, on 18 September 2008, the UK Financial Services Authority (FSA) temporarily prohibited the short-selling of financial companies to protect the integrity of the financial system. The US Securities and Exchange Commission (SEC) followed suit the next day. Additionally, many countries that allow short-selling prohibit or restrict naked short-selling, a practice consisting of short-selling a tradable asset without first borrowing the security or ensuring that it can be borrowed.

8.1.5. Transactional complexity

The mechanics of long-only investing are relatively simple and easy to understand. The investment manager instructs a broker (or uses an electronic platform) to buy stock XYZ. The broker executes the trade on the client's behalf and arranges for the security to be delivered to the client's account. Typically, a custodial bank sits between the investment adviser and the client. In this case, the custodian would deliver the cash for the stock and take possession of the shares of XYZ stock. If the shares are held in a custodial bank, the adviser can liquidate the position at any time (a caveat is that to exercise this flexibility completely, the custodian must be instructed not to lend out the shares). In long-only investing, buying and selling stocks are straightforward, intuitive transactions.

A short-selling transaction is more complex. The investor first needs to find shares of stock to borrow. Although many stocks are easy to borrow, others may be hard to locate, and the cost to borrow these shares can be much higher. Investors must also provide collateral to ensure that they can repay the borrowed stock if the price moves up. Borrowed stock may also be recalled at an inopportune time for the short-seller.

In many regions, regulated investment entities must use a custodian for all the transactions. When a custodian is involved, complicated three-party agreements (between the fund, prime broker, and custodian) are required. The agreements govern the buying and selling of securities as well as the management of collateral. An investor who does not use a custodian is exposed to counterparty risk—the collateral is often held in a general operating account of a prime broker. If the prime broker goes bankrupt, the collateral can vanish (which happened to many investors in the Lehman Brothers bankruptcy). Operational risk is significantly greater with long/short investing.

8.1.6. Management costs

Long-only investing is less expensive, both in terms of management fees and from an operational perspective. Managers of long/short products often charge fees that are a multiple of what long-only managers typically charge. Three categories of long/short products are active extension, market neutral, and directional.[43] As of 2016, management fees on active

---

[43]See Pavilion (2011).

extension strategies usually range from 0.50% to 1.5%, whereas market-neutral and directional strategies typically charge hedge fund fixed fees of 1%–2% and performance fees of 20%. It follows, then, that the investor in a long/short product must have a high degree of confidence in the manager's ability to extract premiums or generate alpha relative to lower-fee, long-only managers.

8.1.7. Personal ideology

Some investors may express a preference for long-only investment for ideological reasons. They may feel that directly gaining from the losses of others is morally wrong, as might be the case in short-selling. Some investors may believe that short-selling requires significantly greater expertise than long-only investing and that such expertise is not reliably available or consistent. And some might argue that short-selling requires significant leverage to achieve the targeted long-term expected return, and they may be unwilling to assume this risk. In short, some investors may "just say no" to anything other than long-only investing.

8.2. Long/Short Portfolio Construction

Investors may be interested in long/short strategies for a variety of reasons. For example, the conviction of negative views can be more strongly expressed when short-selling is permitted than in a long-only approach. In addition, short-selling can help reduce exposures to sectors, regions, or general market movements and allow managers to focus on their unique skill set. Finally, the full extraction of the benefits of risk factors requires a long/short approach (i.e., short large cap and long small cap, short growth and long value, short poor price momentum and long high price momentum, etc.). Long-only investors can profit from only part of the opportunity set.

There are many different styles of long/short strategies, each driven by its own investment thesis. Exhibit 25 presents a range of possible options to structure a long/short portfolio. Implementation of long/short strategies varies with their intended purpose. In a long-only portfolio construction process, the weights assigned to every asset must be greater than or equal to 0 and the weights must sum to 1. In the long/short approach, position weights can be negative and the weights are not necessarily constrained to sum to 1. Some long/short portfolios may even have aggregate exposure of less than 1. The absolute value of the longs minus the absolute value of the shorts is called the portfolio's *net exposure*. The sum of the longs plus the absolute value of the shorts is called the portfolio's *gross exposure*.

A comprehensive use of long/short strategies can also be found in the design of equal-risk-premium products. Such products seek to extract return premiums from rewarded factors, often across asset classes. To do so, the manager must create long/short sub-portfolios extracting these premiums (such as Size, Value, Momentum, and Low Beta) and combine these sub-portfolios using weightings that ensure each component will contribute the same amount of risk to the overall portfolio. The combination may be levered across all sub-portfolios to achieve a specific volatility level. In other words, the manager is using long and short positions as well as leverage (or deleveraging) to achieve the most efficient combination of rewarded factors.

EXHIBIT 25   Illustrative Long/Short Portfolio Structures (as a percentage of capital)

	Long Positions	Short Positions	Cash	Gross Exposure	Net Exposure
Long only	100	0	0	100	100
130/30 long extension	130	30	0	160	100
Market neutral – low risk	50	50	100	100	0
Market neutral – higher risk	100	100	100	200	0
Directional – low risk	80	40	60	120	40
Net short	40	100	160	140	–60

Long/short managers typically define their exposure constraints as part of the portfolio construction process. For example, many equity hedge funds have a strategy of targeting a gross exposure (long plus short) of 150%–200% while targeting a net exposure (long minus short) of 0%–60%. A net exposure greater than zero implies some positive exposure to the Market factor. Regardless of the investment approach, all long/short strategies must establish parameters regarding the desired level of gross and net exposure, and these parameters will provide the investor with meaningful information about the manager's strategy and its expected risk profile.

8.3. Long Extension Portfolio Construction

Long extension strategies are a hybrid of long-only and long/short strategies. They are often called "enhanced active equity" strategies. A particular enhanced active equity strategy called "130/30" was popular until the market decline during the global financial crisis.[44] This strategy is making inroads again as investors better understand the potential pitfalls of shorting and are seeking more return in a low interest rate environment. A 130/30 strategy builds a portfolio of long positions worth 130% of the wealth invested in the strategy—that is, 1.3 times the amount of capital. At the same time, the portfolio holds short positions worth 30% of capital. The long and short positions combined equal 100% of capital. In essence, the short positions are funding the excess long positions, and the resulting gross leverage (160% = 130% + 30%) potentially allows for greater alpha and a more efficient exposure to rewarded factors. Unlike leverage incurred via cash borrowing in a long-only portfolio, which can be used only to exploit *long* insights, the long/short approach allows the portfolio to benefit not only from insights on companies that are forecasted to perform well (the long positions) but also from insights on companies forecasted to perform poorly (the short positions). In theory, this strategy offers the opportunity to magnify total returns. Of course, the long/short approach could also lead to greater losses if the manager is simultaneously wrong on both his long and short picks.

Another benefit of the 130/30 strategy is that long-only managers are limited in their ability to underallocate to securities that have a small initial allocation in the benchmark. For

---

[44] 130/30 strategies can accentuate losses. For example, Value strategies performed poorly during the financial crisis of 2007–2008, whereas Momentum strategies performed poorly after March 2009, as the equity markets rebounded. Many 130/30 products were built on these rewarded factors and performed poorly.

example, if Security X has a 0.25% allocation within the benchmark, a long-only manager can express a negative view on the stock only to the extent of its 0.25% benchmark weight by omitting the security from the portfolio. A 130/30 strategy affords the possibility of sizing the underweight in line with the manager's expectations for the stock. This ability allows the strength of the positive and negative views to be expressed more symmetrically.

8.4. Market-Neutral Portfolio Construction

Market-neutral portfolio construction is a specialized form of long/short portfolio construction. At a very simple, naive level, one might think that in this strategy, the dollars invested in long securities are identical to the dollars associated with short-selling—that is, a portfolio with zero net investment, often called "dollar neutral." But dollar neutral is not the same thing as market neutral, because the economic drivers of returns for the long side may not be the same as the economic drivers for the short side.

True market-neutral strategies hedge out most market risk. They are often employed when the investor wants to remove the effects of general market movements from returns to explicitly focus on the manager's skill in forecasting returns of stocks, sectors, factors, or geographic regions. In essence, the investor wants to remove the "noise" that market movements can create to better focus on the creation of positive abnormal returns. In isolation, this strategy could be considered risky. For example, if stock prices appreciate rapidly (and historically, stock prices do rise), then the investor would miss out on this appreciation. However, some investors might add this type of strategy to their overall portfolio to increase diversification and at least partially offset losses in other parts of the portfolio when stock prices decline.

Market-neutral portfolio construction attempts to exactly match and offset the systematic risks of the long positions with those of the short positions. For example, if one uses beta as the measure of systematic risk, then a market-neutral portfolio, using longs and shorts, would have a Market beta of zero. A simple example of zero-beta investment would be a fund that is long $100 of assets with a Market beta of 1 and short $80 of assets with a Market beta of 1.25. This concept can be extended to include other systematic factors that influence returns, such as Size, Value, and Momentum. In other words, the market-neutral concept can be implemented for a variety of risk factors. The main constraint is that in aggregate, the targeted beta(s) of the portfolio be zero.

A market-neutral strategy is still expected to generate a positive information ratio. Although market neutral may seek to eliminate market risk and perhaps some other risks on an *ex ante* basis, the manager cannot eliminate all risks. If she could—and did—the expected return would likely be equal to the risk-free rate minus the manager's fees. The objective is to neutralize the risks for which the manager believes she has no comparative forecasting advantage, thus allowing the manager to concentrate on her very specific skills.

Given that market-neutral strategies seek to remove major sources of systematic risk from a portfolio, these strategies are usually less volatile than long-only strategies. They are often considered absolute return strategies because their benchmarks might be fixed-income instruments. Even if a market-neutral strategy is not fully successful in its implementation, the correlation of market-neutral strategies with other types of strategies is typically quite low. Thus, some market-neutral strategies may serve more of a diversification role in a portfolio, rather than a high-return-seeking role.

A specific form of market-neutral strategy is pairs trading, where an investor will go long one security in an industry and short another security in the same industry, trying to exploit what the investor perceives as "mispricing." A more quantitatively oriented form of pairs trading called *statistical arbitrage* ("stat arb") uses statistical techniques to identify two securities that are historically highly correlated with each other. When the price correlation of these two securities deviates from its long-term average (and if the manager believes that the deviation is temporary), the manager will go long the underperforming stock and simultaneously short the outperforming stock. If the prices do converge to the long-term average as forecasted, the manager will close the trade and realize a profit.

In other variations of market-neutral investing, one might find portfolios constructed with hundreds of securities identified using systematic multi-factor models that evaluate all securities in the investable universe. The manager will buy the most favorably ranked securities and short the least favorably ranked ones. The manager may impose constraints on exposures of the longs and the shorts to keep gross and net exposures at the desired levels.

Market-neutral strategies have two inherent limitations:

1. Practically speaking, it is no easy task to maintain a beta of zero. Not all risks can be efficiently hedged, and correlations between exposures are continually shifting.
2. Market-neutral strategies have a limited upside in a bull market unless they are "equitized." Some investors, therefore, choose to index their equity exposure and overlay long/short strategies. In this case, the investor is not abandoning equity-like returns and is using the market-neutral portfolio as an overlay.

8.5. Benefits and Drawbacks of Long/Short Strategies

Long/short strategies offer the following benefits:

- Ability to more fully express short ideas than under a long-only strategy
- Efficient use of leverage and of the benefits of diversification
- Greater ability to calibrate/control exposure to factors (such as Market and other rewarded factors), sectors, geography, or any undesired exposure (such as, perhaps, sensitivity to the price of oil)

We've explored the first two benefits of long/short portfolio construction listed above. Let's look more closely at the last one.

A fully invested long-only strategy will be exposed to market risk. To reduce the level of market risk, the manager must either concentrate holdings in low-beta stocks or hold a portion of the assets in cash, an asset that produces minimal return. Conversely, to increase the level of market risk, the long-only manager must own high-beta stocks or use financial leverage; the cost of leverage will reduce future returns. Practically speaking, the portfolio beta of a long-only manager is likely constrained within a range of, say, 0.8–1.2. In contrast, a long/short manager has much more flexibility in adjusting his level of market exposure to reflect his view on the current opportunities.

In long-only portfolios, total portfolio risk is dominated by the Market factor, and the Market factor is a long-only factor. However, all other factor returns can be thought of as long/short portfolios: *Size* is long small cap and short large cap, *Value* is long value and short growth, *Momentum* is long positive momentum and short less positive or negative momentum, and so on. Just like with beta, the ability to tilt a portfolio in favor of these other factors or diversify efficiently across factors is structurally restricted in a long-only portfolio. Because the average of cross correlations among rewarded factors is close to zero or even negative, efficiently allocating across factors could bring significant diversification benefits. But the ability to reduce overall risk and to distribute sources of risk more evenly cannot be optimally achieved without short-selling.

Strategies that short securities contain the following inherent risks, which must be understood:

1. Unlike a long position, a short position will move against the manager if the price of the security increases.
2. Long/short strategies sometimes require significant leverage. Leverage must be used wisely.
3. The cost of borrowing a security can become prohibitive, particularly if the security is hard to borrow.
4. Collateral requirements will increase if a short position moves against the manager. In extreme cases, the manager may be forced to liquidate some favorably ranked long positions (and short positions that might eventually reverse) if too much leverage has been used. The manager may also fall victim to a short squeeze. A short squeeze is a situation in which the price of the stock that has been shorted has risen so much and so quickly that many short investors may be unable to maintain their positions in the short run in light of the increased collateral requirements. The "squeeze" is worsened as short-sellers liquidate their short position, buying back the security and possibly pushing the price even higher.

As previously indicated, to short-sell securities, investors typically rely on a prime broker who can help them locate the securities they wish to borrow. But the prime broker will require collateral from the short-sellers to assure the lenders of these securities that their contracts will be honored. The higher the relative amount of short-selling in a portfolio, the greater the amount of collateral required. A portfolio with 20% of capital invested short may be required to put up collateral equal to 40% of the short positions, whereas a portfolio with 100% of capital invested short could be required to put up collateral equal to 200% of the short positions. In addition, different types of assets are weighed differently in the calculation of collateral value. For example, a US Treasury bill may be viewed as very safe collateral and accorded 100% of its value toward the required collateral. In contrast, a high-yield bond or some other asset with restricted liquidity would have only a portion of its market value counted toward the collateral requirement.

These collateral requirements are designed to protect the lender in the event of adverse price movements. When stock prices are rising rapidly, the lender may recall all the borrowed shares, fearing that the borrower's collateral will be wiped out. If this were to happen, the leveraged long/short manager would be forced to close out his short positions at an inopportune time, leaving significant profits on the table. In the end, long/short investing is a compromise between return impacts, sources of risk, and costs, as illustrated in the table below.

Benefits	Costs
• Short positions can reduce market risk. • Shorting potentially expands benefits from other risk premiums and alpha. • The combination of long and short positions allows for a greater diversification potential.	• Short positions might reduce the market return premium. • Shorting may amplify the active risk (but please note that it does not have to do so). • There are higher implementation costs and greater complexity associated with shorting and leverage relative to a long-only approach.

EXAMPLE 9   Creating a 130/30 Strategy

Alpha Prime has been managing long-only equity portfolios for more than 15 years. The firm has a systematic investment process built around assessing security valuation and price momentum. Each company is attributed a standardized score (F_k) that is based on a combination of quantitative and fundamental metrics. Positions are selected from among those securities with a positive standardized score and are weighted based on the strength of that score. The security weightings within sectors can be significantly different from those of the benchmark, but the portfolio's sector weightings adhere closely to the benchmark weights. Investment decisions are made by the portfolio management team and are re-evaluated monthly. A constrained optimization process is used to guide investment decision-making. Listed below are the objective function and the primary constraints used by the firm.

- *Objective function:* Maximize the portfolio factor score
- *Total exposure constraint:* Sum of portfolio weights must $= 1$
- *Individual security constraint:* Minimum weight of 0% and maximum weight of 3%
- *Sector constraint:* Benchmark weight $\pm 5\%$
- *Constraint on active risk (TE):* Active risk less than 5%

The managers at Alpha Prime have realized that their investment process can also generate a negative signal, indicating that a security is likely to underperform. However, the signal is not quite as reliable or stable when it is used for this purpose. There is much more noise around the performance of the expected losers than there is around the performance of the winners. Still, the signal has value.

1. You are asked to draft guidelines for the creation of a 130/30 strategy. What changes to the objective function and to each of the constraints would you recommend?
2. Discuss the potential challenges of incorporating short positions into the portfolio strategy.

Solution to 1:

- *Objective function:* The objective function would remain the same. Securities with a positive standardized score would be eligible for positive weights, and securities with a negative standardized factor score would receive negative weights (the fund would short these securities).

- *Total exposure constraint:* The portfolio now needs a constraint for gross exposure and one for net exposure. The net exposure constraint in a 130/30 product is constrained to 100%. (The notional value of the longs minus the absolute value of the shorts must be equal to 1.) The portfolio's gross exposure constraint is implicit in the nature of the 130/30 product. (The notional value of the longs plus the absolute value of the shorts cannot exceed 160%.)

- *Individual security constraint:* To take advantage of the negative signals from the model, the portfolio must allow shorting. The minimum weight constraint must be relaxed. Given the issues associated with short-selling, the firm's relative inexperience in this area, and the lower reliability of the short signal, the maximum short position size should be smaller than the maximum long position size. One might recommend that the initial short constraint be set at 1%. Position limits on the long side could stay the same, but that would likely lead to more long positions, given the increase in long exposure to 130%. The manager must assess whether to expand the number of securities held in the portfolio or to raise the maximum position size limit.

- *Sector constraint:* There is no need to change the aggregate sector constraint. The manager now has the ability to offset any overweight on the long side with a short position that would bring the portfolio's exposure to that sector back within the current constraint.

- *Tracking error target:* Sector deviations have a greater bearing on active risk than do security-level differences. Alpha Prime's sector bets are very limited; thus, no change in the tracking error constraint is necessary. The ability to short gives them greater opportunity to exploit investment ideas without changing the firm's approach to sector weightings.

Solution to 2: Shorting adds complexity to both the operational and the risk aspects of portfolio management. Operationally, the firm must establish relationships with one or more prime brokers and ensure that adequate collateral for the short positions remains available. Some securities can be difficult to borrow, and the cost of borrowing some stocks can be prohibitive. This may inhibit Alpha Prime's ability to implement its short ideas and will raise the operational costs of running the portfolio. In addition, shorting introduces a new type of risk: A short transaction has no loss limit. If the stock moves against the manager in the short run, the manager may have to close the position before he is proven right.

EXAMPLE 10   Long Only vs. Long/Short

Marc Salter has been running a long-only unlevered factor-based strategy in the US market for more than five years. He has delivered a product that has all the expected exposure to rewarded risk factors promised to investors. Salter just met with a pension fund investor looking at a multi-factor based approach. However, the pension fund manager indicates they are also considering investing with a competitor that runs a leveraged long/short factor-based strategy. It appears the competitor's product has a significantly higher information ratio. The product of the competitor neutralizes market risk and concentrates on exposure to other rewarded factors.

1. Why would the competitor's long/short product have a higher information ratio?
2. What are its drawbacks?

Solution to 1: Factor returns are usually built from a long portfolio having the desired factor characteristic against a short portfolio that does not. A long-only factor investor is limited in his ability to short (relative to the benchmark) positions that do not have the desired characteristics. Adding the ability to leverage negative as well as positive research insights should improve the transfer coefficient and increase the potential to generate better excess returns.

   In addition, in a long-only strategy, the Market factor dominates all other risks. Adding the ability to short could facilitate a more balanced distribution of risk. Given the similar volatilities and low cross correlations among factors, the more balanced distribution of risk can be expected to reduce the tracking error of the strategy, thereby improving the information ratio.

Solution to 2: Multi-factor products often contain several hundred securities, some of which may be difficult to borrow. The complexity of shorting across this large number of names combined with higher management fees and implementation costs may necessitate more implementation constraints on the short side.

   Removing the risk associated with the Market factor implies that the long/short product would most likely be used as an overlay on long-only mandates. The mandate may also be leveraged (more than 1× long and 1× short) to maximize the potential return per dollar of capital. For example, equal-risk-premium products (that remove the effect of the Market factor) often need three units of leverage long and short to achieve a 10% absolute risk target. Some investors may be uncomfortable with such leverage.

---

9. SUMMARY

Active equity portfolio construction strives to make sure that superior insights about forecasted returns get efficiently reflected in realized portfolio performance. Active equity portfolio construction is about thoroughly understanding the return objectives of a portfolio, as well as its acceptable risk levels, and then finding the right mix of securities that balances predicted returns against risk and other impediments that can interfere with realizing these returns. These principles apply to long-only, long/short, long-extension, and market-neutral approaches. Below, we highlight the discussions of this chapter.

- The four main building blocks of portfolio construction are the following:
    - Overweight, underweight, or neutralize rewarded factors: The four most recognized factors known to offer a persistent return premium are Market, Size, Value, and Momentum.
    - Alpha skills: Timing factors, securities, and markets. Finding new factors and enhancing existing factors.
    - Sizing positions to account for risk and active weights.
    - Breadth of expertise: A manager's ability to consistently outperform his benchmark increases when that performance can be attributed to a larger sample of independent decisions. Independent decisions are uncorrelated decisions.

- Managers can rely on a combination of approaches to implement their core beliefs:
    - Systematic vs. discretionary
        - Systematic strategies incorporate research-based rules across a broad universe of securities.
        - Discretionary strategies integrate the judgment of the manager on a smaller subset of securities.

    - Bottom up vs. top down
        - A bottom-up manager evaluates the risk and return characteristics of individual securities. The aggregate of these risk and return expectations implies expectations for the overall economic and market environment.
        - A top-down manager starts with an understanding of the overall market environment and then projects how the expected environment will affect countries, asset classes, sectors, and securities.

    - Benchmark aware vs. benchmark agnostic

- Portfolio construction can be framed as an optimization problem using an objective function and a set of constraints. The objective function of a systematic manager will be specified explicitly, whereas that of a discretionary manager may be set implicitly.
- Risk budgeting is a process by which the total risk appetite of the portfolio is allocated among the various components of portfolio choice.
- Active risk (tracking error) is a function of the portfolio's exposure to systematic risks and the level of idiosyncratic, security-specific risk. It is a relevant risk measure for benchmark-relative portfolios.
- Absolute risk is the total volatility of portfolio returns independent of a benchmark. It is the most appropriate risk measure for portfolios with an absolute return objective.
- Active Share measures the extent to which the number and sizing of positions in a manager's portfolio differ from the benchmark.
- Benchmark-agnostic managers usually have a greater level of Active Share and most likely have a greater level of active risk.
- An effective risk management process requires that the portfolio manager
    - determine which type of risk measure is most appropriate,
    - understand how each aspect of the strategy contributes to its overall risk,
    - determine what level of risk budget is appropriate, and
    - effectively allocate risk among individual positions/factors.

- Risk constraints may be either formal or heuristic. Heuristic constraints may impose limits on
  - concentration by security, sector, industry, or geography;
  - net exposures to risk factors, such as Beta, Size, Value, and Momentum;
  - net exposures to currencies;
  - the degree of leverage;
  - the degree of illiquidity;
  - exposures to reputational/environmental risks, such as carbon emissions; and
  - other attributes related to an investor's core concerns.

- Formal risk constraints are statistical in nature. Formal risk measures include the following:
  - Volatility—the standard deviation of portfolio returns
  - Active risk—also called *tracking error* or *tracking risk*
  - Skewness—a measure of the degree to which return expectations are non-normally distributed
  - Drawdown—a measure of portfolio loss from its high point until it begins to recover
  - Value at risk (VaR)—the minimum loss that would be expected a certain percentage of the time over a certain period of time given the modeled market conditions, typically expressed as the minimum loss that can be expected to occur 5% of the time
  - CVaR (expected tail loss or expected shortfall)—the average loss that would be incurred if the VaR cutoff is exceeded
  - IVaR—the change in portfolio VaR when adding a new position to a portfolio
  - MVaR—the effect on portfolio risk of a change in the position size. In a diversified portfolio, it may be used to determine the contribution of each asset to the overall VaR.

- Portfolio management costs fall into two categories: explicit costs and implicit costs. Implicit costs include delay and slippage.
- The costs of managing assets may affect the investment strategy and the portfolio construction process.
  - Slippage costs are significantly greater for smaller-cap securities and during periods of high volatility.
  - A strategy that demands immediate execution is likely to incur higher market impact costs.
  - A patient manager can mitigate market impact costs by slowly building up positions as liquidity becomes available, but he exposes himself to greater volatility/trend price risk.

- A well-constructed portfolio exhibits
  - a clear investment philosophy and a consistent investment process,
  - risk and structural characteristics as promised to investors,
  - a risk-efficient delivery methodology, and
  - reasonably low operating costs.

- Long/short investing is a compromise between
  - reducing risk and not capturing fully the market risk premium,
  - expanding the return potential from alpha and other risk premiums at the potential expense of increasing active risk, and
  - achieving greater diversification and higher costs and complexity.

REFERENCES

Amihud, Yakov. 2002. "Illiquidity and Stock Returns: Cross-Section and Time-Series Effects." *Journal of Financial Markets*, vol. 5, no. 1: 31–56.

Asness, Cliff. 2017. "Factor Timing Is Hard." *Cliff's Perspective*, AQR.

Bender, Jennifer, P. Brett Hammond, and William Mok. 2014. "Can Alpha Be Captured by Risk Premia?" *Journal of Portfolio Management*, vol. 40, no. 2 (Winter): 18–29.

Black, Fischer. 1972. "Capital Market Equilibrium with Restricted Borrowing." *Journal of Business*, vol. 45, no. 3: 444–455.

Carhart, Mark M. 1997. "On Persistence in Mutual Fund Performance." *Journal of Finance*, vol. 52: 57–82.

Ceria, Sebastian. 2015. "Active Is as Active Does: Active Share vs. Tracking Error." FactSet 2015 Symposium (March).

Clarke, Roger, Harindra de Silva, and Steven Thorley. 2002. "Portfolio Constraints and the Fundamental Law of Active Management." *Financial Analysts Journal*, vol. 58, no. 5 (September/October): 48–66.

Fama, Eugene F., and Kenneth French. 1992. "The Cross-Section of Expected Stock Returns." *Journal of Finance*, vol. 47, no. 2 (June): 427–465.

Frazzini, Andrea, and Lasse Heje Pedersen. 2014. "Betting against Beta." *Journal of Financial Economics*, vol. 111, no. 1: 1–25.

Frazzini, Andrea, Ronen Israel, and Tobias Moskowitz. 2012. "Trading Costs of Asset Pricing Anomalies." Fama–Miller Center for Research in Finance, University of Chicago Booth School of Business Paper 14–05.

Grinold, R.C. 1989. "The Fundamental Law of Active Management." *Journal of Portfolio Management*, vol. 15: 30–37.

Hasbrouck, Joel. 2009. "Trading Costs and Returns for US Equities: Estimating Effective Costs from Daily Date." *Journal of Finance*, vol. 64, no. 3: 1445–1477.

Ilmanen, Antti. 2011. *Expected Returns: An Investor's Guide to Harvesting Market Rewards*. New York: John Wiley & Sons.

Kahn, Ronald N., and Michael Lemmon. 2016. "The Asset Manager's Dilemma: How Smart Beta Is Disrupting the Investment Management Industry." *Financial Analysts Journal*, vol. 72, no. 1 (January/February): 15–20.

Langlois, Hugues, and Jacques Lussier. 2017. *Rational Investing: The Subtleties of Asset Management*. New York: Columbia Business School Publishing.

MacQueen, Jason. 2007. "Portfolio Risk Decomposition (and Risk Budgeting)." Series of talks presented by R-Squared Risk Management Limited.

Pavilion. 2011. "Long/Short as Long-Only Equity Replacement—Evaluation of Long/Short Strategies: Active Extension, Equity Market Neutral and Directional" (November–December).

Petajisto, Antti. 2013. "Active Share and Mutual Fund Performance." *Financial Analysts Journal*, vol. 69, no. 4 (July/August): 73–93.

Sapra, Steve, and Manny Hunjan. 2013. "Active Share, Tracking Error and Manager Style." PIMCO Quantitative Research and Analytics (October).

Simons, Katerina. 2000. "The Use of Value at Risk by Institutional Investors." *New England Economic Review*, November/December: 21–30.

Taleb, Nassim Nicolas. 1997. *Dynamic Hedging: Managing Vanilla and Exotic Options*. New York: John Wiley & Sons.

Yeung, Danny, Paolo Pellizzari, Ron Bird, and Sazali Abidin. 2012. "Diversification versus Concentration . . . and the Winner Is?" Working Paper 18, University of Technology, Sydney (September).

PRACTICE PROBLEMS

The following information relates to questions 1–8

Monongahela Ap is an equity fund analyst. His manager asks him to evaluate three actively managed equity funds from a single sponsor, Chiyodasenko Investment Corp. Ap's assessments of the funds based on assets under management (AUM), the three main building blocks of portfolio construction, and the funds' approaches to portfolio management are presented in Exhibit 1. Selected data for Fund 1 is presented in Exhibit 2.

EXHIBIT 1   Ap's Assessments of Funds 1, 2, and 3

Fund	Fund Category	Fund Size (AUM)	Number of Securities	Description
1	Small-cap stocks	Large	Small	Fund 1 focuses on skillfully timing exposures to factors, both rewarded and unrewarded, and to other asset classes. The fund's managers use timing skills to opportunistically shift their portfolio to capture returns from factors such as country, asset class, and sector. Fund 1 prefers to make large trades.
2	Large-cap stocks	Large	Large	Fund 2 holds a diversified portfolio and is concentrated in terms of factors. It targets individual securities that reflect the manager's view that growth firms will outperform value firms. Fund 2 builds up its positions slowly, using unlit venues when possible.
3	Small-cap stocks	Small	Large	Fund 3 holds a highly diversified portfolio. The fund's managers start by evaluating the risk and return characteristics of individual securities and then build their portfolio based on their stock-specific forecasts. Fund 3 prefers to make large trades.

EXHIBIT 2   Selected Data for Fund 1

Factor	Market	Size	Value	Momentum
Coefficient	1.080	0.098	−0.401	0.034
Variance of the market factor return and covariances with the market factor return	0.00109	0.00053	0.00022	−0.00025
Portfolio's monthly standard deviation of returns				3.74%

Ap learns that Chiyodasenko has initiated a new equity fund. It is similar to Fund 1 but scales up active risk by doubling all of the active weights relative to Fund 1. The new fund aims to scale active return linearly with active risk, but implementation is problematic. Because of the cost and difficulty of borrowing some securities, the new fund cannot scale up its short positions to the same extent that it can scale up its long positions.

Ap reviews quarterly holdings reports for Fund 3. In comparing the two most recent quarterly reports, he notices differences in holdings that indicate that Fund 3 executed two trades, with each trade involving pairs of stocks. Initially, Fund 3 held active positions in two automobile stocks—one was overweight by 1 percentage point (pp), and the other was underweight by 1pp. Fund 3 traded back to benchmark weights on those two stocks. In the second trade, Fund 3 selected two different stocks that were held at benchmark weights, one energy stock and one financial stock. Fund 3 overweighted the energy stock by 1pp and underweighted the financial stock by 1pp.

In Fund 3's latest quarterly report, Ap reads that Fund 3 implemented a new formal risk control for its forecasting model that constrains the predicted return distribution so that no more than 60% of the deviations from the mean are negative.

1. Based on Exhibit 1, the main building block of portfolio construction on which Fund 1 focuses is *most likely*:
   A. alpha skills.
   B. position sizing.
   C. rewarded factor weightings.

2. Which fund in Exhibit 1 *most likely* follows a bottom-up approach?
   A. Fund 1
   B. Fund 2
   C. Fund 3

3. Which fund in Exhibit 1 *most likely* has the greatest implicit costs to implement its strategy?
   A. Fund 1
   B. Fund 2
   C. Fund 3

4. Based on Exhibit 2, the portion of total portfolio risk that is explained by the market factor in Fund 1's existing portfolio is *closest* to:
   A. 3%.
   B. 81%.
   C. 87%.

5. Relative to Fund 1, Chiyodasenko's new equity fund will *most likely* exhibit a lower:
   A. information ratio.
   B. idiosyncratic risk.
   C. collateral requirement.

6. As a result of Fund 3's two trades, the portfolio's active risk *most likely*:
   A. decreased.
   B. remained unchanged.
   C. increased.

7. What was the effect of Fund 3's two trades on its active share? Fund 3's active share:
   A. decreased.
   B. remained unchanged.
   C. increased.

8. Which risk measure does Fund 3's new risk control explicitly constrain?
   A. Volatility
   B. Skewness
   C. Drawdown

The following information relates to questions 9–15

Ayanna Chen is a portfolio manager at Aycrig Fund, where she supervises assistant portfolio manager Mordechai Garcia. Aycrig Fund invests money for high-net-worth and institutional investors. Chen asks Garcia to analyze certain information relating to Aycrig Fund's three sub-managers, Managers A, B, and C.

Manager A has $250 million in assets under management (AUM), an active risk of 5%, an information coefficient of 0.15, and a transfer coefficient of 0.40. Manager A's portfolio has a 2.5% expected active return this year.

Chen directs Garcia to determine the maximum position size that Manager A can hold in shares of Pasliant Corporation, which has a market capitalization of $3.0 billion, an index weight of 0.20%, and an average daily trading volume (ADV) of 1% of its market capitalization.

Manager A has the following position size policy constraints:

- Allocation: No investment in any security may represent more than 3% of total AUM.
- Liquidity: No position size may represent more than 10% of the dollar value of the security's ADV.
- Index weight: The maximum position weight must be less than or equal to 10 times the security's weight in the index.

Manager B holds a highly diversified portfolio that has balanced exposures to rewarded risk factors, high active share, and a relatively low active risk target.

Selected data on Manager C's portfolio, which contains three assets, is presented in Exhibit 1.

EXHIBIT 1   Selected Data on Manager C's Portfolio

	Portfolio Weight	Standard Deviation	Covariance		
			Asset 1	Asset 2	Asset 3
Asset 1	30%	25.00%	0.06250	0.01050	0.00800
Asset 2	45%	14.00%	0.01050	0.01960	0.00224
Asset 3	25%	8.00%	0.00800	0.00224	0.00640

Chen considers adding a fourth sub-manager and evaluates three managers' portfolios, Portfolios X, Y, and Z. The managers for Portfolios X, Y, and Z all have similar costs, fees, and alpha skills, and their factor exposures align with both Aycrig's and investors' expectations and constraints. The portfolio factor exposures, risk contributions, and risk characteristics are presented in Exhibits 2 and 3.

EXHIBIT 2   Portfolio Factor Exposures and Factor Risk Contribution

	Factor Exposure			Factor Risk Contribution		
	Portfolio X	**Portfolio Y**	**Portfolio Z**	**Portfolio X**	**Portfolio Y**	**Portfolio Z**
Market	1.07	0.84	1.08	103%	82%	104%
Size	–0.13	0.15	–0.12	–2%	7%	–3%
Value	0.04	0.30	0.05	–5%	18%	–6%
Momentum	0.08	0.02	0.07	7%	–3%	7%
Quality	0.10	0.35	0.11	–4%	–21%	–5%
Unexplained	—	—	—	1%	17%	3%
Total	n/a	n/a	n/a	100%	100%	100%

EXHIBIT 3   Portfolio Risk Characteristics

	Portfolio X	**Portfolio Y**	**Portfolio Z**
Annualized volatility	10.50%	13.15%	15.20%
Annualized active risk	2.90%	8.40%	4.20%
Active share	0.71	0.74	0.63

Chen and Garcia next discuss characteristics of long–short and long-only investing. Garcia makes the following statements about investing with long–short and long-only managers:

Statement 1.   A long–short portfolio allows for a gross exposure of 100%.
Statement 2.   A long-only portfolio generally allows for greater investment capacity than other approaches, particularly when using strategies that focus on large-cap stocks.

Chen and Garcia then turn their attention to portfolio management approaches. Chen prefers an approach that emphasizes security-specific factors, does not engage in factor timing, and builds a diversified portfolio.

9. The number of truly independent decisions Manager A would need to make in order to earn her expected active portfolio return this year is *closest* to:
    A. 8.
    B. 11.
    C. 69.

10. Which of the following position size policy constraints is the most restrictive in setting Manager A's maximum position size in shares of Pasliant Corporation?
    A. Liquidity
    B. Allocation
    C. Index weight

11. Manager B's portfolio is *most likely* consistent with the characteristics of a:
    A. pure indexer.
    B. sector rotator.
    C. multi-factor manager.

12. Based on Exhibit 1, the proportion of Manager C's total portfolio variance contributed by Asset 2 is *closest to*:
    A. 0.0025.
    B. 0.0056.
    C. 0.0088.

13. Based on Exhibits 2 and 3, which portfolio *best* exhibits the risk characteristics of a well-constructed portfolio?
    A. Portfolio X
    B. Portfolio Y
    C. Portfolio Z

14. Which of Garcia's statements regarding investing with long–short and long-only managers is *correct*?
    A. Only Statement 1
    B. Only Statement 2
    C. Both Statement 1 and Statement 2

15. Chen's preferred portfolio management approach would be *best* described as:
    A. top down.
    B. systematic.
    C. discretionary.

CHAPTER 8

TECHNICAL ANALYSIS

Aksel Kibar, CMT
Barry M. Sine
Robert A. Strong, PhD, CFA

LEARNING OUTCOMES

The candidate should be able to:

- explain principles and assumptions of technical analysis;
- describe potential links between technical analysis and behavioral finance;
- compare principles of technical analysis and fundamental analysis;
- describe and interpret different types of technical analysis charts;
- explain uses of trend, support, and resistance lines;
- explain common chart patterns;
- explain common technical indicators;
- describe principles of intermarket analysis;
- explain technical analysis applications to portfolio management.

1. INTRODUCTION

Technical analysis has been used by traders, analysts, and investors for centuries and has achieved broad acceptance among regulators and the academic community—particularly with regard to its behavioral finance aspects. This chapter gives a brief overview of the field, compares technical analysis with other schools of analysis, and describes some of the main tools used in technical analysis. Although technical analysis follows predefined rules and principles, the interpretation of results is generally subjective. That is, although certain aspects, such as the calculation of indicators, follow specific rules, the interpretation of findings is often based on a melding of techniques that suit the style and approach of the individual analyst. In this respect, technical analysis is similar to fundamental analysis, which has specific rules for calculating ratios, for example, but introduces increased subjectivity in the evaluation phase.

2. TECHNICAL ANALYSIS: PRINCIPLES, ASSUMPTIONS, AND LINKS TO INVESTMENT ANALYSIS

a. **explain principles and assumptions of technical analysis;**
b. **describe potential links between technical analysis and behavioral finance;**
c. **compare principles of technical analysis and fundamental analysis.**

Vignette

Scene 1

You are a portfolio analyst working at a small sovereign wealth fund (SWF) and reporting to the Deputy Chief Investment Officer (CIO). The SWF has recently implemented an investment in GLD for the purposes of improving the risk-adjusted return of the portfolio. This asset allocation decision was based on extensive analysis and agreed on by the CIO, Head of Risk, Head of Alternative Investments, and other members of the Investment Committee. The benefits of adding gold to the portfolio are due to the low correlation gold has with other asset classes in the portfolio.

The Deputy CIO is on a well-deserved sabbatical for several weeks in Antarctica and left you in charge of monitoring the portfolio. You are looking forward to the opportunity to "be in charge" but also hope that there will be no major decisions to make during this time.

Since the investment in GLD is new, you decide to take a look at gold prices and create a basic graph. You prepare a chart that shows the performance of GLD since the start of the year. The purchase price is the blue point, and the current price is the red point. **You realize that the price of GLD is now below the purchase price.**

There is a knock on the door. The Head of Risk comes into your office and says, ***"The price of gold is now below our purchase price. You're in charge of this position, right? Maybe we should sell now to avoid a bigger loss?"***

You respond to the Head of Risk by saying, ***"Let's not panic. After all, the decision to invest in gold was not a short-term decision but a long-term asset allocation decision. We should not fall into the behavioral finance trap of letting fear guide our decisions."***

The Head of Risk leaves your office. You look at the chart again, and you begin to worry. *Maybe we should sell?* You decide to ask the Technical Analyst to prepare a chart and share her thoughts.

Technical analysis is a form of security analysis that uses price and volume data, often graphically displayed, in decision-making. Technical analysis can be applied to securities in any freely traded market around the globe. A freely traded market is one in which willing buyers trade with willing sellers without external intervention or impediment. Prices are the result of the interaction of supply and demand in real time. Technical analysis allows us to see a battle between buyers and sellers, along with subtle clues as to which side may be winning. Technical analysis is used on a wide range of financial instruments, including equities, bonds, commodity futures, currency futures, and cryptocurrencies.

The underlying logic of technical analysis is simple:

- Supply and demand determine prices.
- Changes in supply and demand—both in price level and volume—cause changes in prices.
- Past price action can be used to anticipate and project potential future prices with charts and other technical tools.

Basic technical analysis of any financial instrument does not require detailed knowledge of that instrument. As long as the chart represents the action in a freely traded market, a technician does not even need to know the name or type of the security to conduct the analysis. Technical analysis can also be applied over any time frame—from short-term price movements to long-term movements of annual closing prices. Trends that are apparent in short-term charts may also appear over longer time frames. While technical analysis is ideal for short-term trading decisions or tactical asset allocation decisions, long-term chart analysis can add value regarding strategic asset allocation or long-term investment decisions. Looking at recurring technical clues on multiple time intervals (monthly, weekly, daily, 60-minute charts, etc.) can be a particularly useful technique.

2.1. Principles and Assumptions

The three main principles of technical analysis are as follows:

- The market discounts everything.
- Prices move in trends and countertrends.
- Price action creates certain patterns that tend to reoccur and may be cyclical.

The market discounts everything.

One of the biggest assumptions in technical analysis is that price already reflects all known factors impacting a financial instrument. This form of analysis assumes that at any point in time, a stock's price is a reflection of everything that affects the organization, including fundamental factors, such as the balance sheet, the income statement, the cash flow, and the management team. Technical analysis also considers broader economic factors and market psychology to be reflected in pricing.

Prices move in trends and countertrends.

The second assumption in technical analysis is that prices follow trends, which move directionally—upward, downward, sideways, or in a combination of these directions. Once a trend is recognized, the expectation is that any future movement in the price of the asset will follow that trend rather than go against it. A trend in motion is more likely to continue than to reverse. An important corollary is that a trend in motion will continue until it reverses. Indeed, a common saying among technical analysts is, "The trend is your friend."

Price action is repetitive, and certain patterns tend to reoccur.

The repetition of price movements, according to technical analysts, is due to market psychology. News is constantly bombarding assets, and how markets react depends upon the technical setup of the market at the time such news hits. News is always important, but the value of any news depends upon the initial market psychology. Because the behavior of investors repeats itself, price movements can be charted, allowing technicians to recognize patterns.

2.2. Technical Analysis and Behavioral Finance

Technical analysis can be thought of as the study of collective investor psychology or sentiment and thus has a direct connection with behavioral finance. Prices in any freely traded market are set by human beings or their automated proxies (such as computerized trading programs), and a price is set at the equilibrium between supply and demand at any given instant. The role of a good technician is to monitor and evaluate the subtle clues in this battle between supply and demand—much like a doctor looking at a patient for subtle clues to that patient's overall health. Various fundamental theorists have proposed that markets are efficient and rational, but technicians believe that humans are often irrational and emotional and that they tend to behave similarly in similar circumstances. The reason chart patterns have predictive value is that they are graphic representations of human trading activity and human behavior is frequently repeated, especially trading activity that is driven by fear (in market sell-offs) or greed (as evidenced in bubbles—that is, rallies that extend well beyond valuation levels derived from fundamental data). In bubbles, investors, driven by hope and greed, push the price of an asset to irrationally high levels, in the expectation that other buyers will be willing to pay an even higher price for the asset. The resulting chart patterns are analyzed and identified by analysts, traders, and investors for decision-making purposes.

Although fundamental data are key inputs for the determination of value, these data are analyzed by humans, who may be driven, at least partially, by motivations that are not rational. Human behavior is often erratic and driven by emotion in many aspects of one's life, so technicians conclude that it is unreasonable to believe that investing is the one exception where humans always behave rationally. Technicians believe that market trends and patterns reflect this irrational human behavior, which can be seen on price charts in the form of volatile price action, such as major sell-offs or strong buying resulting in parabolic advances. Technical analysis is the study of market trends and patterns. And because trends and patterns tend to repeat themselves, they are potentially identifiable and predictable. So, technicians rely on recognition of patterns that have occurred in the past to project future patterns of security prices.

Another tenet of technical analysis is that the market reflects the collective knowledge and sentiment of the many different participants responsible for the buying and selling activity in a particular security. In a freely traded market, only those market participants who actually buy or sell a security have an impact on its price. And the greater the volume of a participant's trades, the more impact that market participant will tend to have on price. Technical analysis relies on market participants that are taking a directional bet in the market and thereby influencing price and volume. Without trading, there will be no meaningful price fluctuations.

Trades determine volume and price. The impact of a trade occurs instantaneously and frequently anticipates or foreshadows fundamental developments. So, by studying market technical data—price and volume trends—the technician is seeking to understand investor sentiment and to detect any fundamental change that is already transpiring behind the scenes or may shortly transpire. The technician benefits from the wide range of knowledge of market participants and their collective conclusion about a security. In contrast, the fundamental analyst must wait for the release of financial statements to conduct financial statement analysis, so a time lag occurs between the market's activities and the analyst's conclusions. Technicians may therefore be ahead of fundamental analysts in their positioning.

Technical analysts believe that human behavior plays a role in the fluctuation of security prices. Investors with a favorable fundamental view may nonetheless sell a financial instrument for other reasons, including pessimistic investor sentiment, margin calls, and a need for capital. Technicians do not care why market participants are buying or selling, just that they are doing so: These actions move prices, forming trends the technician can profit from. Technical moves happen for both fundamental and behavioral reasons.

Some financial instruments have an associated income stream that contributes to the security's intrinsic value. Bonds have regular coupon payments, and equity shares may have underlying cash flows or dividend streams. A fundamental analyst can adjust these cash flows for risk and use standard time value of money techniques to determine a present value. Other assets, such as bushels of wheat, gallons of crude oil, and ounces of silver, do not have underlying financial statements or an income stream, so valuation models cannot be used to derive their fundamental intrinsic values. For these assets, technical analysis may be particularly valuable. So, whereas fundamental analysis is widely used for fixed-income and equity securities, technical analysis is widely used for commodities, currencies, and futures.

Market participants attempt to anticipate economic developments and enter into trades to profit from them. Technicians believe that security price movements occur before fundamental developments unfold—and certainly before they are reported. This belief may be supported by the fact that stock prices are 1 of the 12 components of the National Bureau of Economic Research's index of leading economic indicators.

Market microstructure.

Market microstructure deals with issues of market structure and design, price formation, price discovery, transaction and timing costs, information and disclosure, and investor behavior. It is the process by which buyers find sellers as well as the venues where they meet. The National Bureau of Economic Research (NBER) defines market microstructure as a field of study that is devoted to theoretical, empirical, and experimental research on the economics of security markets. Elements of market microstructure may include minimum tick increments and algorithmic execution interfaces. The field of market microstructure aims to establish connections between activity over the fast-moving short term and the properties that emerge over longer time frames. In this way, market microstructure is a bottom-up approach to understanding financial markets. The recording and analysis of high-quality data that describe the actions and interactions of market participants in the very short term has revealed striking regularities that challenge many theories regarding financial markets.

Market microstructure considers different order types. Every exchange will specify the types of orders that are allowed and how these orders may interact with each other. Some of the important order types are market order, limit order, stop order, good till canceled order, and day order. But hybrid algorithmic orders are also possible and are increasingly prevalent in modern electronic markets (e.g., an order to "participate at 30% of all volume up to a given price limit" or a time-dependent "buy stop close only" order). When placed in the market, orders will have priority depending on such factors as price, time, and size. Buyers with higher bids will have priority over buyers with lower bids. Similarly, sellers with lower asks will have priority over sellers with higher asks. Market orders are executed before limit orders. Orders placed earlier are executed before later orders.

Most trade models assume the presence of both liquidity traders and information traders. Liquidity traders' decisions to buy or sell securities (e.g., for portfolio rebalancing or market making) are assumed to be unrelated to the arrival of new information. Conversely, information traders are cognizant of new information before other market participants during any given trading period. In other words, they have superior knowledge of a security's true equilibrium price. Information traders will buy/sell securities when they can exploit their advantage profitably.

Liquidity traders can be high-frequency traders or market makers on major trading desks. They buy and sell in a tight bid–ask spread with the aim of profiting from small price fluctuations.

Information traders buy and sell because they believe they have sufficient information to predict the next move in a market and thus to beat the market.

2.3. Technical Analysis and Fundamental Analysis

Both technical analysis and fundamental analysis are useful and valid, but they approach the market in different ways. Technicians focus solely on analyzing markets and the trading of financial instruments. Fundamental analysis is a much wider field, encompassing financial and economic analysis as well as analysis of societal and political trends. Technicians analyze market prices. A technician's analysis is derived solely from price and volume data, whereas a fundamental analyst studies a company, incorporating data that are external to the market, and then uses this analysis to predict security price movements. Technical analysis assumes that all of the factors considered by a fundamental analyst are reflected in the price of a financial instrument through buying and selling activity.

A key distinction between technical analysis and fundamental analysis is that the technician has more concrete data, primarily price and volume data, to work with. The financial statements analyzed by fundamental analysts do not contain objective data but rather are the result of numerous estimates and assumptions that have been combined to produce the various line items. Even the cash line on a balance sheet is subject to corporate management's opinion about which assets are liquid enough to be considered "cash." This opinion must be agreed to by auditors and, in many countries, regulators (who sometimes differ with the auditors). Financial statements are subject to restatement because of such issues as changes in accounting assumptions and even fraud. But the price and volume data used in technical analysis are objective. When the data are analyzed, both types of analysis become subjective because judgment is exercised when a technician analyzes a price chart and when a fundamental analyst analyzes an income statement. However, by assigning predefined rules and conditions to their techniques, technical analysts can become more objective.

Fundamental analysis can be considered the more theoretical approach because it seeks to determine the underlying long-term (or intrinsic) value of a security. Technical analysis can be considered the more practical approach because a technician studies the markets and financial instruments as they exist, even if trading activity appears, at times, to be irrational. Technicians seek to project the level at which a financial instrument *will* trade, whereas fundamental analysts seek to predict where it *should* trade.

A drawback of technical analysis is that technicians are limited to studying market movements and do not use other predictive analytical methods, such as interviewing the customers of a subject company to determine future demand for a company's products. Technicians study market trends and are mainly concerned with a security's price trend: Is the security trading up, down, or sideways? Trends are driven by collective investor psychology and generally change gradually, so that the trained technician can spot subtle shifts. However, markets can also change without warning. Additionally, it can take some time for a new trend to become evident. Thus, technicians may make wrong calls and have to change their opinions. Technicians are generally better at identifying market moves when the moves are already underway.

Moreover, trends and patterns must be in place for some time before they are recognizable, so a key shortcoming of technical analysis is that, try as it might to identify clues of an impending trend change, it typically still lags actual price data in such identification. This shortcoming mirrors a key shortcoming of fundamental analysis in that securities often overshoot fundamental fair values in an uptrend and undershoot fundamental fair values in a downtrend. Strictly relying on price targets obtained through fundamental analysis can lead to closing profitable investment positions too early because investors may irrationally bid security prices well above or well below intrinsic value.

Technical analysis and fundamental analysis can be seen as opposing approaches to analyzing securities, but in reality, many investors have experienced success by combining the two techniques. For example, an investor may use fundamental analysis to identify an undervalued stock and then use technical analysis to find specific entry and exit points for that position. Using fundamental and technical analysis together works well, for example, when a security is deemed fundamentally cheap but purchasing the security too early could prove costly. In this instance, technical analysis could help identify an attractive risk/reward entry point and moment in time to express the core fundamental view.

Some technical traders will look at fundamentals to support their trades as well. For example, a trader who is monitoring a **breakout** possibility near an earnings report may look at the fundamentals to get an idea of whether the stock is likely to beat earnings. A breakout refers to when the price of an asset moves above a resistance level.

A good example of a context in which technical analysis can be a superior tool to fundamental analysis is securities fraud. In such cases, fundamental analysts can continue to hold favorable views of a company's equity securities even as its share prices decline.

2.4. The Differences in Conducting/Interpreting Technical Analysis in Various Types of Markets

In general, technical analysis is a trading tool that requires liquidity, so it is best and most easily applied to liquid and deep markets. In other words, the use of technical analysis is limited in illiquid markets, where even modestly sized trades can have an inordinate impact on prices. For example, in considering a thinly traded American Depositary Receipt (ADR), analyzing the more heavily traded local security frequently yields a better analysis—without any potential currency-related distortions. **Gap openings** are more frequent in thinly traded securities and markets. A gap is an area of a chart where a security's price either rises or falls from the previous day's close with no trading occurring in between. A gap opening is the start of a new trading session with a gap.

Technical analysis can be applied to different asset classes, such as equities, commodities, and currencies. The success rate of technical analysis will depend on the nature of the price action in any asset class. Each market has its own character, and the role of the technician is to interpret—but not force—the technical evidence. With regard to equities, in many less-liquid frontier and emerging markets, local retail investors are active traders, whereas developed markets have a higher percentage of institutional investors.

Market participation (institutional vs. retail) can have an impact on technical analysis. The basic difference between retail and institutional investors is that retail investors tend to have less in-depth information (to be more naive) and to be more momentum-centric than institutional investors. As a result, retail investors may depend upon technical analysis and momentum trading somewhat more than institutional investors. Institutional investors also must have enough float/liquidity in a given stock to participate in scale, so are limited in their interest in micro-cap stocks with minimal liquidity. Strong trend periods are the result of inefficiencies, and inefficiencies can be more easily exploited in emerging and frontier markets.

Question 1

Which one of the statements below cannot be stated as a shortcoming of technical analysis?

a. Technical analysts might be late in identifying a trend or pattern because they will require enough data to make a conclusion.
b. Technical analysts might miss a buying opportunity because the fundamental fair value of a company undershoots in a downtrend.
c. Technical analysis will have limited application in the case of an initial public offering (IPO).

Answer: B. The technical analyst will analyze only the price and volume data. If the stock is in a downtrend, the technical analyst will avoid buying it until a new uptrend is established in the analyzed time frame. For that reason, even though a company is fundamentally cheap, the technical analyst will wait for a buy signal that's confirmed by a chart pattern.

A is not the correct answer because being required to wait for confirmation can be viewed as a shortcoming of technical analysis.

C is not the correct answer because an IPO lacks price data, which are required for conducting technical analysis. Not being able to apply technical analysis to securities with limited price history is a shortcoming of technical analysis.

Question 2

Given the behavioral aspects of financial markets, under which conditions and market environments can an investor/analyst apply technical analysis?

a.   Equity markets with poor liquidity and with limited participation
b.   Pegged currency markets
c.   Blue chip technology stocks trading on the NASDAQ Stock Market

Answer: C. For technical analysis to be applied with good results, a market or a stock should have enough participation. Technical analysis measures crowd psychology. An individual's decision-making might be difficult to understand and analyze. However, several individuals acting together produce predictable behavior patterns. Crowd behavior is similar for humans around the world. This is why technical analysis can be applied to different markets as long as there is enough human interaction in the form of buying and selling.

A is not the correct answer because in the case of poor liquidity and limited participation, prices are subject to manipulation. Technical analysis is most effective when prices are determined by demand and supply in free markets.

B is not the correct answer because government intervention is the opposite of what we are looking for in terms of free markets. In such cases, technical analysis will have limited scope.

Question 3

Retail and institutional investors behave differently in the way they invest and trade. Which one of the statements below is NOT one of the basic differences between retail and institutional investors?

a.   Retail investors tend to have less in-depth information when compared to institutional investors.
b.   Retail investors require more float/liquidity in given stocks in order to participate when compared with institutional investors.
c.   Retail investors tend to be more momentum-centric than institutional investors.

Answer: B. Retail traders usually trade with smaller size and can more easily buy and sell shares in less-liquid stocks, such as small-cap and micro-cap stocks.

A is incorrect because it is one of the basic differences between retail and institutional investors. Retail investors typically have limited information, whereas institutional investors typically have dedicated research departments and/or access to significant information.

C is incorrect because it is one of the basic differences between retail and institutional investors. Retail investors are more apt to trade based on market movements and intuition, whereas institutional investors follow a more in-depth investment process.

3. CHARTING

d. describe and interpret different types of technical analysis charts;
e. explain uses of trend, support, and resistance lines;
f. explain common chart patterns.

Vignette

Scene 2

The technical analyst tells you that she can happily provide perspective from a technical point of view. **She prepares the following chart:**

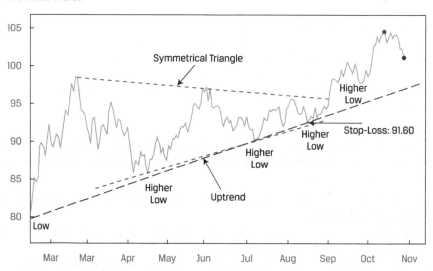

SPDR Gold Shares

She also prepares the following comments:

- Between February and September, the GLD price chart formed a symmetrical triangle chart pattern. The breakout took place in the beginning of September. Following the breakout, the price pulled back to the upper boundary of the chart pattern. The pullback offered an entry opportunity for those who missed the initial breakout in the beginning of September. Following the pullback, the GLD price resumed its upward movement in October.

- Since the beginning of the year, GLD has been in a steady uptrend. The uptrend can be seen in the higher lows. When the higher lows are connected with a trendline, a clear uptrend is visible.
- In late October, the price pulled back and put our long GLD position into an unrealized loss. However, the uptrend was not violated, nor was the chart pattern negated. The minor low at the 91.6 level inside the symmetrical triangle served as the protective stop-loss and the level at which the chart pattern would be negated.

Then she summarizes:

"So, even though the position shows an unrealized loss, there is no reason to change the positive outlook at this point in time."

You breathe a sigh of relief now that you have additional perspective.

The primary tools used in technical analysis are charts and indicators. Charts are a graphical display of price and volume data, and the display may be done in a number of ways. Charts are then subjected to various analyses, including the identification of trends and patterns. Before we discuss several concepts regarding charts, it is important to note that not all price data are suitable for technical analysis. Some instruments (whether equities, futures, commodities, FX, or cryptocurrencies) might not have enough interaction between buyers and sellers to produce meaningful price patterns. Other instruments might become illiquid over time, so that the principles of charting might no longer be applicable.

3.1. Types of Technical Analysis Charts

Charts are an essential component of the technical analyst's toolkit. Charts present information about past price behavior and provide a basis for inferring likely future price behavior. With the help of technology, we have access to financial data through a variety of charts. MetaStock and TradeStation are examples of technical charting and analysis software. A variety of charts can be useful in studying the markets. The selection of the chart to use in technical analysis is determined by the intended purpose of the analysis.

Advanced charting and trading software, utilizing artificial intelligence (AI), can help in simulating trading ideas or strategies as well as in **backtesting** results on historical price data. Backtesting is a method of assessing the viability of a trading strategy by showing how the strategy would play out using historical data.

3.1.1. Line Chart

Line charts are familiar to all types of analysts and are a simple graphic display of price trends over time. Line charts are typically drawn with closing prices as the data points. The vertical axis (*y*-axis) reflects price level, and the horizontal axis (*x*-axis) represents time. Even though the line chart is the simplest kind of chart, an analyst can quickly glean information from this representation of price data. In fact, line charts might be the most effective tool for analyzing price action because they show the closing price of the day, week, or month. The closing price is regarded by traders and investors as the most important data point, as it reflects the final decision for that period's transactions.

Exhibit 1 shows a quarterly chart of the FTSE 100 Index from 1984 through mid-2018. Up years and down years are clearly evident. The strong rally from 1984 through 1999 and the market decline from late 1999 to late 2002 are also clearly visible. The 2003–07 rally did not exceed the high reached in 1999, which suggests that investors were not willing to pay as high a price for stocks on the London Stock Exchange during that rally as they were in the prior rally. The 2007–09 decline didn't reach the lows of 2002, suggesting that investors viewed the prior recessionary period as a support level. From 2009 through mid-2018, the market was in a general uptrend with some pullback in 2015. This visual information in the price chart provides a broad overview of investor sentiment and can lead to further analysis. Importantly, the analyst can access and analyze this information quickly. Collecting and analyzing the full array of data normally incorporated in fundamental analysis would take much longer.

EXHIBIT 1   Line Chart: FTSE 100 Quarterly Price Data, 1984–mid-2018

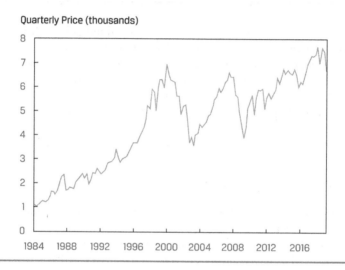

3.1.2. Bar Chart

A line chart has one data point per time interval. A **bar chart**, in contrast, has four bits of data in each entry—the high and low prices encountered during the time interval plus the opening and closing prices. Such charts can be constructed for any time period, but they are customarily constructed from daily data. Traders or investors focusing on longer-term analysis can choose to plot their price data on a weekly or monthly scale. How a chart is interpreted will not depend on its periodicity. However, to get the best results, the analyst/investor or trader should decide on the time frame of operation.

As Exhibit 2 shows, a vertical line connects the high and low prices of the day; a cross-hatch to the right indicates the closing price, and a cross-hatch to the left indicates the opening price. The appeal of this kind of chart is that the analyst immediately gets a sense of the nature of that day's trading. A short bar indicates little price movement during the day; that is, the high, low, and close are near the opening price. A long bar indicates a wide divergence between the high and the low for the day.

EXHIBIT 2   Bar Chart Notation

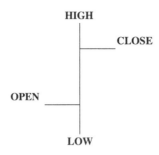

Exhibit 3 shows daily performance of the US dollar (USD) versus the Singapore dollar (SGD) spot FX from early 2018 through late 2018. As we will discuss in the latter sections of this chapter, the analyst can identify an orderly, month-long consolidation between the 1.330 and 1.348 levels during the May–June period. Bar charts become more important in the analysis of short-term price actions, where the identification of support and resistance levels makes a major difference in analysis and trading results. Spikes on the upside and on the downside will form support and resistance levels that can be seen only if the data are plotted as either a bar chart or a candlestick chart (to be discussed shortly). Exhibit 4 shows the same price data plotted as a line chart. With the line chart only, the analyst will not be able to capture the same consolidation period or clearly see the level at which the breakout opportunity will take place. Therefore, it is best to analyze price data that are subject to shorter-term trading by using either bar or candlestick charts.

EXHIBIT 3   Bar Chart: US Dollar/Singapore Dollar, January 2018–August 2018 (daily data)

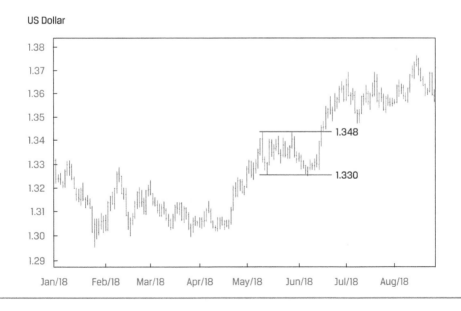

EXHIBIT 4   Line Chart: US Dollar/Singapore Dollar, January 2018–August 2018 (daily data)

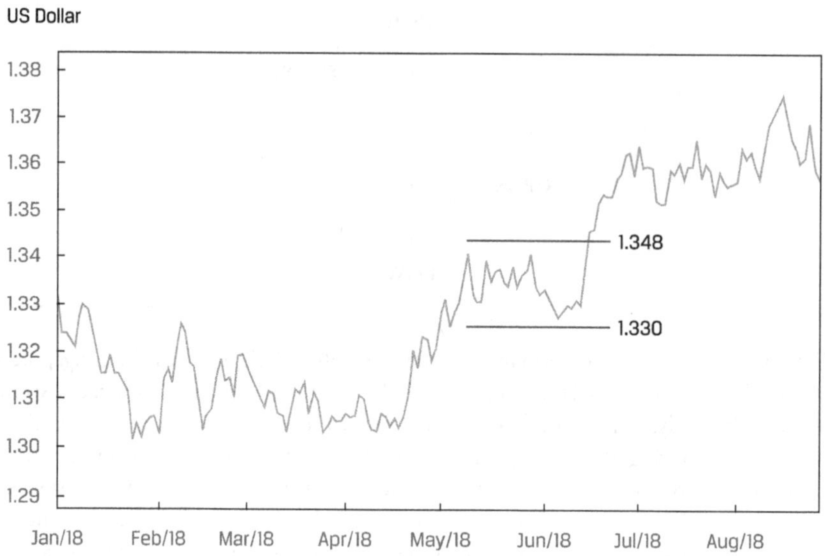

US Dollar

[chart showing line from Jan/18 to Aug/18, with horizontal lines marked 1.348 and 1.330, y-axis from 1.29 to 1.38]

3.1.3. Candlestick Chart

Candlestick charts trace their roots to Japan, where technical analysis has been in use for centuries. Like a bar chart, a **candlestick chart** provides four prices per data point: the opening and closing prices and the high and low prices during the period. As shown in Exhibit 5, a vertical line represents the range through which the security price traveled during the time period. The line is known as the wick or shadow. The body of the candle is white (or clear) if the opening price was lower than the closing price, and the body of the candle is dark if the opening price was higher than the closing price.

EXHIBIT 5   Construction of a Candlestick Chart

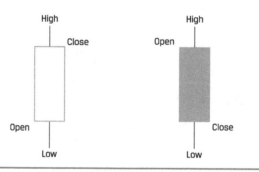

Exhibit 6 shows the US dollar/Singapore dollar daily price chart on a candlestick graph for the period 1 January through 13 July 2018.

EXHIBIT 6   Candlestick Chart: US Dollar/Singapore Dollar, 1 January–13 July 2018 (daily data)

The advantage of the candlestick chart over the bar chart is that price fluctuations are much more visible on the candlestick chart, which allows for better analysis. The bar chart indicates market volatility only by the height of each bar, but on candlestick charts, the difference between opening and closing prices and their relationship to the highs and lows of the day are clearly apparent. Long-legged candlesticks usually indicate the price finding support after meeting sellers during the day. We will discuss interpretation of candlestick chart patterns in subsequent sections. For now, we can highlight the importance of long shadows. In the Japanese terminology used in candlestick charting, one of the widely traded and analyzed candlestick patterns is called a **doji**. The doji signifies that after a full day of trading, the positive price influence of buyers and the negative price influence of sellers exactly counteracted each other—with opening and closing prices that are virtually equal—which suggests that the market under analysis is in balance. If a doji occurs at the end of a long uptrend or downtrend, it signals that the trend will probably reverse. The doji in mid-May 2018 not only marked a short-term trend reversal from the 1.33 level but also strengthened that level, which later became a support level during June 2018. The added value of such interpretation can be gained only by using candlestick graphs.

3.1.4. Scale

For any chart—line, bar, or candlestick—the vertical axis can be constructed with either a **linear scale** (also known as an arithmetic scale) or a **logarithmic scale**, depending on how the analyst wants to view the data. With a logarithmic scale, equal vertical distances on the chart correspond to an equal percentage change. With a linear scale, equal vertical distances on the chart correspond to an equal unit change. A logarithmic scale is appropriate when the analyst is working on longer time frames. A linear scale is better suited for shorter-term price charts. In addition, a logarithmic scale is appropriate when the data move through a range of values representing several orders of magnitude (e.g., from 10 to 10,000); a linear scale is better suited for narrower ranges (e.g., prices from \$35 to \$50). The difference between a logarithmic price chart and an arithmetic (linear) price chart can be small when you are analyzing a short time frame. However, when you look at longer-term charts (more than two years of price data), you will see major differences.

The horizontal axis shows the passage of time. The appropriate time interval depends on the nature of the underlying data and the specific purpose of the chart. An active trader, for instance, may find 10-minute, 5-minute, or even tick-by-tick data useful, but other technical analysts may prefer daily or weekly data. It is important to note that the shorter the time frame, the more random (and thus less meaningful) price action tends to become.

Consider Exhibits 7 and 8, which both show the yearly history of the Dow Jones Industrial Average (DJIA) from 1928 to 2018. Plotting the index on a linear scale, as in Exhibit 7, makes it difficult to gather much information from the first 60 years of the data series. Analysts can see a slight uptrend but not much else. The eye is drawn to the bull market of the 1980s, the subsequent dot-com bubble, the subprime crisis, and the sustained recovery. When the index is plotted on a logarithmic scale, as in Exhibit 8, however, the data tell a more comprehensive story. The Great Depression of the 1930s stands out, but over the following 80 years, the data follow a relatively stable upward trend.

EXHIBIT 7   Dow Jones Industrial Average on Linear Scale, 1920–2018 (US$)

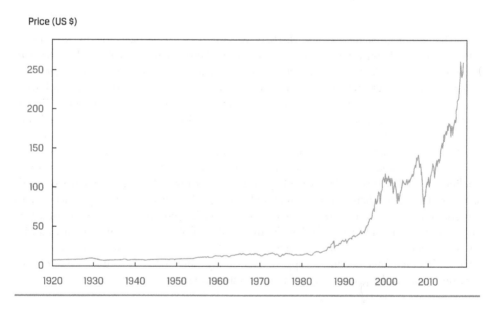

EXHIBIT 8   Dow Jones Industrial Average on Logarithmic Scale, 1920–2018 (US$)

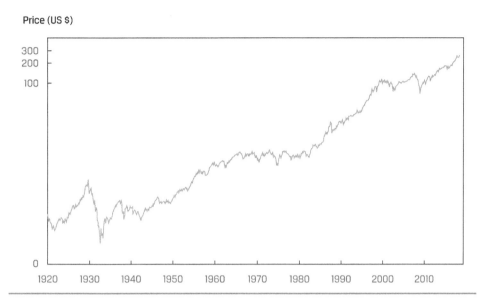

Price (US $)

How you construct your scale will impact the trendlines you draw on your price chart. A good example is the price chart of the Russell 2000 Index ETF (IWM). Exhibit 9 shows a price chart of the Russell 2000 Index for the same time period plotted on a linear scale and on a logarithmic scale.

EXHIBIT 9   Russell 2000 Index Linear and Logarithmic Scales, 2016–2019

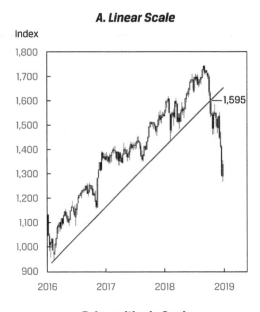

A. Linear Scale

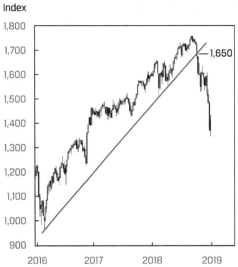

B. Logarithmic Scale

The chart in Panel A is plotted on a linear scale. The chart in Panel B is plotted on logarithmic scale. The upward-sloping trendline breaks down earlier on the logarithmic scale than on the linear scale. Upward-sloping logarithmic trendlines are broken sooner than upward-sloping linear trendlines. The opposite is true for downtrends. Downward-sloping trendlines on logarithmic scale charts are broken later than downward-sloping trendlines on linear scale charts. The **breakdown** signal—and the resulting change in trend—takes place at the 1,650 level on the logarithmic scale chart, whereas the same signal occurs much lower—at the 1,595 level—on the linear scale price chart. A breakdown occurs when the price of an asset moves below a support level.

3.1.5. Volume

Volume is an important characteristic that is included at the bottom of many charts. Volume is used to assess the strength or conviction of buyers and sellers in determining a security's price. For example, on a daily price chart, a bar chart below the price section will show the volume traded for that day.

Some technicians consider volume information to be crucial. If volume increases during a time frame in which price is also increasing, that combination is considered positive and the two indicators are said to "confirm" each other. The signal would be interpreted to mean that over time, more and more investors are buying the financial instrument, and they are doing so at higher and higher prices. This pattern is considered a positive technical development.

Conversely, if volume and price diverge—for example, if a stock's price rises while its volume declines—the implication is that fewer and fewer market participants are willing to buy that stock at the new price. If this trend in volume continues, it is expected that the price rally will soon end because demand for the security at higher prices will cease. However, there are cases where a breakout can take place with low volume. Exhibit 10 shows a price chart for Sunac China Holdings with volume displayed separately.

EXHIBIT 10   Weekly Candlestick Price Chart and Volume Bar Chart: Sunac China Holdings, August 2016–May 2019 (Hong Kong dollars)

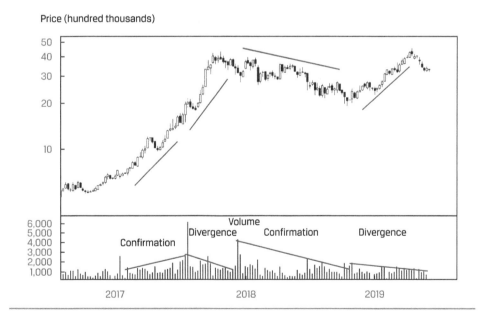

3.1.6. Time Intervals

Charts can be constructed using any time interval. The same principles of technical analysis apply irrespective of the time interval. Using longer intervals allows the analyst to chart longer time periods, for the simple reason that longer intervals contain fewer data points, so a longer time frame can be presented on the chart. A useful step for many analysts is to begin the analysis of a security with the chart for a long time frame, such as a weekly or monthly chart, and then construct charts with shorter and shorter time intervals, such as daily or hourly charts. Over the years, an increase in computerized trading and high-frequency trading (HFT) has resulted in more frequent false and distorted signals in shorter-term analysis. Traders, investors, and analysts should bear in mind the randomness involved in very short-term (intraday) analysis and trading.

3.1.7. Relative Strength Analysis

Relative strength analysis is widely used to compare the performance of a particular asset, such as a common stock, with that of some benchmark—such as, in the case of common stocks, the FTSE 100, the Nikkei 225, or the S&P 500 Index—or with the performance of another security. The intent is to show outperformance or underperformance of the individual issue relative to some other index or asset. Typically, the analyst prepares a line chart of the ratio of two prices, with the asset under analysis as the numerator and with the benchmark or other security as the denominator. A rising line shows the asset is performing better than the benchmark or other stock; a declining line shows the opposite. A flat line shows neutral performance.

Suppose a private investor wants to understand changing market trends for two investment ideas she has read about. Amazon Inc. (AMZN) is a well-known technology-enabled retail company, and Walmart Inc. (WMT) is a US-based multinational retail company. The investor wants to determine which of the two companies' stocks has been the stronger performer (relative to the S&P 500) over the roughly seven-year period ending August 2018. Exhibit 11 shows relative strength lines for the two stocks between 2011 and 2018. For ease of comparison, the ratio of each retail company's price data to the S&P 500 is indexed to 1.00 at the beginning of 2011. A move from 1.00 to 1.50 on the chart in Panel A indicates a 50% outperformance for Amazon versus the S&P 500. Likewise, a drop from 1.00 to 0.80 on the chart in Panel B indicates a 20% underperformance for Walmart versus the S&P 500.

EXHIBIT 11   Relative Strength Analysis of Two Retail Giants: AMZN vs. the S&P 500 and WMT vs. the S&P 500, January 2011–August 2018

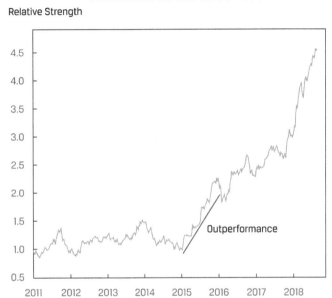

A. Amazon.com Inc. vs. S&P 500

Relative Strength

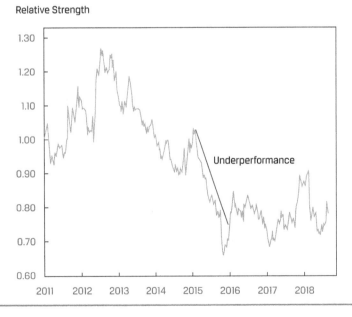

B. Walmart vs. S&P 500

Relative Strength

The units on the vertical axis are not significant; the ratio is a function of the relative prices of the assets under consideration. The important information is how the ratio has changed. This type of chart allows an analyst to make a visual determination of that change.

As Exhibit 11 illustrates, Amazon was a strong performer starting in 2015, but its relative performance wasn't as strong prior to that year. In contrast, the stock of Walmart lost its leadership in the beginning of 2013, and from that point up to mid-2018, its stock has clearly lagged the performance of the S&P 500.

3.2. Trend, Support, and Resistance

The concepts of **trend** and **consolidation** are perhaps the most important aspects of technical analysis. A trend is a long-term pattern of movement in a particular direction. When a security is not trending, it is considered to be in a consolidation. Trend analysis is based on the observations that market participants tend to act in herds and that trends tend to stay in place for some time. A security can be considered to be in an uptrend or a downtrend. The timing of buy and sell decisions will depend on how well we are able to differentiate between a consolidation and a trend phase. Not all securities are in a trend. When a security is not trending, it offers opportunity for traders who buy/sell between well-defined ranges. In the latter part of the chapter, we will discuss how to interpret each consolidation period with the help of chart patterns. Not every chart will have obvious or clear implications, so the analyst must avoid the temptation to force a conclusion from every chart, which may lead to a wrong interpretation.

A security is in an **uptrend** when the price goes to higher highs and higher lows. In an uptrend, the forces of demand are greater than the forces of supply. So, traders are willing to pay higher and higher prices for the same asset over time. Presumably, the strong demand indicates that investors believe the intrinsic value of the security is increasing. As the price of the security moves up, each subsequent new high is higher than the prior high, and each time there is a **retracement**, which is a reversal in the movement of the security's price, it must stop at a higher low than the prior lows in the trend period. To draw an uptrend line, a technician draws a line connecting the lows of the price chart. Major breakdowns in price, however, when the price drops through and below the trendline, indicate that the uptrend is over and may signal a further decline in the price. Minor breakthroughs below previous lows simply call for the line to be moderately adjusted over time. Time is also a consideration in trends: The longer the security price stays below the trendline, the more meaningful the breakdown is considered to be.

In a **downtrend**, a security makes lower lows and lower highs. As the price of the security moves down, each subsequent new high must be lower than the prior high, and each time there is a retracement, the price must stop at a lower low than the prior lows in the trend period. To draw a downtrend line, a technician draws a line connecting the highs of the price chart. Major breakouts above the downtrend line indicate that the downtrend is over and a rise in the security's price may occur. And as with an uptrend, the longer the security price stays above the trendline, the more meaningful the breakout is considered to be.

In a downtrend, supply overwhelms demand. Over time, sellers are willing to accept lower and lower prices to exit long positions or enter new short positions. This seller behavior generally indicates deteriorating investor sentiment about the asset. However, selling may be prompted by factors not related to the fundamental or intrinsic value of the stock. For example, investors may be forced to sell to meet margin calls in their portfolios. From a purely technical standpoint, the reason is irrelevant. The downtrend is assumed to continue until contrary technical evidence appears. Combining fundamental analysis with technical analysis in such a case, however, might reveal a security that has attractive fundamentals but a currently negative technical position.

A security may trade in a fairly narrow range, moving sideways on the price chart without much upward or downward movement. This pattern indicates a relative balance between supply and demand. A technical analyst might not expect to profit from long or short trades in such securities but might devise profitable option strategies for short-term investors with the ability to accept the risks. For position traders and investors, consolidations are pauses in trends. Such pauses also present an opportunity to assess the strength or weakness of that security. Each consolidation period is eventually followed by a trend period. For buyers of that security, it is important to know how the subsequent trend phase will develop. For sellers of the security, it is important to watch for any change in trend.

Exhibit 12 shows the application of trend and consolidation analysis. It is important to note that each trend period will be followed by a consolidation and each consolidation will give rise to a trend period. Most position traders and investors would like to capture these trend periods. Therefore, differentiation or identification of those consolidation and trend periods becomes an important motive of a **chartist**. A chartist is an individual who uses charts or graphs of a security's historical prices or levels to forecast its future trends.

EXHIBIT 12   Trend and Consolidation Analysis: Teladoc Health Price Chart, 2015–2019 (US$)

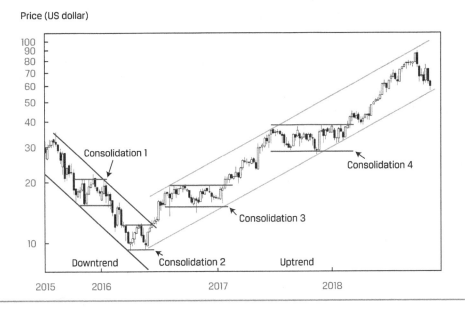

The chart in Exhibit 12 covers roughly four years and would most likely be used by investors with a long time horizon. There are four distinct consolidation periods on the price chart. Identification of those consolidation periods would have helped in making investment decisions. Following its IPO, Teladoc Health started trending lower. In the last quarter of 2015, the stock formed its first consolidation (Consolidation 1). Once the boundaries of the consolidation became clear, the chartist should have asked the question, Which way will the consolidation resolve? If it resolved on the downside, this outcome would suggest that the downtrend would resume. If it resolved on the upside, this outcome would suggest a change in trend, a trend reversal. In the last month of 2015, Teladoc broke down its consolidation to resume its downtrend.

Between March 2016 and May 2016, the stock formed another consolidation (Consolidation 2). This time a breakout on the upside followed. The implication of this breakout was a major trend reversal. It offered a long-term opportunity for investors and traders.

Initial upward thrust pushed Teladoc from around the 12 level to around the 19 level. You will remember that each trend period is followed by a consolidation. Consolidation 3, which took six months to complete, offered an opportunity for traders with short horizons. This was also an opportunity to assess the health of the initial positive change in trend. Once the boundaries of the consolidation became clear, the chartist should have asked the questions, Which way will the consolidation resolve? Would Teladoc offer a new breakout opportunity and a continuation of the existing uptrend? The new breakout occurred in January 2017. At this point, we had an established uptrend with higher lows and higher highs.

The continuation of the uptrend took Teladoc from around the 19 level to around the 38 level. At that point, the stock entered into another consolidation (Consolidation 4). From May 2017 until February 2018, the stock remained in a tight consolidation range, which acted as another opportunity for traders with short horizons. These types of consolidations, once they are identified and mature, offer traders a chance to sell at the upper boundary and buy back their shares at the lower boundary. For position traders and investors, the consolidation is a time to assess the strength of the stock. Consolidation 4 was completed in March 2018 with a breakout above the 38 level, and the uptrend resumed higher, reaching the 89 level by the last quarter of 2018.

Two concepts related to trend are **support** and **resistance**. Support is defined as a low price range in which buying activity is sufficient to stop the decline in price. It is the opposite of resistance, which is a high price range in which selling activity is sufficient to stop the rise in price. The psychology behind the concepts of support and resistance is that investors have come to a consensus about the price of a security. Support and resistance levels can be sloped lines, as in trendlines or horizontal lines.

A key tenet regarding support and resistance as a part of technical analysis is the **change in polarity principle**, which states that once a support level is breached, it becomes a resistance level. The same holds true for resistance levels; once breached, they become support levels.

Support indicates that at some price level, investors consider a security to be an attractive investment and are willing to buy, even in the wake of a sharp decline. (And resistance indicates that at some level, investors are not willing to buy, even in an uptrend.)

In Exhibit 13, we see an example of support and resistance on a widely followed commodity, WTI Light Crude Oil. For more than two decades, this commodity's price fluctuated between $10 per barrel and $37 per barrel. In 2014, the balance between supply and demand changed and pushed the price above the historical resistance at $37. In four years' time, the commodity was trading as high as the $147 level. High commodity prices had significant impact on global economies. During the subprime crisis and related sell-off, the WTI Light Crude Oil price fell back to the $37 level. Previous resistance acted as a strong support. The second time the WTI price tested the $37 support level was in 2016. Even though the price dipped below the support, the close for the quarter was around the $38 level. The price chart formed a long-legged candlestick, suggesting the strong support was still valid.

EXHIBIT 13   Support Level: WTI Light Crude Oil Quarterly Price Chart, 1980–2019 (US$ per barrel)

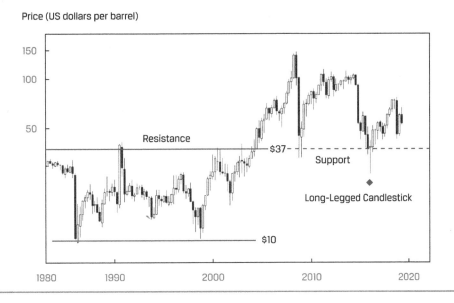

3.3. Common Chart Patterns

Chart patterns are formations that appear in price charts that create some type of recognizable shape over time as the single bar lines accumulate. Common patterns appear repeatedly and often lead to similar subsequent price movements. Thus, the identification and analysis of chart patterns is a basic aspect of how technical analysis is used to predict security prices. An important connection to remember is that because patterns form as a result of the behavior of market participants, these patterns are graphical depictions of the collective psychology of the market at a given time. The recurring patterns that appear in charts can be used as a basis for market analysis.

Chart patterns, while most can be analyzed as a type of consolidation, can be divided into two categories: **reversal patterns** and **continuation patterns**. These terms refer to the trend for the security in question prior to the formation of the pattern (consolidation). The most important concept to understand in using chart patterns is that not every chart will lend itself to easy interpretation. Some charts will be clearer than others, and the analyst should not force an interpretation on any chart. This aspect is frequently forgotten by investors, who are so eager to identify and use patterns that they forget the proper application of charts.

3.3.1. Reversal Patterns
As the name implies, a reversal pattern signals the end of a trend, a change in direction for the financial instrument's price. Evidence that a trend is about to change direction is obviously important, so reversal patterns are noteworthy.

3.3.1.1. Head and Shoulders

Perhaps the most widely recognized reversal pattern is the **head and shoulders pattern**. This pattern consists of three segments. Volume is an important consideration in interpreting this pattern. Because the head and shoulders pattern indicates a trend reversal, it is important to establish the existence of a prior uptrend. Without a prior uptrend to reverse, there cannot be a head and shoulders reversal pattern. Later, we will discuss the *inverse* head and shoulders pattern (preceded by a downtrend).

Exhibit 14 depicts a head and shoulders pattern for Marriott Vacations.

EXHIBIT 14   Head and Shoulders Pattern: Marriott Vacations Weekly Price Chart, January 2016– December 2018 (US$)

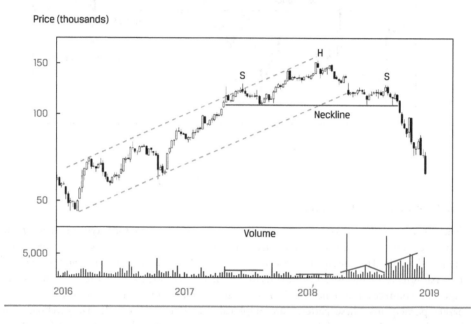

The three parts of the pattern are as follows:

1. Left shoulder: While the security is in an uptrend, the left shoulder forms a peak that marks the high point of the current trend. Often, but not always, this first shoulder may represent the highest volume of the entire pattern. After this peak, a decline ensues to complete the formation of the shoulder.
2. Head: From the low of the left shoulder, an advance begins that exceeds the previous high and marks the top of the head. After this peak, the low of the subsequent decline marks the second point of the neckline. Formation of the head is the first signal that the rally may be coming to an end and that a reversal may be starting. Volume typically will wane a bit into the head high.
3. Right shoulder: The advance from the low of the head forms the right shoulder. This peak is lower than the head (a lower high) and usually in line with the high of the left shoulder. A textbook example should have symmetry between the shoulders in both time and price. The decline from the peak of the right shoulder should break the neckline. It is important that volume be lowest on the second shoulder.

In addition, the following three elements are key for the head and shoulders pattern: neckline, volume, and price target.

- Neckline: The neckline forms by connecting the beginning of the left shoulder and the end of the right shoulder. Depending on the relationship between the two low points, the neckline can slope up, slope down, or be horizontal. A textbook example should have a horizontal chart pattern boundary (neckline) where the lows of both shoulders just touch the horizontal line.
- Volume: As mentioned above, volume plays an important role in the confirmation of a head and shoulders pattern. Ideally, but not always, volume during the advance of the left shoulder should be higher than during the advance of the head. The decrease in volume into the new high of the head then serves as an initial warning sign. The next warning sign comes when volume increases on the decline from the peak of the head, then notably decreases during the advance of the right shoulder. Final confirmation comes when volume increases once again during the decline from the right shoulder.
- Price target: After the price breaks the neckline support, the projected price decline is found by measuring the distance from the neckline to the top of the head. This distance is then subtracted from the neckline to reach a price target. Price targets should be used as guidelines. Price may exceed the chart pattern objective or fall short.

Rarely will an analyst see a perfectly formed head and shoulders pattern; variations include two tops on the shoulders or on the head. The head, however, should rise to a higher price level than either shoulder, whereas the shoulders should be roughly symmetrical. In terms of the neckline price level, the first rally should begin at this level and the left shoulder and head should also decline to roughly this level. But necklines may not always form exactly horizontal lines.

Volume is important in analyzing head and shoulders patterns. A new high in price at the top of the head without a new high in volume signals the presence of fewer bullish market participants. When one indicator is making a new high (or low) but another is not, this situation is called **divergence**.

Once the head and shoulders pattern has formed, the expectation is that the share price will decline through the neckline price. Technicians tend to use filtering rules to make sure that a clear breakdown of the neckline has occurred. These rules may take the form of waiting to trade until the price falls to a meaningful level below the neckline (3% and 5% are commonly used) and/or until the price has remained below the neckline for a specified length of time; when a daily price chart is used, the rule may be several days to a week. Prices commonly rebound to the neckline levels, even after a decline has exceeded the filter levels. Prices generally stop, however, at or around the neckline. The neckline was a support level, and under the change in polarity principle, once a support level is breached, it becomes a resistance level.

3.3.1.2. Inverse Head and Shoulders

The head and shoulders pattern can also form upside down and act as a reversal pattern for a preceding downtrend. Inverse head and shoulders is also referred to as a head and shoulders bottom.

EXHIBIT 15   Inverse Head and Shoulders Pattern: US Dollar/South African Rand Daily Price Chart, December 2017–July 2018

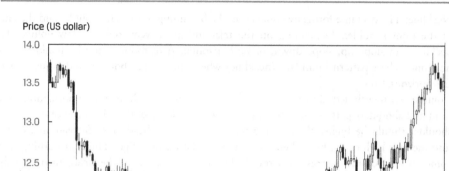

The three parts of the inverse head and shoulders are as follows:

- Left shoulder: This shoulder appears to show a strong decline, with the slope of the decline greater than that of the prior downtrend. The price movement then reverses back to the level where the rally started, forming a V shape.
- Head: The head is a more pronounced version of the left shoulder. Another decline follows, which takes the price to a lower low than the left shoulder by a significant enough margin that it is clearly evident on the price chart. This second decline also reverses, with price rising to the same level at which the left shoulder began and ended. This price level, the neckline, will also be above the downtrend line formed by connecting the high prices in the downtrend preceding the beginning of the inverse head and shoulders pattern. This pattern is the first signal that the decline may be coming to an end and that a reversal may be near. It is possible for the formation of the head to involve a more complex structure. A head can contain two minor lows, as in the US dollar/South African rand example presented in Exhibit 15.
- Right shoulder: The right shoulder is roughly a mirror image of the left shoulder, signifying less selling enthusiasm. The price declines to roughly the same level as the left shoulder, but the rally reverses at a higher low price than the rally that formed the head.

Volume once again is important to watch and should generally diminish into the final reverse shoulder before ideally exploding higher on the subsequent neckline break.

3.3.1.3. Setting Price Targets with the Head and Shoulders Pattern

Like all technical patterns, the head and shoulders pattern must be analyzed from the perspective of the security's long-term price trend. The rally before the formation of the pattern must be large enough for there to be something to reverse. The stronger and more pronounced the rally was, the stronger and more pronounced the reversal is likely to be. Similarly, once the neckline is breached, the security is expected to decline by an amount equal to the change in price from the neckline to the top of the head. If the preceding rally started at a price higher than the neckline, however, the correction is unlikely to bring the price lower than the level at the start of the rally. Because a head and shoulders formation is a bearish indicator (i.e., a technician would expect the previously established uptrend to end and a downtrend to commence), a technician would seek to profit by shorting the security under analysis. When attempting to profit from the head and shoulders pattern, a technician will often use the price difference between the head and the neckline to set a price target, which is the price at which the technician anticipates closing the investment position. The price target for the head and shoulders pattern is calculated as follows:

$$Price\ target = Neckline - (Head - Neckline).$$

For example, in Exhibit 16, the high price reached at the top of the head is roughly $154 and the neckline formed at roughly $108, for a difference of $46. So a technician would expect the price to decline to a level $46 below the neckline—that is, to $62:

$$Price\ target = \$108 - (\$154 - \$108) = \$62.$$

EXHIBIT 16   Calculating a Price Target: Marriott Vacations Weekly Price Chart, January 2016–December 2018 (US$)

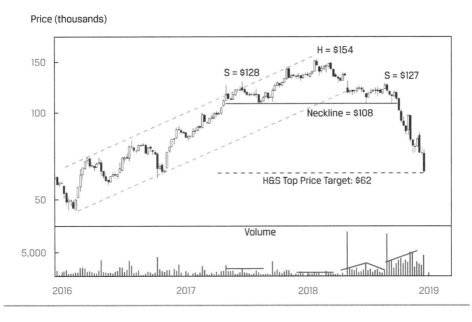

Price targets should be used as guidelines. With stocks in a downtrend and creating bearish chart patterns, a conservative approach to calculating price objectives is warranted. The conservative approach is to take the percentage difference between the high point of the head and the neckline and project it below the breakdown level (the neckline). Note that with a low-priced stock, such as one with a price of $0.50, there is a possibility of projecting price levels below 0. Because negative values for an asset are not possible, measuring price objectives using a percentage decline is more reasonable.

EXAMPLE 1   Determining a Price Target from a Head and Shoulders Pattern

Danielle Waterhouse is the technical analyst at Kanektok Securities. One of the companies her firm follows is LPA Petroleum. Waterhouse believes that a graph of LPA's share prices over the past six months reveals a classic head and shoulders pattern. The share price peaked at US$108, and she estimates the neckline at US$79. At today's close, the shares traded at US$78. Based on the head and shoulders pattern, what price target should Waterhouse estimate?

Solution: Waterhouse estimates the neckline at US$79, which is US$108 minus US $79, or US$29, lower than the head. Her price target is thus US$79 minus US$29, which is US$50. Waterhouse would attempt to sell LPA short at today's price of US$78 and anticipate closing the position at US$50 for a profit of US$28 per share (not accounting for transaction costs).

3.3.1.4. Setting Price Targets with the Inverse Head and Shoulders Pattern
Calculating price targets for inverse head and shoulders patterns is similar to the process for head and shoulders patterns, but because the inverse head and shoulders pattern predicts the end of a downtrend, the technician calculates how high the price is expected to rise once it breaches the neckline. Exhibit 17 illustrates an inverse head and shoulders pattern.

EXHIBIT 17   Calculating a Price Target for an Inverse Head and Shoulders Pattern: US Dollar/South African Rand Daily Price Chart, December 2017–July 2018

For an inverse head and shoulders pattern, the formula is similar to that for a head and shoulders pattern:

$$\text{Price target} = \text{Neckline} + (\text{Neckline} - \text{Head}).$$

For example, in the price chart in Exhibit 17, the low price reached at the bottom of the head is roughly 11.5 and the neckline formed at roughly 12.15. The target can thus be calculated as $12.15 + (12.15 - 11.50) = 12.80$. In this case, a technician might have taken a long position on 23 April, with the strong daily breakout above the neckline at the 12.15 level, and projected a possible exit near the 12.80 level.

3.3.1.5. Double Tops and Bottoms

A **double top** is formed when an uptrend reverses twice at roughly the same high price level. Typically, volume is lower on the second high than on the first high, signaling a diminishing of demand. The longer the time between the two tops and the deeper the sell-off after the first top, the more significant the pattern is considered to be. Price targets can be calculated from this pattern in a manner similar to the calculation for the head and shoulders pattern. For a double top, price is expected to decline below the low of the valley between the two tops by at least the distance from the valley low to the high of the double top.

EXAMPLE 2   Determining a Price Target from a Double Top Pattern

Richard Dupuis is a technician who trades Eurodollar futures for his own account. He analyzes charts based on one-minute intervals, looking for short-term trading opportunities. Eurodollar futures contracts have been trending upward most of the morning, but Dupuis now observes what he believes is a double top pattern: After peaking at US$97.00, the futures contract price falls to US$96.42, climbs again to US $97.02, and then starts a decline. Because of the double top, Dupuis anticipates a reversal from the uptrend to a downtrend. Dupuis decides to open a short position to capitalize on the anticipated trend reversal. What price target should Dupuis estimate for closing the position?

Solution: Dupuis estimates the price target as US$96.42 − (US$97.02 − US$96.42) = US$95.82.

A **double bottom** is formed when the price reaches a low, rebounds, and then declines again to the first low level. Exhibit 18 depicts a double bottom pattern for US 30-year Treasury bond futures (first-month continuation price). Technicians use the double bottom to predict a change from a downtrend to an uptrend in security prices. The neckline for a double bottom is the horizontal line that touches the minor high between the two major troughs. A breakout takes place once the price breaches the neckline. The distance from the resistance breakout to the trough lows can be added to the area above the resistance breakout to estimate a target.

EXHIBIT 18   Double Bottom Pattern: US 30-Year Treasury Bond Daily Price Chart, August 2018– February 2019 (first-month continuation futures, US$)

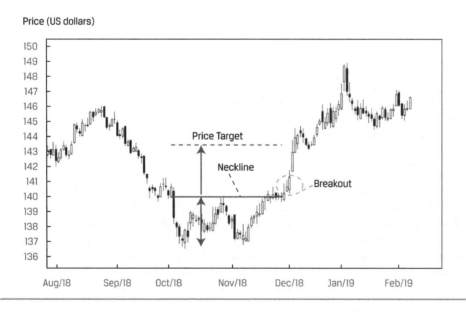

The reason these patterns are significant is that they show that at some price point, investors step in to reverse trends that are underway. For an uptrend, a double top implies that at some price point, enough traders are willing to sell positions (or enter new short positions) that their activities overwhelm and reverse the uptrend created by demand for the shares. A reasonable conclusion is that this price level has been fundamentally derived and that it represents the consensus of investors on the intrinsic value of the security. With double bottoms, if a decline in a security stops at the same price point on two separate occasions, the analyst can conclude that the market consensus is that at that price point, the security is cheap enough to be an attractive investment.

3.3.1.6. Triple Tops and Bottoms

A **triple top** consists of three peaks at roughly the same price level, and a **triple bottom** consists of three troughs at roughly the same price level. A triple top for Odfjell Drilling during 2018 is shown in Exhibit 19.

EXHIBIT 19   Triple Top Pattern: Odfjell Drilling Weekly Price Chart, January 2017–January 2019 (Norwegian krone)

One of the challenges with double top and triple top patterns—and one of the valid criticisms of technical analysis in general—is that an analyst cannot know which pattern will result until after the fact. There is no evidence that market corrections must end with a double bottom or that rallies must end with a double top, and there is no generally accepted technical theory that predicts whether a low will be repeated once or even twice before a reversal occurs. A double bottom is considered to be a more significant pattern than a single bottom because traders have stepped in on two occasions to halt declines. However, traders have no way to determine whether a double top or bottom will be followed by a third top or bottom. The goal of a trader, investor, or analyst is not to predict possible price action but to identify well-defined levels for decision-making. It is the breach of these levels—the breakout—that matters most because it completes the lengthy consolidation and gives rise to a new trend period. Triple tops and triple bottoms are rare, but when they occur, they are more significant reversal patterns than double tops or double bottoms. On three separate occasions, traders stepped in to sell or buy shares with enough volume to end a rally or decline underway at the time. Nevertheless, the greater the number of times the price reverses at the same level, and the greater the time interval over which this pattern occurs, the greater the significance of the pattern. Note that a bottoming process, whatever the reversal chart pattern, tends to be more predictable than a topping process. This is because in a bottoming process, market forces are capitulating, whereas in a topping process, irrational exuberance can always take prices to higher levels before ultimately reversing.

Some securities, due to either their volatility or their active trader/investor profile, offer similar well-defined chart pattern opportunities. Exhibit 20 shows a triple bottom chart pattern for Odfjell Drilling prior to the strong uptrend that pushed the stock price from around the 3.5 level to the high teens.

EXHIBIT 20   Triple Bottom Pattern: Odfjell Drilling Weekly Price Chart, January 2017–January 2019 (Norwegian krone)

When identifying chart patterns, we should remind ourselves of the importance of trends and consolidations. Regardless of the chart pattern in question, the formation of a price range is a *consolidation*, which, once completed with a confirmed breakout in either direction, will be expected to give rise to a trend period. For optimal decision-making, traders, investors, and analysts should focus on successfully identifying and differentiating those two phases.

Exhibit 21 shows the Odfjell Drilling price chart between September 2013 and January 2019. The downtrend that started in the last quarter of 2013 reached a bottom in the second half of 2015. A yearlong sideways consolidation offered a trading opportunity for short-term traders between well-defined chart pattern boundaries. Traders, investors, and analysts with a slightly longer horizon should be asking: What type of price action can follow after the yearlong consolidation? If the chart pattern acts as a triple bottom with a breakout above the chart pattern boundary, can it reverse the two-year-long downtrend? In the second half of 2016, Odfjell Drilling completed the triple bottom with a strong weekly breakout and started a new uptrend. The triple bottom reversed the existing trend from down to up.

EXHIBIT 21   Trend and Consolidation: Odfjell Drilling Weekly Price Chart, September 2013–January 2019 (Norwegian krone)

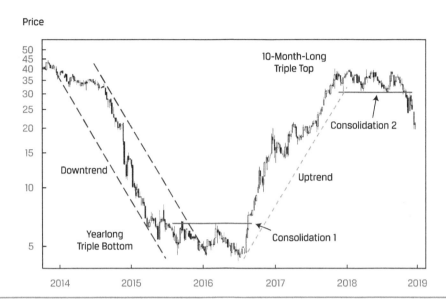

Similar analysis was required from the technician in the last quarter of 2017. Consolidation 2 was a triple top and acted as a top reversal. The uptrend was followed by a consolidation that reversed the existing trend from up to down.

3.3.2. Continuation Patterns

A **continuation pattern** is used to predict the resumption of a market trend that was in place prior to the formation of a pattern. From a supply and demand standpoint, a continuation pattern often indicates a change in ownership from one group of investors to another. For example, if a positive trend was in place prior to a pattern and then one group of investors begins selling, the negative impact on price is quickly offset by other investors buying, so the forces of supply and demand go back and forth in terms of their impact on price. But neither has an overwhelming advantage. This type of pattern is often called "a healthy correction" because the long-term market trend does not change and because while one set of investors is seeking to exit, they are replaced by another set of investors willing to take their positions at roughly the same share price. Continuation patterns can take various forms, including triangles, rectangles, and flags, which are detailed in the rest of this section.

3.3.2.1. Triangles

Triangle patterns are a type of continuation pattern. They come in three forms: symmetrical triangles, ascending triangles, and descending triangles. A triangle pattern forms as the range between high and low prices narrows, visually forming a triangle. In the older terminology, triangles were referred to as "coils" or "springs" because a triangle was considered analogous to a spring being wound up tighter and tighter, storing energy that would at some point be released. In a triangle, a trendline connects the highs and another trendline connects the lows. As the distance between the highs and lows narrows, the trendlines meet, forming a triangle.

In a daily price chart, a triangle pattern usually forms over a period of several weeks. In a weekly price chart, a triangle pattern can extend over several months.

In a symmetrical triangle, the trendline formed by the highs slopes down and the trendline formed by the lows slopes up, both at roughly the same angle, forming a symmetrical pattern.

Exhibit 22 contains a symmetrical triangle formed on the price chart of Diös Fastigheter AB during 2018. This triangle indicates that buyers are becoming more bullish while, simultaneously, sellers are becoming more bearish, so buyers and sellers are moving toward a market-clearing point of consensus. Because the sellers are often dominated by long investors exiting positions (as opposed to short sellers creating new short positions), the pressure to sell diminishes once the sellers have sold the security. Thus, the pattern ends with an ongoing move in the same direction as the trend that preceded it, either up or down.

EXHIBIT 22   Symmetrical Triangle: Diös Fastigheter AB Weekly Price Chart, March 2017–March 2019 (Swedish krona)

The possible price target is derived by calculating the difference in price from the two trendlines at the start of the triangle. Once the pattern is completed and the price breaches one of the trendlines that forms the triangle, the analyst expects the price to move by at least the amount of the calculated difference in price from the two trendlines at the start of the triangle above or below the trendline. Typically, price breaks out of a triangle pattern between halfway and three-quarters of the way through the pattern. The longer the triangle pattern persists, the more volatile and sustained the subsequent price movement is likely to be.

In an ascending triangle, as shown in Exhibit 23, the trendline connecting the high prices is horizontal and the trendline connecting the low prices forms an uptrend. This pattern means that market participants are selling the stock at the same price level over a period of time and putting a halt to rallies at the same price point, but buyers are getting more and more bullish and stepping in at increasingly higher prices to halt sell-offs instead of waiting for further price declines. An ascending triangle typically forms in an uptrend. However, there are several cases where an ascending triangle can form as a bottom reversal. The bullish implication of the pattern is more important than where the pattern forms on a price chart. The horizontal line represents sellers taking profits at around the same price point. The fact that the breakout pushes through the horizontal boundary is usually a bullish signal suggesting that buyers have overcome the selling pressure around the horizontal boundary. Irrespective of where the ascending triangle is identified, occasionally as a reversal chart pattern or more frequently as a continuation chart pattern, it should be considered a *consolidation* with bullish implications, and the breakout above the well-defined horizontal boundary should alert traders, investors, and analysts to act accordingly.

EXHIBIT 23   Ascending Triangle Pattern

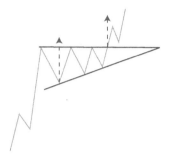

Exhibit 24 contains an ascending triangle formed on the price chart for bitcoin versus the US dollar during 2016. This ascending triangle indicates that buyers are becoming more bullish while sellers are acting around the same price level. The buyers are able to bid the price higher at every correction attempt. Eventually, the sellers lose the battle and the price breaks through the horizontal boundary. The prior trend was up, and the seven-month-long ascending triangle was a consolidation. A breakout above the 470 level completed the consolidation and resulted in a new uptrend. The ascending triangle acted as a bullish continuation chart pattern. The calculation for a chart pattern price target is similar to that for a symmetrical triangle. The possible price target is derived by calculating the difference in price from the two trendlines at the start of the triangle. Once the pattern is broken and the price breaks through one of the trendlines that form the triangle, the analyst will expect the price to move by at least the amount of the breakthrough above or below the trendline.

EXHIBIT 24   Ascending Triangle: Bitcoin/US Dollar Daily Price Chart, September 2015–June 2016 (US$)

In a descending triangle, as shown in Exhibit 25, the low prices form a horizontal trendline and the high prices form a series of lower and lower highs. Typically, a descending triangle will form in a downtrend. However, there are several situations in which a descending triangle acts as a top reversal. The bearish implication of this pattern is more important than where the pattern forms on a price chart. At some point during the rebounds from the horizontal support, sellers appear with enough supply to halt the countertrend recoveries each time they occur. Sellers push the price to lower levels at each rebound, thereby gaining the upper hand against the buyers who bid the price around the same level. The downward-sloping upper boundary of the descending triangle gives the pattern its bearish bias. Irrespective of where the descending triangle is identified, occasionally as a reversal chart pattern or more frequently as a continuation chart pattern, it should be considered a *consolidation* with bearish implications, and the breakdown below the well-defined horizontal boundary should alert traders, investors, and analysts to act accordingly.

EXHIBIT 25   Descending Triangle Pattern

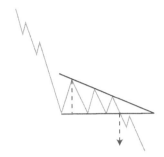

Exhibit 26 shows a descending triangle formed on the price chart of Sibanye Gold Ltd. during 2017. This descending triangle indicates that sellers are becoming more bearish while buyers are acting around the same price level. The sellers are able to push the price lower at every recovery attempt. Eventually, the buyers lose the battle and the price breaks down the horizontal boundary. The prior trend was down, and the yearlong descending triangle was a consolidation. The breakdown below the 1,365 level completed the consolidation and resulted in a downtrend. The descending triangle acted as a bearish continuation pattern. The calculation for a descending triangle pattern price target is slightly different with price charts in a downtrend, partly because of the zero boundary. It is important to note that chart pattern price objectives should be used as guidelines only. Price may reach the projected target, or it may fall short. It is always best to pick the most conservative approach. The possible price target is derived by calculating the percentage change from the two trendlines at the start of the triangle. Sibanye Gold formed a minor high at the 2,200 level. The horizontal boundary was around 1,365. This difference translates roughly into a 38% drop. Once the pattern is completed with a breach of the horizontal support, we can extend the price objective by another 38% on the downside. Please note that we are not taking the absolute price change. A 38% drop from the lower boundary of the descending triangle is equivalent to the 850 level.

Following breakdowns or breakouts, the price can pull back to the chart pattern boundary in an attempt to retest it. Sibanye Gold rebounded to test the previous support at the 1,365 level. The previous support became the new resistance—that is, there was a change in polarity.

EXHIBIT 26   Descending Triangle: Sibanye Gold Ltd. Weekly Price Chart, March 2016–May 2018 (South African rand)

3.3.2.2. Rectangle Pattern

A rectangle usually develops as a continuation pattern formed by two parallel trendlines, one connecting the high prices during the pattern and the other connecting the lows. Exhibit 27 shows two rectangle patterns. Like other patterns, the rectangle pattern is a graphical representation of what has been occurring in terms of collective market sentiment. The horizontal resistance line that forms the top of the rectangle shows that investors are repeatedly selling shares at a specific price level, bringing rallies to an end. The horizontal support line forming the bottom of the rectangle indicates that traders are repeatedly making large enough purchases at the same price level to reverse declines. The support level in a bullish rectangle is natural because the long-term trend in the market is bullish. The resistance line may simply represent investors taking profits. Conversely, in a bearish rectangle, the support level may represent investors buying the security. Again, the technician is not concerned with why a pattern has formed, only with the likely next price movement once the price breaks out of the pattern.

EXHIBIT 27   Rectangle Patterns

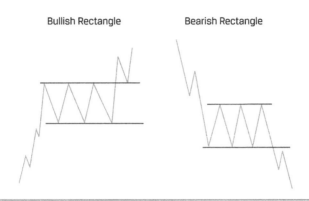

Rectangle patterns, due to their configuration, are much easier to identify on price charts than other classical chart patterns. Two horizontal boundaries and a clearly visible consolidation period on a price chart allows the analyst to detect the pause in trend periods with ease. This looks similar to a triple top pattern, but a rectangle pattern is a pause in a trend while a triple top pattern is a reversal of a trend.

Exhibit 28 shows a bullish rectangle pattern formed on the price chart of Vitrolife AB between 2017 and 2018. A 15-month-long sideways consolidation formed after a steady uptrend. After several tests of pattern boundaries both on the upside and on the downside, Vitrolife AB cleared the upper boundary that was acting as a strong resistance at the 142 level. The breakout was followed by a pullback, a retesting of the previous resistance. Several weeks of pullback eventually found support at the chart pattern boundary, and the uptrend resumed. The price objective was met in a matter of a few months. It is important to note that Vitrolife AB started a new strong uptrend following the lengthy consolidation. As a result, the price objective was exceeded during the uptrend. The longer the consolidation takes, the stronger the breakout is. The price objective is calculated by taking the width of the rectangle in absolute price terms and adding it to the breakout level.

EXHIBIT 28   Bullish Rectangle: Vitrolife AB Weekly Price Chart, December 2016–April 2019
(Swedish krona)

Exhibit 29 shows a bearish rectangle pattern formed on the price chart of Société Générale SA during 2018. A five-month-long sideways consolidation formed after a steady downtrend. After several tests of pattern boundaries, both on the upside and on the downside, Société Générale breached the lower boundary of the rectangle pattern that was acting as a strong support at the 35 level. This breakdown was followed by a pullback, a retesting of the previous support. A short pullback found resistance at the pattern boundary, and the downtrend resumed. The price objective was exceeded during the downtrend. The price objective is calculated by taking the width of the rectangle in percentage terms and projecting it lower from the breakdown level. The difference between the 38.5 and 35 levels translates into a 9% drop. Extending the price objective by 9% from the breakdown level of 35 gives us 31.85.

EXHIBIT 29   Bearish Rectangle: Société Générale SA Daily Price Chart, April 2018–December 2018
(Price in Euro)

3.3.2.3. *Flags and Pennants*

Flags and **pennants** are considered minor continuation patterns because they form over short periods of time—for example, on a daily price chart, typically over a week. However, flags or pennants may form on weekly price charts over slightly longer durations. Flags and pennants are similar and have the same uses. A flag is formed by parallel trendlines, in the same way that most countries' flags are rectangular and create a parallelogram. Typically, the trendlines slope in a direction opposite to the trend up to that time; for example, in an uptrend, the flag's trendlines slope down. A pennant formation is similar except that the trendlines converge to form a triangle. The key difference between a triangle and pennant is that a pennant is a short-term formation whereas a triangle is a long-term formation.

The expectation for both flags and pennants is that the trend will continue after the pattern in the same direction it was going prior to the pattern. The price is expected to change by at least the same amount as the price change from the start of the trend to the formation of the flag or pennant. In Exhibit 30, an uptrend begins at point A, which is €70.5. At point B, which is €111, a flag begins to form. The distance from point A to point B is €40.5. The flag ends at point C, which is €104.5. The price target is €104.5 plus €40.5, which is €145, the line labeled D.

As one added note, volume should ideally be high in the left "flagpole" part of a flag pattern, diminish as the flag forms, and then increase again on the subsequent breakout from the flag pattern. It is not unusual to see chart "gaps" near flag patterns, particularly during the continuation breakout period.

EXHIBIT 30   Flag Formation: Nemetschek SE, October 2016–May 2019 (Price in Euro)

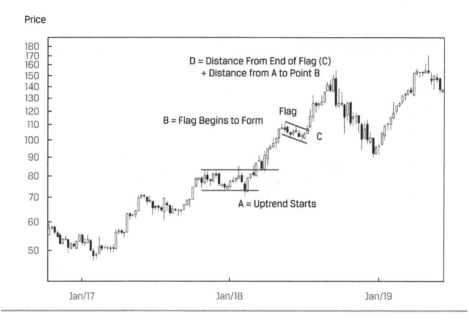

Price

Question 4

Which charting style takes into consideration *only* the closing prices?

a. Candlestick charts
b. Line charts
c. Bar charts

   B is correct. Line charts connect the closing prices of each period. Both candlestick charts and bar charts include each period's opening, high, low, and closing prices.

   Neither A nor C is the correct answer because both bar charts and candlestick charts take into consideration opening, high, low, and closing values.

Question 5

   A trader is looking at long-term charts and wants to exit some of his long positions. In doing so, he wants to confirm major trendline breaks to decide when to exit the positions. Which price scale will generate an earlier breakdown alert?

a. Linear scale
b. Logarithmic scale
c. Scale will not impact this

   B is correct. A trendline plotted on a logarithmic scale will be steeper in an uptrend when compared to the same trendline plotted on a linear scale. As a result, a reversal will breach the trendline earlier on a logarithmic scale than on a linear scale.

A is not correct because a trendline plotted on a linear scale will be less steep in an uptrend than the same trendline plotted on a logarithmic scale. As a result, a reversal will breach the trendline later on a linear scale than on a logarithmic scale.

C is not correct because scale will indeed impact the timing of either a breakdown below or a breakout above a trendline.

Question 6

The chart below shows the price of Amana Insurance on Saudi Arabia's Tadawul stock exchange between 2011 and 2015. Over the analyzed period, the stock formed three major classic chart patterns. Each one of those patterns (labeled 1, 2, and 3 on the chart) resulted in a strong trend period following the breakout. Which choice below lists the correct chart patterns in the correct order?

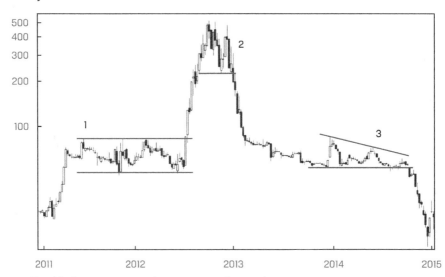

a.   Double bottom, rectangle, symmetrical triangle
b.   Rectangle, double top, descending triangle
c.   Rectangle, head and shoulder top, ascending triangle

B is correct.

The first chart pattern, which formed between 2011 and 2012, is a rectangle. A rectangle is a continuation pattern. Prior to the rectangle, the stock had been in an uptrend. The rectangle acted as a "rest" period in the strong uptrend. A breakout from the rectangle was followed by another strong upward move. In the second half of 2012, the price formed a double top. A double top is a bearish reversal and should come after an advance. The third chart pattern is a descending triangle. A descending triangle is a bearish continuation pattern. Prior to a descending triangle, the price should be in a downtrend. A descending triangle is usually a "rest" period in a steady downtrend. Following the breakdown, the stock resumed its downtrend.

A is incorrect because chart pattern 1 is not a double bottom. For a double bottom, the prior trend should be downward. In this case, the price moved upward prior to the consolidation. A double bottom is a reversal chart pattern that reverses an existing downtrend. Chart pattern 2 is not a rectangle. Chart pattern 3 is not a symmetrical triangle. A symmetrical triangle has two converging boundaries.

C is incorrect because chart pattern 2 is not a head and shoulders top. For a head and shoulders top, there needs to be three peaks, with the head being the highest and the two shoulders being lower than the head. Both head and shoulders and double top are reversal chart patterns, but in this case, pattern 2 can be classified as a double top due to its two peaks. Chart pattern 3 is not an ascending triangle. An ascending triangle has a horizontal upper boundary and an upward-sloping lower boundary. Both symmetrical triangles and ascending triangles can act as continuation patterns, but in this case, chart pattern 3 has a downward-sloping upper boundary and a horizontal lower boundary and is clearly a descending triangle.

Question 7

The chart below shows the Ericsson daily price chart between January 2018 and February 2019. The stock is listed on the Stockholm Stock Exchange, and the price is quoted in Swedish krona. Between October 2018 and February 2019, the Ericsson price chart formed a four-month-long symmetrical triangle. The stock is breaking out of a symmetrical triangle chart pattern, and the analyst wants to calculate the price target. Calculate the price target given the reference levels for the chart pattern boundaries.

a.   98.4
b.   94.9
c.   88.3

B is correct.

The price target is calculated by taking the width of the widest point in the symmetrical triangle and adding it to the breakout level at the upper boundary of the symmetrical triangle.

$$85.6 - 72.8 = 12.8$$

$$12.8 + 82.1 = 94.9$$

A is incorrect because it is not correct to add the width of the widest point (85.6 – 72.8 = 12.8) to the minor high where the symmetrical triangle started forming (12.8 + 85.6 = 98.4).

C is incorrect because it is not correct to add the width of the widest point (85.6 – 72.8 = 12.8) to the level of the lower chart pattern boundary (12.8 + 75.5 = 88.3).

4. TECHNICAL INDICATORS

g.   explain common technical indicators.

Vignette

Scene 3

A few days pass. You update your basic price chart for GLD and note that the price has been rising. The current price is the yellow point.

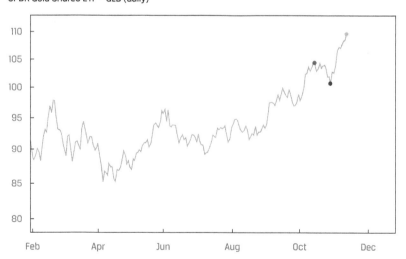

SPDR Gold Shares ETF – GLD (daily)

There is a knock on the door. The Head of Alternatives comes into your office and says, *"Hey, gold has rallied and is well above our purchase price. I'm thinking it might be time to sell and take some profits on the investment."*

You respond by saying, *"Remember, this investment in gold is a long-term asset allocation decision. We should not fall into the behavioral finance trap of letting greed guide our decisions."*

You decide to ask the technical analyst to again share her perspective.

The technical analyst prepares the following chart:

SPDR Gold Shares ETF – GLD (daily)

She also prepares the following comments:

- The symmetrical triangle price target has been met at the 109 level. The price target for the symmetrical triangle is calculated by taking the width of the chart pattern at the widest point and adding it to the breakout level.
- However, it is important to note that price can exceed calculated chart pattern price targets. The best way to capture long-term trends is either to use long-term averages to trail the price or to use trendlines to monitor the uptrend for a possible breakdown and a change in trend.

Then, she summarizes:

"So, even though the symmetrical triangle chart pattern price objective is met, the uptrend is still strong and is not violated. A new trendline (a steeper one) can be drawn, and the stop-loss can be raised to the most recent minor low of 101.15. In addition, the price continues to record higher lows, which is an indication of a steady uptrend."

You appreciate the additional perspective.

4.1. Technical Indicators

The technical analyst typically uses a variety of other technical indicators to supplement the basic information gleaned from chart patterns. A technical indicator is any measure based on price, market sentiment, or funds flow that can be used to predict changes in price. These mathematically calculated indicators often have a supply and demand underpinning. The moving average is the simplest of these techniques and has been used by statisticians to smooth data since the early 1900s.

4.1.1. Price-Based Indicators

Price-based indicators incorporate information contained in current and historical market prices. Indicators of this type range from simple (e.g., a moving average) to complex (e.g., a stochastic oscillator).

4.1.1.1. Moving Average

A **moving average** is the average of the closing prices of a security over a specified number of periods. Moving averages smooth out short-term price fluctuations, giving the technician a clearer image of market trends. Technicians commonly use a simple moving average, which weights each price equally in the calculation of the average price. Some technicians prefer to use an exponential moving average (also called an exponentially smoothed moving average), which gives the greatest weight to recent prices while giving exponentially less weight to older prices.

The number of data points included in the moving average depends on the intended use of the moving average. A 20-day moving average is commonly used because a month contains roughly 20 trading days. Also, a 60-day average is commonly used because it represents a quarter year (three months) of trading activity.

Moving averages can be used in conjunction with a price trend or in conjunction with one another. Moving averages are also used to determine support and resistance levels.

Because a moving average is less volatile than price, this tool can be used in several ways. First, whether a price is above or below its moving average is important. As a general guideline, if the price is above a moving average, the trend is up. If the price is below a moving average, the trend is down. Second, the distance between the moving-average line and the price is also significant. Once price begins to move back up toward its moving-average line (in a reversion to the mean), this line can serve as a resistance level. Similarly, when price begins to move down after an upward trend, the moving average can serve as a support level. Even though moving averages for certain time periods (e.g., 200 days) are discussed and widely followed in the financial media, there is no ideal moving-average periodicity. It is important to note that the analyst, trader, or fund manager should pick the time period that is the best fit for the trading/investment horizon.

Two or more moving averages can be used in conjunction. A 5-day moving average is often used as a proxy for short-term momentum, while a 20-day or 60-day moving average can be an indicator of the intermediate trend. The 5-day moving average breaking up through the longer-term moving average can be used as a buy signal, indicating that momentum and trend are changing to the upside, and conversely, the 5-day breaking down through the longer-term moving average can be used as a sell signal.

Longer-horizon investors may want to simply focus on two intermediate-term moving averages. Exhibit 31 shows the price chart of Microsoft Corporation on the NASDAQ stock exchange overlaid with 20-day and 60-day moving averages during 2018–2019. Note that the longer the time frame used in the creation of a moving average, the smoother and less volatile the line will become. Investors often use moving-average crossovers as buy or sell signals. When a short-term moving average (e.g., one month) crosses a longer-term average (e.g., three months) from underneath, this movement is considered bullish. This crossover is called a **bullish crossover**. Conversely, when a short-term moving average crosses a longer-term moving average from above, this movement is considered bearish. This crossover is called a **bearish crossover**. In the case shown in Exhibit 31, a trading strategy of buying on bullish crosses and selling on bearish crosses would have been profitable.

A widely followed moving-average crossover signal is the one that takes place between the 50-day moving average and the 200-day moving average. Financial networks (such as Bloomberg and Reuters) refer to this crossover signal as either a **golden cross** or a **death cross**. When the short-term (50-day) moving average crosses above the long-term (200-day) moving average, this movement is called a golden cross and is a bullish signal. Conversely, when the short-term average crosses below the long-term average, this movement is called a death cross and is a bearish signal.

Moving averages, while reducing noise by smoothing out day-to-day fluctuations, are useful for keeping the trader or investor on the right side of the price action and are key to trend-following strategies often used by commodity trading advisers (CTAs). When a short-term moving average is above the long-term average or the price is clearly above the average, traders and investors know that the trend in the given period of analysis is up, and therefore they should remain invested in the overall direction of the trend.

EXHIBIT 31   Daily Price Chart with 20-Day and 60-Day Moving Averages: Microsoft Corporation, April 2018–April 2019 (US$)

Moving averages are easy to construct, and simple trading rules can be created for using them. Computers can optimize the time lengths to set when using two moving averages. This optimization may take the form of changing the number of days included in each moving average or adding filter rules, such as waiting several days after a trade signal is given, or waiting until a minimum penetration distance is achieved, to make a trade. Reasons for optimization include the desire to minimize false signals and thereby manage capital drawdowns (maximize gains and minimize losses). Once the moving average is optimized, even if a profitable trading system is devised for that security, the strategy is unlikely to work for other securities, especially if they are dissimilar. Also, as market conditions change, a previously optimized trading system may no longer work. For that reason, one should not focus too much on the optimization of moving averages because this practice risks "overfitting" past data that may not necessarily repeat in the future. Moving averages should be used as trend filters.

When the price is above the moving average, this scenario suggests that the trend is upward. When the price is below the average, this scenario should warn the analyst of further weakness. When the short-term moving average is above the long-term moving average, the analyst should be alert for the continuation of that uptrend. When the short-term moving average is below the long-term average, this scenario should signal caution. It may suggest that any initial long exposure should be closed and that the investor should step to the sidelines in expectation of further weakness.

4.1.1.2. Bollinger Bands

Market veteran John Bollinger combined his knowledge of technical analysis with his knowledge of statistics to create an indicator called **Bollinger Bands**. Bollinger Bands consist of a moving average (middle band), a higher line (upper band) representing the moving average plus a set number of standard deviations from the average price (for the same number of periods used to calculate the moving average), and a lower line (lower band) that is a moving average minus the same number of standard deviations. This indicator can help define a statistically reasonable range that the market is expected to trade within. Exhibit 32 depicts Bollinger Bands for Microsoft Corporation.

EXHIBIT 32   Bollinger Bands Using 20-Day Moving Average and Two Standard Deviations: Microsoft Corporation Daily Price Chart, September 2018–April 2019 (US$)

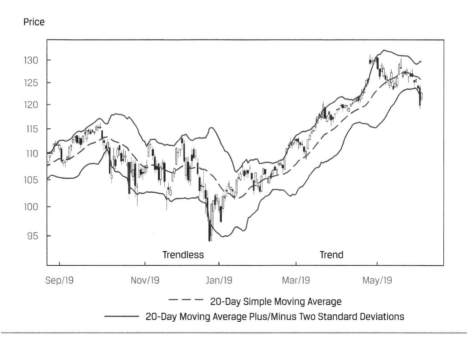

The more volatile the security being analyzed becomes, the wider the range becomes between the two outer lines or bands. Like moving averages, Bollinger Bands can be used to create trading strategies that can be easily computerized and tested. A common use is as a contrarian strategy, in which the investor sells when a security price reaches the upper band and buys the security back when the price reaches either the middle band (if within a perceived uptrend) or the lower band (when within a perceived range). This strategy assumes that the security price will stay within the bands. During trendless periods, this strategy works well. This type of strategy is likely to lead to a large number of trades, but it also limits risk because the trader can quickly exit unprofitable trades. In the event of a sharp price move, investors might instead buy on a significant breakout above the upper band because a major breakout would imply a change in trend that is likely to persist for some time.

The long-term investor would sell on a significant breakdown below the lower band in an attempt to limit downside risk. In this strategy, statistical significance would be defined as breaking above or below the band by a certain percentage (say, 5% or 10%) and/or for a certain period of time (say, a week for a daily price chart). Again, such rules can easily be computerized and tested. In the example of Microsoft, October 2018–February 2019 was a trendless period. A death cross took place in October 2018, and the stock remained choppy within a wide trading range. During this period, a trader could have applied the Bollinger Band strategy to buy at the touch of the lower band and sell at the touch of the upper band. This strategy would have worked well until the stock experienced a change in trend.

In February 2019, Microsoft experienced a bullish moving-average crossover resulting in a golden cross. Following the bullish signal, the price touched the upper Bollinger Band, suggesting a continuation of the uptrend. Selling at the touch of the upper band and waiting for prices to return to the lower band was not the right strategy; buying at the touch of the middle band would have worked better.

4.1.1.2.1. *Bollinger Band Width Indicator*

Bollinger Band width is an indicator derived from Bollinger Bands. Band width measures the percentage difference between the upper band and the lower band. Band width decreases as Bollinger Bands narrow and increases as Bollinger Bands widen. Because Bollinger Bands are based on standard deviation, falling band width reflects decreasing volatility and rising band width reflects increasing volatility.

$$\text{Bollinger Band width} = [(\text{Upper band} - \text{Lower band})/\text{Middle band}] \times 100$$

When calculating band width, the first step is to subtract the value of the lower band from the value of the upper band. The result is the absolute difference. This difference is then divided by the value of the middle band to normalize the value. This normalized band width can then be compared across different time frames or with the band width values for other securities.

Band width is relative. Band width values should be gauged relative to prior band width values over a period of time. It is important to use an adequate look-back period to define the band width range for a particular ETF, index, or stock.

Bollinger Band width is best known for identifying a "squeeze." A squeeze occurs when volatility falls to a very low level, as evidenced by the narrowing bands.

The theory is that periods of low volatility are followed by periods of high volatility. Relatively narrow band width can foreshadow a significant advance or decline. After a squeeze, a price surge and a subsequent band break signal the start of a new move. A new advance starts with a squeeze and a subsequent break above the upper band. A new decline starts with a squeeze and a subsequent break below the lower band.

EXHIBIT 33   Bollinger Band Width and Squeeze: Diös Fastigheter AB, March 2017–March 2019 Weekly Scale Price Chart (Swedish krona)

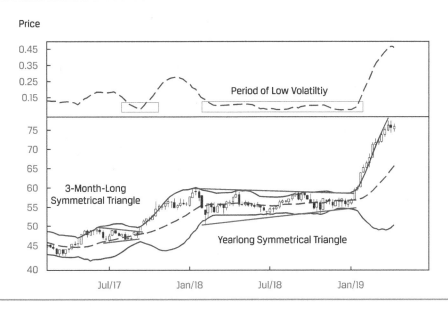

Exhibit 33 shows the Diös Fastigheter AB price chart that was featured earlier in this chapter (see Exhibit 22). Every time the stock entered into a consolidation period, the volatility dropped to low levels. Low volatility was an indication of a possible high-volatility period to come. Low volatility begets high volatility, and vice versa. A breakout from low-volatility conditions can be seen on the Bollinger Band width indicator: Bollinger Bands start expanding, and Bollinger Band width starts rising from extremely low levels.

When combined with classical charting tools (such as a breakout above a predefined chart pattern boundary), Bollinger Bands have significant value. A breakout from a consolidation period at a time of historical low volatility suggests that the trend period that follows will have the strength to resume toward much higher levels. The two breakouts shown in Exhibit 33, one from a three-month-long symmetrical triangle and the other from a yearlong symmetrical triangle, both started from extreme low-volatility conditions.

4.1.2. Momentum Oscillators

One of the key challenges in using indicators overlaid on a price chart is the difficulty of discerning changes in market movements that are out of the ordinary. **Momentum oscillators** are one tool intended to alleviate this problem. They are constructed from the rate of change in price data, but they are calculated so that they either oscillate between a low and a high (typically 0 and 100) or oscillate around a number (such as 0 or 100). Because of this construction, extreme highs and lows are easily discernible. These extremes can be viewed as graphic representations of market sentiment when selling or buying activity is more aggressive than has been historically typical. Because they are price based, momentum oscillators can be analyzed by using the same tools technicians use to analyze price, such as the concepts of trend, support, and resistance. It is important to note that indicators that are derived from price will lag price. An analyst will be able to calculate the latest value for the indicator only after the relevant day's, week's, or month's price data are recorded.

Technicians also look for **convergence** or **divergence** between oscillators and price. Convergence occurs when the oscillator moves in the same manner as the security being analyzed, and divergence occurs when the oscillator moves differently from the security. For example, when price reaches a new high, this sign is considered bullish, but if the momentum oscillator being used does not also reach a new high at the same time, the result is divergence. Divergence is considered to be an early warning of weakness, an indication that (in this case) the uptrend may soon end because momentum (or the rate of change in prices) is actually waning despite the new highs.

Momentum oscillators should be used in conjunction with an understanding of the existing market (price) trend. Oscillators alert a trader to **overbought** or **oversold** conditions. In overbought conditions, market sentiment is considered unsustainably bullish. In oversold conditions, market sentiment is considered unsustainably bearish. In other words, the oscillator *range* must be judged separately for every security. Some securities may experience wide variations, and others may experience only minor variations.

Oscillators have three main uses:

1. Oscillators can be used to determine the strength of a trend. Extreme overbought levels are warning signals for uptrends, and extreme oversold levels are warning signals for downtrends. We should note, however, that occasionally an indicator can stay overbought or oversold for an extended period of time. As a result, just because the indicator reached an overbought level doesn't mean we should anticipate a sudden change in trend. Uptrends and downtrends can sometimes resume despite overbought/oversold readings on oscillators.

2. When oscillators reach historically high or low levels, they may be signaling a pending trend reversal. For oscillators that move above and below zero, crossing the zero level signals a change in the direction of the trend. For oscillators that move above and below 100, crossing the 100 level signals a change in the direction of the trend.

3. In a trendless market, oscillators can be used for short-term trading decisions—that is, to sell at overbought levels and to buy at oversold levels.

4.1.2.1. Rate of Change Oscillator

The rate of change (ROC) oscillator is a pure momentum oscillator and is sometimes referred to as simply the momentum oscillator. The ROC oscillator is calculated by taking the most recent closing price, subtracting the closing price from a date that is a set number of days in the past, and multiplying the result by 100:

$$M = (V - Vx) \times 100,$$

where

M = momentum oscillator value
V = most recent closing price
Vx = closing price x days ago, typically 10 days

When the ROC oscillator crosses zero in the same direction as the direction of the trend, this movement is considered a buy or sell signal. For example, if the ROC oscillator crosses into positive territory during an uptrend, this movement is a buy signal. If it enters into negative territory during a downtrend, the crossover is considered a sell signal. The technician will ignore crossovers in opposition to the trend because when using oscillators, the technician must *always first* take into account the general trend.

An alternative method of constructing this oscillator is to set it to oscillate above and below 100, instead of 0, as follows:

$$M = \frac{V}{Vx} \times 100$$

This approach is shown in Exhibit 34 for Microsoft Corporation.

EXHIBIT 34   ROC Oscillator with 100 as Midpoint: Microsoft Corporation, April 2018–April 2019 (US$)

In Exhibit 34, the ROC oscillator for Microsoft stock, traded on the NASDAQ stock exchange, is set to move around 100, and *x* is 12 days. An extreme high means that the stock has posted its highest gain in any 12-day period, and an extreme low reading means it has posted its greatest loss over any 12-day period. When investors bid up the price of a security too rapidly, the indication is that sentiment may be unduly bullish and the market may be overbought. Exhibit 34 shows that overbought levels of the ROC oscillator coincide with temporary highs in the stock price. So, those levels would have been signals to sell the stock. We analyzed the moving-average crossovers and the trend and consolidation periods in preceding sections of this chapter. It is important to incorporate that information in analyzing the price chart. During trend periods, we can see that the ROC oscillator moves approximately between 100 and 110. So once the uptrend is confirmed with a bullish crossover, we can use the ROC oscillator to time the minor peaks and troughs in the uptrend. A good strategy would be to take profits as the ROC approaches the 110 level and initiate new long positions as it falls back to the 100 level. During a trendless period (consolidation), we can see that the ROC oscillator moves in a wide range between 80 and 110. Following the bearish crossover, we should be aware that the trend period might be over and that we might see choppy price action. The timing of entry and exit might be more difficult in such a market environment.

However, with the help of Bollinger Bands and ROC oscillators, the analyst can capture overbought/oversold levels in the consolidation range. In the beginning of 2019, the ROC oscillator once again climbed above the 100 level, and the trend was confirmed with a bullish crossover, suggesting a new uptrend. In February 2019, the ROC oscillator found support around 100, the low level for the indicator during an uptrend. It was a good time to initiate a long position as the stock was entering a new uptrend period. In previous sections, we have seen that the Microsoft price also touched the upper Bollinger Band following the bullish crossover signal and generated a buy signal based on the Bollinger Band strategy. The other notable aspect of Exhibit 34 is the divergence when the share price hit a new high in October 2018 but the ROC oscillator did not reach its July high. This divergence would have been a bearish signal and would have been interpreted to mean that, although the share price hit a new high, market momentum was actually lower than it had been previously. In itself, this information would not have been enough to warrant selling the shares because an uptrend in price was still in place, but it alerted the technician to the fact that the trend might end soon. The technician could then look for further indications of the trend's end—such as a moving-average crossover to the downside—and with such confirmation, decide to sell the stock.

4.1.2.2. Relative Strength Index

Another tool often used to measure momentum is a **relative strength index (RSI)**, which is computed over a rolling time period. The RSI graphically compares a security's gains with its losses over the set period. The creator of the RSI, Welles Wilder, proposed a 14-day time period, and this is the period used by most technical analysis software. The technician should understand that this variable can be changed and that the optimal time range should be determined by how the technician intends to use the RSI information. Factors that influence the selection of a time period for the RSI are similar to those that influence the selection of a time period for moving averages.

The RSI is a momentum oscillator and provides information on whether or not an asset is overbought—in other words, whether an asset has advanced too quickly relative to a chance to digest recent advances. The formula is as follows:

$$RSI = 100 - \frac{100}{1 + RS}$$

where

$$RS = \frac{\sum(\text{Up changes for the period under consideration})}{\sum(\text{Down changes for the period under consideration})}$$

The RSI indicator is primarily used to analyze the inner momentum of a security. The analysis is performed by identifying divergences. A positive divergence takes place when the security price records a new low but the RSI records a higher low. This scenario suggests that while the price is reaching a new low, the inner momentum is improving; in other words, the selling pressure is decreasing.

A negative divergence takes place when the security price reaches a new high but the RSI fails to reach a new high. This scenario suggests that while the price is reaching a new high, the inner momentum is deteriorating; in other words, buying pressure is decreasing. Divergences are early signs of reversal that may foreshadow and anticipate a subsequent moving-average crossover reversal.

Note: The RSI is not to be confused with the "relative strength analysis" charting method. The RSI measures the internal strength of a single asset in terms of a ratio of the magnitude of "up days" to the magnitude of "down days" of that asset across a given period, whereas relative strength analysis compares the ratio of two security prices plotted over time or the relative performance of two assets.

EXHIBIT 35   Candlestick Chart with RSI: WTI Light Crude Oil First-Month Continuation Futures Price, June 2014–April 2019 (US$)

The candlestick chart of the WTI Light Crude Oil futures price in Exhibit 35 illustrates several aspects of the use of an RSI. For example, because the RSI oscillator was lower than 30 in the beginning of 2015, so the commodity was oversold at that time, a simple reading of the chart might have led to the conclusion that the trader should buy the commodity because an "oversold" indicator reading suggests the price is likely to rebound in the near term. However, this decision would have resulted in further losses as the price slid to new lows. A more careful technical interpretation that took the general trend into account would have indicated that the commodity was in a downtrend, as can be seen by the trendline and the fact that the price was trading below its long-term average, so further RSI readings below 30 could be expected. In other words, using the RSI alone may identify short-term reversal levels but risk early bottom-picking or top-picking that can still prove problematic. Buying at the time of an oversold condition might not be the best timing tool for trend reversals. Likewise, an overbought reading above the 80 level alone is not sufficient to conclude that price will reverse. It is best to combine the momentum indicator with elements of trend analysis, such as a trendline break.

Even if a stock, commodity, or currency is showing an oversold reading on the RSI, there is often not enough information to conclude that it is a good time to buy that security. In the second half of 2015, WTI reached a new low, but this time the RSI didn't reach a new low. Again, just because we have seen the first positive divergence (RSI lows labeled 1 and 2 in Exhibit 35) doesn't mean that a trend reversal is taking place. We need to see confirmation of the change in trend in the form of a breach of a trendline or a long-term average (confirmation by price action). In the beginning of 2016, the WTI price reached a new low but the RSI generated its second positive divergence. It was after this low that the price managed to breach the downtrend line and the long-term moving average on the upside, confirming a change in trend. A technician should be patient enough to wait for such periods of clear divergence late in the trend of a given asset.

Similarly, the top that formed during 2018 on the WTI price chart followed the same sequence of divergences. This time, the price continued to reach new highs but the RSI warned of a possible eventual change in trend direction. Only after the second negative divergence (RSI peaks labeled 2 and 3 in Exhibit 35) did the price of WTI break down the trendline (confirmation by price action) and the long-term average, resulting in a change in trend.

4.1.2.3. Stochastic Oscillator

The **stochastic oscillator** is a momentum indicator that compares a particular closing price of a security to a range of its prices over a certain period of time. The stochastic oscillator is based on the observation that in uptrends, prices tend to close at or near the high end of their recent range and in downtrends, they tend to close near the low end. The logic behind these patterns is that if the shares of a stock are constantly being bid up during the day but then lose value by the close, continuation of the rally is doubtful. If sellers have enough supply to overwhelm buyers, the rally is suspect. If a stock rallies during the day and is able to hold on to some or most of those gains by the close, that sign is bullish.

The stochastic oscillator oscillates between 0 and 100 and has a default 14-day period, which may be adjusted for the situation, as we discussed for the RSI. The oscillator is composed of two lines, called %K and %D, that are calculated as follows:

$$\%K = 100\left(\frac{C - L14}{H14 - L14}\right)$$

where

C = the latest closing price
$L14$ = the lowest price in the past 14 days
$H14$ = the highest price in the past 14 days
and where
%D = the average of the last three %K values calculated daily

Analysts should think about %D in the same way they would a long-term moving-average line in conjunction with a short-term line. That is, %D, because it is the average of three %K values, is the slower-moving, smoother line and is called the signal line. And %K is the faster-moving line. The %K value means that the latest closing price (C) was in the %K percentile of the low–high range ($L14$ to $H14$).

The default oversold–overbought range for the stochastic oscillator is based on reading the signal line relative to readings of 20 and 80. The shorter the time frame is, the more volatile the oscillator becomes and the more false signals it generates.

The stochastic oscillator should be used with other technical tools, such as trend analysis, pattern analysis, and RSI analysis. If several methods suggest the same conclusion, the trader has convergence (or confirmation), but if they give conflicting signals, the trader has divergence, which is a warning signal suggesting that further analysis is necessary.

The absolute level of the two lines should be considered in light of their normal range. Movements or changes in trend in the middle of an 80–20 indexed range can most often be deemed short-term noise. To a technician, movements above this range indicate an overbought security and are considered bearish; movements below this range indicate an oversold security and are considered bullish. But it is important to note that an overbought indicator doesn't warrant selling the security. Likewise, an oversold reading is not an indication to buy. One should generally look for changes in trend with the help of the %K line changing direction or a trendline break or a breach of moving average.

Crossovers of the two lines can also give trading signals, the same way crossovers of two moving averages give signals. When %K moves from below the %D line to above it, this move is considered a bullish short-term trading signal; conversely, when %K moves from above the %D line to below it, this movement is considered bearish. In practice, a trader can use technical analysis software to adjust trading rules and optimize the calculation of the stochastic oscillator for a particular security and investment purpose (e.g., short-term trading or long-term investing). While optimization can help to achieve better results for a certain period, as conditions change, the parameters might need to be revised.

The reason technicians use historical data to test their trading rules and find the optimal parameters for each security is that each security is different and may have its own natural rhythm. The group of market participants actively trading also differs from security to security. Just as each person has a different personality, so do groups of people. In effect, the group of active market participants trading each security is imparting its personality on the trading activity for that security. As this group changes over time, the ideal parameters for a particular security may change. The choice of either optimizing the indicator or following the default set of parameters is a continuous trade-off.

There are benefits as well as disadvantages to optimization. Exhibit 36 provides a good example of how the stochastic oscillator can be used together with trend analysis. The exhibit provides the daily price chart and stochastic oscillator for Total SA, which is traded on the Paris stock exchange, from July 2018 through April 2019. Note that during the sideways movement between July and October, the stochastic oscillator moved between 20 and 80 from one boundary to the other. It was one of the best times to trade the stock with the help of overbought/oversold conditions identified by the oscillator. Each time the oscillator reversed from the 80 level, it provided a valid sell signal, and each time it reversed from the 20 level, it provided a valid buy signal. These reversals coincided with reversals from horizontal support/resistance levels on the price chart. When the downtrend started in October, the stochastic oscillator reached oversold levels and hardly recovered above 50. Technicians should be able to identify the trend period (sideways, upward, or downward) and then adjust their expectations as to the levels the indicator can reach. During the downtrend, the oversold level remained around 20 but the overbought level shifted down to 50. Selling the rally around the 50 level in the established downtrend proved to be a good strategy. When the uptrend started at the beginning of January, the stochastic oscillator reached overbought levels. However, during the uptrend, the oscillator didn't reach oversold levels. While the overbought level remained around 80, the oversold level during the uptrend shifted up to 50. Buying the pullback when the indicator reached the 50 level proved to be a good strategy.

EXHIBIT 36   Daily Price Chart and Stochastic Oscillator: Total SA, July 2018–April 2019 (€)

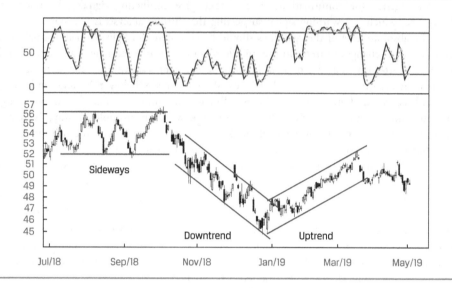

4.1.2.4. Moving-Average Convergence/Divergence Oscillator (MACD)

The **moving-average convergence/divergence oscillator** is commonly referred to as the MACD. The MACD is the difference between short-term and long-term moving averages of the security's price. The MACD is constructed by calculating two lines, the MACD line and the signal line:

- The MACD line is the difference between two exponentially smoothed moving averages, generally over periods of 12 and 26 days.
- The signal line is the exponentially smoothed average of the MACD line, generally over 9 days.

The indicator oscillates around zero and has no upper or lower limit. Rather than using a set overbought–oversold range for the MACD, the analyst compares the current level with the historical performance of the oscillator for a particular security to determine when a security is out of its normal sentiment range.

The MACD is used in technical analysis in three ways:

1. to note crossovers of the MACD line and the signal line, as discussed for moving averages and the stochastic oscillator. Crossovers of the two lines may indicate a change in trend.
2. to look for times when the MACD is outside its normal range for a given security.
3. to use trendlines on the MACD itself. When the MACD is trending in the same direction as price, this pattern is in convergence, and when the two are trending in opposite directions, the pattern is in divergence.

Exhibit 37 shows a weekly price chart for Palladium (at the top) with the MACD oscillator for August 2016 through April of 2019. The chart shows the effectiveness of MACD crossover signals when used in conjunction with trendline breakouts. This example highlights once again the importance of confirming any indicator signal with price action. During the uptrend between October 2016 and December 2018, the MACD generated several crossover signals. The early 2018 crossover signal was confirmed by a breakdown of the uptrend channel. Similarly, the trend reversal that took place in the last quarter of 2018 was confirmed by both the MACD crossover signal and a trend channel breakout. In August 2018, we can also identify the long-legged doji candlestick that marked the bottom. The uptrend that started in the last quarter of 2018 pushed the MACD to historical high levels when compared with previous readings. The reversal not only generated a MACD crossover but also broke down the upward trend channel.

EXHIBIT 37   MACD and Weekly Price Chart: Palladium, August 2016–April 2019 (US$)

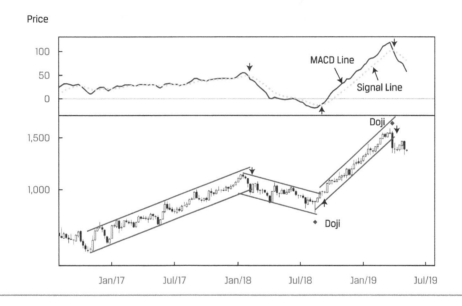

4.1.3. Sentiment Indicators

Sentiment indicators attempt to gauge investor activity for signs of increasing bullishness or bearishness. Sentiment indicators come in two forms—investor polls and calculated statistical indexes.

4.1.3.1. Calculated Statistical Indexes

Statistical indexes are sentiment indicators that are calculated from market data, such as security prices. The two most commonly used are derived from the options market; they are the put/call ratio and the volatility index. Additionally, many analysts look at margin debt and short interest.

The **put/call ratio** is the volume of put options traded divided by the volume of call options traded for a particular financial instrument. Investors who buy put options on a security are presumably bearish, and investors who buy call options are presumably bullish. The volume of call options traded is greater than the volume of put options over time, so the put/call ratio is normally below 1.0. The ratio is considered to be a contrarian indicator, meaning that higher values of put volume relative to call volume are considered bullish and lower values are considered bearish. But the ratio's usefulness as a contrarian indicator is limited, except at extreme low or high levels (relative to the historical trading level) of the put/ call ratio for a particular financial instrument. The actual value of the put/call ratio and its normal range will be different for each security or market, so no standard definitions of overbought and oversold levels exist.

The **CBOE Volatility Index (VIX)** is a measure of near-term market volatility calculated by the Chicago Board Options Exchange. Since 2003, the VIX has been calculated from option prices on the stocks in the S&P 500. The VIX rises when market participants become fearful of an impending market decline. These participants bid up the price of puts, and the result is an increase in the VIX level. Technicians use the VIX in conjunction with trend, pattern, and oscillator tools, and it is interpreted from a contrarian perspective. When other indicators suggest that the market is oversold and the VIX is at an extreme high, this combination is considered bullish. Exhibit 38 shows the VIX from March 2005 to April 2019.

EXHIBIT 38   VIX, March 2005–April 2019

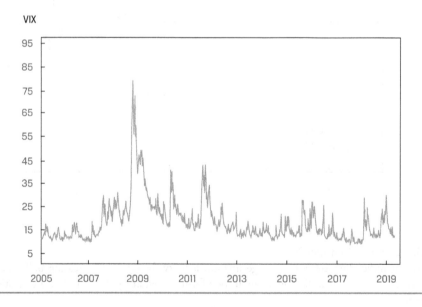

Margin debt is also often used as an intermediate- to long-term indication of sentiment. As a group, investors have a history of buying near market tops and selling at the bottom. When the market is rising and indexes reach new highs, investors are motivated to buy more equities in the hope of participating in the market rally. A margin account permits an investor to borrow part of the investment cost from the brokerage firm. This debt magnifies the gains or losses resulting from the investment.

Investor psychology plays an important role in the concept of margin debt as an indicator. When stock margin debt is increasing, investors are aggressively buying, and stock prices will move higher because of increased demand. Eventually, the margin traders use all of their available credit, so their buying power (and, therefore, demand) decreases, which fuels a price decline. Falling prices may trigger margin calls and forced selling, which drive prices even lower.

Brokerage firms must report activity in their customers' margin accounts, so keeping track of borrowing behavior is relatively easy. Exhibit 39 provides a 22-year comparison of margin debt with the S&P 500. The correlation is striking: Rising margin debt is generally associated with a rising index level, and falling margin debt is associated with a falling index level. In fact, for the two decades shown in Exhibit 39, the correlation coefficient between the level of margin debt and the S&P 500 is 80.2%. When margin debt peaked in the summer of 2007, the market also topped out. Margin debt dropped sharply during the latter part of 2008 as the subprime crisis took the market down. Investors began to use borrowed funds again in the first half of 2009, when heavily discounted shares became increasingly attractive. Margin debt was still well below the average of the last decade, but in this instance, the upturn would be viewed as a bullish sign by advocates of this indicator. Over the past decade, both margin debt and the S&P 500 have climbed to new highs. This outcome has been bullish for the market in the short term but is concerning in the longer term.

EXHIBIT 39   Margin Debt in US Market vs. S&P 500, 1997–2019

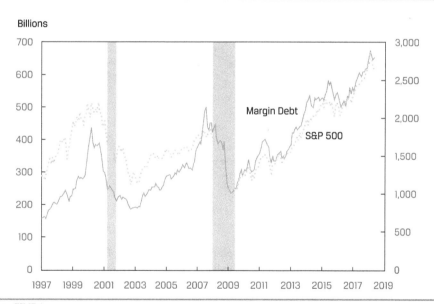

Source: FINRA.

Question 8

A trader wants to buy WTI Crude Oil futures. She wants to build a sizable position and is willing to enter a long position after the uptrend is underway. In other words, the trader aims to invest once the uptrend is established. For this reason, the trader wants to utilize moving-average crossovers as a trend filter and wants to buy after the bullish crossover. In addition to utilizing moving averages, she wants to utilize momentum as a timing tool to enter long positions. The trader knows that in uptrends, a pullback to the 100 level on the momentum indicator offers a buying opportunity. Find three points on the chart that meet those two criteria for a buying opportunity: an uptrend and a pullback to the 100 level.

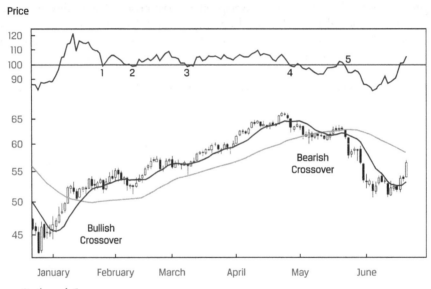

a. 3, 4, and 5
b. 1, 4, and 5
c. 1, 3, and 4

Answer: C. The bullish crossover took place in the middle of January 2019. At the time, the momentum indicator was above 110—an overbought level. Later, the indicator pulled back to the 100 level. The points labeled 1, 2, 3, and 4 were all buying opportunities in a steady uptrend. Even though point 4 met both criteria, the move failed to materialize into a new uptrend, and the indicator fell below the 100 level, indicating a change in trend. Weakness in momentum was followed by a bearish crossover on the moving averages.

Neither A nor B is the correct answer because at point 5, the momentum indicator was pulling back to the 100 level but the moving averages had already had a bearish crossover, suggesting a downtrend. All points except 5 were buying opportunities in an uptrend.

Question 9

When a stock price moves to a new high but the momentum indicator records a lower high, the analyst labels the divergence as a:

a. positive divergence.
b. negative divergence.
c. positive reversal divergence.

Answer: B. A negative divergence takes place when a stock price moves to a new high but the momentum indicator fails to keep up with the price and records a lower high.

A is not the correct answer because a positive divergence takes place when a stock moves to a new low but the indicator records a higher low.

C is not the correct answer because a positive reversal divergence takes place when the indicator reaches a new low but the price fails to record a new low.

Question 10

A trader wants to take a long position in WTI Crude Oil. He wants to utilize the RSI indicator to check for positive divergence as an early trend reversal signal but also wants to time his entry with a chart pattern breakout signal. Which number on the chart below is sufficient to make a trade decision based on the above requirements?

a. 1
b. 2
c. 3

Answer: C. At point 3, the RSI has already reached an oversold level, rebounded, and formed a positive divergence. Meanwhile, the price holds at its previous low, forming a double bottom. Double bottom breakout confirmation takes place when the price breaches the neckline at point 3.

A is not the correct answer because at point 1, the price is in a steady downtrend and the indicator is at an oversold level. The price can continue to fall, and the indicator can remain in oversold territory.

B is not the correct answer because at point 2, the price is testing a support (previous low) and the indicator is showing a positive divergence. However, we don't have confirmation on the price chart in the form of a reversal chart pattern completion or a downtrend breakout. The trend reversal confirmation takes place at point 3.

Question 11

The chart below shows the price of bitcoin versus the US dollar between August 2015 and December 2015. In November 2015, bitcoin had a sharp advance, which turned into a buying frenzy and reached the 500 level. After the sharp advance, the price of bitcoin sold off to test 295. In late 2015, the bitcoin/US dollar price chart tested the November 2015 highs. During the uptrend between November and December, the stochastic oscillator reached overbought levels. An overbought indicator can remain overbought while price continues to move higher. Based on support/resistance levels and the stochastic oscillator, what would be your strategy at point 3?

a Buy more, because the price is in an uptrend and the indicator is overbought.
b Sell, because the price has reached an important resistance-level overbought reading on the stochastic oscillator.
c Sell, because the indicator has formed its fifth negative divergence.

Answer: B. The stochastic oscillator can reach overbought levels and stay in the overbought range (above 80). This scenario doesn't mean one should sell because of the overbought reading. Point 1 is an overbought reading on the stochastic oscillator, but the price is still far from the strong resistance area. Point 2 is similar. The stochastic oscillator is at an overbought level once again, but the price is below the strong resistance. At point 3, price meets both conditions: an overbought reading on the oscillator and a test of the strong resistance level. From a risk/reward perspective, it is a better decision to sell at the resistance with overbought conditions.

A is not the correct answer because the price of bitcoin is reaching the resistance level formed by the minor high at the 470 level. The test of the resistance takes place after the stochastic oscillator reaches an overbought level. The probability of a reversal is higher at point 3 than at 1 and 2. As a result, buying more bitcoin at the resistance is not the best strategy.

C is not the correct answer because the indicator hasn't formed its fifth negative divergence. Between the minor highs of points 2 and 3, the indicator forms its first negative divergence.

Question 12

A trader is looking to trade breakout opportunities as she thinks the cyclical nature of the markets suggests a strong trend period approaching. She knows that volatility is cyclical and that low volatility begets high volatility and vice versa. She opens charts with three different indicators: Bollinger Band width, the MACD, and the RSI. Which indicator and condition will guide her in identifying breakout opportunities by capturing low-volatility conditions?

a.   The MACD line crossing over the signal line when the indicator is below the zero level
b.   The RSI crossing above the 30 level after generating a positive divergence
c.   The Bollinger Band width indicator reaching its lowest level over a three-year look-back period

Answer: C. Bollinger Band width measures volatility with the help of Bollinger Bands. Band width is narrow and the indicator reaches low levels when price goes through a low-volatility condition. Low-volatility periods are usually followed by high-volatility periods, and these are usually trend periods that emerge from lengthy consolidations.

Neither A nor B is the correct answer because both the MACD and the RSI are price-based trend indicators. They don't have a volatility component in their calculation.

5. APPLICATIONS TO PORTFOLIO MANAGEMENT

h.   describe principles of intermarket analysis;
i.   explain technical analysis applications to portfolio management.

Vignette

Scene 4

A few days pass, and the Deputy CIO is back from her Antarctic vacation. She thanks you for your efforts while she was away. She mentions that while viewing the penguins in Antarctica, she was thinking that although the gold investment was put in place for long-term asset allocation, she should find out about any tactical asset allocation opportunities. She asks you to look at gold versus oil. Before doing an in-depth analysis, you ask the technical analyst to provide perspective using intermarket analysis.

The technical analyst prepares the following chart:

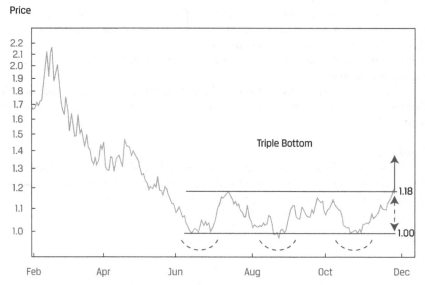

She also prepares the following comments:

- For ease of understanding, the GLD/WTI ratio is indexed to 1.0 at the low in June 2009.
- Between February and June, GLD underperformed WTI. However, since June 2009, the GLD/WTI ratio has started forming a bottom. The GLD/WTI ratio has fluctuated between the 1.0 level and the 1.18 level.
- The sideways consolidation of the GLD/WTI ratio formed a triple bottom. A triple bottom can act as a major reversal and could result in a strong outperformance period for GLD.

Then, she summarizes:

"So, now is not the time to allocate from GLD to WTI because GLD could start outperforming WTI. In addition, a breakout on the relative performance chart of GLD/WTI would put the gold price on the radar of many investors."

You thank the technical analyst for her support. You are also glad that you had a chance to work with the technical analyst and feel that you better understand the role technical analysis can play in investment management. You are also happy that the Deputy CIO is back in the office! Well, mostly...

5.1. Principles of Intermarket Analysis

Intermarket analysis is a field within technical analysis that combines analyses of major categories of securities—namely, equities, bonds, currencies, and commodities—to identify market trends and possible inflections in a trend. Intermarket analysis also looks at industry subsectors and their relationship to sectors and industries. In addition, it measures the relative performance of major equity benchmarks around the globe.

In intermarket analysis, technicians often look for inflection points in one market as a sign or clue to start looking for a change in trend in a related market. To identify these intermarket relationships, a commonly used tool is relative strength analysis, which charts the price of one security divided by the price of another or the ratio of the values of two assets. A subtle shift may show up first in this kind of ratio analysis, where it may be clearer than in either individual chart pattern. Compared to traditional global macro analysis, using technical analysis to conduct intermarket analysis is considerably less time-consuming.

Exhibit 40 shows the price of 10-year US Treasury bonds compared with the S&P 500. Major trends can be clearly seen in periods of both outperformance and underperformance of the T-bond price relative to the S&P 500. The inflection points in this chart occur in 2000, 2003, 2007, and 2009. At each of these points, the relative performance ratio signaled that the time had come to move investments between these asset classes.

EXHIBIT 40   Relative Strength of 10-Year T-Bonds vs. S&P 500, 1999–2018

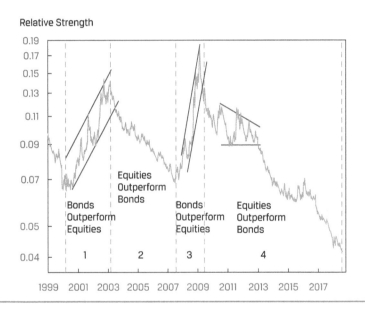

Exhibit 41 is a relative strength chart depicting the ratio of the S&P 500 to commodity prices. The chart shows a clear reversal of trend in mid-2008 from outperformance by commodities to outperformance by equities. This inflection point shows US stocks strengthening relative to commodities and indicates that moving funds away from commodities and into US equities might be appropriate. Of course, promptly interpreting such a sudden "V-reversal" in trend is still difficult to do, but a ratio chart may still help in the identification of a macro inflection point.

EXHIBIT 41   Historical Example: S&P 500 Index vs. Commodity Prices, 2007–2010

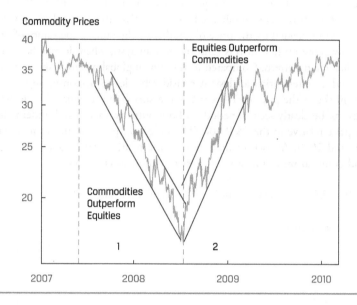

In addition to the preceding comparisons, once an asset category has been identified, relative strength analysis can be used to identify the best-performing securities in a sector. For example, if commodities look promising, an investor can analyze each of the major commodities relative to a broad commodity index in order to find the strongest commodities.

Exhibit 41 shows the relative price performance of Palladium versus commodities from 2009 to 2019. The ratio is constructed and indexed to 1.0 at the beginning of 2019. As of May 2019, the ratio is at the 13 level, meaning that Palladium outperformed commodities by a factor of 13. The year 2015 marked the acceleration of Palladium's outperformance versus the commodity index.

EXHIBIT 42   Palladium vs. Commodity Prices, 2009–2019

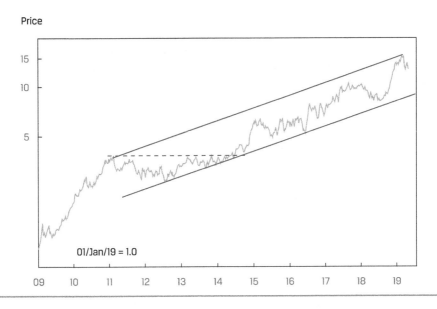

Intermarket analysis can also be used to identify sectors of the equity market to invest in —often in connection with technical observations of the business cycle at any given time. The equities of certain industry sectors tend to perform best at the beginning of an economic cycle. These sectors include financials, consumer non-durables, and transportation. As an economic recovery gets underway, retailers, manufacturers, health care, and consumer durables tend to outperform. Lagging sectors sometimes include those tied to commodity prices, such as energy and basic industrial commodities, which may catch up only in late-cycle, increasingly inflationary periods. In the final stage of a waning expansion, utility and consumer staple stocks may outperform because of their perceived safety, while transportation stocks often lead early market weakness in anticipation of a softening economy.

Observations based on intermarket analysis can also help in allocating funds across national markets. Certain countries' economies—for example, those of Australia, Canada, and South Africa—are closely tied to commodities. As economies evolve, these relationships change. So, the relationships must be monitored closely. For instance, a strong performance in industrial and precious metals can benefit mining stocks. The economies of Australia, Canada, and South Africa depend on the mining industry's performance, and as a result, strong metal prices can have a positive impact on the performance of these countries' equity markets.

5.2. Technical Analysis Applications to Portfolio Management

A technician acts very much like a doctor, who analyzes a patient for signs of wellness or sickness and then uses the clues discovered to formulate a composite opinion about fundamental changes in that patient's health. In this way, technical analysis complements fundamental analysis, whether the approach is top-down or bottom-up.

The top-down approach focuses on how the overall economy is affecting different sectors or industries. Analysts who apply a top-down approach believe that if a sector is doing well, stocks in that sector should also perform well.

Intermarket analysis is a key technical analysis tool that helps put the "big picture" into perspective. Intermarket analysis and relative strength analysis help the technician identify trends in countries, sectors, and industries and even among stocks within the same industry.

The bottom-up approach to identifying investment opportunities depends on rules and conditions. The analyst, trader, or investor starts his or her research with an *opportunity set* and tries to pick stocks that meet the *predefined criteria* irrespective of country, sector, or industry trends, which are sometimes considered as extraneous unknowable factors most easily considered as "All else being equal." Sometimes several opportunities in the same sector or industry will point to a developing overall *theme*. For example, finding several investment opportunities in mining stocks will alert the analyst, trader, or investor that metals (precious or industrial) might have strong performance. Or breakdowns in small-cap stocks might alert the analyst, trader, or investor that a possible "risk-off" environment is around the corner for the major equity benchmarks.

5.2.1. Technical Analysis Applications to Portfolio Management: Top-Down Approach

Analysts, traders, or investors whose focus is global equity markets often start their top-down approach by analyzing global benchmarks, such as MSCI and FTSE. The relative performance of major indexes will reveal important investment themes for investors with a long-term focus.

The same principles of charting and technical analysis discussed in the earlier sections of this chapter can be applied to relative strength analysis. The aim is to identify consolidation periods and then participate in major trends once these consolidations are completed, whether on the upside or on the downside. In other words, the technician attempts to capture trend periods by focusing on major inflection points on price charts.

Exhibit 43 shows the relative strength of the MSCI Emerging Markets Index and the MSCI All Country World Index between 1997 and 2019. The highest point reached in 2010 is indexed to 1.0 for ease of analysis. Starting in July 1997, the Asian financial crisis was a period of turmoil in currency and equity markets that gripped much of East Asia and Southeast Asia and raised fears of a worldwide economic meltdown through financial contagion.

The relative strength chart for the Emerging Markets Index and the All Country World Index shows that 1997–1999 was a period of strong underperformance for the Emerging Markets Index. Indonesia, South Korea, and Thailand were the countries most affected by the crisis. Hong Kong SAR, Malaysia, and the Philippines were also hurt by the slump. These were all countries classified as emerging markets.

However, in 2001–2002, the performance ratio tested the 1998–99 lows and formed a double bottom chart pattern. Retesting of the previous lows and a reversal from the support area were the first signs of a change in trend. The actual change took place in 2003, when the ratio cleared its long-term average and the horizontal boundary (resistance) of the double bottom chart pattern. This movement signaled the beginning of a period of outperformance for the Emerging Markets Index against the All Country World Index. For investors, it was a time to focus on emerging market opportunities.

Strong outperformance for the Emerging Markets Index continued until 2012, when the ratio started challenging its long-term average and the upward-sloping trendline. A new trend was established: Since 2012, the developed markets have been outperforming the emerging markets. Global asset allocators would have captured much better performance by investing in developed market equities over the past six years.

In Exhibit 43, the two major inflection points are the breakout from the double bottom chart pattern with the breach of the long-term average in 2003 and the breakdown of the trendline and long-term average in 2012. These inflection points are labeled as "trend change" on the price chart.

EXHIBIT 43   MSCI Emerging Markets Index vs. MSCI ACWI, 1997–2019

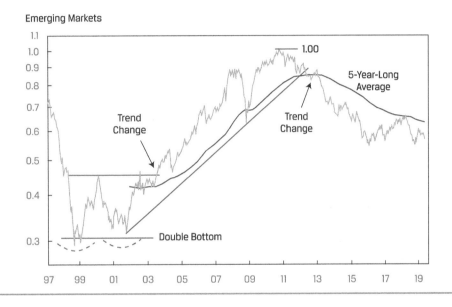

Exhibit 44 shows the relative strength of the MSCI Frontier Markets Index and the MSCI All Country World Index between 2002 and 2019. The highest point reached in 2005 is indexed to 1.0 for ease of analysis.

The charted ratio shows a strong outperformance for frontier market equities between 2002 and 2005. The ratio moved from the 0.35 level to as high as 1.00. This is almost 3 times outperformance during the three-year period. However, 2005 marked the highest point for the ratio over the analyzed period. In 2008, the ratio reached the previous highs and formed a double top. This chart pattern is the exact opposite of the one identified on the MSCI Emerging Markets versus MSCI ACWI chart during the 1998–2002 period.

A double top warns of a change in trend from up to down. At the beginning of 2009, the ratio not only breached the long-term average but also broke down the horizontal support formed by the neckline of the double top chart pattern.

Investors who had benefited from the outperformance of frontier market equities during 2002–2008 started allocating their funds out of frontier markets due to a change in trend. The following decade was a period of underperformance for the Frontier Markets Index. The ratio dropped from 0.7 to 0.35.

EXHIBIT 44   MSCI Frontier Markets Index vs. MSCI ACWI, 2002–2019

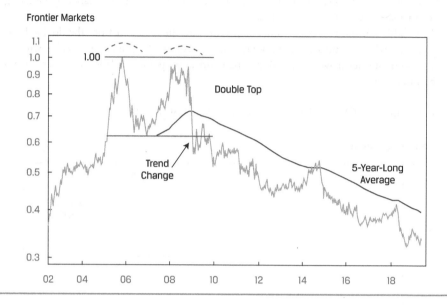

Out of the three major MSCI benchmarks—the developed, emerging, and frontier market indexes—both the Emerging Markets Index and the Frontier Markets Index started underperforming the All Country World Index after 2009–2010. At the same time, developed markets started outperforming the All Country World Index. The intermarket analysis suggested an allocation to developed markets.

However, not all developed markets performed well after the 2009–10 period. The analyst or investor should also have been selective in picking the outperforming countries.

Intermarket analysis can be used to advantage in asset allocation decisions. **Tactical asset allocation (TAA)** is a portfolio strategy that shifts the percentages of assets held in various asset classes (or categories) to take advantage of market opportunities. Allocation shifts can occur within an asset class or across asset classes. This strategy allows portfolio managers to add value by taking advantage of certain situations in the marketplace.

Technical analysis and intermarket analysis help the portfolio manager make discretionary TAA decisions. In preparing to make these decisions, the portfolio manager studies trends and possible changes in the relationships on relative strength charts.

Exhibit 45 shows the relative strength of the S&P 500 Index and the Goldman Sachs Commodity Index on a daily scale. The ratio of these indexes was trending down between May 2007 and July 2008. The downtrend in the ratio signaled an outperformance for commodities. The ratio formed a head and shoulders bottom reversal during 2008. Completion of the head and shoulders bottom took place at the same time as a breach above the 200-day average. These two signals confirmed the change in trend, which favored equities over commodities. From a TAA perspective, intermarket analysis suggested shifting assets from commodities to equities.

EXHIBIT 45.   S&P 500 Index vs. GSCI (Equities vs. Commodities), May 2007–August 2010

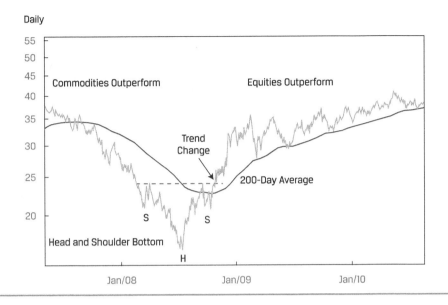

Short-term charts such as the daily scale help us identify changes in trends at the early stages. Longer time frames will alert us to major shifts in demand and supply.

Exhibit 46 shows the relative performance of the S&P 500 Index and the Goldman Sachs Commodity Index on a weekly scale. Following the initial trend change in the last quarter of 2008, equities outperformed commodities until 2010. The ratio moved sideways between 2010 and 2012. In the first half of 2012, the S&P 500 to GSCI ratio cleared the horizontal resistance, suggesting a new phase of outperformance. Asset allocators would have higher conviction for increasing equity allocations following the renewed strength and breakout in the second half of 2012.

EXHIBIT 46.   S&P 500 Index vs. GSCI (Equities vs. Commodities), 2007–2019

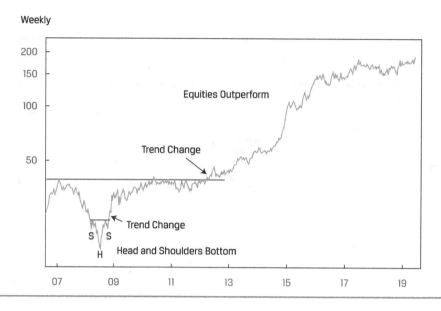

A similar relative strength chart can be drawn to compare bonds and commodities. Exhibit 47 shows the ratio of the 30-year US Treasury bond to the Goldman Sachs Commodity Index. Bonds started outperforming commodities in the second half of 2008. From the first quarter of 2009 till the last quarter of 2014, the ratio remained sideways and formed a symmetrical triangle. Consolidation periods are usually followed by trends. The breakout and trend change took place in the last quarter of 2014. Renewed strength in the ratio suggested outperformance for bonds versus commodities. From a TAA perspective, the intermarket analysis suggested shifting allocations from commodities to bonds.

EXHIBIT 47.   30-Year US Treasury Bond vs. GSCI (Bonds vs. Commodities), 2006–2019

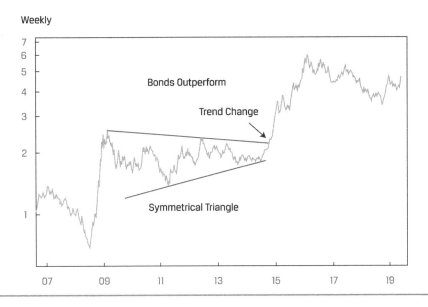

Exhibit 48 shows the relative strength of the S&P 500 Index and the 30-year US Treasury bond. Starting at the beginning of 2009, intermarket analysis suggested outperformance for equities versus bonds. Classical charting principles would have helped the asset allocator to identify the change in trend at the beginning of 2013, when the ratio completed a symmetrical triangle.

EXHIBIT 48.   S&P 500 Index vs. 30-Year US Treasury Bond (Equities vs. Bonds), 2006–2019

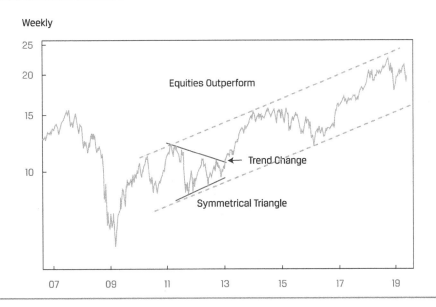

We started our intermarket analysis with global equity markets. With the help of relative strength analysis and classical charting principles, we have identified trends favoring emerging and frontier markets and then developed markets.

As another example, Exhibit 49 shows the relative strength of Microsoft Corporation and the MSCI USA Index. Microsoft is a large holding in this benchmark. It is important for fund managers and portfolio managers to have a view on large holdings in the index. The only significant technical analysis signal was triggered when the ratio completed a multi-year-long symmetrical triangle consolidation at the beginning of 2016. The inflection point is labeled "trend change" on the chart and is indexed to 1.0. After the breakout, the ratio pulled back to test the previous support/resistance area formed by the apex of the symmetrical triangle. Microsoft entered a period of strong outperformance between 2016 and 2019. The ratio moved from 1.00 to 1.90 over the three-year period. The intermarket analysis suggested an overweight position for Microsoft.

EXHIBIT 49   Microsoft Corporation vs. MSCI USA Index, 2000–2019

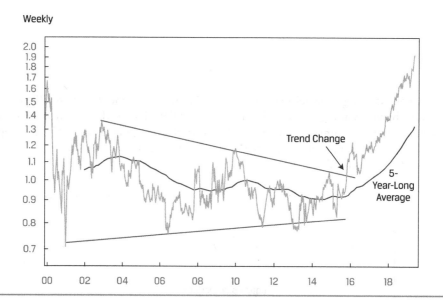

While the price ratio was generating a positive technical signal in favor of Microsoft, one would have questioned how to build positions in the stock. At this point, the analyst or investor would refer to the company's price chart to see trend and consolidation periods and the possibility to capture one of those well-defined breakout opportunities.

Exhibit 50 shows the price chart for Microsoft between October 2014 and May 2019. At the time when Microsoft started outperforming the MSCI USA Index, the price chart was trying to complete the yearlong rectangle labeled "Consolidation 1." The upper boundary of this yearlong consolidation acted as resistance at the 49.5 level. In the last quarter of 2015, Microsoft broke out of its rectangle chart pattern with a strong weekly candlestick. At the same time, the ratio of Microsoft to the MSCI USA (Exhibit 49) broke out of its multi-year-long symmetrical triangle consolidation.

The breakout on the Microsoft price chart was followed by a pullback and another multi-month-long consolidation. During this new consolidation, labeled "Consolidation 2" in

Exhibit 50, previous resistance acted as support at the 49.5 level. Consolidation periods are price ranges in which investors with a longer-term focus assess the strength of the company and accumulate shares. If demand overcomes the supply, price eventually breaks out of the consolidation, and the trend resumes. Microsoft completed the second rectangle chart pattern in the second half of 2016 and resumed its uptrend. "Breakout 1" and "Breakout 2" are two inflection points on the price chart where Microsoft generated technical buy signals.

EXHIBIT 50   Microsoft Corporation, October 2014–May 2019 (US$)

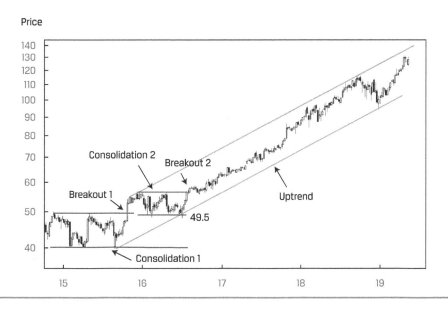

5.2.2. Technical Analysis Applications to Portfolio Management: Bottom-Up Approach

A bottom-up investing approach focuses on the analysis of individual stocks. In bottom-up investing, the investor focuses his or her attention on a specific company's technicals rather than on the industry or index in which that company is classified. A bottom-up approach focuses on stock picking irrespective of market, industry, or more macro trends. It is possible that a thorough analysis of individual stocks will reveal investment themes in different sectors and industries. For example, several bottom reversals on individual health care stocks might suggest a turnaround in that sector due to anticipated news or a change in fundamentals.

To use the bottom-up approach, first, the investor or analyst needs an investment universe—a group of instruments to make a selection from. Second, the investor or analyst needs a method for selecting instruments using predefined criteria.

We will focus on momentum and breakout strategies. A breakout trader enters a long position after the stock price breaks above resistance or enters a short position after the stock breaks below support.

In our analysis, we will follow the following criteria, or trading rules, for stock selection:

1. The breakout should take place above the 200-day exponential moving average (long-only strategy).
2. Price should be in a low-volatility condition prior to the breakout.

3. The breakout should take place from a well-defined classical chart pattern between 3 and 24 months in duration.
4. Breakout confirmation should be a weekly close above the chart pattern boundary.

Our opportunity set will be developed market equities.

The examples below highlight breakout opportunities that were possible to identify during 2016. These breakouts not only captured directional movements on price charts but also pointed analysts and investors to a specific theme.

Our initial requirement for a stock is that it be going through a low-volatility period. We would like to capture those stocks that are in consolidation periods. If the opportunity set is large, the analyst can use filtering criteria to identify stocks with low Bollinger Band readings, as discussed in preceding sections. Following the initial screening, the analyst will use the **visual technique** to select one of the well-defined classical chart patterns.

Before we proceed to the examples below, we should clarify one important point. To use a bottom-up approach to stock selection, an analyst should have a method for identifying potential trades. Focusing on breakout and momentum is one of many different approaches to stock selection and investment decision-making. Each analyst, investor, or trader can implement his or her own approach to identifying opportunities.

In our simplified scenario, these are the commonsense technical rules that we choose to apply:

*   The breakout should take place above the 200-day exponential moving average (long-only strategy).

It is important to identify stocks that are already in a steady uptrend or are entering into an uptrend. Breakouts from consolidation periods in or preceding an uptrend are usually followed by a continuation of the existing trend. Investing in the overall direction of the trend is the *path of least resistance*.

*   Price should be in a low-volatility condition.

Low-volatility conditions are usually followed by high volatility, and vice versa. Stocks that break out from low-volatility conditions are likely to experience high volatility, and high volatility in the direction of the existing trend will usually help the trend to pick up momentum.

*   The breakout should take place from a well-defined classical chart pattern between 3 and 24 months in duration.

The longer the consolidation, the stronger the breakout and the subsequent trend period will be.

*   Breakout confirmation should be a weekly close above the chart pattern boundary.

In an attempt to avoid premature breakout decisions, we will wait for a decisive weekly close above the chart pattern boundary.

Exhibit 51 shows the price chart for Belo Sun Mining Company from July 2013 to February 2017. The stock is listed on the Toronto Stock Exchange. The price chart formed a multi-month-long ascending triangle between 2014 and 2015. An ascending triangle is a bullish chart pattern. Its upward-sloping boundary gives this triangle its bullish bias. This pattern suggests that buyers are able to bid the price to higher levels after each correction.

Prior to the formation of an ascending triangle, the stock was in a steady downtrend. The ascending triangle acted as a consolidation and represented a period of low volatility. The breakout above the chart pattern boundary at 0.28 took place at the beginning of 2016. At this point, the stock was above its long-term average and ready for a new trend period. The breakout took place with a strong weekly candlestick. The bullish ascending triangle acted as a bottom reversal for the silver mining company, and a strong trend period followed. According to the bottom-up approach, in the last quarter of 2015, Belo Sun Mining should have been on our watch list for a possible breakout opportunity.

EXHIBIT 51   Belo Sun Mining Company, July 2013–February 2017 (Price in Canadian Dollars)

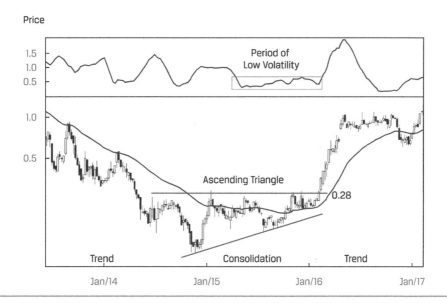

Exhibit 52 shows the price chart for Pan American Silver Corporation between January 2014 and September 2016. The stock is listed on the Toronto Stock Exchange. Pan American Silver formed a double bottom chart pattern, a bullish reversal, around the same time some of the silver mining companies formed consolidations. The double bottom formed in the second half of 2015. At the beginning of 2016, a breakout from the bullish reversal chart pattern above the 11.2 levels took place with a strong weekly candlestick.

Because these two stocks were going through low-volatility conditions and forming one of the well-defined chart patterns, they would have been on our watch list. Bullish bias in all the chart pattern developments would have alerted us to a possible reversal on silver prices and possibly other precious/industrial metal prices. This example shows how one can start with individual stocks and end up finding an investment theme.

EXHIBIT 52   Pan American Silver Corporation, January 2014–September 2016 (Price in Canadian Dollars)

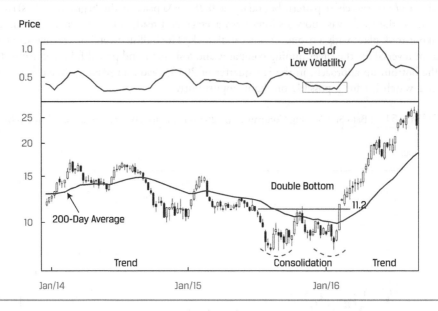

In this instance, strength in silver mining equities happened to lead the breakout in commodity prices.

Exhibit 53 shows the silver (per ounce) price between April 2014 and August 2016. Silver mining equities bottomed or completed bullish continuation chart patterns in the beginning of 2016. Silver prices formed an inverse head and shoulders chart pattern from the second half of 2015 to the first quarter of 2016. A breakout from the inverse head and shoulders chart pattern took place in April 2016, when price cleared the horizontal resistance at the 16 level. Following the breakout, price pulled back to the chart pattern boundary and resumed the uptrend.

EXHIBIT 53   Silver (per Ounce) Price, April 2014–August 2016 (US$)

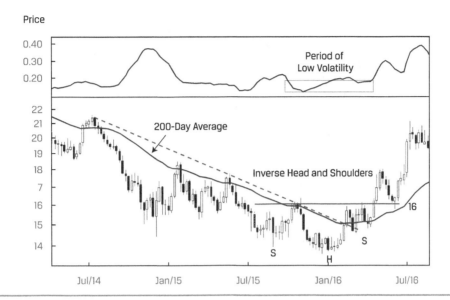

5.3. The Role of the Technical Analyst in Fundamental Portfolio Management

A technical analyst can serve a supporting role in a team of investors. The technician can conduct research and find investment opportunities by applying different strategies. As mentioned in the examples above, the technical analyst goes through the opportunity set and provides trade and investment ideas to the portfolio/fund managers.

The key value-added input would be in the form of timing of the purchase or sale of that security. The technical analyst should provide the rationale as well as potential price targets for the expected move and the price level at which the analysis would be invalidated. The technical analyst should follow a purist approach and follow the results of the research without being influenced by other inputs, such as news and fundamental data on the specific company—though news confirming the development of a technical trend is always welcome.

The technical analyst will typically not be directly involved in position sizing decisions, such as how much of the portfolio to allocate to a certain idea or by what margin the fund should overweight or underweight the specific stock. However, the portfolio manager may well use high-conviction inputs from the technical analyst in weighting decisions.

Question 13
A trader identifies an inverse head and shoulders chart pattern on the commodity XYZ. He plans to buy 100 units of the commodity at the time of the breakout. However, he only manages to get filled for 20 units because the price moves quickly. Over the next few weeks, the price moves close to the chart pattern price target at the 18.6 level but then reverses back to the breakout level. What should the trader do, given the price movement, assuming the chart pattern will hold?

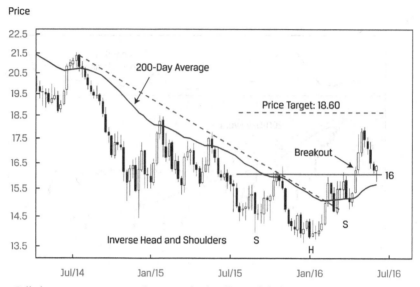

a. Sell the existing 20 units because the breakout failed.
b. Buy the remaining 80 units (of the initial 100-unit purchase plan) because the price is giving another opportunity with a pullback.
c. Wait for further correction toward the next support between 14.5 and 15.0.

Answer: B. The price pullback to the chart pattern boundary provides an opportunity to complete the purchase of the planned quantity.

A is not the correct answer because the breakout didn't fail: The price held above the chart pattern boundary.

C is not the correct answer because a correction toward the 14.5–15.0 area would put the bullish interpretation in question and the chart pattern might lose its validity.

Question 14

A fund manager has been trading ABC stock between the horizontal chart pattern boundaries throughout 2018. Every time the price reached the 60 level (support), she was overweighting the stock, and every time it reached the 70 level (resistance), she was underweighting it. This strategy worked well until October 2018, when the stock price slipped below the horizontal support at the 60 level. The fund manager's mandate is to beat a benchmark, and the stock is one of the blue chips in the index with a high weighting. What should the fund manager do?

a. Buy more of the ABC stock and remain overweight because the stock is now cheaper.
b. Sell part of the exposure and remain underweight because the stock might be breaking down a lengthy consolidation.
c. Expect the stock to remain sideways and maintain a market-weight position.

Answer: B.

The stock is completing a yearlong rectangle pattern, and the volatility measured by the Bollinger Band width is about to break out from a two-year-long consolidation. Therefore, there is a high probability that a trend period will follow and the stock will underperform. Selling part of the exposure and going underweight the benchmark at a time when the stock is likely to trend downward would result in outperformance versus the benchmark, adding value to the portfolio.

A is not the correct answer because buying more of the stock and overweighting the position at a time when the stock is likely to trend downward would result in underperformance versus the benchmark.

C is not the correct answer because maintaining a market-weight position at a time when the stock is likely to trend downward would result in a lost opportunity to outperform the benchmark by underweighting the position.

SUMMARY

• Technical analysis is a form of security analysis that uses price data and volume data, typically displayed graphically in charts. The charts are analyzed using various indicators in order to make investment recommendations.

- Technical analysis has three main principles and assumptions: (1) The market discounts everything, (2) prices move in trends and countertrends, and (3) price action is repetitive, with certain patterns reoccurring.
- Increasingly, analysts, fund managers, and individual investors are studying the basic principles of technical analysis to support their decision-making in financial markets. Behavioral finance, which is the study of the influence of psychology on the behavior of investors, focuses on the fact that investors are not always rational, have limits to their self-control, and are influenced by their own biases. This relatively new field of finance is motivating more practitioners to consider technical analysis as a tool for understanding and explaining irrationalities in financial markets.
- Technical analysis can be used on any freely traded security in the global market and is used on a wide range of financial instruments, such as equities, bonds, commodities, currencies, and futures. However, in general, technical analysis is most effectively applied to liquid markets. Therefore, technical analysis has limited usefulness for illiquid securities, where a small trade can have a large impact on prices.
- The primary tools used in technical analysis are charts and indicators. Charts are graphical displays of price and volume data. Indicators are approaches to analyzing the charts. While the tools can be used on a standalone basis, many analysts, fund managers, and investors will find added value in combining the techniques of chart analysis with their own research and investment approach.
- Charts provide information about past price behavior and provide a basis for inferences about likely future price behavior. Basic charts include line charts, bar charts, and candlestick charts.
- Charts can be drawn either to a linear scale or to a logarithmic scale. A logarithmic scale is appropriate when the data move through a range of values representing several orders of magnitude (e.g., from 10 to 10,000), whereas a linear scale is better suited to narrower ranges (e.g., $35 to $50).
- Volume is an important element of technical analysis and is often included on charts. Volume can be viewed as a confirmation in that it indicates the strength or conviction of buyers and sellers in determining a security's price.
- One of the most important steps in successfully applying technical analysis is to define the time period being analyzed. Technical analysis and charting become more reliable as the time scale increases from intraday to daily, weekly, and even monthly. Analysts and investors whose primary research method is fundamental analysis will find more value in charting instruments on a weekly and/or a monthly scale. Longer time frames will allow analysts and investors to better identify the consolidation and trend periods and time their purchases or sales of securities.
- Several basic concepts can be applied to charts. These include relative strength analysis, trend, consolidation, support, resistance, and change in polarity.
- Relative strength analysis is based on the ratio of the prices of a security and a benchmark and is used to compare the performance of one asset with the performance of another asset.
- The concept of trend is an important aspect of technical analysis. An uptrend is defined as a sequence of higher highs and higher lows. To draw an uptrend line, a technician draws a line connecting the lows on the price chart. A downtrend is defined as a sequence of lower highs and lower lows. To draw a downtrend line, a technician draws a line connecting the highs on the price chart.

- Support is defined as a low price range in which the price stops declining because of buying activity. It is the opposite of resistance, which is a price range in which price stops rising because of selling activity.
- Chart patterns are formations appearing on price charts that create some type of recognizable shape. There are two major types of chart patterns: reversal patterns and continuation patterns.
- Reversal patterns signal the end of a trend. Common reversal patterns are head and shoulders (H&S), inverse H&S, double top, double bottom, triple top, and triple bottom.
- Continuation patterns indicate that a market trend that was in place prior to the pattern formation will continue once the pattern is completed. Common continuation patterns are triangles (symmetrical, ascending, and descending), rectangles (bullish and bearish), flags, and pennants.
- Technical indicators are used to derive additional information from basic chart patterns. An indicator is any measure based on price, market sentiment, or fund flows that can be used to predict changes in price. Mathematically calculated indicators usually have a supply and demand underpinning. Basic types of indicators include price-based indicators, momentum oscillators, and sentiment indicators.
- Price-based indicators incorporate information contained in market prices. Common price-based indicators include the moving average and Bollinger Bands.
- The moving average is the average of the closing prices of a security over a specified number of periods. Moving averages are a smoothing technique that gives the technical analyst a view of market trends. So, a moving average can be viewed as a trend filter. Long-term moving averages can provide important signals. A price move above the long-term moving average is a sign of an uptrend. A price move below the long-term moving average is a sign of a downtrend.
- When a short-term moving average crosses over a longer-term moving average from underneath, this movement is considered a bullish indicator and is called a "bullish crossover." When a short-term moving-average crosses over a longer-term moving average from above, this movement is a bearish indicator and is called a "bearish crossover."
- Bollinger Bands combine the concept of a moving average with standard deviations around the moving average. This tool is useful in defining a trading range for the security being analyzed. The Bollinger Band width indicator provides an indication of volatility. The idea is that periods of low volatility are followed by periods of high volatility, so that relatively narrow band width can foreshadow an advance or decline in the security under analysis.
- Momentum oscillators are constructed from price data, but they are calculated so that they fluctuate between a low and a high, typically between 0 and 100. Some examples of momentum oscillators include rate of change (ROC) oscillators, the relative strength index (RSI), stochastic oscillators, and the MACD (moving-average convergence/divergence oscillator).
- Momentum oscillators can be viewed as graphical representations of market sentiment that show when selling or buying activity is more aggressive than usual. Technical analysts also look for convergence or divergence between oscillators and price. For example, when the price reaches a new high, this outcome is usually considered "bullish." But if the momentum oscillator does not also reach a new high, this scenario is considered divergence and an early warning sign of weakness.
- Momentum oscillators also alert the technical analyst to overbought or oversold conditions. For example, in an oversold condition, market sentiment is considered unsustainably bearish.

- Sentiment indicators attempt to gauge investor activity for signs of increasing bullishness or bearishness. Commonly used calculated statistical indexes are the put/call ratio, the VIX, and margin debt.
- Intermarket analysis combines technical analysis of the major categories of securities— namely, equities, bonds, currencies, and commodities—to identify market trends and possible inflections in trends. Intermarket analysis also looks at industry subsectors and their relationship to sectors and industries. In addition, it measures the relative performance of major equity benchmarks around the globe.
- Technical analysis can use either a top-down approach or a bottom-up approach to analyze securities. The top-down method is useful for identifying outperforming asset classes, countries, or sectors. This approach can add value to asset allocation decisions. Allocation shifts can occur within an asset class or across asset classes. The bottom-up method is useful for identifying individual stocks, commodities, or currencies that are outperforming, irrespective of market, industry, or macro trends.
- The technical analyst can add value to an investment team by providing trading/investment ideas through either top-down or bottom-up analysis, depending on the nature of the investment firm or fund. In addition, technical analysis can add value to a fundamental portfolio approach by providing input on the timing of the purchase or sale of a security.

PRACTICE PROBLEMS

1. Technical analysis relies *most importantly* on:
   A. price and volume data.
   B. accurate financial statements.
   C. fundamental analysis to confirm conclusions.

2. Which of the following is *not* an assumption of technical analysis?
   A. Security markets are efficient.
   B. The security under analysis is freely traded.
   C. Market trends and patterns tend to repeat themselves.

3. Drawbacks of technical analysis include which of the following?
   A. It identifies changes in trends only after the fact.
   B. Deviations from intrinsic value can persist for long periods.
   C. It usually requires detailed knowledge of the financial instrument under analysis.

4. Why is technical analysis especially useful in the analysis of commodities and currencies?
   A. Valuation models cannot be used to determine fundamental intrinsic value for these securities.
   B. Government regulators are more likely to intervene in these markets.
   C. These types of securities display clearer trends than equities and bonds do.

5. Technical analysis is a form of security analysis that:
   A. assesses past price action to project future prices.
   B. requires in-depth knowledge of financial instruments.
   C. is ineffective when evaluating long-term price movements.

6. One principle of technical analysis is that a security's price:
   A. tends to move in a random fashion.
   B. moves in patterns that tend to reoccur.
   C. does not reflect all known factor information relating to the security.

7. A daily bar chart provides:
   A. a logarithmically scaled horizontal axis.
   B. a horizontal axis that represents changes in price.
   C. high and low prices during the day and the day's opening and closing prices.

8. A candlestick chart is similar to a bar chart *except* that the candlestick chart:
   A. represents upward movements in price with X's.
   B. also graphically shows the range of the period's highs and lows.
   C. has a body that is light or dark depending on whether the security closed higher or lower than its open.

9. In a candlestick chart, a shaded candlestick body indicates that the opening price was:
   A. equal to the closing price.
   B. lower than the closing price.
   C. higher than the closing price.

10. A chart constructed with a single data point per time interval is a:
    A. bar chart.
    B. line chart.
    C. candlestick chart.

11. In analyzing a price chart, high or increasing volume *most likely* indicates which of the following?
    A. Predicts a reversal in the price trend.
    B. Predicts that a trendless period will follow.
    C. Confirms a rising or declining trend in prices.

12. In constructing a chart, using a logarithmic scale on the vertical axis is likely to be *most useful* for which of the following applications?
    A. The price of gold for the past 100 years.
    B. The share price of a company over the past month.
    C. Yields on 10-year US Treasuries for the past 5 years.

13. A linear price scale is:
    A. inappropriate for a candlestick chart.
    B. better suited for analysis of short-term price movements.
    C. constructed with equal vertical distances corresponding to an equal percentage price change.

14. A downtrend line is constructed by drawing a line connecting:
    A. the lows of the price chart.
    B. the highs of the price chart.
    C. the highest high to the lowest low of the price chart.

15. Relative strength analysis typically compares the performance of an asset with that of a benchmark or other security using a:
   A. bar chart that reflects the two assets' price history.
   B. line chart that reflects the ratio of the two assets' prices.
   C. candlestick chart that reflects ratios measuring the magnitude of each asset's up days versus down days.

16. Exhibit 1 depicts ABC Co., Ltd., ordinary shares, traded on the Shenzhen Stock Exchange, for the months of November through September in renminbi (RMB).

EXHIBIT 1   Candlestick Chart: ABC Co., Ltd. Price Data, November–September (Price Measured in RMB × 10)

   Based on Exhibit 1, the uptrend was *most likely* broken at a price level nearest to:
   A. 7 RMB.
   B. 8.5 RMB.
   C. 10 RMB.

17. The "change in polarity" principle states which of the following?
   A. Once an uptrend is broken, it becomes a downtrend.
   B. Once a resistance level is breached, it becomes a support level.
   C. The short-term moving average has crossed over the longer-term moving average.

18. Exhibit 2 depicts XYZ Co. ordinary shares, traded on the London Stock Exchange, in British pence.

EXHIBIT 2   Candlestick Chart: XYZ Co. Price Data, January–January (Price Measured in British Pence)

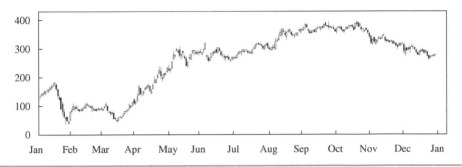

Based on Exhibit 2, Barclays appears to show resistance at a level nearest to:
A. 50p.
B. 275p.
C. 390p.

19. When a security is not trending, it is considered to be in a:
A. breakout.
B. retracement.
C. consolidation.

20. A technical analyst who observes a downtrending security break out of a consolidation range on the downside will *most likely* predict that the downtrend will:
A. resume.
B. reverse trend with an upside breakout.
C. retrace back to the consolidation range.

21. Which of the following statements regarding technical support and resistance is correct?
A. A breached support level becomes a new level of resistance.
B. Support is a price range where selling activity is sufficient to stop a rise in price.
C. Resistance is a price range where buying activity is sufficient to stop a decline in price.

22. Exhibit 3 depicts DGF Company common shares, traded on the New York Stock Exchange, for five years in US dollars.

EXHIBIT 3   Candlestick Chart: DGF Company, five years, February–February

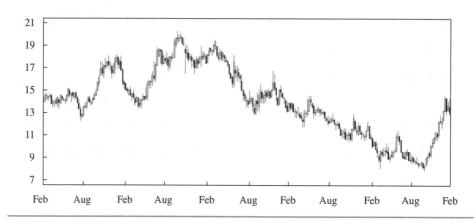

Exhibit 3 illustrates *most clearly* which type of pattern?
A. Triangle
B. Triple top
C. Head and shoulders

23. A triangle chart pattern that indicates a consolidation period and has bullish trading implications would *most likely* be classified as a(n):
A. ascending triangle.
B. descending triangle.
C. symmetrical triangle.

24. In an inverted head and shoulders pattern, if the neckline is at €100, the shoulders at €90, and the head at €75, the price target is *closest* to which of the following?
A. €50.
B. €110.
C. €125.

25. Which of the following chart patterns signals the end of an uptrend in price?
A. Bearish rectangle
B. Head and shoulders
C. Symmetrical triangle

26. An inverse head and shoulders acts as a reversal pattern for a preceding:
A. uptrend.
B. downtrend.
C. consolidation.

27. A fully formed head and shoulders pattern is *most likely* an indicator to:
A. buy.
B. sell.
C. hold.

28. To profit from a head and shoulders formation, a technician often sets a price target below the neckline price by an increment equal to the:
    A. head minus neckline.
    B. head minus top of right shoulder.
    C. top of right shoulder minus neckline.

29. A "healthy correction" chart pattern:
    A. is classified as a type of reversal pattern.
    B. does not change long-term price trends since supply and demand remain in balance.
    C. is formed when the price reaches a low, rebounds, and then sells off back to the first low level.

30. Which flow-of-funds indicator is considered bearish for equities?
    A. A large increase in the number of IPOs.
    B. Higher-than-average cash balances in mutual funds.
    C. An upturn in margin debt but one that is still below the long-term average.

31. If the 5-day moving average for AZB Company crossed over its 60-day moving average from underneath, it would be considered a:
    A. bullish indicator.
    B. bearish indicator.
    C. new level of resistance.

32. A trader observes that the 50-day moving average for the S&P 500 Index recently crossed below its long-term 200-day moving average. This situation is referred to as a:
    A. death cross.
    B. golden cross.
    C. Bollinger Band.

33. Bollinger Bands are constructed by plotting:
    A. a MACD line and a signal line.
    B. a moving-average line with an uptrend line above and downtrend line below.
    C. a moving-average line with upper and lower lines that are at a set number of standard deviations apart.

34. A Bollinger Band "squeeze" occurs when volatility:
    A. falls to low levels as the Bollinger Band widens.
    B. falls to low levels as the Bollinger Band narrows.
    C. rises to high levels as the Bollinger Band narrows.

35. Which of the following is *not* a momentum oscillator?
    A. MACD
    B. Stochastic oscillator
    C. Bollinger Bands

36. Which of the following is a continuation pattern?
    A. Triangle
    B. Triple top
    C. Head and shoulders

37. Which of the following is a reversal pattern?
    A. Pennant
    B. Rectangle
    C. Double bottom

38. Which of the following is generally true of the head and shoulders pattern?
    A. Volume is important in interpreting the data.
    B. The neckline, once breached, becomes a support level.
    C. Head and shoulders patterns are generally followed by an uptrend in the security's price.

39. Intermarket analysis focuses on the:
    A. valuation drivers of intermarket asset price relationships.
    B. bottom-up economic fundamentals of intermarket relationships.
    C. identification of inflection points in intermarket relationships using relative strength indicators.

40. A technical analyst following a bottom-up investing approach focusing on momentum and breakout strategies should favor long positions in stocks with:
    A. shorter consolidation periods.
    B. high Bollinger Band readings.
    C. low volatility prior to an upside breakout.

GLOSSARY

Abnormal return   The amount by which a security's actual return differs from its expected return, given the security's risk and the market's return.

Active investment   An approach to investing in which the investor seeks to outperform a given benchmark.

Active return   The return on a portfolio minus the return on the portfolio's benchmark.

Active risk   The annualized standard deviation of active returns, also referred to as *tracking error* (also sometimes called *tracking risk*).

Active Share   A measure of how similar a portfolio is to its benchmark. A manager who precisely replicates the benchmark will have an Active Share of zero; a manager with no holdings in common with the benchmark will have an Active Share of one.

American depository receipt   A US dollar-denominated security that trades like a common share on US exchanges.

American depository share   The underlying shares on which American depository receipts are based. They trade in the issuing company's domestic market.

Arbitrage   1) The simultaneous purchase of an undervalued asset or portfolio and sale of an overvalued but equivalent asset or portfolio, in order to obtain a riskless profit on the price differential. Taking advantage of a market inefficiency in a risk-free manner. 2) The condition in a financial market in which equivalent assets or combinations of assets sell for two different prices, creating an opportunity to profit at no risk with no commitment of money. In a well-functioning financial market, few arbitrage opportunities are possible. 3) A risk-free operation that earns an expected positive net profit but requires no net investment of money.

Backtesting   With reference to portfolio strategies, the application of a strategy's portfolio selection rules to historical data to assess what would have been the strategy's historical performance.

Bar chart   In technical analysis, a bar chart that plots four bits of data for each time interval—the high, low, opening, and closing prices. A vertical line connects the high and low prices. A cross-hatch left indicates the opening price and a cross-hatch right indicates the closing price.

Basket of listed depository receipts   An exchange-traded fund (ETF) that represents a portfolio of depository receipts.

Bearish crossover   A technical analysis term that describes a situation where a short-term moving average crosses a longer-term moving average from above; this movement is considered bearish. A **death cross** is a bearish crossover based on 50-day and 200-day moving averages.

Behavioral finance   A field of finance that examines the psychological variables that affect and often distort the investment decision making of investors, analysts, and portfolio managers.

Best-in-class   An ESG implementation approach that seeks to identify the most favorable companies and sectors based on ESG considerations. Also called *positive screening*.

Blue chip   Widely held large market capitalization companies that are considered financially sound and are leaders in their respective industry or local stock market.

Bollinger Bands   A price-based technical analysis indicator consisting of a line representing the moving average, a higher line representing the moving average plus a set number of standard deviations from the average (for the same number of periods as was used to calculate the moving average), and a lower line representing the moving average minus the same number of standard deviations.

Breadth The number of truly independent decisions made each year.

Breakdown A breakdown occurs when the price of an asset moves below a support level.

Breakout A breakout occurs when the price of an asset moves above a resistance level.

Buffering Establishing ranges around breakpoints that define whether a stock belongs in one index or another.

Bullish crossover A technical analysis term that describes a situation where a short-term moving average crosses a longer-term moving average from below; this movement is considered bullish. A **golden cross** is a bullish crossover based on 50-day and 200-day moving averages.

Candlestick chart A price chart with four bits of data for each time interval. A candle indicates the opening and closing price for the interval. The body of the candle is shaded if the opening price was higher than the closing price, and the body is white (or clear) if the opening price was lower than the closing price. Vertical lines known as wicks or shadows extend from the top and bottom of the candle to indicate, respectively, the high and low prices for the interval.

Cash drag Tracking error caused by temporarily uninvested cash.

CBOE Volatility Index (VIX) A measure of near-term market volatility as conveyed by S&P 500 stock index option prices.

Change in polarity principle A tenet of technical analysis that states that once a support level is breached, it becomes a resistance level. The same holds true for resistance levels: Once breached, they become support levels.

Chartist An individual who uses charts or graphs of a security's historical prices or levels to forecast its future trends.

Closet indexer A fund that advertises itself as being actively managed but is substantially similar to an index fund in its exposures.

Common shares A type of security that represent an ownership interest in a company.

Completion overlay A type of overlay that addresses an indexed portfolio that has diverged from its proper exposure.

Consolidation The movement of a stock's price within a well-defined range of trading levels for a period of time. The price consolidates between a support level and a resistance level.

Continuation pattern A type of pattern used in technical analysis to predict the resumption of a market trend that was in place prior to the formation of a pattern.

Convergence The tendency for differences in output per capita across countries to diminish over time. In technical analysis, the term describes the case when an indicator moves in the same manner as the security being analyzed.

Convertible preference shares A type of equity security that entitles shareholders to convert their shares into a specified number of common shares.

Cumulative preference shares Preference shares for which any dividends that are not paid accrue and must be paid in full before dividends on common shares can be paid.

Cumulative voting A voting process whereby each shareholder can accumulate and vote all his or her shares for a single candidate in an election, as opposed to having to allocate their voting rights evenly among all candidates.

Currency overlay A type of overlay that helps hedge the returns of securities held in foreign currency back to the home country's currency.

Data mining The practice of determining a model by extensive searching through a dataset for statistically significant patterns. Also called *data snooping*.

Data snooping See *data mining*.

Death cross See **Bearish crossover**.

Depository bank A bank that raises funds from depositors and other investors and lends it to borrowers.

Depository receipt A security that trades like an ordinary share on a local exchange and represents an economic interest in a foreign company.

Divergence In technical analysis, a term that describes the case when an indicator moves differently from the security being analyzed.

Dividend capture A trading strategy whereby an equity portfolio manager purchases stocks just before their ex-dividend dates, holds these stocks through the ex-dividend date to earn the right to receive the dividend, and subsequently sells the shares.

Doji In the Japanese terminology used in candlestick charting, the doji signifies that after a full day of trading, the positive price influence of buyers and the negative price influence of sellers exactly counteracted each other—with opening and closing prices that are virtually equal—which suggests that the market under analysis is in balance.

Double bottom In technical analysis, a reversal pattern that is formed when the price reaches a low, rebounds, and then declines back to the first low level. A double bottom is used to predict a change from a downtrend to an uptrend.

Double top In technical analysis, a reversal pattern that is formed when an uptrend reverses twice at roughly the same high price level. A double top is used to predict a change from an uptrend to a downtrend.

Downtrend A pattern that occurs when the price of an asset moves lower over a period of time.

Earnings surprise The portion of a company's earnings that is unanticipated by investors and, according to the efficient market hypothesis, merits a price adjustment.

Efficient market A market in which asset prices reflect new information quickly and rationally.

Exhaustive An index construction strategy that selects every constituent of a universe.

Expected shortfall The average loss conditional on exceeding the VaR cutoff; sometimes referred to as *conditional VaR* or *expected tail loss*.

Expected tail loss See *expected shortfall*.

Flag A technical analysis continuation pattern formed by parallel trendlines, typically over a short period.

Foreign exchange gains (or losses) Gains (or losses) that occur when the exchange rate changes between the investor's currency and the currency that foreign securities are denominated in.

Free float The number of shares that are readily and freely tradable in the secondary market.

Fundamental analysis The examination of publicly available information and the formulation of forecasts to estimate the intrinsic value of assets.

Fundamental value The underlying or true value of an asset based on an analysis of its qualitative and quantitative characteristics. Also called *intrinsic value*.

Gap opening A gap is an area of a chart where a security's price either rises or falls from the previous day's close with no trading occurring in between. A gap opening is the start of a new trading session with a gap.

Global depository receipt A depository receipt that is issued outside of the company's home country and outside of the United States.

Global registered share A common share that is traded on different stock exchanges around the world in different currencies.

Golden Cross See **Bullish crossover**.

Head and shoulders pattern In technical analysis, a reversal pattern that is formed in three parts: a left shoulder, a head, and a right shoulder. A head and shoulders pattern is used to predict a change from an uptrend to a downtrend.

Herding Clustered trading that may or may not be based on information.

High-water mark A specified net asset value level that a fund must exceed before performance fees are paid to the hedge fund manager.

Impact investing Investment approach that seeks to achieve targeted social or environmental objectives along with measurable financial returns through engagement with a company or by direct investment in projects or companies.

Information cascade The transmission of information from those participants who act first and whose decisions influence the decisions of others.

Information coefficient Formally defined as the correlation between forecast return and actual return. In essence, it measures the effectiveness of investment insight.

Informationally efficient market A market in which asset prices reflect new information quickly and rationally.

Initial public offering (IPO) The first issuance of common shares to the public by a formerly private corporation.

Intermarket analysis A field within technical analysis that combines analysis of the major categories of securities—namely, equities, bonds, currencies, and commodities—to identify market trends and possible inflections in trends.

Intrinsic value See *exercise value.*

January effect Calendar anomaly that stock market returns in January are significantly higher compared to the rest of the months of the year, with most of the abnormal returns reported during the first five trading days in January. Also called *turn-of-the-year effect.*

Leveraged buyout A transaction whereby the target company's management team converts the target to a privately held company by using heavy borrowing to finance the purchase of the target company's outstanding shares.

Line chart A type of graph used to visualize ordered observations. In technical analysis, a plot of price data, typically closing prices, with a line connecting the points.

Linear scale A scale in which equal distances correspond to equal absolute amounts. Also called an *arithmetic scale.*

Logarithmic scale A scale in which equal distances represent equal proportional changes in the underlying quantity.

Loss aversion The tendency of people to dislike losses more than they like comparable gains.

Management buyout A leveraged buyout event in which a group of investors consisting primarily of the company's existing management purchases at least controlling interest in its outstanding shares. At the extreme, they may purchase all shares and take the company private.

Market anomaly Change in the price or return of a security that cannot directly be linked to current relevant information known in the market or to the release of new information into the market.

Market value The price at which an asset or security can currently be bought or sold in an open market.

Momentum oscillator A graphical representation of market sentiment that is constructed from price data and calculated so that it oscillates either between a low and a high or around some number.

Moving average The average of the closing price of a security over a specified number of periods. With each new period, the average is recalculated.

Moving-average convergence/divergence oscillator A momentum oscillator that is based on the difference between short-term and long-term moving averages of a security's price.

Negative screening An ESG implementation approach that excludes certain sectors or companies that deviate from an investor's accepted standards.

Non-cumulative preference shares Preference shares for which dividends that are not paid in the current or subsequent periods are forfeited permanently (instead of being accrued and paid at a later date).

Non-participating preference shares Preference shares that do not entitle shareholders to share in the profits of the company. Instead, shareholders are only entitled to receive a fixed dividend payment and the par value of the shares in the event of liquidation.

Optional stock dividends A type of dividend in which shareholders may elect to receive either cash or new shares.

Overbought A market condition in which market sentiment is thought to be unsustainably bullish.

Overlay A derivative position (or positions) used to adjust a pre-existing portfolio closer to its objectives.

Oversold A market condition in which market sentiment is thought to be unsustainably bearish.

Packeting Splitting stock positions into multiple parts.

Participating preference shares Preference shares that entitle shareholders to receive the standard preferred dividend plus the opportunity to receive an additional dividend if the company's profits exceed a pre-specified level.

Passive investment A buy and hold approach in which an investor does not make portfolio changes based on short-term expectations of changing market or security performance.

Pennant A technical analysis continuation pattern formed by trendlines that converge to form a triangle, typically over a short period.

Portfolio overlay An array of derivative positions managed separately from the securities portfolio to achieve overall intended portfolio characteristics.

Positive screening An ESG implementation approach that seeks to identify the most favorable companies and sectors based on ESG considerations. Also called *best-in-class*.

Preference shares A type of equity interest which ranks above common shares with respect to the payment of dividends and the distribution of the company's net assets upon liquidation. They have characteristics of both debt and equity securities. Also called *preferred stock*.

Private equity securities Securities that are not listed on public exchanges and have no active secondary market. They are issued primarily to institutional investors via non-public offerings, such as private placements.

Private investment in public equity (PIPE) An investment in the equity of a publicly traded firm that is made at a discount to the market value of the firm's shares.

Program trading A strategy of buying or selling many stocks simultaneously.

Put/call ratio A technical analysis indicator that evaluates market sentiment based on the volume of put options traded divided by the volume of call options traded for a particular financial instrument.

Rebalancing overlay A type of overlay that addresses a portfolio's need to sell certain constituent securities and buy others.

Relative strength analysis A comparison of the performance of one asset with the performance of another asset or a benchmark, based on changes in the ratio of the two assets' prices over time.

Relative strength index (RSI) A technical analysis momentum oscillator that compares a security's gains with its losses over a set period.

Resistance In technical analysis, a price range in which selling activity is sufficient to stop the rise in the price of a security.

Retracement In technical analysis, a reversal in the movement of a security's price such that it is counter to the prevailing longer-term price trend.

Return on equity (ROE) A profitability ratio calculated as net income divided by average shareholders' equity.

Reversal pattern A type of pattern used in technical analysis to predict the end of a trend and a change in the direction of a security's price.

Risk aversion The degree of an investor's inability and unwillingness to take risk.

Securities lending A form of collateralized lending that may be used to generate income for portfolios.

Selective An index construction methodology that targets only those securities with certain characteristics.

Semi-strong-form efficient market A market in which security prices reflect all publicly known and available information.

Short selling A transaction in which borrowed securities are sold with the intention to repurchase them at a lower price at a later date and return them to the lender.

Special dividends A dividend paid by a company that does not pay dividends on a regular schedule, or a dividend that supplements regular cash dividends with an extra payment.

Sponsored A type of depository receipt in which the foreign company whose shares are held by the depository has a direct involvement in the issuance of the receipts.

Statutory voting A common method of voting where each share represents one vote.

Stochastic oscillator   A momentum indicator that compares a particular closing price of a security to a range of the security's prices over a certain period of time.

Stock lending   Securities lending involving the transfer of equities.

Strong-form efficient market   A market in which security prices reflect all public and private information.

Support   In technical analysis, a price range in which buying activity is sufficient to stop the decline in the price of a security.

Tactical asset allocation (TAA)   A portfolio strategy that shifts the percentages of assets held in various asset classes (or categories) to take advantage of market opportunities. Allocation shifts can occur within an asset class or across asset classes.

Technical analysis   A form of security analysis that uses price and volume data, often displayed graphically, in decision making.

Thematic investing   An investment approach that focuses on companies within a specific sector or following a specific theme, such as energy efficiency or climate change.

Transfer coefficient   The ability to translate portfolio insights into investment decisions without constraint.

Trend   A long-term pattern of movement in a particular direction.

Triangle pattern   In technical analysis, a continuation chart pattern that forms as the range between high and low prices narrows, visually forming a triangle.

Triple bottom   In technical analysis, a reversal pattern that results when the price forms three troughs at roughly the same price level. A triple bottom is used to predict a change from a downtrend to an uptrend.

Triple top   In technical analysis, a reversal pattern that results when the price forms three peaks at roughly the same price level. A triple top is used to predict a change from an uptrend to a downtrend.

Turn-of-the-year effect   Calendar anomaly that stock market returns in January are significantly higher compared to the rest of the months of the year, with most of the abnormal returns reported during the first five trading days in January.

Unsponsored   A type of depository receipt in which the foreign company whose shares are held by the depository has no involvement in the issuance of the receipts.

Uptrend   A pattern that occurs when the price of an asset moves higher over a period of time.

Venture capital   Investments that provide "seed" or startup capital, early-stage financing, or later-stage financing (including mezzanine-stage financing) to companies that are in early development stages and require additional capital for expansion or preparation for an initial public offering.

Visual technique   The most common and readily available method of initial data assessment. Experts in pattern recognition maintain that the visual (or "eyeball") technique is still the most effective way of searching for recognizable patterns.

Vote by proxy   A mechanism that allows a designated party—such as another shareholder, a shareholder representative, or management—to vote on the shareholder's behalf.

Weak-form efficient market hypothesis   The belief that security prices fully reflect all past market data, which refers to all historical price and volume trading information.

ABOUT THE AUTHORS

Ryan C. Fuhrmann, CFA, is at Fuhrmann Capital LLC (USA).

Asjeet S. Lamba, PhD, CFA, is at the University of Melbourne (Australia).

Sean Cleary, PhD, CFA, is at Queen's University (Canada).

Howard J. Atkinson, CIMA, ICD.D, CFA, is at Horizons ETF Management (Canada) Inc. (Canada).

Pamela Peterson Drake, PhD, CFA, is at James Madison University (USA).

James Clunie, PhD, CFA, is at Jupiter Asset Management (United Kingdom).

James Alan Finnegan, CAIA, RMA, CFA (USA).

David M. Smith, PhD, CFA, is at the University at Albany, New York (USA).

Kevin K. Yousif, CFA, is at LSIA Wealth & Institutional (USA).

Roger G. Clarke, PhD, is at Ensign Peak Advisors (USA).

Harindra de Silva, PhD, CFA, is at Analytic Investors, Wells Fargo Asset Management (USA).

Steven Thorley, PhD, CFA, is at the Marriott School, BYU (USA).

Bing Li, PhD, CFA, is at Yuanyin Asset Management (Hong Kong SAR).

Yin Luo, CPA, PStat, CFA, is at Wolfe Research LLC (USA).

Pranay Gupta, CFA, is at Allocationmetrics Limited (USA).

Jacques Lussier, PhD, CFA (Canada).

Marc R. Reinganum, PhD (USA).

Aksel Kibar, CMT, is at Tech Charts Research & Trading (Bulgaria).

Barry M. Sine is at Drexel Hamilton, LLC (USA).

Robert A. Strong, PhD, CFA, is at the University of Maine (USA).

ABOUT THE
CFA PROGRAM

If the subject matter of this book interests you, and you are not already a CFA Charterholder, we hope you will consider registering for the CFA Program and starting progress toward earning the Chartered Financial Analyst designation. The CFA designation is a globally recognized standard of excellence for measuring the competence and integrity of investment professionals. To earn the CFA charter, candidates must successfully complete the CFA Program, a global graduate-level self-study program that combines a broad curriculum with professional conduct requirements as preparation for a career as an investment professional.

Anchored in a practice-based curriculum, the CFA Program body of knowledge reflects the knowledge, skills, and abilities identified by professionals as essential to the investment decision-making process. This body of knowledge maintains its relevance through a regular, extensive survey of practicing CFA charterholders across the globe. The curriculum covers 10 general topic areas, ranging from equity and fixed-income analysis to portfolio management to corporate finance—all with a heavy emphasis on the application of ethics in professional practice. Known for its rigor and breadth, the CFA Program curriculum highlights principles common to every market so that professionals who earn the CFA designation have a thoroughly global investment perspective and a profound understanding of the global marketplace.

www.cfainstitute.org

INDEX

Note: An n after a page number indicates a footnote.

A

Abnormal returns, 44
Absolute objectives, 296–297
Absolute return strategies, 337
Absolute risk, 302–305, 317
Accounting constraints, 118
Accounting information, cascade due to, 59
Accounting return on equity, 23–28
Accruals anomaly factor, 223
Active equity investing strategies, 197–263
  activist, 228–235
  approaches to active management, 198–203
  bottom-up, 204–211
  comparing, 176
  costs associated with, 83–84
  creating fundamental strategies, 239–245
  creating quantitative strategies, 246–253
  event-driven, 238
  factor-based, 214–228
  and investment style classification, 253–261
  management fees with, 81
  manager selection for, 36
  market microstructure-based arbitrage, 237
  passive vs., 107
  statistical arbitrage, 235–238
  top-down, 211–214
Active equity portfolio construction, 271–344
  alpha skills, 277–279
  approaches to, 284–301
  breadth of experience, 281–283
  building blocks of, 272–284
  characteristics of well-constructed portfolios, 328–332
  fundamentals of, 273–275
  implicit cost-related considerations in, 321–327
  with long extension strategies, 336–337
  with long-only strategies, 333–335, 342
  with long/short strategies, 335–336, 338–342
  with market-neutral strategies, 337–338

  position sizing, 279–281
  rewarded factor weightings, 275–277
  risk budget allocation in, 301–314
  risk measures used during, 314–321
Active extension strategies, 334–335
Active portfolio management, 141–186
  added value from, 142–147
  comparing strategies for, 176
  in efficient markets, 37, 50
  ex ante measurement of skill in, 183–184
  with fixed-income strategies, 177–182
  fundamental law of, 158–185
  with global equity strategy, 169–176
  independence of investment decisions in, 184–185
  risk–return trade-off for, 147–158
Active returns, 36. *See also* Value added
  and active weight sizing, 161–162
  generating, 273–274
  from global equity strategy, 171
  mathematical expression of, 272–273
  measuring, 143–145
  variance of, 168, 305–306
Active risk:
  and active share/factor exposure, 290–291
  calculating, 289–290
  causes and sources, 305–307
  defined, 316
  and fundamental law of active management, 158
  and information ratio, 150, 152–153
  with optimal portfolio, 153–154, 156
  and portfolio construction, 288–295
  scaling of, 308
  strategy classification based on, 291–293
  and volatility, 280–281
Active share, 151, 288–295
  and active risk/factor exposure, 290–291
  calculating, 289
  defined, 285
  strategy classification based on, 291–293
Active weights, 144, 161–162, 171